# The Psychology of False Confessions

# Wiley Series in the

# Psychology of Crime, Policing and Law

Series Editors

## Graham M. Davies[1] and Ray Bull[2]

*[1]University of Leicester, UK*
*[2]University of Derby, UK*

---

The Wiley Series in the Psychology of Crime, Policing and Law publishes concise and integrative reviews on important emerging areas of contemporary research. The purpose of the series is not merely to present research findings in a clear and readable form but also to bring out their implications for both practice and policy. In this way, it is hoped the series will not only be useful to psychologists but also to all those concerned with crime detection and prevention, policing and the judicial process.

For other titles in this series please see www.wiley.com/go/pcpl

# The Psychology of False Confessions

## Forty Years of Science and Practice

Gisli H. Gudjonsson

# WILEY

The right of Gisli H. Gudjonsson to be identified as the author of this work has been
asserted in accordance with law.

*Registered Offices*
John Wiley & Sons, Inc., 111 River Street, Hoboken, NJ 07030, USA
John Wiley & Sons Ltd, The Atrium, Southern Gate, Chichester, West Sussex,
PO19 8SQ, UK

*Editorial Office*
The Atrium, Southern Gate, Chichester, West Sussex, PO19 8SQ, UK

For details of our global editorial offices, customer services, and more information about
Wiley products visit us at www.wiley.com.

Wiley also publishes its books in a variety of electronic formats and by print-on-
demand. Some content that appears in standard print versions of this book may not be
available in other formats.

*Library of Congress Cataloging-in-Publication Data*

Names: Gudjonsson, Gisli H., author.
Title: The psychology of false confessions : forty years of science and practice /
   by Gisli H. Gudjonsson.
Description: Hoboken, NJ : John Wiley & Sons, Inc., [2018] | Series: Wiley series
   in the psychology of crime, policing and law | Includes index. |
   Identifiers: LCCN 2017057204 (print) | LCCN 2017059019 (ebook) |
   ISBN 9781119315698 (pdf) | ISBN 9781119315681 (epub) |
   ISBN 9781119315667 (cloth) | ISBN 9781119315674 (pbk.)
Subjects: LCSH: Police questioning–Psychological aspects. |
   Confession (Law)–Psychological aspects. | Criminal psychology.
Classification: LCC HV8073 (ebook) | LCC HV8073 .G888 2018 (print) |
   DDC 363.25/4–dc23
LC record available at https://lccn.loc.gov/2017057204

Cover image: (left) © g-stockstudio/Shutterstock; (right) © RichLegg/Getty Images;
(background) © chrupka/Shutterstock
Cover design by Wiley

Set in 10/12pt NewCenturySchlbk by SPi Global, Pondicherry, India

Printed and bound by CPI Group (UK) Ltd, Croydon, CR0 4YY

10  9  8  7  6  5  4  3  2  1

*To my dear brother*
*Gudmundur Gudjónsson MBE*
*With love*

# Contents

# About the Author

Gisli Hannes Gudjonsson is an Emeritus Professor of Forensic Psychology at the Institute of Psychiatry, Psychology & Neuroscience, King's College London, and a Professor in the Psychology Department at Reykjavík University. Prior to his retirement from King's College on 1 January 2012 he was the Head of Forensic Psychology Services for the Lambeth Forensic Services and Medium Secure Unit at the South London and Maudsley NHS Trust. Professor Gudjonsson is a Fellow of the British Psychological Society and a registered practitioner (clinical and forensic) with the Health Care Professions Council.

Professor Gudjonsson pioneered the empirical measurement of interrogative suggestibility and has published extensively in the areas of psychological vulnerabilities, false confessions, and police interviewing. He has provided expert evaluation in a number of high profile cases, including the Guildford Four, the Birmingham Six, Judith Ward, Engin Raghip, Stephen Miller, Donald Pendleton, Andrew Evans, Ian Lawless, and Raymond Gilmour. He has also testified in high profile cases in the USA, Canada, Norway, Iceland, and Israel.

Professor Gudjonsson was awarded an Honorary Doctorate in Medicine in 2001 by the University of Iceland for services to forensic psychiatry and psychology. In April 2009 the British Psychological Society presented him with a Lifetime Achievement Award. He was awarded The European Association of Psychology and Law Life Time Achievement Award for 2012, and received the 2017 Tom Williamson (iIIRG) Life Time Achievement Award 'In recognition for his outstanding lifetime achievement to the area of investigative interviewing' (iIIRG is the International Investigative Interviewing Research Group). He was appointed a Commander of the Order of the British Empire (CBE) in the Queen's Birthday 2011 Honours List for services to clinical psychology.

Professor Gudjonsson is the author of *The Psychology of Interrogations, Confessions and Testimony* (John Wiley & Sons, 1992), *The Psychology of Interrogations and Confessions, A Handbook* (John Wiley & Sons, 2003), *The Gudjonsson Suggestibility Scales Manual* (Psychology Press, 1997), *The Causes and Cures of Criminality* (Plenum Press, 1989, jointly written with Hans Eysenck), and *Forensic Psychology: A Guide to Practice* (Routledge, 1998, jointly written with Lionel Haward).

# Series Preface

The Wiley Series in the Psychology of Crime, Policing and Law publishes both single and multi-authored monographs and edited reviews of important and emerging areas of contemporary research. The purpose of this series is not merely to present research findings in a clear and readable form, but also to bring out their implications for both practice and policy. Books in this series are useful not only to psychologists, but also to all those involved in crime detection and prevention, child protection, policing, and judicial processes.

The author of this new volume, Professor Gisli H. Gudjonsson, CBE, is pre-eminent in the field of false confession, a subject of concern to all criminal justice systems. Professor Gudjonsson has devoted much of his professional career to studying this issue, both as a researcher and as an expert witness in cases where contentious confessions are an issue, not only in the United Kingdom but throughout the world. His first book *The Psychology of Interrogations, Confessions and Testimony* launched this book series in 1992. It described how psychological pressures induced by then accepted interrogation techniques could lead to false and sometimes self-incriminating testimony, which in turn could result in miscarriages of justice. He illustrated this thesis with reference to a number of the high-profile cases in which he had given evidence, notably those of the 'Birmingham Six' and the 'Guildford Four', where coercive interview tactics had resulted in innocent suspects confessing while in police custody to involvement in these shocking crimes. Despite their subsequent retractions of involvement, all defendants were found guilty at trial and sentenced to lengthy prison terms. Their eventual release by the Court of Appeal owed in part to Professor Gudjonsson's expert testimony. He demonstrated through systematic analyses of the personal vulnerabilities of some of the defendants high levels of 'interrogative suggestibility', which in turn made their confessions an unsafe basis for conviction.

His second book *The Psychology of Interrogations and Confessions: A Handbook* appeared in the series in 2003 and summarized developments in the concept of interrogative suggestibility, again illustrated by many new cases in which he had given expert evidence. Much of that evidence was derived from administration of the *Gudjonsson Suggestibility Scales*, a psychometric tool he developed to tease out the potential effects of suggestibility and compliance in cases of contested confession evidence. The handbook also summarized the growing research literature on false confessions, much of which had been sparked by his pioneering work. His demonstration of the impact on evidence of coercive interview procedures led in turn to major changes being introduced to police interviewing procedures in England and Wales, although sadly, not in the United States, where disputed confessions remain a major concern for justice (Kassin, 1997).

Professor Gudjonsson's new book describes two murder cases in his native Iceland following the disappearance of two young men, Gudmundur Einarsson and Geirfinnur Einarsson, in 1974. No trace of the men was ever found, but police investigations led eventually to the arrest and subsequent trials for murder of six young persons. The evidence against them rested almost entirely on their confessions and no forensic evidence was offered at trial. The confessions themselves, secured in many instances after long periods of solitary confinement and intensive interrogation, were contradictory. In an effort to iron out such contradictions, the authorities involved a former senior investigator with the German police who conducted a further round of interrogations, which in turn led to further unreliable admissions. In the subsequent trial, the investigator's findings were used by the prosecution, while the defendants, now freed from oppressive detention, retracted their earlier confessions. All were found guilty and sentenced to lengthy prison terms.

As Professor Gudjonsson explains, when he examined the evidence in these cases, they showed the same pattern of coerced confession followed by subsequent retraction, reminiscent of many other proven cases of false confessions that he had investigated. His careful and detailed examination of the evidence and the experiences and personality of the accused led him to conclude that all six were innocent and that a serious miscarriage of justice had taken place. By a curious quirk of fate, he had met five of the six accused as a young police officer conducting research for a psychology dissertation. In 2012, he returned to Iceland as an internationally renowned expert, to assist with an official enquiry into the disputed convictions. Sadly, for two of the six, this development came too late, but the remaining four and the families of the two deceased men now await the decision of the Iceland Supreme Court to see whether their names will finally be cleared.

*The Psychology of False Confessions: Forty Years of Science and Practice* is a fascinating and personal account of the mysterious disappearances, and their subsequent investigation and the fight of the accused and their supporters for justice. In addition, Gudjonsson uses the opportunity to look back over his own career and to review the latest research on false confessions, with particular relevance to the travails of the Icelandic six. It is a story that can be read with profit by psychologists, criminologists, and lawyers and indeed, all those concerned with the prosecution of crime and the importance of justice.

Graham Davies
*University of Leicester*

# Preface

This book would not have been written had it not been for my becoming involved as a 'confession expert' in two Icelandic cases in 2011. The cases involved the disappearances of two unrelated men, *Gudmundur Einarsson* and *Geirfinnur Einarsson*, in January and November 1974, respectively. At the end of December 1975 and beginning of January 1976, the Reykjavík Criminal Investigation Police commenced murder investigations without the victims' bodies, a known crime scene, or credible leads. Despite the investigations floundering on numerous occasions, after eliciting confessions that were massively contradictory and could not be independently corroborated, six young people were convicted and imprisoned on the basis of their confessions. The convicted persons *Saevar Ciesielski*, *Kristján Vidarsson*, *Tryggvi Leifsson*, *Gudjón Skarphédinsson*, *Erla Bolladóttir*, and *Albert Skaftason* all claimed to be innocent and alleged that their confessions were coerced by the police. Saevar and Tryggvi are now dead, but the other four convicted persons and the families of the two dead men are currently fighting to have their convictions overturned.

In the summer of 1976 while working as a detective in Reykjavík, I met four of the six suspects and they participated while in custody in an experiment I was conducting into lie detection for an MSc dissertation in clinical psychology. I was not involved in the criminal investigation and was oblivious to what was really going on behind the closed doors at Sídumúli [Holding] Prison, where most of the interrogations took place. These were to become the biggest murder investigations in Iceland's history and the Minister of Justice, Ólafur Jóhannesson, sought help from Karl Schütz, a retired, senior, and high profile investigator with the German Federal Criminal Police Office (Bundeskriminalamt; BKA). Karl Schütz dominated the Geirfinnur investigation in the summer and autumn of 1976 and helped the

Icelandic judiciary to convict the six defendants by his strong presumption of guilt and forthright assertions. The bodies of the two men were never found and no forensic evidence linked the suspects to the alleged murders.

In early 1997, Saevar Ciesielski contacted me and asked whether I could help him with his pending appeal application before Iceland's Supreme Court. He was fighting a desperate battle to seek justice for himself and the others. Sadly, I had to turn him down, not only for practical reasons to do with other commitments, but I did not think that the Icelandic judiciary was ready to consider any psychological or other grounds for appeal. At the time, the psychological evidence base for investigating disputed confessions was still modest, but it was growing fast. In the 1990s, interest in the psychology of false confessions had gained momentum after the publication of my first Wiley book, *The Psychology of Interrogations, Confessions and Testimony* in 1992, followed ten years later by *The Psychology of Interrogations and Confessions. A Handbook*.

At the end of September 2011, an Icelandic journalist, Helga Arnardóttir, contacted me and asked me to look at three diaries that Tryggvi Leifsson had written while in solitary confinement in Síðumúli Prison in 1976 and 1977. The diaries were never used at trial and their contents were unknown to anybody, apart from Tryggvi, his wife, and his daughter. Reading the diaries had a profound effect upon me; they seemed authentic and Tryggvi came across as very sincere when describing his immense mental suffering during lengthy solitary confinement and compelling claims of innocence. Knowing from my extensive involvement in cases of disputed confessions in the UK, the USA, and elsewhere, and the growing and by now well-established empirical evidence base, I was in no doubt that the convictions in the Gudmundur and Geirfinnur cases needed to be reviewed, a view I repeated in an Icelandic television documentary on the cases. Within days of the broadcast, Iceland's Minister of the Interior, Mr Ögmundur Jónasson, contacted me and asked me to act as an expert to a Committee he was setting up to look into the cases. The Committee referred to in this book as the 'Working Group' reported its findings in March 2013 and concluded that the confessions of all six convicted persons were wholly unreliable. The Government then established the Icelandic Court Cases Review Commission, which concluded in February 2017 after two year's work that there were good grounds for appeal regarding the manslaughter convictions and Albert's conviction for participating in interfering with the crime scene (removal of the body) in the Gudmundur case. The appeal has already been lodged with the Supreme Court.

My experience as a detective in Iceland in the summers of 1975 and 1976 inspired me to become a forensic psychologist after completing my clinical psychology training in 1977. I remained fascinated by the psychology of confessions and in the early 1980s it became one of my principal areas of research interest and endeavour. I never envisaged that almost 40 years later I would become involved in the Gudmundur and Geirfinnur cases as a 'confession expert' and able to bring back to Iceland the science that had evolved during that period. This book shows the development of the science behind the psychology of false confessions, building on my two previous books, with minimum overlap, and describes how I have applied the science to the two Icelandic cases.

# Acknowledgments

A large number of people have contributed to the completion and success of this book. Professor Graham Davies, the Series Editor, and my wife Julia have read and commented on drafts of all the chapters. Their comments have been invaluable and improved the quality of the book. They have also provided me with continued support and encouragement throughout. With regard to Parts II and III of the book, Erla Bolladóttir, Sigurthór Stefánsson, and Ragnar Adalsteinsson provided me with important material regarding the Gudmundur and Geirfinnur cases. Sigurthór gave me his hard copy of all the 'Books of Evidence'. This made it easier for me to read and access the voluminous and complex material. Gudmundur Gudjónsson and Haraldur Steinthórsson suggested helpful background material. Erla, Gudjón, and Albert agreed to further interviews and this strengthened the psychological analysis of their individual cases and gave me deeper insights into their interrogation, confinement, and mental state in the 1970s. Hafthór Saevarsson provided me with his father's 'Social Journal' where I discovered that Saevar had been diagnosed in Denmark in 2010 with attention deficit hyperactivity disorder (ADHD), just over a year prior to his early tragic death at the age of 56. ADHD has featured in my individual analyses of the cases of Saevar, Tryggvi, and Albert. Emma-Louise Bush assisted with the production of some of the figures. The following people have read and provided comments on one or more of the chapters: Erla Bolladóttir, Gudjón Skarphédinsson, Kristín Tryggvadóttir, Sjöfn Sigurbjörnsdóttir, Tryggvi Rúnar Brynjarsson, Júlia Marinósdóttir, Hafthór Saevarsson, Sigurthór Stefánsson, Helga Arnardóttir, Arndís Sigurdardóttir, Haraldur

Steinthórsson, Gudmundur Gudjónsson, Helen Grady, Dr John Pearse, and Professor Susan Young. Cathryn Primrose-Mathisen, commissioned by Wiley, provided diligent and efficient copy-editing.

—Gisli H. Gudjonsson

# Icelandic Names

Icelandic names can be difficult and in order to simplify matters, I generally avoid giving middle names, which are very common in Iceland, unless it has a specific purpose (e.g. differentiating people with the same first names). Icelandic names are patronymic, indicating the father of the child and not the historic family lineage (i.e. son or daughter being added to the father's Christian name, becoming the child's surname). Therefore, people with the same surnames are not necessarily related (e.g. Gudmundur Einarsson and Geirfinnur Einarsson). It is customary in Iceland to address people by their first name rather than their surname and I generally keep to this tradition. With regard to my own name, I have kept the English spelling, Gisli Gudjonsson, rather than Gísli Guðjónsson, in order not to confuse the reader with regard to the citations of my international publications. I have replaced the consonants ð and þ with 'd' and 'th' respectively.

# The Psychology of False Confessions

# Introduction

*The only thing necessary for the triumph of evil is for good men to do nothing*[1]

It was a beautiful midsummer afternoon in Reykjavík. The year was 1975. I was a detective with the Reykjavík Criminal Investigation Police, which was situated close to the seafront in Reykjavík and in the same building as the Reykjavík Criminal Court. My detective badge had been recently issued by the head of the Criminal Court and the Reykjavík Criminal Investigation Police, officially my boss, Halldór Thorbjörnsson. I was full of enthusiasm for my new job, investigating criminal offences. A large part of the job was taking witness statements from complainants and victims of crime, and interrogating suspects. A new complaint had just arrived at my desk. A young woman, I will call Anna, wanted to report a theft of her purse, and the suspect was a man whom the evening before she had met at a club in Reykjavík. They had subsequently gone back to her flat and continued to drink. The man then left and Anna went to sleep. The following morning Anna could not find her purse and assumed the man she had met the night before had stolen it. I then contacted the suspect, who I will call David, and requested that he attend for questioning. David attended the police station and was fully cooperative. He said that he could recall meeting

---

[1] From Edmund Burke, Irish statesman, 18th century.

*The Psychology of False Confessions: Forty Years of Science and Practice*, First Edition.
Gisli H. Gudjonsson.
© 2018 John Wiley & Sons Ltd. Published 2018 by John Wiley & Sons Ltd.

Anna at the discotheque and later that evening going to Anna's home for drinks. He said he could not recall much of what had taken place at Anna's flat.

When confronted with Anna's allegation, David soon admitted taking the purse but claimed not to recall actually taking it or knowing what had happened to it. Nevertheless, he accepted that he must have taken it and wanted to settle the matter as soon as possible.

David was full of apology and remorse and wanted to make amends for the 'theft'. He explained that he was prone to alcohol blackouts after heavy drinking, which in those days typically consisted of Icelandic 'Brennivín': a strong spirit commonly referred to as 'black death'. Until the 1980s the importation and brewing of beer was prohibited and people typically drank spirit. As a result of his memory blackouts after drinking he had developed a distrust of his memory and accepted responsibility for his 'crime'. 'An open and shut case' I initially thought. How wrong I was. David had made a false admission to a crime that had never taken place. Fortunately for David and justice, Anna found the purse with its full contents; it had never been stolen in the first place. I was flabbergasted. I had unwittingly elicited a false admission which could have resulted in a wrongful conviction. Why did I not see this coming? Why had I not asked Anna whether she had carefully checked that the purse was nowhere in the flat? I had wrongly assumed David's guilt and sought to extract a confession, a painful reminder that I had to be more careful and open-minded in the future when interviewing complainants and suspects. At the time, I had never come across a case of a false confession and knew nothing about it. This case influenced my thinking about the role of memory distrust in cases of false confession, which is discussed in this book.

All three participants had acted in good faith. Anna genuinely thought that David had stolen the purse and reported it to the police as the duty of a responsible citizen. I had in good faith uncritically accepted Anna's assumption of David's guilt. David being prone to alcohol blackouts and bad behaviour when intoxicated, accepted responsibility and wanted to make amends.

Many miscarriages of justice start off with the good intentions of police investigators (e.g. genuinely wanting to solve the case), which become misguided once 'tunnel vision' and 'confirmation bias' set in. Indeed, 'the road to hell is paved with good intentions', with unforeseen lasting consequences for victims and suspects and their families and often leaving ruined lives behind. This has been the most difficult part of my work to experience as a forensic psychologist. The human suffering in cases of miscarriages of justice is grossly underestimated and under researched.

In the summer of 1976 I was back as a detective in the Reykjavík Criminal Investigation Police and this was to be one of the most remarkable periods in my life. It was packed with challenges and adventures that shaped my path as a future forensic psychologist and Professor of Forensic Psychology at King's College London. My professional career, whether in terms of research or clinical/forensic practice, continued to be stimulated and guided by real-life forensic cases over the next 40 years. It demonstrated over and over again the lessons that practitioners and academics can learn from case studies and by conducting empirical research.

My mission was set in stone in 1980, soon after I took up a post as a lecturer in psychology at the Institute of Psychiatry and became an honorary clinical psychologist at the Maudsley and Bethlem Royal Hospitals: *the development of forensic psychology as a scientific discipline*. The specific field of expertise I particularly wanted to develop related to understanding better the impact of custody and different police interrogation techniques on the reliability of confession evidence, pertinent psychological vulnerabilities of witnesses and suspects, and false confessions.

## A BRIEF REVIEW OF MY CASES ON DISPUTED CONFESSIONS (1980–2016)

I received my first referral of a case involving a disputed confession in 1980, and until the mid-1980s many such cases were referred to me by psychiatrist colleagues, who themselves had been instructed by lawyers. Up to 1986 I had only worked on 16 disputed confession cases, but from 1986 onward the number of referrals from solicitors grew exponentially following the implementation of the Police and Criminal Evidence Act (PACE; Home Office, 1985) in January 1986. By now, I had begun to work with Michael Mansfield, one of England's leading defence lawyers, who has described the early expert work on disputed confessions in the following terms:

> During these years there was a gradual recognition and appreciation that there were a multitude of subtle forces at work that might result in a false confession. These forces might not be obvious and could easily be missed by judges, juries and interrogators alike. There were three outstanding experts who pioneered advances and moved the frontiers of understanding, often in [the] face of scepticism, disbelief and even hostility. They were Gisli Gudjonsson, James MacKeith and Olive Tunstall. Together they embraced psychology and psychiatry, with

particular regard for social and educational development. They were able to demonstrate the myriad of different mental, social and educational factors that have a diffuse and subtle effect upon the person being questioned. Even an interview being conducted in seemingly proper conditions, with contemporaneous recording, access to legal advice and the presence of a solicitor or appropriate adult where necessary, could not be guaranteed to produce reliable statements.

(Mansfield, 2009, p. 217)

There was considerable hostility towards me during those early years, expressed by both judges and prosecutors and noted by Michael Mansfield who has commented on my persistence in overcoming the initial judicial resistance (Hildibrandsdóttir, 2001). This made me even more determined to fight for the emerging science of forensic psychology. I had one huge advantage over other experts; I had developed empirical tests of interrogative suggestibility and compliance that seemed of relevance to cases of disputed confessions, accompanied by extensive research endeavour (Gudjonsson, 1997, 2003a, 2003b).

By the end of 2016, I had accepted instructions in 486 cases where confession evidence was disputed. There were a total of 504 individuals involved as in some cases there was more than one person evaluated. Of the individuals evaluated, 441 (87.5%) were male and 63 (12.5%) were female. The mean age was 31.4 (range 11–82 years). The great majority of the referrals were from the UK, followed by the USA, Canada, Ireland, Norway, Iceland, Jersey, the Isle of Man, Israel, and New Zealand. These represent cases where the evidence against the client was based either entirely or substantially on a confession or some self-incriminating admission not amounting to a full confession.

## THE STRUCTURE AND CONTENT OF THE BOOK

This book is in three parts and comprises 18 individual chapters. Part I, 'The emerging science and practice', focuses on the era of early enquiry and development, the impact of real-life cases on legal changes, police practice, and science, and the key theories and empirical studies that have shaped the current thinking about false confessions. It provides the scientific foundation for Parts II and III, where the knowledge is applied to two real-life cases.

The early conceptualization of Hugo Münsterberg (1908) laid the foundation for understanding different types of false confession, but further tangible theoretical developments did not take place until the 1980s. However, in the 1970s two miscarriage of justice cases, one in the USA and another in the UK, set the scene for better understanding the vulnerabilities of young people when manipulated by the police to extract a confession, which in both cases turned out to be false.

These were the cases of 18-year-old Peter Reilly (Barthel, 1976; Connery, 1977), and three innocent young persons in London who were convicted of murdering Maxwell Confait and later exonerated (Irving & McKenzie, 1989; Price & Caplan, 1977), leading to the setting up of the Royal Commission on Criminal Procedure and followed by the implementation of PACE in January 1986 (Gudjonsson, 2003a).

The Reilly case was discussed by Kassin and Wrightsman (1985) in their influential chapter on the threefold psychological classification of false confessions ('voluntary', 'coerced-compliant', and 'coerced-internalized'). It was an excellent illustration of a coerced-internalized false confession, a model for the analysis of similar future cases.

After allegedly failing a polygraph test and being subsequently interrogated, Reilly was persuaded that he had murdered his mother, of which he was innocent, using words like: 'Maybe I did do it', 'I believe I did it', 'It really looks like I did it', and then saying 'Yes' when asked directly, 'You did it?'. Reilly then signed his written confession statement (Connery, 1977, pp. 65–67; Gudjonsson, 2003a). What is apparent is that Reilly had become confused by the result of the 'failed' polygraph test and intensive interrogation, believing that he might have murdered his mother, but he always remained unsure (i.e. he was never completely confident that he had murdered his mother; in fact, he harboured serious doubts about it).

Reilly's wording has turned out to be a 'red flag' for identifying internalized false confessions. I have repeatedly come across similar expressions in other cases and it fits well with our early conceptual framework of 'memory distrust syndrome' (Gudjonsson & MacKeith, 1982) and the more recent development of a heuristic model of internalized false confessions, which will be discussed in detail in this book with case illustrations.

Importantly:

> Whatever the appalling deficiencies of Peter's interrogation, it was at least recorded on tape. Indeed, it might be said that one of the factors leading to Peter Reilly's eventual vindication was the audiotape made during his ruthless grilling; it clearly revealed the browbeating methods of coercion used upon an exhausted boy, and helped many people make up their minds about the police and their subtle brutality.
> (Styron, 1996, p. xvi)

The above quote highlights something I have repeatedly seen during my 40-year career as a clinical psychologist. It shows the importance of electronic recording of the entire interrogation. Without it, investigators will almost certainly deny any coercion or wrongdoing and get away with it. There is general reluctance among judiciaries internationally to criticize the police or their methods. In contrast, defendants' allegations of threats or inducements are typically viewed as 'self-serving' and not to be believed. There is a need for a greater balance of attitudes and fairness, which would be facilitated by the mandatory audio and video recording of interrogations in their entirety (Kassin et al., 2010a, 2010b), although alone it will not be sufficient to eradicate false confessions from the interrogation room (Lassiter, Ware, Lindberg, & Ratcliffe, 2010).

In the 1980s the main obstacle to preventing and correcting miscarriages of justice involving confession evidence was that people found it hard to believe that anyone would confess to a serious crime of which they were innocent (Gudjonsson, 2003a). That misguided attitude changed considerably after the acquittal of the 'Guildford Four' in October 1989 (Ewing & McCann, 2006; Gudjonsson & MacKeith, 2003), a case that opened the gate to other miscarriage of justice cases involving disputed confessions in the UK (Gudjonsson, 2010a). The case represented a long and hard battle (Kee, 1989; McKee & Franey, 1988), but justice prevailed in the end (Victory, 2001). Persistence does pay. I am pleased to have had the opportunity of playing a part in that landmark victory.

A part of the early battle was to change negative attitudes and misconceptions by educating police officers, lawyers, and judges about the growing evidence base of false confessions and the need for improved police interview training and practice (Gudjonsson, 1992a, 2003a). The science of the psychology of false confession emerged in the 1980s and 1990s and has continued to develop over time. It has paid dividends in the form of changing the legal landscape in the UK and Norway, but other countries have been slower to respond (Walsh, Oxburgh, Redlich, & Myklebust, 2016).

A solid theoretical foundation, supported by empirical evidence and case studies, helps us understand the underlying causes of false confessions and how they may be identified, researched, and prevented. This book shows the scientific advances that have been made over the past 40 years.

## THE GUDMUNDUR AND GEIRFINNUR CASES

In Part II, I discuss in detail how political and societal pressures, combined with seriously flawed and misguided investigation, resulted in the convictions of six young people who had confessed to knowledge or involvement in the disappearances of two men: Gudmundur Einarsson (age 18) and Geirfinnur Einarsson (age 34), on 27 January and 19 November 1974, respectively. These cases involved the largest murder enquiry in Iceland's history and a scandal that the judiciary has fought hard to bury.

On 24 February 2017, the Icelandic Court Cases Review Commission, which I refer to in this book as the 'Commission', concluded that there were strong grounds for appeal with respect to the manslaughter convictions and referred the cases back to the Supreme Court for consideration. I discuss in detail the Commission's conclusions and 40 years of struggle for justice to begin to prevail.

In Part III, I provide a detailed psychological analysis of the confessions of each of the six convicted persons: Saevar Ciesielski, Erla Bolladóttir, Kristján Vidarsson, Tryggvi Leifsson, Gudjón Skarphédinsson, and Albert Skaftason. I will show that five of these young persons suffered from memory distrust syndrome as a result of their frequent, lengthy, and intense interrogations. The impact on their memory was profound and with regard to one of the men, it was permanent and continues to impair his quality of life.

These cases represent the most extreme custodial confinement and interrogation I have come across in my 40-year psychology career. It happened in a country with remarkably advanced police codes of practice at the time and an extremely low homicide rate (Gudjonsson & Petursson, 1982). So what went so drastically wrong? This book will tell the story and it will be an invaluable lesson to criminal justice systems worldwide.

In the summer of 1976, when the Gudmundur and Geirfinnur investigations were at their peak, I was a detective in Reykjavík. I soon discovered the 'tunnel vision' and guilt-presumptive attitude of the investigators and prosecutor. Thirty-six years later I was brought back to Iceland to assist with a review of the cases and discovered that the convicted persons had not stood a chance in 1975–1977, such was the ferocity of the methods used to break down their resistance and attempt to harmonize the confessions so that they could be convicted. As a result, five of the convicted persons made massive 'source monitoring' errors in their statements that led to memory illusions and false confessions. Rather than unburdening the Icelandic nation of a nightmare, the investigators and judiciary had created a nightmare that still has not ended.

This book represents my personal account of how cases I came across while working as a detective in Iceland in the 1970s influenced my psychology career and research endeavours. In turn, my professional expertise in the area of false confessions later proved invaluable in helping me almost 40 years later to demonstrate the injustices that had occurred to the six young people, whose lives and those of their families have been severely adversely affected. In the case of Saevar Ciesielski it destroyed him. This has been a remarkable journey for me and I tell it through the development of the science of the psychology of false confession.

# Part I

# The Emerging Science and Practice

# 1

# An Era of Enquiry and Development

I was born in Reykjavík in the early hours of 26 October 1947, following my identical twin brother Gudmundur, who had been born an hour earlier. We were constant companions and in our late teens were actively involved in athletics and talked about joining the police. Some of the men we were training with were police officers. We were looking for an exciting and challenging career and the idea of keeping Reykjavík 'safe' appealed to us. Unlike Gudmundur, who spent 40 years as a policeman in Iceland and became a Chief Superintendent in the Office of the National Commissioner of the Icelandic Police, I did not become a career policeman. I had strong cravings to travel abroad and explore different opportunities. Part of the reason was that I wanted to establish my own identity and independence, because throughout our childhood and adolescence we were usually referred to as 'the twins' and I did not like it. In addition, I had developed a thirst to learn and went to study in England. The intention was always to bring back that knowledge to Iceland. I loved my country of origin and still do.

At first, I was aiming for a career in commerce, being influenced by my grandfather and father who had both been businessmen. In 1971 I began to study economics at Brunel University. I had the opportunity of attending some classes in psychology and law, which I found more interesting than economics. I developed a keen interest in the observation, understanding, and measurement of behaviour and changed to psychology while in my second year.

*The Psychology of False Confessions: Forty Years of Science and Practice*, First Edition.
Gisli H. Gudjonsson.
© 2018 John Wiley & Sons Ltd. Published 2018 by John Wiley & Sons Ltd.

The four-year sandwich degree course at Brunel University, which was conveniently situated for Heathrow Airport with direct flights to and from Iceland, enabled me to combine my academic studies with practical placements relevant to psychology and law, each one of six month's duration. These included my working as a deputy warden in a young offenders' hostel in Bristol (1972), a uniformed police constable with the Reykjavík Police Department (1973), and a counsellor with the Reykjavík Social Services Department (1974). I then worked as a detective with the Reykjavík Criminal Investigation Police during the summers of 1975 and 1976. These 'work placements' were instrumental in my wanting to become a forensic psychologist and in developing a keen and lasting interest in the psychological processes and factors relevant to offending, police interviewing, and false confessions.

I was particularly interested in understanding offending behaviour and this formed a part of my BSc dissertation (Gudjonsson, 1975, 1982). My study was conducted in Iceland and 30 years later my dissertation became influential in a public enquiry into alleged abuse in a care home for behaviourally disturbed youngsters, called 'Breidavík' (Spano, Sigurdsson, & Gudjonsson, 2016). In 1975, my findings had raised serious concerns about the persistent offending of the majority of the 72 boys from Reykjavík who had been placed in Breidavík in the period 1953 to 1970. Undoubtedly, largely due to the negative findings from my study, which the Social Services kept confidential, Breidavík was closed down permanently (see Chapter 13). One of the participants in my study was Saevar Ciesielski, the alleged main perpetrator in connection with the disappearances of Gudmundur Einarsson and Geirfinnur Einarsson in 1974.

After graduating in social sciences (psychology major) in 1975 with a first class honours degree, I was offered a place to study criminology at the Institute of Criminology (University of Cambridge), which interested me greatly, but I made the pragmatic decision that a better career plan was to enrol in an MSc clinical psychology training programme. After attending an interview, I was offered a place at the University of Surrey, which I accepted. This was based on my belief at the time, and confirmed by my later experience, that clinical training is the best foundation for the practice of forensic psychology (Gudjonsson & Young, 2015). The late Professor Lionel Haward, the father of forensic psychology in Britain (Haward, 1981), was the head of the clinical psychology course at the University of Surrey and he further inspired my interest in forensic psychology. This led to his supervising my PhD on lie detection and to our writing a book together about the development and practice of forensic psychology (Gudjonsson & Haward, 1998). My clinical training involved applying psychological principles and theory to a range of clinical problems.

I collected data for my MSc dissertation in clinical psychology while working as a detective in Reykjavík during the summer of 1976. At the time, the Gudmundur and Geirfinnur investigation, which was briefly outlined in the Introduction and will be discussed in detail in Part II of this book, was at its peak and four of the suspects in the cases participated in my research into lie detection. In addition, at the request of the police, I conducted a 'real-life' lie detection test on Gudjón Skarphédinsson on 31 December 1976, who had seven weeks previously become a suspect in the disappearance and alleged murder of Geirfinnur (see Chapter 17 and Gudjonsson, 2017).

## MY EARLY RESEARCH ON LIE DETECTION

In September 1975, after returning to England from my work as a detective in Reykjavík, I commenced clinical training at the University of Surrey. Soon I had to find a research project which would meet the course's criteria but could be conducted in Iceland during the summer of 1976 where I was going to work full-time as a detective to fund my studies, as I had done the previous summer. Then on 14 December 1975, I read an article in the *Sunday Times* about the work Alan Smith had been conducting on 'lie detection' in the UK. Alan was based at Powick Hospital, where he had begun work in September 1971 (Smith, 2011). In December 1972 Alan had gone to Washington on a five-day training course on lie detection using the 'Psychological Stress Evaluator' (PSE), a machine developed by three former US Army intelligence officers. According to Alan:

> They had expertise in polygraph lie detection and in electronics, and wished to produce a better type of lie detector. By analysing the voice, the whole process would be recorded for analysis (together with any confessions) and there might even be occasions when it could be done covertly ... over the phone.... The original [PSE] version used a multi-speed reel-to-reel tape machine to record the interview, which was fed into PSE equipment.... The operator played each of the subject's replies at slow speed into the PSE, which used a heat pen on a rolling paper strip to draw a voice chart. This showed the voice electronically in terms of its fundamental frequency activity, and the aim was to detect a microtremor in the voice.... A stressed voice will therefore cease to show any modulation, and the PSE chart will show straight or square patterns.
>
> (Smith, 2011, p. 56)

The *Sunday Times* article demonstrated the use of the PSE as a lie detector in the case of a man called George Davis, who had been convicted of robbery at the Ilford branch of the London Electricity

Board in April 1974, and there was at the time a big campaign to clear his name after his appeal failed in December 1975 (Smith, 2011). The *Sunday Times* headline was 'Lie detector okays George Davis alibi'.

On 8 April 1976 Alan gave a 10-minute speech in the House of Commons about the results from the George Davis case. One of those attending the presentation was Michael Heseltine, a Member of Parliament, who later became the Secretary of State for the Environment. In May 1976, the Home Secretary Roy Jenkins exercised his royal prerogative of mercy and freed Mr Davis because of serious doubts concerning his conviction.

The work Alan was doing with the PSE was getting a lot of attention in the UK. He was contacted by the solicitors of both Peter Hain, who spent 11 hours in police detention on 24 October 1975 being wrongly accused of snatching money from a cashier at Barclays Bank in Putney (Hain, 2012), and John Stonehouse, a British politician, who in 1974 had unsuccessfully faked his own death. In neither case did Alan think it was appropriate to use his new PSE machine to assist with their cases. In the case of Stonehouse:

> His solicitor rang me and asked if I could help, but I couldn't see how lie detection could be applied even if you believed that it worked. It seemed that Mr Stonehouse was more or less willing to admit that he had behaved in various illegal ways, but he wished to demonstrate that his motivations were good and honest ones. I excused myself on the grounds that this is technically not feasible.
>
> (Smith, 2011, p. 71)

What is important from Alan Smith's experience with the PSE is the public's naive belief about the accuracy of lie detectors and how they are seen as the ultimate tool for determining the veracity of suspects' accounts. At the time, a similar misconception also centred on the use of 'truth drugs' to elicit the truth in criminal cases, a procedure that has been demonstrated to have no validity (Gudjonsson, 1992a; Gudjonsson, Kopelman, & MacKeith, 1999).

While having Christmas with my parents and brother in Iceland in 1975, I kept thinking about the *Sunday Times* article and was mulling over the possibility of doing research into lie detection. 'Surely this could be conducted in Iceland', I kept telling myself. 'What about testing whether offenders are better at beating the lie detector than clergymen?' These are two extreme groups and I reasoned at the time that clergymen with their religious beliefs and strong moral sense would find it difficult to beat the machine, whereas offenders, who are used to lying, might have weaker consciences. This kind of experiment had never been published before and I thought it was innovative and might throw up interesting findings, which it did!

Unknown to me at the time, during my Christmas vacation in Iceland in 1975, Saevar Ciesielski and Erla Bolladóttir were being interrogated by the police in connection with Post and Telecommunication fraud and became implicated in the Gudmundur and Geirfinnur cases, and three further suspects, Kristján Vidarsson, Tryggvi Leifsson, and Albert Skaftason, had now been arrested and were beginning their lengthy solitary confinement prior to trial; their nightmare was beginning. I did not know that the following summer most of them would be participating in my research.

Upon returning to university in England after the Christmas vacation, I wrote to Alan Smith to ask him about training courses in the UK on lie detection. I was keen to be properly trained in the use of the polygraph before I conducted my MSc research project. Alan replied to my letter on 15 January 1976:

> In reply to your questions, I do not know of any training courses in the UK. There is at least one private investigation business which uses lie detectors, but they do not welcome enquiries. Nor do I know of any police facilities of this kind. The USA would be the place to go for specific training.

## My MSc Dissertation

I took up Alan's offer to visit him to see his PSE machine. He impressed me by his skill and enthusiasm; here was a real scientist at work, I thought. I did not know that a year after his letter to me, he would be analysing the microtremor in Gudjón Skarphédinsson's voice when asked questions about the disappearance of Geirfinnur Einarsson (see Chapter 17).

I was disappointed that there were no training courses on lie detection available in the UK. I enquired about courses in the USA but these were time consuming and costly. In addition, the most widely used polygraph at the time was the Lafayette, a portable machine which measured blood pressure, respiration, and galvanic skin response (GSR) (Reid & Inbau, 1977), and it was too costly for me to purchase. I settled for a compromise with regard to my MSc dissertation: no training course and a simple meter measuring the GSR. This obviously limited the type of experiment I could conduct and the generalizability of the findings to real-life cases. I knew that research could not involve asking people about their crime. It would need to involve either a 'mock crime', where half of the participants are asked to commit a designated 'crime' and then try to conceal it during a lie detection procedure, or card tests (participants pick a numbered card out of a pack, note what is written on it, and then deny that they know it for each card in turn).

Conducting a 'mock crime' experiment was impractical because most of the offenders were in custody, so I decided on simple card tasks.

The participants were to be asked to 'lie' about a card they had picked and their date of birth. My research was accepted at the University of Surrey and was supervised by Dr Jeremy Thorpe, Epsom District Hospital, and Dr Sandra Canter from the University of Surrey. Neither supervisor was an expert on lie detection, but they turned out to be helpful supervisors. After submission, the examiners concluded:

> This piece of work has been well organized and is well reasoned and presented. It could be regarded as an adequate pilot study, having both theoretical interest (e.g. for Eysenck's theory of the biological bases of personality and Davis's conditioned response theory) and possibly some practical implication in the light of Peter Hain's recent ordeal by identification parade.

The supervisors' reference to the Peter Hain case is particularly interesting both in terms of the date and his cognitive processes while in police custody. Hain had spent his childhood in South Africa and was an anti-apartheid activist who went on to become a British Cabinet Minister and served 12 years in the Labour government. In his autobiography (Hain, 2012), Hain describes spending 11 hours in police detention on 24 October 1975, being accused of snatching a bundle of five pound notes from a cashier at Barclays Bank in Putney, London. After the guilt-presumptive interrogation, he was locked up in a cell for the rest of the day during which time 'a confusing swirl of thoughts increasingly mesmerised me as the long hours dragged by, nothing happening, no explanations, nobody to speak to' (p. 97). He went on:

> I began to wonder whether perhaps I had done it. Perhaps I was a bank robber? For a moment I considered the possibility that I had 'flipped' – but then what had I done with the money I was supposed to have stolen?
>                                                      (Hain, 2012, pp. 97–98)

Hain's case, which involved a high profile Old Bailey trial in 1976 where he was acquitted of the robbery, illustrates the vulnerabilities to 'memory distrust' during presumptive questioning and solitary confinement, which is a powerful factor in making a false confession (Gudjonsson & MacKeith, 1982).

The main aim of my MSc study was to investigate to what extent responsivity to lie detection on card tasks (i.e. failure to lie successfully regarding a number picked prior to the procedure and the denial of the participant's month of birth) was related to personality factors and whether offenders would respond differently to other groups of citizens.

The hypothesis was that offenders would prove 'better liars' than policemen or clergymen. This was the first study to compare the responses of these three groups of participants. I measured skin resistance to a mild electric current during the administration of the card tasks and measured the change from baseline when the participants were denying each card in turn. The tasks were as follows:

*Number task.* The participant was asked to pick one card from a pile, write down the number he/she had picked, and while wired up to the machine deny each number presented to them in a random order: 'Did you pick number ...?' The numbers used in the experiment (3, 5, 7, 10, 11, 14, and 16) were presented twice in order to eliminate order effects and so increase the validity of the findings. A textbook on interrogation methods by Reid and Inbau (1977) had recommended the use of this test with suspects prior to the administration of the formal lie detector test, to demonstrate the effectiveness of the machine in detecting their lies.

*Month of birth task.* The participant chose a card representing his/her month of birth from cards of all months of the year. Six cards were subsequently put aside and the participant was required to place the chosen card with the remaining cards, leaving a total of seven cards as in the number task. The participant was asked, 'Were you born in ...?'.

*Word task.* The participant had to pick out a card from a list of words: table, house, candle, light, paper, chair, and bag. The procedure was the same as for the number task.

For the purpose of the experiment I had purchased an Omega 2 Meter in a nice mahogany case, which cost £69 (plus VAT), and was advertised as 'a new versatile skin resistance meter designed to advance existing techniques' and was mainly aimed at therapists using it for biofeedback during therapy; the idea was that as patients became more relaxed during therapy they would show increased skin resistance as measured by a needle moving more slowly across a meter scale (i.e. the change in ohms from the baseline). In contrast, the PSE machine Alan Smith had purchased cost over £1,000 at that time (Smith, 2011).

I was able to recruit four different groups of participants – uniformed police officers; detectives; clergymen; and offenders – 12 in each group. As far as the offenders were concerned, there were eight suspects of murder and four who had allegedly committed serious thefts. All the murder suspects were tested while in custody and four of the suspects in the Gudmundur and Geirfinnur cases were included: Erla Bolladóttir, Tryggvi Leifsson, Kristján Vidarsson, and Saevar Ciesielski. All participants were friendly and cooperative. Each examination lasted for over an hour. Saevar took the longest to complete the test, because he

**Table 1.1**  The efficacy of the machine to detect lies among the participants on the three card tasks

| Group | Number task | Month of birth task | Word task | Total |
|---|---|---|---|---|
| Clergymen | 12 (100%) | 12 (100%) | 10 (83%) | 34 (94%) |
| Uniformed police | 11 (92%) | 12 (100%) | 10 (83%) | 33 (92%) |
| Detectives | 10 (83%) | 10 (83%) | 10 (83%) | 30 (83%) |
| Offenders | 9 (75%) | 10 (83%) | 7 (58%) | 26 (72%) |
| *Total detection* | 42 (87.5%) | 44 (92%) | 37 (77%) | 123 (85%) |

From Gudjonsson (1977).

wanted to share his wisdom about lie detectors and expressed great interest in them. Within a week, I was asked to perform a real-life lie detection test on Saevar, which I suspect was at his instigation (see Chapter 13).

While doing the experiment, some of the prison officers in the Sídumúli [Holding] Prison, where most of the tests on the 'offenders' were conducted, asked whether they could try to beat the machine, and they were much impressed by the machine's ability to 'detect lies'. At the time, the police had virtually taken over the prison as their work base for the Gudmundur and Geirfinnur investigation. My lie detection research was generating a great deal of interest among the police and the prison officers. Almost half of all the detectives in Reykjavík took part in my lie detection experiment.

Table 1.1 gives the results of the efficacy of the machine in detecting lies for the three card tests. The overall detection rate in the experiment was 85%, which impressed me. The word task gave the worst overall results (77%), and the month of birth task the best (92%). With regard to the different groups of participants, rates were 94% for clergymen, 92% for the uniformed police officers, 83% for the detectives, and 72% for the offenders. With such powerful findings it was easy to become overconfident in the effectiveness of lie detectors. However, real-life detection is not as straightforward as these simple card tests might suggest.

## THE *SUNDAY TIMES* EXPERIMENT

The result of the lie detection experiment was published in the *British Journal of Social and Clinical Psychology* (Gudjonsson, 1979) and attracted the attention of Isabel Hilton, a journalist with the *Sunday*

*Times.* As a consequence, in November 1979, almost four years after the publication of the article in the *Sunday Times* of Alan Smith's work with the PSE, I was asked to perform lie detection tests on a number of celebrities in an office of the *Sunday Times*; there was a great deal of background noise and the participants had been offered a hospitality drink beforehand. I was worried that the noise and alcoholic drink might undermine my findings. After all, Isabel Hilton, and Harold Evans the editor of the *Sunday Times*, wanted me to prove that I could detect lying in nine out of ten people as I had claimed in my recent article in the *British Journal of Social and Clinical Psychology*. My level of performance anxiety was high and afterwards I went to a pub myself for a drink, to settle my nerves, where Isabel Hilton proved a calming influence. The people I tested included the celebrity chef and liberal politician Clement Freud, playwright and screenwriter Michael Pertwee, Winston Fletcher, who was a leader in the advertising industry, clergyman Lord Donald Soper, actor Derek Nimmo, and actress Francesca Annis. The results were published in the *Sunday Times* on 25 November 1979 demonstrating the effectiveness of the procedure in detecting lies. I detected lies in four of the participants on both tests, but failed to detect the lies of Derek Nimmo and Francesca Annis on one of the two tests. Francesca Annis beat the machine on the number task and Derek Nimmo the month of birth test. When Isabel Hilton asked me about the failure to detect the lies of Annis and Nimmo, I commented, 'It could mean that in their profession they learn to simulate and control bodily reactions.'

Isabel Hilton and Harold Evans also took the test and both failed to lie successfully. Ms Hilton concluded her article by stating: 'Since I did not lie successfully the reader may assume this story is as true as I can make it.'

Prior to completing the lie detector test, Clement Freud, the grandson of psychoanalyst Sigmund Freud, told me that he had taken several lie detector tests before and had always 'beaten the test' and this occasion was not going to be any different. He was full of confidence and approached the test with fierce competitiveness. Yes, I felt intimidated by his behaviour and celebrity status, but I was determined not to show it and carried out the procedure with confidence and determination. He failed both the number and month of birth tasks. After the procedure, Freud was very quiet and left the room more humbly than he had entered. Perhaps failing the lie detector test made him realize he was not such a good liar after all.

I also tested an even more difficult celebrity, who must remain nameless in view of the fact that he never completed the experiment and did not feature in the article. He was a journalist and broadcaster known for his relaxed bonhomie. However, this was not evident during the experiment. He looked very anxious before and during the procedure and kept sipping his alcoholic hospitality drink. After the number task, he wanted to know the outcome of the test before we proceeded to the month of birth task. I told him he had picked the number 14, which was correct. He then began to accuse me of having been hired by the *Sunday Times* to discredit him. I kept reassuring him that this was not the case but he kept arguing with me. After a while I terminated the experiment and politely showed him out of the room.

About 17 years after the *Sunday Times* lie detection experiment, I was giving evidence in a criminal trial at the Old Bailey. After leaving the witness box and walking out of the courtroom, I was followed by Derek Nimmo, who said, 'Sorry, don't I know you?' He had forgotten that we had met in 1979 but he recognized my appearance and voice and wanted to know where he had encountered me previously. I reminded him of our meeting at the *Sunday Times* experiment and he laughed when I told him that he had not been a perfect liar, having failed to beat the machine on one of the two tests. He said that he knew the trial judge who had invited him to attend court for interest's sake. A few years later I heard that Derek Nimmo had died at the age of 68, a sad loss indeed.

## BRITISH PSYCHOLOGICAL SOCIETY COMMITTEES ON LIE DETECTION

During my clinical training and the early years of my clinical career I was enthusiastic about the use of the polygraph for lie detection purposes and had confidence in its effectiveness. This was to change. Following the Geoffrey Prime spy case in the early 1980s, the UK government announced its intention to undertake pilot studies of the use of polygraph tests for the purpose of security vetting. In the meantime, the British Psychological Society (BPS) set up a committee on the effectiveness of the polygraph, chaired by Professor Anthony Gale. The published report concluded that the use of polygraph tests for lie detection purposes in the context of criminal investigation, security vetting, and personnel selection was problematic and contrary to the spirit of the Society's Code of Conduct (Gale, 1988).

The government review on the polygraph was conducted by Levey (1988), who concluded that:

1. 'Laboratory studies on the polygraph suggest that its accuracy as an instrument of detection is not high enough to meet conventional psychometric standards'. (p. viii)

2. 'The most puzzling feature of the polygraph literature is the discrepancy between the modest accuracy observed in the laboratory and the high levels reported in the field'. (p. viii)
3. 'It is a simplification to assume that real-life detection of misdemeanours is more accurate than laboratory detection of games and play-acting'. (p. 63)

Levey (1988) emphasizes the importance of population differences:

> Gudjonsson (1979), for example, comparing Icelandic clergymen, policemen and offenders found a detection rate of 94 per cent among clergymen, but only 72 per cent among offenders. Reassuringly, the police sample fell significantly closer to the clergymen than to the criminals. The point to be observed is that the experimental literature has tended to neglect serious considerations of its sample population.
>
> (pp. 62–63)

From Levey's comment, it seems that this Icelandic study made a unique contribution to knowledge in terms of highlighting possible, and sometimes expected, population differences. This made me feel that the project had been worthwhile.

In 2004, the BPS commissioned a second committee to review the scientific status and the application of the polygraph, including clinical forensic applications (British Psychological Society, 2004, p. 7). The report's main conclusions were:

1. 'Most published research on polygraph deception detection has been concerned with its possible use in criminal investigations. The results of better quality research studies demonstrate that while the correct classification of deceivers can sometimes be fairly high, incorrect decisions about who is or is not being deceptive occur at rates that are far from negligible'.
2. 'The use of the polygraph in employment and security screening is not justified by the available research evidence'.
3. 'The use of the polygraph in the clinical setting, with specific reference to its use with sex offenders, has received too little research attention'.
4. 'More research is needed on other possible methods to detect deception, honesty and integrity'.
5. 'Over confidence in the ability of any procedure designed to detect deception can have serious consequences, especially if the deceivers are few among many non-deceivers'.

I was a member of both the BPS committees on the use of polygraph for lie detection purposes (Gudjonsson & Young, 2015). I lost some confidence in the value of the polygraph for lie detection in real-life cases in the mid-1980s after reviewing the evidence with the first

BPS committee and I had become concerned about the ways it was sometimes used by American investigators to elicit confessions (Gudjonsson, 1992a). In my early career I testified in an American military case that involved an alleged offence in the UK, in which a serviceman had confessed to the murder of his friend after failing a polygraph test (Gudjonsson & Lebegue, 1989). It had the hallmarks of a false confession (i.e. presumption of guilt by his interrogators and persuasive interviewing; very poor recollection of the event by the suspect; grief over losing a close friend; and my testing showed him to be highly suggestible and compliant). I testified and the serviceman was acquitted. Similar abuse of the use of the polygraph to extract confessions has been reported in other American cases (Kassin, 2007).

## ONWARD AND UPWARD

After completing my clinical training in September 1977, I was appointed as a 'basic grade' clinical psychologist at Epsom District Hospital in Surrey. By then I was in a serious relationship with Julia, who was at the time the head of art therapy at Netherne Hospital in Hooley. We married in February 1979 and Julia has always been whole-heartedly supportive of my work. We had met in October 1976 while I was on a clinical placement at Netherne Hospital and we soon began courting. Julia was a single mother with two adorable daughters from a previous marriage, Rowena and Rhiannon, aged 7 and 6 years, respectively, who like their mother were intellectually gifted with a loving nature. Our relationship changed my plan to return to Iceland after my clinical training. In fact, after the exciting and challenging summer of 1976 as a detective, I had considered going back to the Reykjavík Criminal Investigation Police after completing my studies in England. I had enjoyed my time as a detective immensely and liked the police officers with whom I had worked.

I worked in Epsom for just over two years. In January 1980, I was appointed to a lecturership in psychology at the Institute of Psychiatry, which at the time was a part of the University of London, but later merged with King's College London. I had an honorary contract to provide a clinical forensic service at the Maudsley and Bethlem Royal Hospitals. In the autumn of 1980, I was appointed to the newly established medium secure unit at the Bethlem Royal Hospital in Beckenham, where I became the head of the clinical/forensic psychology services and remained there for 32 years. In 2000 I was promoted to a professor of forensic psychology at King's College London.

It was during my early clinical career that I was able to apply psychological theory to a range of forensic cases, including psychogenic amnesia, blood injury phobia, suggestibility in a police interview, and disputed confessions (Gudjonsson, 1992a). My interest in suggestibility, and its concept as an individual differences variable, arose in 1980 from my involvement as an expert witness for the prosecution in a case of an intellectually disabled woman who had been the victim of a gang rape (Gudjonsson & Gunn, 1982). At the time I was aware of Loftus's (1979) experimental work into memory and suggestibility, but I found no test of suggestibility that could be applied to the performance of victims, witnesses, and suspects during police questioning and during cross examination in court. In early 1982 I decided to develop such a test, the Gudjonsson Suggestibility Scale (GSS 1), which in 1987 was followed by the parallel version (GSS 2) and in 1989 by the Gudjonsson Compliance Scale. The validation of the GSS was mainly conducted in the 1980s and 1990s, accompanying a detailed model of interrogative suggestibility, published in 1986 (Gudjonsson & Clark, 1986), which unlike Loftus's experimental work focused on the role and measurement of individual differences in suggestibility.

Extensive research has been conducted into the Scales and their application (Gudjonsson, 1983, 1984a, 1989a, 1992a, 1997, 2003a, 2010b, 2013, 2014; Gudjonsson, Vagni, Maiorano, & Pajardi, 2016). There have been two rigorous independent reviews of the Scales. The first review was completed by Grisso (1986) about the early development of the GSS 1, which led to the development of the GSS 2, and a more recent review in Buros's *Mental Measurement Yearbook* (Janoson & Frumkin, 2007).

The idea of constructing the GSS 1 came to me in early 1982 (see Chapter 3). I wanted to develop an experimental test, like a mini-interrogation, which was subtle and with which people would not know that their susceptibility to suggestion was being measured. I was familiar with the Wechsler Memory Scales and thought that a similar narrative to that used to measure immediate and delayed recall would provide the foundation for the Scale. It had to measure the two basic components of 'interrogative suggestibility', the susceptibility to give in to leading questions, labelled 'Yield', and giving in to interrogative pressure, labelled 'Shift'. I completed the construction of the Scale one Sunday afternoon and the following week I tested it out on a few of my colleagues and found that it worked exactly as I had hoped. I then collected empirical data on the Scale.

The scales have been translated into many different languages and are used internationally for research and forensic purposes. They measure vulnerabilities to being misled during questioning and cross-examination and not false confessions directly. They typically form one important part of the forensic evaluation in cases of disputed confessions (DeClue, 2005; Frumkin, 2016; Frumkin, Lally, & Sexton, 2012; Gudjonsson, 2003a).

My interest in false confessions commenced while serving as a detective with the Reykjavík Criminal Investigation Police. As discussed in the Introduction to this book, the year of 1975 was a turning point when I became aware of the risk of false confession. A few years later, while working at the Institute of Psychiatry in London, I met a forensic psychiatrist, James ('Jim') MacKeith, who described a couple of cases where similar memory distrust had occurred during interrogation at English police stations. We decided to present our findings at The Stockholm Symposium on Witness Psychology, which was organized by Professor Arne Trankell between 16 and 19 September 1981. The title of our presentation was 'False admission, psychological effects of interrogation. Ethical, clinical and research implications. A discussion paper'.

Many eminent scientists attended this conference including Ray Bull, Graham Davies, Helen Dent, Lionel Haward, Astrid Holgerson, Elizabeth Loftus, David Raskin, Max Steller, Udo Undeutsch, and Daniel Yarmey. This was one of the first conferences to bring together researchers from several countries working on the psychological aspects of witness testimony.

Jim and I introduced the term 'memory distrust syndrome' as a general description of the phenomenon (Gudjonsson & MacKeith, 1982), which subsequently became embedded in the scientific literature as a valid and useful concept (e.g. Schacter, 2007; Van Bergen, 2011; Van Bergen, Jelicic, & Merckelbach, 2008, 2009). The High Court's acceptance of memory distrust syndrome as a valid descriptive concept in cases of disputed confessions is found in the case of Andrew Evans in England and Birgitte Tengs in Norway (Gudjonsson, 2003a).

## CONCLUSIONS

My interest in the psychology of false confessions dates back to my work as a detective with the Reykjavík police. I was lucky that in the early 1970s the Reykjavík Uniformed Police and the Criminal Investigation Police had begun to employ teachers and university students as policemen during the summer vacation (Jónsson & Gudjónsson, [Gudmundur] 1997). There is no doubt that working as a uniformed police officer and then as a detective shaped my future professional career and provided me with an insight into human behaviour and legal processes that proved invaluable in my work as a forensic psychologist.

According to Blackburn (1996), Lionel Haward 'pioneered the application of psychology to legal questions in this country [the UK]' (p. 7) and this was the position I started from in the early 1980s. The court cases I worked on often raised issues that led to research questions. I wanted answers and conducted the relevant research, which then generated a scientific knowledge base that could be used to apply psychology to other relevant legal issues. The focus was primarily on identifying psychological vulnerabilities associated with the outcome of police interviews, as well as understanding the impact of custody and certain interview techniques on the reliability of confessions. I soon discovered that science and practice were closely intertwined. Observations from cases can lead to the development of a theory, which can then be empirically tested and hopefully provide a better understanding of a particular phenomenon, such as risk factors relevant to false confession. Scientific principles can assist with the development of psychological tests that can be used in forensic practice. Although such developments are rare, they do happen and can impact hugely on practice (Gudjonsson, 2003a). Blackburn (1996) identified the development of the GSS 1 and GSS 2 as an exceptional contribution to forensic psychology.

In the 1970s and 1980s the admissibility of expert psychiatric and psychological evidence was restrictive, because following the judgement in the case of *Regina v. Turner* in 1975 there had to be evidence of the defendant's mental illness in order for expert evidence to be admitted in court. The reasoning was that 'Jurors do not need psychiatrists to tell them how ordinary folks who are not mentally ill are likely to react to the stresses and strains of life' (Fitzgerald, 1987).

According to Fitzgerald (1987), the evidence of psychologists was particularly problematic because they were typically focusing on cognitive processes, emotional reactions, and mental development of people who did not have a mental disorder. Fitzgerald concluded:

> It is, therefore, important that lawyers and psychologists begin the process of challenging the approach to psychologists' testimony which sees the science of psychology as merely a subdivision of psychiatry in order to change it to one which insists instead on the expertise of psychologists being valid for the interpretation of the mental processes and experiences of all human beings to judges and juries. Otherwise, the courtrooms will continue to be deprived of the whole area of scientific expertise which can make a valuable contribution to the determination of the issues of such aspects as reliability and suggestibility.
>
> (p. 44)

# 2

# The Impact of Real-Life Cases on Legal Changes, Police Practice, and Science

*Perjury is a double-edged sword. It boxes witnesses in to a story that, once given, leads to fear of prosecution and makes retraction unlikely*[1]

Nowhere in the world have cases of miscarriage of justice involving confession evidence impacted on legal changes, police practice, and science more than in the UK. This is largely due to the receptiveness of the English legal system to cases of miscarriage of justice and the willingness to learn lessons from the cases in order to improve legal practice, fairness, and justice. I am pleased to have had the opportunity of being a part of that important and exciting process.

In this chapter, I briefly review the six key early cases that influenced the law, legal practice, police practice, science, and the attitude of the judiciary towards the admissibility and receptiveness ('weight') of expert psychological evidence. These are the 'Confait' case, the 'Guildford Four', the 'Birmingham Six', the 'Tottenham Three' (i.e. the defence submission in the case of Engin Raghip), the case of Judith Ward, and the 'Cardiff Three' (i.e. the interviewing and confessions of Stephen Miller). A consequence of these cases was a change in the way suspects were interviewed by the police and that expert psychological evidence began to be accepted as a serious discipline.

---

[1] Sekar (2012) with reference to the acquittal of the 'Cardiff Three' and the subsequent collapsed corruption trial (p. 189).

*The Psychology of False Confessions: Forty Years of Science and Practice*, First Edition.
Gisli H. Gudjonsson.
© 2018 John Wiley & Sons Ltd. Published 2018 by John Wiley & Sons Ltd.

I also present a brief overview of the PEACE Model of interviewing (PEACE is an acronym for Preparation and planning, Engage and explain, Account, Closure, and Evaluation), which was implemented in 1993 following cases of miscarriage of justice and evidence of poor interview performance (Williamson, 1994, 2006, 2007).

## THE CONFAIT CASE

The basic facts in the Confait case are as follows (Irving & McKenzie, 1989; Price & Caplan, 1977; Williamson, 2007). Three boys, Colin Lattimore (18), Ronald Leighton (15), and Ahmet Salih (14) had been arrested within two days of the murder of Maxwell Confait (26) on 22 April 1972. Within two and a half hours of their arrest and detention, the three boys had made a confession. Lattimore had a significant intellectual disability, was illiterate and suggestible, and had attended three special schools; Leighton was of borderline intelligence and had attended a school for behaviourally disturbed boys; and Salih was of a Turkish Cypriot background and spoke English as a second language. All three boys were convicted on 24 November 1972 on the basis of their confessions alone (Irving & McKenzie, 1989). Their convictions were quashed three years later.

According to Williamson (2007):

> Exceptionally for Court of Appeal acquittals at the time, a government inquiry was conducted by a retired judge, the Hon. Sir Henry Fisher, who published his report in December 1977. In his findings Fisher was at pains to point out that the youths had not been physically assaulted by the police and that no police officer had deliberately falsified the record of oral answers given by the three youths to questions. All three youths gave evidence to the inquiry, and Fisher was concerned that they had personal characteristics which rendered them vulnerable during police questioning.
>
> (p. 71)

This case was important to the development of science and practice in relation to confession evidence. Barrie Irving, a social psychologist, attended the enquiry and gave evidence about the mental and social processes that might impact on the reliability of confessions (Williamson, 2007). As a social psychologist, Irving was particularly interested in the inherent coercion of the custodial environment and how this impacted on the suspect's decision-making. Fisher rejected Irving's proposed explanations for the confessions in terms of custodial coercion and chose to focus on their vulnerabilities and the absence of a solicitor in relation to all three boys, and the failure to interview two of the younger boys in the presence of their parents. Of course, Irving had not assessed the three wrongfully convicted persons himself, but he nevertheless had a good insight into their vulnerabilities to the custodial interrogation and giving false confessions. His detailed analysis of the case is as follows (Irving & McKenzie, 1989):

- Lattimore's confession was successfully used to extract confessions from Leighton and then Salih. In psychological terms, Lattimore was the most intellectually impaired and suggestible. Within two and a half hours of their detention on 24 April 1972 all three had made verbal confessions, which were then written down. The written confessions were detailed and consistent across the three boys suggesting contamination: 'Was it because interviewing officers in fact went backwards and forwards between suspects, even talking among themselves in the hearing of the suspects?' (pp. 221–222)
- Irving and McKenzie noted that false confessions can be extracted after a very short time in police custody and during reasonably short police interviews.
- The absence of proper custody records and the lack of electronic, verbatim, or contemporaneous recording made it impossible to produce anything 'but hypothetical reconstructions of what might have happened to produce false confessions in this case' (p. 222).
- After giving their confessions, all three boys subsequently reiterated their confessions in front of their parents in the presence of the police.
- The interrogator admitted using some leading questions but 'insisted that vital substantive detail in the confessions was spontaneous. They were referring in particular to details of the supposed murder weapon (a length of electric flex) and other details about the murder scene' (p. 223). This allegedly implied 'special knowledge', implying guilt.
- The police had suggested that the boys could go home after their interviews.

   'At the inquiry the case for the boys having made false confessions was not based on the overt use of interrogation tactics but on their vulnerability to the ordinary run of custodial interrogation. The tactics issue was obscured by the absence of paper records.' (Irving & McKenzie, 1989, p. 223)

Lord Fisher made one serious mistake in his conclusions, which is very common in cases of miscarriages of justice. He assumed that the boys' incriminating details of the crime (i.e. 'special knowledge') had originated from them, implying their guilt on the balance of probabilities, rather than the police, and hence his suggestion that one or more of the youngsters had been involved in Confait's death. It was this alleged special knowledge which most incriminated the three boys and undoubtedly led to their convictions. That special knowledge most probably originated from the police, but the police will hardly ever admit to such transmission of knowledge (known as 'contamination'). Typically, police and prosecutors will argue in court that the special knowledge could only have come from the suspect (Garrett, 2011; Gudjonsson, 2003a). The advent of electronic recording of all police interviews in a case helps to prevent such contamination and provides a record of it, when it occurs (Kassin et al., 2010a).

Within the Police and Criminal Evidence Act (PACE), which came into effect in January 1986 (Gudjonsson, 2003a), all three boys would have required the support of an 'appropriate adult', but no such support was provided, none of them had a lawyer, and in the case of Lattimore, the questioning was deemed to be leading. There was also evidence of an inducement at the critical phase of the questioning: the senior interviewer commented that the youngsters would be allowed to go home after the interview. This kind of inducement is commonly seen in cases of miscarriage of justice and is a powerful factor in encouraging suspects to make a confession (Gudjonsson, 2003a).

## The Main Impacts of the Confait Case

- The case led to the setting up of the Royal Commission on Criminal Procedure (1977–1981). The focus was on the rights and duties of the police and suspects, and the process and responsibility of the prosecution. Importantly, there was a Research Committee, focusing on the formulation of a research programme, which resulted in a series of important empirical research studies that assisted the Royal Commission on Criminal Procedure to evaluate the existing police practice and legislation and make future recommendations (Irving & McKenzie, 1989).
- The Royal Commission on Criminal Procedure found the Judges' Rules to be ineffective in controlling police practice during custodial questioning and recommended that the term 'voluntary' (i.e. the statement had not been obtained 'by fear of prejudice or hope of advantage, exercised or held out by a person in authority, or by oppression') should be replaced by whether or not the statement was 'reliable' (Williamson, 2007).
- The recommendations of the Royal Commission on Criminal Procedure led to the creation of PACE, accompanied by the Police Codes of Practice, and the creation of an independent Crown Prosecution Service. The Codes of Practice have been amended at various times over the years and now include 'fitness to be interviewed' (Gudjonsson, 2016; Home Office, 2017).

## THE GUILDFORD FOUR

Ewing and McCann (2006) describe the case of the Guildford Four as:

> ... one of the most infamous occurrences of wrongful conviction based on a false confession and one of the worst miscarriages of justice in recent history.
>
> (p. 54)

On 5 October 1974, members of the Irish Republican Army (IRA) planted bombs in two public houses in Guildford, England. Five people were killed and a further 57 were injured. Eight people were initially charged with the bombings, but only four of them had confessed (Patrick Armstrong, Gerry Conlon, Paul Hill, and Carole Richardson), and the four were convicted on 22 October 1975 (Gudjonsson & MacKeith, 2003). My psychiatrist colleague, Jim MacKeith, and I were originally commissioned by the Prison Medical Service in early 1986 to evaluate the mental state of Carole Richardson and this involved evaluating the reliability of her confession statements to the police in 1974. We subsequently assessed the remaining three Irishmen, but the key focus of our work was on Miss Richardson's confessions. On the basis of the psychological evaluation in April 1986, I found her to be an anxious introvert, of good intelligence with excellent memory capacity, but highly suggestible. I concluded in my psychological report:

> ... bearing in mind the circumstances of the lengthy interrogations and the likelihood that she was exceptionally vulnerable at the time (e.g. low self-esteem, drug withdrawal, highly suggestible) the validation of the confessions made in 1974 must be seriously questioned.

Of particular interest to Jim and I was that Miss Richardson reported that after having given her confession and been in custody for a few days and questioned intensively, she had begun to believe that perhaps she had been involved in the Guildford bombing and was blacking it out of her memory (i.e. her confession had become internalized because of memory distrust). What was crucial, according to Miss Richardson, who was only 17 years of age at the time, was that the police officers were so confident that she was involved, and she could not at the time recall exactly where she had been on 5 October 1974. She produced four statements (4, 5, 6, and 9 December 1974) after having been arrested on the 3 December, and confessed within 48 hours of her arrest. After being remanded to Brixton Prison, the pressure eased so she was no longer in a confused state and regained her belief in her innocence. It was the combination of the intense questioning, custodial confinement, not recalling what she was doing on the day of the bombing, and the confidence of the police officers of her involvement (i.e. Gerry Conlon had implicated her and her boyfriend Patrick Armstrong) that increased her sense of confusion, making her distrust her own memory of her innocence. By this time she had already implicated herself and claimed at the time of the trial that she had been subjected to police brutality and that her statements were dictated to her.

Our reports on Miss Richardson were used to persuade the Home Secretary to reopen the case. The Avon and Somerset Police then conducted a review of the case and discovered discrepancies between detention sheets and police interview records regarding time and duration of police interviews. The case was taken up by the Court of Appeal in London on 19 October 1989.The four persons were acquitted. The Lordships concluded:

> It follows that any evidence which casts a real doubt upon the reliability or veracity of the officers who were responsible for the various interrogations must mean that the whole foundation of the prosecution case against them disappears and that the confessions will in those circumstances be obviously unsafe.
> (Court of Appeal Judgement, 19 October 1989, p. 5)

A few days prior to the appeal, the Crown informed the court that it 'would no longer seek to uphold these convictions' (p. 2), which meant that the appeal was not contested. If the Crown had contested the appeal, the outcome might have been different.

### The Main Impacts of the Guildford Four Case

* The psychiatric and psychological evidence was successful in helping to persuade the Home Secretary to reopen the case in January 1988. Prior to the appeal Jim and I met with Miss Richardson's defence counsel with a view to giving evidence at the appeal. In the end we did not have to testify at the appeal. An enquiry conducted by the Avon and Somerset Police had discovered police impropriety during the original investigation, which clinched the successful appeal.
* The case emphasized the importance of a close working relationship between the two professions: psychiatry and psychology. Jim and I had a very successful partnership and worked on a number of cases together, both nationally and internationally (Gudjonsson, 2003a).
* The case provided the means to further our understanding of memory distrust syndrome, a concept Jim and I had first described at a conference in 1981 (Gudjonsson & MacKeith, 1982). This was our first joint case involving the syndrome. It showed that a coerced

compliant confession can turn into an internalized confession when the pressure persisted over several days. It also illustrated the importance of lengthy custody (i.e. several days) in leading to memory distrust syndrome and an internalized false confession.

- The case raised awareness of psychological and mental health vulnerabilities during police interviews and of the risk of false confessions, and opened the way for other similar appeals.
- It showed that public and media pressure on the police in notorious cases can lead to coercive police tactics.

### Carole Richardson and the Battle at the Hospital Gate

After the acquittal of the Guildford Four at the Old Bailey on the morning of 19 October 1989 I went back to the Bethlem Royal Hospital in Beckenham where I worked. For security reasons, the appeal took place at the Central Criminal Court (Old Bailey) rather than in the Royal Court of Justice in the Strand, where appeals normally take place. There was a heavy armed police presence both within and outside the building. Jim MacKeith and I had arrived early and were there to look after the welfare of Carole Richardson and Patrick Armstrong. The successful outcome of the appeal was anticipated because of the fact that the prosecution was not contesting it. I had never before or since seen Jim so excited, his speech was exceptionally fast and he could not keep still. I was more controlled, taking nothing for granted, and tried unsuccessfully to calm him down. The courtroom was packed full, and immediately after the acquittals were pronounced there was a loud eruption of cheers as people jumped out of their seats. The atmosphere was electric and I have never experienced anything like it. Carole Richardson and Patrick Armstrong left court through the back entrance to avoid the media, Paul Hill remained in custody temporarily in relation to another case, and Gerry Conlon left the court through the front entrance and shouted to the crowd: 'I have been in prison for something I did not do. I am totally innocent.... Let's hope the Birmingham Six are freed.'

I went to a nearby car park, picked up my car and drove to work, 21 km (13 miles) away. The journey took me just over an hour. I had lunch in the canteen and then went to the Denis Hill Unit, where I was based for my clinical and forensic practice. In the latter part of the afternoon Jim telephoned me and said that he was with Carole Richardson in a chauffeur driven car and was being followed by news reporters. Carole was being driven to a safe house at a secret location and they needed to lose the paparazzi. They were taking a detour towards Beckenham and I was to go to the big metal gates in front of this historic hospital and once they were through close the gates behind them. I went with Frank Hardiman, a senior nurse from the Denis Hill Unit, and waited. After about 20 minutes the chauffeur driven car entered the hospital grounds, we could see Jim in the front seat with the driver and Carole was sitting in the back with a female companion. Frank and I attempted to shut the gates behind them but the car immediately following would not stop and pushed against the gates. We did not give in and after a while the driver stopped pushing against the gates, which we had not been able to shut properly. At one point I felt I was about to fall under the car such was the determination of the news reporter to get through. I suddenly had a flashback of falling on my back onto snow, feeling very cold and frightened, and that a car was reversing over me. I could hear children shouting in Icelandic, *Stoppiði bílinn, stoppiði bílinn* ('Stop the car, stop the car'). I could not make any sense of this experience.

My mother later told me what had really happened. She was coming out of the block of flats where we lived in the west part of Reykjavík at Blómvallagata 11 and could hear children shouting, and she saw a car reversing over a child. It was me, aged about 7. I had been trying to catch a lift in the snow by holding on to the car's rear bumper. Unfortunately the car reversed and I went under it, being left with some bruises and in a state of shock. I had no memory of it until the battle at the hospital gate, 34 years later; even then it was not a complete memory (i.e. I still cannot remember the broader context of what I was doing before I went under the car or what happened afterwards). What triggered the memory of the children shouting and the strong sensory and emotional reaction at the gates was the similarity of the stimulus propensities of the two events (i.e. perception of falling under a car). For me this was evidence of the importance of 'context dependent memory' (Baddeley, 1995).

Once the gates were closed, I met up with Jim and Carole. We decided we needed a decoy while Carole would travel in my car to a rendezvous point. I had a clinical psychology trainee with me on placement, Sue Rutter, who looked similar to Carole in terms of her hair and body build. Sue dressed up in Carole's jacket and used her headscarf. The chauffeur drove around Beckenham, Shirley, and West Wickham for a while as a decoy. In the meantime, I had hidden Carole in the boot of my car. I drove out through the gates of the hospital, turned right into Monks Orchard Road to the end of the road, then left into West Wickham High Street. I kept looking in the mirror to see whether we were being followed, but I did not see any cars following us. I then drove into a garage at Corkscrew Hill, let Carole out of the boot of my car and she came and sat in the front passenger seat. We then drove to my home in a small town in Surrey, where my wife Julia had cooked us prawns with rice, Carole's first meal out of prison after 14 years. Carole was then taken to her secret address to begin her adjustment to life outside prison.

## THE BIRMINGHAM SIX

On 21 November 1974 the IRA bombed two public houses in the centre of Birmingham. 21 people died and many were injured. Six Irishmen (Hugh Callaghan, Paddy Hill, Gerry Hunter, Richard McIlkenny, Billy Power, and Johnny Walker) were charged with multiple murders. In June 1975 they were all convicted (Mansfield, 2009; Mullin, 1989).

After their arrest, Dr Frank Skuse, a civil service forensic scientist, concluded that there was evidence of nitroglycerine on the hands of Paddy Hill and Billy Power, and he told the police he was 99% sure they had been in contact with that substance. He had used the 'Griess' test, which was later found to be unreliable because it lacked specificity (Court of Appeal Judgement [1991] 93 Cr App R, 287). Nevertheless, his conclusions undoubtedly misled the investigators and gave them a false sense of confidence that they had arrested the right people. As five of the men were travelling together on 22 November 1974 on a ferry to Ireland they were assumed to be co-conspirators and placed under enormous pressure to confess (Mullin, 1989).

In 1987 the case was referred by the defence lawyers to Jim MacKeith and I. We thoroughly assessed all six persons and wrote detailed reports. The most interesting finding from the psychological evaluation was that the two persons who did not give a signed confession in the case (Paddy Hill and Gerry Hunter) were found to score very low on both suggestibility and compliance, in great contrast to the other four convicted men (Gudjonsson & MacKeith, 2003), emphasizing the importance of individual differences within a case and reflecting their ability to resist interrogation under extreme pressure. These tests were conducted 13 years after their interrogation, showing stability in their suggestibility and compliance over time.

Mansfield (2009) argues that there were two key events that led to the successful application for appeal in the case. Firstly, in 1989 the West Midlands Police, which had been responsible for the Birmingham investigation, announced that it was disbanding the Serious Crime Squad, which had been accused of fabrication of confessions and other evidence, and violence and intimidation. 'The second straw was the release in October 1989 of the Guildford Four. Both cases relied on false confessions, allegations of violence by the police, and fraud and perjury to cover it up, all in a climate of anti-IRA hysteria' (p. 309).

In August 1990, the Home Secretary referred the case to the Court of Appeal, after a police enquiry had found discrepancies in a police interview record of one of the men.

According to the defence barrister Michael Mansfield (2009), prior to the successful appeal:

> Every surviving police document was subjected to intense scrutiny.... The results were stark. Tests showed that some of the notes of interviews claimed to be contemporaneous cannot have been, and therefore their integrity was demolished.
>
> (p. 311)

All six appellants were acquitted after the appeal on 14 March 1991. As in the case of the Guildford Four, the Crown did not resist the appeal. According to the Court of Appeal 1991 judgement:

> It was Superintendent Reade's inability to explain the ESDA test of the McIlkenny interview, and the refusal by D.S. Morris and D.C. Woodwiss to answer any questions, which led the Home Secretary to refer the case back to the Court of Appeal.
>
> (Court of Appeal Judgement [1991] 93 Cr App R, 287, p. 16)[2]

### The Main Impacts of the Birmingham Six Case

- Flawed forensic evidence, in this case based on the Griess test, which lacked specificity (i.e. false positive findings could easily have been caused by the playing cards they used on the ferry journey), seriously misled the investigation and placed the suspects under great pressure to confess. For example, 'Power confessed almost at once, when told of Dr Skuse's findings' (Court of Appeal Judgement, p. 4).
- The British government set up the Royal Commission on Criminal Justice immediately following the release of the Birmingham

---

[2] ESDA stands for Electro-Static Deposition Analysis, which is a technique used to measure impressions made from handwriting on any paper beneath. It has been used successfully in a number of criminal cases to show that notes of police interviews with suspects had been altered (Mansfield, 2009). It successfully overturned the convictions of three appellants in Northern Ireland in the case of the UDR Four (Gudjonsson, 2003a).

Six and completed its report in 1993. Twenty-two research studies were commissioned, and they produced many important results (Gudjonsson, 2003a). One of the studies (Gudjonsson, Clare, Rutter, & Pearse, 1993) showed that custody sergeants were poor at detecting mental health issues in suspects requiring the services of an 'appropriate adult'.

- The Royal Commission on Criminal Justice made 352 recommendations. One of the recommendations led to the setting up of the Criminal Cases Review Commission, which was established by Section 8 of the Criminal Appeal Act 1995 and started work investigating possible miscarriages of justice on 31 March 1997.
- The two persons who did not give a signed confession in the case (Paddy Hill and Gerry Hunter) were found to score very low on both suggestibility and compliance, in great contrast to the other four convicted persons, emphasizing the importance of individual differences within a case and reflecting their ability to resist interrogation under extreme pressure.

## THE TOTTENHAM THREE (ENGIN RAGHIP)

Following a major public disturbance on Broadwater Farm Estate on 6 October 1985, a police officer, Keith Blakelock, was attacked by a mob of people and murdered. By May 1986, 359 people had been arrested in connection with the case and 167 were charged with a range of offences, mainly public disturbance offences. Most of those detained were denied access to a lawyer or to their family. Six defendants were charged with murder, and three were convicted (Winston Silcott, Mark Braithwaite, and Engin Raghip).

Engin Raghip was 19 years of age at the time of his arrest. A pretrial report showed that he had an IQ of 73. I was commissioned by the defence after Raghip's conviction in 1987. I found him abnormally suggestible and compliant on testing. He was of borderline intelligence, was a very anxious man and had poor self-esteem. After hearing fresh psychological evidence, Raghip's conviction was overturned on 27 November 1991. No retrial was ordered.

### The Main Impacts of the Tottenham Three Case

- This was the first case where expert psychological evidence was influential in the UK in overturning a conviction in a case of disputed confession. The judgement broadened the criteria for the admissibility of psychological evidence to cases of personality, more specifically interrogative suggestibility, and suggested that the lower courts should not confine admissibility to scores below an arbitrary IQ point of 70.

- Importantly, the Court of Appeal warned that suggestibility and intellectual deficits could not be satisfactorily detected by observations of the defendant's performance in the witness box.
- The case also showed how feelings of suspiciousness and anger can temporarily reduce suggestibility (Gudjonsson, 1989b, 2003a). The pretrial psychologist had tested Mr Raghip under conditions likely to reduce his suggestibility scores.
- The case showed that changes in attitudes over time are important:

> By the time of the second appeal in 1991 there had been a sea-change in attitude. Two experts from the time of the original trial changed their minds in light of Gisli's work.
>
> (Mansfield, 2009, p. 218)

- After this landmark victory for psychology and justice, Mansfield (2009) concluded:

> Gisli developed a series of tests that could be objectively applied by different psychologists, and these are now widely accepted: for example, he was able to measure susceptibility and suggestibility. Many of the tests are set out in his authoritative work, *The Psychology of Interrogations, Confessions and Testimony*.
>
> (p. 218)

## THE CASE OF JUDITH WARD

Judith Ward was arrested in February 1974 and charged with serious terrorist offences (Gudjonsson, 2003a; Ward, 1993). Jim MacKeith and I assessed her in Holloway Prison for the defence in 1990. The psychological assessment showed Miss Ward to be of average intelligence, highly extraverted, suggestible, exhibiting hysterical reactions under stress, and with an abnormal tendency to confabulate. The defence psychiatrist, Jim MacKeith, and the prosecution psychiatrist, Paul Bowden, concluded that Miss Ward was suffering from 'a personality disorder with histrionic features' (Gudjonsson & MacKeith, 1997, p. 8). All three of us testified at the appeal in May 1992 and Miss Ward was acquitted.

## The Main Impact of the Judgement in the Judith Ward Case

Personality disorder was now a condition that psychiatrists and psychologists could testify about in cases of disputed confessions. The concept of confabulation was introduced as a relevant factor in Miss Ward's diagnosis and the unreliability of her confession. The psychometric test results provided support, if not partly the basis, for the psychiatric evidence tendered regarding personality disorder.

Their Lordships concluded:

> We agree with what Lawton LJ said in Turner, that *Lowery* is not an authority for the proposition that in all cases psychologists and psychiatrists can be called to prove the probability of the accused's veracity. Nor is the decision of this court in Raghip authority for such a wide-ranging proposition. But we conclude on the authorities as they now stand that the expert evidence of a psychiatrist or a psychologist may properly be admitted if it is to the effect that a defendant is suffering from a condition not properly described as mental illness, but from a personality disorder so severe as properly to be categorised as mental disorder.
>
> (R v Ward [1993] 1 WLR 619, 96 Cr App Rep 1, p. 89)

## THE CARDIFF THREE (STEPHEN MILLER)

This case involved the murder of Lynette White, a sex worker in Wales, on 14 February 1988. Lynette was Stephen Miller's girlfriend. Mr Miller was questioned the following day and left alone in a room with the post-mortem photographs of his girlfriend's butchered body, which distressed him greatly (Sekar, 1997). Miller was released without charge but was arrested nearly 10 months later along with four other men (Yusef Abdullahi, John and Ronnie Actie, and Tony Paris) and subjected to 19 taped interviews, almost 13 hours in total, over five days, because he had been falsely implicated by two sex workers, who claimed to have seen the murder and then went into protective custody. These two witnesses were to testify against the five men during two trials, apparently under police duress, and three defendants were convicted (Sekar, 1997, 2012).

In August 1989 I was commissioned by the defence to assess Stephen Miller and study the 19 police interview tapes. My main conclusions were that Mr Miller was of borderline intelligence, proved abnormally suggestible and compliant on testing, was prone to symptoms of anxiety, had his self-esteem severely manipulated by the interviewing officers, was placed under extreme pressure to confess, and his distress was clearly evident from the interview tapes. His solicitor was present, except for the first two interviews, but did not intervene with the oppressive interviewing. I concluded in my psychological report:

> In view of Mr Miller's marked psychological vulnerabilities he would have been ill-prepared at the time of the interviews to cope psychologically with the pressure and demand characteristics of the situation. There is no doubt in my mind that bearing in mind the type, intensity and duration of the police pressure during the interviews and his psychological vulnerabilities, the reliability of the interviews must be considered to be unsafe and unsatisfactory.

These were strong conclusions. It is extremely rare for me to give such firm conclusions regarding disputed confessions in a court report, but I had found the situational and personal risk factors overwhelming. The severity of the pressure and manipulation during those interviews, which were so clear from the taped interview, are still fresh in my mind after 27 years.

There were two trials. The first trial commenced at Swansea Crown Court in October 1989. I attended court during the legal arguments. Judge McNeill ruled my evidence inadmissible and allowed the oppressive interviews into evidence. The two main witnesses testified that they had been present during the murder and implicated the five defendants. The prosecutor highlighted parts of Miller's interview where he had not agreed with the officers to show that he was not suggestible. On 26 February 1990, five months into the trial, judge McNeill suffered a fatal heart attack.

A retrial commenced on 2 May 1990 before Mr Justice Leonard. I testified during the legal arguments before the judge and then again before the jury six months later. I was the only defence witness called. For some reason, the defence only asked me questions about Mr Miller's vulnerabilities. Defence counsel did not ask me any questions about the police interviews or about the reliability of Miller's confession. In contrast, the prosecution counsel did not ask me any questions about Miller's vulnerabilities, but instead focused on the police interviews and tried to demonstrate that Miller had not agreed with all suggestions offered by the police. I found the cross-examination aggressive, with the prosecutor trying to rattle me by asking me to look at the gruesome post-mortem photographs while I was testifying in the witness box. I explained to the jury that although Miller was abnormally suggestible, he would not be expected to agree with everything the police officers suggested to him. I also explained that Miller had told me that two of the officers had been 'nasty' to him, whereas one of the officers had been 'nice' to him. This 'Mr Nice and Mr Nasty' interview tactic has sometimes been used to break down resistance and get a confession, although it is no longer considered acceptable police practice (St-Yves, 2014).

It was bizarre that both the prosecution and trial judge Mr Justice Leonard 'seemed to expect Miller to agree with absolutely everything that was put to him in order to qualify as suggestible' (Sekar, 1997, p. 118).

'Miller denied involvement in the murder over three hundred times and expressed anger that Vilday [one of the prosecution witnesses in the case] had implicated him in a crime he insisted he did not commit, but his denials were not believed by police. They stated Vilday's account as if it was a fact and told him that they had witnesses; why should they lie? Miller did not know why they were lying but insisted that they were lying. Once again the police did not believe him' (Sekar, 1997, p. 39).

As a part of his PhD in 1997, John Pearse, a competent researcher and a police officer of the highest integrity, factor analysed the tactics used to break down Miller's resistance (Pearse, 1997; Pearse & Gudjonsson, 1999, 2003). He found that there were five main interview tactic factors during Tape 7, which was highly coercive and laid the foundation for the false confession:

1. *Mr Nasty factor*. Repeatedly challenging Mr Miller's version of events as his being a liar, continued dispute, raised voices, threats, maximizing Miller's anxiety.
2. *Mr Nice factors*. Low tone and reassurance, accompanied by multiple assertions and implying the existence of evidence.
3. *Manipulation factor*. Emphasizing the experience of the officers, manipulating details, minimizing responsibility, and challenging Miller's version of events with information provided by coerced witnesses.
4. *Poor delivery factor*. The use of multiple questions and assertions.
5. *Persistent pressure factors*. Questioning by multiple officers, emphasizing the serious nature of the offence, and use of inducements.

John's sophisticated factor analysis echoed my more basic evaluation of the interview tactics. It was the first and only study to scientifically demonstrate the use of the 'Mr Nasty' and 'Mr Nice' technique and showed the cumulative buildup of pressure over time, particularly during Tape 7. Once Miller's resistance began to break in Interview (Tape) 7, 'Mr Nasty's' job was done, he was out of the interviews, and 'Mr Nice' took over to obtain Miller's confessions by subtle and persuasive interrogation, presented in a quiet but forceful manner. In the following two interviews Miller began to distrust his own memory and began to incorporate the officers' suggestions and scenario into his own memory recollection (see Table 2.1).

**Table 2.1** Evidence for memory distrust syndrome in Miller's case (extracts from Pearse, 1997)

| Day: (Tapes) | Tactics | Miller's reaction | Comment |
|---|---|---|---|
| 1: (1 & 2) | Mr Nice tactic and psychological manipulation dominate with manipulation reaching high peaks in Tape 2. | Seeks information, provides an account and some angry denials in Tape 2. | Two peripheral admissions (i.e. living off immoral earnings and uses drugs). |
| 2: (3 to 5) | There is persistent cumulative pressure evident in Tapes 3 and 4, accompanied by an increase in manipulation and Mr Nice tactics. The Mr Nice tactic dominates Tape 5. | Miller provides an account and seeks to know the information against him, accompanied by angry denials. | There are new interviewers. There is one new peripheral admission. |
| 2: (6 & 7) | The officers introduce new evidence from witnesses by reading directly from their statements. In Tape 7 the Mr Nasty tactic reaches an extreme level, followed by persistent pressure and manipulation. | There are continued angry denials, which reach an extreme level towards the middle of Tape 7. The peak of angry denials corresponds to the peak of the Mr Nasty tactic. | The first pair of interviewers (Mr Nice and Mr Nasty) is back. There is an admission at the beginning of Tape 7 (i.e. Miller accepts he may have taken drugs on the day of the murder). |
| 2: (8 & 9) | After the bombardment in interview 7 there is a change of tactics. There is a Mr Nice tactic accompanied by persistent pressure, emphasizing the seriousness of the offence. Mr Nice voice is soft and has a hypnotic quality to it. | Miller reacts by giving multiple admissions relating to the theme of the officers that he had been high on drugs and might have been at the crime scene. | Miller is now expressing doubts ('I could have been there') and has become confused and is beginning to accept the police scenario. He begins to cry towards the end and has developed a serious distrust of his memory. The Mr Nasty tactic and angry denial have now disappeared and do not feature in the case any longer. Miller's resistance has been substantially broken down. |

| | | |
|---|---|---|
| 3: (10 & 11) | This is a consolidation interview where Miller is not allowed to deviate from the previously agreed story. The main tactic is Mr Nice exerting persistent pressure and takes Miller through the sequence of events at the murder scene and names the persons present. The questioning is very leading and capitalizes on Miller's extreme trait and state susceptibility to suggestions. | A striking feature is Miller's vagueness in his replies and accounts, continually seeking information, because in reality he had nothing to do with the murder. |
| 3: (12 & 13) | There is persistent pressure in these two interviews, and the officers explain his poor recollection in terms of his having been high on alcohol and drugs at the time and therefore not recalling what he did to the victim. Mr Nice is particularly effective in getting Miller to agree with him. | Miller makes a number of admissions about being present in the flat when the murder took place. He is continuously seeking information, because in reality he had not been at the crime scene. |
| 4: (14 to 17) | Mr Nice features in this interview and is joined by a new interviewer. The main tactic is the use of closed and leading questions. | There is general acceptance of the suggestions and scenarios presented. |
| 5: (18 & 19) | The officers have been provided with new evidence of what allegedly happened at the murder scene and Miller is presented with an inducement regarding a reduced sentence ('... lesser sentences or lesser charges ... we are now in a position of power ...'). | Miller now makes a confession to participating in the stabbing, accepting the accounts and scenarios presented to him. He is still giving tentative replies ('Yeah most probably, I don't know, I just don't know'). | Miller does not accept all the suggestions offered and now refused to accept that he was a heavy user of drugs, which he had admitted to on numerous occasions before. |

Unfortunately, defence counsel had made a serious tactical error in his submission in only requesting that a part of that tape was played to the jury and thereby failing to back up its claim 'that Miller had been the victim of cumulative bullying' (Sekar, 1997, p. 156).

The other defence counsel error, which surprised me greatly at the time, was that he did not ask me any questions about the police interviews, leaving my evidence focusing exclusively on Miller's low IQ and high suggestibility. In addition to analysing the police tactics, John also analysed Miller's responses, and it was evident that the 'Mr Nasty' tactic made him very angry and this temporarily reduced his level of suggestibility and compliance, which supported the prosecution's argument that Miller was capable of resisting suggestions, but he broke down towards the end of Tape 8. At this point 'Mr Nice' came in with the 'softly softly approach' and Miller then made multiple admissions (Pearse, 1997, p. 83). It was the combination of these 'Mr Nasty' and 'Mr Nice' tactics that resulted in his breaking down and making a false confession to the murder. John's PhD methodology provided an impressive scientific evaluation of the manipulative and oppressive process.

## The Main Impacts of the Cardiff Three Case

In spite of the new PACE legislation, which was implemented in England and Wales in January 1986, in the late 1980s the police were still using coercive interview tactics, heavily influenced by the American Reid Technique (Inbau, Reid, & Buckley, 1986; Walkley, 1987), and this was documented by a scientific approach from analysis of tape-recorded interviews, including the 19 tape-recorded interviews of Stephen Miller in the presence of his solicitor in all but the first two interviews. Tape 7 was the most oppressive (Pearse, 1997; Pearse & Gudjonsson, 1999, 2003).

- The case shows that the mere presence of a lawyer in a police interview is no guarantee that the confession is reliable, or in fact true, and in the case of Miller may have made matters worse for the suspect, as pointed out by Lord Chief Justice Taylor in the judgement.
- If it had not been for the implementation of the electronic recording of suspects' interviews, in accordance with PACE, the extent of the pressure Miller was placed under would never have been fully evident. It demonstrated the importance of the electronic recording of suspect interviews.
- Early analysis of electronically recorded interviews had shown ineptness in interviewing skills (Baldwin, 1992) and Stephenson and Moston (1994) found that the great majority of the interviewers

entered a suspect interview with a presumption of guilt and thought that the main purpose of the interview was to get a confession.

- In December 1992, the appeal judges were very critical of the police interview techniques used to elicit a confession from Stephen Miller and stated:

    'In our view, those responsible for police training and discipline must take all necessary steps to see that guidelines are followed' (see Gudjonsson, 2003a, p. 517).

- According to Tom Williamson (1994, p. 109), the Cardiff Three Court appeal judgement set the standards 'against which all future interviews will be assessed' and the case became important for police training in the early 1990s. Williamson argued for more open-minded and ethical interviewing of suspects.

- We know now that Miller's confession was false. DNA evidence after his acquittal on appeal identified the real murderer and led to his conviction. Table 2.1 shows that Mr Miller's false confession was of the internalized type, precipitated by the development of memory distrust syndrome following subtle manipulative interviewing after his resistance had been broken down during interview 7.

The case demonstrates how vulnerable witnesses can be manipulated by police and coerced into giving false statements. Their statements were then used to coerce a vulnerable man to give a false confession (Sekar, 1997).

Importantly, the convicted men, Abdullahi, Miller, and Paris, had their convictions quashed on 10 December 1992, on the basis of the oppressive interviewing of Miller. The real murderer, Jeffrey Gafoor, was convicted on DNA evidence and made a guilty plea in July 2003 (Sekar, 2012). There followed a corruption trial in 2011 that collapsed because of the belief of the trial judge that documents had been destroyed when they had not – an error that has hampered the vindication of the innocent men implicated in Lynette White's murder (Sekar, 2012, 2017).

## THE PEACE MODEL OF INTERVIEWING

Tom Williamson was a senior police officer conducting research into police interviewing with Professor Geoffrey Stephenson at the University of Kent in the late 1980s, where he was awarded a PhD in 1990. He later became very influential in the development and implementation of the PEACE Model, focusing heavily in his work on 'ethical policing' (Williamson, 1994). After retiring in 2001 he became an academic and edited several books. I first met Tom in December

1985 and we remained friends until his death in 2007. I always found him supportive of my work and inspirational.

The PEACE Model has been in continuous use in the UK since 1993, when it was rolled out as part of a national training package for police officers (Bull, 1999, 2013; Bull, Valentine, & Williamson, 2009; Bull & Soukara, 2010; Clarke & Milne, 2016; Griffiths & Milne, 2006; Shawyer, Milne, & Bull, 2009; Shepherd & Griffiths, 2013). Bull and Soukara (2010) reviewed four studies involving the PEACE Model and suggested that the findings 'could be taken to suggest that police organizations around the world actively consider adopting the PEACE approach and associated training programs' (p. 94). It is now also being employed in New Zealand (Cain, Westera, & Kebbell, 2016) and Norway (Fahsing, Jakobsen, & Öhr, 2016), and other countries around the world are urged to follow (Walsh, Redlich, Oxburgh, & Myklebust, 2016).

The implementation of the PEACE Model in Norway was the direct result of an acquittal in a murder case where I testified as a court appointed expert in June 1998, concluding that the confession was 'false' on psychological grounds because of the development of memory distrust syndrome (Gudjonsson, 2003a). The false confession was obtained by a detective who at the time 'was regarded as one of the best interviewers in Norway' (Fahsing et al., 2016, p. 181). The acquittal of the appellant and my criticism of the Norwegian police interrogation technique in court had huge positive benefits in terms of improved police interviewing and the creation of a Norwegian Criminal Cases Review Commission. It was not an easy fight for justice; I received a great deal of hostility when I testified, in contrast to the Swedish psychiatrist who testified that the confession was 'true'. He was allowed to testify for almost two days, although he had not examined the appellant and indeed declined to do so. I was allowed about half of that time and the chief judge kept rushing me through my evidence, but I stood my ground, and fortunately the jury came to the right decision (Gudjonsson, 2003a; Jahr, 2015).

The PEACE Model was developed on sound psychological principles, which followed valuable collaborative work between academics, psychologists, police practitioners, and lawyers. It was intended to take into account the vulnerabilities of some interviewees, with the aim of minimizing the risk of a false confession (Shawyer et al., 2009). The focus is on fairness, openness, workability, accountability, and fact (truth) finding rather than merely obtaining a confession. Leading questions, heavy pressure, and psychological manipulation are avoided, thereby potentially reducing the risk of false confession while still producing true confessions (Shawyer et al., 2009).

In contrast to the PEACE Model, the Reid Technique, which is influential in the USA, encourages interviewers to use a two-stage interview process (Gudjonsson & Pearse, 2011; Inbau, Reid, Buckley, & Jayne, 2013). The first stage is a nonaccusatory interview, in which general background information about the suspect is obtained, rapport and trust are built, and a determination is made about whether or not the suspect is lying about the offence. If the suspect is judged to be lying, then the interview progresses to a nine-step accusatory (presumption of guilt) approach, typically referred to as 'interrogation' (Inbau et al., 2013). Kassin and Gudjonsson (2004) argue that the nine-step Reid Technique can be reduced to three general phases: 'custody and isolation' (i.e. the suspect is detained and isolated, anxiety and uncertainty are generated in order to weaken resistance); 'confrontation' (i.e. the suspect's guilt is assumed and he or she is confronted with alleged incriminating evidence that may or may not be genuine, denials are rejected, even if they happen to be true, and the consequence of continued denial is emphasized); and 'minimization' (i.e. the interrogator tries to gain the suspect's trust and provides face-saving excuses for the crime, including suggesting that it was an accident or that the victim deserved it). In contrast to the PEACE Model, the Reid Technique has been associated with increased risk of false confession (Gudjonsson & Pearse, 2011; Kassin et al., 2010a; Meissner, Redlich, Bhatt, & Brandon, 2012; Pearse & Gudjonsson, 1999; Snook, Luther, & Barron, 2016).

Of relevance is the fact that in 1956, Darrel Parker, a forester for the city of Lincoln in the USA, was wrongfully convicted of the murder of his wife Nancy, based upon a false confession obtained by John E Reid, one of the originators of the Reid Technique. Mr Parker's innocence has now been accepted by the relevant authorities.[3]

Snook et al. (2016), Oxburgh, Fahsing, Haworth, & Blair (2016), and Vrij, Hope, and Fisher (2014) provide helpful descriptions of the two interview styles typically associated with the UK and the USA respectively (i.e. the PEACE Model vs the Reid Technique): (a) the information-gathering ('truth finding') style used to establish rapport with interviewees and the use of open-ended exploratory questions to elicit information and establish evidence of guilt or innocence; and (b) the accusatorial style, which is guilt-presumptive, uses closed-ended confirmatory questions to elicit confessions.

---

[3] http://www.exonerated.org/index.php?option=com_content&view=category&layout=bl og&id=41&Itemid=94&tmpl=component&type=raw&limitstart=110 (last accessed 24 January 2018).

Oxburgh, Myklebust, Grant, and Milne (2016) describe the improved professionalism in 'investigative interviewing' over the past 25 years, which has been accompanied by much greater collaboration between academics and practitioners and the setting up of various international organizations committed to improving the standards of interviewing worldwide, including the International Investigative Interviewing Research Group (iIIRG).[4]

## SUMMARY AND CONCLUSIONS

1. These six landmark cases broadened the legal, police practice, and science landscape. The Confait case led to the setting up of the Royal Commission on Criminal Procedure and the creation of PACE and its codes of practice. The new legislation and police practice were based in part on an impressive research evidence base from the late 1970s (Gudjonsson, 2003a).
2. The acquittals of the Guildford Four raised awareness of police impropriety, psychological vulnerabilities during questioning, high-lighted in the case of Carole Richardson, and false confessions. It opened the way to justice in other cases, including the Birmingham Six. Following the acquittal of the Birmingham Six in 1991, the Home Secretary set up the Royal Commission on Criminal Justice, and the subsequent creation of the Criminal Cases Review Commission followed.
3. In the case of Engin Raghip, for the first time, expert psychological evidence was influential in the UK in overturning a conviction in a case of disputed confession. The judgement broadened the criteria for the admissibility of psychological evidence to cases of personal-ity, more specifically interrogative suggestibility and compliance scores, and suggested that the lower courts should not confine admissibility to an arbitrary IQ point of 69. This landmark judgement has been influential in the successful appeal of many subsequent cases (Gudjonsson, 2010a). It was a major victory for clinical forensic psychology (Gudjonsson & Young, 2015).
4. The Raghip judgement was followed six months later by the judge-ment in the case of Judith Ward, in which psychologists and psychia-trists were now allowed for the first time to testify about personality disorder in cases of disputed confessions. Psychometric test results provided the support, if not partly the basis, for the psychiatric

---

[4] https://www.iiirg.org/ (last accessed 24 January 2018).

diagnosis, and findings regarding suggestibility and confabulation were accepted into evidence.

5. The acquittal of Stephen Miller in the Cardiff Three case raised the profile of oppressive police interviewing, and made legal history. It influenced police interview training in the UK (Williamson, 1994, 2007). It demonstrated the importance of electronic recording of police interviews in correcting injustices. As a part of his PhD dissertation, John Pearse analysed in detail the police tactics used and Miller's responses to the tactics, employing a new and innovative methodology. It showed the cumulative pressure within the interviews and how it led Miller to develop memory distrust syndrome.

6. Barrie Irving was a social psychologist, who specialized in understanding the custodial environment. In the late 1970s he had applied a methodologically sound approach in both the Confait and Guildford Four cases. In spite of this, he did not testify at the appeal of the Guildford Four case in 1977, and in the Confait case, Lord Fisher rejected his evaluation of the police tactics. There were two issues here. Firstly, Irving was not clinically trained and focused more on the situational rather than personal vulnerability factors, which limited the scope of his enquiries. Secondly, in those days, and until the acquittal of the Guildford Four in October 1989, prosecutors and judges were very sensitive to any criticism of the police, even when well supported and justified. As Irving and Williamson have both pointed out, Lord Fisher went out of his way to avoid any criticism of police behaviour. Irving was a victim of the times both in terms of negative judicial attitudes towards psychologists and the limited evidence base he had to work from. In spite of this, he was an early pioneer, whose work for the Royal Commission on Criminal Procedure in the late 1970s and his subsequent setting up of the Police Foundation in the UK stimulated research and impacted on police practice and justice.[5]

7. In conclusion, the general themes from my analysis of the six cases are that defendants need to be listened to (i.e. their claims of innocence should not be dismissed without an open-minded enquiry), police evidence cannot always be relied upon (i.e. sometimes police use oppressive and coercive tactics and wittingly or unwittingly feed suspects with information that later becomes wrongly attributed to them), and electronic recording of all police interviews contributes to fairness and justice. When mistakes and injustices occur, they should not be covered up and the lessons learned should be used to

---

[5] https://www.theguardian.com/law/2013/feb/27/barrie-irving (last accessed 24 January 2018).

improve practice. My extensive court experience, supported by these cases, is that a key obstacle to fairness and justice in the 1980s was the old fashioned and negative attitude of the police and prosecutors towards people claiming innocence, and hostility towards the expert witnesses who supported them. Criticism of the Criminal Justice System does not necessarily lead to it being undermined; in fact it can strengthen it (Gudjonsson, 2010a).

I will now turn to the theories that have shaped our understanding of interrogative suggestibility.

# 3

# Interrogative Suggestibility

*The influence of the stronger mind upon the weaker often produces, by persuasion or suggestion, the desired result*[1]

The concept of 'interrogative suggestibility' is intrinsic in all the theories of false confessions and will therefore be reviewed, with a particular emphasis upon the Gudjonsson and Clark (1986) model.

There are two complementary approaches available for measuring interrogative suggestibility. Schooler and Loftus (1986) have referred to these as the 'individual differences' and 'experimental' approaches. They represent the measurement of 'immediate' and 'delayed' suggestibility, respectively (Ridley & Gudjonsson, 2013). Immediate suggestibility refers to the instant effects of asking leading questions and interrogative pressure and is typically measured by the Gudjonsson Suggestibility Scales (GSS 1 and GSS 2; Gudjonsson, 1984a, 1987, 1997, 2013). In contrast, delayed suggestibility refers to the extent to which the person subsequently incorporates misleading post-event information into their recollection ('misinformation' effects) and follows the experimental paradigm of Loftus, Miller, and Burns (1978).

---

[1] Borchard (1932, p. xviii).

---

*The Psychology of False Confessions: Forty Years of Science and Practice*, First Edition.
Gisli H. Gudjonsson.
© 2018 John Wiley & Sons Ltd. Published 2018 by John Wiley & Sons Ltd.

## THE EXPERIMENTAL APPROACH

Binet (1900) first introduced the idea of 'interrogative suggestibility' and it was used by Stern (1939) to show that leading questions can produce distorted responses due to being phrased in such a way as to suggest the wanted or expected answer. Later researchers have employed a similar or modified procedure to that of Stern in order to elicit this type of suggestibility (e.g. Loftus, 1979; Loftus et al., 1978; Stukat, 1958; Tousignant, Hall, & Loftus, 1986).

Powers, Andriks, and Loftus (1979) define the experimental approach in the following terms:

> ... the extent to which they [people] come to accept a piece of post-event information and incorporate it into their recollection.
>
> (p. 339)

This definition emphasizes the importance of memory processing in suggestibility. It identifies two separate processes: the acceptance of the suggested information (i.e. believing that it is true, or may be true), and then the subsequent incorporation of the suggestion into memory (i.e. the misleading or false information being stored in memory).

According to the experimental approach, suggestibility is mediated by a central cognitive mechanism, referred to as 'discrepancy detection' (Loftus, 1991; Schooler & Loftus, 1986; Tousignant et al., 1986), also known as 'source monitoring errors' (Chrobak & Zaragoza, 2013). The discrepancy detection principle stipulates that:

> Recollections are most likely to change if a person does not immediately detect discrepancies between post-event suggestions and memory for the original event.
>
> (Schooler & Loftus, 1986, pp. 107–108)

Discrepancy detection is thought to be affected by two factors: (a) 'the strength of the original information in memory', and (b) 'the manner in which the post-event suggestion is influenced' (Schooler & Loftus, 1986, p. 108).

> The notion of detection of discrepancies can help us to understand, and even predict in advance, the likely influence of a number of situational and individual difference variables that could potentially lead to a misinformation effect.
>
> (Tousignant et al., 1986, p. 337)

Ayers and Reder (1998) reviewed 20 years of research into the misinformation effect and discussed several theoretical perspectives, including the following:

- *Trace* (i.e. the misinformation changes the structure of the memory, altering or replacing the original memory).
- *Blocking* (i.e. the misinformation blocks access to the original information because of retroactive interference).
- S*trategic effects* (i.e. strategic bias to select the misinformation in the absence of other memories, or remembers the event but gives the experimenter the information he/she thinks is wanted – in the early experiments strategic effect was reportedly more powerful than memory impairment in explaining the findings).
- S*ource monitoring* (i.e. difficulties determining the source of their memory and may respond on the basis of familiarity, or the misinformation is the only alternative presented – the evidence indicates greater memory impairment when there have been multiple exposures to the misinformation).
- *Activation-based semantic memory account* (i.e. labelled 'source of activation confusion', which most resembles the source monitoring model, but focuses more on whether or not the semantic concept is active and its associations with other concepts).

Ayers and Reder suggest that the activation-based model of memory most comprehensively explains the research findings and conclude:

> One of the most important developments is a consensus among researchers that no single factor is responsible for the [misinformation] effects. Whereas in its infancy, researchers explained the misinformation effect as either a memory-based phenomenon or an artefact of the testing situation, most researchers today would agree that both of these factors – as well as others – are responsible for the observed effects.
>
> (p. 19)

Loftus (2005a, 2005b) provides a review of the development of the science in relation to the misinformation effect over the previous 30 years, following groundbreaking neuroimaging research that revealed the underlying mechanism of the misinformation effect (Okado & Stark, 2005). However, neural activity methodology is a long way from being able to assist with the discrimination between true and false memories in actual criminal cases.

Loftus (2005b) outlined the most important questions and answers in relation to the misinformation effect. These are as follows:

1. 'Under what conditions are people particularly susceptible to the negative impact of misinformation?' (Answer: short exposure time to the relevant information, longer retention interval when original memory has faded with the passage of time, when made to believe they had been drunk, and when people have been hypnotized. Also trivial and peripheral detail is more likely to be accepted than salient and central detail: see Hammersley & Read, 1986).

2. 'Can people be warned about misinformation, and successfully resist its damaging influence?' (Answer: warnings may assist with resistance to misinformation, but it depends on the circumstances – a warning is much less effective when misinformation has high accessibility, for example, when it is presented multiple times. See also Szpitalak (2017) on recent evidence of the limitations of warnings. Awareness of discrepancies does not fully protect people from the misinformation effect, suggesting a non-memory misinformation effect: Polak, Dukala, Szpitalak, & Polczyk, 2016).

3. 'Are some types of people particularly susceptible?' (Answer: young children, the elderly, those with previous lapses in memory and attention, and those with personality traits of 'empathy, absorption, and self-monitoring', Loftus, 2005b, p. 362).

4. 'When misinformation has been embraced by individuals, what happens to their original memory?' (Answer: this question has resulted in a lively debate and stimulated research, focusing on the different ways people come to report misinformation items as their memory. Loftus and Hoffman (1989) argue that irrespective of whether 'integration' or 'coexistence' of the memory occurs, witness testimony is adversely affected).

5. 'What is the nature of misinformation memories?' (Answer: the content of real memories may be different to those of false ones, but there are no tangible discriminative criteria to use in practice).

6. 'How far can you go with people in terms of the misinformation you can plant in memory?' (Answer: misinformation, particularly when there is a strong form of suggestion, can lead to 'the creation of very rich false beliefs and memories' about a non-existent event, Loftus, 2005b, p. 364).

## THE INDIVIDUAL DIFFERENCES APPROACH

In January 1980 I was appointed as a Lecturer in Psychology at the Institute of Psychiatry, University of London, with clinical responsibilities to the Maudsley and Bethlem Royal Hospitals. I was a part of Professor John Gunn's forensic psychiatry team and in October 1980 I was appointed as the lead clinical psychologist at the newly established interim secure unit based at the Bethlem Royal Hospital. Dr James ('Jim') MacKeith was the consultant psychiatrist with whom I worked most closely both clinically and on cases of miscarriage of justice in the UK and abroad. We remained friends and close colleagues until his death on 4 August 2007.

Jim and I had different strengths and we complemented each other well when we worked on cases together. Jim was an exceptionally talented clinician, who showed great compassion for the victims of miscarriages of justice, and he frequently referred them to me for post-release prison anxiety management and trauma therapy. As a result, I learned a great deal about the suffering and psychological damage caused by wrongful conviction and imprisonment, an experience that I have never forgotten. Jim was highly extraverted, had an endless list of professional contacts, and was patient and diplomatic in all our dealings with the Home Office, Prison Service, Court, and lawyers. I found his creative thinking, enthusiasm, and positive demeanour inspiring and empowering. In contrast to Jim, I was introverted and reserved but brought to the team rigorous methodology, research focus, and academic productivity and credibility.

When working on cases of disputed confession, we used to do joint assessments, closely watching each other at work and providing helpful feedback. It was a good learning experience for both of us. Jim remained particularly vigilant when I administered my suggestibility scales in the early years, making sure I was being consistent in the amount of interrogative pressure I placed on the participants to measure Shift. On 30 April 1986, after administering the GSS 1 to Carole Richardson, one of the Guildford Four, in Styal Prison, Jim told me that I was now 'perfect' at administering my own test. I felt a sense of achievement and thanked him for his evaluation! Personally I thought Jim got carried away by the fact that Carole had proved to be very suggestible on testing in spite of her high IQ and excellent immediate and delayed recall. After all, it was our first 'high profile' case together and my suggestibility scale later proved helpful in persuading the Home Office to reopen the case.

My own research career has been partly devoted to exploring the individual differences approach to suggestibility and false confessions. The individual differences approach to suggestibility that I developed in 1982 with the construction and validation of the GSS 1 and GSS 2 has been my most unique and influential contribution to the science of forensic psychology.

The background to the development of the scales is as follows. On 14 November 1980 I evaluated a 22-year-old woman with a history of intellectual disability, who was alleging sexual assault by several defendants (Gudjonsson & Gunn, 1982). The Assistant Director of Public Prosecutions had referred the case to John Gunn who asked me to conduct a psychological evaluation on the 'victim', focusing on her IQ and the reliance that could be placed on her testimony in court. The woman, who I refer to as 'Mary', obtained a full-scale IQ of 47.

I conducted an experiment on how she would respond to leading questions and interrogative pressure. I interviewed Mary in the morning and tested her IQ. In the afternoon I asked her a number of leading questions about the morning session and then tried to shift her answers with interrogative pressure. My findings showed that she was extremely suggestible over matters she recalled poorly or had no interest in, but could not be shifted on facts she clearly remembered (e.g. she recalled that the blocks on one of the tests I had shown her in the morning were white and red and not black and green, as I suggested. She would not change her answer under pressure). Furthermore, Mary was able to give an accurate basic account of the morning session. John Gunn and I gave evidence at the Old Bailey in December 1981. In my testimony I suggested that since Mary was capable of giving a reliable account of basic facts, she should be asked to give an account of what happened to her without leading questions (e.g. 'Just tell me what happened'), and any challenges during cross-examination she resisted would be an indicator of her reliability. As a result of our testimony, the prosecution strategy was to rely upon Mary to provide a simple and basic account of the events during the evening in question without expecting her to identify the individuals responsible for specific acts. Mary successfully testified in court and five defendants were convicted. What I learned from this case was that *uncertainty* is a key component to suggestibility, challenging previous answers can provide a useful measure of susceptibility to interrogative pressure in addition to leading questions, and there was a need for an objective individual differences measure of interrogative suggestibility.

As early as February 1982 John Gunn and I were beginning to draft a scientific paper on the case, which was published later that year in the *British Journal of Psychiatry* (Gudjonsson & Gunn, 1982). It was around that period that the idea of developing a test of suggestibility became crystallized in my mind. Mary's case had given me innovative ideas, which had proved helpful to the prosecution, and writing the article with John made me reflect back on my experience as a police interrogator in Iceland and how to test susceptibility to suggestions and interrogative pressure.

When I developed the GSS 1 in early 1982, I decided on the following:
- The test had to have similar characteristics to a real-life interrogation (i.e. people are questioned about an event they had either heard or experienced) and procedure that did not require any equipment. All that was required was a test form and a quiet room.
- It was based on a short story that was read out to the participant, followed by misleading questions. The story I developed was similar to that found in the Wechsler Memory Scale but was longer so that a

sufficient number of leading questions could be asked for a wide range of suggestibility scores to be obtained. I wanted the test to be applicable to a range of witnesses and suspects, including older children and adults, and people with mild intellectual disability. The main challenge was to determine the right length of the narrative and number of leading questions.

- I decided on 15 misleading questions and interspersed five 'true' questions where the right answer was an affirmative one. These were used to conceal the real purpose of the test. Participants were told that this was a memory test, which in fact it was in part. Telling them that their suggestibility was being measured would have made them guarded about the questions and would have defeated the purpose of the test (Gudjonsson, 2003a).

- Two different types of suggestibility needed to be measured: (a) 'Yield' (i.e. giving in to leading questions, and (b) 'Shift' (i.e. participants being told they have made errors and that the questions had to be repeated, monitoring the number of changes and type of changes, which produces interrogative pressure). The measure of Shift was unique and I had added this to the test on the basis of Kelman (1950) finding that feedback of failure will increase suggestibility in line with the principle of reinforcement and related principles of learning.

Shortly after constructing the GSS 1, I tested it out on several colleagues, including John Gunn and Jim MacKeith, none of whom realized their suggestibility was being measured. I was excited that my new scale seemed to be sufficiently subtle for practical purposes and I started collecting the empirical data to test out its reliability and validity. Within a year my first paper on interrogative suggestibility was published (Gudjonsson, 1983).

In summary, the GSS 1 and GSS 2 comprise a short story, followed by 20 questions, 15 of which are misleading. The Scales provide a score of immediate and delayed recall (usually 40–50 minutes), each comprising a maximum of 40 items; Yield 1 (i.e. the number of leading questions to which the participant yields, the maximum score being 15); Yield 2 (i.e. the number of leading questions to which the participant yields after being provided with negative feedback, the maximum score being 15); Shift (i.e. the number of questions to which the participant changes the answer after negative feedback, the maximum score being 20); and Total Suggestibility (i.e. the sum of Yield 1 and Shift, the maximum score being 35).

I incorporated the GSS 1, on a trial basis, into my forensic evaluations from July 1982 onward. The first case involved a 24-year-old man, charged with murder, referred to me by a London-based firm of lawyers at the request of John Gunn, who by now knew about my research into interrogative suggestibility. The defence was concerned about the inconsistent answers the defendant had given during his statement to police, which looked incriminating, and the fact that their client seemed 'mentally slow', although a forensic medical examiner thought he was of normal intelligence when examining him at the police station prior to the police interview.

On testing, the defendant obtained an IQ of 72 and in spite of a poor recollection on both immediate (score of 9) and delayed (score of 6) recall, he proved resistant to suggestion, obtaining a score of 4 on Yield and 1 on Shift. I testified at the Old Bailey in November 1982 about the results, the primary focus being on the low IQ. The defendant was acquitted. What I learned from this case was that people with a significant intellectual limitation are not necessarily suggestible. The key issue in this case was the defendant's poor verbal skills, particularly comprehension, which could explain the inconsistencies in the police statement.

A measure of confabulation was subsequently added to the Scales (Clare & Gudjonsson, 1993; Clare, Gudjonsson, Rutter, & Cross, 1994; Gudjonsson, 1997). More recently, delayed suggestibility was incorporated into the GSS 2 (i.e. the number of misleading suggestions that were incorporated into memory narrative after one week) and was found to be poorly correlated with immediate suggestibility (Gudjonsson, Vagni, et al., 2016; Vagni, Maiorano, Pajardi, & Gudjonsson, 2015).

I have defined confabulation within an interrogative context as 'problems in memory processing where people replace gaps in their memory with imaginary experiences that they believe to be true' (Gudjonsson, 2003a, p. 364). The confabulations in cases of false confessions typically do not arise in the context of neurological disease (Kopelman, 2010) but are due to subtle psychological processes in situations of high emotional intensity (Gudjonsson, Sigurdsson, Sigurdardottir, Steinthorsson, & Sigurdardottir, 2014).

Kopelman (1987) provides some evidence for the distinction between 'spontaneous confabulation', which is rare and may have an organic basis, and 'provoked confabulation', which is more common and usually temporary. According to Kopelman, 'provoked confabulation' 'resembles the errors produced by healthy subjects and at prolonged retention intervals, and may represent a normal response to a faulty memory' (p. 1486). 'Provoked confabulation' is particularly relevant to cases of false confession resulting from the development of memory distrust syndrome (Gudjonsson, 2003a; Gudjonsson et al., 1999). According to Kopelman (2010), provoked confabulation 'appears to result from a "normal" response to a "weak" memory trace' (p. 32).

## THE GUDJONSSON AND CLARK MODEL

Following my early work on the GSS 1 and its validation, I wanted to develop a detailed theory of interrogative suggestibility. The foundation for the theory had already been laid by the time I devised the GSS 1 (Gudjonsson, 1983) and continued for the next three years. Some of the most creative ideas came to me while swimming in Iceland. The creation of the final model was a lot harder and took longer than the development of the GSS 1, but my empirical work on the Scale, as well as my experience as a police interrogator in Iceland in the summers of 1975 and 1976 helped me to formulate the theory. I wrote a comprehensive article and submitted it to the editor of *Social Behaviour*, Professor Geoffrey Stephenson, who asked his colleague Noel Clark to review it. Noel provided constructive comments which improved the presentation of the theoretical model of the article and became a co-author. The article was published in the first issue of *Social Behaviour* (Gudjonsson & Clark, 1986), along with an innovative commentary from Schooler and Loftus (1986), followed in the second issue by a commentary from another leading expert, Barrie Irving (1987).

In our article, we defined interrogative suggestibility:

> as the extent to which, within a closed social interaction, people come to accept messages communicated during formal questioning, as a result of which their subsequent behavioural response is affected.
>
> (Gudjonsson & Clark, 1986, p. 84)

An abbreviated version of the Gudjonsson and Clark model is shown in Figure 3.1. The essence of the model is that suggestibility arises from the way the individual interacts with others within the social and physical environment. This is a dynamic and interactive process, the outcome of which is determined by the coping strategies that people can generate and implement when faced with leading questions and interrogative pressure. When questioned, people have to cognitively process the question and context in which the questioning takes place. This process involves the interviewee having to cope with *uncertainty* and *interpersonal trust* on the one hand and *expectations* on the other. These three components are seen as essential prerequisites for the suggestibility process and can be manipulated during an interview in order to influence the answers given.

The Gudjonsson and Clark model provides detailed information about studies that have successfully tested different aspects of the model (e.g. raising expectations, the use of warnings regarding leading questions, types of coping strategies used during the questioning)

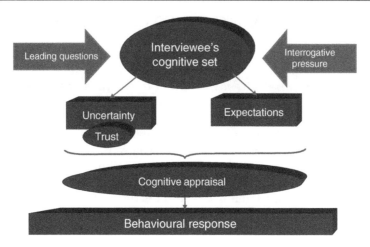

**Figure 3.1**   An abbreviated version of the Gudjonsson and Clark model of
interrogative suggestibility

(Gudjonsson, 2003a). Szpitalak and Polczyk (2016) provide empirical
support for the model by demonstrating the importance of experimentally induced self-confidence in reducing suggestibility using the GSS
2. In accordance with the Gudjonsson and Clark model, feelings of suspiciousness and anger can temporarily reduce the susceptibility to suggestions (Gudjonsson, 1989b).

Mastroberardino and Marucci (2013) raise an important issue
regarding the extent to which the Yield and Shift scores on the GSS
reflect internalization and compliance. They found, using a source
identification task that Yield 1 was associated with both internalization and compliance, whereas Shift was only related to compliance.
Sigurdsson and Gudjonsson (1996a) found that internalized false confessions were associated with elevated Yield 1, Total Suggestibility, and
confabulation, but not Shift.

I have summarized the extensive empirical evidence for the model
elsewhere (Gudjonsson, 2003a, 2013).

The Gudjonsson and Clark model differs in several respects from the
typical Loftus paradigm (Gudjonsson, 2003a). Schooler and Loftus
(1986) argue that the principal differences represent two complementary approaches: the 'individual differences' and 'experimental'
approaches. The experimental approach focuses on the timing (i.e.
length of time after observing the event) and the nature of the questions (e.g. the precise wording of the question), in which suggestibility
is seen to be principally mediated by a central cognitive mechanism
referred to as 'discrepancy detection' (i.e. the ability of the individual to

detect discrepancies between what is observed and what is suggested). The individual approach, in contrast, construes suggestibility as a potential vulnerability during questioning in terms of giving in to leading questions and interrogative pressure. Here, suggestibility is seen as being moderated by factors such as low IQ, poor memory, anxiety, low self-esteem, and history of life adversity, which impair the ability of the person to cope with the uncertainty and expectations contained within questioning (Drake, 2010, 2014; Gudjonsson, 2003a; Vagni et al., 2015).

What the experimental and individual differences approaches have in common is poor source monitoring (discrepancy detection) errors, but they differ in terms of how the interviewee processes the flawed source monitoring over time. Discrepancy detection errors can be measured by the 'don't know' replies provided to the GSS questions. People with attention deficit hyperactivity disorder (ADHD) give a disproportionately large number of 'don't know' replies to the interrogative questions on the GSS 2, while not appearing unduly suggestible on testing (Gudjonsson, Young, & Bramham, 2007). This type of 'don't know' response style makes suspects susceptible to developing memory distrust syndrome when interrogated (Gudjonsson, 2003a).

## CONCLUSIONS

In this chapter I have outlined the development of my suggestibility scales and the model that helps explain the mechanism of interrogative suggestibility. The model has been particularly powerful in generating testable hypotheses. The focus has been on understanding individual differences in terms of vulnerability to give in to leading questions and interrogative pressure, referred to as Yield and Shift, respectively. This individual differences approach, which tests immediate suggestibility, has recently been used to also measure delayed suggestibility (Gudjonsson, Vagni, et al., 2016). The current evidence is that the individual differences approach and the traditional experimental approach both rely on a common cognitive mechanism, discrepancy detection, but differ in the way people process the suggestion over time.

In the next chapter, I will focus on theories of false confessions and show that interrogative suggestibility, both immediate and delayed, is a key element in all of the theories.

# 4

# The Psychology of False Confessions: The Theories

*Although it may seem inconceivable to many people that anyone would come to believe and remember that they committed a crime of which they are in fact innocent, such cases – however rare – do exist*[1]

In the 1980s the main obstacle to preventing and correcting miscarriages of justice involving confession evidence was that people found it hard to believe that anyone would confess to a serious crime of which they were innocent (Gudjonsson, 2003a). A solid theoretical foundation can help us to understand the underlying causes of false confessions and how they may be identified, researched, and prevented.

Research has highlighted that there are a number of different causes of false confessions: even within a given case, there is often a combination of situational and personal factors (Gudjonsson, 2003a; Kassin & Gudjonsson, 2004; Kassin et al., 2010a). In this chapter, after defining false confessions, I will discuss theoretical developments, commencing with the early conceptualization of Hugo Münsterberg (1908), Kassin and Wrightsman's (1985) threefold psychological classification of false confessions, and our own work on memory distrust syndrome (Gudjonsson, 2003a; Gudjonsson & MacKeith, 1982) and a heuristic model of internalized false confessions (Gudjonsson, 2017; Gudjonsson et al., 2014).

---

[1] A quote from Henkel and Coffman (2004, p. 584).

*The Psychology of False Confessions: Forty Years of Science and Practice*, First Edition.
Gisli H. Gudjonsson.
© 2018 John Wiley & Sons Ltd. Published 2018 by John Wiley & Sons Ltd.

## DEFINITIONS OF FALSE CONFESSION

The most basic definition of a false confession occurs when a person confesses to a crime for which he or she is completely innocent (Gudjonsson, 2003a). In real-life cases certainty of innocence is difficult to establish without DNA or other forensic evidence exonerating the false confessor and, hopefully, identifying the real culprit (Garrett, 2011; Leo, 2008).

However, there is one circumstance when a confession may be considered false on psychological grounds. This happens when the confession is not based on the interviewee's actual knowledge or memory of the facts (Gudjonsson, 2003a; Ofshe, 1989). This is the essence of the definition used in this book in relation to the Gudmundur and Geirfinnur cases, where 'memory' problems were pervasive, both among witnesses and suspects.

Ofshe and Leo (1997a) and Leo and Ofshe (1998) make an important distinction between the initial admission ('I did it') and the 'post-admission narrative' that follows the admission, the latter building on the former. Through the 'post-admission narrative' the suspect provides details about his involvement and motivation. This 'special knowledge' is often used in court as evidence of the defendant's guilt and typically results in a conviction (Garrett, 2011).

The main problem with alleged 'special knowledge' in cases of disputed confession is that the police may either wittingly or unwittingly have communicated it to the suspect and then claim it all originated voluntarily and independently from him or her (Gudjonsson, 2003a). In his analysis of 250 cases of DNA exonerations in the USA, Garrett (2011) found that out of those 40 suspects who had falsely confessed, 38 (95%) provided detailed special knowledge that must have originated from the police: 'The police officers went further and also claimed they assiduously avoided contaminating the confession by not asking leading questions, rather, they allowed the suspect to volunteer each of the crucial facts' (p. 20).

## AN EARLY CONCEPTUAL FRAMEWORK

Hugo Münsterberg, who was a German–American psychologist, was one of the early pioneers in both experimental and applied psychology. In 1908 he published *On the Witness Stand*, a book which brought together a collection of magazine articles that he had published in the area of forensic psychology. The book included chapters on witness

memory, false confessions, and the impact of suggestion in police interviews and in court (Münsterberg, 1908). Rather than talking about
'false confessions', which is the modern terminology, Münsterberg
described these as 'untrue confessions'.

In my view, the psychology of false confessions started with
Münsterberg, who described the broad motivation behind false
confessions in the following terms:

> The untrue confessions from hope or fear, through promises and threats,
> from cunning calculations and passive yielding thus shade off into others
> which are given with real conviction under pressure of emotional excite-
> ment or under the spell of overpowering influences.
>
> (p. 147)

This statement and a careful reading of Münsterberg's chapter on
'Untrue Confessions' reveals that he anticipated the three distinct
types of false confession which are recognized today: the *voluntary
confession* ('The self-sacrificing desire to exculpate others' – p. 144), the
*coerced-compliant confession* ('The untrue confessions from hope or
fear, through promises and threats' – p. 147), and the *coerced-internalized confession* ('given with real conviction under pressure of emotional
excitement or under the spell of overpowering influences' – p. 147).

Münsterberg described a case of the internalized type, illustrating
the importance of the police presumption of guilt, the use of suggestion
during questioning, and the emergence of increased confabulation in
the narrative as it was repeated over and over again:

> When he came to the [police] station, he was told at once that he was the
> guilty man; but the accused denied everything. Now the police began to
> press him and to suggest more and more impressively to him his guilt.
> Suddenly he began to confess, and he was quite willing to repeat his
> confession again and again. Every time it became richer in detail.
>
> (pp. 164–165)

In psychological terms, Münsterberg described such internalized cases
as resulting from an 'emotional shock or a captivating impression'
that resulted in dissociation and imaginative thoughts. The key
elements are distortions in emotion and memory.

Münsterberg noted the importance of suggestion in the contamination of the memory process:

> And yet we have not even touched one factor which, more than anything
> else, devastates memory and plays havoc with our best intended
> recollections: that is, the power of suggestion.
>
> (p. 69)

Münsterberg's conceptualization of false confessions was basic and rather superficial, but it had the essence of a psychological process, particularly in relation to internalized false confession where intense emotions, memory flaws, and suggestions are the key psychological factors.

Another important contribution of Münsterberg's work was his proposition that false confessions can occur in healthy individuals who are caught up in an unusual circumstance (i.e. being arrested and accused of a serious crime). He did not view mental disorder, labelled 'mental disease' in the book, as generally being of primary importance in cases of false confession. Of greater importance in Münsterberg's theorizing was the fallibility of memory and he has been proved to be right! Münsterberg did have a remarkable insight into the psychology of false confessions in spite of the limited empirical evidence available at the time: he was an important pioneer.

## THE KASSIN AND WRIGHTSMAN THREEFOLD CLASSIFICATION

Professor Saul Kassin, a formidable social and experimental psychologist at John Jay College of Criminal Justice in New York, has made a number of major contributions to the understanding of the psychology of false confessions since the mid-1980s (Kassin, 2005, 2015, 2017; Kassin & Gudjonsson, 2004; Kassin & Kiechel, 1996; Kassin et al., 2010a; Wrightsman & Kassin, 1993). In this chapter I will focus on his classification of false confessions into three distinct types – 'voluntary', 'coerced-compliant', and 'coerced-internalized' (Kassin & Wrightsman, 1985) – and the identification of the key components that facilitate the process of internalization in cases of false confession (Kassin, 2007).

Kassin and Wrightsman (1985) arrived at their threefold classification on the basis of a review of the anecdotal literature and social-psychological theories of attitude change. *Voluntary confessions* were made in the 'absence of elicitation' and the main motives were a 'morbid desire for notoriety', 'the unconscious need to expiate guilt over previous transgressions via self-punishment', 'the hope for a recommendation of leniency', 'a desire to aid and protect the real criminal', and those 'unable to distinguish between fantasy and reality' (pp. 76–77). The voluntary type is distinct from the police coerced false confessions, which result from suspects' reactions to 'social control' attempts (Kelman, 1958).

The suspect's reaction to the social control pressure can either lead to a *coerced-compliant* or *coerced-internalized* false confession.

The compliant type is caused by the suspect giving in to custodial and interrogative pressure, knowing that he is innocent, but being motivated by short-term gains (for instance, an attempt to terminate the interrogation, hope of release from custody). The key element is the desire to escape from an intolerable situation. It persists as long as it is perceived to have an instrumental gain (i.e. the confession is likely to be retracted once the police pressure is off and the suspect feels safe). The key mechanism is *dysfunctional / maladaptive coping* (Gudjonsson, 1988, 2003a; Gudjonsson & Sigurdsson, 2003).

In contrast, the internalized type results from an *acceptance* of the allegations presented by the police, may persist over time and across situations (e.g. at the police station, in consultation with a lawyer, in court). The two key facilitating factors are: firstly, the conditions of the interrogation produce a trance-like state similar to that found in hypnosis (Ofshe, 1992), leading to distortions in reality, heightened capacity for imagination, and increased suggestibility and confabulation; and secondly, following the prediction of 'self-perception theory' (Bem, 1966, 1967), reiterating a lie makes people come to believe it. In a later publication, Kassin (2007) adds a *source monitoring* framework as an additional factor (i.e. people make attributions concerning the sources, contexts, or origins of their memories). He cites the work of Henkel and Coffman (2004), which suggests that source monitoring errors in cases of coerced false confessions are most likely to occur when the imagined material is plausible, vivid, easy to imagine, repeated, and similar to previously experienced actions or events. There is experimental evidence that the misinformation effect, which occurs when information presented subsequently interferes with the ability of the witness to retain previously encoded information, is more marked when people are hypnotized (Scoboria, Mazzoni, Kirsch, & Milling, 2002).

According to Kassin and Wrightsman, internalized false confessions involve a transition from an initial denial to a state of confusion, self-doubt, and acceptance. These authors emphasize the potential deleterious impact of internalization on subsequent memory retrieval:

> What is frightening under this stronger form of false confession is that the suspect's memory of his or her own actions may be altered, making its original contents potentially irretrievable.
>
> (p. 78)

The suggestion from this quote is that in internalized false confession cases memory may be altered to the extent that the original memory (e.g. the suspect's clear recollection that he/she had nothing to do with the offence) becomes inaccessible (i.e. the effect on memory is profound and permanent). Ofshe and Leo (1997a) have strongly challenged this proposition and Kassin (2007) has provided a robust response.

I have found the Kassin–Wrightsman classification helpful both in terms of clinical forensic practice and guiding research. Their single most important contribution is the theoretical distinction between compliant and internalized false confessions (Gudjonsson, 2003a; Sigurdsson & Gudjonsson, 1996a, 1996b). In addition, the classification has generated important research questions (Gudjonsson, 1992a, 2003a), and has been relied upon by confession experts, including its most vocal and high profile critics, Richard Ofshe and Richard Leo (Leo & Ofshe, 1998; Ofshe, 1989; Ofshe & Leo, 1997a, 1997b). This shows that the classification has withstood the passage of time, despite requiring some refinements.

## CRITIQUE OF THE KASSIN–WRIGHTSMAN CLASSIFICATION

At the time that Kassin and Wrightsman published their classification, the literature on false confession was in its infancy. False confessions were poorly understood and generally not accepted as genuine in the absence of mental disorder, such as intellectual disability or mental illness (see Gudjonsson, 1992a, 2003a; Gudjonsson & MacKeith, 1982). In view of this, it is not surprising that the typology has come under criticism. This includes observations that not all police-induced false confessions are coerced (Davison & Forshaw, 1993) and that coercion can occur from sources other than the police (McCann, 1998).

These are important and justified criticisms. To overcome the first criticism, I have recommended that the word 'coerced', which is a legal concept in this context, be replaced by the word 'pressured' (Gudjonsson, 2003a). The pressure may arise from detention, or fear of detention, interrogative pressure that does not amount to 'coercion', or a suspect desperately wanting to get out of the police station, which is common among drug addicts (Gudjonsson, 2003a; Pearse, Gudjonsson, Clare, & Rutter, 1998).

Even innocence itself may in some cases be sufficient to make suspects waive their legal rights at the police station (Kassin, 2005; Kassin & Norwick, 2004). I have come across many cases where suspects did not think they needed a lawyer because they were innocent. This is a naive perspective to take and mostly these suspects did not have an intellectual disability. In fact, short-sighted decision-making is a common reason suspects give for having made a false confession (Gudjonsson, 2003a). They believe that in spite of giving a self-incriminating statement to the police, somehow the truth of their innocence will eventually emerge (e.g. they think that their innocence will be self-evident).

In one case, a highly intelligent suspect developed a false sense of security after being told by his lawyer that the courts do not convict innocent people (he had asked his lawyer 'Do they convict innocent people' and the lawyer replied 'No'). Two weeks later the suspect gave a detailed pressured-internalized false confession to murder, which led to his conviction. His naivety and that of his lawyer had played a role in his false confession. I testified in the case on appeal and the man was acquitted and DNA later exonerated him (see Chapter 23, Gudjonsson, 2003a). The outcome of this case led to improved interviewing techniques in Norway (Fahsing et al., 2016).

## The 'Coerced-Reactive' Type

In some cases people may be pressured by other than police officers to make a false confession to a crime they did not commit. Such a confession is most likely to arise from a relationship pressure (e.g. peer, friend, relative, family). McCann (1998) argues that it is not adequately recognized by Kassin and Wrightsman's typology and recommends a separate coerced confession category, labelled 'coerced-reactive'. He suggests that in spite of some similarities with police coerced confessions (e.g. giving in to pressure), the coerced-reactive type is more likely to involve a close emotional relationship between the false confessor and the coercer and should therefore be conceptualized separately. McCann's re-conceptualization was stimulated by a case he had been consulted on involving a woman who had volunteered to police a false confession to having murdered one of her children. Later, it emerged that her husband had coerced her to do so.

When publishing his article in 1998, McCann stated:

> At this point, the coerced-reactive false confession remains at a theoretical and conceptual level of development and future research is required to examine ways in which various sources of coercion impact on the interrogation and confession process.
>
> (p. 450)

An English case having components of this type of false confession is that of Timothy Evans, who was found guilty of murdering his infant daughter and executed on 9 March 1950 (Kennedy, 1988). He went voluntarily to the police station having been manipulated by his landlord at 10 Rillington Place, John Christie, who was a serial murderer. Christie later told a psychiatrist: 'I could make Evans do or say anything I wanted' (Kennedy, 1988, p. 84).

What also sometimes happens is that people are tricked into a confession by a person with whom they have a relationship and it is secretly tape-recorded and then handed over to the police.

In one English case, a drug addict was used by police to put pressure on a fellow drug addict to confess to a murder he was suspected of having committed. The police then used self-incriminating comments from the tape-recording to try to elicit a confession from the suspect during formal questioning, but without success. Nevertheless, the man was convicted on the basis of the comments to the other drug addict but had his conviction quashed six years later on the basis of expert psychological testimony (Gudjonsson, 2006a, 2010a; see Case number 29 in the articles).

McCann's main contribution is that he raised awareness of an important group of false confessors that had been previously neglected. It is likely that the coerced-reactive type is largely confined to young persons and that such confessions are generally treated as voluntary confessions, because they are probably less likely to be retracted than police coerced confessions.

McCann also raises the potential importance of emotional connection between the coerced person and the coercer. The assumption is that the existing interpersonal (emotional) relationship produces an additional pressure on the coerced person. Is there any evidence for this? Interestingly, yes there is evidence to support this supposition from our own research. In 2008 we published a paper entitled 'Personal versus impersonal relationship compliance and their relationship with personality' (Gudjonsson, Sigurdsson, Einarsson, & Einarsson, 2008). The participants were 1,461 students in further education in Iceland, who had completed a specially constructed 15-item 'Situation Compliance Scale' (SCS) and some personality tests, including the Gudjonsson Compliance Scale (GCS). A principal component analysis of the SCS items showed that 'personal' and 'impersonal' items loaded on separate factors, which were moderately correlated (medium effect size). Both were significantly related to general compliance, anxiety proneness, and low self-esteem, suggesting an overlap in vulnerability to compliance in personal and impersonal relationships.

However, there are likely to be differences in the perceived outcome of a refusal to comply with a request or command with regard to personal and impersonal relationships. In police interviews, resistance often results in increased interrogative pressure and fear of detention (Gudjonsson & Sigurdsson, 1999). The key weapon of influence is the power of the interrogator over the suspect and his or her freedom (Hilgendorf & Irving, 1981). In contrast, a refusal to comply with a request from a close friend or partner, even if it is unreasonable, may result in a fear of emotional rejection (Cialdini, 1993). Of course, as in the case McCann described, fear of violence in an abusive relationship is also a powerful factor to induce compliance.

### The Ofshe–Leo Critique

Ofshe and Leo (1997b) provide the most vocal critiques of the Kassin–Wrightsman classification, describing it as 'in some ways inadequate' and based in part on 'erroneous assumptions' (p. 209). They express three criticisms:

- There is no need to have separate models for true and false confessions because 'both are driven by the same underlying logic and arise from interrogations that are to a considerable degree similar' (p. 209). Ofshe and Leo (1997b) then introduce their own theory and classification, which encompasses both true and false confessions.
- The classification fails to encompass the police-induced confessions that do not involve coercion (i.e. those that occur in the absence of police threats or inducements), citing Davison and Forshaw (1993), forensic psychiatrists at the Maudsley Hospital in London who focused primarily on the capacity of mentally disturbed people to act rationally and give voluntary confessions.
- The 'classification scheme misapplies the concept of internalization to the phenomenon of false confessions' (Ofshe & Leo, 1997b, p. 209) by suggesting that it is stable and can permanently distort memory.

Their most crucial attack on Kassin and Wrightsman concerns the latter's suggestion that internalization in cases of false confession may be stable and permanent. Ofshe and Leo (1997b) argue that from their experience and knowledge of the case literature that 'police-induced belief change during interrogation is temporary, inherently unstable, and situationally adaptive' ... 'Ordinary police interrogation is not sufficient to produce transformative or internalized belief change' (p. 209).

However, Ofshe and Leo (1997b) accept that in the case of Sheriff Officer Paul Ingram, who had confessed to sexual abuse of his daughters, he believed over a period of about six months that he was a leader of a satanic cult.

> Once the social structure (police, authority figures and family) supporting and shoring up Mr. Ingram's fragile belief system was withdrawn, his confidence ebbed, he realized that his new beliefs were unsupportable by

fact and he rejected them. Although Mr. Ingram's belief endured for an exceptionally long time, so did his interrogation. The beliefs he developed crumbled once his six-month long series of interrogations ended.

(p. 243, Note 26)

Ofshe and Watters (1994) have described this case in detail and the most relevant points are as follows:

- Paul Ingram was interrogated by policemen whom he knew and trusted.
- When denying any wrongdoing, he was pressed to agree that his daughters would not lie about something as serious as sexual allegations. The confidence in his memory began to crumble (i.e. changing his denial from 'I didn't do it' to 'I don't remember doing it') and he began to make admissions but was not able to provide any details.
- He was persuaded that he may have 'repressed' the memory of the abuse. The police brought in a local clinical psychologist to assist with the interrogation and convince Mr Ingram that it was possible to repress the memory of a serious criminal activity. The detectives became angry when Mr Ingram was unable to provide details of the alleged sexual offences, because he did not have any to reveal.

During the second day of interrogation the detectives played on Mr Ingram's feelings of guilt and the safety of his daughters. One of the detectives instructed him in a softly spoken voice:

> Just let yourself go and relax. No one's gonna hurt you. We want to help. Just relax.... Try not to think about anything. Ask yourself what you need to do. An answer will come, because I don't think that you ever wanted to hurt your kids. I know you want to provide a life for your children that is not filled with pain. You can still do that.... Why don't you tell us what happened to Julie, Paul – what happened at the poker games ...
> (p. 169)

Mr Ingram then suddenly began to visualize the scenes that the detectives had suggested to him. He subsequently repeatedly visualized the scenes without much encouragement – 'The process was motivated by his own desire to find the memories in question and augmented by an environment in which his memory search was strongly encouraged' (p. 174).

The crucial issues of the profoundness and duration of the internalized false confession will be comprehensively discussed in the second part of this book in relation to the convicted persons in the Gudmundur and Geirfinnur cases. It will go some way to resolving the disputes between Kassin and Ofshe and Leo.

## KEY COMPONENTS THAT ELICIT AND FACILITATE
## THE INTERNALIZATION PROCESS

Ofshe (1989), on the basis of four cases, argues that the primary mechanism for internalized false confessions consists of inducing self-doubt and confusion in the mind of the suspects, which permits the alteration of their perception of reality and belief system. This involved the interrogator convincing the suspects of the following:

- There is incontrovertible evidence that they committed the crime of which they are accused, even though they have no recollection of it.
- There is a good and valid reason why they have no memory of having committed the crime.

The four participants had been psychologically assessed. None were mentally ill, but all had the following dispositional traits: *good trust of people in authority*, *lack of self-confidence*, and *heightened suggestibility*.

Based on the analysis of case studies, Kassin (2007) identified five key components that facilitate the process of internalization (these overlap with those provided by Ofshe, 1989):

- There is a suspect with certain dispositional characteristics (e.g. young, naive, has low IQ, is suggestible) that makes him or her susceptible to police manipulation, as well as transient factors associated with custody and interrogation (e.g. social isolation, extreme stress, sleep deprivation).
- The police, wittingly or unwittingly, confront the suspect with false incontrovertible evidence of his or her involvement in the crime (e.g. alleged eyewitness, a false statement of a co-accused, failed polygraph test).
- Often with the assistance of the police, the suspect begins to believe that he has blacked out the memory of the crime (e.g. police suggest amnesia for the offence and provide an explanation such as experience of trauma or substance misuse).
- The suspect makes a tentative admission of guilt, typically using a language of inference rather than direct experience (e.g. 'I must have done it', 'I may have done it', 'I probably did it'). Even a shift from 'I didn't do it' (denial) to 'I don't remember doing it' (neither a denial nor an admission) may represent the first step in the admission process (see Ofshe & Watters, 1994, p. 167).
- The suspect converts the simple admission into a detailed confession where there has been confabulation from second-hand sources of information (e.g. suggestions from police, overheard conversation, crime scene photos, and visits to the crime scene). The confabulation process is facilitated by imaginational exercises (e.g. 'How could I have done it?').

Kassin and Wrightsman (1985) argue that compliance is most effectively elicited by forceful and blatant interrogation techniques, whereas internalization is more likely to result from subtle and manipulative methods, citing the work of Lepper (1983). This is consistent with my extensive experience with real-life cases of both types (Gudjonsson, 2003a).

Henkel and Coffman (2004) provide a source monitoring framework for understanding the cognitive processes that are involved in pressured-internalized false confessions, based on the work of Johnson and Raye (1981) and Johnson, Hashtroudi, and Lindsay (1993). Source monitoring involves a judgement process, which can be either *heuristic* or *systematic*. Heuristic judgements rely primarily on the qualitative features associated with the remembered event such as: (a) perceptual characteristics (e.g. visual detail, sound, or tactile sensations); (b) contextual characteristics (e.g. spatial and temporal information); (c) semantic detail (e.g. the distinctiveness and meaning of the item); (d) affective information (e.g. the emotional reaction to the event); and (e) information about the cognitive operations involved in the creation of a memory (e.g. information about the use of retrieval, identification, or organization when the event was first remembered). In addition to the automatic and qualitative features of heuristic judgements, deliberate and systematic judgement processes may take place, which require effort and energy to evaluate the source of a memory or its plausibility (e.g. on reflection the person realizes that the suggested event is far too unrealistic to have happened).

According to Henkel and Coffman:

> Many of the interrogation tactics widely used and advocated involve the creation of vivid mental imagery in suspects, a practice that according to principles of the source monitoring framework can result in misattributions of the imagery to actual perception.
>
> (p. 575)

## MEMORY DISTRUST SYNDROME

In September 1981 Jim MacKeith and I presented a paper on false confessions and psychological effects of interrogation at The Stockholm Symposium on Witness Psychology based on real-life cases (Gudjonsson & MacKeith, 1982). I discussed the background to this conference in Chapter 1.

The participants at the conference were sceptical about false confessions in the absence of mental disorder. This scepticism about false confessions remained among the English legal establishment until the release of the Guildford Four in October 1989 and has improved from then to the present day through a series of legal judgements focusing on police interviewing and psychological vulnerabilities (Gudjonsson, 2003a, 2003b, 2010a, 2012).

At the Stockholm Conference we introduced the concept of memory distrust syndrome, which we described at the time but did not define:

> The term 'memory distrust syndrome' may have some usefulness as a simple and memorable general description of some persons' tendencies to be persuaded that they might have committed a crime because they do not trust their own memory due to previous memory impairment.
> (Gudjonsson & MacKeith, 1982, p. 265)

This description was based on three case studies, one involving my eliciting of a false confession as a police detective in 1975 from a man with a history of alcoholic blackouts, which I described in the Introduction, and two cases from Jim MacKeith's case files. The first of Jim's cases involved a man suspected of murder, and when Jim was allowed to see him after three days in custody, he was in a 'very distressed state', but his anxiety was greatly reduced after seeing Jim, with whom he was familiar. He had a history of alcoholic blackouts and had nine months previously completed a seven-year sentence for manslaughter. He had been arrested again because certain aspects of the murder were similar to the offence of which he had been convicted. After intensive interrogation and three days in detention he contemplated whether he could have committed the murder and did not remember it. At one point *plausibility* of his involvement had set in and he was tempted to confess but managed to stop himself from doing so. Dr MacKeith arrived just in time to give him the support he needed.

The other case involved a man who was in police custody being interrogated about thefts from the Post Office, where he had worked. Two months before he had been wrongfully detained in police custody for three days in connection with an armed robbery, which had left him traumatized. When arrested for the alleged theft offences he could not tolerate the thought of another long interrogation and custody. He confessed after beginning to doubt his memory. He subsequently retracted his confession and was acquitted at trial.

This early work on memory distrust syndrome was preliminary and over the next two decades I came across several cases that further developed the model, and I collected the empirical evidence to support it (Gudjonsson, 2003a). I defined memory distrust syndrome as:

> A condition where people develop profound distrust of their memory recollections, as a result of which they are particularly susceptible to relying on external cues and suggestions.
>
> (p. 196)

Based on a number of cases I have assessed following our conference presentation, memory distrust syndrome is associated with three distinct conditions:

1. The suspect has no memory of the offence, even if he or she committed it. This may be due to psychogenic amnesia or alcohol-related memory problems. Those who are innocent may not recall what they were doing at the time the offence was committed, which weakens their resistance to police pressure and suggestions because of the *absence of a memory trace* to guide them.

2. The suspect has a poor recollection of what he or she was doing at the material time (i.e. *a weak memory trace*), typically due to the length of time since the alleged offence and not having at the time of their arrest and interrogation access to their diary or other material that could assist their recollection. For example, when Carole Richardson was arrested on 3 December 1974 in connection with the two Guildford bombings, she could not recall what she was doing on the day of the bombings. She knew the answer would be in her diary, but the police would not allow her access to it. It was later discovered that on the evening of the bombing on 5 October 1974, Carole had been at a concert at South Bank Polytechnic (Victory, 2001).

3. The suspect has a clear recollection of what he or she was doing at the time of the offence (i.e. in their mind they have a clear alibi – *a strong memory trace*), but the recollection of the alibi is undermined over time by subtle manipulative influences. The confidence in the alibi is eroded and new beliefs are created by the police, either wittingly or unwittingly.

The weaker the original memory trace, the easier it is for the police to extract an internalized false confession, but even in cases of a strong memory trace, suspects may eventually succumb to pressure in police interview (Gudjonsson, 2003a). In addition to this quantitative aspect of memory during retrieval, the qualitative nature of the memory is also important (Gallo, Meadow, Johnson, & Foster, 2008). Suspects may recall some aspects of their alibi well and other parts poorly (e.g. clearly recalling returning home after a night out but not recalling precisely the time when doing so). This suggests a failure in 'memory binding', where the individual components of the suspect's memory of the experience do not form a unitary whole, or a workable sequence (Schacter, 2007). The police can then use the vagueness about the timing to undermine the suspect's confidence in his alibi. People who distrust their own memory are particularly likely to accept misinformation, although they did not score higher on the GCS or the Gudjonsson Suggestibility Scale (GSS) than those with memory confidence (Van Bergen, Horselenberg, Merckelbach, Jelicic, & Beckers, 2010). Probably a better measure of memory distrust than Yield 1 and Shift scores are the number of 'don't know' replies given to the leading questions (Gudjonsson, 2003a; Gudjonsson et al., 2007). This should be the lead measure in future research.

## THE FIVE SEQUENTIAL STEPS

Episodic false memories of committing a crime have been reported in real-life cases (Gudjonsson, 2003a) and in a controlled experimental setting (Shaw & Porter, 2015), supporting the theory of memory distrust syndrome. In a previous publication (Gudjonsson et al., 2014), we outlined five sequential steps of how such memories may happen:

*A trigger.* False beliefs can be provoked by something people see, hear, are told, or dream about. In one case the trigger was a confrontation by police about errors in a person's memory, followed by a dream that he might be involved (Gudjonsson et al., 1999).

*Plausibility.* The incident is perceived as if it could have happened. The threshold for a plausibility shift can be quite low for it to be accepted and incorporated into memory (Mazzoni, Loftus, & Kirsch, 2001). The more serious the incident (crime), the higher the threshold needed for acceptance of plausibility (i.e. the person needs to be able to see him/herself as capable of having committed the act).

*Acceptance that the event may have happened.* After contemplating the plausibility that the material event occurred, unless a 'distinctiveness heuristic' is successfully activated, source monitoring errors occur and the witness or accused accepts that the event may have happened (Schacter, 2007). The more plausible the accusation the greater the likelihood that the accused will accept it, internalize it, and give a false confession (Horselenberg et al., 2006).

*Reconstruction.* Once acceptance has taken place, the person then tries to make sense of it by constructing in their imagination what could or may have happened. This reconstruction may be assisted by information provided by the police, co-accused, crime scene visits, or what the individual has heard or read about the case (Gudjonsson et al., 2014). Encouraging suspects to visualize what they think happened and using hypnotic suggestions substantially increases the risk of the production of false memories (Schacter, 2007).

*Resolution.* When does the person realize that they had a false belief/ memory and have given a false confession? In some instances the person may continue to believe it for a long time and usually the resolution is associated with: (a) the person was in a state of confusion and once the pressure is removed and they have had time to think constructively, the true memory comes back (Gudjonsson, 2003a; Ofshe & Leo, 1997a; Ofshe & Watters, 1994); or (b) the person goes through the evidence in the case and realizes that they had nothing to do with the offence – it facilitates the return of their remembering that they are innocent (Gudjonsson et al., 2014).

Table 4.1 shows a three-level process of internalized false confession (i.e. police making the suspect doubt his/her innocence, creating a false belief of guilt, and then assisting the suspect with the reconstruction), the technique used (challenges, suggestions, minimization, providing crime-related details), and pre-existing vulnerabilities. The pre-existing vulnerabilities for eroding existing memory of innocence may include a history of substance misuse, memory problems, lack of memory confidence, poor discrepancy detection, trust in the police, and suggestibility and compliance.

In serious criminal cases, interrogation that breaks down denials and resistance typically involves lengthy, manipulative, and repeated interviews (Pearse & Gudjonsson, 1999).

The initial process of internalized false confession consists of two distinct phases. Firstly, where some memory trace of innocence exists, the memory of the alibi, and knowledge and confidence in their genuine memory is eroded by police presumption of guilt, persuasive interviewing, and a possible explanation as to why their memory is flawed (e.g. alcohol or drug problem, poor memory, the trauma associated with the crime). Suggesting that the suspect has memory problems increases the likelihood of the development of memory distrust during questioning (Van Bergen et al., 2008). There is then a gradual development of confusion regarding the original recollection. The comments the suspect makes may go from 'I remember not doing it' to 'I don't remember doing it'. This is a strong indication to the police that resistance is beginning to break down and they take advantage of it (Ofshe & Watters, 1994). This shift is caused by a failure in the 'distinctiveness heuristic', a key mechanism in internalized false confessions (see section below).

**Table 4.1**   The process of internalized false confession, type of technique used by the police, and pre-existing vulnerabilities

| The process | Type of technique | Pre-existing vulnerabilities |
|---|---|---|
| Causing suspects to doubt existing memory of innocence | • Guilt-presumptive questioning<br>• Police challenging the accuracy of the original memory and suggesting memory problems<br>• Presentation of false evidence<br>• Police providing an explanation for the apparent absence of memory<br>• Told will not get out until they 'tell the truth'<br>• Solitary confinement<br>• Sleep deprivation | • Substance misuse<br>• Memory problems<br>• Lack of confidence in memory<br>• Poor ability for discrepancy detection<br>• Trust in police<br>• Suggestibility<br>• Compliance |
| Creating the false belief of guilt ('plausibility', 'acceptance') | • Establish good rapport with suspect and build up feelings of trust<br>• Gentle interrogation, using a softly spoken voice<br>• Use of 'minimization' (e.g. 'You didn't mean to do it', 'Was it an accident?', 'The victim was being unreasonable and provocative', 'I would have done the same') | • Trust in police<br>• Poor self-image/ low self-esteem<br>• Suggestibility<br>• Compliance<br>• Good imagination<br>• Tendency towards confabulation |
| Reconstruction – the suspect's replies to questions are vague and tentative – the outcome may resemble a *screenplay* with a combination of suggested and imagined material | • Police provide details of crime<br>• Shown crime scene photographs<br>• Visits to crime scene<br>• Leading and hypothetical questions<br>• Guided imagery technique<br>• Hypnosis<br>• Truth drugs | • Trust in police<br>• Poor self-image/ self-esteem<br>• Suggestibility<br>• Compliance<br>• Good imagination<br>• Tendency towards confabulation |

Once the original memory trace has been weakened or has serious doubt cast over its accuracy, the second stage involves the police implanting the belief that the suspect committed the offence. This process is easy to demonstrate experimentally when people are falsely accused of having touched the wrong key on a computer by mistake (Kassin & Kiechel, 1996), but persuading suspects that they have committed a serious crime that is completely 'out of character' is far more challenging for the interrogator. The Reid Technique of 'minimization' is commonly used for this purpose (Kassin & Gudjonsson, 2004), where the suspect's role in the offence is initially minimized and some justification provided (e.g. they did not mean to do it, it was an accident, or the victim was being unreasonable and provocative). The key psychological vulnerability here is low or 'fragile' self-esteem, which makes the suspect accept that he committed an offence of which he is innocent.

The police may assist the suspect with the reconstruction of what happened, for example by providing crime-related knowledge and using leading and hypothetical questions (Gudjonsson, 2003a). Unless the entire interview is audio and/or videotaped, the extent of the incriminating information the police communicate to the suspect to incorporate into his statement is difficult to verify. Where police contamination takes place, it is almost invariably denied by the police, claiming 'they assiduously avoided contaminating the confession by not asking leading questions, but rather allowing the suspect to volunteer each of the crucial facts' (Garrett, 2011, p. 20).

Table 4.2 shows the factors involved in the process of resolution. A number of factors can prevent resolution, including continued interrogation and social isolation. This increases the likelihood that the suspect remains in a state of confusion. Once the interrogation stops and the pressure no longer exists, the state of confusion is typically resolved. However, in some cases the state of confusion does not spontaneously resolve and may continue for several months or even

**Table 4.2**  The process of resolution

| Preventative factors | Facilitating factors |
|---|---|
| • Social isolation<br>• Continued solitary confinement<br>• Continued interrogation over a long time period<br>• Lack of social/legal support<br>• No access to case material that shows weakness in the evidence | • Pressure of interrogation is over<br>• Being released from custody<br>• Resolution of the confusional state<br>• The suspect/defendant/appellant carefully scrutinizing the evidence<br>• Good social/legal support<br>• Having others believe in their innocence<br>• New evidence of innocence<br>• Passing a polygraph test |

years (Gudjonsson, 2003a, 2017). In one such case, passing a polygraph test helped the defendant to believe in his innocence, whereas in another case it was speaking to a lawyer about the lack of evidence against him (Gudjonsson, 2003a). A strong motivating factor is derived from the knowledge that significant others (e.g. lawyers, family, friends, mental health professionals, journalists) believe in their innocence.

There is evidence for the importance of suggestibility and compliance in relation to memory distrust and internalized false confessions. It is mainly based on anecdotal case histories (Gudjonsson, 2003a; Kassin, 2007; Ofshe, 1989; Ofshe & Watters, 1994; Sigurdsson & Gudjonsson, 1996a), but laboratory evidence has emerged to validate the application of the concept in relation to suggestibility, compliance, and false confessions (Blair, 2007; Redlich & Goodman, 2003; Thorley, 2013; Van Bergen et al., 2009), although contradictory findings have been reported (Blair, 2007; Horselenberg, Merckelbach, & Josephs, 2003; Horselenberg et al., 2006; Van Bergen, 2011). There is anecdotal evidence that proneness to fantasy or confabulation is associated with internalized false confessions (Gudjonsson, 2003a), which is supported by experimental evidence (Horselenberg et al., 2006). An experimental study has shown that suggesting memory problems and providing false technical evidence has a significant impact on memory distrust (Van Bergen et al., 2008). Presenting participants with faked video evidence increases the risk of internalized false confessions (Nash & Wade, 2009).

The Sigurdsson and Gudjonsson (1996a) study is particularly informative of the role of suggestibility and compliance in relation to false confessions. Out of 509 Icelandic prisoners interviewed and tested psychometrically, 62 (12%) reported that they had given a false confession to police at some time in their lives. The false confessors scored significantly higher on the GCS than the other prisoners. Nine (14.5%) of the 62 false confessions were of the internalized type and those confessors scored significantly higher on suggestibility and confabulation on the GSS 1 than the other types of false confessors.

## IMMEDIATE VERSUS DELAYED SUGGESTIBILITY

When reviewing the evidence of a relationship between suggestibility and memory distrust, it is important to distinguish between 'immediate' and 'delayed' suggestibility (Ridley & Gudjonsson, 2013). Immediate suggestibility refers to the immediate effects of leading questions and interrogative pressure and is generally measured by the GSS 1 and GSS 2; Gudjonsson, 1984a, 1987, 1997). In contrast, delayed suggestibility refers to the extent to which the person incorporates misleading post-event information into their subsequent recollection, typically labelled 'misinformation' effects, and follows the experimental paradigm of Loftus et al. (1978). It generally follows a three-stage misinformation paradigm (Chrobak & Zaragoza, 2013; Ridley & Gudjonsson, 2013): (1) witnessing an event, (2) exposure to misleading post-event information, and (3) a delayed test to see whether the misleading post-event information presented earlier leads to a suggestible response. Unlike immediate suggestibility it is measured in a subsequent test to that of the initial suggestion (Chrobak & Zaragoza, 2013; Lee, 2004; Loftus, 1979). The central cognitive mechanism that appears to drive both immediate and delayed suggestibility is faulty 'discrepancy detection' (Gudjonsson, 2003a; Schooler & Loftus, 1986), also known as 'source monitoring' error (Chrobak & Zaragoza, 2013; Johnson et al., 1993).

There is a poor relationship between immediate and delayed suggestibility (Vagni et al., 2015). Furthermore, unlike immediate suggestibility, delayed suggestibility is not related to the original memory trace of the event or the age of the child (range 7–16). As far as I am aware, there is no comparable data available for adults.

Delayed suggestibility appears more related to memory distrust syndrome than immediate suggestibility (Gudjonsson et al., 2014), although anecdotally a lack of effective source monitoring on the GSS, indicated by vague, hesitant, and a disproportionate number of 'don't know' replies to the leading questions have been noted in cases of memory distrust (Gudjonsson, 2003a).

## A HEURISTIC MODEL OF INTERNALIZED FALSE CONFESSIONS

In 2014 my colleagues and I published a paper in *Applied Cognitive Psychology* on a heuristic model of memory distrust that described the antecedents and processes involved in producing internalized false confessions (Gudjonsson et al., 2014). The background behind this article is that the Icelandic government Working Group on the Gudmundur and Geirfinnur cases published its report in March 2013, which cast serious doubts on the reliability of the confessions of the six convicted persons. Having acted as an expert to the Working Group, I believed that the lessons learned regarding the psychology of false confessions warranted a scientific analysis of the case and suggested to the four

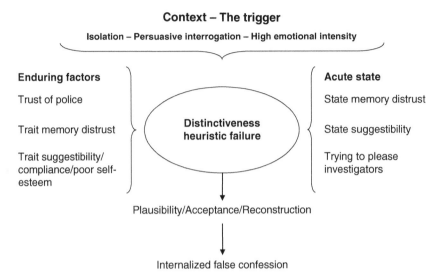

**Figure 4.1**  Heuristic model of pressured-internalized false confessions

members of the Working Group that we should write a joint paper on the case. Two years later I refined the model in an article in *Cortex* (Gudjonsson, 2017), which lays the foundation for this section.

Figure 4.1 provides an outline of the model. The 'context' of the arrest and confinement provided the potential 'trigger' for altering suspects' belief systems regarding the alleged offence. The three key triggers are *social isolation*, *persuasive interrogation*, and *high emotional intensity*, which feed directly into the suspect's cognitive appraisal of the situation and are viewed as contextual 'risk factors'. These do not inevitably lead to a false confession, but they are important prerequisites for internalized false confessions to occur.

Whether or not the contextual risk factors elicit an internalized false confession depends on the nature, duration, and intensity of the custodial confinement and interrogation, the effects of which are mediated by two sets of vulnerability factors: *enduring characteristics* (i.e. general trust of the police, trait memory distrust, high suggestibility and compliance, poor self-esteem) and an *acute state* generated by the contextual trigger factors (i.e. state memory distrust, state suggestibility, and compliance – attempts to please the investigators). The enduring and acute state factors lead to failure to evoke or maintain the *distinctiveness heuristic*, which is the primary mechanism whereby internalized false confessions arise.

The phenomenon of the distinctiveness heuristic has been well established by experimental work in the field of memory. Schacter (2007, p. 102) defines it as:

> a rule of thumb that leads people to demand recollections of distinctive details of an experience before they are willing to say that they remember it.

It represents a state of mental confusion where the person is no longer able to distinctively recall that he/she had not committed or witnessed the crime. For example, when being falsely accused of a serious crime, the immediate instinctive reaction is likely to be: 'I didn't do it', sometimes followed by the explanation 'If I had done it, I would remember it'.

According to the heuristic model, the custodial risk factors activate both enduring and state factors. In some instances, there may not necessarily be salient enduring factors. For example, Davis and Leo (2012, 2013) describe how acute factors (i.e. emotional distress, reduced glucose intake, and fatigue/sleep deprivation) may cause failure in 'self-regulation' (i.e. an inability to control emotion, cognition, and behaviour). The implication is that healthy suspects of good intelligence may in some circumstances succumb to pressures in a police interview due to depletion of self-regulatory resources.

The distinctiveness heuristic is easier to evoke in relation to recent events than those that took place a long time ago because memory deteriorates over time. If arrested on suspicion of a serious offence like murder or a sexual offence, it is likely to cause a great deal of emotional distress even if suspects are fully aware of their innocence. The more serious and bizarre the offence the greater the likelihood that the distinctiveness heuristic will be evoked, because the perceived plausibility will be low. In those circumstances the police might attempt to erode the belief that 'If I had done it, I would remember it'. This is sometimes done by persuading the suspect that the event was so traumatic that he/she must have 'repressed' it from memory, or that their memory is faulty. Once the suspect begins to comment, 'I don't remember doing it', then this is a clear sign that their distinctiveness heuristic is failing. The police might then say, 'If you don't remember doing it, how can you be sure you didn't do it?', further undermining the suspect's confidence in his innocence. The suspect now begins to accept the plausibility that he committed the crime ('I may have done it'), followed by acceptance ('I did it') and attempts at reconstruction of the alleged crime. The internalized false confession is now complete.

Memory distrust and suggestibility have both trait and state like features. A high trait component of either memory distrust or suggestibility makes people potentially vulnerable to pressured-internalized false confessions, but this does not exclude the possibility that such confessions can be elicited in the absence of trait vulnerabilities. A suspect may enter the interrogation with pre-existing distrust of their memory, which may be manipulated by the interrogator to induce state memory distrust, or the memory distrust may be entirely induced during the interrogation and confinement (i.e. state dependent). In either case, the interrogation would typically involve challenging the suspect's existing memory of innocence (e.g. alibi), providing a plausible explanation of why the event was apparently forgotten (e.g. because of substance misuse, history of memory problems, amnesia), causing them to wonder whether he or she committed the offence ('Perhaps I did do it'), and getting him/her to make a full ('I did it') or tentative ('I may have done it', 'I could have done it') admission, leading to a full admission ('I did it'). Once the admission has been obtained, the police may assist the suspect in generating a plausible crime-related scenario and forming a mental image of what may have taken place, which in turn becomes his or her confession.

## CONCLUSIONS

In this chapter I have outlined the development of theories of false confessions and interrogative suggestibility. It is evident that many advances have been made since Münsterberg's (1908) publication *On the Witness Stand*. In spite of criticisms and its limitations, the Kassin and Wrightsman (1985) threefold classification for the psychology of false confessions has stood up well to the passage of time. In the early 1980s, the literature on false confession was in its infancy. The introduction of the Kassin and Wrightsman classification, our concept of memory distrust syndrome, innovative research into interrogative suggestibility, and the publication in 1992 of *The Psychology of Interrogations, Confessions, and Testimony* (Gudjonsson, 1992a) have had a huge impact on the knowledge of false confessions and relevant psychological vulnerabilities. This chapter shows the impact. The greatest advance has been made in furthering the understanding of internalized false confessions. The heuristic model provides a unique insight into their cause and mechanism of formation.

# 5

# The Development of the Science: The Evidence Base

*My first reflection is that it does not take much skill to beat a confession out of a suspect detained in police custody*[1]

In this chapter I will discuss the key empirical findings and show that major advances have been made in terms of understanding the dynamic process of interrogation, the negative impact of certain tactics, the frequency with which false confessions occur, the reasons for false confessions, and the processes and risk factors involved. The focus in this chapter is on 'What does the evidence tell us?' The beginning of the science of the psychology of false confessions did not properly commence until the 1980s and continues to develop to the present day.

In 1980, Irving and Hilgendorf (1980, pp. 25–26) pointed to the limited knowledge about false confessions:

> Although we can argue from the psychological literature that in princi-ple, false confessions can be elicited by the application to an innocent suspect of techniques which may also be successful in obtaining true con-fessions from the guilty, the state of knowledge is not sufficient to assist in detecting false confessions when they have been obtained (assuming that there is no other evidence which casts doubt on their reliability). At present it is not even possible to be certain about how a confession which is known to be false came to be made.

---

[1] The words of a senior English police officer who was instrumental in introducing the PEACE Model in the early 1990s (Williamson, 1994, p. 107).

*The Psychology of False Confessions: Forty Years of Science and Practice*, First Edition.
Gisli H. Gudjonsson.
© 2018 John Wiley & Sons Ltd. Published 2018 by John Wiley & Sons Ltd.

I will summarize the principal areas of development, which are based on:
* Models of interrogation and confessions.
* Observational field studies of suspects interrogated by police.
* In-depth analysis of interrogation tactics.
* Anecdotal case studies of false confessions.
* Interviews and psychological evaluations of suspects and convicted prisoners.
* Surveys of students, juveniles, those with mental illness, and police officers regarding false confessions.
* Laboratory (experimental) studies.


## BRIEF SUMMARY OF THEORETICAL DEVELOPMENTS

### Interrogation

A number of models have been developed to help explain the mechanisms and processes that facilitate a confession during custodial interrogation. These focus primarily on true confessions but are also relevant to false confessions. I will briefly review six of these models.

1. *The Reid model of confession* (Inbau et al., 2013).

Also known as the Reid Technique. The authors recommend a three-stage process. Stage one involves a factual analysis of the offence and circumstances prior to interviewing the suspect. Stage two involves a nonaccusatory interview, referred to as a *Behavioural Analysis Interview* (BAI) where the interviewer determines, on the basis of observational clues, whether or not the suspect is guilty of the alleged offence. It is recommended at this stage that suspects are interviewed in a noncustodial environment, because it 'eliminates the need to advise the suspect of his constitutional rights under *Miranda*' (p. 74). Once the suspect's guilt 'seems definite or reasonably certain' (Inbau et al., 2013, p. 187), stage three, the 'nine steps' of interrogation, commence.

The ability of investigators to accurately determine guilt or innocence influences the base rate of guilt among those interrogated. Inbau and his colleagues place a great deal of weight on the ability of investigators to detect deception on the basis of the BAI. They claim that trained investigators can achieve an 85% level of accuracy regarding the detection of deception through verbal clues, nonverbal clues, and behavioural attitudes (Kassin et al., 2007).

The problem is that there is no behavioural or verbal cue that is uniquely related to deception (Vrij, 2008). In fact, Vrij devotes an entire chapter in his book on the BAI and concludes that the principles underlying it are 'questionable' (p. 193). In addition, the empirical research and experimental studies that have attempted to validate the BAI have generally not produced favourable results.

Vrij concludes:

> The situation is worrying for innocent suspects who are submitted to the BAI protocol. Investigators may base their impressions about the suspect's guilt on the outcome of a BAI interview. Although there is no guarantee that their impressions will be correct, BAI users may be confident that they are. Police investigators who are reasonably certain of a suspect's guilt may submit a suspect to persuasive interrogation techniques meant to break down the suspect's resistance [...] once innocent suspects are mistakenly identified as guilty, they run the risk of being submitted to an interview style that is even more grilling than the interview style that guilty suspects are subjected to. This may lead to false confessions.
>
> (p. 199)

Vrij et al. (2014) review different techniques for identifying deception in police interviews, including the recent Strategic Use of Evidence approach (Granhag & Hartwig, 2008, 2015) and the cognitive lie detection approach (Vrij, Granhag, Mann, & Leal, 2011). Both these new approaches consider the different frame of mind of truth-tellers and liars and are based on the principle that interviewers can elicit differences in response strategies between truth-tellers and liars through asking specific questions.

A high false negative error rate means police are eliminating many guilty people from enquiries, whereas a high positive error rate indicates that many innocent people are interrogated as suspects, increasing the risk of false confessions. In an experimental study, Meissner and Kassin (2002) found that while investigators have higher confidence than students in distinguishing between true and false denials, they were significantly more likely to make false positive errors, suggesting an 'investigator bias' towards perceiving deception when there is none. Narchet, Meissner, and Russano (2011) have shown experimentally how investigator bias leads to more frequent use of minimization tactics and thereby increases the risk of false confession.

The Reid nine-step model is guilt-presumptive, using direct confrontation, deception, psychological manipulation, suggestions, and theme development to break down resistance. The authors make a bold statement justifying their technique: 'It must be remembered that none of the steps is apt to make an innocent person confess and that all the steps are legally as well as morally justified' (Inbau et al., 2013, p. 187). Pérez-Sales (2017) describes the Reid Technique as 'the most well-known coercive interrogation paradigm' (p. 199).

Kassin and McNall (1991) argue that the main deception and manipulation of the technique involves 'maximization' (i.e. exaggerating the strength of the evidence against the suspect and the seriousness of his/her predicament) and 'minimization' (i.e. playing down the seriousness of the offence and providing the suspect with face-saving excuses through the use of theme development). Kassin and McNall provide experimental evidence that raises serious concerns about the use of the Reid Technique (see also Gudjonsson, 1992a, 2003a; Gudjonsson & Pearse, 2011; Kassin & Gudjonsson, 2004; Kassin et al., 2010a; Leo, 2008; Meissner, Russano, & Narchet, 2010; Meissner et al., 2014; Ofshe & Leo 1997a, 1997b; Pérez-Sales, 2017).

Pearse and Gudjonsson (1999, 2003) found that in the late 1980s and early 1990s police officers in the UK sometimes used aspects of the Reid Technique to break down resistance in serious cases (i.e. intimidation, robust challenges, psychological manipulation), leading to unreliable confessions. This is perhaps not surprising when one considers that at the time Walkley (1987) produced a handbook of interviewing for British police officers endorsing many of the elements of the Reid Technique, including psychological manipulation.

2. *Decision-making model of confession* (Hilgendorf & Irving, 1981; Irving & Hilgendorf, 1980).

This includes false confessions, although it is not a model of false confessions. The model is closely linked to the legal concepts of 'voluntariness' and 'oppression' and postulates that suspects' decisions are determined by their perceptions of available courses of action, their estimates of the likely consequences attached to these courses of action, and the gains attached to them. The authors point out that:

> The problems with confessions made to police is that they are frequently retracted with the same spontaneity and conviction with which they were first uttered, leaving the prosecution and defence all too often with two conflicting statements and no corroborative evidence to back either of them.
>
> (Hilgendorf & Irving, 1981, pp. 67–68)

Within their framework, Hilgendorf and Irving argue that threats and inducements, stated or implied, can markedly influence the decision to confess due to the power the police have over suspects in custody. Importantly, interrogators jeopardize the reliability (validity) of the confession when they manipulate social and self-approval utilities and the suspect's perception of different courses of action within the interview. Anxiety, fear, and discomfort impair the suspect's decision-making ability.

The potential contribution of applied psychologists in evaluating the reliability of confession evidence was seen at the time to be hampered by three factors:

- Lack of reliable information about the circumstances in which the confession was obtained, or that the available information was disputed.
- Where reliable information is available, 'the state of psychological knowledge about the relative power of the relevant variables and their possible interactions is insufficient because interrogation *per se* has not been extensively studied' (p. 68).
- Even where the information is available and the state of psychological knowledge is present (e.g. in cases of sleep deprivation), the expert opinion must fit in with the pre-existing legal framework.

3. *Psychoanalytic models of confession* (e.g. Berggren, 1975; Reik, 1959).

These models are based on the assumption that feelings of guilt are fundamental causes of both true and false confessions. Berggren argues that for satisfactory cathartic effects to occur the person has to confess to a person in authority, such as a priest or policeman.

Many sex and violent offenders report strong feelings of guilt and shame regarding their offences (Gudjonsson & Petursson, 1991), but feelings of shame need to be first overcome in order to obtain a confession, particularly in sex offender cases (Gudjonsson, 2006b). Items relating to feelings of guilt and shame load on separate factors and these should be viewed as distinct concepts (Wright & Gudjonsson, 2007).

4. *An interactional process model of confession* (Moston, Stephenson, & Williamson, 1992).

The model postulates that the suspect's initial reaction to the allegations, irrespective of his or her involvement in the crime, is influenced by three main factors:

- Background characteristics of the suspect and the offence (e.g. type of offence, its severity, age and gender of the suspect, and the suspect's pre-existing personality).
- Contextual characteristics of the case (e.g. access to legal advice, the strength of the police evidence).
- The interview technique utilized.

Moston and colleagues showed that the strength of the police evidence significantly predicted whether or not the suspect confessed. For example, where the evidence was rated as 'weak', only 23.4% confessed, in contrast to 66.7% where it was rated as 'strong'. Viljoen, Klaver, and Roesch (2005) found that this was also true among young defendants (age range 11–17) with the exception of those in the youngest age group (11–13).

The strength of the model is that it looks at the outcome of the interview as an interaction process of a number of factors, rather than looking at each factor in isolation. An important implication of the model is that background characteristics of the suspect and the case, in tandem with contextual factors, influence the interviewer's beliefs, attitudes, and style of questioning, which in turn influence the suspect's behaviour.

The main limitation of the model is that it does not focus on the mental state and cognitive processes of the suspect.

5. *A cognitive-behavioural model of confession* (Gudjonsson, 1989c, 2003a).

This model postulates that both true and false confessions are best construed as arising through the existence of a particular relationship between the suspect, the environment and significant others within that environment. In order to understand that relationship, we need to look closely at the *antecedents* and *consequences* of confessing behaviour within the framework of behavioural analysis.

The antecedents to confessions are discussed in terms of 'social' (i.e. isolation, police pressure), 'emotional' (i.e. distress), 'cognitive' (i.e. functional vs dysfunctional thinking), 'situational' (i.e. arrest, interrogation, confinement, access to a lawyer), and 'physiological' (i.e. high physical arousal, effects of alcohol and drugs) events.

The consequences of confession are immediate (e.g. police providing positive reinforcement if a confession is obtained, terminating the interview, the suspect getting out of the police station) and long term (e.g. conviction, imprisonment, having to come to terms with being viewed as a criminal).

When under the stress of interrogation and confinement, suspects tend to focus on the immediate consequences of the situation rather than the long-term consequences (Gudjonsson, 2003a). This is supported by empirical evidence, which shows that not realizing the long-term consequences of the confession loads strongly on a factor of 'external' (i.e. police and custodial) pressure to confess (Sigurdsson & Gudjonsson, 1996b).

In a lecture at the Medico-Legal Society in London on 12 January 1989, I stated:

> A frequent comment among people who have retracted their confession is that they thought that the truth would somehow come out, that their solicitor would sort it out when he arrives, if he or she is not present during the interview, and that the case against them will not proceed. This is clearly a very naive assumption, since in reality a self-incriminating admission to a serious crime, even if disputed at trial, results in a conviction in a great majority of cases. In exceptional circumstances innocent

criminal suspects may through subtle police questioning begin to wonder if they could have committed the offence after all.

(Gudjonsson, 1989c, p. 98)

Kassin and Norwick (2004) confirmed my clinical observation 15 years later in a laboratory experiment involving a mock theft, which showed that 'innocent' suspects were significantly more likely to waive their rights than the 'guilty' suspects, suggesting that innocence itself is a potential risk factor during police interviews due to the naivety associated with their innocence.

The *cognitive-behavioural model* led to me developing a 'confession questionnaire' (Gudjonsson Confession Questionnaire, GCQ), which could be used for understanding both 'true' and 'false' confessions (Gudjonsson & Petursson, 1991). It consisted of 36 items and was first validated on 74 convicted Icelandic prisoners. A principal component analysis revealed three key factors that facilitate a confession and one factor that inhibited offenders from confessing to the crime they had committed (e.g. thoughts of their family and friends and finding it difficult to accept what they had done). Importantly, the GCQ identifies reasons for confession that are translatable into interrogation techniques (Kelly, Miller, Redlich, & Kleinman, 2013).

The three facilitating confession factors were:
- 'External pressure' (i.e. fear of police, pressure during interview, feeling bullied, and being frightened of being locked up).
- 'Internal pressure' (i.e. feeling guilty about the offence, wanting to 'get it off their chest', and a sense of relief after giving a confession).
- 'Perception of proof' (i.e. believing that there was no point in denying it and thinking that the police would eventually prove they were responsible).

*Perception of proof* was the most commonly reported reason for giving a true confession, followed by feelings of remorse about the offence, but typically suspects confessed because of a combination of factors.

*External pressure* was found to be particularly high among those interrogated in relation to property offences. The strongest *internal* need to confess was found among sex and violent offenders, but before being able to do so their feelings of shame had to be overcome (Gudjonsson, 2006b).

At the time of completing the GCQ the participants completed a number of psychological tests. These were a nonverbal measure of IQ (the Standard Progressive Matrices, Raven, 1960), the Eysenck Personality Questionnaire (EPQ, Eysenck & Eysenck, 1975), and the Gudjonsson Blame Attribution Inventory-Revised (BAI-R, Gudjonsson & Singh, 1989). The results are shown in Table 5.1. *External pressure*

**Table 5.1** The correlations of the three facilitating confession factors with age and psychological variables

| Variable | External pressure | Internal pressure | Perception of proof |
|---|---|---|---|
| Age | −0.34** | 0.06 | 0.01 |
| IQ (Raven) | −0.19 | −0.10 | 0.04 |
| EPQ Psychoticism | 0.23* | −0.14 | −0.21 |
| EPQ Neuroticism | 0.45*** | −0.10 | −0.06 |
| BAI-R Mental element attribution | 0.15 | 0.49*** | 0.14 |
| BAI-R Guilt | 0.07 | 0.70*** | 0.21 |

BAI-R = Blame Attribution Inventory-Revised; EPQ = Eysenck Personality Questionnaire.
*$p < 0.05$ (two-tailed).
**$p < 0.01$ (two-tailed).
***$p < 0.001$ (two-tailed).

was correlated with younger age (medium effect size), and EPQ Psychoticism (low effect size) and Neuroticism (medium effect size), whereas *internal pressure* correlated with how much the prisoners attributed their offence to mental factors (medium effect size) and reported feelings of guilt (large effect size).[2]

This study was subsequently replicated in a much larger sample of Icelandic prisoners (n = 411) and 108 juvenile offenders given a conditional discharge (Gudjonsson & Sigurdsson, 1999), revealing the same three key factors. The Gudjonsson Confession Questionnaire-Revised (GCQ-R) was used containing 52 rather than the 36 original items (see Gudjonsson, 2003a, Appendix, pp. 628–630).

In both samples, *external pressure* was significantly correlated with EPQ Psychoticism (low and medium effect sizes). *Internal pressure* correlated with Neuroticism and compliance (Gudjonsson Compliance Scale). Both correlations were of medium effect size, whereas in the juvenile sample, the correlation with compliance was of large effect size (r = 0.55). The findings suggest that personality is related to how prisoners rate *external* and *internal* pressure in police interviews. The most pertinent finding is that both neuroticism and compliance are significantly associated with *internal pressure* to confess (i.e. the need to get the offence 'off their chest').

This study also showed that the three confession factors were associated with different reactions to the confession. *External pressure* was

---

[2] Effect sizes are based on Cohen's d (Cohen, 1992).

associated with regrets about having confessed, in haste, feeling unable to cope with the interrogation, and the belief that they would not have confessed had they fully realized the consequences of doing so.

*Internal pressure* was associated with having felt remorse about the offence and experiencing a sense of relief after confessing. Participants in this group were pleased they had confessed and had no regrets about it.

Confessing because of *perception of proof* was associated with being caught committing the offence, seeing no point in denying it, and their perception that it was obvious to the police that they had committed the offence.

Experimental evidence suggests that the decision to confess or not is based on different factors for guilty and innocent participants (Horgan, Russano, Meissner, & Evans 2012). Horgan et al. found that guilty participants more commonly confessed due to the perceived proof of evidence against them and feelings of guilt (i.e. internal factors), whereas innocent participants confessed due to the perceived consequences of doing so and the amount of external pressure to confess (i.e. external factors).

6. *The Ofshe and Leo decision-making model of interrogation* (Ofshe & Leo, 1997a). This police-induced confession model describes the process of modern American interrogation in which suspects are moved from denial to admission. The first step involves repeatedly accusing the suspect of the offence, vigorously refuting their denial, attacking their alibi and memory, and presenting them with 'supposedly *incontrovertible* evidence of guilt' (p. 990), which may be real or fabricated. The purpose is to undermine suspects' confidence and lead to a state of hopelessness and despair from which they cannot escape. The second step involves offering inducements in order to obtain a confession. These range from 'weak' (e.g. suggesting feelings of relief, of being seen as courageous) to 'strong' (e.g. offering leniency, a lesser sentence).

Once an admission ('I did it') has been achieved, the officer is faced with the task of turning the admission into a confession, which consists of a 'post-admission narrative'. The better the 'fit' between the details the suspect gives and the known facts, the more convincing is the confession evidentially.

According to Ofshe and Leo, the content of the 'post-admission narrative' can be used to determine guilt or innocence, which is true provided it can be shown that the details did not originate from the police. Unfortunately, in spite of what police and prosecution commonly allege at trial, it seems that often the 'special knowledge' details must have originated from the police either wittingly or unwittingly (Garrett, 2011; Gudjonsson, 2003a).

Ofshe and Leo (1997b) suggest that the techniques used to break down denials are the same for guilty and innocent suspects. In my view, the main difference is that unlike truly guilty suspects, innocent suspects are not prepared for the confrontation and accusations, which leaves them at a disadvantage during interrogation.

## False Confession

As discussed in Chapter 4, the key theoretical development commenced with the early work of Münsterberg (1908), followed by Irving and Hilgendorf's (1980) decision-making model of confessions; the introduction to the concept of memory distrust syndrome (Gudjonsson & MacKeith, 1982); and Kassin and Wrightsman's (1985) threefold classification of false confessions into 'voluntary', 'coerced-compliant', and 'coerced-internalized' types, which, in turn, led to critiques of the threefold classification (McCann, 1998; Davison & Forshaw, 1993; Ofshe & Leo, 1997a, 1997b; Gudjonsson, 2003a).

On the whole, the Kassin and Wrightsman classification has stood up well to the passage of time and has been successful in several respects. I am in no doubt that most false confessions can be incorporated into the threefold classification, with a few exceptions. Pressure, inducements, and threats from other than police, including the real offender or their associates (peers, spouses, friends), is the main exception, and in some instances cases where drug addicts falsely confess in order to escape from custody.

In some cases, stress and persuasion may be more important in eliciting a false confession than coercion, suggesting that use of the term 'coercion' may be problematic (Gudjonsson, 2003a; Ofshe & Leo, 1997a). In view of this, I recommended the term 'pressured-compliant' and 'pressured-internalized'. Even vocal critics of the classification, such as Ofshe and Leo (1997a, 1997b), have accepted that it has generated a series of research questions and has proved useful in practice.

Secondly, the classification can accommodate the 'Mr Big' scenario reasonably well: undercover police officers pose as members of a powerful and sophisticated criminal organization, under the direction of 'Mr Big', who is presented as the commanding and all-powerful boss of the criminal gang (e.g. Gudjonsson, 2003a; Moore & Keenan, 2013; Smith, Stinson, & Patry, 2009). These are coerced confessions, even if they are not elicited officially in the name of the police (i.e. the suspect does not know at the time that he is being tricked and manipulated by an undercover policeman).

Thirdly, I have found the descriptions of the three psychological types helpful in my evaluation of cases both in terms of clinical practice and research (Gudjonsson, 2003a).

More recent developments have focused on a heuristic model of internalized false confessions (Gudjonsson et al., 2014; Gudjonsson, 2017), reviewed and discussed in Chapter 4 and developed further through a detailed and careful analysis of the 'Reykjavík confessions' in Parts II and III of this book. The analysis of the cases shows that in exceptional circumstances, the influence of beliefs formed during interrogation can be enduring.

It is not known what proportions of false confession typically fall into each of the three groups. The first systematic study into false confessions (Gudjonsson & Sigurdsson, 1994; Sigurdsson & Gudjonsson, 1996a) found that nine out of 62 (14.5%) were of the pressured-internalized type.

## LANDMARK EARLY STUDIES ON POLICE INTERROGATION

### The Brighton Police Station Studies

In 1979, Irving (1980) conducted an observational study of the interrogation of 60 suspects at Brighton Police Station, on the south coast of England. The principal aims were to describe how suspects were interviewed, identify what specific techniques were used to obtain information from suspects, how the techniques affected suspects, and the outcome of the interview.

As far as the type of crime the suspects were arrested for, 45 (75%) involved property offences and 15 (25%) crime against a person (i.e. violent and sexual offences).

The average length of time suspects were kept in custody was 12 hours (ranging from 50 minutes to 26 hours and 45 minutes). The mean interview time was 76 minutes (range 5–382 minutes).[3] Out of the 60 suspects, 35 (58%) made admissions during the interview. As far as interview tactics were concerned, in 16 (27%) cases no 'identifiable tactics were used' (p. 146). In the remaining cases the most common tactics were:

- Persuading the suspect that he/she has no decision to make because of the evidence against him/her.
- Exercising police discretion and providing expert knowledge.

---

[3] Irving (1980) concluded that it is very rare in England for suspects to be held in custody for more than three days, even in the most serious cases.

• Influencing the suspect's own evaluation of the consequences of confessing, including utilitarian, social, and self-esteem consequences.
• Using conditions of custody and police authority.

Irving and Hilgendorf (1980) concluded:

> The results of our observations at Brighton confirm that the kinds of
> techniques which were predicted from a review of the psychological
> literature, are in fact used, and that there are many similarities between
> what is taught to American detectives and what happens in the inter-
> view rooms at Brighton Police Station.
>
> (p. 150)

In relation to confessions:

> Confession appeared to reduce anxiety by creating an acceptable level
> of certainty about the immediate future. It is interesting to note that
> the change occurred in connection with the admission rather than with
> later detailed discussion of the suspect's criminal behaviour.
>
> (p. 133)

Irving's original research at Brighton Police Station was replicated
twice following the implementation of the Police and Criminal
Evidence Act (PACE; Home Office, 1985) in January 1986. Irving and
McKenzie observed suspects in 1986 and then again in 1987. The
studies (Irving & McKenzie, 1989) showed that following PACE, there
was a large drop in the use of manipulative and persuasive interrogation tactics by the police at Brighton Police Station, except in the most
serious cases.

These findings support the findings of Pearse and Gudjonsson (1996,
1999, 2003), who identified very little manipulation in 'run-of-the-mill'
cases, but in the more serious cases police officers in the late 1980s and
early 1990s sometimes used the manipulative elements of the Reid
Technique to break down resistance. With mandatory tape-recording,
the interviews became much shorter, with almost three-quarters being
concluded within 30 minutes and only 7% lasting more than one hour
(Baldwin, 1992, 1993). However, Baldwin noted a 'general ineptitude'
with regard to interview tactics used.

### North American Police Stations Study

Leo (1994, 1996, 2008) conducted an observational study in three
North American police stations. He observed the interrogation of 182
suspects in relation to theft (5%), burglary (12%), robbery (43%), assault
(24%), homicide (12%), and other (4%) offences.

One-hundred and thirty-seven out of 175 (78%) waived their Miranda rights (there were seven cases where it was not relevant – see Leo, 1994, p. 264). The number of interrogation tactics across the cases ranged between 0 and 15 (mean = 5.6). In total there were 24 tactics, the 10 most commonly used being (n = 153 cases)[4]:

- 'Appeal to the suspect's self-interest' (88%)
- 'Confront suspect with existing evidence' (85%)
- 'Undermining suspect's confidence in denial of guilt' (43%)
- 'Identify contradictions in suspect's story' (42%)
- 'Any Behavioural Analysis Interview questions' (40%)
- 'Appeal to the importance of cooperation' (37%)
- 'Offer moral justification/psychological excuses' (34%)
- 'Confront suspect with false evidence of guilt' (30%)
- 'Use of praise or flattery' (30%)
- 'Appeal to detective's expertise/authority' (29%).

Over 70% of the interrogations lasted less than one hour. Only 8% lasted more than two hours. Out of the total sample, 64% made incriminating statements.

This was a groundbreaking study and showed that manipulative tactics were commonly used during interrogation. It is noteworthy that the great majority of the interrogations were short.

Leo (1994, pp. 258–259) states with regard to his methodology: 'The quantitative data that I describe and analyze in this chapter are drawn from my direct or indirect participant observations [...] I had no control over which video-taped interrogations the Southville or Northville Police Departments provided me'.

In another early study, Softley (1980) observed the interrogation techniques used at four police stations in England. This study, too, found that suspects rarely exercised their rights to silence, and persuasive interrogation was found in 60% of the interviews.

## FALSE CONFESSIONS IN MISCARRIAGES OF JUSTICE RESEARCH

The greatest battle in the 1980s and 1990s was persuading prosecutors, judges, and jurors that false confessions do sometimes occur and are more common than generally thought (Gudjonsson, 2003a). There was general reluctance among the judiciary to accept that people make

---

[4] In 29 cases the suspect had invoked his/her *Miranda* rights and no interrogation took place.

false confessions to serious crimes without the presence of serious mental illness or intellectual disability. Changing such misconceptions was crucial to the successful appeals of people wrongfully convicted in the UK, commencing with the Guildford Four and Birmingham Six (Gudjonsson & MacKeith, 1997, 2003).

Wrongful convictions are the most serious form of miscarriage of justice, but wrongful arrests that do not end in a conviction can also cause enormous harm to innocent people and their families (Forst, 2013; Gudjonsson & MacKeith, 1982). In the 1980s, the topic of wrongful convictions was apparently a controversial area of research in America due to government policies on the death penalty (Norris, 2017). Norris quotes recent data from the National Academy of Sciences, suggesting that the rate of wrongful convictions in death penalty cases is 4.1%. Gross's (2013) 'tentative estimate' is 1%–5% regarding serious felonies (p. 57).

In *The Psychology of Interrogations and Confessions* (Gudjonsson, 2003a), I discussed in detail cases of miscarriage of justice in connection with false confessions. Drizin and Leo (2004) have conducted an important review of the key USA studies and also analysed in detail 125 'proven' cases of false confession. It is a compelling review.

Drizin and Leo (2004) concluded that 'only a few studies have systematically aggregated, quantified, and analyzed the causal role of false confession in wrongful conviction cases' (p. 906), citing Bedau and Radelet (1987) as the first such.[5] The studies Drizin and Leo rely on are shown in Table 5.2. In view of methodological flaws, they excluded the

**Table 5.2**  The percentage of false confessions in studies of wrongful convictions

| Author | Number of false confessions | Percentage |
|---|---|---|
| Bedau & Radelet (1987)* | 49/350 | 14% |
| Connors, Lundregan, Miller, & McEwen (1996)* | 5/28 | 18% |
| Scheck, Neufeld, & Dwyer (2000)* | 15/62 | 24% |
| Innocence Project (2003)* | 35/140 | 25% |
| Garrett (2011) | 40/250 | 16% |

*Cited in Drizin & Leo (2004) – Footnote 61 (Innocence Project, 2003, case files, at https://www.innocenceproject.org – last accessed 24 January 2018).

[5] The Bedau and Radelet (1987) findings were ferociously attacked in the death penalty debate (Norris, 2017).

study of Huff, Rattner, and Sagarin (1996), where only 8% of the wrongful confessions were attributed to false confession as the primary cause. The methodological flaws they identified were: the authors only included false confessions where they thought it was the primary cause, thereby probably not giving the full rate of false confession in their sample, and they failed to list the names of the cases they included in their study, which made it impossible to verify their findings.

Table 5.2 shows that false confession is the main cause of wrongful conviction in 14%–25% of cases derived from four studies. I have added the study of Garrett (2011), which looked at the content of 40 false confessions from 250 DNA exoneration cases. The 16% rate cited in Garrett's book is substantially below the 24%–25% in the other two DNA exoneration studies (Scheck et al., 2000 and Innocence Project, 2003, a case file study, respectively). All three studies are based on data sets from the Innocence Project, reflecting different inclusion criteria for what constituted a 'false confession'. Garrett's study included more stringent criteria where suspects gave detailed narratives of the crime.

Leo's (1994) study shows that a substantial proportion of incriminating statements involve a 'partial admission' rather than a 'full confession' or other 'incriminating statement'. Importantly, Leo pointed out that 'implausible or contradictory denials' can also be incriminating and called for consistency in the operational definition of a false confession (p. 270). I have shown elsewhere how a lie in the form of a denial was used at trial in a murder case as incriminating evidence (Gudjonsson, 1995a, 2003a).

Until the DNA exoneration studies, there always remained an uncertainty about whether all the cases included involved genuinely false confessions. Even in the presence of compelling DNA evidence, the police and prosecution sometimes continue to play the 'blame game', which is compellingly illustrated in the UK 'Cardiff Five' case (Sekar, 1997, 2012, 2017).

In a Norwegian murder case, DNA evidence was marginalized by the police and prosecution because there was a 'confession' and as a result the defendant was convicted, but later acquitted (Gudjonsson, 2003a). Garrett (2011) reported a similar experience in the USA:

> In eight cases, the suspects had confessed, but DNA tests conducted at the time had already excluded them, providing powerful evidence of innocence. Yet police and prosecutors continued to insist that the defendants had committed the crimes. Judges and jurors presumably believed the confessions and discarded the DNA evidence.
>
> (p. 35)

In Garrett's study, 38 (95%) of the 40 false confessions were based on richly contaminated accounts, which 'were so persuasive, detailed, and believable that judges repeatedly upheld the convictions during appeals and habeas review' (p. 21). This appears to be a stringent criterion for defining a false confession. In contrast, the 350 DNA exonerations listed by the Innocence Project website includes both 'confessions' and 'admissions':

> Astonishingly, more than 1 out of 4 people wrongfully convicted but later exonerated by DNA evidence made a false confession or incriminating statement.[6]

Garrett's research shows that in 13 (32.5%) of the cases the police brought the suspect to the crime scene and 17 (42.5%) not only confessed to the crime, but implicated others. Thirty (75%) produced salient inconsistencies with the known facts, which should have alerted the police to the possibility of their innocence; all waved their Miranda rights, and to Garrett's surprise 'several of the people who falsely confessed no longer challenged their confessions' (p. 185). Many had not even challenged their confession at trial, because they had perceived themselves in a hopeless, no-win, situation and entered into a plea bargain for a more lenient sentence (pp. 151–153).

This phenomenon of not challenging the confession at trial or after conviction was recently seen in a murder case from Wales, UK.[7] In 1976, Mr Noel Jones, who was 18 at the time, was arrested and wrongly convicted of the murder of a 15-year-old girl after having been 'coerced' into giving a false confession. He stated in court at the trial of the real murderer in July 2017: 'I was just lost … I didn't know what was going on … everything was going so fast and they were just saying to me "you done it, you done it, you done it" … it seemed like forever.'

The police were 'bombarding' him with questions and he was simply 'agreeing to whatever they wanted me to say'. The questioning continued 'until they got what they wanted … I happened to fit the bill'.

Mr Jones said: 'I was like a scapegoat. That's what it felt like.'

A statement that Mr Jones had made in 1976, in which he confessed to killing Janet, was read to the court. When he was asked whether any of it was true, he replied: 'No sir, 100% not true.'

He told the jury: 'I did not know this person and I would not commit this crime. I had no reason to commit this crime […] I had a girlfriend

---

[6] https://www.innocenceproject.org/cases/ (last accessed 24 January 2018).
[7] http://www.bbc.co.uk/news/uk-wales-north-east-wales-40497416 (last accessed 24 January 2018).

at the time and we were happy together,' he added. 'I had plenty of friends. I had no reason to do this.'

Referring to Mr Jones's trial in 1976 where he was convicted of manslaughter, the defence barrister asked him: 'If you made a bogus confession, why not get the barrister to say so?'

Mr Jones replied: 'I don't know sir'.

### Internalized Versus Compliant Types of False Confession

Studies have generally not separated out the type of false confession. The *pressured-compliant* type is most common in cases of miscarriage of justice, followed by the *pressured-internalized* type, which from my case files of 46 successful appellants in 34 UK cases, involved six (13.0%) individuals (Gudjonsson, 2003a, 2006a, 2010a). The appellants who had made *internalized* false confessions were: Carole Richardson, David MacKenzie, Stephen Miller, Andrew Evans, Ian Hay Gordon, and Shane Smith.

In our study of 62 false confessors among Icelandic prisoners, nine (14.5%) were of the *internalized* type and it was associated with heightened suggestibility and confabulation (Sigurdsson & Gudjonsson, 1996a).

## RATE OF INTERROGATION, BASE RATE OF GUILT, AND FALSE CONFESSIONS[8]

There are no databases that can provide a base rate of guilt of those interrogated in criminal cases within or across jurisdictions. Nor is it known what proportion of cases involves true confessions, false confessions, true denials, and false denials. Leo (2008) argues that there are currently three major logistic reasons why it is not possible to estimate the frequency of false confessions in the USA. Firstly, no government or private organization in America keeps a record of the number of interrogations conducted. Secondly, even if all cases could be identified, locating the relevant and sufficient primary case material would be impossible (e.g. in the USA, many interrogations are not electronically recorded). Thirdly, even if interrogations are electronically recorded, determining that a confession is false is inherently problematic (e.g. it is almost impossible for those who make a false confession to prove their innocence).

---

[8] The studies focus on lifetime prevalence rates unless otherwise specified.

Leo rightly points out that documented cases of police-induced false confessions are an underestimate of the 'true' rate of false confessions. They focus almost exclusively on the most serious cases (e.g. murder and rape where DNA evidence is more readily available for exoneration) and only represent the 'tip of the iceberg' regarding false confessions.

Data from a number of research studies conducted since the early 1990s show that false confessions are commonly reported for lesser offences as a consequence of police interrogation and pressure (Gudjonsson, 2010c).

## Community Studies

Table 5.3 reviews the findings from nine community-based studies of students in compulsory ('pupils') and further education ('college' or 'university' students). Seven of the studies were conducted in Iceland, one in Denmark, and one across seven countries in Europe (Iceland, Norway, Finland, Latvia, Lithuania, Russia, and Bulgaria).

The results of these surveys show that more of the Icelandic college and university students had been interrogated by the police (19%–25%) than the pupils in the last three years of compulsory education (10%–11.5%). Of those interrogated, the base rate of guilt was 44% for the seven European countries, 51% among Danish college students, and 65%–67% in four Icelandic studies.

The European study shows that the base rate of guilt varied considerably across the seven countries (Gudjonsson, 2010c): Iceland (71%), Finland (64%), Norway (59%), Bulgaria (47%), Lithuania (37%), Latvia (36%), and Russia (35%). The highest base rate of guilt was found in the Icelandic samples, which is consistent with the rate from the other studies cited in the table. A high base rate of guilt is desirable, because it suggests that the police are largely targeting guilty suspects for interrogation and the expected risk of false confession would be lower.

Table 5.3 shows that the rate of false confession among those interrogated is lowest for university students, followed by college students, and is highest among the younger age group (i.e. pupils). Worryingly, the rate of false confessions in Iceland has apparently increased over time. This refers to whether or not they had at some time in their lives confessed to police to an offence that they had not committed.

Since the methodology in the different studies is similar, it suggests that either false confessions are on the increase in Iceland or that they are becoming more readily reported by the participants. The two most recent studies show reported false confession rates of

**Table 5.3**    Reported false confessions among student and pupil samples

| Sample | N | Mean age (years) | Interrogated (%) | Base rate of guilt (%) | Rate of false confession (%) |
|---|---|---|---|---|---|
| 1. Icelandic college students | 1,080 | 18 | 25 | 67 | 3.7 |
| 2. Icelandic university students | 666 | 24 | 25 | 66 | 1.2 |
| 3. Icelandic college students | 10,472 | 18 | 19 | 67 | 7.3 |
| 4. Danish college students | 717 | 19 | 10 | 51 | 6.8 |
| 5. Icelandic college students | 10,363 | 18 | 20 | – | 8.8 |
| 6. Icelandic pupils | 7,149 | 15.5 | 11 | 65 | 11.3 |
| 7. European pupils | 24,627 | 15.5 | 11.5 | 44 | 13.8 |
| 8. Icelandic college students | 11,388 | 18 | 21 | – | 12.4 |
| 9. Icelandic pupils | 10,838 | 15 | 10 | – | 19.9 |

Study 1: Gudjonsson, Sigurdsson, Bragason, Einarsson, & Valdimarsdottir (2004).
Study 2: Gudjonsson, Sigurdsson & Einarsson (2004).
Study 3: Gudjonsson, Sigurdsson, Asgeirsdottir, & Sigfusdottir (2006).
Study 4: Steingrimsdottir, Hreinsdottir, Gudjonsson, Sigurdsson, & Nielsen (2007).
Study 5: Gudjonsson, Sigurdsson, Sigfusdottir, & Asgeirsdottir (2008).
Study 6: Gudjonsson, Sigurdsson, & Sigfusdottir (2009b).
Study 7: Gudjonsson, Sigurdsson, & Sigfusdottir (2009a).
Study 8: Gudjonsson, Sigurdsson, Sigfusdottir, & Young (2012a).
Study 9: Gudjonsson, Sigurdsson, Sigfusdottir, Asgeirsdottir, González & Young (2016).

12.4% and 19.9% among college students and pupils, respectively.[9] These are very high rates of reported false confessions and should be a warning to police officers to take an open-minded approach when interviewing young persons.

A consistent pattern across these studies is that many of the participants reported having given more than one false confession, which suggests that for many individuals, false confessions are a pattern of behaviour when interrogated by the police. For example, in Studies

---

[9] Drizin and Leo (2004) noted a similar apparent increase over time in the rate of false confessions in their wrongful conviction study of 125 US cases between 1971 and 2002 (pp. 929–930), suggesting that false confessions are on the increase or are more frequently reported.

8 and 9, out of a combined total of 434 participants claiming to have given a false confession, 60.8% said it had happened once, 18.9% said twice, 9.2% three times, and 11.1% more than three times (serial false confessors) (Gudjonsson, Sigurdsson, et al., 2016).

The European study shows large differences between countries. Taken as a whole, 11.5% reported having been interrogated by the police and of these, 13.8% reported giving a false confession. Russia had the lowest rate of interrogation (6.4%) but the highest rate of false confession (19.0%). Lithuania had the lowest rate of false confession (10.9%), followed by Iceland and Latvia (both at 12.1%).

## Prison and Police Station Studies

Table 5.4 provides data on the false confession rates in three Icelandic prisons, one study of suspects interrogated at police stations, and one study of prisoners in Scotland. Study 2 incorporates the 229 participants from Study 1 and shows an overall false confession rate of 12.2%. Study 3 was conducted over 10 years later, using the same methodology, and the rate of false confession had doubled (24.4%). Gudjonsson, Sigurdsson, Bragason, Newton, and Einarsson (2008) explained the differences over time in terms of false confessions either being on the increase in Iceland or that participants are now more aware of it and more willing to report it.

The police station study, conducted two years prior to Study 3, showed a false confession rate of 19.1%; 8.6% said they had falsely confessed regarding the current interrogation, but the psychological evaluation immediately followed the interrogation, which is an

**Table 5.4**  Reported false confessions among prisoners/suspects at police stations

| Sample | N | Mean age (years) | Rate of false confession (%) |
|---|---|---|---|
| 1. Icelandic prisoners | 229 | 30 | 11.8 |
| 2. Icelandic prisoners | 509 | 31 | 12.2 |
| 3. Icelandic prisoners | 90 | 30 | 24.4 |
| 4. Suspects interrogated | 47 | 31 | 19.1 |
| 5. Scottish prisoners | 386 | 30 | 33.4 |

Study 1: Gudjonsson & Sigurdsson (1994).
Study 2: Sigurdsson & Gudjonsson (1996a).
Study 3: Gudjonsson, Sigurdsson, Bragason, Newton, & Einarsson (2008).
Study 4: Sigurdsson, Gudjonsson, Einarsson, & Gudjonsson (2006).
Study 5: Gudjonsson, González, & Young (in preparation).

advantage in terms of clear recall. The 19.1% rate is most similar to that found in Study 3 (24.4%).

The last study in Table 5.4 shows the rate of false confession among Scottish prisoners (33.4%), which is much higher than that found in the last Icelandic prison study. This sample had a high rate of substance misuse and dependence (Gudjonsson, González, & Young, in preparation), which may partly explain the high confession rate.

## Other Studies

Table 5.5 shows studies of false confessions in three countries: England, Iceland, and the USA. For the three groups of juveniles, the false confession rates were 0% (Iceland), 23% (England), and 6% (USA). Richardson's (1991) study involved 60 young male offenders who were residents in a specialized facility for those with serious behavioural difficulties.

The Sigurdsson and Gudjonsson (1996a) study comprised 108 young 'first offenders', 87% of whom were male. They had all admitted the alleged offence, which in 97% of cases involved theft, pleaded guilty to the offence, and received a conditional discharge of between one and five years. One of the conditions of their discharge was that they attended supervision sessions with a probation officer during the period of their discharge (Sigurdsson, 1998). It was their probation officer who arranged their appointment with the psychologist. Both were employed by the Prison and Probation Administration and were close colleagues.

A five-year follow-up of the juveniles' criminal records showed that 41% reoffended (Sigurdsson, Gudjonsson, & Peersen, 2001). Considering the nature of the sample, it is very surprising that none of them had

**Table 5.5** Reported false confessions among other groups

| Sample | N | Mean age (years) | Rate of false confession (%) |
| --- | --- | --- | --- |
| 1. English forensic juveniles | 60 | 15 | 23 |
| 2. Icelandic offender juveniles | 108 | 18 | 0 |
| 3. US forensic juveniles | 152 | 15 | 6 |
| 4. Persons with mental illness | 1,249 | 36.5 | 22 |

Study 1: Richardson (1991).
Study 2: Sigurdsson & Gudjonsson (1996a).
Study 3: Viljoen, Klaver, & Roesch (2005).
Study 4: Redlich, Summers, & Hoover (2010).

claimed a false confession in the original study. Were they merely an unusual group of young offenders who had not made any false confessions in their lives, or were they for some reason reluctant to reveal a history of false confession? My concern, with the benefit of hindsight, is that members of this group might have been reluctant to admit to cases of false confession if they thought it might jeopardize the status of their conditional discharge (which in reality it would not have).

The Viljoen et al. (2005) study included 152 defendants in a pretrial detention facility in Washington, 52% of whom were males and 48.0% were females between the ages of 11 and 17 years. Nine of the participants (5.9%) said they had at some time in their lives made a false confession to police, seven of whom (77.8%) said they had done so to 'protect others' (p. 264).

The Redlich, Summers, and Hoover (2010) study investigated the lifetime prevalence rate of false confession and guilty pleas among 1,249 persons with mental illness involved in the criminal justice system. The participants were recruited from courts and prisons across six locations in the USA and interviewed. The majority (86%) had a history of serious mental illness (i.e. schizophrenia/psychosis, bipolar disorder, major depression). The false confession and false guilty plea rate across the six sites were 22.0% and 36.5%, respectively. The respective rates per each interrogation were 4.4% and 7.7%.

This study is important in that it investigated both the lifetime prevalence rate of false confessions and the rate per interrogation. The 4.4% rate per interrogation is similar to the rate of 4.8% that has been estimated from surveying North American police officers regarding their views of innocent suspects providing a false confession (Kassin et al., 2007). The study also draws attention to the very high rate of false guilty pleas, which is of great concern. It is unique in the number of participants reported to have serious mental illness.

## TYPE OF OFFENCE FALSELY CONFESSED TO

Table 5.6 shows the type of offence to which the participants said they had confessed falsely. The five studies represent prisoners (Studies 1–3), mentally ill offenders (Study 4), and young persons from a large national community study (Study 5). Property offences (21%–62%) were the most commonly reported offences in all but Study 4 where 'person' offences were most frequent.

The Redlich et al. (2010) study refers to 'person' offences (not defined but presumably including violent and sexual offences) comprising over

**Table 5.6**   Type of offence to which they confessed falsely

| Type of offence | Study 1 (%) (n = 62) | Study 2 (%) (n = 22) | Study 3 (%) (n = 129) | Study 4 (%) (n = 274) | Study 5 (%) (n = 314) |
|---|---|---|---|---|---|
| Property offences | 58 | 62 | 29 | 32 | 21 |
| Serious traffic violation | 19.5 | – | 8 | – | 20 |
| Violent offence | 6.5 | – | 14 | – | 14 |
| Sex offences | 3.0 | – | 2 | – | 9 |
| 'Person' offences | – | – | – | 34 | – |
| Criminal damage | 6.5 | 9 | 13 | – | 13 |
| Drug offences | 6.5 | 29 | 15 | 25 | 14 |
| Public order | – | – | – | 9 | – |
| Other | – | – | 19 | – | 9 |
| Total | 100 | 100 | 100 | 100 | 100 |

Study 1: Sigurdsson & Gudjonsson (1996a) – Icelandic prisoners.
Study 2: Gudjonsson, Sigurdsson, Bragason, Newton, & Einarsson (2008) – Icelandic prisoners.
Study 3: Gudjonsson, González, & Young (in preparation) – Scottish prisoners.
Study 4: Redlich, Summers, & Hoover (2010) – US mentally ill offenders.
Study 5: Gudjonsson, Sigurdsson, Sigfusdottir, & Young (2012a) – Icelandic students (15–25 years).

one-third (34%) of the cases. The authors state that confessions to murder and rape accounted for only 3.3% of the cases. Drug offences accounted for 25% of the cases, but the figure fluctuated widely across the other studies: 6.5%, 29%, 15%, and 14% in Studies 1, 2, 3, and 5, respectively. Criminal damage ranged between 6.5% and 13% in the four studies where it was reported.

In Studies 1 and 5, consisting of Icelandic prisoners and national community samples respectively, person offences (violent and sexual offences combined from Table 5.6) involved 9.5% and 23% of the two samples, respectively. These findings suggest that property, drug, 'person' offences, and criminal damage are the most common offences to which suspects falsely confess.

## REASONS GIVEN FOR THE FALSE CONFESSION

In order to understand the psychology of false confessions it is essential
to know the reasons why they are made. One way of finding out is to ask
people why they made them either by the use of open-ended questions
(e.g. 'Tell me in your own words, why you confessed', Redlich, Kulish, &
Steadman, 2011), a structured interview (Sigurdsson & Gudjonsson,
1996a), or the use of questionnaires (Gudjonsson, Sigurdsson,
Sigfusdottir, & Young, 2012a; Sigurdsson & Gudjonsson, 1996b).

In cases of disputed confessions, I often ask the person I am evaluating why he or she made the confession. The most common answer in
cases of voluntary confessions was the need for attention and notoriety,
whereas in police-pressured confessions, which was by far the largest
category, the typical answers related to alleged police threats or inducements, sometimes physical violence, the inability to cope with the police
pressure or custody, and thinking that the transparency of their false
confession would be recognized and that their lawyer would sort it all
out. In a minority of cases they claimed to have been persuaded over
time that they had committed the offence, even though they had not
remembered it. I have discussed several of these cases elsewhere
(Gudjonsson, 2003a).

I have learned from cases in which I have been involved that when
experiencing severe distress, the suspect's focus is principally on ways
of relieving the mental pain and uncertainty (e.g. how long the interrogation and detention will go on), and on occasions the confessions
serve the purpose of immediate relief. Irving (1980) had also noticed
this in his observational study.

Table 5.7 shows five studies where participants had been asked to
give the reasons for their false confession. The first three studies
involved interviewing prisoners, two in Iceland and one in Scotland,
followed by a US study of mentally ill prisoners, and a large epidemiological study of an Icelandic student population. Some of the studies
vary in terms of methodology: the American study used slightly different questions than those used in the other studies, and in Studies 1, 2,
and 4 participants were able to give more than one reason, rather than
the single most important reason as in Studies 3 and 5.

What is most striking about the findings in Table 5.7 is the high
proportion of participants (29%–62%) who report having given a false
confession in order to protect somebody else. Viljoen et al. (2005) in
their study of 152 detained young persons (age 11–17), nine (6%)
reported a false confession, seven of whom (78%) reported having
falsely confessed to protect another person. In my experience, these
types of cases are almost unheard of in disputed confession cases that

**Table 5.7**  Reasons given for the false confession

| Type of offence | Study 1 (%) | Study 2 (%) | Study 3 (%) | Study 4 (%) | Study 5 (%) |
|---|---|---|---|---|---|
| Protecting somebody else | 48 | 29 | 62 | 53 | 29 |
| Avoiding custody | 40 | 43 | – | – | 12 |
| Police pressure | 51 | 19 | 14 | 48 | 17 |
| Threats | 4 | – | 1 | – | 12 |
| Taking revenge on police | 2 | – | 0 | – | 3 |
| Influence of substance use / withdrawal symptoms | – | 29 | 2 | – | 3 |
| Wanted to get away from police | – | – | 4 | – | – |
| Wanted the police questioning to stop and to go home | – | – | – | 65 | – |
| Initially thought had committed the crime | – | – | – | 26 | – |
| Other / Could not recall | – | 34 | 17 | – | 24 |
| Total | – | – | 100 | – | 100 |

Study 1: Sigurdsson (1998); Sigurdsson & Gudjonsson (1996a) – Icelandic prisoners.
Study 2: Gudjonsson, Sigurdsson, Bragason, Newton, & Einarsson (2008) – Icelandic prisoners.
Study 3: Gudjonsson, González, & Young (in preparation) – Scottish prisoners.
Study 4: Redlich, Kulish, & Steadman (2011) – US mentally ill offenders.
Study 5: Gudjonsson, Sigurdsson, Sigfusdottir, & Young (2012a) – Icelandic students (15–25 years).

go before the court in the UK, presumably due to the confession most commonly not being retracted and not officially disputed. Neither of these types of cases features in published cases of wrongful convictions.

Sigurdsson and Gudjonsson (1996a), who were the first to systematically investigate the reasons given for false confessions, found that the type of person being protected was: (a) friend/peer (60%), (b) relative (20%), (c) fiancée/spouse (10%), and (d) some other person (10%). However, we found that only three (5%) of the false confessors had voluntarily gone to the police station. This was done in order to protect a friend who had committed a serious traffic violation. A third (33%) of the false confessors claimed that they had not retracted or disputed the confession and this was most common among those who had falsely confessed to protect another person.

It is also noteworthy that confessing as a way of avoiding custody was commonly found in the Icelandic studies (12%–43%). This may be due to Iceland historically making more use of solitary confinement than the UK for interrogation purposes. As explained in Part II of this book, solitary confinement was used to an extreme extent in the Gudmundur and Geirfinnur cases.

Also noteworthy in Table 5.7 is the finding that 65% of the participants in the Redlich et al. (2011) study 'Wanted the police questioning to stop and to go home'. This suggests that suspects with serious mental problems may have a particularly strong urge to terminate questioning as soon as possible and go home. They will have had fewer cognitive and emotional resources to cope with their predicament. We found a similar phenomenon in cases of drug addicts, who confessed more readily than the other suspects (Pearse et al., 1998).

One of the Icelandic prisoners in Study 1 confessed to murder and was subsequently convicted of wasting police time and sentenced to 45 days imprisonment (Sigurdsson, 1998, Case 41). When in police custody in the 1980s for a minor forgery offence, he asked to speak to the State Criminal Investigation Police and declared that he knew where the bodies of Gudmundur and Geirfinnur were hidden. The police did not believe him and then later that evening he confessed to having murdered a man whose body had been found on the west shore of Reykjavík more than a year previously. His false confession was corroborated by official records. The motive, he said, was to provoke and confuse the police and take revenge on them, because he was arrested when he was having a good time at a party.

Table 5.7 also shows that police pressure is a common reason given for a false confession (14%–51% across the five studies), but importantly suspects typically give more than one reason (Redlich et al., 2011; Sigurdsson & Gudjonsson, 1996a). We know from Study 1 that two (4%) of the cases where data was available involved threats from the real culprit. The finding regarding Study 5 is more ambiguous because the question did not ask where the threat had come from. Nevertheless, this provides some support for the existence of McCann's (1998) *coercive-reactive* type.

## Studies Using the GCQ-R

Sigurdsson and Gudjonsson (1996b) used the GCQ-R to investigate differences in the motivation behind true and false confessions, using a within-subject design. Fifty-one prisoners completed the GCQ-R in relation to a false confession offence and the current offence that they claimed they had committed. The main findings were that with regard to the false confession offence, there was more *external pressure* (low effect size), less *internal pressure* (medium effect size), less *perception of proof* (large effect size), and less understanding of their *legal rights* (low effect size).

Differences also emerged with regard to the type of false confession using a between-subject design. When compared with other false confessors, those who confessed to protect another person experienced less *external pressure* (large effect size), less *internal pressure* (medium effect size), less *perception of proof* (large effect size), more *drug intoxication* during questioning (large effect size), and exercised much less *resistance* (large effect size).

A comparison was also made between the pressured-compliant and pressured-internalized false confessors. There was no significant difference in relation to *external pressure, perception of proof*, and *resistance*, but the pressured-internalized false confessors reported greater *internal pressure* and *drug intoxication* (medium effect size). The limitation with this comparison is that there were only nine pressured-internalized false confessors in the study.

Redlich et al. (2011) compared 30 'true' and 35 'false' confessors with serious mental illness, using the GCQ-R with some added items, and some open-ended questions. The authors found that the false confessors were interrogated more often than the true confessors, took longer to confess, perceived the evidence against them as weaker (*perception of proof*), and reported significantly more *external pressure* and less *internal pressure*, replicating our own findings. However, no difference was found between the groups in relation to understanding their *legal rights*. Open-ended questions showed that the false confessors were over three times more likely than true confessors to explain the confession in terms of short-term gain.

With regard to the outcome of the case, 90% of the true confessors and 83% of the false confessors were convicted, showing the power of confession. When convicted, the false confessors were four times more likely to receive a prison sentence than the true confessors. The reason for this difference did not appear to be related to the type of crime to which they had confessed. The authors speculated that the reason might have been due to the false confessors more often retracting their confession statement than the true confessors.

## 'I'D KNOW A FALSE CONFESSION IF I SAW ONE'

Police officers, judges, and jurors are not good at identifying false confessions when they occur. Leo and Ofshe (1998) analysed 60 proven or probable false confession cases and found that 73% of defendants tried on the basis of their confessions were convicted. In view of this, it is important that genuine false confessions, when they do occur, are identified prior to trial. At times, a comprehensive psychological evaluation helps with this process (Gudjonsson, 2003a).

In an innovative experimental study, Kassin, Meissner, and Norwick (2005) tested the common assumption that 'I'd know a false confession if I saw one'. College students and police investigators watched or listened to 10 prisoners confessing to crimes. Half of the confessions were false. There were two experiments. In Experiment 1, the participants were told that some of the statements were true and others false without specifying the precise base rate, which was 50/50. The students were significantly more accurate in discriminating the true from the false confessions compared with the police investigators, who were more confident in their judgements and prone to judge the confessors as guilty, suggesting a presumption of guilt bias. This police bias was reduced in Experiment 2 when participants were told before the experiment that half of the statements were true and half false. The implication is that when the rate of false confessions is not known, investigators focus more on guilt than innocence.

Another important finding in this study was that participants in Experiment 1 were on average 11.5% more accurate in the audio tape than videotape condition, which raises important issues about possible misleading effects of visual information (Lassiter et al., 2010). However, even when relying on the audio tapes, the overall judgement accuracy was low in both groups (i.e. 64.1% and 54.5% for students and investigators, respectively). The findings challenge the belief that lay people and investigators are good at spotting false confessions when they occur.

## RISK FACTORS

Risk factors are those that increase the likelihood of a particular outcome, such as a false confession. Any factor that impairs the suspect's capacity to cope with the interrogation and confinement, including informed decision-making, can be construed as reducing the reliability of the confession given. These fall into the broad categories of 'situational' and 'personal' risk factors (Kassin & Gudjonsson, 2004).

Brandon and Davies (1973) reviewed 70 UK cases of 'wrongful imprisonment' of people determined to be 'innocent' (the exonerations took place between 1950 and 1970). Those who had given a false confession possessed three types of vulnerabilities, which the authors associated with high suggestibility: (a) low intelligence and/or illiteracy,

(b) young age, and (c) mental health issues (e.g. depression). Some of the 'false confessors' were said to be of normal intelligence but had psychological problems. This was an insightful lead into how we now understand some of the personal risk factors involved in producing false confessions.

In terms of vulnerabilities, one of the essential parts of any police interview is the ability of the suspect to communicate effectively and reliably, and includes being able to make informed decisions (Gudjonsson & Joyce, 2011).

There are a number of risk factors that may need to be considered when evaluating the reliability of a confession, including the following:
1. *Context* (e.g. pressure on police to solve the case, the relationship of the suspect with the victim and other suspects, having responsibility for dependents at the time of interrogation and confinement, undergoing loss or bereavement with regard to the victim) (Davis & Leo, 2012, 2013; Gudjonsson, 2003a; Gudjonsson & Lebegue, 1989).
2. *Interrogation and custodial factors* (i.e. the length and number of interviews, tactics used, the nature and duration of custody/solitary confinement) (Drizin & Leo, 2004; Gudjonsson, 2003a; Leo, 2008; Leo & Ofshe, 1998; Ofshe & Leo, 1997a, 1997b; Pearse & Gudjonsson, 1999, 2003; Perske, 2008).
3. *Not understanding the police caution / Miranda rights* (DeClue, 2010; Fenner, Gudjonsson, & Clare, 2002; Fulero & Everington, 2004; Grisso, 1980; Gudjonsson, 2003a, 1995a, 2016; Viljoen et al., 2005).
4. *Youth* (typically under 18 years, but may be older in real-life cases) (Drizin & Leo, 2004; Feld, 2006; Gudjonsson, Sigurdsson, Asgeirsdottir, & Sigfusdottir, 2006; Gudjonsson, Sigurdsson, et al., 2016; Redlich & Goodman, 2003).
5. *The 'mind set' of the suspect.* Innocence itself may be a risk factor when suspects focus primarily on the immediate effect of confessing (e.g. being released from custody) and naively waiving their legal (Miranda) rights, believing that truth and justice will always prevail and their solicitor will sort it out (Clare & Gudjonsson, 1995; Gudjonsson, 2003a; Kassin & Norwick, 2004; Viljoen et al., 2005).
6. *Physical and mental health problems,* including mental illness, anxiety, depression, and specific phobias (e.g. claustrophobia) (Gudjonsson, 2003a, 2016; Gudjonsson & MacKeith, 1997; Gudjonsson, Sigurdsson, Sigfusdottir, & Asgeirsdottir, 2008).
7. *Developmental disorders* (i.e. intellectual disability, attention deficit hyperactivity disorder (ADHD), autism, literacy problems) (Gudjonsson, 2003a; Gudjonsson, González, & Young, in preparation; Gudjonsson & Joyce, 2011; Gudjonsson & MacKeith, 1994; Hayes, Shackell, Mottram, & Lancaster, 2007; Perske, 2008).

8. *Lack of access to prescribed medication while in custody* (Gudjonsson & MacKeith, 1997).
9. *A history of suffering from sexual abuse, violence, bullying, and other traumatic life events* (Drake, 2010; Drake, Bull, & Boon, 2008; Drake, Gonzalez, Sigurdsson, Sigfusdottir, & Gudjonsson, 2017; Drake, Gudjonsson, Sigfusdottir, & Sigurdsson, 2015; Drake, Sigfusdottir, Sigurdsson, & Gudjonsson, 2016; Gudjonsson, Sigurdsson, & Sigfusdottir, 2009a, 2009b, 2010; Gudjonsson, Sigurdsson, Sigfusdottir, & Asgeirsdottir, 2008; Gudjonsson, Sigurdsson, Sigfusdottir, & Young, 2012a; Gudjonsson, Sigurdsson, & Tryggvadottir, 2011; Gudjonsson, Vagni, et al., 2016; Vagni et al., 2015).
10. *Delinquent peers* (Gudjonsson et al., 2006; Gudjonsson, Sigurdsson, Sigfusdottir, & Asgeirsdottir, 2008).
11. *Conduct disorder and antisocial personality traits* (Gudjonsson, Sigurdsson, Bragason, Einarsson, & Valdimarsdottir, 2004; Gudjonsson, Sigurdsson, et al., 2016; Sigurdsson & Gudjonsson, 2001).
12. *Frequent contact with the police and involvement in delinquency/ criminal activity* (Gudjonsson et al., 2009a; Redlich et al., 2011; Sigurdsson & Gudjonsson, 2001).
13. *Substance abuse history* (Davison & Forshaw, 1993; Gudjonsson et al., 2009a, 2009b; Sigurdsson & Gudjonsson, 1994, 2001).
14. *Alcohol or substance misuse intoxication or withdrawal at the time of the alleged offence or when in custody* (Gudjonsson, 2003a; Gudjonsson et al., 1993; Gudjonsson, Hannesdottir, Petursson, & Tyrfingsson, 2000; Pearse et al., 1998; Sigurdsson & Gudjonsson, 1994).
15. *Personality* (e.g. suggestibility, compliance, acquiescence) (Blair, 2007; Davis & Leo, 2012, 2013; Gudjonsson, 1984b, 1990, 2010a, 2003a; Redlich & Goodman, 2003; Sigurdsson & Gudjonsson, 1996a; Thorley, 2013; Van Bergen, 2011; Van Bergen et al., 2008, 2009).
16. *Cognitive abilities* (i.e. low IQ, memory problems) (Gudjonsson, 2003a; Gudjonsson, Murphy, & Clare, 2000).
17. *Absence of support while in custody and during interviews* (e.g. no legal advice, no appropriate adult when one is required, lack of access to a doctor) (Medford, Gudjonsson, & Pearse, 2000, 2003). The most extreme form is solitary confinement, which may involve no outside social contact, a small and uncomfortable cell, no access to reading or writing material, and no stimulation, apart from that provided by police interrogators (Pérez-Sales, 2017).

The outcome of the interview involves an interactive and dynamic process (Gudjonsson, 2003a). Situational and personal vulnerabilities do not act in isolation and these have to be interpreted within the totality of the relevant material available in the case. Generally speaking, the larger the number of relevant risk factors, the greater the risk of false confession.

Suspects' reactions to interrogation and confinement vary immensely, highlighting the importance of individual differences (Gudjonsson, 2003a). Borchard (1932) has alluded to the fact that 'The influence of the stronger mind upon the weaker often produces, by persuasion or suggestion, the desired result' (p. xviii).

Borchard's comments draw attention to the importance of 'psychological vulnerabilities', which I have defined in the context of police interviewing and testifying in court as: 'psychological characteristic or mental state which renders a witness prone, in certain circumstances, to providing information which is inaccurate, unreliable or misleading' (Gudjonsson, 2006c, p. 68). In this context, psychological vulnerabilities represent potential risk factors rather than definitive markers of unreliability. The stronger the explanatory power of the individual risk factors, whether acting individually or in combination, the greater the likelihood of a certain outcome (e.g. unreliable/false confessions).

The identification of vulnerabilities early in the investigative process helps ensure fairness and justice, provided police take appropriate action to protect the integrity of the statement taken (Gudjonsson, 2016). Police using psychological vulnerabilities to manipulate suspects to confess (e.g. sensitivities regarding sexuality) has resulted in false confessions (Gudjonsson, 2003a). For example, Gudjonsson and MacKeith (1990) describe a case study of a proven case of coerced-compliant false confession of a 17-year-old youth of average intelligence, who confessed to a double murder and sexual assault after lengthy interrogation and psychological manipulation regarding his self-esteem and sexuality. He repeated the confession in front of his lawyer the following day when pressured again by police, after a retraction at the beginning of the interview. A few days later he succumbed to pressure by another prisoner to confess. The main vulnerability was the young man's inability to cope with interrogative pressure, desperately wanting the questioning to stop, and telling the police what he thought they wanted to hear. His innocence and naivety about his predicament were also vulnerability factors. The real murderer was apprehended when attempting to kill another woman, while the false confessor was on remand.

## SITUATIONAL RISK FACTORS

### Interrogation Tactics

Since Irving's (1980) and Softley's (1980) observational studies for the Royal Commission on Criminal Procedure, followed by Leo's (1994) study in the USA, a large number of other studies have investigated police interviewing/interrogation and confessions (Bull & Soukara, 2010; Gudjonsson, 2003a; Kelly et al., 2013; Kelly, Miller, & Redlich, 2016; Moston & Stephenson, 1993a, 1993b; Pérez-Sales, 2017; Pearse & Gudjonsson, 1999; Soukara, Bull, Vrij, Turner, & Cherryman, 2009).

Oxburgh, Fahsing, et al. (2016) suggest that how suspects are interviewed is 'an acid test' of the professionalism of the police (p. 153). These authors recommend the 'science-based search-for-the-truth' approaches, exemplified by the PEACE Model and related approaches.

There is no doubt that persuasive interrogation techniques, including the Reid Technique, are effective in breaking down resistance during interrogation, but when innocent suspects are wrongly classified as guilty then they are at heightened risk of giving a false confession. Usually interrogators use several techniques in combination (Kelly et al., 2013), which makes it difficult to determine which specific technique was most effective in producing a confession, whether true or false. Kassin et al. (2010a) suggested that *false-evidence* ploys were most commonly seen in cases of false confession in America.

Unfortunately, despite the large potential for false confessions when false-evidence ploys are used, jurors are only marginally less likely to convict a defendant who confessed after a false-evidence ploy (Woody & Forrest, 2009). The authors suggested that jurors are not likely to be effective gatekeepers who prevent confessions in response to false-evidence ploys.

Importantly, guilty suspects who report they were tricked and pressured into giving a confession most strongly regret having confessed (Gudjonsson & Sigurdsson, 1999), which may lead to a lasting resentment towards the police. The level of resentment may be even greater in cases where false confessions are coerced (Sigurdsson & Gudjonsson, 1996a, 1996b). In contrast, humanitarian interviewing, where the focus is on understanding the needs and feelings of the suspect and treating him/her with respect, is more likely to lead to a truthful outcome (Bull, 2013; Holmberg & Christianson, 2002; Holmberg, Christianson, & Wexler, 2007). Tom Williamson (1994) was the strongest police advocate for ethical interviewing in the early 1990s (Williamson, 1994) and was influential in the development of the PEACE Model (Williamson, 2006). Ede and Shepherd (2000) were also strong early advocates of the ethical approach to investigative interviewing.

There is some evidence that there is a relationship between police interview style and personality. Officers who score high on 'perspective taking' and 'agreeableness' tended to use more active listening techniques and rapport building, respectively (Wachi, Watanabe, Yokota, Otsuka, & Lamb, 2016).

Appleby, Hasel, and Kassin (2013) subjected 20 proven police-induced false confessions to content analysis and found that all involved vivid details of the crime and crime scene; 95% of the suspects made references to co-perpetrators, witnesses, and others; 85% reflected on their own thoughts and feelings while committing the crime; 80% described what the victims had said; 80% gave a motive for the crime; and 40% expressed sorrow or remorse for the offence. The authors tested the impact of confessions in another study, which was published within the same article, using an experimental approach, and showed that 'mock jurors' found confession evidence persuasive, even in the face of contradictory evidence, particularly when it contained vivid detail. The findings suggest that it is essential to understand the conditions under which confessions are produced.

In addition, recent research shows how prosecutors' speculative theories at trial may mitigate the mismatch between confessions and exculpatory DNA, leading to wrongful convictions (Appleby & Kassin, 2016).

Meissner et al. (2012) and Meissner et al. (2014) conducted a systematic and comprehensive review of experimental and observational studies into the effectiveness of interviewing (information-gathering) and interrogation (accusatorial) methods. The findings from the experimental studies support the information-gathering method in terms of increasing the likelihood of true confessions, while reducing the likelihood of false confessions.

What has been largely neglected in the literature is the sophisticated interplay between interrogation tactics and suspects' reactions (Bull & Soukara, 2010). This important relationship was first comprehensively illustrated by the factor analytic models of our work on the tactics that break down resistance during interrogation in 18 serious cases, using 5-minute time intervals for analysis of audio and videotapes throughout the duration of the interviews (Pearse & Gudjonsson, 1999). John Pearse and I subsequently added two further cases, which involved false confessions where legal representatives were present during lengthy interviews, making a total sample of 20 cases (Pearse & Gudjonsson, 1999, 2003).

Half (50%) of the cases involved an acquittal. This method allowed us to discriminate between the tactics used, including between 'overbearing' tactics (e.g. intimidation, 'browbeating', persistent pressure, psychological manipulation, and exaggeration of evidence) and the more 'sensitive' style of interviewing (e.g. appeal and soft challenges). The greater the number and frequency of 'overbearing' tactics, the significantly more likely it was that the outcome resulted in acquittal. The findings suggested, for example, that what legitimately breaks down resistance in sex offences cases is reassurance and shame reduction delivered in a low tone yet firmly emphasizing the evidence in the case.

As far as I am aware, this was the first study to investigate time sequence with regard to tactics and suspects' reactions, showing how these varied and fluctuated over time, and demonstrating the dynamic and interactive nature of police interviews. It showed that it is not merely a question of what tactics are used, when and how they are used also matters. Sometimes this involves two interviewers working in pairs to break down resistance, using the 'Mr Nice and Mr Nasty' technique (Pearse & Gudjonsson, 1999, 2003; St-Yves, 2014), which is very coercive.

Subsequent studies in England have shown that following the implementation of the PEACE Model there has been a substantial reduction in the 'overbearing' tactics that John Pearse and I had previously identified, although leading questions are still commonly used (Bull & Soukara, 2010).

According to Kelly et al. (2013), in view of the concerns that have been raised about interrogation and false confessions, '... the amount of academic scholarship on interviewing and interrogation has increased exponentially in the past 25 years, creating a vast, if disparate, literature on effective techniques' (p. 165). They cite 47 primary studies in their reviews, from the following countries: the USA (21), the UK (20), Canada (2), Finland (1), Sweden (1), Australia (1), and China (1). These are mostly empirical studies based on case file reviews, direct observation, surveys, and audio/videotape analysis.

The basic premise behind their taxonomy is that research on interrogation has focused primarily on either broad categories (e.g. information-gathering vs accusatory models, minimization and maximization, humane vs dominant) or specific techniques (e.g. open-ended questions, and appealing to the suspect's conscience). The purpose was to identify conceptually meaningful clusters of interrogation techniques, through a careful review of the literature.

In order to integrate the broad categories from the 'macro level' and numerous 'micro level' techniques, Kelly and his colleagues identified 71 techniques and assigned them to one of six domains: (a) *rapport and relationship building* (14 techniques); (b) *context manipulation* (11 techniques); (c) *emotion provocation* (12 techniques); (d) *confrontation/competition* (19 techniques); (e) *collaboration* (7 techniques); (f) *presentation of evidence* (8 techniques).

This six domain taxonomy is then discussed in terms of a theoretical process model that helps explain how the domains relate to one another in an interrogation session. Rapport is in the centre of the model (first level) and interacts with 'Emotion', 'Confront', 'Evidence', and

'Collaborate' (second level), while the Context Manipulation (third level) domain envelops the model because the physical setting and other non-interpersonal factors (e.g. the physical surroundings, the time of day the interview is conducted) need to be considered in all interrogation sessions.[10] These factors can contribute to the success or failure of the interrogation, and the authors argue that the context can affect any of the other domains, starting with Rapport and Relationship Building.

I like this gestalt approach to interrogation, which combines either narrow- or broad-based approaches typically used in previous research. The strength is that it describes interrogation as an interactive process and identifies the key domains. Rapport and Relationship Building does meaningfully interact with the four second-level domains within the model, but I found the arrows that link the four domains themselves unclear. The authors do not provide data to validate their model, nor do they put forward ideas about how the model could be tested or applied.

In a recent study of 29 interrogations involving 21 adult suspects, Kelly et al. (2016) combined the interrogation taxonomy, a measure of suspect cooperation (Feld, 2013), and the coding of the dynamics between the interrogator and suspect in 5-minute time intervals (Pearse & Gudjonsson, 1999). The findings showed that four of the domains (i.e. *rapport and relationship building*, *emotion provocation*, *presentation of evidence*, and *confrontation/competition*) varied across each interrogation and differed significantly when suspects confessed as opposed to giving denials. The more subtle the presentation of evidence (e.g. not using it right at the beginning of an interview and avoiding intensity that makes suspects go on the defensive), the greater the likelihood of a confession. Regression models showed that suspect cooperation was positively affected by rapport building and negatively by presentation of evidence and confrontation. It shows the importance of effective rapport building, supporting the views of St-Yves (2009, 2014). Finally, the study clearly demonstrated the dynamic nature of interrogations, which John Pearse and I had identified in our original study.

## The Custodial Environment

Irving (1980) noted during his observational study that anxiety, fear, and discomfort impair the suspect's decision-making ability, all of which may be associated with detention. As far as the suspects' reactions are concerned, it was noted that reactions to confinement

---

[10] None of the contextual tactics refer to threats of custody or solitary confinement, perhaps with the exception of tactic 4 ('Isolate source before interrogation').

varied considerably, ranging from 'withdrawal', which was common, to the violent reaction of those with claustrophobia:

> In summary, we believe that under-arousal caused by confinement before interview is a significant factor in the suspect's pre-interview experience and probably has a significant effect on his performance in an interview. Claustrophobic reactions are significant to the interview process because the mere fact of terminating an individual interview could constitute a threat to suspects who react in this way [...] A powerfully built man suspected of burglary, apparently with severe claustrophobia, went berserk in his cell. His frenzy brought on a *grandmal* epileptic seizure and when the jailer and other officers opened his cell to investigate he viciously attacked them. Six officers were needed to restrain him.
>
> (pp. 132–133)

In our study for the Royal Commission on Criminal Justice (Gudjonsson et al., 1993), we identified only one suspect who showed evidence of claustrophobia, but many expressed distress at being locked up, asking us questions like, 'When am I going to be let out?', 'When am I going to be interviewed?', and 'What is going to happen to me?' (p. 15). The researchers noted that many of the suspects expressed relief about seeing the psychologist, because it took their mind off their current predicament and provided them with stimulation that was welcomed. In spite of this, when compared with anxiety normative data from prisoners, 19% of the suspects had an abnormally high level of *state anxiety*, whereas their *trait anxiety* was very similar to that found from normative data of prisoners. The findings suggest that being detained for an interview at a police station is extremely stressful for about one-fifth of suspects.

On the basis of a brief clinical interview, we found that 35% of the suspects were not in a normal mental state due to extreme distress or a mental disorder, which could impair their capacity for rational decision-making or coping effectively with the interview and confinement.

In England and Wales, police can detain suspects in custody for up to 24 hours before they have to charge them. Police can then apply to hold suspects for up to a maximum of 36 hours, extended to 96 hours if they are suspected of a serious crime, such as murder. In terrorist cases, suspects can be held for up to 14 days without charge.[11]

Much has been written about stress arising from confinement, including early experimental studies (Irving, 1980). Shalev (2008) describes three main causes for the deleterious effects of solitary confinement: *social isolation, reduced environmental stimulation*, and

---

[11] https://www.gov.uk/arrested-your-rights/how-long-you-can-be-held-in-custody (last accessed 24 January 2018).

*loss of control* over daily activities, which have a number of physical and psychological effects. According to this report: 'The extent of the physical and psychological damage of solitary confinement will depend on the individual prisoner, his background, the context of placement in isolation, its duration, conditions of confinement and degree of mitigation' (p. 23). This shows the importance of context and individual differences.

Pérez-Sales (2017) provides a comprehensive review of the field with regard to the effects of solitary confinement on mental health, which is more commonly associated with a form of legal punishment of serving prisoners rather than police detainees.

However, the literature on solitary confinement is relevant to this book in relation to the Gudmundur and Geirfinnur cases and therefore merits some discussion. In their Report to the Icelandic Government on 28 June 1994, the European Committee for the Prevention of Torture and Inhuman or Degrading Treatment or Punishment (CPT, 1993), was extremely concerned about the regular use by police of solitary confinement. Until 1992, suspects remanded in custody were 'systematically placed in solitary confinement. The regime could be applied for extended periods – often several months and in rare cases, more than a year' (p. 25):

> This situation has been the subject of criticism and the CPT notes that the report of the committee set up by the Minister for Justice states that 'psychiatrists, psychologists and other specialists have stressed that solitary confinement as practised in Sidumúli Prison has a harmful effect on prisoners' mental and physical health, particularly in the case of those detained for long periods'.
>
> (Footnote, p. 25)

Pérez-Sales views social isolation in itself as a strategic process during detention and interrogation that prevents the suspect from interacting with people other than the police. In the context of coercive interrogation it causes a number of problems, including:

- The basic human feeling of belonging is exploited. The suspect is left with his/her own fears, including uncertainty.
- Prolonged isolation increases the need for contact with the interrogators, increasing the suspect's need to talk.
- Over time, emotional dependence on the interrogator may occur.
- The detainee is likely to repeatedly go over in his/her mind what was said during interrogation, increasing the likelihood of memory problems and confusion.
- The lack of basic stimulation reduces the mental strength to resist suggestions.

In his review of the literature, Pérez-Sales lists the most common symptoms associated with solitary confinement:

- The inability to distinguish facts (reality) from fantasy.
- Hyper-responsivity to external stimuli and increased inability to tolerate ordinary stimuli.
- Experiencing perceptual distortions, illusions, and hallucination.
- Anxiety and panic attacks.
- Helplessness and feelings of despair.
- Major difficulties with thinking, concentration, and memory.
- Intrusive thoughts.
- Obsessional thoughts.
- Difficulties with impulse control.

Suspects with ADHD find it more difficult than others to tolerate confinement (Young et al., 2009; Young, Goodwin, Sedgwick, & Gudjonsson, 2013).

Interrogators may also use sleep deprivation as an additional form of coercion, which over a 72-hour period linearly increases negative mood, cognitive difficulties, and waking dreams (Mikulincer, Babkoff, Caspy, & Sing, 1989).

Blagrove and his colleagues have conducted a number of studies, which show that sleep deprivation increases suggestibility, particularly after negative feedback ('Shift'), and the longer the sleep deprivation the more suggestible people become (Blagrove, 1996; Blagrove & Akehurst, 2000; Blagrove, Cole-Morgan, & Lambe, 1994).

## PERSONAL RISK FACTORS

### Age

Age is a risk factor for false confessions. Drizin and Leo (2004) found that more than half (63%) of their false confessors were under the age of 25 years when they made their confession, and a third (33%) were under the age of 18 (i.e. juveniles). Drizin and Leo explained the young persons' vulnerabilities in terms of being less mature and having had less life experience than older suspects, leaving them feeling more intimidated and coerced and less able to cope with the demand characteristics of the police interrogation. There is evidence that juveniles give in more easily to interrogative pressure than adults (Gudjonsson & Singh, 1984) and on occasions give voluntary confessions (Aebi & Campistol, 2013).

The younger the person, the greater the likelihood that he/she will waive their right to legal advice (Viljoen et al., 2005) and give a false confession (Gudjonsson et al., 2006; Gudjonsson, Sigurdsson, et al., 2016; Redlich & Goodman, 2003).

## Gender

The overwhelming majority of people wrongfully convicted on the basis of confession evidence are males, but this is undoubtedly due to the fact that murders and sexual crimes are dominated by males. Drizin and Leo (2004) found that 93% of their sample was males. Out of 46 successful appellants, Gudjonsson (2010a) found that 43 (93%) were males. The three females were Carole Richardson, Jacqueline Fletcher, and Judith Ward (Gudjonsson, 2006a). These cases of wrongful conviction only represent the tip of the iceberg regarding false confession, because they focus primarily on cases of murder and therefore give a wrong impression regarding gender.

In two large surveys, males were more likely to be interrogated by the police and report a history of false confession than females. In the first survey, involving 24,627 students in the last three years of compulsory education in seven countries in Europe, 16% of the boys and 7% of the girls had been interrogated by the police, and of those interrogated, 15.8% and 11.6%, respectively, reported having given a false confession to the police (Gudjonsson et al., 2009a).

In a more recent survey of 21,260 Icelandic students (14–24), males were significantly more likely to have been interrogated than females, 19.8% and 8.7%, respectively, and of those interrogated, 16.2% of the males and 11.4% of the females reported a history of false confession (Gudjonsson, Sigurdsson, et al., 2016).

Redlich et al. (2011) found that participants claiming false confession and false pleas were more likely to be males than females, although the effects were not strong.

## Ethnic Minorities

Redlich et al. (2011) found that ethnic minorities were more likely to report a false confession and false pleas than non-minorities. The authors pointed out that ethnic minorities may be particularly vulnerable to making false confessions, and wrongful convictions more generally. One reason may be their higher level of suggestibility in police custody (Gudjonsson, Rutter, & Clare, 1995).

## Suggestibility and Compliance

I have already discussed the concepts of suggestibility and compliance and their relevance to interrogation and confessions in Chapters 3 and 4. These are the two key concepts that are particularly relevant to police-induced false confessions. Indeed, in real-life cases of false confession, the susceptibility of the false confessor to suggestion is often a common feature (Borchard, 1932; Davis & Leo, 2013; Gudjonsson, 2003a, 2010a; Kassin, 2007; Ofshe, 1992).

Sigurdsson and Gudjonsson (1996a) showed that compliance differentiated overall between 'false confessors' and 'non-false confessors', whereas suggestibility and confabulation in memory were higher in pressured-internalized false confessions than other false confessions, which is consistent with the Gudjonsson and Clark model of interrogative suggestibility (see Chapter 3). The limitation of the Sigurdsson and Gudjonsson study is that almost half of the false confessions were due to the motivation to protect somebody else rather than being police-induced, which reduced the effect size. The strongest effects of suggestibility and compliance are undoubtedly where there is lengthy and intense interrogation. For example, Gudjonsson (1984b) found a large effect size (Cohen's $d = 2.77$) in total suggestibility between 'false confessors' and persistent 'deniers' in very serious cases where there was a great deal of pressure to confess. This shows that suggestibility does not act in isolation to the interrogative pressure in the interview. Under those circumstances, a high level of trait suggestibility places interviewees at increased risk of giving a false confession.

According to Davis and Leo (2012, 2013), within the context of interrogation, suggestibility can be viewed either as an enduring personality trait, leaving some suspects vulnerable to leading questions and interrogative pressure during questioning, or an acute state associated with the circumstances of the interrogation (i.e. depletion of self-regulatory resources due to such acute situational factors as emotional distress, glucose depletion, and sleep deprivation). This implies that some interviewees who do not score highly on the Gudjonsson Suggestibility Scales (GSSs) may have been uncharacteristically suggestible during interrogation due to the unusual circumstances. There is evidence from individual case studies to support this view (Davis & Leo, 2012, 2013; Gudjonsson, 2003a).

Laboratory studies into false confessions help us to understand the conditions under which a false confession is elicited and the moderating/mediating effect of state and trait variables (Meissner et al., 2010; Russano, Meissner, Narchet, & Kassin, 2005). However, for ethical reasons, laboratory studies are extremely limited in the amount of manipulation, types of tactics, pressure, and duration of interrogation that can be applied. In major real-life cases, interrogation that breaks down denials and resistance often involves lengthy, manipulative, and repeated interviews (Pearse & Gudjonsson, 1999), which is likely to greatly increase the risk of false confessions, particularly in psychologically vulnerable suspects. In addition, laboratory studies do not sufficiently capture the role and complexity of mental state and personality factors that commonly occur in real-life settings and the persistence of memory distrust over time.

## Intellectual Disability

In terms of psychological vulnerability, a common theme across real-life studies is that many of the exonerated people who falsely confessed had intellectual disabilities, although authors typically do not present systematic evidence for this claim. However, in a study of 40 DNA exonerated men who had falsely confessed in the USA, 35% were known to have an intellectual disability or were borderline disabled (Garrett, 2011). Drizin and Leo (2004) identified 28 (22%) of their false confessors as having intellectual disability but pointed out that there might have been more due to absence of data in the records. Schatz (2018) estimated a rate of 25.7% in his analysis of 245 exonerated false confession cases. Gross et al. (2005) found in a study of 340 exonerations that the rate of false confession was disproportionately high among suspects who were mentally ill or had intellectual disability.

It would be expected that suspects with intellectual disability had lower cognitive capacity to cope with police interviews. For this reason, they are entitled to the presence of an 'appropriate adult' in the UK, who is there to give advice, further communication, and ensure the interview is conducted fairly (Medford et al., 2003). Gudjonsson and Clare (1994) found a strong correlation (large effect size) between IQ and understanding of the police caution and suggested that those with intellectual disabilities would be most affected. Viljoen et al. (2005) found that those defendants with poor legal understanding were most likely to waive their legal protection. IQ has not been found to be associated with the general rate of confession (Pearse et al., 1998; Viljoen et al., 2005).

Satisfactory understanding of the police caution is highly relevant to the fitness for interview (Gudjonsson, 2016). Those with intellectual disability are most affected (Fulero & Everington, 2004; Gudjonsson & Joyce, 2011).

In an experimental study of a mock police interview, Clare and Gudjonsson (1995) compared the perceptions of participants with intellectual disability (IQ score 60–75) with those of participants with 'average' intelligence (IQ score 90–118) in terms of their understanding of the implications of being interviewed by police in connection with a murder and making a false confession. It showed that those with intellectual disability were more likely to believe that the suspect did not need legal advice, since he was innocent, would be allowed to go home after confessing, and that his retraction would be believed.

Gudjonsson and MacKeith (1994) have shown how the naivety of a man with intellectual disability (IQ score of 65) resulted in his making a false confession to a double murder in the face of subtle police manipulation and inducement. The case study highlighted the dangers of officers offering subtle inducements outside the video-recorded interview.

Perske (2008) provides a brief review of 53 persons with moderate/ mild or borderline intellectual disability who had given a false confession to serious offences, including murder, rape, arson, and robbery. All had been legally exonerated. IQ scores were provided for 18 (34%) of the exonerated persons. Only four had an IQ of 70 or above. One who was described as 'with foetal alcohol effect' was coerced into confessing falsely to setting fire to his high school (p. 468). People with foetal alcohol syndrome disorder are known to be very susceptible to suggestions (Brown, Gudjonsson, & Connor, 2011), and are at risk of giving false confessions (Young, Absoud, et al., 2016).

Another exonerated person was said to have autism and confessed falsely to a bank robbery (p. 470). The relationship between autism and false confessions is unknown. North, Russell, and Gudjonsson (2008) compared the suggestibility and compliance scores of high functioning patients with autism (autism spectrum disorder) with those of normal controls. The two groups were matched for IQ: no significant group differences were found in immediate recall, confabulation, and suggestibility scores on the GSS 2, but the autism spectrum disorder group were significantly more anxious, depressed, and compliant than the controls.

Perske's (2008) article showed that in 11 of the cases the interrogation lasted between six and 50 hours (no specific length of interrogation was provided for the other cases, but in two further cases there were references to '5 days' and 'hours of intensive questioning'). In one murder case the suspect 'was arrested, shackled to the floor, beaten, and threatened with the electric chair until he confessed' (p. 469), while another was threatened with the death penalty. In other cases there was eagerness to please the investigators and promises that they could go home if they signed a confession. Perske concluded (p. 468):

- 'Almost half had been exonerated by DNA'.
- 'In some cases, the real perpetrator finally confessed to the crime in question'.
- 'Most of the exonerations took place since 1990'.
- 'In all cases, a defense lawyer was not present during the interrogations'.
- 'These cases cry out for the nonstop videotaping of suspects in interrogation rooms'.
- 'Officers need to learn how easy it is to get false confessions from some suspects with intellectual and related disabilities'.

What these studies do not show is whether the rate of intellectual disability merely reflected the nature of suspects interrogated by the police, which surveys have shown to have a mean Full Scale IQ of about 82–83 (Gudjonsson et al., 1993; Viljoen et al., 2005), or whether they were more intellectually disadvantaged than other police detainees or prisoners. This is an important research question. Gudjonsson et al. (1993) found that 8.6% of the sample had an IQ below 70, which is a figure commonly used to define intellectual disability, and 33.7% had an IQ of 75 or below (i.e. bottom 5% of the general population).

Hayes et al. (2007) investigated the prevalence of intellectual disability among UK prisoners, which included objective measurement of both IQ and social functioning. The mean IQ was 87.10 (SD = 12.5, range 62–122) and the composite standard score on the Vinland Adaptive Behaviour Scales was 82.5 (SD = 13.2, range 36–111). On the Wechsler Adult Intelligence Scale-III, 7.1% of the prisoners had an IQ score below 70, and a further 23.6% had scores between 70 and 79 (borderline range).

Young et al. (2013) used the Learning Disability Screening Questionnaire (McKenzie, Michie, Murray, & Hales, 2012; McKenzie, Sharples, & Murray 2015) to estimate the rate of intellectual disability among 195/196 adult suspects detained at a large London Metropolitan Police Station. Only 13 (6.7%) were found to meet the intellectual disability criteria on the test, in contrast to 46 (23.5%) who met screening diagnosis of ADHD.

The current evidence for answering the question of whether the rate of intellectual disability merely reflects the nature of suspects interrogated by police is somewhat contradictory. Sigurdsson and Gudjonsson (1996a) found no significant difference in nonverbal IQ, measured by the Standard Progressive Matrices, between 'false confessors' and other prisoners. In contrast, Gudjonsson (1990) found that alleged 'false confessors' referred for a psychological assessment had a significantly lower Full Scale IQ than other forensic referrals (i.e. 80.0 vs 91.4 IQ points). There could have been a selection bias in that lawyers may have been more inclined to refer disputed confession cases for a psychological evaluation where they were having problems taking instructions from their client. This was particularly common in the early cases where intellectual difficulties were often raised.

Gudjonsson, González, and Young (in preparation) investigated this gap in the literature by comparing the rate of mild intellectual disability of prisoners who report a history of false confessions with those who do not. Intellectual disability was measured by the Learning Disability Screening Questionnaire (McKenzie et al., 2012, 2015). IQ was estimated from the Vocabulary subtest of the Wechsler Abbreviated Scale of Intelligence (Wechsler, 1999). Intellectual disability among the 'false confessors' (n = 129) and 'non-false confessors' (n = 257) was 8.1% and 8.3%, respectively. Prorated IQ did not discriminate between the two groups.

I have reviewed the IQ scores of successful appellants whose convictions were overturned in cases of disputed confessions in the UK between 1989 and 2009 (Gudjonsson, 2010a). There were 34 cases involving 46 appellants. IQ scores were available for 36 (78%) appellants. The mean IQ was 89 (SD = 14.6, range 51–113). One had an IQ below 70, and 16.7% had scores of 75 or below (i.e. bottom 5%) of the general population. Eleven (30.6%) had an IQ score of below 80 (i.e. either intellectual disability or borderline).

In conclusion, many suspects interviewed by police have a low IQ score (i.e. mean about 82–83), and about 6%–9% have intellectual disability in contrast to 2% of persons in the general population. The evidence shows that a low IQ score (or intellectual disability) impairs the capacity of suspects to understand their legal rights, and their ability to exercise their rights, and to make informed decisions. The relationship between intellectual disability and giving a false confession is complex, reflecting coexisting vulnerabilities such as suggestibility, compliance, acquiescence, and proneness to confabulation, how they are interviewed, and the support they receive while at the police station (e.g. access to a lawyer and an appropriate adult).

Some people with intellectual disability may have impaired capacity to give evidence in court. Gudjonsson, Murphy, and Clare (2000) found that 75% of people with an IQ score of 60 or above had a basic understanding of the oath, whereas none of those with IQ scores of below 50 understood the oath. Gudjonsson and Gunn (1982) published the details of an early landmark case where competency of a victim to give evidence against suspects was a key issue.

The issue of malingering must of course always be considered in forensic evaluations, including cases of disputed confessions (Gudjonsson & Young, 2009).

## Mental Illness

Garrett (2011) found that three (7.5%) of the 40 false confessors had a history of mental illness. Drizin and Leo (2004) reported 12 (10%) cases of mental illness in their sample. In 34 UK cases where convictions were overturned on appeal, only two (6%) were mentally ill (Gudjonsson, 2010a). These were George Long who suffered from clinical depression and Stefan Kiszko who had schizophrenia (Gudjonsson, 2003a). These rates are very similar to those found for suspects detained at police stations for questioning (Gudjonsson et al., 1993; Gudjonsson, 2003a; Irving, 1980; Irving & McKenzie, 1989).

Gudjonsson et al. (2006), in a large epidemiological study of Icelandic youth, found that the extent of involvement in delinquent activities, the involvement of friends in delinquency, and depression were most strongly associated with reported false confession.

Sigurdsson, Gudjonsson, Einarsson, and Gudjonsson (2006) raised concerns about the high rate of anxiety, depression, hopelessness on psychometric testing, and history of substance abuse, among suspects interviewed by police in Iceland.

As noted earlier in this chapter, in the study for the Royal Commission on Criminal Justice, about a third of suspects were not in a normal mental state while in police custody due to extreme distress or a mental disorder, which could impair their capacity for rational decision-making or coping effectively with the interview and confinement. The evidence suggests that many suspects interviewed at police stations have mental health issues / psychological problems, even if it does not amount to mental illness or a disorder, which leaves them potentially vulnerable to giving misleading or unreliable statements.

### ADHD and False Confession

ADHD is a neurodevelopmental disorder with childhood onset and occurs in about 5% of children and 2.5% of adults (American Psychiatric Association, 2013). It is highly prevalent among prisoners, with a prevalence estimate of 26% for adult and 30% for youth prisoners (Young, Moss, Sedgwick, Fridman, & Hodgkins, 2015). Young et al. (2013) found that 23.5% of suspects at a London Metropolitan police station met screening diagnosis of ADHD. In view of the vulnerabilities of suspects with ADHD, a consensus statement has been produced with regard to their identification and management (Young et al., 2011), and recommendations made for cost-effective screening (Young, Absoud, et al., 2016; Young, Gonzalez et al., 2016).

Four studies have been conducted into the reported rate of false confessions among people who have screened positive for ADHD. The studies have focused on prisoners (Gudjonsson, Sigurdsson, Bragason, et al., 2008; Gudjonsson, González, & Young, in preparation) and community samples of young persons in mandatory and further education (Gudjonsson, Sigurdsson, Sigfusdottir, & Young, 2012a; Gudjonsson, Sigurdsson, et al., 2016). These studies suggest that persons who are symptomatic for ADHD are two to three times more likely than their 'peers' to give false confessions during police questioning.

Drake et al. (2017) investigated critical susceptibility factors for reported false confessions across three age bands (14–16, 17–19, and 20–24). Latent hyperactivity predicted false confessions across all three age bands, whereas inattention was found to be a significant predictor in only the youngest group. This is consistent with the findings of Gudjonsson, González, and Young (in preparation), who found that hyperactivity/impulsivity was better related to false confession than inattention among adult prisoners.

## Substance Abuse

Pearse et al. (1998) found that the odds of suspects making a confession, irrespective of its veracity, were more than three times greater (odds ratio = 3.37) if they reported having taken illicit drugs within 24 hours of their arrest. The implication was that they had confessed as a way of getting out of the police station as quickly as possible in order to feed their drug habit, thus increasing the risk of a false confession (Gudjonsson, 2003a).

Sigurdsson and Gudjonsson (1994) investigated the reported effects of alcohol and drug intoxication and withdrawal during interrogation on suspects' mental state. Although substance intoxication and withdrawal symptoms were not found to have impaired the participants in coping with the police interview, it was consistently reported as having made them feel confused.

There is evidence that a history of substance abuse and addiction increases the risk of false confession (Gudjonsson et al., 2009a; Sigurdsson & Gudjonsson, 2001). Gudjonsson et al. (2009b) found that having a history of substance abuse substantially increased the likelihood of the reporting of false confession. Having received substance abuse therapy increased the likelihood of a false confession by over four times (odds ratio = 4.13).

## Negative Life Events

There is growing evidence that a history of negative life events (e.g. witnessing or experiencing physical violence, sexual abuse, death in the family) increases the likelihood of a false confession. In the first study in this area, Gudjonsson et al. (2006) concluded that multiple exposure to negative life events is associated with the reporting of false confessions during interrogation.

Table 5.8 shows the differences with regard to key negative life events between those who made no false confession during interrogation and those who falsely confessed. The odds ratio is given for each event in the two studies (Gudjonsson et al., 2009a, 2009b).

**Table 5.8**   Differences in experience of key negative life events between those who made no false confession during interrogation and those who falsely confessed

| Type of negative life event | Study 1 (Europe) odds ratio | Study 2 (Iceland) odds ratio |
| --- | --- | --- |
| Witnessed serious violence at home involving adults | 1.69 | 3.36 |
| Experienced serious violence at home involving adults | 2.09 | 3.15 |
| Sexually abused by an adult within the family | 2.99 | 6.73 |
| Sexually abused by an adult outside the family | 3.70 | 3.61 |
| Parent or sibling dies | 1.82 | 4.13 |
| Friend died | 1.43 | 2.46 |
| Group attacked you and hurt you when you were alone | 2.54 | – |
| Expelled from school | 1.89 | 2.58 |

Study 1: Gudjonsson, Sigurdsson, & Sigfusdottir (2009a).
Study 2: Gudjonsson, Sigurdsson, & Sigfusdottir (2009b).

A history of sexual abuse, followed by witnessing or experiencing violence, and death within the family, were the most salient negative life events. The odds ratios were consistently higher in the Icelandic sample than the European sample, with the exception of 'Sexually abused by an adult outside the family', suggesting possible cultural differences.

In a separate article, Gudjonsson, Sigurdsson, and Sigfusdottir (2010) showed that group bullying was reported by 23% and 43% of Icelandic and European samples, respectively. These were all students in the final three years of their compulsory education. Combining the two studies, false confessions were most common in the 'bully-victims' (18.5%) and 'pure victims' (16.5%) groups and least in the 'pure bullies' (9.5%) and 'neither bullies nor victim' (9.1%) groups.

These findings are consistent with those of Gudjonsson et al. (2006) and Gudjonsson, Sigurdsson, Sigfusdottir, and Asgeirsdottir (2008) with an older student group (15–24), which showed a significant relationship between being a victim of bullying and giving false confessions.

Drake and her colleagues have in a number of studies found a significant relationship between negative life events and suggestibility

(Drake, 2010, 2014; Drake et al., 2008). Drake et al. (2015) and Drake et al. (2016) found that 'latent stress sensitivity' (i.e. stress symptoms and history of negative life events) significantly and directly predicted the likelihood of false confessions.

In a study of patients attending outpatient treatment for substance misuse, Gudjonsson et al. (2011) found a significant relationship between compliance and history of childhood neglect and physical and sexual abuse (all medium effect size).

From the evidence available, a history of negative/traumatic life events is associated with an increased level of suggestibility, compliance, and false confession.

## THE PSYCHOLOGICAL EFFECTS OF INTERROGATION

Little is known about the psychological effects of interrogation and detention in cases of miscarriage of justice. Gudjonsson and MacKeith (1982) described two cases where interrogation led to post-traumatic stress disorder (PTSD), which was 'characterised by severe anxiety symptoms, impotence, insomnia with nightmares about their interrogation experience, undue suspiciousness and fearfulness' (p. 266).

Grounds (2004, 2005) provides an important explanatory model of outcomes of wrongful imprisonment. He completed a psychiatric assessment of 18 males with 16 (89%) of the referrals from the UK, which included all four of the 'Guildford Four' and one of the 'Birmingham Six'. None of the 18 men had a previous psychiatric history, but 14 (78%) met a diagnosis for 'enduring personality change following catastrophic experience', and 12 (67%) met criteria for PTSD, often accompanied by depressive disorder, panic disorder, and paranoid symptoms. Consistently there were major problems with psychological adjustment, particularly within the family. The author recommended that a system of support be set up to help the wrongfully convicted and their families after release.

## CONCLUSIONS

A number of major scientific advances have been made over the past 40 years in understanding the psychology of false confessions. Irving and Hilgendorf's (1980) quote from 37 years ago that 'At present it is not even possible to be certain about how a confession which is known to be false came to be made' (p. 26) has been replaced by gradual accumulation of scientific knowledge. The electronic recording of interrogations and greater access to interrogations for research has hugely improved our understanding of the dynamics of interrogation and the risk of certain tactics in producing false confessions. We now know that the outcome of an interrogation involves a subtle dynamic and interactive process, which under certain circumstances results in false confessions. False confessions are typically caused by a combination of factors, which is broadly made up of 'situational' and 'personal' risk factors.

We now know that false confessions occur in about 14%–25% of cases of miscarriage of justice in the USA. There have been 350 DNA exonerations since 1989 and about 25% of those involve false admissions or confessions. These comprise almost exclusively murder and rape cases, where DNA evidence is most readily available. Similarly, reviews of anecdotal cases in the USA and UK where convictions are based on confessions show that these consist mostly of murder. These types of miscarriage of justice cases only represent the 'tip of the iceberg' of overall false confessions.

What is impressive is that in order to understand false confessions, researchers have used a wide range of methodologies, including observational field studies, in-depth interviews, survey research, and laboratory experiments.

Most investigations and surveys into false confessions have been conducted in Iceland because of my collaborative work with Jón Fridrik Sigurdsson and other colleagues at Reykjavík University. Studies have also been conducted in other countries, including Denmark, Finland, Norway, Bulgaria, Lithuania, Latvia, Russia, England, Scotland, and the USA.

Nine studies conducted among pupils in their final three years of compulsory and further education show that the rate of reported false confession of those interrogated by police was on average over 9%. This was the lifetime prevalence, with many participants reporting having confessed falsely more than once. The lowest rates were found among university students (1.2%), followed by other college students (3.7%–8.8%), and the highest among pupils (11.3%–19.9%).

A consistent finding from anecdotal and research studies is that young persons, particularly juveniles, are more likely to confess falsely than older suspects. The main reason appears to be that they are less robust in resisting police pressure due to their relative immaturity and inexperience. It is also known that juveniles are more susceptible to interrogative pressure than older persons. They are also vulnerable to false confession because they readily 'take on' a case for a peer.

There have been four prison studies, three in Iceland and one in Scotland, where the lifetime prevalence rates of reported false confessions have ranged between 11.8% and 33.4%, with many reporting more than one false confession. One similar American study among mentally ill 'offenders' found a lifetime prevalence rate of 22%, with 4.4% occurring per interrogation. There was a high rate of false pleas in this study, which Drizin and Leo (2004) also noted in their ground-breaking anecdotal study of false confessions. Innocent defendants sometimes pleaded guilty to serious crimes because of plea bargaining or that they could see no other way out of their predicament.

The reasons given for those false confessions across the community and prison/custody studies typically consist of protecting the real perpetrator, which do not feature in cases of wrongful convictions, and giving in to police pressure. It is also evident from our research that both the base rate of guilt and false confessions varied considerably across countries. Fear of custody was commonly reported in Iceland as a reason for the false confession. This may relate to the ready availability of solitary confinement of suspects in Iceland, which the CPT has criticized (CPT, 1993).

There is now extensive evidence that many people detained at police stations for questioning are psychologically vulnerable to giving a false confession, under certain circumstances, due to low IQ, ADHD, a history of substance misuse, past trauma, and disturbed mental state, which typically increase their level of suggestibility and/or compliance. I have identified 17 areas of situational and personal vulnerabilities in this chapter that increase the risk of false confession. Innocence itself may be a risk factor when suspects focus primarily on the immediate effect of confessing (e.g. completing the interrogation, being released from custody) and naively waive their legal (Miranda) rights, believing that truth and justice will always prevail and their solicitor will sort it out for them.

The presence of personal vulnerabilities needs to be interpreted within the context of the totality of evidence in the case, particularly the situational factors associated with the interrogation and confinement. The fact that the suspect has a low IQ, a history of trauma, and is suggestible does not by itself necessarily undermine the reliability of the confession.

When there is little or no tangible evidence against the suspect, the interrogation techniques found to be successful in breaking down resistance among guilty suspects are similar to those that are associated with eliciting false confessions. The risks of false confession are greatest when the police are guilt-presumptive and use psychological manipulation, deception, and coercive techniques to break down denials in psychologically vulnerable suspects.

The post-admission narrative is a potentially powerful discriminant between true and false confessions, provided the police have not either wittingly or unwittingly communicated the 'special knowledge' to the suspect. Unfortunately, cases of proven false confession show that they typically include salient details that must have originated from the police, something the police invariably deny at trial. The most powerful 'special knowledge' is when the suspect reveals information that the police did not know, such as the location of the murder weapon or the body of the victim.

There are no definitive markers of false confessions that can be applied across all cases. Each case needs to be considered on its own merit. The larger the number of risk factors involved, and the greater their salience, the higher the risk of false confession.

# Part II

# The Gudmundur and Geirfinnur Cases

# 6

# Icelandic Society in the 1970s

*A place to dwell for the ghosts of those lost in the network of crevasses and fissures, some of them going down 30 metres, deep enough to swallow a person, to make them disappear*[1]

The purpose of this chapter is to provide a brief overview of key elements of Icelandic society and the national character of Icelanders so that readers will understand better the context within which the Gudmundur and Geirfinnur cases were investigated and the defendants convicted and sentenced.

## BRIEF HISTORY AND LANDSCAPE

Iceland is a volcanic island in the middle of the North Atlantic. The total land mass is 103,000 square kilometres (40,000 square miles). In 1976, at the time the suspects were detained in custody in relation to the disappearances of Gudmundur and Geirfinnur, the population was only just over 220,000, which made it a very sparsely populated country and it remains so. The capital, Reykjavík, had a population of about 80,000 at that time. The national language, Icelandic, is based on old

---

[1] *The Reykjavik Confessions*, BBC 15 May 2014 (http://www.bbc.co.uk/news/special/2014/newsspec_7617/index.html, last accessed 24 January 2018).

*The Psychology of False Confessions: Forty Years of Science and Practice*, First Edition.
Gisli H. Gudjonsson.
© 2018 John Wiley & Sons Ltd. Published 2018 by John Wiley & Sons Ltd.

western Norwegian dialects with Icelanders having preserved the language much as it was when Iceland was settled in the 9th century (Rosenblad & Sigurdardottir-Rosenblad, 1993).

It is a land of 'fire and ice' mainly settled by people from around Bergen in Norway. It has constant volcanic and geothermal activity with many people undoubtedly remembering the extensive disruption to flights across Europe in April 2010 following the eruption of Eyjafjallajökull volcano, the name few foreigners were able to pronounce correctly.

Rosenblad and Sigurdardottir-Rosenblad (1993) provide a good description of the erratic Icelandic weather and character of Icelanders:

> There are few places in the world where storms can blow up with such unexpected force as in the waters around Iceland.... During the space of twenty-four hours all types of weathers may be experienced ...
>
> (p. 240)

> ... the long struggle for independence, inherited national spirit, strong family ties, and the pronounced individualism of the Icelanders [have shaped their character and political system.] They like to manage their lives with the aid of the family, relatives, good friends, and neighbours, but without the interference of the authorities.
>
> (p. 257)

In the 1970s Iceland, along with Greenland and the Faroe Islands, was experiencing a huge growth in its population, while population growth had stagnated in Denmark, Finland, and Sweden (Rosenblad & Sigurdardottir-Rosenblad, 1993). The reason for this difference was thought to reflect the heavy dependence of the three islands on fisheries and other primary production, which had 'created a stronger link between man and nature' (p. 232). There was also during this time a rapid movement of people from the rural areas into the cities.

Iceland was heavily dependent on its fish for export and domestic consumption. Between 1958 and 1976 Iceland was involved in three disputes with Britain over fisheries. Feelings of the necessity of extending the fishing limit were strongly held in Iceland during the three cod wars. Ólafur Jóhannesson, one of Iceland's toughest politicians (Jóhannesson, 2013), fought hard during two of the cod wars and defeated the British government on both occasions. According to a BBC Four documentary on the cod wars in the Storyville series, Iceland had won a 'historically unique' victory.[2]

In his memoirs, Henry Kissinger (2011) recalls during the second 'cod war' in 1973 the courage with which this remote land of no apparent geopolitical consequence dared to defend its waters.

---

[2] https://www.bing.com/videos/search?q=BBC+Four+documentary+on+the+cod+wars+in+the+Storyville+series&view=detail&mid=FC282F7E8E7C3E8C6C2EFC282F7E8E 7C3E8C6C2E&FORM=VIRE (last accessed 24 January 2018).

The Icelandic ministers were uttering dire threats of escalating military action while Nixon and Rogers implored them to withhold the final sanction … I sat there in wonderment. Here was an island with a population of 200,000 threatening to go to war with a world power of 50 million over codfish … [it] said volumes about the contemporary world and of the tyranny that the weak can impose on it. (pp. 172–173)

In February 1976, the *Guardian* newspaper carried an article which questioned the motives of Ólafur Jóhannesson and suggested that domestic tensions might lie behind his aggressive stance on foreign affairs (see Box 6.1).

---

**Box 6.1**  Ólafur Jóhannesson – Profile

Ólafur Jóhannesson was the Minister of Justice during the Gudmundur and Geirfinnur investigation. He was the Chairman of the Progressive Party (1968–1979) and Iceland's Prime Minister in 1971–1974 (First Term) and 1978–1979 (Second Term). He was a key fighter against the British government in the first (1972–1973) and second (1975–1976) 'cod wars'.

On 30 January 1976, an Icelandic journalist (Vilmundur Gylfason), writing in the *Vísir* newspaper, accused Mr Jóhannesson of having twice interfered in connection with the nightclub, Klúbburinn, which featured extensively in the Geirfinnur investigation. In October 1972 Mr Jóhannesson had lifted a ban on alcohol at the club, and again in 1975 he had allegedly stopped an interrogation of a suspect in the case, accusing the investigators of harassment. This was used against him both domestically and abroad. The same journalist had written a similar article on 10 October 1975.

On 2 February 1976 there was a heated discussion in Parliament about an alleged financial link between the Progressive Party and Klúbburinn.

Writing in the *Guardian* newspaper on 4 February 1976, Alan Smith, a journalist based in Iceland 'assessed the motives of Ólafur Jóhannesson, the hard man behind the cod war talks', concluding that:

Jóhannesson is … the plain speaking uncle of Icelandic politics and the key to the present situation. He is also the Minister responsible for the coastguards, who have taken such a notably tough line while negotiations were continuing.

Smith suggested that domestic tensions may have had some bearing on Jóhannesson's antagonistic stance on foreign affairs, referring to a political 'cover up' in Iceland:

Jóhannesson has also recently been playing hard to get in the gallery to protect his own position after allegations of a cover-up … in a case involving one of Iceland's recent murders.

Smith was referring to the case of Geirfinnur Einarsson, at the time the most high profile murder investigation in Iceland's history. Ólafur Jóhannesson was under political pressure to solve the Gudmundur and Geirfinnur cases. Forty years on, it is still the subject of conspiracy theories (Latham & Gudjonsson, 2016).

Following the release of the 'four wrongly accused' from Sídumúli Prison on 9 May 1976, and the potential jeopardy to the entire investigation, Mr Jóhannesson had asked ambassador Pétur Eggerz to arrange for a well-qualified German criminal investigator to assist with the Gudmundur and Geirfinnur investigation. At the beginning of June, Mr Eggerz met in Athens with Dr Siegfried Fröhlich, the director of West Germany's Ministry of the Interior. Dr Fröhlich recommended a recently retired German lead investigator with the German Federal Office of Criminal Investigation, Karl Schütz.

In February 1977, after Mr Schütz's Task Force had completed its work, Mr Jóhannesson publicly stated that 'The nation had been unburdened of a nightmare', expressing a particular gratitude to Mr Schütz.

## THE CONSTITUTION AND GOVERNMENT

Iceland had for centuries been ruled by Nordic monarchs. On 17 June 1944 Iceland finally gained full independence from Denmark and became a republic with its own constitution. The head of state was no longer the Danish king. Iceland now had its own elected president. The constitution stipulates that Iceland is a republic with a parliamentary government. Iceland's national parliament was founded at Thingvellir in 930 and the president jointly exercises legislative power with the parliament, whereas judges exercise judicial power. The government has executive function and needs the legislative power of Parliament.

Iceland has a proud tradition on women's rights, which has included Iceland's fourth president, Vigdís Finnbogadóttir, who from August 1980 served for 16 years as head of state. After the financial crisis in 2008, Jóhanna Sigurdardóttir became the first female prime minister in Iceland in February 2009 and remained in power until May 2013. In the summer of 1994, Jóhanna lost her bid to become the head of the Social Democratic Party (Leósdóttir, 2013). Afterwards she raised her fist in Parliament and declared *Minn tími mun koma!* ('My time will come!'), as indeed it did. Jóhanna Sigurdardóttir was prime minister throughout the time that the 'Working Group' was reviewing the Gudmundur and Geirfinnur cases. I know Jóhanna well and have always respected her honesty and integrity. She is my first cousin on my father's side of the family (Valsson, 2017).

The Minister of Justice is in overall charge of the police and judiciary. At the time of the Gudmundur and Geirfinnur investigation, Ólafur Jóhannesson was the Minister and he played an important role in the political background to the cases and influenced the direction of the investigation.

## THE POLICE

According to the comprehensive history of the Icelandic police (Jónsson & Gudjónsson [Gudmundur], 1997), the first two uniformed policemen were Danes, both appointed in Reykjavík in 1803. The first Icelandic-born policeman was appointed in 1814, replacing one of the Danes (Gudjónsson [Gudmundur], 2004). After 1859 the force was staffed entirely by Icelanders.

The Office of the Chief of Police was created by law in 1917 and the first Chief of Police in Reykjavík was Jón Hermannsson, who was appointed in 1918. Erlingur Pálsson, a swimming champion, was appointed to be the first Chief Superintendent in 1920, after studying at a police college in Copenhagen. He was responsible for the uniformed officers and criminal investigations, but in later years, investigations were taken over by two other officers (Jónsson & Gudjónsson [Gudmundur], 1997). By 1937 there were 60 uniformed police officers in Reykjavík (Gudjónsson [Gudmundur], 2004).

In 1938, Sveinn Saemundsson was appointed as Chief Superintendent in charge of the Reykjavík Criminal Investigation Police (*Rannsóknarlögreglan í Reykjavík*), which had now become fully separated from the uniformed police. At the time it consisted of five detectives. A technical division was created in 1946 starting with just two people, with a further post being added in 1963. In 1956, Ragnar Vignir, a qualified photographer, took over as the Head of the Technical Division and remained in charge of the Division during the Gudmundur and Geirfinnur investigation and took the 'crime scene' photographs (Latham & Gudjonsson, 2016). The two other members of the Technical Division were Saevar Jóhannesson and Haraldur Árnason. Haraldur Árnason became a member of the 'Reykjavík Task Force', set up in early August 1976 by Karl Schütz, the retired senior policeman from the German Federal Office of Criminal Investigation who had been brought in to strengthen the investigating team.

In 1962 there were 167 policemen in Reykjavík, which included some 23 detectives working in the Reykjavík Criminal Investigation Police under the direction and management of the Reykjavík Criminal Court

(Working Group Report, 2013). Staffing remained at similar levels into the 1970s.

An important feature of the Reykjavík Criminal Investigation Police during the Gudmundur and Geirfinnur investigation is that it was headed by the Chief Judge of the Reykjavík Criminal Court, Halldór Thorbjörnsson, who had overall supervision of the investigation. Both the Police and the Criminal Court (*Sakadómur Reykjavíkur*) were housed on different floors in the same building at Borgartún 7. The Criminal Court oversaw criminal investigations; in serious cases their designated legal representative (*fulltrúi*) was responsible for the investigation of cases and directed the conduct of the investigation. He had the power to detain people in solitary confinement for a month or more, which could then be repeatedly extended by a court. Indeed, the six suspects in the Gudmundur and Geirfinnur cases were detained in solitary confinement for between 88 and 741 days in total (ICCRC Report, 2017), and there were many lengthy interrogations (Gudjonsson et al., 2014).

An investigative prosecutor, Hallvardur Einvardsson, was also allocated to the Gudmundur and Geirfinnur cases before charges were laid, and he too took an active part in the investigation. Hallvardur Einvardsson was at the time the Deputy Director of Prosecutions in Iceland and his name will feature in this book. I got to know him quite well in 1976 and liked him. We worked together on cases in Iceland after the Gudmundur and Geirfinnur investigation was completed. To me, he came across as a conscientious and focused person with academic interests.

Once charges were laid against the suspects in the Gudmundur and Geirfinnur cases, three criminal judges at the Reykjavík Criminal Court were allocated to the cases. They acted both as investigative and trial judges. As will be shown in this book, the lack of separation between the police and the judiciary created serious problems with the investigation.

In July 1977, police investigations were separated from the judiciary by the opening of the State Criminal Investigation Police (*Rannsóknarlögregla ríkisins* or RLR), who later moved to Kópavogur, a small town next to Reykjavík. Hallvardur Einvardsson became the first head of the State Criminal Investigation Police when it became operational. His deputy was Thórir Oddsson, who in 1979 with the assistance of Detective Gudmundur Gudjónsson, conducted a 'duress investigation' (*Harðræðisrannsókn*) into an assault by the chief prison officer at Sídumúli Prison on Saevar Ciesielski during a supervised *face-to-face confrontation* meeting between three suspects in the Geirfinnur case on 5 May 1976.

In 1997, the RLR closed with the creation of the Office of the Commissioner of Police, which had a more national and international focus (Gudjónsson [Gudmundur], 2004).

## The Police Legal Framework

Extracts from the code of legal practice in criminal cases at the time of the Gudmundur and Geirfinnur investigation are provided in Box 6.2. These show that at that time: adverse inferences could be drawn from suspects not answering questions about the suspected offence; all investigations should be approached with an open mind; offering inducements and lying to suspects was illegal; and the questions asked should be 'clear, short and unequivocal' and not likely to confuse suspects. This legal framework that dated back to the early 1950s shows a remarkably advanced police code of practice in terms of its emphasis on open-mindedness and fairness. The risk of false confession would be substantially reduced, provided the codes were properly applied and enforced.

## Employing Students and Teachers

In the early 1970s the Reykjavík Uniformed Police and the Criminal Investigation Police began to employ teachers and university students as policemen during the summer vacation (Jónsson & Gudjónsson [Gudmundur], 1997). This was an innovative idea, but not without

---

**Box 6.2**  Extracts from the code of legal practice in criminal cases at the time of the Gudmundur and Geirfinnur investigation (74/1974)

Police officers shall always investigate cases with an open mind, focusing both on matters that support guilt and innocence. (Section 39)

An accused person, questioned by police, shall be informed that he does not have to answer questions related to the offence he is suspected of, but that his silence can be used against him. (Section 40)

Policemen should ask questions that are 'clear, short and unequivocal'. They may not in any way attempt to confuse a person with lies or in other ways such that he did not know what he was answering, or resulted in his giving wrong answers. They may not offer the 'accused person promises, favours or perks if he confesses ...'. (Section 40)

It is not permitted to question a person for more than six hours continuously and he shall be allowed sufficient sleep and rest. (Section 40)

Each time a suspect is interviewed it shall be recorded when the questioning started and is concluded. (Section 40)

controversy in view of the limited police training they received before going out 'on the beat'.[3] However, when these officers went out 'on the beat' or in police cars, they were usually accompanied by qualified and experienced officers. It improved the transparency of the police, and provided students with an invaluable experience that assisted them in their future careers. On occasion, these students applied to become fully qualified police officers, something I considered doing myself. For example, in 1976 there were four summer detectives employed with the Reykjavík Criminal Investigation Police. Two were law students (Bjarni Stefánsson and Ágúst Jónsson), one was a theology student (Pálmi Matthíasson), and the fourth was a psychology student (Gisli Gudjonsson – myself). After qualifying as a lawyer, Bjarni Stefánsson went back into the police and became the Chief of Police in Blönduós, a town in the northern part of Iceland. After qualifying in clinical psychology, I went on to become a clinical forensic psychologist with a special interest in false confessions (see Chapter 1). Pálmi Matthíasson became a priest and Ágúst Jónsson a lawyer. A photograph of the four of us with Superintendent Kristmundur Sigurdsson appeared in the History of the Icelandic Police (Jónsson & Gudjónsson [Gudmundur], 1997).

## THE COURTS

The defendants in the Gudmundur and Geirfinnur cases were sentenced in both of the two levels of court in Iceland, the District Court and the Supreme Court. The District Court of Reykjavík hears both civil and criminal cases. The Reykjavík Criminal Court is a branch of the District Court. In May 2016, the Icelandic parliament passed a bill bringing major changes to its judicial system.[4] It introduced a three tier system, adding 'Land's Court' (*Landsréttur*) between the District Courts and Supreme Court. The aim is to reduce the unsustainable work load on the Supreme Court and have a fairer and more efficient judicial system.

The Supreme Court of Iceland, by contrast to the District Courts, covers the entire country, and hears all appeals in Iceland, in a similar way to the appeal courts in the other Nordic countries (Gudjonsson, Sigurdsson, Sveinsdottir, Arnardottir, & Jonsson, 2010). Depending on

---

[3] I worked as a 'uniformed officer' in Reykjavík during the summer of 1973 and as a detective in the summers of 1975 and 1976.

[4] http://icelandreview.com/news/2016/05/26/three-tier-judicial-system-approved (last accessed 24 January 2018).

the case, three or five judges sit to hear a case before the Court: there are no citizen juries. Typically, cases are presented orally before the Court. The judges then retire to confer and vote on the outcome of the case. One judge is allocated the responsibility to review the key elements in the case and provides legal arguments for an outcome. Each of the other judges will then in turn explain their position and discuss the case during meetings.

## PRISONS

The suspects in the Gudmundur and Geirfinnur cases were detained for a long time in solitary confinement at Sídumúli Prison, one of four prisons in Iceland in the 1970s. The 'Workhouse' at *Litla-Hraun*, which was the largest prison in Iceland, is located outside the town at Eyrarbakki, 65 kilometres southeast of Reykjavík, near the seafront. It was established in 1929, but a new building in the 1990s added a further 55 beds to the prison, housing a total of 87 inmates (Sigurdsson, 1998). The *Hegningarhúsið* (Penitentiary) was built in 1873, was located very close to the centre of Reykjavík at Skólavördustígur 9, and held 16 inmates. *Kvíbryggja*, a small prison 250 kilometres from Reykjavík on the west coast of Iceland, housed 14 inmates (Sigurdsson, 1998). *Síðumúlafangelsi* (Sídumúli Prison) was a remand prison at Sídumúli 28 in Reykjavík.

The Sídumúli [Holding] Prison building was originally a storage building and car wash for police cars, which had been converted into a prison (Working Group Report, 2013). There were 19 cells in the building located in three parallel rows between two corridors. Each cell was only furnished with a chair, a small table, and a bed. Row 1 consisted of seven cells (1–7), Row 2 of five cells (8–12) and one toilet, and Row 3 of seven cells (13–18, 22) (there were no cells 19–21) and one toilet. The size of each cell was between 5 and 5.5 square metres (CPT, 1993), apart from Cell 22, which was at the far end of Row 3 in the corner and next to a prison officers' room. It was therefore likely to be noisier than the other cells. This cell was considerably larger than the other cells and not connected to any of the other cells. It was a storage room that was converted to a custody cell. It also differed to all the other cells in that the light switch was on the outside. The detainee in Cell 22 had no direct control over the light switch. The description and position of this cell is important in relation to the detention of Saevar Ciesielski and allegations of abuse, which will be discussed in Chapter 13.

There were no washing or toilet facilities in the cells. The detainee had to ring a bell located in the cell to get attention and request a visit to the toilet. Close to the entrance there were three rooms: an office, a meeting room, and an interview room in the corner, which the police and prison officers referred to as *hornið* ('the corner'), and it was used for interrogations. The interrogation room was on the immediate right of the entrance to the prison, which made it easy for the police to bring witnesses from outside for questioning, a practice they used frequently during the Gudmundur and Geirfinnur investigation. Interrogating witnesses in this coercive setting subtly acted as a sharp reminder of what might happen if they were seen not to be fully cooperating. In addition to detention and interrogation, this prison was used extensively for bringing the co-accused together in one room for suspects' face-to-face confrontations (*samprófun*), where two or more suspects were put together in a room, supervised by police, in an attempt to improve the consistency in their accounts of what had happened. This greatly increased the risk of contamination (Gudjonsson et al., 2014).

## DRUG ABUSE PROBLEMS AND SMUGGLING

Suspected smuggling was a key aspect to the investigation into Geirfinnur Einarsson's disappearance on 19 January 1974. In the 1960s, Iceland was beginning to experience problems with drug abuse and smuggling. In 1969, Kristján Pétursson, a divisional manager of the Customs at Keflavík Airport conducted an informal survey and discovered that many young people, particularly those who had lived in Denmark, England, and the USA, regularly consumed cannabis and LSD, a habit that they brought back with them to Iceland (Jónsson & Gudjónsson [Gudmundur], 1997).

In his biography, Haukur Gudmundsson (Jónsdóttir, 2010) states that he and Kristján Pétursson wrote a report in 1969 about the seriousness of smuggling offences at Keflavík Airport. The smuggling of alcohol into Iceland was an important problem identified in the report. In the 1970s, the retail of alcohol in Iceland was a government monopoly and bottles were specially labelled in order to distinguish them from alcohol smuggled into the country. Illegal home brewing and the smuggling of alcohol were commonplace, with many taxi drivers being suspected of selling and distributing alcohol illegally (Jónsdóttir, 2010). There was a prohibition of alcohol in Iceland from 1915 until 1935. In 1935, wines and spirits were allowed, but it was not until 1 March 1989 that beer with an alcohol content exceeding 2.25% was permitted.[5]

In order to combat this problem, a Committee was set up comprising several key officials, including Kristján Pétursson, to review the position and find a solution (Jónsson & Gudjónsson [Gudmundur], 1997, p. 569). The Committee reported to the Ministry of Justice in the summer of 1970. It concluded that drug abuse was beginning to become an issue in Iceland and the Committee recommended increases in staff numbers at customs and police to combat substance use and distribution. The Committee also concluded that doctors were too freely prescribing tranquilizers and sleeping tablets. This finding is relevant in relation to the detention of the suspects in the Gudmundur and Geirfinnur cases, who were heavily medicated during their lengthy period in custody, impairing their capacity for clarity of thought and decision-making (Working Group Report, 2013).

On 27 November 1970, the Reykjavík Chief of Police, Sigurjón Sigurdsson, arranged a meeting between the police committee, Kristján Pétursson, divisional manager at Keflavík Airport, and the Head of Customs, Ólafur Jónsson. The purpose of the meeting was to discuss a new proposed regulation regarding drugs and their importation and distribution. Kristján Pétursson said it was essential to create full-time designated police posts to deal with the problem and the Chief of Police agreed.

In 1971 a Working Group was set up at the request of the Ministry of Justice in order to improve information and detection of drug abuse and distribution offences. Kristján Pétursson from Keflavík Customs, Rúnar Sigurdsson from the Reykjavík police, and Detective Haukur Bjarnason were all in the Working Group. The results proved impressive and resulted in the setting up of a special division within the police dealing with drug-related offences. The narcotics police division began work on 9 February 1972 (Jónsson & Gudjónsson [Gudmundur], 1997). The first Icelandic sniffer dog, Prins, was purchased and an officer went to London for training in the use of the dog. The dog proved very effective at Keflavík Airport, where smuggling of drugs was considered rife (Jónsdóttir, 2010). In 1973, a special court was set up to deal with substance misuse offences for the entire country, headed by judge Ásgeir Fridjónsson.

In the early 1970s, Kristján Pétursson fought hard against drug offences and he was a pioneer in this area in Iceland (Jónsson & Gudjónsson [Gudmundur], 1997). In late1974, Kristján Pétursson and

---

[5] http://www.bbc.com/news/magazine-31622038, 1 March 2015 (last accessed 24 January 2018).

Rúnar Sigurdsson both became part of the Geirfinnur Einarsson disappearance investigation, because the case was thought to be associated with smuggling, an area of huge interest to both officers. In fact, smuggling and drug dealing were an integral part of the Geirfinnur investigation from the beginning to the end. It made Geirfinnur's disappearance look very mysterious and added fuel to the frenzy of the media.


## MEDIA FRENZY

No criminal cases had ever received such phenomenal media attention in Iceland as the Gudmundur and Geirfinnur cases (Working Group Report, 2013). A review by Gudrún Sesselja Baldursdóttir, cited in the Working Group Report, shows that there were over 950 articles on the cases in Iceland's main newspapers between 1974 and 1980. Most of the articles were published between 1975 and 1977, with *Dagbladid* publishing the greatest number of articles – over 200 during that period – followed by the *Morgunbladid* and *Vísir*.

Haukur Gudmundsson, the first detective to work on Geirfinnur's disappearance in November 1974, has stated that during that time, newspapers were selling more than ever before and the Icelandic nation was 'obsessed with justice', with each piece of news escalating the rumours (Jónsdóttir, 2010, p. 85). Certainly, rumours of smuggling became an important feature of the Geirfinnur case. There soon spread a rumour that a certain nightclub in Reykjavík, Klúbburinn, was linked to Geirfinnur's disappearance (Working Group Report, 2013). Rumours were now fuelling speculation and apparently influencing the police investigation.

A good brief review of the influence of the media is provided by Ómar Ragnarsson, a renowned television reporter (Karlsson, 1994, pp. 143–144). He was in a good position to provide an understanding of the circumstances and mood of the Icelandic nation at the time. He recalls how the Geirfinnur investigation had a huge impact on Icelandic citizens: a mysterious disappearance, threats, and the clay 'likeness' of the head of the man seen making a phone call at the Harbour Café (*Hafnarbúðin*) on the evening of 19 November 1974. The apparent murder mystery fuelled the imagination of the public and media alike. The public wanted to be kept up to date with new information, and the newspapers were ready to provide news bulletins and articles to feed the public's thirst for news. Ómar Ragnarsson described how normally scrupulous and calm journalists lost all sense of proportion in their reporting of the case. No media outlet could afford to stand by when 'everybody' was talking about the case. The newspapers were also competing against one another. Accounts of the police investigation and persons allegedly involved presented an absorbing mystery that drew the public's interest.

Ómar Ragnarsson described the media as being partly responsible for the 'horrifying witch-hunt' that followed against 'innocent suspects', but he reckoned that the 'witch-hunt' became institutionalized from the government to the Supreme Court. It seemed that nobody was immune from allegations of involvement in the case. As an example, he discussed how the Minister of Justice, Ólafur Jóhannesson, came under fire in Parliament and was accused of involvement in the case, and there were calls for his resignation.

## HOMICIDE IN ICELAND

In the early 1980s, my psychiatrist colleague Hannes Pétursson and I began to conduct empirical research into homicides in Iceland from the beginning of the 20th century. The impetus for this research was an interest I had developed in homicide investigations when I worked with the Reykjavík Criminal Investigation Police in 1975 and 1976. I wanted to understand homicides in Iceland because they were so rare at the time. What made people commit murder? How relevant are psychological factors? These were the kinds of questions I kept asking myself and I wanted to know the answers. One case influenced my early thinking more than any other.

### The Murder at Miklubraut

On 26 August 1976 a brutal murder was committed in a beautiful part of Reykjavík, Miklubraut 26, overlooking a park and close to the city centre. Lovísa Kristjánsdóttir, a woman in her late fifties who lived about a 15-minute walk away, had entered a house at Miklubraut to water the plants on the morning of 26 September 1976 while the occupants were on holiday abroad. The murderer had entered the house with the intention of stealing a valuable stamp collection that he knew was there in the house. He carried with him a toolbox, which included a crowbar, which became the murder weapon. While in the house he was confronted by Lovísa who had just entered the house to look after the plants. The murderer allegedly begged her not to tell if he returned the stolen possessions, asking her twice. She refused and he went into a rage and beat the woman on the head several times.

I was one of the detectives that Chief Superintendent Magnús Eggertsson appointed to work on the investigation. I was deeply excited and honoured. This was my first murder case. I was determined to help my colleagues find the murderer and we did within days. The chief suspect was a well-known journalist and newsreader on Icelandic TV and radio, Ásgeir Ingólfsson, aged 42.

I visited the crime scene the day after the murder with retired German policeman Karl Schütz. At the time, Mr Schütz was assisting the police with the Gudmundur and Geirfinnur investigation, having been brought in by the Minister of Justice, Ólafur Jóhannesson. The crime scene looked horrendous and the apparent ferocity of the attack made me think that the murder had been committed by a mentally disturbed person. Ásgeir Ingólfsson did have psychological problems and had sought help from a psychiatrist (*Morgunbladid*, 2 September 1976, p. 20).

One strand of the investigation was to interview people who knew the occupants of the house. Several people were interviewed. Ásgeir was interviewed about his whereabouts at the time of the murder. He knew one of the women living in the house and was a possible suspect. We conducted 'house to house' enquiries and found evidence that Ásgeir had been seen near the murder spot. His alibi did not stand up to scrutiny. He was now our prime suspect and was remanded in custody on 28 August, two days after the murder. The evidence against him was mounting, but he still would not confess to the murder. The three most senior investigators on the case were Njördur Snaehólm, Haukur Bjarnason, and Gísli Gudmundsson. Njördur had had a colourful experience during the Second World War as a Chief Superintendent with the Norwegian Air Force and returned to Iceland on 8 July 1946 to become 'one tired, small number in the Reykjavík police' (Snaehólm, 1949, p. 128).

On 1 September 1976 a photograph appeared on the front page of the *Dagbladid* newspaper with me in the company of Njördur Snaehólm and Haukur Bjarnason at the Gufunes rubbish dump, where a search had started for the murder weapon.

Ásgeir proclaimed his innocence and his father allegedly commented that his son 'couldn't kill a fly' – a typical description of somebody who is naturally soft and gentle, but in some cases it may also suggest a personality pattern known as 'over-controlled hostility' (Gudjonsson, Petursson, Sigurdardottir, & Skulason, 1991). The importance of Ásgeir's personality explained what had precipitated the murder: when Lovísa refused to keep silent about his breaking into the house, Ásgeir's anger spilled over into extreme violence.

On 1 September 1976 Detective Bjarni Stefánsson and I went to collect Ásgeir Ingólfsson from Sídumúli Prison in the morning. We handcuffed him and brought him to Borgartún 7, the Headquarters of the Reykjavík Criminal Investigation Police and the Criminal Court, for interrogation with Karl Schütz.

Mr Schütz had been assisting the murder team with the investigation into Lovísa Kristjánsdóttir's murder. He had interviewed Ásgeir twice after his original alibi statement, but he did not confess to the murder. On the morning of 1 September he was ready to confess and left a message for Schütz that he wanted to speak with him. I suspected that he wanted to confess to Schütz because of vanity or to distance himself from the murder by initially confessing to it in German, or perhaps some combination of both. The interview was conducted in German, which Ásgeir spoke fluently. Ásgeir confessed to the murder and was then able to confess in Icelandic and a statement was taken. After the confession and a visit to the rubbish dump where Ásgeir said he had disposed of the murder weapon, Njördur Snaehólm and I took him back to Sídumúli Prison, arriving there at 19.35.

I had been intrigued by the motivation behind Ásgeir Ingólfsson's murder of Lovísa Kristjánsdóttir at Miklubraut on 26 September 1976 and the 'psychological markers' he had left at the horrific crime scene. I figured out that psychology and psychiatry were relevant to understanding some homicides.

There was another important aspect to this case: I came across my first voluntary false confession. The day after the murder, which had been reported in the media, a young man went to the police and gave a voluntary confession to Lovísa's murder. He was interrogated but what he said did not match the facts and he was ruled out of the case, having been drunk at the time.[6]

## Our Homicide Research

When I started work at the Institute of Psychiatry in January 1980, I met the psychiatrist Hannes Petursson, who later was to become an eminent psychiatrist in Iceland. Hannes and I instantly got on and we have always remained good friends. Hannes is a kind, fair man of great integrity and intellect. I invited him to join me in my research into homicide in Iceland and he accepted. We investigated homicides in Iceland between 1900 and 1979 and discovered that during this 80-year period there had been 45 murders (Gudjonsson & Petursson, 1982, 1990; Petursson & Gudjonsson, 1981). There had been only two known homicides during the first 40 years, representing an annual rate of 0.052 per 100,000 inhabitants. In contrast, there were 43 murders

---

[6] *Vísir*, 30 August 1976, p. 1.

between 1940 and 1979, a rate of 0.72 per 100,000 inhabitants. Furthermore, between 1970 and 1979, there had been an increase in the homicide rate to 0.97 per 100,000 inhabitants. The sharp increase in the rate in the 1970s to about two murders a year may have given rise to considerable concern in such a small community.

It is of interest to note that an increase in the murder rate in the 1970s was also seen in the other Nordic countries, with the greatest increase being in Greenland, Finland, and Sweden (Gudjonsson & Petursson, 1990). Iceland and Norway had the overall lowest homicide rate. The general trends noted in the Nordic countries were primarily due to an increase in non-domestic homicides and the growing role of alcohol and drug abuse in violent deaths.

In spite of the rapid increase in the homicide rate in Iceland in the 1970s, the number was only two per year. The consequence was that detectives and judges had very limited experience of murder investigations. This was of considerable importance to the Gudmundur and Geirfinnur investigation, which may explain why the Minister of Justice, Ólafur Jóhannesson, turned to Karl Schütz for assistance.

## The Case of the Missing Confession

One 'unsolved' murder case from 1968 may have subtly influenced the attitude of the detectives in the Gudmundur and Geirfinnur cases in obtaining confessions. Out of 43 homicides in Iceland between 1940 and 1979, four (9.3%) remained unsolved (Gudjonsson & Petursson, 1982). One of these 'unsolved' cases involved the murder of a 43-year-old Reykjavík taxi driver, Gunnar Tryggvason, who had been found shot dead in his taxi in the early hours of 18 January 1968. The murder weapon was an automatic pistol. A man was later found in possession of the weapon and charged with the murder. He was detained in custody for about a year but never confessed. The police were accused of inexperience in the investigation of murders (Einarsson, 2007). The legacy from this case was that confessions in murder cases are not always forthcoming and this may jeopardize the chance of a conviction (i.e. if the suspect had confessed, he would undoubtedly have been convicted).

I was living in Iceland at the time the taxi driver was murdered and I remember it and its aftermath well. The newspapers were whipping up fear that a new and horrific crime wave was happening in our peaceful country – the use of a firearm in a suspected robbery painted an ominous picture for the future. The headline in Iceland's largest national newspaper, *Morgunbladid* (20 January 1968, p. 1), read: 'Murderer among us ...', followed by 'Many have said: Reykjavík is not the same town after the brutal murder of the taxi driver on Thursday morning'.

## CONCLUSIONS

Since settlement began in the 9th century, Icelanders have struggled for survival in a harsh physical environment. During the early part of the 20th century they fought a long campaign for independence. These factors shaped their national character. Icelanders fight hard for their cause as they showed in the cod wars against the UK: they do not give up easily. This is also relevant to the individuals who instigated and took part in the Gudmundur and Geirfinnur investigation in the 1970s. All showed these qualities: from the Minister of Justice to the detectives on the ground, the suspects who persisted in proclaiming their innocence to no avail, and the prosecutor and judges who were determined to convict the suspects. The fight is now for fairness and justice, which has continued for over 40 years.

The murder of Gunnar Tryggvason in 1968 and the increase in the homicide rate in the 1970s generated a fear among the peaceful Icelandic population, which was accompanied by contemporary concerns about drug and alcohol smuggling. This provided the background to the media frenzy and political pressure in early 1976 to solve the Geirfinnur case, combined with the police and judiciary's limited experience with homicide investigations and the belief that confessions were essential for a successful conviction in a murder case.

I now turn to the disappearance of Geirfinnur Einarsson on 19 January 1974, the Keflavík police investigation that followed, and the first false confession.

# 7

# The Keflavík Investigation and the First Confession

*I'm convinced of the innocence of those convicted persons*[1]

This chapter describes the disappearance of Geirfinnur Einarsson on Tuesday 19 November 1974 and the investigation carried out by the Keflavík Sheriff's Department. The circumstances of Geirfinnur's disappearance were suspicious and the investigation was carried out by a small team of investigators with some assistance from the Reykjavík police. The focus of the investigation soon turned into trying to establish a link between Geirfinnur's disappearance and the smuggling of alcohol.

The popular Reykjavík bar and music venue, Klúbburinn, situated at Borgartún 32, overlooking the southern seafront and picturesque mountain of Esja, soon featured in the case through rumours and media speculation. Within a year, the rumours were to lead to a voluntary false confession that set the scene for the subsequent 'Reykjavík Confessions' of *Erla Bolladóttir, Saevar Ciesielski, Kristján Vidarsson,* and *Gudjón Skarphédinsson.*

---

[1] A declaration made by ex-detective Haukur Gudmundsson in his biography (Jónsdóttir, 2010).

---

*The Psychology of False Confessions: Forty Years of Science and Practice*, First Edition.
Gisli H. Gudjonsson.
© 2018 John Wiley & Sons Ltd. Published 2018 by John Wiley & Sons Ltd.

## THE INVESTIGATION AND PRINCIPAL CHARACTERS

In order to place this chapter in context, there were four phases in the investigation into the disappearances of Gudmundur and Geirfinnur. These are shown in Table 7.1 with the names of the main investigators involved during each phase. Many of these names will appear throughout Parts II and III of this book.

Less than two days after the disappearance of Geirfinnur on 19 November 1974, the Keflavík investigation commenced, but it stopped in June 1975 without having officially identified any suspects (Phase I). This was followed by three investigators, 'The Reykjavík Team', starting an investigation in early December 1975 into Gudmundur's disappearance after a tip-off from an undisclosed source, but about 40 years later he was identified and shown to have been a wholly unreliable informant (Chapter 12). Once confessions were obtained in the Gudmundur case, the Reykjavík investigators zoomed in to solve Geirfinnur's disappearance (Phase II), which had looked mysterious and through public rumours was associated with alcohol smuggling, something that was rife in Iceland at the time. The case soon created frenzy among journalists and the police were under pressure to solve the case.

By early summer in 1976, the Gudmundur and Geirfinnur investigations were in jeopardy due to the absence of any corroborative evidence to support the vague and inconsistent confessions. The Minister of Justice, Ólafur Jóhannesson, hired Karl Schütz to help with the investigation. Mr Schütz had previously led an investigation against the *Spiegel* magazine for treason and worked extensively on the Baader-Meinhof group investigation (Chapter 10). He set up the 'Reykjavík Task Force' (Phase III) and in practical terms took control of the investigation over a six-month period. Karl Schütz, who was German and spoke no Icelandic, interrogated witnesses and suspects through an interpreter. Six people were subsequently convicted: *Saevar Ciesielski, Kristján Vidarsson, Tryggvi Leifsson, Gudjón Skarphédinsson, Erla Bolladóttir*, and *Albert Skaftason*.

In January 1977, the three Criminal Court trial judges appointed to the Gudmundur case identified a number of limitations with the investigation and asked Detective Gísli Gudmundsson, who was assisted by two other detectives, to conduct further enquiries (Phase IV), which he did (Chapter 8).

At the beginning of the Reykjavík investigation into the Geirfinnur case in early 1976, Erla, Saevar, and Kristján falsely implicated four older men as being responsible for Geirfinnur's disappearance. Their names were *Einar Bollason* (teacher/sportsman), *Magnús*

**Table 7.1**   The four phases of the investigation and the names of the principal investigators

**Phase I. The Keflavík Team (November 1974 – June 1975)**

*Geirfinnur case*

Valtýr Sigurdsson – Sheriff's lawyer – in overall charge of the investigation
Haukur Gudmundsson – Detective
Kristján Pétursson – Customs officer
Rúnar Sigurdsson – Police officer

**Phase II. The Reykjavík Team (December 1975 – July 1976)**

*Gudmundur and Geirfinnur cases*

Örn Höskuldsson – Criminal Court lawyer – in overall charge of the
investigation
Eggert Bjarnason – Detective
Sigurbjörn Vídir Eggertsson – Detective

**Phase III. Reykjavík Task Force (August 1976 – February 1977)**

*Gudmundur and Geirfinnur cases*

Karl Schütz – Retired German Federal Officer
(Pétur Eggerz – Schütz's interpreter)
Örn Höskuldsson – Criminal Court lawyer – in overall charge of the
investigation
Birgir Thormar – Criminal Court lawyer – briefly allocated judicial
supervision of Gudjón Skarphédinsson (see Chapter 17)
Eggert Bjarnason – Detective
Sigurbjörn Vídir Eggertsson – Detective
Ívar Hannesson – Detective
Grétar Saemundsson – Detective
Jónas Bjarnason – Detective
Haraldur Árnason – Detective
Rúnar Sigurdsson – Police officer

**Phase IV. The Follow-up Enquiry Team (January – October 1977)**

*Gudmundur case*

Gísli Gudmundsson – Detective
Hellert Jóhannesson – Detective
Njördur Snaehólm – Detective

**Prosecutor**
Hallvardur Einvardsson

*Leópoldsson* (managing director of Klúbburinn), *Sigurbjörn Eiríksson* (director of Klúbburinn), and *Valdimar Olsen* (office worker). The men were arrested and kept in solitary confinement for between 90 and 105 days but were released on 9 May 1976, leaving the investigation in crisis.

## THE DISAPPEARANCE OF GEIRFINNUR EINARSSON

Geirfinnur Einarsson, age 32, was last seen by his wife at about 22.30 on the evening of 19 November 1974, when he left their home after receiving a telephone call, telling his wife that he had to go out but would be back soon. The Reykjavík Criminal Court provided details of Geirfinnur's character and the circumstances surrounding his disappearance. The basic known facts were as follows.

Geirfinnur was born on 7 September 1942 in Vopnafjördur in the northwest of Iceland, but in 1960 he moved to Keflavík. He left school after completing his mandatory education. He met his wife Gudný in 1963 while they were working together in a fishing factory, and they married in December 1964. They had two children, a son born in August 1964 and a daughter born in January 1970. Geirfinnur had various jobs but prior to his disappearance had worked for a few years with a construction company in a nearby town. He worked with heavy machinery, including diggers. He was described as an excellent worker. Of medium height (1.75 m or five feet and nine inches) and build, he was described as rather reserved and secretive, but he became less shy and more talkative when under the influence of alcohol. He was a modest drinker and in good health. The family were comfortably off financially; Geirfinnur was a good provider. He did not have many friends and had brewed alcohol at home with a friend solely for their own use, a common pastime in Iceland at the time. He had no criminal record.

It is known that at the time of Geirfinnur's disappearance, his wife was having an affair with a young man and had seen him in Keflavík shortly before Geirfinnur disappeared. The young man was interviewed by the police, including the Reykjavík police, but does not seem to have been treated as a serious suspect.

According to his wife, Geirfinnur had gone to see a film with his workmates at 19.00 on Sunday 17 November 1974. Returning home, he told his wife that he wanted to go to Klúbburinn with his mates. He invited her to come along; she declined but was happy for him to go. He went to Klúbburinn with his workmates, Thórdur, who drove, and Björn. Geirfinnur returned home at 02.00 and was a little intoxicated, according to his wife, who had offered him food. He did not mention anything unusual happening at Klúbburinn.

According to Thórdur, Geirfinnur had no money on him; the three men spent most of the time in Klúbburinn together, although at one point he remembered Geirfinnur speaking with somebody he seemed to know. They had stayed in Klúbburinn from 22.00 to 01.00, which would have left Geirfinnur sufficient time to be at home again by 02.00.

According to Gudný, on 19 November 1974, Geirfinnur went to work as usual and returned home at 18.00. Just after finishing dinner at 19.00 the telephone rang and Geirfinnur answered it. It was a short call and Geirfinnur did not talk about it, but it seemed to cause him concern.

Gudný went out at about 20.00 and when she returned between 20.30 and 21.00, Geirfinnur was at home with his friend, Thórdur, watching television. At about 22.00 Geirfinnur and Thórdur went out. Gudný asked her husband to buy her some cigarettes, for which she gave him money. Geirfinnur returned at 22.15, having been to the nearby Harbour Café (*Hafnarbúðin*). Shortly afterwards his 10-year-old son Sigurdur answered the phone and the person at the other end of the phone asked whether 'Geirfinnur Einarsson' was home, which suggested, having used his full name, that the person was not well acquainted with Geirfinnur. Gudný heard her husband say (translated from Icelandic): 'I've already come', followed by 'I'll come'.

Geirfinnur took his pipe and tobacco, put on his coat, and drove away in his Ford Cortina. He did not tell Gudný where he was going, but this was not unusual when Geirfinnur went out. He never returned home and has not been seen since.

Thórdur told the police that he had arrived at Geirfinnur's house at about 21.00 on 19 November. He wanted Geirfinnur to go with him to the local cinema that evening. Geirfinnur said he could not go because he had to meet some men at 22.00 by the Harbour Café. Geirfinnur told Thórdur that he did not know these men and he said he did not want his wife or anybody else to know. He did not explain the purpose of the meeting. Thórdur drove Geirfinnur to the meeting and dropped him off a short distance from the Harbour Café. Geirfinnur purchased a packet of cigarettes and returned home at 22.15. What is known is that shortly after Geirfinnur returned home he received a call and left the house in his car. His car was later found parked close to the Harbour Café.

## THE KEFLAVÍK INVESTIGATION INTO GEIRFINNUR'S DISAPPEARANCE

Table 7.2 provides a brief overview of the case's chronology during the Keflavík investigation.

The Criminal Court Judgement shows that Geirfinnur's employer, Ellert Skúlason, officially reported him missing at 09.00 on 21 November 1974, although concerns had been raised about his disappearance the

**Table 7.2** Brief chronology regarding the Keflavík investigation

| Date | Event |
|---|---|
| 17 November 1974 | Geirfinnur Einarsson visits Klúbburinn for an evening out with two friends and stays there between 22.00 and 01.00. This was seen as a key link between Geirfinnur's disappearance, Klúbburinn, and the smuggling of alcohol. |
| 19 November 1974 | 22.00: Geirfinnur buys a packet of cigarettes in the Harbour Café and appears to be in a hurry. 22.15: An unknown man enters the Harbour Café, looks agitated, and asks to use the phone, then leaves. He later became the 'prime suspect'. Around 22.15: Geirfinnur received a phone call at home – his wife heard him say 'I've already come', followed by 'I'll come'. Geirfinnur Einarsson leaves his home after receiving this telephone call, apparently to meet one or more people at the Harbour Café. He was never seen again. His car was later found abandoned close to the Harbour Café. |
| 21 November 1974 | At 09.00 Geirfinnur's employer reports him missing to the police. The criminal investigation starts, headed by Valtýr Sigurdsson from the Keflavík Sheriff's Office, and lead Detective Haukur Gudmundsson. They are soon joined by Kristján Pétursson, Keflavík Airport Customs, and Reykjavík police officer Rúnar Sigurdsson. The Reykjavík police provide advice and facilities. |
| 26 November 1974 | A decision is made to publicize a 'clay head' of the suspect who made the phone call in the Harbour Café, labelled 'Leirfinnur'. Soon afterwards rumours start to spread that the disappearance of Geirfinnur Einarsson was connected with Klúbburinn. |
| 13 December 1974 | The Keflavík Sheriff's Department reports being under public and media pressure to solve the case, and a suspected link has developed between Geirfinnur's disappearance and the smuggling of alcohol. Haukur Gudmundsson, Kristján Pétursson, and Rúnar Sigurdsson are commissioned to focus on this aspect of the case. |
| 03 February 1975 | Sigurbjörn Eiríksson and Magnús Leópoldsson, the director and managing director of Klúbburinn, respectively, make a formal written complaint about the rumours to the Ministry of Justice, politely informing them to either 'Put up or shut up'. About four weeks later the Ministry of Justice sends a letter to the Sheriff in Keflavík regarding the complaint, which formally stops the investigation into the Klúbburinn aspect of the case. |
| 04 June 1975 | The Ministry of Justice writes a letter to the Keflavík Sheriff's Department recommending that Haukur Gudmundsson be released from the case, effectively closing the Keflavík investigation. Officially, no known suspects had been identified. Leirfinnur's identity remained unknown. |

previous day. The Harbour Café soon became the focus of the investigation. Two witnesses reported having seen Geirfinnur come into the Harbour Café at about 22.00 on 19 November and later, after a public appeal, three further witnesses who had seen Geirfinnur in the café came forward. There was an extensive search conducted over a wide area, which included divers going into the Keflavík harbour and surrounding areas. A sniffer dog found that his smell trace was lost by the Harbour Café.[2]

The Keflavík investigation was headed by Valtýr Sigurdsson, who had been with the Sheriff's Department since June 1971 (Gunnlaugsson, 2014, p. 375). Haukur Gudmundsson was the lead investigator (see Box 7.1), but several other police officers assisted with the investigation, including customs officer Kristján Pétursson and senior officers

---

**Box 7.1**   Haukur Gudmundsson – Profile

Haukur Gudmundsson had just turned 30 when he became involved in the Geirfinnur investigation in November 1974. He had been a policeman since 1965 and worked in Keflavík and the surrounding area. According to his biography, published in 2010, his early police work had much to do with the smuggling of alcohol. In 1970 he was appointed as the first detective in Keflavík. This included investigating burglaries, road traffic accidents, assaults, and smuggling offences.

Haukur worked closely with divisional customs manager, Kristján Pétursson, who 'many thought had a horrifying talent for finding those who had something to hide with regard to smuggling and other property offences' (Jónsdóttir, 2010, p. 42). In 1969 Haukur and Kristján wrote a joint report of the problems associated with the smuggling of drugs into Iceland. They were close colleagues and specialized in smuggling and black market offences.

Haukur was the first detective to work on the Geirfinnur case and operated under the direction of Valtýr Sigurdsson, a legal representative from the Keflavík Sheriff's Department. Kristján Pétursson was soon brought into the investigation and Reykjavík police officer Rúnar Sigurdsson also joined the team. The investigation was supported by senior members of the Reykjavik Criminal Investigation Police and the team was provided with facilities at the Uniformed Police Headquarters at Hverfisgata.

The Keflavík investigation did not officially identify any suspects and in June 1975 the case was handed over to the Ministry of Justice.

In his biography, Haukur concluded in relation to the Geirfinnur case: 'I'm convinced of the innocence of those convicted persons' (Jónsdóttir, 2010, p. 243).

---

[2] ICCRC Report, 2017, Saevar Ciesielski, Paragraph 545.

from the Reykjavík Criminal Investigation Police (Jónsdóttir, 2010). These included Chief Superintendent Magnús Eggertsson, Superintendent Kristmundur Sigurdsson, and Chief Inspector Njördur Snaehólm.

Facilities were provided at the main Reykjavík Police Station at Hverfisgata from 28 November, a five-minute walk away from the Reykjavík Criminal Court and Criminal Investigation Police. Rúnar Sigurdsson, a Reykjavík police officer who specialized in investigating drug/smuggling offences, was seconded to the Keflavík police to work on the Geirfinnur case (Jónsdóttir, 2010).

According to Haukur Gudmundsson's memoirs (Jónsdóttir, 2010), Valtýr Sigurdsson directed the investigation from the beginning. At that time, the Keflavík police were ill-prepared for this kind of investigation. From the outset, Geirfinnur's disappearance was treated as suspicious and investigated as a likely criminal offence. The investigators decided to involve the media, a decision which caused controversy.

Within hours of the investigation starting, it was decided that it was likely that one or more men were responsible for Geirfinnur's disappearance, or at least knew what had happened to him. A detailed background investigation was conducted on Geirfinnur, but nothing was found to explain his disappearance. He appeared to have no enemies and no motive could be established.

Gudlaug, who worked in the Harbour Café, said that Geirfinnur, whom she knew, had come into the Harbour Café at around 22.00 and bought a packet of cigarettes. He seemed to be in a hurry: usually when he came into the café he stopped for a chat. About 10–15 minutes after Geirfinnur left the café, a stranger entered, who kept pacing around the café, said he did not want to buy anything, and looked agitated. After a short while he had asked to use the phone. It was a short call; he paid for the call, and walked out of the café. The man was described as being about 180 cm (five feet and 11 inches) in height, with rather broad shoulders, and wore a brown leather jacket. When Gudlaug asked him whether she could help, he replied 'I don't want to buy anything, I want to wait a bit' (Supreme Court Judgement, p. 164). This man was to become a central figure in the investigation of Geirfinnur's disappearance. A crucial investigative lead was to trace the telephone call to Geirfinnur's home, but the police failed to do this. It was assumed that the call had come from the Harbour Café.

It proved difficult to obtain a consistent description from witnesses of the stranger's appearance. The artists' sketches were not thought to be a good likeness, and one of the artists suggested producing a clay model of the man's head, which was done. After the clay head was produced there was a meeting on 26 November, exactly one week after Geirfinnur's disappearance, with key specialists from Reykjavík, which included the Criminal Investigation Police, and a legal representative from the Ministry of Justice. The outcome of the meeting was to publicize the 'clay head', referred to as 'Leirfinnur': the first part of Geirfinnur's name 'Geir' being substituted by 'Leir'. The *Tíminn* newspaper published a photograph of the clay model on its front page on 27 November 1974 with a photograph of Valtýr Sigurdsson and Haukur Gudmundsson.

Magnús Leópoldsson, the managing director of Klúbburinn, explains in his biography (Jónasson, 1996) that in 1975 Haukur Gudmundsson and Rúnar Sigurdsson interviewed him informally about his likeness to the Leirfinnur clay head and about his car ownership. They also asked him about a delivery van, which Magnús did not own.

The key witness from the Harbour Café, Gudlaug, later said that she had been shown a number of photographs of people before the production of the clay head, including one of Magnús Leópoldsson. She suspected that the clay head had been made from Magnús's photograph (Supreme Court Judgement, p. 165). This suggests that the Keflavík police had Magnús as a possible suspect in mind from the beginning of the investigation, although the investigators have always denied this.

Soon after pictures of the clay model appeared in the media, rumours started to spread that the disappearance of Geirfinnur was connected with Klúbburinn where he had been seen two days before his disappearance. Sigurbjörn Eiríksson was the director of Klúbburinn and Magnús Leópoldsson was the managing director. On 3 February 1975 both men wrote to the Ministry of Justice and requested either an investigation into the source and validity of the rumours, or a public announcement be made officially denying the rumours, in other words: 'Put up or shut up' (Jónasson, 1996). About four weeks later, the Ministry of Justice sent a letter to the Sheriff in Keflavík requesting that consideration should be given to the deleterious impact the unsubstantiated rumours were having on the lives and work of Sigurbjörn and Magnús. According to Magnús, there is evidence that Haukur Gudmundsson interpreted this Ministry of Justice intervention to be a request that interrogations and investigations into this aspect of the case should cease (Jónasson, 1996). All interrogations of Magnús were stopped, until he was arrested by the Reykjavík police on 26 January 1976 following the reopening of the case (see Chapter 9).

There is evidence that Kristján Pétursson had a long-standing interest in Klúbburinn, suspecting Sigurbjörn and Magnús of illegal alcohol transactions: in the autumn of 1972 he had persuaded the

Reykjavík Chief of Police to close the place down, but the Minister of Justice intervened to overturn the decision within a few days. In early 1976 this caused a political backlash for Ólafur Jóhannesson and his Progressive Party (*Morgunbladid*, 30 January 1976, p. 9; Jónasson, 1996). Mr Pétursson's preoccupation with Klúbburinn was evident when the Reykjavík Criminal Investigation Police commenced their investigation into Geirfinnur's disappearance in January 1976 (see Box 7.2).

Mr Pétursson has published two books about his investigative work and the back cover of his second book describes his work in the following terms (Pétursson, 1994):

> His work was very controversial since he did not use conventional methods for solving criminal cases. The secrecy that often surrounded his investigations caused fear and horror, not only among criminals but also officials and politicians.

The 1972 incident may have fuelled rumours that there was a political and financial link between Sigurbjörn Eiríksson, the owner of Klúbburinn, and the Progressive Party. The investigation into the working of Klúbburinn was completed in February 1976. No evidence was found of smuggling or illegal sales of alcohol (Jónsdóttir, 2010).

On 13 December 1974 the Keflavík Sheriff's Department reported being under public and media pressure to solve the case, and a possible link had emerged between Geirfinnur's disappearance and the smuggling of alcohol. Haukur Gudmundsson, Kristján Pétursson, and Rúnar Sigurdsson, the three smuggling offences experts, were commissioned to focus on this aspect of the case (Working Group Report, 2013).

By Christmas 1974 the investigation was no further forward in finding Geirfinnur or solving the case. At the suggestion of veteran Reykjavík Detective Inspector Njördur Snaehólm, the Keflavík investigation team sought the services of a renowned Dutch psychic, Gerard Croiset (Jónsdóttir, 2010). Croiset suggested that Geirfinnur's body was in water close to the Harbour Café, but a careful search gave no support for this view. According to Haukur Gudmundsson, several other psychics were consulted, but without success. Geirfinnur's wife travelled abroad to see another psychic, but neither Geirfinnur nor his body were ever found.

Officially, the Keflavík investigation lasted until 5 June 1975 when the Ministry of Justice formally took over the case (Jónsdóttir, 2010). The previous day, the Ministry of Justice had written to the Keflavík

**Box 7.2**   Kristján Pétursson – Profile

Kristján Pétursson was divisional manager at Keflavík Airport Customs. He completed police training in 1954 and subsequently attended a number of workshops and training courses abroad on security and drug and alcohol offences. He worked at Keflavík Airport from 1950 and became a divisional manager in 1967. In 1969 he wrote a joint report with Haukur Gudmundsson about drug problems in Iceland and the seriousness of smuggling offences at Keflavík Airport. He was a strong advocate for increased training and resources to cope with the growing threat from drug and alcohol smuggling.

At the end of January 1974 the Narcotics Police placed Saevar Ciesielski under surveillance and on 4 February Kristján Pétursson arrested him at his home at Hamarsbraut 11 and took him to Reykjavík Police Headquarters. Saevar was later to claim that Kristján periodically put him under surveillance, including on the evening of Geirfinnur's disappearance.

Kristján often worked on investigations outside his own jurisdiction, but it is unclear under which legal authority he was working. He was a maverick who liked to work in the shadows. His tactic was to spy on people and in 1972 he placed Klúbburinn under observation every Saturday morning for six weeks and produced a report on suspected illegal alcohol transfer, which was discussed at a meeting between senior members of Customs, Inland Revenue, Prosecution, Reykjavík Criminal Court, and the Public Accountant. Kristján attended the meeting, which he had requested. Following this meeting the Chief of Police banned the consumption of alcohol on Klúbburinn premises, effectively closing the club. Kristján's allegations against Klúbburinn were taken seriously, apparently mainly driven by the efforts of prosecutor Hallvardur Einvardsson. The owner of Klúbburinn made an official complaint and the Minister of Justice, Ólafur Jóhannesson, intervened and lifted the ban on alcohol at the club, leaving the Chief of Police and Hallvardur Einvardsson unhappy about the decision.

Kristján was seconded to the Keflavík investigation into Geirfinnur's disappearance. After the Reykjavík Criminal Investigation Police officially took over the investigation in January 1976, Kristján soon requested a meeting with the top officials involved in the investigation. He claimed to be in possession of a considerable amount of important information on the Geirfinnur case, but as it turned out, this mainly involved an alleged link of Klúbburinn to the smuggling of alcohol prior to the Geirfinnur case (i.e. in 1972).

Sheriff's Department recommending that Haukur Gudmundsson be released from the case, although there is evidence that he continued to work on it after this date (Working Group Report, 2013). This effectively closed down the Keflavík investigation.

## THE FIRST CONFESSION TO GEIRFINNUR'S DISAPPEARANCE

Rumour that the director and managing director of Klúbburinn were involved in smuggling and the disappearance of Geirfinnur Einarsson flared up again in October 1975. The seeds had been sown during the Keflavík investigation and the case now took a sinister turn.

Shortly after 22.00 on 20 October 1975, a 42-year-old hospital worker, Gudmundur Agnarsson, turned up intoxicated at his daughter's house in Reykjavík. His daughter was working and his son-in-law let him in. When his daughter arrived home around midnight she challenged her father about his affair with a middle-aged woman, named Gróa. The relationship had started earlier that year and led to her parents separating: his daughter was not happy about the affair. Gróa had previously been cohabiting with Sigurbjörn Eiríksson, the director of Klúbburinn, and they had had two children together. When pressed by his daughter to explain why he was continuing with the affair, Mr Agnarsson began to cry and said that he could not break it off because he was 'involved' in the disappearance of Geirfinnur Einarsson. He said he had been with Geirfinnur when he disappeared into the sea near Keflavík harbour and Sigurbjörn Eiríksson was also involved, hence the incriminating link with his girlfriend and his need to keep her happy.

Mr Agnarsson described how he had met Sigurbjörn Eiríksson while they were patients together at a psychiatric hospital in the 1960s. Sigurbjörn had allegedly expressed an interest in the fact that Gudmundur Agnarsson had been a ship's engineer and offered him a job that 'paid very well'. Then in 1974 Sigurbjörn asked him to go with Geirfinnur Einarsson to collect contraband which had been dropped in the sea near Keflavík. At the time the smuggling of alcohol into Iceland was common and was of concern to the customs and police authorities. Mr Agnarsson said he had borrowed a boat from his cousin and sailed from Keflavík slipway to a nearby place where the contraband had been dropped into the sea for collection. Geirfinnur dived into the sea in his diving suit and recovered the contraband. Mr Agnarsson was paid kr. 70,000 (about £580 at the time) for assisting Geirfinnur.[3]

Then in November 1974, Mr Agnarsson allegedly had a phone call from Sigurbjörn while he was on night shift at the hospital asking him to go to Keflavík, meet up with Geirfinnur, and collect more contraband from the sea. Mr Agnarsson met Sigurbjörn Eiríksson and Magnús Leópoldsson in Keflavík by the Harbour Café, but they were late and

---

[3] This precise amount was to appear later in the confession statement of Saevar Ciesielski, dated 7 December 1976, as the amount he was going to offer Geirfinnur for the smuggled alcohol. Mr Agnarsson's false confession appears to have contaminated the subsequent Reykjavík investigation (see Chapters 9 and 12).

Geirfinnur was not there as arranged. Magnús went into the Harbour Café and telephoned Geirfinnur, who soon arrived. Mr Agnarsson and Geirfinnur then went on a boat to retrieve the contraband hidden in the sea near the harbour. Again, Geirfinnur's role was to dive to recover the contraband. He had made two successful dives and brought up parts of the load, which they had taken ashore, where Sigurbjörn and Magnús and two other men were waiting. However, on the third dive, Geirfinnur disappeared. Mr Agnarsson waited four hours at sea to no avail. When he arrived back on shore Sigurbjörn Eiríksson was waiting for him, but the others were gone. Mr Agnarsson explained Geirfinnur's disappearance in terms of an accident but did not have the courage to speak out, feeling under pressure from Sigurbjörn and his associates to keep quiet.[4]

Mr Agnarsson's family believed his story and encouraged him to go to the police. Gudmundur Agnarsson said the case had been a heavy burden on him and made him feel very anxious. When he did not go to the police, his family contacted Detective Haukur Bjarnasson from the Reykjavík Criminal Investigation Police.

In the meantime, Mr Agnarsson was getting into arguments with his girlfriend. At one point after making a reference to the Geirfinnur case, he made a chilling comment to her:

'Doomsday has arrived'.

Later that day (21 October 1975) he met Gróa again and they began arguing. She called the police and Mr Agnarsson was taken to a Reykjavík police station. He told the police he wanted to give a statement regarding the disappearance of the man in Keflavík, but he was told to come back the following day when he was sober. The next day Mr Agnarsson did not have the courage to go to the police, but when he arrived home that evening the police were waiting for him. They took him into custody at Síðumúli Prison and interrogated him.

In addition, witness statements were taken from members of Mr Agnarsson's family. His daughter and son-in-law both found Mr Agnarsson's confession convincing. On the face of it, it looked like a credible confession. His daughter told Detective Haukur Bjarnasson two days after the confession:

I personally believe the story since after Geirfinnur disappeared my father has not been able to relate to anybody unless he was drunk and he has been using a lot of tranquilizers.

---

[4] I have found no evidence that Geirfinnur was a diver or had the equipment or skills to recover the contraband from the seabed. In fact, there is evidence that he could not swim (ICCRC Report, 2017, Saevar Ciesielski, Paragraph 19).

Detective Haukur Bjarnasson interviewed Mr Agnarsson under caution for over two hours on 22 October 1975, but the signed statement
only consisted of one short paragraph:

> It is not correct as has been revealed in this case that I had gone with
> Geirfinnur out to sea, rather this is pure fantasy and it's not true what I
> told my children the night before last or last night. I know nothing about
> this case and cannot provide any information.

Mr Agnarsson was kept in custody at Sídumúli Prison and Haukur
Bjarnasson interviewed him again under caution between 14.20 and
15.30 the following day. The three-page statement reveals that Mr
Agnarsson confirmed the stories he had told his family members. He
had a reasonably clear recollection of what he had told his daughter
and son-in-law two days before.

Regarding the motivation for the confession Mr Agnarsson stated:

> 'I say finally that there was no other reason for these made up stories but
> my making myself a bigger man and I'm now aware of what I was doing'.

On 23 October 1975 Detective Haukur Bjarnasson interviewed a
colleague of Mr Agnarsson at the hospital where they worked. He
acknowledged that Mr Agnarsson sometimes left the hospital during
his night shift for, for example, up to two hours, but:

> 'It is impossible that he could have disappeared from the shift overnight,
> because I would have remembered that'.

The colleague's statement appears to have satisfied the police that Mr
Agnarsson was not involved in Geirfinnur's disappearance. As far as one
can tell from the evidence available, Mr Agnarsson was subsequently
never treated as a suspect. In fact, nothing further happened regarding
Mr Agnarsson's confession until 14 February 1976, St Valentine's Day,
when Chief Inspector Njördur Snaehólm took a detailed witness statement from Mr Agnarsson's girlfriend, Gróa. This appears to have been
due to the fact that her previous partner, Sigurbjörn Eiríksson was now
in police custody, implicated in the suspected murder of Geirfinnur
Einarsson. During the interview, Mr Agnarsson's name came up in relation to the confession and it left a loose end that could have jeopardized
the Reykjavík investigation into Geirfinnur's suspected murder.

Three days after Chief Inspector Njördur Snaehólm took the witness
statement of Gróa, one of the Reykjavík detectives, Eggert Bjarnason,
interrogated Mr Agnarsson in relation to the confession he had made
in October 1975. Mr Agnarsson confirmed his statement of 23 October
1975 that he had made up the smuggling incident. He had not been

involved in Geirfinnur's disappearance, but now explained the 'false confession' in terms of his having been angry towards Gróa and wanted to take revenge on her. He said that he had made up the entire story from rumours circulating about Geirfinnur's disappearance, such as smuggling, the location at Keflavík harbour, the Harbour Café's telephone call to Geirfinnur, and the suspected involvement of Sigurbjörn Eiríksson and Magnús Leópoldsson. His confession was substantially based on these rumours.

### A Voluntary False Confession

Gudmundur Agnarsson's confession to his relatives on 21 October 1975 was of the voluntary type. That is, it was not coerced by police, nor did he confess to police when interviewed on three occasions about the confession. It was not coerced by his relatives and did not meet the criteria for the 'coerced-reactive' type discussed in Chapter 4. False confessions of this type result from a combination of circumstances and psychological vulnerabilities. The basic psychological vulnerability involves feelings of inadequacy, poor self-esteem, self-centred focus, and disregard for the truth (Gudjonsson, 2003a).

Sometimes a voluntary confession arises during alcohol intoxication, which can lead to behavioural disinhibition. This is what happened in the British case of Ian Lawless (Gudjonsson, 2010a). Lawless had a history of alcoholism and while drinking one evening he confessed to his daughter and others in a public house that he had been involved in a local murder of a man, Alfred Wilkins. An accelerant had been poured through the letter box of his home and ignited. The victim died as a result of smoke inhalation. Three months previously, Wilkins had been acquitted of an indecent assault on a child and he was subsequently harassed by one or more persons. The case was described by one witness in the case as the 'talk of the town'. Lawless did not repeat the confession to the police and coped well with the interrogation, but he was nevertheless convicted of the murder. He did not confess to starting the fire himself, but said he had acted as 'a look out man' when the fire was started at Mr Wilkins's house, hence his being complicit in his death. Seven years later Lawless's conviction was quashed on appeal after psychological evidence showed him to have poor self-esteem and a pathological need for attention. The Court of Appeal stated:

> Professor Gudjonsson also expressed the view that the fact that Mr Lawless had apparently expressed distress, and even cried, whilst claiming involvement in the murder of Mr Wilkins should not be viewed as evidence of his guilt; it was likely that the expression of distress was part of his pathological attention-seeking behaviour.
> (Court of Appeal Judgement, Paragraph 26; [2009] EWCA Crim 1308)

Mr Agnarsson's confession had some similarities with Ian Lawless's confession. Both men had alcohol problems and made a confession to their daughter while intoxicated and cried to make their confession sound more authentic. This is typical attention-seeking behaviour. Both cases were the 'talk of the town' in their respective communities. Unlike Ian Lawless, Mr Agnarsson was not assessed psychologically so his mental state at the time is a matter of conjecture. However, Mr Agnarsson's wife provides an important insight into his psychological problems in her witness statement. In the 1950s, Mr Agnarsson had been an engineer on a boat, *Drífa*, that stranded by the Reykjanes peninsula. A media search showed that this happened in the early hours of the morning of 6 February 1953. All six crew members survived, but witnesses to the incident said that they were only saved 'in the nick of time', as soon afterwards the ship capsized and sank (*Visir*, 6 February 1953).

Mr Agnarsson was apparently traumatized by the incident. According to his ex-wife, her husband never recovered from this:

> After this Gudmundur became nervous and I did not recognize him as the same man, because before he was calm and even-tempered. It is as if he could not control his temper afterwards, and had terrifying claustrophobia.

On the basis of the material available it seems that following this incident Mr Agnarsson was left traumatized and was still having problems over 20 years later when he made the confession to his family. In the late 1960s he became a hospital worker with responsibilities for hospital vehicles. His mental state appears to have deteriorated in 1975, with increased alcohol consumption. His affair with Gróa was creating problems within his family and he was under pressure to stop it. His confession is most likely to have been due to his drinking, low self-esteem, and need for attention in the context of an affair that appears to have been turbulent. He implicated two men who had been rumoured to be involved in Geirfinnur's disappearance. One of these men, Sigurbjörn Eiríksson, had been in the past Gróa's long-standing partner. Mr Agnarsson also expressed an element of anger towards Gróa and this added a possible revenge motive. The case illustrates the fact that false confessions are usually precipitated by a combination of factors, rather than one factor acting in isolation, even when given voluntarily.

## CONCLUSIONS

The disappearance of Geirfinnur Einarsson on 19 November 1974 was suspicious from the beginning because of the mysterious meeting he had arranged with one or more people at the Harbour Café that evening. His car was later found abandoned nearby and a sniffer dog found that his smell petered out near the Harbour Café. The Keflavík police failed to investigate the source of the telephone call to Geirfinnur's home on the evening of 19 November, but it was assumed that it had come from the Harbour Café. This assumption was never independently corroborated.

The Keflavík investigation was headed by Valtýr Sigurdsson from the Keflavík Sheriff's Department and the two main investigators, Haukur Gudmundsson and Kristján Pétursson, specialized in smuggling offences. Rúnar Sigurdsson, who had been on the working group that helped set up the Reykjavík narcotics police in February 1972 (Jónsson & Gudjónsson [Gudmundur], 1997), was seconded to the investigating team, apparently due to his specialism in the field of drug and alcohol offences. These three officers focused primarily on the assumption that there was a link between Geirfinnur's disappearance and the smuggling of alcohol. This hypothetical link drove the investigation and rumours soon spread in the media, possibly through loose talk by one or more members of the investigative team. The strength and persistence of the rumours suggest that they were driven by a source inside the investigation. It is known that Kristján Pétursson was at that time in close contact with the media (Jónasson, 1996), and had the opportunity and motivation, although I am not aware of any evidence directly linking him to the rumours. The evidence is circumstantial, including his apparent obsession with Klúbburinn's alleged link to smuggling, dating from as early as August 1972 when he had placed the Klúbburinn under surveillance every Saturday morning for several weeks. Magnús Leópoldsson reports often seeing Kristján Pétursson 'sniffing around Klúbburinn' and had been informed that he thought Magnús and Sigurbjörn were 'big smugglers' (Jónasson, 1996, p. 118).

The official complaint that Sigurbjörn Eiríksson and Magnús Leópoldsson made to the Ministry of Justice on 3 February 1975 regarding the harmful impact of the rumours on their lives, and the running of Klúbburinn, temporarily stopped that aspect of the investigation after the Ministry of Justice intervened. Officially the Keflavík police identified no suspects and the Reykjavík police later took over the investigation. Unknown to Sigurbjörn and Magnús at the time, this was just the beginning of their nightmare. Worse was to come, including solitary confinement for three months.

The rumours that the director and managing director of Klúbburinn were involved in smuggling and the disappearance of Geirfinnur Einarsson sowed the seeds for the voluntary false confession in October 1975 from a man with mental health issues. This false confession, investigated by the Reykjavík police and discarded, later became incorporated into the confessions obtained from Erla Bolladóttir, Saevar Ciesielski, and Kristján Vidarsson. It showed how early police assumptions and rumours, generated during the Keflavík investigation, later influenced the Reykjavík police investigation, leading to the 'Reykjavík Confessions'.

# 8

# The Confessions
# in the Gudmundur Einarsson Case

*They [the investigators] formed a crack in my mind and then they just got in there*[1]

In this chapter, I focus on the investigation into the disappearance of Gudmundur Einarsson, who went missing in the early hours of Sunday 27 January 1974. This was not at the time treated as suspicious.

Around the middle of December 1975 a young couple, Saevar Ciesielski and Erla Bolladóttir, were arrested and detained in custody for suspected fraud offences. After seven days in solitary confinement Erla confessed to the fraud offences and gave a statement, but investigators then started questioning her about Gudmundur's disappearance. The investigators 'had heard' that Saevar might know something about Gudmundur's disappearance and they were determined to extract confessions. After intense questioning and further time in detention, Erla implicated Saevar and his friend Kristján. Saevar, in turn, implicated two further people, Tryggvi Leifsson and Albert Skaftason. The material relied on in this chapter is derived from the Court's Books of Evidence (referred to as 'Evidence Books'), the Supreme Court Judgement, extracts from the custody record diary held at Síðumúli Prison (i.e. the prison kept a detailed daily diary of

---

[1] A comment Erla Bolladóttir made about her experience during the interrogation in the Gudmundur and Geirfinnur cases on Mosaic Films' *Out of Thin Air*, shown on BBC Four Television (Storyville Series) on 14 August 2017 and available on Netflix.

*The Psychology of False Confessions: Forty Years of Science and Practice*, First Edition.
Gisli H. Gudjonsson.
© 2018 John Wiley & Sons Ltd. Published 2018 by John Wiley & Sons Ltd.

who entered the prison, the duration of their visit, and their interactions with prisoners), and information from the Working Group Report (2013) and the Icelandic Court Cases Review Commission Report (ICCRC Report, 2017).

## THE POST AND TELECOMMUNICATION FRAUD

At the beginning of January 1974 Erla Bolladóttir returned to her job as a telex operator with Iceland's Post and Telecommunication Company. She continued to work there until October 1974. In August 1974 Saevar and Erla forged five telecommunication cheques, worth a total of kr. 475,000 (about £4,000). A similar fraud for the same amount took place the following October. Chief Inspector Njördur Snaehólm initially investigated the two fraud cases and by December 1974 he had found several witnesses who identified from photographs of four women Erla Bolladóttir as the person who most resembled the person who had cashed the cheques in the second fraud.[2] In fact both Erla and Saevar were treated as the prime suspects, but for some unknown reason they were not formally interviewed about it until mid-December 1975 and then by the 'Reykjavík Team'. Considering Njördur Snaehólm's extensive detective experience and the serious nature of the fraud offences, this seems most extraordinary. According to one of Erla's police statements, Njördur interviewed her in the summer of 1975 about the fraud, but the interview was informal and not recorded.

On 6 December 1975, Njördur Snaehólm took a statement from a farmer who recalled that in September 1974, he had employed a 20-year-old woman, who had participated in the first fraud with Erla and Saevar. The farmer remembered that when the woman arrived in the southeast of Iceland on 26 September for work in the farmhouse, she looked 'extremely shattered and it was obvious that something was wrong'.[3] Subsequently, the farmer had had a long conversation with her and found her knowledgeable and intelligent, but she seemed particularly interested in discussing what happened after death, an ominous sign as it turned out. A few days later the young woman was found dead on the shore in Vík in Mýrdal, having apparently drowned herself.

There is no evidence that Saevar had anything to do with the death of the young woman in Vík in Mýrdal, but there were rumours and two

---

[2] Evidence Book VII, pp. 155–156.
[3] Evidence Book VII, pp. 107–109. The police report on the investigation, dated 29 November 1974, identifies both Erla and Saevar as prime suspects in the two frauds.

officers took them seriously.[4] In June 1976 Keflavík customs officer Kristján Pétursson and Reykjavík narcotics officer Gísli Pálsson were interviewing a female suspect in Spain in connection with the smuggling of cannabis. The woman repeated the rumour, naming an Icelandic source, that Saevar had strangled the young woman who was found drowned in Vík in Mýrdal and thrown her into the sea to cover it up. Saevar had also, among other things, allegedly been hired to burn down the summer house of the then prime minister, Bjarni Benediktsson, who died in a fire at Thingvellir with his wife and grandson on 11 July 1970.

The two officers produced a joint report with these pieces of information and it was forwarded by prior agreement to Hallvardur Einvardsson, the prosecution representative in the Gudmundur and Geirfinnur cases. The report, dated 16 June 1976, is included in the court papers[5]; no evidence was ever found to support these rumours. Nevertheless, this shows how some investigators were giving credence to unsubstantiated claims and senior prosecutor Hallvardur Einvardsson was taking an interest.

According to the Supreme Court Judgement (pp. 143–144), the most significant development regarding the fraud allegations occurred on 8 December 1975, when a woman, whose lost identity card had been used in one of the frauds, told police that 'she had heard' through a third party that Saevar was responsible for the fraud.

This starting point has been superseded by more recent evidence that suggests the involvement of SSA as the police informant in both the fraud and Gudmundur disappearance cases (see Chapter 12).[6]

On 11 December a statement was taken from Kristján, a serving prisoner and Saevar's friend. This interview lasted almost three hours and was conducted in Sídumúli Prison. Kristján incriminated Saevar by informing the detectives that he had seen Saevar with a lot of money in August 1974, which Saevar later told him he had obtained fraudulently using a young woman to collect the money for which she was allegedly paid kr. 100,000. The following day Saevar was arrested, and the day after that Erla was arrested.

The 'Reykjavík Team' comprised Detectives Eggert Bjarnason and Sigurbjörn Vídir Eggertsson, and the Criminal Court's legal representative, Örn Höskuldsson, started at the beginning of December 1975, and possibly before. These investigators have consistently been

---

[4] ICCRC Report, 2017, Saevar Ciesielski, Paragraph 463.
[5] Evidence Book XIII, pp. 284–286.
[6] ICCRC Report, 2017, Saevar Ciesielski, Paragraphs 47–49, 1909, 2396, 2892 and 2893.

extremely reticent about explaining the beginning of their investigation, but in spite of their resistance and claimed memory lapses the
truth is beginning to emerge.

After Erla had denied the fraud offences on 13 December 1974 she
was remanded in custody for 30 days (see Table 8.1). At that time she
was 20 years of age and had an 11-week-old daughter, Julia, Saevar
being the baby's father. Erla had been kept in solitary confinement for
several days before she was interrogated on 17 December for over five
hours by Detectives Eggert Bjarnason and Sigurbjörn Vídir, and later
in the evening they were joined by Örn Höskuldsson for a further
interrogation. Over the following two days she was interrogated on
several occasions and gave two confession statements regarding the
fraud cases.

In her autobiography, published in 2008, Erla explains the motive for
the fraud in the following terms:

> One of Saevar's dreams was to commit a major crime and get away with
> it. He said that Vilhjálmur Knudsen [a film producer] needed a loan for
> up to kr. 300,000 and the idea emerged of committing fraud to gain the
> money. If Saevar could lend Vilhjálmur the money, he would in turn lend
> Saevar a motion picture camera and other film equipment on extended
> loan [at the time Saevar fancied himself becoming a film producer].
> We discussed this over and over again and got very excited about it. We
> decided that I would investigate this at work over the next few days.
>
> (Bolladóttir, 2008, p. 138)

Once arrested Erla did not want to confess to the fraud, fearing that
if she did so, her infant daughter would be taken into care. She also had
the belief at that point that policemen were bad people and that she
should not cooperate with them. Importantly, she did not want to betray
Saevar by informing on him regarding the fraud and drug-related
offences that he was suspected of having committed. The three investigators tried hard to persuade her that they cared about her welfare
and that they understood how difficult it was to live with a man like
Saevar. They knew that not all was well in their relationship, because
when searching their home in December 1975, the officers had found a
letter signed by Saevar indicating a problem in their relationship and
they used this to get her to confess.

Erla told me in 2017 that this was a declaration statement concerning her being allowed to keep all their domestic possessions after their
intended separation in January 1976 – she had kept the declaration
letter inside the telephone directory.

According to Erla the investigators reassured her that her daughter
would not be taken away from her if she confessed. After her full and

**Table 8.1**   Key chronology regarding the arrests, detention, and interrogation of Erla Bolladóttir and Saevar Ciesielski in connection with the Post and Telecommunication fraud

**Event**

At the beginning of December 1975, SSA implicates Saevar and Erla in the fraud case and mentions Kristján as a potential witness.

**11 December 1975**
Kristján Vidarsson, a serving prisoner and a friend of Saevar, is questioned by Detective Eggert Bjarnason for almost three hours at Sídumúli Prison regarding his knowledge of Saevar having committed fraud in August 1974 and being in possession of a lot of money.

**12 December 1975**
Saevar Ciesielski is interrogated in connection with a Post and Telecommunication fraud (16.30–17.05). He denies any involvement and is taken to Sídumúli Prison where he is remanded in custody for 30 days.

**13 December 1975**
Erla Bolladóttir is interrogated in connection with a Post and Telecommunication fraud (14.55–16.23). She denies any involvement and is taken to Sídumúli Prison where she is remanded in custody for 30 days.

**17 December 1975**
09.40–10.30. Erla speaks with her solicitor, Jón Oddsson.
11.15–16.30. Detectives Eggert Bjarnason and Sigurbjörn Vídir interview Erla at Sídumúli Prison. (From the custody record: 'Erla is put into her cell after a long and rigorous interview'.)
21.40–00.35. Detectives Eggert Bjarnason and Sigurbjörn Vídir interview Erla, joined by investigative judge Örn Höskuldsson at 23.05.
**Note:** There are no reports regarding these interviews.

**18 December 1975**
Erla is interrogated and gives a detailed statement in connection with the first Post and Telecommunication fraud (13.00–19.30). She confesses and reports that Saevar had pressured her into committing the fraud. The interrogation continues without it being recorded, but it was noted that Örn Höskuldsson took over the interrogation between 22.05 and 22.30. The interrogation that day lasted for nine and a half hours.
**Note:** Police informant SSA was brought to Sídumúli Prison at 15.00 that same day, after having been released from Litla-Hraun Prison six days previously and was kept in Sídumúli Prison there until the following day (ICCRC Report, 2017, Kristján Vidarsson, Paragraphs 56–57).

**19 December 1975**
Erla is interrogated in connection with the second Post and Telecommunication fraud, committed two months later, and gives a detailed confession statement (19.50–21.20).

(Continued)

**Table 8.1**   (*Continued*)

**20 December 1975**

Erla is released from custody at Síðumúli Prison at 16.54, after having been
    interviewed as a witness in the Gudmundur Einarsson case. The police had
    apparently heard from an informant (SSA) that the convicted persons
    might be implicated in the case (see Chapter 12). At the beginning of
    December SSA had implicated Saevar and Erla in the fraud case.

**11 January 1976**

13.50–15.00. Saevar is interrogated regarding the first Post and
    Telecommunication fraud and gives a detailed confession statement,
    stating that he instigated the offence.

15.05–15.45. Saevar is interrogated regarding the second Post and
    Telecommunication fraud and gives a detailed confession statement,
    stating that he instigated the offence.

frank fraud confessions, she was expecting to be released from solitary
confinement and looked forward to seeing her infant daughter, who she
missed desperately. When Örn Höskuldsson asked her whether she
knew Gudmundur Einarsson and showed her a photograph of him
(Bolladóttir, 2008), she recognized Gudmundur as a man she had met
at a party a few years previously. Örn Höskuldsson kept asking her
questions about him and Erla recalled that on the night of his disappearance she had had a nightmare. According to Erla, Örn suggested
that she had witnessed some horrible event at Hamarsbraut 11, her
home, that night. He went on:

> I know that this is difficult but we are going to help you. You will now go
> back into your cell and continue to recall this period and we will speak
> again tomorrow. You will not leave this place until you have managed to
> recall what happened that night.
>
> (Bolladóttir, 2008, p. 185)

## THE DISAPPEARANCE OF GUDMUNDUR EINARSSON

Meanwhile another investigation was taking place behind the scenes
involving the disappearance of a young man, Gudmundur Einarsson,
two years previously. The name of Saevar Ciesielski had apparently
cropped up as a suspect in this new case via the police informant, SSA
(see Chapter 12). It cannot be assumed that SSA necessarily implicated Saevar first in the fraud case, if he was an informant in both
cases. The two cases may be intrinsically linked.

Gudmundur Einarsson, age 18, went to a dance hall at Alþýðuhúsið, in Strandgata, Hafnarfjördur, on the evening of Saturday 26 January 1974. He was seen in the street outside the dance hall at about 02.00 on Sunday morning in the company of another man. Hafnarfjördur is an old fishing town located on the southwest coast of Iceland, about 10 kilometres (6 miles) from the capital Reykjavík. There is evidence that Gudmundur intended to walk home to Reykjavík in the snow and icy weather, but he never reached it. His father, Einar Baldursson, formally reported his son missing on 29 January. He last saw him at 20.00 on 26 January. Gudmundur had long dark hair and was 180 cm (five feet and 11 inches) in height and had no criminal convictions. His disappearance was reported in the media and the search for him lasted for several days: no trace of him has ever been found.

A preliminary police investigation revealed that Gudmundur had left his home after dinner on 26 January. He went to his friend's house in Gardabaer between 21.00 and 22.00, which is on the way from Reykjavík to Hafnarfjördur. They sat drinking for about two hours after which he went with friends to Alþýðuhúsið and arrived there around midnight. According to witnesses, Gudmundur was wearing a jacket and no overcoat. He seems to have become separated from his friends at the dance hall.

On the night of Gudmundur's disappearance, snow had been falling and the temperature was close to freezing. The subsequent search for Gudmundur was hampered by the fact that the whole area between Hafnarfjördur and Reykjavík was covered by 60 cm (approximately two feet) of snow. It was not possible to search the adjacent lava field or areas outside the main roads (*Morgunbladid*, 30 January 1974, p. 2). It is also important that Gudmundur was known to be intoxicated when he left Alþýðuhúsið. Witnesses had seen him at the dance hall looking unsteady on his feet.

In the early evening of 29 January a woman, Elínborg, telephoned the police and said that she had been with a friend driving through Strandgata at 02.00 on 27 January, when she saw Gudmundur, whom she recognized, on the road with another man, who was older, trying to catch a lift. The other man was wearing a yellow shirt and she did not recognize him. He looked intoxicated and excitable and in view of this they did not bother to stop.

On 31 January the Chief Superintendent in Hafnarfjördur, Sveinn Björnsson, telephoned the Reykjavík Criminal Investigation Police to say that he had received a phone call from a man, who reported seeing an intoxicated man trying to catch a ride on the main road out of Hafnarfjördur (Reykjanesvegur) after 02.00 on 27 January. The man was described as tall with long hair. This account and description was confirmed by another man in the car. Both described the man on the road as looking intoxicated. One of the men had seen a photograph of Gudmundur Einarsson and he was in no doubt that it was the same person he had seen on the Reykjanesvegur on the night of 27 January 1974.

Chief Inspector Njördur Snaehólm investigated Gudmundur's disappearance and found no trace of him. There was apparently nothing suspicious about his disappearance and it was at the time treated as a 'missing person' enquiry. The Gudmundur case lay dormant until late December 1975 when it surfaced as a murder enquiry in Reykjavík, instigated by the Reykjavík Team, following a rumour that the police had heard from an undisclosed source, which is now known to have been police informant Sigurdur Almarsson.


## THE GUDMUNDUR EINARSSON INVESTIGATION

The Gudmundur Einarsson murder investigation was initiated by a rumour from an undisclosed source that Saevar 'could possibly be involved in the disappearance of Gudmundur Einarsson'. The Reykjavík Team – headed by investigative judge Örn Höskuldsson and assisted by Detectives Eggert Bjarnason and Sigurbjörn Vídir – started the investigation on the basis of this rumour, but later none of them could recall why: they have consistently failed to provide details of the source of this rumour, the context within which it emerged, and the likely validity of the accusation.

Örn Höskuldsson was a lawyer with the Reykjavík Criminal Court, a position he had held since June 1970, immediately after qualifying as a lawyer (Haraldsson, 1993, p. 645). He was in his early thirties and had the authority to remand suspects into custody, which he used freely during the Gudmundur and Geirfinnur investigation. I remember him as a tall man of heavy build, with a beard and dark glasses and receding hair. When our paths crossed, he always looked serious and I rarely saw him smile. He had a certain intensity about him. I could see how people might feel intimidated in his company.

Eggert Bjarnason was a detective in his late thirties with 11 years' experience as a detective with the Reykjavík Criminal Investigation Police (Jónsson & Gudjónsson [Gudmundur], 1997, p. 126). He qualified from business school in 1955 and worked for a while in an office before joining the police in April 1961. Eggert was vigilant and observant. I recall once being with him in an unmarked police car when he suddenly spotted a wanted criminal in the far distance. He was driving and we were fully engaged in a conversation at the time. Eggert could be determined and forceful.

Sigurbjörn Vídir Eggertsson, the most junior of the Reykjavík Team, was in his late twenties and had only been in the Reykjavík Criminal Investigation Police since November 1973, having entered the uniformed branch in 1969 (Jónsson & Gudjónsson [Gudmundur], 1997, p. 473). I remember him as an ambitious and enthusiastic detective. He was likeable, full of energy, and had a sense of confidence about him. He came across as a smooth operator who could establish good rapport with people. After having not seen him for 40 years, I met him inside the Reykjavík District Court on 28 January 2016 and he was as chatty and friendly as I had remembered him.

In August 1976, Karl Schütz set up a Task Force, which involved a number of additional police officers being appointed to the investigation (see Chapters 9 and 10).

## The Further Enquiries

Karl Schütz and his Reykjavík Task Force completed their investigation into the Gudmundur case in October 1976 (Working Group Report, 2013). In December that year the case was placed in the hands of three criminal court judges who discovered a number of deficiencies with regard to the investigation. As a result, lead judge Gunnlaugur Briem appointed Detective Gísli Gudmundsson to investigate a number of outstanding issues, including Saevar's possible alibi.[7] Detective Gudmundsson found a new witness in the case (Gunnar Jónsson – see below), discovered that the telephone at Hamarsbraut 11 had been disconnected at the time of Gudmundur's disappearance, and found that Saevar might have had an alibi. Gísli Gudmundsson was assisted, when required, by Detectives Hellert Jóhannesson and Njördur Snaehólm.

## The Suspects and Witnesses

On the basis of a witness statement Erla had made in custody after confessing to the Post and Telecommunication fraud in December 1975, a murder investigation into Gudmundur's disappearance commenced. The alleged crime scene was Hamarsbraut 11, which is situated in the centre of Hafnarfjördur and close to where Gudmundur had been last seen. There were three suspects (Saevar Ciesielski, Kristján Vidarsson,

---

[7] Evidence Book II, pp. 31–35.

and Tryggvi Leifsson) and three witnesses (Erla Bolladóttir, Albert Skaftason, and Gunnar Jónsson) to what allegedly took place at Hamarsbraut 11 in the early hours of 27 January 1974.

Erla implicated Saevar and Kristján and in a later interview also Tryggvi. This officially started the investigation. In his first interview Saevar implicated Kristján and Tryggvi, and mentioned having telephoned Albert, who had access to his father's car, to take Gudmundur Einarsson's body to the Hafnarfjördur lava field. Gunnar Jónsson's name was first mentioned in a statement Saevar made on 3 March 1977.

### Gunnar Jónsson

Gunnar's incriminating witness statement against the three defendants was elicited during three days of intense questioning in court, after having told police he knew nothing about Gudmundur's disappearance (see Box 8.1). It shows the judiciary's determination to convict the defendants after Saevar, Kristján, and Tryggvi had retracted their confession statements. Erla did not retract her confession in the Gudmundur case for several years, because the Reykjavík Team had persuaded her that the event had taken place and she was for a very long time unsure about whether it was real or not, suggesting long lasting memory distrust syndrome (Working Group Report, 2013, Chapter 14).

## THE CONFESSIONS TO GUDMUNDUR EINARSSON'S MURDER

### General Background

The confessions obtained during the investigation into Gudmundur's disappearance were extremely poorly recorded. Most interrogations took place at Sídumúli Prison and its detailed daily custody record (diary) log shows a large number of interrogations that were never recorded (Working Group Report, 2013). For example, according to the Prison diary, Saevar was interrogated for over 10 hours on 21 December 1975, where nothing was recorded. The following day he was interrogated for seven hours and a one page summary of the interrogation that day gave just a brief outline of his confession. No contemporaneous notes were kept of interviews, and the questions asked to elicit confessions were not recorded.

In Iceland, investigators typically typed a statement once the suspect had given an account of what had happened, or provided some new information to advance the case. The interviewee was then asked to

**Box 8.1**   Gunnar Jónsson – Witness in the Gudmundur case

At the time of the Gudmundur investigation Gunnar Jónsson was a 20-year-old man who was travelling abroad.

Gunnar's name was first mentioned in a statement Saevar made on 3 March 1977. Saevar said that Albert had driven to Hafnarfjördur in the early hours of 27 January 1974 with Kristján and Tryggvi and a 'third man' called Gunni, a nickname for Gunnar. The following day the police took a statement from Albert who identified Gunnar.

On 8 March 1977, the police made a request to the Ministry of Justice that Gunnar be located. He was located in Spain.

On 20 April 1977 a court summons was issued to Gunnar Jónsson to give a witness statement about a fight he witnessed at Hamarsbraut 11 on 27 January 1974.

On 23 April 1977 two detectives went to Spain and brought Gunnar back on 29 April. Detective Gísli Gudmundsson took a statement from Gunnar that evening and he made it clear that he did not know anything about Gudmundur's disappearance or his death. He stayed in a hotel overnight under police supervision.

On Saturday 30 April, Gunnar spent most of the day in court being taken through the defendants' statements implicating his presence at Hamarsbraut 11 on the night of Gudmundur's alleged death. He was too tired for a statement to be taken. The case was postponed until Monday 2 May. After Court on 30 April Gunnar was placed under police guard and taken to Hamarsbraut 11.

Gunnar spent the Monday to Wednesday, 2–4 May, being questioned in court. His account over the three days was very vague and incomplete, but it was all the prosecution and court needed to help secure a conviction against the three alleged perpetrators: Saevar, Kristján, and Tryggvi, who had all retracted their confessions by the time of the trial in December 1977. The prosecution was satisfied with Gunnar's vague confession and announced that 'as the case now stands' he would not be prosecuted. The implication was that if Gunnar tried to retract his witness statement, he could face charges of some kind (e.g. perjury).

The linchpin to Gunnar's testimony was on the final day of giving evidence when he said he had tried to recall the previous night what had happened at Hamarsbraut 11, and now 'firmly remembers' that he was told that 'the man fell on a table and was knocked out'. On the basis of the content of Gunnar's evidence in court, it seems a real possibility that at the time he was suffering from memory distrust syndrome.

sign the statement in front of a witness, usually another police officer, who should not have been present during the interrogation.

The absence of electronic, verbatim, or contemporaneous recording makes it impossible to know exactly what happened during these long interrogations to produce confessions. In these types of cases, police officers invariably deny any allegations of coercion or impropriety, and the accounts subsequently given by defendants are typically treated as being self-serving and unreliable (Gudjonsson, 2003a). As a result, defendants claiming they were coerced into giving a false confession are seriously disadvantaged when their case goes to court, even if they are telling the truth. In making allegations against police officers, even if true, they risked being charged with perjury.

### The Sequence of Statements and Key Content of the Confessions

I will give a brief summary of the written statements that the suspects gave to the police concerning Gudmundur Einarsson's disappearance. This is not an exhaustive list but it includes the most salient statements.

It is important to note that there were a large number of unrecorded interviews conducted, which means that the statements presented below do not tell the full story (Working Group Report, 2013). For example, Tryggvi Leifsson's lawyer, Hilmar Ingimundarsson, noted in a letter to judge Gunnlaugur Briem on 14 September 1977 that his client had been interviewed over 30 times but had only provided two short written statements.[8]

In addition to the police interviews, there were a large number of face-to-face confrontations (*samprófun*) where two or more suspects were put together in a room, supervised by police, in order to improve consistency in their accounts of what had happened to Gudmundur and Geirfinnur (Gudjonsson et al., 2014; Working Group Report, 2013). Sometimes the purpose of these confrontations was to pressure one or more suspects to agree with the incriminating account given of another and obtain a confession (i.e. hypothesis driven guilt-presumption account – police pressure by proxy).

The Commission Report (ICCRC Report, 2017) showed that these suspects' face-to-face confrontations were much more frequent early in the Gudmundur and Geirfinnur investigation and declined in the autumn of 1976.

### Erla Bolladóttir (20 December 1975)

Erla was questioned as a witness for over six hours and implicated Saevar and Kristján in the death of Gudmundur Einarsson, after which she was released from Síðumúli Prison. She reported that when she had arrived home at around 03.30 to 04.00 on 27 January 1974, she

---

[8] Evidence Book III, pp. 41–57.

noticed that her bed sheet had gone missing and thought it was strange. She described how she had been woken up at Hamarsbraut 11 on the night of Gudmundur's disappearance by a scuffle outside her bedroom window. She later saw Saevar and Kristján and a third man (later identified as Tryggvi) inside the basement flat carrying between them something big and heavy covered in a bed sheet, which she thought was a human body. She noticed a bad smell coming from the sheet, similar to that of excrement. Erla went back to sleep and in the morning found the sheet of her bed in the dustbin outside the house covered in human faeces.

**Note:** In her autobiography Erla (Bolladóttir, 2008) revealed that she had soiled the sheet herself and placed it in the dustbin but was too embarrassed to tell the investigators. The bed sheet was to become a key feature in the confessions of the suspects.

### Saevar Ciesielski (21/22 December 1975)

Saevar was interrogated for over 10 hours on 21 December, without any record being kept, and the following day (22 December) for a further seven hours (i.e. 11.00–13.00; 14.00–19.00), which resulted in a one page unsigned confession statement. Investigative judge Örn Höskuldsson and Saevar's defence lawyer Jón Oddsson were present during most of the afternoon interview. Saevar was repeatedly asked about his knowledge of Gudmundur Einarsson's disappearance, but at first persistently denied any knowledge of it. He confessed after a part of Erla's witness statement was read out to him. He mentioned that on the night in question, Gudmundur, Kristján, and Tryggvi came to Hamarsbraut 11 and a fight broke out. Saevar said that he had telephoned Albert to help with the transportation of Gudmundur's body, because Albert had access to his father's car. They moved Gudmundur's body and hid it in the lava field south of Hafnarfjördur. Saevar remained in custody on an existing court order.

**Note:** At this time, Saevar now introduced two additional people not mentioned by Erla: Tryggvi Leifsson and Albert Skaftason. It was much later discovered that at the time of Gudmundur's disappearance the telephone at Hamarsbraut 11 had been disconnected and Saevar could not have made the call from there as he claimed in his statement.

### Albert Skaftason (23 December 1975)

Albert arrived at Sídumúli Prison at 05.00, having been collected from Seydisfjördur by detectives in connection with the disappearance of Gudmundur Einarsson. Technically he was not under arrest, but the inherently coercive effects on him were the same. If he had refused to accompany the detectives to Reykjavík he would have been arrested. He was locked up at Sídumúli Prison for eight hours, not knowing exactly what was going on, but he had been informed it was in connection with the disappearance of Gudmundur and that it was serious. His detention activated a 'softening up' process. He was informed that Saevar had given a statement with regard to what had happened at Hamarsbraut 11. Albert was questioned for over three hours in the afternoon (13.55–17.10), having the status of a witness, and a statement was taken. Albert said that at the time he had access to his father's yellow Toyota car, but could not recall whether he drove the others to Hafnarfjördur or whether they telephoned him and asked him to meet them there. He did not recall why he was at Hamarsbraut 11 but recalled being parked outside the house. Saevar asked him to open the boot of the car, which was facing the house, and he thought that one or more bags were put in it, which rocked the car. Saevar, Kristján, and Tryggvi got into the car and Albert drove them south out of Hafnarfjördur, past the aquarium, and on the road towards Keflavík, passing the aluminium factory at Straumsvík on the way. Saevar was directing where to go and then told him to stop the car. Saevar, Kristján, and Tryggvi went out of the car and took the baggage with them. When they returned, Albert thought he drove them to Kristján's address at Grettisgata 82, Reykjavík, but was not sure.

When Albert appeared in court that evening he stated that he 'recognized' (kannast við) having driven Saevar, Kristján, and Tryggvi with something they had put in the boot of his car, implying he did not properly recall it. Albert now had the status of a suspect and was remanded in custody for 45 days.

**Note:** Albert's statement is vague and superficial and suggests serious memory problems with regard to what allegedly happened that night. The police later discovered that at the time of Gudmundur Einarsson's disappearance Albert's father had a Volkswagen Beetle car, not a yellow Toyota (which he did not own until later in 1974).

The Sídumúli Prison diary shows that during the period the statement was taken, Albert was taken out of the prison at 14.25 on an 'expedition trip', presumably a scene visit, accompanied by five detectives and the investigative judge.[9] This is not mentioned in the statement taken, highlighting the absence of transparency with regard to the police investigation and the heavy handed approach taken.

---

[9] ICCRC Report, 2017, Albert Skaftason, Paragraph 24.

### Kristján Vidarsson (23 December 1975)

Kristján was transferred to Sídumúli Prison from Litla-Hraun Prison, where he was serving a prison sentence, and questioned about the disappearance of Gudmundur Einarsson. He admitted knowing Gudmundur from school, but denied having knowledge about his disappearance. He refused to sign the written statement.

Kristján appeared in 'court' in the evening and denied any knowledge of Gudmundur's disappearance. He was remanded in custody for 90 days.

**Note:** Investigative judge Örn Höskuldsson often used the interrogation room at Sídumúli Prison as a 'virtual court' where he remanded suspects in custody or extended their detention rather than taking them to Reykjavík Criminal Court at Borgartún 7, which was a few minutes' drive away.

### Tryggvi Leifsson (23 December 1975)

Tryggvi Leifsson was arrested and brought to Sídumúli Prison at 14.15 in connection with the disappearance of Gudmundur Einarsson. He was briefly interviewed but denied knowing anything about Gudmundur's disappearance.

At 19.35 that day Tryggvi appeared in 'court' and was remanded in custody for 90 days.

### Kristján Vidarsson (28 December 1975)

On 28 December, Kristján was interrogated for almost six hours (19.45–01.42). He declared from the beginning that at the time of Gudmundur's disappearance, he was under the influence of alcohol and did not remember much about what happened. He said that he had gone to Hamarsbraut 11 that night with Saevar and Tryggvi and a third man whom he did not recognize. He said Erla was not in the house when they arrived. Kristján used tentative language when describing what happened (e.g. 'I think', 'probably', 'I think it is most likely'). He thought that Tryggvi and the unknown man may have engaged in a fight. They left the unknown man in the flat and drove around Hafnarfjördur (there was no mention of who was driving or in whose vehicle); when they returned to Hamarsbraut 11, Erla had come home. Kristján remembered Albert arriving in a yellow Japanese car. The boot of the car was facing the house and Saevar and Tryggvi put something heavy in the boot, which rocked the car, and they all drove off towards the aluminium factory. When the car stopped,

Saevar and Tryggvi took something out of the boot of the car and returned after about 15 minutes. He thought he was then driven home and did not connect this event with the disappearance of Gudmundur Einarsson, which was reported in the newspapers a few days later.

**Note:** Kristján now introduced new elements to the story. After the fight with Gudmundur Einarsson they left the flat, drove around Hafnarfjördur, and when they returned Erla had come home. This helped explain the two-hour gap between Gudmundur's disappearance and Erla arriving home at about 04.00, which must have bothered the investigators. It also helped to explain why Erla had discovered her bed sheet was missing when she arrived home. The reference to the car having 'rocked' reiterates that referred to previously in Albert's statement, suggesting cross-suspect contamination.

### Kristján Vidarsson (3 January 1976)

Kristján was interrogated again (13.45–17.25) and gave a statement. He said he had thought a lot about the case since his last statement. He gave a more detailed account of the altercation but still did not recall why he was at Hamarsbraut 11 that night. He said that Saevar was having a fight with a man, who he now identified as Gudmundur Einarsson. Saevar was losing the fight and called for help. Kristján and Tryggvi went to assist him. Saevar repeatedly kicked Gudmundur in the head while he was on the floor. Kristján had a vague recollection of being in a car with Saevar and Tryggvi and driving around Hafnarfjördur. He could not recall whose car it was or whether they were in a taxi. He stated that he 'believed' the reason for the attack at Saevar's home was that Gudmundur called them 'drug addicts' (*dóbista*). He saw Saevar and Tryggvi wrap something light around something bulky, and imagined that it could be a bed sheet. He refused to assist the other two with carrying the baggage out of the house. While sitting in Albert's car he heard the others put something in the boot of the car. He now thinks, 'on reflection' (*við nánari umhugsun*), that Albert's car was not a yellow Japanese car, but a black Volkswagen.

**Note:** Kristján still had serious problems with his memory of what had allegedly taken place. He now gave a motivation for the attack on Gudmundur. It is not clear from the records whether the change in the type of car Albert drove originated from the investigators or from Kristján. The reference to the bed sheet suggests cross-suspect contamination.

## Saevar Ciesielski (4 January 1976)

Saevar was interrogated for over four hours. He explained that one night early in 1974 he found Kristján and Tryggvi waiting outside his home at Hamarsbraut 11. Erla was not at home. They all went in and shortly afterwards Saevar heard a 'bump' (*dynk*) coming from the storeroom and went in there to inspect. He saw a man covered in a bed sheet. Saevar hid in the toilet for a while and when he returned to the storeroom he found Kristján and Tryggvi with the man, who had been fully covered in a sheet and tied up. Erla then suddenly appeared and looked perturbed. The man was placed between Kristján and Tryggvi in the back seat of Albert's car, and they drove south out of Hafnarfjördur and towards Keflavík. They stopped close to the aluminium factory at Straumsvík and got out of the car. He saw the others carrying the man away. After a while they reappeared and Saevar could not recall where he was dropped off.

**Note:** Saevar's new statement corroborated Kristján's claim that Erla had arrived home after the attack on Gudmundur, explaining the disappearance of her bed sheet.

## Saevar Ciesielski (6 January 1976)

Saevar gave a further statement, wanting to add to his previous statement. He stated that when he arrived at Hamarsbraut 11, sometime after midnight, Kristján and Tryggvi were waiting on the steps outside the basement flat at Hamarsbraut 11. With them was a man Saevar did not recognize. They all went inside and Kristján hit the man (Gudmundur) in the face. Saevar later heard a 'bump' from the bedroom and he heard Kristján say the man was dead. Kristján ordered him to telephone Albert and ask him to come, promising him cannabis in return. After doing so he noticed that the bed sheet from the bedroom had been taken. When Albert arrived in his father's Volkswagen, they drove around Hafnarfjördur, and then returned to Hamarsbraut 11. He heard Erla speaking and realized she had come home while they were out. He saw Kristján and Tryggvi carry something heavy covered in a bed sheet from the washroom and out of the flat. He stayed with Erla, who looked upset, and after a while Albert returned alone. Albert drove him to the staff accommodation at Kópavogur Hospital (where Saevar had a friend, Helga).

**Note:** This is the first statement where Saevar refers to the type of car (Volkswagen), and he gets it right; the police may have known by now what type of car Albert's father had at the time. Saevar's lawyer, Jón Oddsson, and Örn Höskuldsson were present when the report was read out to Saevar.

### Tryggvi Leifsson (9 January 1976)

Tryggvi was questioned for one and a half hours about Gudmundur's disappearance and gave a statement. He said he had thought a lot about the case since his previous interrogation on 23 December 1975, and now wanted to give a new statement. In brief, his story was now as follows: At the material time he found himself in a house somewhere with Saevar and Kristján, and a third man who he did not recognize. He could not recall whose house it was or why they were there. He thinks there was some disagreement between Kristján and the unknown man in one of the living rooms and the altercation moved into another room. Saevar now entered the fight and shouted for help. Tryggvi went between Saevar and the unknown man with the latter hitting him, and Tryggvi thinks he hit him back. The man fell down and looked dazed. Saevar then kicked the man in the head. Tryggvi could not recall much of what happened after that.

**Note:** This statement shows that Tryggvi had serious problems recalling what had allegedly happened at the time of Gudmundur's disappearance. Throughout this statement he makes qualifying comments, such as 'I think', 'It's unclear', 'Seems to me', ending the statement by saying that he cannot recall the antecedent to his being in the flat, or what happened after the man had been put in the storeroom.

### Albert Skaftason (7 March 1976)

Albert appeared in the 'court' setting at Sídumúli Prison, having previously given a statement on 23 December 1975, and reported that he was now certain that there were two separate trips with Gudmundur Einarsson's body (i.e. it being removed after the first burial), accompanied by Saevar, Kristján, and Tryggvi. He said he could not remember where it was taken the first time, but thinks it might have been subsequently moved south to Kúagerdi, Reykjanes. His detention was extended for a further 30 days.

**Note:** The idea of two trips helped explain why he mixed up his father's two cars (i.e. his father replaced the Volkswagen with a Toyota several months after Gudmundur's disappearance).

### Albert Skaftason (19 March 1976)

Albert was questioned again about Gudmundur's disappearance and gave a statement. He is said to have requested the interview, having thought a great deal about what had happened that night in January 1974. He explained that he was wrong about the reference to his father's Toyota car in his previous statement and dates it to another event in September 1974 (this refers to the subsequent removal of Gudmundur's body from the Hafnarfjördur lava field). He now introduced his father's Volkswagen car and described how on 27 January Saevar had telephoned him at about 01.00 and asked him to come to Hafnarfjördur for a cannabis cube, which he did. He met with Saevar, Kristján, and Tryggvi and the latter two carried a long bag, tied together at both ends, and tried to fit it into the boot, but the boot was too small so they put the body in the back behind the front seats (not referred to in this statement is the fact that in the Volkswagen Beetle, the boot was in the front, not the back).

Kristján and Tryggvi then sat in the back seat with their legs on Gudmundur's body. Saevar told him where to drive. They drove out of Hafnarfjördur towards the aquarium, but found the gate there closed. They drove towards Hafnarfjördur but then turned back towards the aquarium again and on the way stopped the car. Saevar, Kristján, and Tryggvi then took the body out of the car and carried it across the road, into the lava field, in the direction of the aluminium factory. They returned after a while and Albert dropped them all back at Hamarsbraut 11. Saevar then gave him the cannabis cube, as he had promised.

Albert's lawyer, Örn Clausen, was present during the interview. After giving his statement, Albert was released from custody.

**Note:** On the night of Gudmundur Einarsson's disappearance there was heavy snow on the roads, there were allegedly five people packed into a Volkswagen Beetle, and they were driving in the dark in the middle of the night. This is a highly improbable story.

### Kristján Vidarsson (7 April 1976)

Kristján was questioned again and gave a detailed statement. He stated that his two previous reports were largely correct, but he now wanted to provide the full truth as he remembered it. He said that there was a fight, but Gudmundur died after he had stabbed him. He said that on Saturday evening on 26 January 1974, Saevar and Tryggvi were at his home and wanted to go out and enjoy themselves. They took a taxi to the staff residence at Kópavogur Hospital. They left Saevar there and agreed to meet later in Hafnarfjördur. Kristján had with him a large 'soldier's knife'. They were walking about in Hafnarfjördur, having failed to meet up with Saevar, and met Gudmundur Einarsson as he was walking towards Reykjavík. They all walked towards Hamarsbraut 11 and found nobody at home, but Saevar soon arrived and all four of them went inside. Saevar and Gudmundur then got into a fight and Saevar came running out of the bedroom with Gudmundur following him.

Kristján said he did not know why they started fighting but thought it was because Gudmundur had called Saevar a drug addict. Gudmundur refused to leave the house when told to do so and attacked Kristján from behind and tried to strangle him. Kristján got frightened and reached for the knife and stabbed Gudmundur somewhere, he did not know exactly where. Gudmundur did not fall and chased Kristján across the room and tore off one of the buttons of Kristján's overcoat, before he fell on the floor. While this was going on Saevar was hiding in the toilet and came out when Kristján called him and they moved Gudmundur into the storeroom. Kristján suggested telephoning the police, but in the end they decided against it. They all three then left the house, took a taxi, and drove around Hafnarfjördur. They then returned to the flat and decided to get rid of the body. They covered Gudmundur's body with a sheet of some light material. Saevar telephoned Albert, offered him cannabis, and he arrived in his father's black Volkswagen. Erla suddenly arrived home. Gudmundur was put on the floor in the back of the car. He thinks they drove towards the aquarium and then towards the aluminium factory. Saevar and Tryggvi took the body out of the car, Kristján followed them and helped them carry the body. They placed the body into a deep crack in the lava.

**Note:** This is the first account of where they allegedly met Gudmundur Einarsson and the use of a knife to kill him. Kristján told me in an interview in 2012 that Detective Sigurbjörn Vídir had suggested the use of the knife.

### Tryggvi Leifsson (30 April 1976)

On 30 April, Tryggvi appeared in court and confirmed his statement from 9 January. He repeated what was in his confession statement and did not recall having moved Gudmundur's body to Albert's car. Nor did he recall in which house the material event happened and why he was there.

**Note:** Tryggvi was still having memory problems and this undoubtedly explained why the police were not able to obtain a detailed statement from him.

### Kristján Vidarsson (22 June 1976)

Kristján was questioned at his own request about Gudmundur's disappearance. He stated that it was not correct what he had said in his previous statement (7 April) regarding having stabbed Gudmundur, but pointed out that it was correct that Saevar got into a fight with Gudmundur that led to his death. He could not recall whether he took the knife with him to Hafnarfjördur on 27 January 1974. He thought the fight with Gudmundur started because Gudmundur called them drug addicts. He said he did not know why he talked about the knife in his previous report, but at the time of giving the statement he thought he had used the knife, implying a false belief/memory.

**Note:** In this statement Kristján referred to being taken by the police to several areas south of Hafnarfjördur, searching for places where they had allegedly taken Gudmundur's body. One area he specifically referred to was a place called *Fjárborg*, which was an old sheep shelter. This same place was suggested to Tryggvi when he was interviewed on 8 March 1977 and he thought he remembered being there with Saevar and Kristján.

### Albert Skaftason (7 August 1976)

Karl Schütz met with Albert in the office of Örn Höskuldsson at Borgartún 7. The interview lasted four and a half hours. Mr Schütz told Albert that he did not think he was really a criminal, which pleased Albert. However, he told Albert that he did not think he had been entirely honest and was sure he knew where Gudmundur's body was hidden. He said that soon there would be a large and costly search party sent out to locate the body and Albert would be responsible for this (i.e. a threat). Albert said he was very confused about the location of the body, particularly after having been out with the police looking for the body. Mr Schütz told him that this would be his last chance to change his previously wrong statements and doing so would improve his position regarding his standing with the authorities (i.e. an inducement).

Albert complained about his poor memory of events and said that when he was arrested he could not remember anything about it, but his memory of what happened at Hamarsbraut 11 came later. Mr Schütz said he found it strange that Albert could not recall the reason why he went to Hafnarfjördur and points to various discrepancies in his previous statements. Albert said that he had gone on two errands for Saevar and the others and had confused the two occasions. He thought at first that during the first trip he had gone in his father's Toyota car but later realized that this was impossible since his father did not have the Toyota car at the time, but had it later in 1974. Schütz told him that it was obvious that he went from Saevar's house at Hamarsbraut 11 in the Volkswagen car, and also in the Toyota car. Albert said that in the Volkswagen car they drove by the aquarium but the gates were closed. They turned round and dumped the bag in the lava field nearby. Albert was not sure how long a time there was between the two trips, in the Volkswagen and Toyota cars, respectively.

Albert was taken to the aquarium through the old Keflavík road at Kúlugerdi and Lónakotsgryfjan, accompanied by Eggert Bjarnason, Karl Schütz, and Pétur Eggerz. Albert did not recognize the place.

**Note:** Karl Schütz had arrived in Iceland just over a week before. It is evident from this statement that there was a presumption of guilt: he was sceptical about Albert's memory problems, and Schütz placed him under considerable pressure to disclose the location of Gudmundur's body, which confused him even more. In order to break down resistance, Schütz's strategy was to point out previous discrepancies in Albert's statements and make him feel that he was hindering the investigation, hence being responsible for unnecessary costs.

### Saevar Ciesielski (30 September 1976)

Saevar gave a statement claiming that he was with Albert on the evening of 26 January 1974. Saevar wanted to go to Kópavogur Hospital to meet his friend, Helga,[10] but Albert said he was too busy to drive him there. About an hour later Kristján and Tryggvi arrived at Kópavogur Hospital in a taxi wanting to borrow money from Saevar. Saevar lied that he did not have any money and after they left he worried that they would go to his home at Hamarsbraut 11 to look for money, so he took a taxi home.

When he arrived at Hamarsbraut 11 he found Kristján and Tryggvi there with a man who he learned was Gudmundur Einarsson. Kristján attacked Gudmundur and Saevar locked himself in the toilet. Tryggvi and Kristján came looking for him and told him that Gudmundur was dead. They discussed what to do, including calling the police, but decided to move Gudmundur into the storeroom in case Erla came home. Gudmundur's body was covered in a sheet. Saevar noticed a bad smell coming from Gudmundur, like that of excrement. They went out after having telephoned for a taxi, drove around Hafnafjördur, and when they later returned to Hamarsbraut 11, Erla was there.

Kristján told Saevar to telephone Albert and offer him a cannabis cube if he came. While waiting for Albert, the three of them decided to dump Gudmundur's body in the lava field south of Hafnafjördur. Tryggvi and Albert carried the body out and into the car, while Saevar spoke with Erla. When Saevar got out of the house, he saw Albert shut the boot of the car, then Kristján and Tryggvi got in on the left-hand side and sat in the back. Saevar sat in the front with Albert. They then

---

[10] In her witness statement, Helga said she had a relationship with Saevar over a 10-day period in January 1974 and he used to visit her at her Kópavogur Hospital accommodation (Evidence Book I, pp. 272–274).

drove towards the aquarium and the aluminium factory, but he did not recall the order regarding these two locations. Kristján and Tryggvi carried Gudmundur into the lava field and returned with the bed sheet, which Saevar then threw into the dustbin at Hamarsbraut 11. Saevar also told the officers that when Kristján met him at Kópavogur Hospital he had a knife with him, which he recognized as the knife that Kristján had bought when they were together in Copenhagen in 1973. It was an old bayonet, 40–45 cm long.

**Note:** At this point the police had not discovered that the telephone at Hamarsbraut 11 was disconnected, and Saevar claiming to have brought Erla's bed sheet back home and disposing of it in the dustbin now matched her statement, suggesting contamination.

### Saevar Ciesielski (5 October 1976)

Saevar informed the police that at the beginning of August 1974 he and Kristján met and discussed removing Gudmundur Einarsson's remains from the Hafnarfjördur lava field to a cemetery, and decided on the Fossvogur Cemetery in Reykjavík. They went home to Albert and discussed this with him. They went in Albert's yellow Toyota car and took with them two big black plastic bags. They found the body and put the body in the bags and brought it back to the car, putting it in the boot. They then went to Kristján's home at Grettisgata 82 and stayed there until midnight. They then got two shovels from the basement and drove to Fossvogur Cemetery, where they buried Gudmundur's remains. Saevar was questioned again the following day. He was adamant that the body had been buried in the cemetery. Later, the police took Saevar to the cemetery, where he pointed out a particular grave where he said the body had been buried. The caretaker said the grave had not been tampered with, but Saevar was adamant that this was where the body had been buried. He also said that Kristján's long knife had been buried with Gudmundur.

**Note:** Saevar at this time revealed that Gudmundur's body had been removed from its original burial site, helping to explain Albert's confusion over his father's two cars.

### Albert Skaftason (5 October 1976)

Albert was questioned extensively (11.15–15.30), and on this occasion said that Saevar had telephoned him one night in January 1974 and said he wanted him to collect a corpse. Albert refused but Saevar persuaded him to help in exchange for a cannabis cube. Kristján and Tryggvi tried to put something bulky and heavy, covered in a sheet, in the boot of the car, but it was too big so they put it inside the car behind the front seats. They drove to the aluminium factory and turned into the road opposite and stopped. The car was facing the aluminium factory and Saevar, Kristján, and Tryggvi took the object they were carrying with them. They returned to the car with the bed sheet and put it in the boot of the car. Albert now thinks he may have gone to the same spot again and the three co-accused brought something in black bin bags, which they took to Álftanes, where the bags were buried. Albert commented that 'This is all very unclear to me'.

The following day, Albert was questioned further (08.45–09.45 and 11.30–12.15) about the current location of Gudmundur's body. Albert stated that he thought he had given the police the wrong location of the body on the previous day. He recalled Saevar visiting him at home in the summer of 1974 and wanting him to use his father's Toyota car to drive him somewhere. They picked up two black plastic bags and two shovels from Kristján's home and then went to pick up something, took it to the graveyard, and buried it. He did not recall whether Tryggvi was with the other two. Albert said he could not explain why he was remembering this now but thought it had to do with fear of punishment. He stated:

> I think that following these last interrogations, there is something wrong with my head. I know that I took part in this and that I should be able to explain it all, but even though I try hard, I find it difficult to distinguish between imagination and reality.[11]

Albert said that Kristján and Saevar had come to his home some months after taking Gudmundur's body to the Hafnafjördur lava field. He thought he brought the shovels, which belonged to his father, and they went to Kristján's home to collect the plastic bags. They then drove to the lava field to collect Gudmundur's remains. He believed that Tryggvi was with them. He waited in the car, possibly with Kristján, while the others collected the remains. The bags were then put in the boot of his car and taken to Grettisgata 82. Later that night they moved the body from Kristján's home to the Fossvogur Cemetery, where Saevar and Kristján buried the remains. He was unsure whether Tryggvi was also with them at that point. He still recalled a grave being made in Álftanes, as he mentioned before, but now was not sure whether any body was put in it.

On 6, 8, and 10 October, Albert was taken to the Fossvogur Cemetery. He remembered for certain a particular place where they had taken

---

[11] Evidence Book I, p. 285.

Gudmundur's body. 'He said that after he had started to recollect this, he was now sure that they had gone to the Fossvogur Cemetery, but previously this had been completely erased from his memory'.[12]

**Note:** During the interview on 5 October, Albert recalled bringing back the bed sheet, which Saevar had revealed to the police the week before (30 September). Gudmundur's remains were now allegedly kept at Kristján's home for a few hours before being removed to the Fossvogur Cemetery.

### Erla Bolladóttir (20 February 1977)

A statement was taken from Erla in order to clarify a few points in relation to the Gudmundur case. Erla said that her previous statements were correct and she had nothing to add. She said she did not recognize Tryggvi before the events at Hamarsbraut 11, but thinks it was him who was with Saevar and Kristján. The three of them had not told her who was inside the bed sheet. When she went to Hamarsbraut 11 in the early hours after having spent the evening clubbing, she had no key so climbed through the washroom window. She did not think anybody was in there. She said she was not aware of Albert coming to the house that night. She said the three men made a lot of noise while carrying the man in the sheet. She said Kristján had been very drunk when he was in the house, but not the other two. She did not see Kristján with a knife, nor did she recall seeing any blood. She thinks she saw the bed sheet in the dustbin outside the house. She said she moved into her father's basement flat at Hamarsbraut 11 in November 1973 and Saevar was living there with her on and off. At the end of the interview she said that she had never heard Saevar mention Gudmundur Einarsson before or after the event.

### Saevar Ciesielski (27 February 1977)

Detective Gísli Gudmundsson interviewed Saevar, who told him that it was not correct what he had said in his previous statements that he had made a phone call to Albert from Hamarsbraut 11. The line was disconnected because of failure of payment. The police confirmed this with the telephone company.

On 3 March, Saevar was interviewed and changed his story about 27 January 1974. He now said that Albert had driven him, Kristján, and Tryggvi to Hafnarfjördur that night, along with the third man, named

---

[12] Evidence Book I, p. 294.

Gunni (Gunnar Jónsson). When asked why he had not mentioned this before he said he had not seen the point since his story was generally not believed.

### Albert Skaftason (4 March 1977)

Albert was interviewed and stated that he wanted to 'wipe the slate clean and tell the full truth in the case'.[13] The main points in his statement are as follows:

• He went with Gunnar Jónsson to Grettisgata 82 to meet Kristján. Tryggvi was there.

• Albert recalled that Saevar asked for a lift to the staff accommodation at Kópavogur Hospital, but he refused to go there because he had previously got into a fight there.

• None of them had any money, so they drove to Kópavogur to borrow money from Saevar. Kristján went in while Tryggvi and Gunnar waited in the car. Saevar did not want to lend them money.

• They decided to go to Hafnarfjördur to rob people's wallets as they were leaving dance places. Kristján and Tryggvi got out of the car and after a little while brought back with them a man, who later turned out to be Gudmundur Einarsson. He looked intoxicated. Kristján suggested they go to Hamarsbraut 11 for a 'party'. Nobody was in the house and they all went in.

• They decided to buy a bottle of alcohol, but Gudmundur did not want to contribute to that. As a result, Kristján and Tryggvi attacked Gudmundur. Saevar then came home and joined them. He did not see Saevar hit or kick Gudmundur. While this was going on, Albert and Gunnar sat on the sofa in the front room and did not see the fight.

• Albert looked into the inner room and saw Gudmundur lying still on the floor on his back. He did not see any blood. Albert and Gunnar soon left the house. Albert then drove Gunnar home. He did not recall anybody else in the car. Albert then returned to Hamarsbraut 11 and Saevar, Kristján, and Tryggvi first tried to put the body in the boot of his car but then put it in the back behind the front seats.

• Saevar directed where to go. They drove south of Hafnarfjördur and stopped by the aquarium, but the gate was locked. They then drove along the old Reykjanesbraut road, opposite the aluminium factory, and the three of them took the body out. Albert waited in the car. They came back in about half an hour.

• Some time later, around August time, they moved Gudmundur's body from the lava field to Hafnarfjördur Cemetery (he had previously

---

[13] Evidence Book II, pp. 140–147.

said it was the Fossvogur Cemetery in Reykjavík). He said he participated in digging the grave but did not put Gudmundur in it.
**Note:** Albert now introduces a new motive for Gudmundur's murder –
that Gudmundur had refused to contribute to the purchase of alcohol.

### Saevar Ciesielski (9 March 1977)

Saevar was interviewed and reported that on the evening of 26 January
1974 he went by taxi to the staff accommodation at Kópavogur Hospital
to meet a friend, Helga, arriving there around midnight. Shortly afterwards, Kristján arrived asking him for money. He noticed Albert waiting
outside in a Volkswagen car with Gunnar Jónsson. Kristján told him that
Tryggvi was also in the car. At around 02.00 he went to Hamarsbraut 11
and found Kristján, Tryggvi, Gunnar, Albert, and Gudmundur there (he
said the house had been left unlocked). He saw Kristján hit Gudmundur
in the face and there was a fight, which did not involve him or Gunnar.
  **Note:** Saevar provided four pieces of new information, which contradicted his previous statements: (1) Albert and Gunnar had been inside
the basement flat when Gudmundur was killed, supporting Albert's
recent statement. (2) Erla's bed sheet had not been used at all to wrap
around Gudmundur's body – this had been a consistent feature in
Erla's, Saevar's, and Kristján's statements. (3) They carried the body
straight out to the car and put it on the floor behind the front seats. The
body was not removed or kept in the storeroom as previously claimed.
(4) Saevar could not recall seeing Erla in the flat that night, having not
met her until the following (Sunday) evening.

### Tryggvi Leifsson (11 March 1977)

Tryggvi was asked only one question: Did he know whether Gudmundur
Einarsson's remains were buried in Hafnarfjördur Cemetery? He
replied: 'I know nothing about it, because I'm not involved'.[14]
  **Note:** That day Saevar was asked the same question and said he did
not know.

### Erla Bolladóttir (14 March 1977)

Erla said she could not explain why she had not been able to identify
all the men (i.e. Albert and Gunnar) who were at Hamarsbraut 11 in
the early hours of 27 January 1974.

---

[14] Evidence Book II, p. 166.

## Kristján Vidarsson (14 March 1977)

Kristján said that he had not stabbed Gudmundur as he had previously claimed. He had made it up, thinking perhaps he wanted to take the blame for Gudmundur's death. He said that the story of the bad smell coming from the body came from Erla and the investigators at the beginning of the investigation. Asked about other men at Hamarsbraut 11, Kristján recalled Albert and Gunnar being present, but they did not participate in the assault on Gudmundur. The purpose of going to Hamarsbraut 11 was to borrow money from Saevar. He admitted hitting Gudmundur four times and claimed, but could not recall, that the body was wrapped in a bed sheet, which contradicted his previous statements.

## Saevar Ciesielski (13 April 1977)

Saevar asked to speak with Detective Gísli Gudmundsson, who had not been a part of the Reykjavík Task Force, and was carrying out follow-up enquiries for the Criminal Court. He told the detective that he had an alibi for the time of Gudmundur's disappearance and had first seen Erla at Hamarsbraut 11 on the evening of Sunday 27 January 1974, after having been away for a while, seeing another woman. Erla had suspected this and challenged him about it, but he kept denying it and tried to persuade her that he had been abroad and had arrived on a flight that same day.

## Erla Bolladóttir (14 April 1977)

Detective Gísli Gudmundsson interviewed Erla and she independently confirmed Saevar's story and gave up the name of the girl with whom Saevar was having an affair and where she lived. Gísli thought this possible alibi should be investigated, but two of the trial judges told him it was unnecessary.[15]

**Note:** Within six weeks of his retirement at the end of August 1996, former Detective Chief Superintendent Gísli Gudmundsson came forward publicly claiming that in early 1977, the District Court judges responsible for concluding the investigation had prevented him from investigating a possible alibi for Saevar for the night of Gudmundur Einarsson's disappearance (Working Group Report, 2013).

---

[15] Evidence Book III, pp. 63–66.

## THEMATIC ANALYSIS OF THE SUCCESSIVE ACCOUNTS

I used thematic analysis (Braun & Clarke, 2006) to identify, analyse, and report pertinent themes within the statements, using a 'bottom up' approach (i.e. themes derived from the data rather than theory). A thematic analysis of the statements in the Gudmundur case showed four key themes: *Fight*, *Motive*, *Body*, and *Memory Problems*.

### Fight

The consistent theme is that there was a fight with Gudmundur at Hamarsbraut 11 as a result of which he died. The three participants, Saevar, Kristján, and Tryggvi provided different accounts about who was involved in the fight and what exactly happened, but all the accounts were vague and kept changing. Kristján, followed by Tryggvi, claimed that Saevar had kicked Gudmundur in the head as he lay on the floor. Saevar claimed to have hidden in the toilet while the fight was going on, and Kristján confirmed this in one of his later statements (7 April 1976). In this same interview Kristján admitted to stabbing Gudmundur with a big hunting knife, but later retracted this. Saevar could not confirm the use of the knife, but said he had seen Kristján with the knife earlier in the night. The Supreme Court did not rely on Kristján having stabbed Gudmundur and attributed responsibility for his death equally among Saevar, Kristján, and Tryggvi.

The focus in the statements is on what happened at Hamarsbraut 11 and to Gudmundur's body. There is striking absence in the suspects' early statements about the antecedents leading to Gudmundur being at Hamarsbraut 11. Where did the suspects meet Gudmundur and why did they take him to Erla's home? These are important questions that were apparently never asked, or satisfactorily answered.

In his statement on 4 March 1977, well over a year into the investigation, Albert said that they decided to go to Hafnarfjördur to rob people's wallets as they were leaving dance places. Kristján and Tryggvi allegedly got out of the car and after a little while brought back with them a man, who later turned out to be Gudmundur Einarsson. He looked intoxicated and Kristján suggested they go to Hamarsbraut 11 for a 'party'.

All the suspects gave fragmented accounts of what had allegedly happened at Hamarsbraut 11, with important information missing. None were able to give a detailed, comprehensive, or credible account of the sequence of events that allegedly led to Gudmundur's death.

## Motive

The suspects were very vague about describing the motive for the assault on Gudmundur Einarsson. This was another striking feature from the thematic analysis: the absence of an expected theme. In one of his earliest interviews, Kristján 'believed' the reason for the attack was that Gudmundur called them drug addicts. There is also a reference to Gudmundur refusing to leave the flat when Saevar told him to, but the Supreme Court settled on the motive that Gudmundur did not want to contribute to the purchase of a bottle of alcohol (Box 8.2).

The apparent lack of focus on the motivation for the attack on Gudmundur is a serious flaw in the investigation. The occasional casual references to a possible motive are vague and lack credibility, including the motive accepted by the Supreme Court.

## Body

The general theme is that Saevar had telephoned Albert from Hamarsbraut 11 and asked him to come and collect Gudmundur's body because they needed transport. In exchange, Albert would get a cannabis cube. Much later it transpired that the telephone in the flat had been disconnected at that time because of failure of payment, which

---

**Box 8.2**   The Supreme Court's version of the facts in the Gudmundur Einarsson case

1. The man seen outside the dance hall in Hafnarfjördur with Gudmundur in the early hours of 27 January 1974 was Kristján Vidarsson.
2. Kristján Vidarsson, Saevar Ciesielski, and Tryggvi Leifsson all violently assaulted Gudmundur at Hamarsbraut 11, the house where Saevar lived with his girlfriend, Erla Bolladóttir. Gudmundur was killed and his body taken to an unknown location.
3. The motive was Gudmundur's alleged failure to contribute to the purchase of a bottle of alcohol.
4. Erla was present in the house at the time but did not witness the attack. An acquaintance of the three killers, Albert Skaftason, did. Albert's friend, Gunnar Jónsson was present at Hamarsbraut 11 at the time of the assault. The Court relied on their testimony against the other three men.
5. The Court considered it important that Erla had not retracted her statements in the Gudmundur case. Kristján, Saevar, and Tryggvi all retracted their confessions, but the Court did not accept their retractions.

meant that Saevar could not have made that phone call. This required a change in the story, and in March 1997 Albert obliged by giving a statement saying that he had given Kristján, Tryggvi, and Gunnar Jónsson a lift into Hafnarfjördur.

This new story was in great contrast to his previous statements, including the one on 7 August 1976 when Karl Schütz interviewed Albert and told him that he found it strange that he could not recall the reason why he had gone to Hafnarfjördur.

Another related theme is that Albert had transported Gudmundur in his father's car to the Hafnarfjördur lava field. The first story was that he had been in his father's yellow Toyota car and that Gudmundur's body had been put in the boot of the car; he described the car shaking when something heavy was put in the boot. The police later discovered that his father had a Volkswagen car at that time and did not purchase the Toyota until later that year, although it is not clear whether this change in the story first came from the investigators or Kristján. The story now changed to the Volkswagen car and that Gudmundur's body had been put in the back of the car, not the boot, because the boot in this type of car was too small for the body. In order to explain the reference to the Toyota car, there were now two trips described. The first trip, in the Volkswagen car, involved taking Gudmundur's body to the lava field, and the second trip, about eight months later, involved removing Gudmundur's remains from the lava field to a cemetery, either Reykjavík or Hafnarfjördur. No motive was given for moving the body from its original burial site.

Erla's first statement set the scene for what might have happened at Hamarsbraut 11. She had come home at about 04.00 and discovered her bed sheet was missing. She went to sleep and then was woken up by noise and saw Saevar, Kristján, and a 'third man' (Tryggvi) carrying something heavy in a bed sheet, which could have been a human body (Gudmundur). In his first confession (28 December 1975), Kristján provided an apparent explanation for the disappearance of the bed sheet, adopted in part by Saevar's subsequent statements. The bed sheet had been used to cover up Gudmundur's body, which was then left in the washroom while they drove around Hafnarfjördur, either in a taxi or in Albert's borrowed car (the story varied). When they arrived back at the flat, Erla had arrived, or she arrived a little later (the story varied), and saw them carrying Gudmundur's body out of the flat. In later statements, they claimed to have brought back the bed sheet and put it in the dustbin to corroborate Erla's story.

Gudmundur's body being carried in a bed sheet, and the presence of a bad smell, featured in the story throughout, except in Saevar's statement on 9 March 1977, when he contradicted many of the central components in the story, including stating that the bed sheet had not been used at all, that the body had not been kept in the washroom as previously claimed, and that Erla had not been in the flat that night. This seriously undermined the credibility of the earlier stories, but it had no effect on the case's outcome (i.e. convictions). The Court chose which statements to rely upon, thereby being very selective in their approach.

## Memory Problems

Kristján, Tryggvi, and Albert repeatedly complained of serious problems with recalling what had taken place. Their statements were typically vague, hesitant, and tentative. Albert's memory problems were so severe that the police hired a psychologist 'to facilitate recovery of his memory regarding the details of the car trip' with his co-accused, Saevar, Kristján, and Tryggvi (Working Group Report, 2013, p. 418). The memory enhancement sessions took place on 11, 13, 15, and 19 March 1976. Iceland's most prominent expert on hypnosis at the time, Dr Jakob Jónason, was hired to hypnotize Albert with little success (i.e. apparently he was not responsive to the hypnotic induction procedure). As discussed in Chapter 5, there is empirical evidence available to suggest that hypnosis results in increased misinformation and contamination (Scoboria et al., 2002).

## THE SUPREME COURT'S VERSION OF THE FACTS IN THE GUDMUNDUR EINARSSON CASE

On 22 February 1980, the Supreme Court judges put forward their version of what had happened at Hamarsbraut 11 in the early hours of 27 January 1974. They ruled that Kristján, Saevar, and Tryggvi had all violently assaulted Gudmundur at Hamarsbraut 11 and hidden his body in an unknown location. The defendants' retractions of their confessions were not believed and they were sentenced to imprisonment.

## CONCLUSIONS

Erla Bolladóttir's incriminating statement in the Gudmundur case on 20 December 1975 needs to be viewed in the context of three important contextual factors. Firstly, she had been in solitary confinement for seven days in relation to the fraud offences, away from her 11-week-old daughter, and she expected to be released from custody once she had given her frank confessions regarding the fraud. She was extensively interrogated about the fraud over three days.

Secondly, the Gudmundur Einarsson murder investigation was initiated by a rumour from an undisclosed source that Saevar 'could possibly be involved in the disappearance of Gudmundur Einarsson'. Erla was prevented from leaving prison and told to think about it overnight. The following day she was interrogated for most of the day. She knew she was going nowhere until she told the investigators what they wanted to hear. According to Erla, Örn Höskuldsson had made this very clear to her the evening before when she was first questioned about Gudmundur's disappearance (Bolladóttir, 2008). In view of what I have seen of the investigators' methods, I find Erla's allegation credible.

Thirdly, Erla was having serious difficulties in her relationship with Saevar and was intending to leave him. The investigators knew this, having found her letter to Saevar referring to her plan during a house search. It would have been easy to persuade her that Saevar was capable of participating in murder, this being the first step towards her implicating him in the disappearance of Gudmundur Einarsson.

I used thematic analysis to identify, analyse, and report pertinent themes within the confession statements. Reading the statements within the context of the numerous unrecorded interviews and face-to-face confrontations between interviewees, documented in the prison custody diary, it is evident that the accounts twist and turn to fit the latest police theories and information. There was considerable cross-suspect contamination, as interviewees were presented with the latest evidence of a co-accused, rather than representing a free narrative of their uncontaminated recollections. What is consistently striking about the content of the interviews is the vagueness of what had allegedly happened to Gudmundur at Hamarsbraut 11 and subsequently to his body. There appeared to be no solid substance to any of the salient details provided. The police tried to corroborate new pieces of information, but found that it did not advance the case at all, and then turned to the suspects for clarification or new information, leading to changes in the accounts and further statements that could not be corroborated either. My general overall impression of the content of the statements and how they changed over time, as the police failed to corroborate anything of substance, is that the interviewees were describing a hypothetical rather than a tangible event.

The idea that on the night of Gudmundur's disappearance five people were packed into a Volkswagen Beetle, driving in the dark in the middle of the night and in heavy snow, is ludicrous. If the event did happen, why did Albert, Saevar, Kristján, and Tryggvi not make any reference to ferocious weather conditions that night? An omission that strongly indicates they were not there.

Another ludicrous idea was the removal of Gudmundur's body from the Hafnarfjördur lava field to a cemetery, either Reykjavík or Hafnarfjördur. This idea was first triggered during an interview with Albert and then became further developed. No motive was ever given for moving the body from its original burial site, probably because it never happened. Its only purpose was to explain the mistake the suspects made regarding the model of car originally used to remove Gudmundur's body from Hamarsbraut 11. Importantly, if Saevar and Kristján were able to locate the original burial site several months after the alleged murder, they would have been able to take the police to that location after giving their confessions.

The investigators took a big leap in the dark on the basis of a 'rumour', whose origin, substance, and credibility they have never revealed or substantiated. The case had no investigative potential. There was no body, no crime scene, and no credible witnesses. What we know now is that it was built on information from a wholly unreliable prison informant (see Chapter 12), which is probably the reason the investigators have always avoided disclosing his identity. There was no solid foundation for commencing their questioning of Erla Bolladóttir: she should have been released from custody after giving her confession statements in the fraud case. In spite of this, all three defendants were convicted and sentenced to imprisonment.

On 20 December 1975, after incriminating Saevar and Kristján in the murder of Gudmundur Einarsson, Erla was released from solitary confinement, but the investigators kept in close contact with her and before long they were asking her about Saevar's possible involvement in the disappearance of Geirfinnur Einarsson on 19 November 1974 (Bolladóttir, 2008).

# 9

# The Confessions in the Geirfinnur Einarsson Case

*You use your influence to 'soften him up' from the beginning…. You control who he is allowed to have contact with, and in that way prevent him receiving psychological support from others.*[1]

In this chapter I discuss the two-stage Reykjavík investigation into Geirfinnur's disappearance and the confessions that were elicited by the police. In January 1976, within a month after Erla Bolladóttir had been released from Sídumúli Prison having implicated Saevar and Kristján in the Gudmundur case, she was being questioned in connection with Geirfinnur's disappearance and began to implicate a large number of people. These included four men, which in this chapter I will refer to as the 'four wrongly accused'. This part of the investigation was conducted by the 'Reykjavík Team' (investigative judge Örn Höskuldsson and Detectives Eggert Bjarnason and Sigurbjörn Vídir Eggertsson).

Then, after the 'four wrongly accused' were released from Sídumúli Prison on 9 May 1976, the case against Saevar and Kristján appeared to be in jeopardy and the Minister of Justice hired Karl Schütz to work on the case. At the beginning of August, shortly after he arrived in Iceland, Schütz set up a special Task Force, which included the

---

[1] A mission statement of the National Norwegian Criminal Investigation Service, cited in Fahsing et al. (2016, p. 182), which had in 1997 obtained a pressured-internalized false confession arising from such methods (Gudjonsson, 2003a).

*The Psychology of False Confessions: Forty Years of Science and Practice*, First Edition.
Gisli H. Gudjonsson.
© 2018 John Wiley & Sons Ltd. Published 2018 by John Wiley & Sons Ltd.

Reykjavík Team and five new investigators. The Reykjavík Task Force, under Schütz's leadership, completed its investigation by the beginning of February 1977, and Schütz announced at a press conference that the Geirfinnur case was solved. In return, the Minister of Justice, Ólafur Jóhannesson, thanked Schütz for 'unburdening the Icelandic nation of a nightmare'. By this time, convictions of the 'prime suspects' seemed inevitable. This chapter shows how the story unfolded during the investigation.

## THE PROSECUTION REQUEST FOR THE KEFLAVÍK PAPERS

On 5 January 1976, the Keflavík Sheriff's Department had delivered reports and documents concerning the Geirfinnur investigation to Hallvardur Einvardsson, Deputy Director of the State Prosecutor's Office. The papers had been requested on 31 December, the day after Erla had been brought to Síðumúli Prison and spent five hours there (see Table 9.1). This all took place before Erla Bolladóttir complained to the police about nuisance phone calls that subsequently led to her being questioned at Síðumúli Prison as a witness on 21, 22, and 23 January 1976.[2]

Within days of the Keflavík Sheriff's Department delivering the papers to the State Prosecutor's Office, speculation began to circulate about a link between the Gudmundur and Geirfinnur cases, suggesting a leak to the media, a common feature of this investigation.

On 9 January 1976, the newspaper *Althýdubladid* published an article on its front page entitled: 'Is Gudmundur's disappearance related to the Geirfinnur case?'. The journalist speculated about a possible link between the Gudmundur and Geirfinnur cases and spoke to one of the Keflavík detectives, most probably Haukur Gudmundsson, who said nothing new had emerged in the case, but they would be looking for a possible link between the two cases after receiving further information from the Reykjavík authorities. The detective said the Geirfinnur investigation had remained open in the hope that new information would emerge to help solve the case.

Table 9.1 provides a basic chronology of the Reykjavík Team investigation, which highlights the crucial time points and events. There were a large number of interviews, many of which were not recorded (Working Group Report, 2013). Detective Eggert Bjarnason conducted

---

[2] ICCRC Report, 2017, Erla Bolladóttir, Paragraphs 114, 116, 119, and 120.

**Table 9.1**   Key chronology of the Reykjavík investigation into the Geirfinnur case

**Late December 1975 / early January 1976**
The Reykjavík Team and Erla were in contact after her release from custody on 20 December and, according to Erla's autobiography, at the end of December 1975 the investigators began to ask her about Saevar's possible involvement in Geirfinnur's disappearance, following her meeting with Detective Sigurbjörn Vídir Eggertsson in order to get into her sealed flat to collect her daughter's possessions.

**28 December 1975**
At 13.35 Erla telephoned Sídumúli Prison and spoke with Sigurbjörn Vídir. It is not known what this conversation was about, but it coincides with Erla's request to get into her sealed flat at Thverbrekka 4.

**30 December 1975**
At 13.25 Eggert Bjarnason went from Sídumúli Prison to collect Erla. Erla left the prison with Eggert at 18.45. According to the Commission (ICCRC Report, 2017, Erla Bolladóttir, Paragraphs 74 and 2439), there are no records available about the nature or content of this five-hour visit.

**31 December 1975**
According to Keflavík Detective Haukur Gudmundsson, on this day the state prosecution office requested the papers in the Geirfinnur case 'because of new information in the case' (*Morgunbladid*, 15 January 1977, p. 5).

**5 January 1976**
At the request of prosecutor Hallvardur Einvardsson, on this day the Keflavík Sheriff's Department delivered reports and documents concerning the Geirfinnur investigation to his office.

**6 January 1976**
At 12.05 Erla telephoned Sídumúli Prison and asked to speak to Sigurbjörn Vídir or Eggert Bjarnason as soon as possible but neither was available at the time. It is not known what this conversation was about.

**9 January 1976**
*Althýdubladid* newspaper published an article on its front page entitled: 'Is Gudmundur's disappearance related to the Geirfinnur case?'. The journalist speculated about a possible link between the Gudmundur and Geirfinnur cases and spoke to one of the Keflavík detectives.

**'Mid-January' 1976**
Eggert Bjarnason's retrospective notes, dated 10 March 1976, reveal that as a result of frightening phone calls around the 'middle of January' the investigators took Erla to Sídumúli Prison for questioning on 21 January. He makes no reference to the five-hour session there with Erla on 30 December 1975. This omission is curious, especially since Eggert Bjarnason had collected her from her home and then taken her back home.

**19 and 20 January 1976**
The Sídumúli Prison diary shows that Saevar was extensively interviewed on both of these days, but there are no records of those interviews. Saevar claimed in a letter to his lawyer in June 1979 that the investigators asked him about Einar Bollason, Magnús Leópoldsson, Sigurbjörn Eiríksson, and Valdimar Olsen, claiming that they had proof (*sannanir*) that Saevar had gone to Keflavík with Einar Bollason on the evening of 19 November 1974 (ICCRC Report, 2017, Erla Bolladóttir, Paragraph 2450).

(Continued)

**Table 9.1**   *(Continued)*

**21 January 1976**
At 19.50 Sigurbjörn Vídir went to collect Erla Bolladóttir for Örn Höskuldsson and brought her to Síðumúli Prison 10 minutes later. She was questioned until 23.55, after which she was taken home. The Commission (ICCRC Report, 2017, Erla Bolladóttir, Paragraph 116) has revealed an eight page handwritten investigative note from the interview, written in the first person, describing the journey to Keflavík, referring to the presence of Einar Bollason, Magnús Leópoldsson, Sigurbjörn Eiríksson, Geirfinnur Einarsson, and Kristján. There was one person there Erla did not recognize but said it could have been Jón Ragnarsson. She described a boat trip to collect the contraband and all the men present wore gloves. Erla was frightened and ran away, hid in a nearby building, hitched a lift the following morning to the Grindavík junction in an old Moskvitch car, and from there caught a lift to Hafnarfjörður in an oil van.
**Note:** Saevar was questioned in the same prison between 20.15 and 02.00. The ICCRC Report (2017, Saevar Ciesielski, Paragraph 114) outlined handwritten points from his interview, which made references to Erla probably being frightened of Einar Bollason, Jón Ragnarsson (referred to as 'JR' in the Report), and Magnús Leópoldsson in connection with Geirfinnur. Saevar had heard that 'Valdimar', who had allegedly worked in Klúbburinn, also went to Keflavík.

**22 January 1976**
At 19.45 Sigurbjörn Vídir went to collect Erla and brought her to Síðumúli Prison 10 minutes later. At 21.45 Sigurbjörn Vídir and Eggert Bjarnason left the prison with Erla. The Icelandic Court Cases Review Commission commented that no investigative notes were available about this visit, but it is important that the interview with Erla followed shortly after an interview with Saevar between 14.15 and 19.05, during which he had mentioned the names of Einar Bollason, Magnús Leópoldsson, Geirfinnur Einarsson, Valdimar Olsen, and Jón Ragnarsson, raising the real possibility of a contamination effect.

**23 January 1976**
A police officer left Síðumúli Prison at 10.10 to collect Erla and they arrived 15 minutes later. An interrogation took place between 10.30 and 13.30 during which a statement was taken. This was Erla's first official statement in the Geirfinnur case.

**23–25 January 1976**
Erla, Saevar, and Kristján implicated a number of men in the disappearance of Geirfinnur, which led to the arrest and detention of Magnús Leópoldsson, Einar Bollason, and Valdimar Olsen on 26 January, followed by the arrest of Sigurbjörn Eiríksson on 11 February. All four men denied knowing anything of Geirfinnur's disappearance and were released from custody on 9 May 1976. On 3 March 1983 the Supreme Court awarded the four men compensation for their wrongful arrest and detention.

**25 January 1976**
At 14.40 Erla telephoned Síðumúli Prison and spoke to one of the detectives in the case, but it is not known what this conversation was about. Later that day armed police officers arrived at her place and stayed there overnight because of a possible revenge attack on Erla (ICCRC Report, 2017, Erla Bolladóttir, Paragraph 2468).

**Table 9.1**    *(Continued)*

**25 January 1976**
Saevar was taken to Keflavík and identified the slipway as the most likely location.

**26 January 1976**
At 06.00 Magnús Leópoldsson, Einar Bollason, and Valdimar Olsen were arrested in connection with the Geirfinnur case and taken to Síðumúli Prison.

**3 February 1976**
Erla identified Vatnsstígur, located in downtown Reykjavík, as the place where Kristján was picked up on the way to Keflavík. She remembered her brother Einar being in Keflavík, but 'thought' (*halda*) Valdimar Olsen was also there, but she was apparently not sure. She was shown a picture of Sigurbjörn Eiríksson but said she could not confirm (*fullyrða*) it at this point in time that he was there (ICCRC Report, 2017, Erla Bolladóttir, Paragraph 146).

**11 February 1976**
Sigurbjörn Eiríksson was arrested in connection with the Geirfinnur case.

**3-4 May 1976**
Erla was taken to Síðumúli Prison at 20.30 on 3 May for questioning as a witness. She was kept in custody overnight and the following day gave a statement that she had shot Geirfinnur. She was detained in solitary confinement until 22 December 1976.

**7 May 1976**
Kristján was interviewed and referred to a tropical (southern) – 'foreign looking' – man on the slipway, which he later identified as Gudjón Skarphéðinsson.

**9 May 1976**
Magnús Leópoldsson, Sigurbjörn Eiríksson, Einar Bollason, and Valdimar Olsen were released from solitary confinement.

**28 July 1976**
Karl Schütz came to Iceland to work full-time on the Gudmundur and Geirfinnur cases. He set up the Reykjavík Task Force, and after a while focused primarily on the Geirfinnur case.

**28 October 1976 – Gudjón Skarphéðinsson is implicated**
Saevar implicated Gudjón Skarphéðinsson, who was arrested on 12 November and detained in custody. Saevar also implicated himself, for the first time, in the assault on Geirfinnur.

**9 November 1976**
Kristján implicated himself, Saevar, and Gudjón in attacking Geirfinnur on the slipway. He said he was pretty sure that Sigurbjörn Eiríksson was also there and held Geirfinnur by the neck during the struggle, identifying Mr Eiríksson as the 'chubby' man referred to in other statements.

**28 November 1976**
Gudjón was taken to the Keflavík slipway (*Dráttarbrautin*) and Harbour Café (*Hafnarbúðin*), but could not recall anything about Vatnsstígur and was reminded that he had earlier mentioned a Volkswagen car connected to Vatnsstígur. He replied: 'Yes I once went to Keflavík in a Volkswagen car.'

*(Continued)*

**Table 9.1** (*Continued*)

He said he was the driver but could not give the date in November 1974 when it took place.

**30 November 1976**
Saevar was interviewed about delivery vans to which he had had access in 1974. He referred to Kristján's cousin, Sigurdur Óttar Hreinsson, having had access to a delivery van.

**30 November 1976**
Erla appeared in Court before Örn Höskuldsson and informed him that Saevar had told her to mention the names of Magnús, Sigurbjörn, Valdimar, and Einar, and others, if implicated in the case, in order to draw attention away from the truly guilty persons (i.e. Saevar, Kristján, and Gudjón).

**8 December 1976**
Gudjón stated during interrogation that Sigurbjörn Eiríksson, Magnús Leópoldsson, Einar Bollason, and Valdimar Olsen were all innocent.

**8 December 1976**
The charges against the suspects were issued in the cases with further charges being laid in the Geirfinnur case on 16 March 1977.

**9 December 1976 – Sigurdur Óttar Hreinsson is implicated**
Saevar implicated Sigurdur Óttar as the delivery van driver. Sigurdur Óttar was placed in custody overnight on 13 December after a long interrogation and denial. Karl Schütz interrogated him the following day and he confessed to being the van driver. Sigurdur Óttar became an important material witness in the case against Saevar, Kristján, and Gudjón.
Saevar said that in July 1975, he, Erla, Kristján, and Gudjón had met and agreed that if they were arrested in connection with the case they would implicate the Klúbburinn men and bootleggers from Reykjavík.

**13 December 1976**
Erla told the police that a few days after Geirfinnur was killed on the slipway and his body hidden in the Red Hills, Saevar told her that if anybody asked, then tell them the Klúbburinn men were responsible.

**31 December 1976**
Psychology student Gisli Gudjonsson gave Gudjón a lie detector test at the request of investigative judge Birgir Thormar.

**23 January 1977**
There was a staged re-enactment at Keflavík slipway of what allegedly took place there on 19 November 1974.

**2 February 1977 – Press conference**
Karl Schütz had completed his final report and spoke at length at the press conference, which became the foundation for the District and Supreme Courts' alleged sequence of events in the Geirfinnur case.

**19 December 1977**
Convictions in the District Court.

**22 February 1980**
Convictions in the Supreme Court.

almost all of the early recorded interviews of the suspects, being the senior detective in the team.

## CONFESSIONS OBTAINED BY THE REYKJAVÍK TEAM

On 26 November 1974 the clay model head based on witness reports of the man seen in the Harbour Café on 19 November 1974 was released to the media. Shortly afterwards a rumour started to spread that the disappearance of Geirfinnur Einarsson was connected with Klúbburinn, where Geirfinnur had been seen two days before his disappearance. Sigurbjörn Eiríksson was the director of Klúbburinn and Magnús Leópoldsson was the managing director. On 3 February 1975 both men wrote to the Ministry of Justice and requested an investigation into the source of this rumour and the substance of it.[3] The importance of this is that Sigurbjörn Eiríksson and Magnús Leópoldsson were connected to the disappearance of Geirfinnur for over a year before Erla, Saevar, and Kristján implicated them and Einar Bollason and Valdimar Olsen[4] in January 1976 (see Box 9.1).

According to the police, the antecedents to the incriminating statements of Erla, Saevar, and Kristján were as follows. In early to mid-January 1976, Erla started receiving phone calls that had frightened her. (There is a record of her telephoning Síðumúli Prison on 6 January and urgently wanting to speak to the detectives in the case, which may be linked to this.) Erla was living at her mother's home at the time and most of the calls were silent, but one involved a threatening male voice. Erla contacted the police, which led to her being interviewed on 21 January at Síðumúli Prison and being repeatedly asked the names of people who frightened her, but no statement was taken from her. She allegedly mentioned three people: Einar Bollason, her half-brother, Sigurbjörn Eiríksson, and Jón Ragnarsson, the managing director of the Reykjavík Harbour Cinema, and said that the phone calls were linked to the Geirfinnur case. Erla made no mention of Kristján in her first statement.

However, the accuracy of this police recollection of events needs to be interpreted with caution, because it first appeared in Detective Eggert Bjarnason's summary notes on 10 March 1976, almost two months after the interrogation. Importantly, handwritten notes of the interview

---

[3] Referred to in the Supreme Court Judgement of the two men for compensation, dated 3 March 1983.

[4] Erla never properly implicated Valdimar Olsen (see Daníelsson, 2016, and Chapter 12).

**Box 9.1**   The arrest and detention of the 'four wrongly accused'

At 06.00 on 26 January 1976, Magnús Leópoldsson, Einar Bollason, and Valdimar Olsen were arrested in connection with the Geirfinnur case, taken to Sídumúli Prison, and remanded in custody for 45 days. Custody was extended twice and these three men spent 105 days in solitary confinement.

Sigurbjörn Eiríksson was arrested in connection with the Geirfinnur case on 11 February. He spent 90 days in solitary confinement.

The 'four wrongly accused' all denied their involvement in Geirfinnur's disappearance and were released from custody on 9 May 1976, but restrictions on their movements remained until 1 July 1976. They were later exonerated and awarded compensation (Supreme Court Judgement, 3 March 1983).

Two of the men, Einar Bollason and Magnús Leópoldsson, have discussed their arrest, detention, and the damaging impact on their lives in their biographies (Jónasson, 1996; Karlsson, 1994).

The Working Group Report (2013) noted the small number of written reports in relation to the interrogation of the four men, which was presumably due to their persistent denials.

with Erla on 21 January exist and show that she was claiming that she and Saevar were driven to Keflavík harbour to collect alcohol, which Geirfinnur and the others were going to collect from the sea.[5] She referred to all the men wearing gloves and recognized her brother Einar and made a reference to Sigurbjörn Eiríksson, Magnús Leópoldsson, and Kristján also being there. She said that the one person she did not recognize 'could have been [Jón Ragnarsson]'. Erla referred to running away, fearing for her life, hiding in a building overnight, then hitching a lift to Grinadvík junction in an old Moskvitch car and then in an oil tanker to Hafnarfjördur.[6] There is a reference in the handwritten notes about a problem having arisen, which Saevar said he was going to discuss with Gudjón Skarphédinsson. This was the first reference to Gudjón's name, although at this point Erla did not identify him as having been in Keflavík.

The importance of these handwritten notes is that Erla's story had in broad terms emerged two days prior to her first written police statement on 23 January.[7]

---

[5] ICCRC Report, 2017, Erla Bolladóttir, Paragraph 116.
[6] While this interview took place, Saevar was also being interrogated within the same prison without it being recorded.
[7] ICCRC Report, 2017, Erla Bolladóttir, Paragraph 116.

Saevar was interviewed on 22 January and was told of Erla's fears. He gave the names of Einar Bollason, who was the alleged driver into Keflavík, Magnús Leópoldsson, Valdimar Olsen, and Jón Ragnarsson. The purpose of the trip according to Saevar was to collect alcohol from the sea with Geirfinnur's help. Saevar's role was to distribute the alcohol afterwards. He made no mention in this first statement of Erla or Kristján being involved. Saevar claimed that he and Einar drove around Keflavík while the others collected the alcohol from the sea. When they returned to the harbour, Magnús told them that there had been an accident and that Geirfinnur had fallen overboard and drowned.

In this statement, Saevar claimed that a few days prior to the trip to Keflavík, he had met Einar, Magnús, and Geirfinnur at Laugavegur, Reykjavík; they wanted to discuss with him the distribution of smuggled alcohol because of his reputation for distributing illegal drugs. This part was soon dropped from the story.

The following day, 23 January, Erla gave a statement during a three-hour interview. She was told that the reason for the interview was that the police believed she might be in possession of information concerning Geirfinnur's disppearance. She said that on the evening of 19 November 1974 she was in Klúbburinn with Saevar and went from there to Keflavík in a car driven by Magnús Leópoldsson. In the car, Saevar firmly held her hand and she had the feeling that there was a plan to kill her. She heard a discussion of making somebody (Geirfinnur) 'disappear', because he was being 'uncooperative'. When they arrived in the Keflavík harbour she saw 'seven men', including Einar Bollason and Kristján. She thought she recognized her father's red Fiat car and saw a large van. Once on the slipway, Erla ran away and hid in a nearby house, which had discarded timber inside, later identified as the 'Red Mill' (*Rauða Millan*). The following day she hitched a lift from two separate drivers: first in an old Moskvitch car with an elderly driver from the Westman Islands to the junction at Reykjanesbraut and Grindavík, and from there in a large lorry to Hafnarfjördur, where she caught a bus to Reykjavík.

After Erla's interview on 23 January, Kristján was interviewed for over four hours. At the beginning, he declared: 'I do not consider myself involved or to know anything about the disappearance of Geirfinnur Einarsson'.

Later in the interview he accepted that he had been to Keflavík around the time Geirfinnur disappeared but had problems recollecting any detail because of his extensive use of stimulants and sedatives that affected his memory at the time. He recalled one evening getting into a large Mercedes-Benz delivery van outside Klúbburinn and going to

Keflavík, where he noticed a small boat in the harbour. There were at least two passenger cars there too, in addition to the delivery van. He recognized Saevar, Erla, and Einar Bollason. He declared:

> I cannot say anything further about this case, at least not at present, but it is possible that my memory of the incident will recover later. I cannot confirm whether this incident or trip was about the time Geirfinnur disappeared, but I consider it possible.

On 25 January, Saevar was interrogated again after being taken to Keflavík harbour and shown around. He identified the 'slipway' (*Dráttarbrautin*) as the most likely location. Later the slipway became the 'crime scene' where Geirfinnur was said to have been killed.

Saevar made a correction to his previous statement, describing how contact was made with those going to Keflavík on 19 January 1974. He now claimed that he was collected by a car containing Einar Bollason, Magnús Leópoldsson, and Erla; instead of Valdimar Olsen, Kristján was in the car. He no longer thought it was a Fiat. He claimed the purpose of the trip was to collect alcohol and when they arrived in Keflavík harbour he saw two other cars: a passenger car and a large delivery van. There was a small motor boat by the pier and several people went on board, including Erla, and the boat sailed away. Saevar and Einar did not go on board, but drove around. When they returned, they saw merchandise being transferred from the boat to the delivery van. Magnús told them that there had been an accident and Geirfinnur had fallen into the sea and drowned. Saevar described the slipway as being in darkness with poor visibility but thought that some light might have come from nearby buildings and ships.

**Note:** Saevar's description about the lighting was very vague, but it looks as though it arose from a response to a direct question.

In further interviews on 27 January, both Saevar and Kristján implicated Sigurbjörn Eiríksson in their statements. They allege that he had gone on board the boat with Geirfinnur on the slipway to collect the alcohol.

Saevar, who allegedly was present on the boat, said that there had been a fight and he saw Kristján, Sigurbjörn, and Magnús assault Geirfinnur, who fell overboard. When Geirfinnur was brought back on board he appeared to be dead. They got the alcohol on board the boat. It had been wrapped in sails and nets, attached to floats, and it was in large, 50 litre containers. The merchandise was put in the delivery van, driven by either Valdimar Olsen or Jón Ragnarsson, and taken to Klúbburinn. Magnús and Einar took Saevar home to his mother's house at Grýtubakki, whereas Erla got a lift home in one of the cars.

Saevar was unsure whether it was Einar or Magnús who had driven them back to Keflavík.

Kristján, in his statement on 27 January, mentioned that he, Saevar, Magnús Leópoldsson, and Sigurbjörn Eiríksson had gone on board the boat, and when shown a photograph of Geirfinnur, said he was also on board the boat, but Erla, Valdimar Olsen, and Jón Ragnarsson stayed behind. On reflection, he thought that one of the passenger cars was a red Fiat, driven by Einar, which fitted with what Saevar had said in his first statement. He said the other car was a Mercedes-Benz. He thought Valdimar drove the delivery van. Kristján described a fight breaking out on the boat, in which Einar hit Geirfinnur in the head, while Sigurbjörn held him by the neck. After the fight, Geirfinnur lay motionless on the deck. They went ashore and transferred the merchandise to the delivery van. He thought Geirfinnur was wrapped in plastic and put in the van, but he was not sure.

In her statement dated 3 February, Erla said she had tried to remember more about the trip to Keflavík. She now recalled having met Saevar at Klúbburinn and had got into a car, whose driver was Magnús Leópoldsson. They drove to Vatnsstígur, located in downtown Reykjavík, and picked up Kristján who also got into the car, and possibly another man. This alleged pick up point – Vatnsstígur – became an important feature of the accounts of the alleged trip to Keflavík (see Karl Schütz's press conference statement, below).

Erla also identified Einar Bollason, Geirfinnur Einarsson, Valdimar Olsen, Sigurbjörn Eiríksson, and Ásgeir Eiríksson, as having been on the slipway. (There is a reference to her being shown photographs of several men and selecting these as having been present.) However, her references to Valdimar, Sigurbjörn, and Ásgeir were tentative. Erla said that all the men on the slipway had one thing in common: they were all wearing gloves, a comment she had first made in her interview on 21 January.

On 10 February, Erla, Saevar, and Kristján were also shown a large number of photographs of men, and all identified, among others, Sigurbjörn Eiríksson as having been on the slipway. The following day Sigurbjörn Eiríksson was arrested and remanded in custody.

On 2 March, Kristján retracted his confession, claiming that he had nothing to do with the Geirfinnur case, claiming he had made it all up after being told others had described the trip. On 9 March, he took back his retraction in a further statement, which contained a vague reference to it being dark on the slipway.

Following the arrests of the 'four wrongly accused' the Reykjavík Team focused on interviewing them and other witnesses without much success, and they had to release them from custody on 9 May 1976.

According to Magnús Leópoldsson, prosecutor Hallvardur Einvardsson raised strong objections to his being released and insisted on a further 90 days in custody 'in view of the seriousness of the accusations', but investigative judge Örn Höskuldsson did not agree (Jónasson, 1996, p. 158).

### Erla's Confession to Shooting Geirfinnur

According to the Síðumúli Prison diary, Erla was brought there at 20.30 on 3 May 1976 and questioned for over two hours, mainly by prosecutor Hallvardur Einvardsson. When she was kept in custody overnight she became extremely distressed and during the night saw the prison chaplain. The prison staff gave her chloral hydrate to help her sleep.

The following day, Erla was interviewed in Síðumúli Prison and described the journey to Keflavík in similar terms as before. On the slipway she saw Magnús Leópoldsson and Saevar talking to a 'rustic' looking man (later identified as Geirfinnur), who did not seem to fit in there and was arguing with the other two men. Saevar handed Erla something heavy, which she should use on the man. This was a rifle and she shot the man while closing her eyes. Erla said that she was standing so close to the man that she 'clearly saw his facial expression' and 'He seemed to realize what was happening and there was horror in his expression and eyes'.[8]

**Note:** Erla's clear description of the man's face is surprising as she had stated that it was dark on the slipway, with poor visibility, and she claimed to have shut her eyes. She said Saevar took the rifle from her and she managed to escape to a nearby house when people were attending to the man (i.e. the Red Mill).

### The 'Slap in the Face' Incident

This took place on 5 May 1976 during suspects' face-to-face confrontation (*samprófun*), which was a commonly used method in the case (Gudjonsson et al., 2014). The incident was staged in the interrogation room at Síðumúli Prison in the evening and involved the three suspects – Saevar, Kristján, and Erla – being brought together in order to improve the consistency in their version of events concerning the disappearance of Geirfinnur. The reason was probably Erla's confession the previous day that she had shot Geirfinnur, and that Saevar had the previous month retracted his confession. In contrast, Kristján had recently given

---

[8] Evidence Book XII, p. 198.

a further confession statement about the trip to Keflavík, now being confident that Einar Bollason, Valdimar Olsen, and Sigurbjörn Eiríksson had all been on the slipway. The confrontation focused on Saevar's denials, using Erla and Kristján as protagonists to break down his resistance.

On occasions, like this one, there were instances where police and court were putting one or more suspects under pressure to agree an apparently accepted account (i.e. a hypothesis-driven confrontation-police interrogation by proxy).

There were nine people sitting in an irregular circle around the room, which was only about 12 metres square. Gunnar Gudmundsson, the chief prison officer at Sídumúli Prison was present, together with Örn Höskuldsson, Detectives Eggert Bjarnason and Sigurbjörn Vídir, Njördur Snaehólm, and senior prosecutor Hallvardur Einvardsson.[9] The conversation inside the room became very heated when Saevar would not accept that he was involved in the Geirfinnur case. He became angry and argumentative and it reached a point where Gunnar slapped Saevar in the face. Saevar subsequently reported the incident to his lawyer and the prison chaplain.

According to the witness statement of Hallvardur Einvardsson, Örn Höskuldsson instigated the meeting and the primary focus was on a confrontation between Saevar and Erla, at a time when the investigation had entered a 'very difficult point'. Erla did indeed confront Saevar about his denials and she became very emotional during an angry exchange between them.

In the autumn of 1979, Thórir Oddsson, the deputy head of the State Criminal Investigation Police, was appointed to investigate Saevar's claims of coercion and being assaulted by Gunnar Gudmundsson. Thórir Oddsson was assisted by Detective Gudmundur Gudjónsson, my twin brother, who conducted most of the interviews. The interviews were conducted mostly in the presence of Saevar's defence lawyer, Jón Oddsson, and a prosecution representative, Pétur Gudgeirsson. All nine persons present at the meeting were interviewed and gave statements. Eggert Bjarnason said that he could not recall Gunnar slapping Saevar, Sigurbjörn Vídir claimed that he was not aware that the incident had taken place, and Örn Höskuldsson said that it must have taken place when he was out of the room attending to a phone call, although nobody else referred to his having left the room. He did not

---

[9] In his witness statement during the subsequent duress investigation, dated 26 November 1979, Mr Einvardsson said that he sometimes discussed the progress of the case with Njördur Snaehólm, whose advice he valued (Duress Investigation Report, 1979, pp. 124–126). (Cited as Case number 2875/79.)

recall the incident ever having been mentioned. Neither could he recall who was in charge of the meeting but accepted that it was either him or Hallvardur Einvardsson. Saevar, Erla, and Kristján all vividly recalled the slapping incident. Importantly, both Hallvardur Einvardsson and Njördur Snaehólm stated that they had observed Gunnar slap Saevar in the face. Gunnar had difficulties accepting what he had done and stated: 'After hearing the testimony of Hallvardur Einvardsson and Njördur Snaehólm and finding it impossible to believe that they are wrong, I regret that this incident took place, although I find it a mystery that the incident happened'.[10]

The Supreme Court accepted that the incident had happened but considered that it did not undermine the reliability of Saevar's previous confessions in the case.

After the duress investigation was completed, Saevar's lawyer gave a statement describing its work as 'exemplary'. However, he expressed great disappointment about the narrow scope of the remit that Thórir Oddsson had been asked to investigate (i.e. some of Saevar's complaints were specifically excluded from the remit because they had been previously investigated and rejected by the District Court). For these reasons the duress investigation has come under criticism (Daníelsson, 2016).

## The 'Foreign Looking Man'

On 7 May 1976, Kristján was interviewed and referred to a tropical (southern) – 'foreign looking' – man on the slipway, who spoke good Icelandic, which fitted the description of Gudjón Skarphédinsson.

The Reykjavík Team had first shown an interest in Gudjón on 10 February 1976 when Detective Eggert Bjarnason questioned him about Saevar. Gudjón said it was difficult to know whether Saevar was telling the truth or not. He thought that Saevar was bright but had a poor memory. The previous summer Saevar had told him that it was not difficult to kill people in Iceland and ensure that their bodies were never found. All that had to be done was to take the body to the lava field and cover it up (urða). Saevar also claimed to know a lot about the Geirfinnur case.

On 14 May 1976, Detective Eggert Bjarnason interviewed Gudjón as a witness at Sídumúli Prison and asked him whether he had been standing by a delivery van at Vatnsstígur in November 1974 with Saevar. Gudjón said he did not remember that at all, which meant

[10] Witness statement, dated 1 October 1979, p. 136 (Duress Investigation Report, 1979; Case number 2875/79).

he could not exclude it as a possibility, subsequently leaving him vulnerable to the development of memory distrust in the Geirfinnur case (Chapter 17).

Gudjón said he had taught Saevar at Reykjanes, in the west part of Iceland, either in 1970 or 1971. He had met him at various times and places since. Twice they had been on fishing trips together. During the summer of 1974, Saevar asked Gudjón more than once to participate in a Post and Telecommunication fraud, which Gudjón thought was ridiculous. He saw Saevar in October 1974, when Saevar showed him a Land Rover he had bought. He invited Gudjón to test drive it, which he did. In the summer of 1975, Saevar mentioned to Gudjón that he knew all about the Geirfinnur case.

It is of importance that while Gudjón was being interviewed in Sídumúli Prison, Kristján was removed from his cell and taken to the room next door to the interrogation room. He observed Gudjón twice through the door and confirmed that Gudjón was the 'foreign looking' man he had previously referred to seeing on the slipway.

The following day Kristján gave a statement where he stated that he was convinced that the man he saw in the Sídumúli interrogation room (i.e. Gudjón Skarphédinsson) was the man he had seen speaking with Saevar by the delivery van at Vatnsstígur. He said that later that night he had seen Gudjón at the slipway, where some men had surrounded another man (Geirfinnur). Gudjón was now on the police radar as a possible suspect, six months prior to his ultimate arrest.

## THE REYKJAVÍK TASK FORCE

The 'four wrongly accused' men had reasonable access to lawyers while in custody, unlike the other suspects (Daníelsson, 2016, p. 250), and denied any involvement in the Geirfinnur case. The release of the four men created a problem for the Geirfinnur investigation, which resulted in the Minister of Justice, Ólafur Jóhannesson, seeking support from abroad (Working Group Report, 2013). The motivation may have been twofold: to seek an authoritative, investigative expert not available in Iceland, and to appoint an independent investigator to assist with the case, which had become political. Karl Schütz, a retired German senior officer with the German Federal Police, was appointed by the Icelandic Ministry of Justice in the summer of 1976 to work on the Gudmundur and Geirfinnur cases. He soon set up a Task Force, focusing on Geirfinnur's disappearance (see Chapter 10 regarding Schütz's background, appointment to the cases, and his behaviour).

The Reykjavík Task Force was set up by Karl Schütz in August 1976 in collaboration with the Head of the Reykjavík Criminal Court, Halldór Thorbjörnsson, and the Criminal Investigation Police. It apparently comprised 12 members; Karl Schütz was the acting head of the Task Force, along with Örn Höskuldsson, who was the designated overall chief investigator (*Morgunbladid*, 3 February 1977, p. 20).

The Working Group Report (2013) noted that Schütz's appointment letter and the minutes of the numerous meetings he had with the Task Force members could not be located, which is very unfortunate since they would undoubtedly have been informative. A formal list of the members could not be found, but there is a photograph of its members (Latham & Gudjonsson, 2016) and newspaper articles identify the following persons as comprising the Task Force.

Pétur Eggerz was Schütz's interpreter. Pétur was a qualified lawyer and secretary to the first president of the republic of Iceland, Sveinn Björnsson (Eggerz, 1971). He worked for the foreign office and prior to the Geirfinnur case had been an attaché to the Icelandic embassies in London, Washington DC, and Bonn, as well as a former ambassador to the European Council in Strasbourg. He was a very eminent man, who had been asked by Iceland's Minister of Justice, Ólafur Jóhannesson, to find a well-qualified German policeman to assist with the Gudmundur and Geirfinnur cases, resulting in Schütz being appointed. (It is unknown why he especially wanted a German policeman.) Given his own professional standing, Pétur Eggerz's appointment as Schütz's interpreter seems extraordinary.

There were also two registered female translators employed to assist Schütz with the urgent translation of documents and, occasionally, interpretation during interrogation.

The three members of the Reykjavík Team – Örn Höskuldsson, Eggert Bjarnason, and Sigurbjörn Víðir – who were described in Chapter 8, were transferred to the Task Force and a further five police officers added: Ívar Hannesson, Grétar Saemundsson, Jónas Bjarnason, Haraldur Árnason, and Rúnar Sigurdsson. Undoubtedly, these five investigators were carefully selected for their specialist skills.

Ívar Hannesson was in his mid-forties and had been a policeman for over 20 years, five of which he had served in the Reykjavík Criminal Investigation Police (Jónsson & Gudjónsson [Gudmundur], 1997). In his youth he had been a keen sportsman and in the mid-1960s he sang with the police choir and served on its committee. He appeared reserved and somewhat stern but was an experienced and competent detective. My understanding at the time was that he had had some experience with murder investigations, although these were very rare in Iceland in the 1970s (see Chapter 6). He had responsibility for investigating Geirfinnur's background and prepared the testimony of suspects and witnesses for court.

On the Task Force, Eggert Bjarnason had special responsibility for Saevar, but also for the alleged driver of the delivery van who drove to the Keflavík slipway, who was not convicted (Sigurdur Óttar Hreinsson – see Box 9.2). Sigurbjörn Vídir was given special responsibility for Erla, presumably because he had established a rapport with her after she was released from custody on 20 December 1975 and he remained in regular contact with her (Bolladóttir, 2008).

Grétar Saemundsson was in his early thirties and had been with the Reykjavík Criminal Investigation Police for five years (Jónsson &

---

**Box 9.2**    Sigurdur Óttar Hreinsson – Witness in the Geirfinnur case

At the time of the Geirfinnur investigation, Sigurdur Óttar was a 20-year-old technical college student.

Sigurdur Óttar's name was first mentioned in a statement Saevar made on 9 December 1976. Saevar alleged that he had asked Kristján to find a delivery van driver to transport the merchandise from the Keflavík slipway. Saevar had been reluctant to reveal Sigurdur Óttar's name during the six-hour interview but eventually relented.

On the evening of 13 December, Sigurdur Óttar was placed in overnight custody at Sídumúli Prison after Eggert Bjarnason had interrogated him for five hours as a witness. During the interrogation he denied any involvement in the Geirfinnur case.

On 14 December, Karl Schütz interrogated him and after a long conversation Sigurdur Óttar said 'I will tell the truth'. His confession statement is vague and tentative. He is then released from custody.

On 23 January 1977, Sigurdur Óttar participated with Erla, Saevar, Kristján, and Gudjón in a reconstruction at the slipway. Sigurdur Óttar positioned the delivery van 30 metres further east than the others.

Sigurdur Óttar formally retracted his confession in a police statement on 12 October 1977. He said he had told his lawyer the day after his release from custody the previous December that he had made a false confession but did not want his lawyer to do anything about it, because he was frightened of the police and at the time was not entirely sure whether he had been at the slipway or not.

On 12 October, Sigurdur Óttar appeared in Court and refused to withdraw his retraction. Sigurdur Óttar was remanded in custody and three days later he was subjected to three and a half hours of interrogation in which he answered 27 questions related to his retraction and the reasons for it. It seems that during his interrogation by Karl Schütz, he developed memory distrust syndrome, which lasted for a while after he was released from custody (see Appendix 1).

In spite of the retraction, the Supreme Court ruled that on 22 February 1980 he had driven the delivery van to Keflavík on 19 November 1974 and was a material witness.

Gudjónsson [Gudmundur], 1997). I found him a very likeable person, always calm, persuasive in his arguments, and an excellent communicator. After Gudjón Skarphédinsson was arrested in November 1976, Grétar was allocated the job of interrogating him and generally 'looking after' his welfare while in custody (e.g. getting him reading material, staying in contact). Grétar soon established very good rapport with Gudjón and was able to use his skills as an interrogator to get Gudjón talking about the Geirfinnur case. They were of the same age.

Jónas Bjarnason, in his early fifties, was the oldest of the detectives and had been a policeman for over 25 years. He was an expert on accident investigations and did not commence work in the Reykjavík Criminal Investigation Police until 1 July 1976, but early in his career he had worked for a year in the technical division (Jónsson & Gudjónsson [Gudmundur], 1997). It is possible that he was selected for the Task Force when Karl Schütz visited Iceland at the end of June 1976. On the face of it, he was an unusual choice because he did not appear to have had much experience of criminal investigations. He was allocated special responsibility for Saevar and took over his interrogation from October 1976 (see Schütz's final report).

Haraldur Árnason was a detective in his mid-thirties. He entered the police in 1963 and transferred to the Reykjavík Criminal Investigation Police in 1973 (Jónsson & Gudjónsson [Gudmundur], 1997). In late 1968 and until the end of 1969 he did security work at the main headquarters of the United Nations. At the time of the Gudmundur and Geirfinnur investigation he was attached to the technical division of the Criminal Investigation Police and had a special responsibility for Kristján. I remember him as an intelligent, cheerful, and entertaining man.

Rúnar Sigurdsson was in his late twenties but had had experience in investigating drug-related and smuggling offences. He was the first drug offences investigator appointed in Iceland (Jónsdóttir, 2010), taking up a position in the Narcotics Police in 1971 (Jónsson & Gudjónsson [Gudmundur], 1997). He assisted the Keflavík investigation into the disappearance of Geirfinnur from early on (see Chapter 7). He was seconded to the Task Force from the Reykjavík uniformed police and allocated special responsibility for Saevar's care.

The fact that three Task Force officers were allocated special responsibility and supervision of Saevar (*Morgunbladid*, 3 February 1977, p. 20) shows the importance of his status as the 'prime suspect' in the case. My impression in 1976 was that Saevar was seen as the most oppositional, defiant, manipulative, and cunning of the suspects and was thought to have the answers to where the bodies of Gudmundur and Geirfinnur were hidden, but he chose not to tell.

His silence on these matters undoubtedly infuriated Schütz, the prosecutor Hallvardur Einvardsson, as well as the detectives.

The Task Force worked closely as a team. Karl Schütz met with the investigators first thing in the morning, when tasks were set, and then the following day the investigators had to report back on the progress they had made with their designated tasks. My impression was of a hard-working Task Force who were set clear goals that they had to complete to Schütz's satisfaction. He was a demanding leader and the investigation moved forward very quickly.

Ragnar Vignir, the head of the technical division of the Criminal Investigation Police, was responsible for technical aspects of the Gudmundur and Geirfinnur cases, including taking crime scene photographs, but he was apparently not officially a member of the Task Force.[11] His importance is shown by his presence at the press conference on 2 February 1977, where Karl Schütz and Örn Höskuldsson presented the 'official' version of what had supposedly happened to Geirfinnur. Ragnar was a qualified photographer prior to entering the police in 1952. In the mid-1950s he studied in the technical division of the Danish Police and attended courses and conferences in England and West Germany (Jónsson & Gudjónsson [Gudmundur], 1997).

My recollection is that prior to Karl Schütz taking over the investigation in August 1976, the three members of the Reykjavík Team kept information about the cases very much to themselves. Karl Schütz finished his work with the Reykjavík Criminal Court by Saturday 5 February 1977 when he left Iceland for good (*Morgunbladid*, 3 February 1977, p. 20).

## KEY TASK FORCE STATEMENTS

In a letter to investigative judge Örn Höskuldsson, dated 3 August 1976, Erla complained that he had not come to see her as he had promised, describing her distress and requesting that he visit her immediately (Working Group Report, 2013).

Karl Schütz interviewed Erla on 11 August 1976. She complained that she had not been allowed to see her child and told that she would not be allowed to do so until she had seen Karl Schütz. She complained that she had seen her lawyer only once, the previous June. Schütz reproached her for having given a great number of statements that she

---

[11] He does not appear in the picture of the members of the Task Force when it was set up in August 1976 (Latham & Gudjonsson, 2016).

had subsequently changed or retracted. He said nobody knew when or whether she was telling the truth, or whether she was deliberately lying. She was encouraged to think carefully about whether she could provide proof that she was telling the truth. Erla said she was trying to tell the truth but had lied in an attempt to be allowed to go home. She was confronted with the contradictions in her statements. When pressured with providing proof of what she was saying, she said she had left her red coat in a car belonging to a man called 'Bjarni', who had driven them to Keflavík on 19 November 1974. It was wrong what she had said before that Magnús Leópoldsson had been the driver to Keflavík. She had now introduced a new driver who was soon excluded from the case.

On 1 September 1976, Erla gave a detailed statement, retracting her admission of shooting Geirfinnur, but still admitting to having gone to Keflavík with the others. She referred to a car and a delivery van having been on the Keflavík slipway. Erla said that Magnús, Valdimar, Sigurbjörn, and Einar were on the slipway, in addition to other people not previously mentioned, but she had not seen Gudjón on the slipway. However, she made a point of saying that Saevar had mentioned the names of these people; the names did not come directly from her.[12]

The fact that she was being asked about Gudjón suggested that he was on the police radar as the 'fourth man' (i.e. the driver of the car to Keflavík – with the 'four wrongly accused' being out of the case, a new driver was needed to complete the story).

On 7 September 1976 detectives took Kristján to Vatnsstígur for him to explain the preparation of the trip to Keflavík. He was then taken to Keflavík and said that he had arrived there with Saevar, Erla, and an unknown driver (later to be identified as Gudjón). When the police took Kristján to the Harbour Café, he thought he recognized it. He said that when they had arrived in Keflavík on 19 November 1974, Saevar had asked him to go into the Harbour Café and telephone somebody (Geirfinnur), whose name he could not remember. The man's name and telephone number were written on a piece of paper and when he phoned a child answered, who called for his father. This was his first reference to the Harbour Café and his having telephoned Geirfinnur's home, but the day before, Kristján had been taken to Vatnsstígur and told police about Saevar stopping the car outside a café in Keflavík and asking Kristján to call somebody, whose name could have been Geirfinnur.[13]

On 15 October 1976, Karl Schütz interrogated Erla and she attempted to retract her confession. Schütz pointed out contradictions regarding

[12] Evidence Book XIV, pp. 545–548.
[13] ICCRC Report, 2017, Kristján Vidarsson, Paragraph 615.

her testimony. Erla then said 'she had not been in Keflavík, she was insistent about that'. She said nobody believed her and she no longer knew what to say. When asked to reveal who had given her the detailed special knowledge information she possessed, she insisted that she had used her imagination, claiming that she had 'made it all up'. When told that she could not have made up these specific details, she became 'mentally disturbed' and insisted that she had not gone to Keflavík. When pressed to give details regarding the source of her special knowledge, she replied: 'Well, then I was in Keflavík, but I remember nothing about it'. When told the interrogation was over, she became 'hysterical and repeatedly banged the table, shouting out crying: Nobody here believes me'. On her way into Síðumúli Prison, Detective Sigurbjörn Vídir overheard Erla threatening suicide. She was undoubtedly very frustrated and distressed by the fact that nobody was prepared to consider her claims of innocence.[14]

On 21 October 1976, Kristján described what happened on the slipway. He, Saevar, and Geirfinnur had left the car, while Erla waited in the car. They were approached by a 'foreign looking man' (later to be identified as Gudjón), who asked whether they had ever been to sea. The man asked Kristján to wait by a boat. Geirfinnur approached Kristján, called him bad names, and was threatening in his demeanour. Geirfinnur was very angry and came quickly towards Kristján as he was on the cliff edge. Kristján moved out of the way and Geirfinnur fell over the cliff by accident on to the beach. He saw Geirfinnur lying three metres below the cliff and his head was covered in blood. Kristján did not tell anybody what had happened at the top of the cliff. He returned to Reykjavík, but Erla was not with them in the car. In this version, Kristján explained Geirfinnur's alleged death as an accident, a version Schütz was definitely not prepared to accept (see his comments below – press conference).

On 27 October 1976 Saevar was extensively interviewed and said that Kristján telephoned him the day before they went to Keflavík and asked him to go with him to collect smuggled alcohol. Saevar told Kristján that he would be at Kjarvalsstadir Museum on the evening of 19 January and would meet him after the film show, which ended at 21.00. Saevar and Erla were collected by car at about 21.30 and then picked up Kristján. They drove to the Harbour Café, met Geirfinnur, and drove to the slipway, where Saevar saw a delivery van. A fight started close to the delivery van. Kristján hit Geirfinnur while somebody else, an older man (later to be identified as Sigurbjörn Eiríksson), held Geirfinnur by the neck. The two men then carried Geirfinnur's

---

[14] Evidence Book XIV, pp. 587 and 650–651.

body into the back of the delivery van. He did not know what subsequently happened to Geirfinnur. Then suddenly Erla disappeared, which supported her first statement in the case.

On 28 October, Saevar implicated Gudjón Skarphédinsson and himself as perpetrators in the Geirfinnur case. The intention was to sell Geirfinnur alcohol, rather than buying it from him, which had been the previous version.[15] *This was a very major change in the story and without an explanation, undermining its entire credibility.* Gudjón said he had arranged to meet Geirfinnur in Keflavík. Geirfinnur wanted to buy about 60 litres of alcohol and that Saevar and Kristján would get a percentage. At 21.00 Saevar and Erla met Gudjón and he was driving a Citroen car. They stopped to collect Kristján from Laugavegur in the centre of Reykjavík. When they arrived in Keflavík, they went to the Harbour Café. The time was about 22.15, later than they had arranged with Geirfinnur. Gudjón handed Kristján a piece of paper with Geirfinnur's telephone number. Soon Geirfinnur arrived and they went to the slipway. There was a delivery van there, which contained the smuggled alcohol. On the slipway, Geirfinnur did not want to keep his end of the deal, stating that he knew Sigurbjörn from Klúbburinn. Geirfinnur intended to walk away and pushed Kristján out of the way, who hit Geirfinnur in the face. A 'chubby' man (later to be identified as Sigurbjörn Eiríksson) put his arm around Geirfinnur's neck from behind, and Gudjón hit Geirfinnur with a large piece of wood. Kristján then hit Geirfinnur twice in the head, leaving him unconscious. They looked for Erla and could not find her. Geirfinnur's body was taken to Grettisgata 82 in the delivery van along with the alcohol. Gudjón suggested a place east of Grafningur by Thingvallavatn, where Geirfinnur's body could be covered in plastic bags and hidden by stones. Another idea they had was to hide Geirfinnur in Thingvallavatn, which is a rift valley lake in the southwestern part of Iceland.

On 30 October, Karl Schütz and Detective Sigurbjörn Víðir interrogated Erla, who started by saying that she had not gone to Keflavík on 19 January 1974 and that she could prove it, because that night she was with the Knudsen family, who were in the film production business and associated with Saevar and Erla. After she had been directed to her previous testimony, she eventually admitted that she had been on the trip, along with Saevar, Kristján, and another man, who remained unknown (known as 'the fourth man'). Again, Schütz did not accept Erla's claims of innocence and confronted her with her previous statements. Erla was pressed regarding the identity of 'the fourth man' and

---

[15] Evidence Book XIV, pp. 662–669.

became distressed, claiming to be frightened of him. She mentioned Jósep, Saevar's stepfather, then Gudjón Skarphédinsson. She gives a description of the man (35–40, 1.80 cm tall, dark hair), which matched Gudjón.

On 2 November, Detective Sigurbjörn Vídir and Karl Schütz went with interpreter Audur Gestsdóttir to Sídumúli Prison to interview Erla. Erla said she did not recall the name of the 'fourth man' in the car to Keflavík, but recalled Saevar having a piece of wood, which he used to hit Geirfinnur.

On 3 November, Kristján was interviewed and claimed to have remembered more. On the evening of 19 November 1974 he met Saevar at Vatnssígur, where they got into a Moskvitch car, but he did not recognize the driver. When they arrived in Keflavík, Kristján telephoned Geirfinnur from the Harbour Café and he soon arrived and they drove to the nearby slipway. He thought that a fight broke out between Saevar and Geirfinnur on board a boat, and he saw Saevar holding a club.[16] He now remembered that Geirfinnur's body was kept in the washroom at Grettisgata 82, where Kristján lived, for a few days without his knowledge until Saevar later showed it to him. Saevar then moved the body out of the house in a bag. Kristján said he could not recall whether he had been at Klúbburinn on 17 January 1974, and claimed he had never spoken with Geirfinnur until the evening of 19 January.

On 4 November, Schütz interviewed Saevar. He said Gudjón had collected him in his Citroen car. Kristján had Erla shoot Geirfinnur in the slipway. Saevar was presented with Erla's testimony that she had seen Sigurbjörn Eiríksson repeatedly hit Geirfinnur with a club. When asked where Geirfinnur's body had been moved to, he said to Thingvallavatn. He said he had been buried before in Grafningur. He was repeatedly challenged and complained that the police did not believe him, claiming that he had told the truth in his previous statements. On the way to Sídumúli Prison, Detectives Grétar Saemundsson and Ívar Hannesson told Saevar that he needed to produce something tangible, for example the location of Geirfinnur's body, to be believed, but was unable to do so.

On the same day, Schütz interviewed Erla, who had told Detective Sigurbjörn the day before that she had made the decision to receive three more months in custody because she was not ready to name the 'fourth man'. Erla asked: 'When can I see my child again?' She was told firmly that visits to see her daughter had nothing to do with her testimony

---

[16] Evidence Book XIV, pp. 694–695.

and 'She was reminded that these kinds of accusations could result in her being charged with making false accusations'.[17]

On 5 November, Kristján said he recalled that he could have been at Klúbburinn with Saevar on 17 November 1974. Saevar asked him to approach a man, who he thought was Geirfinnur, to sell him smuggled alcohol. Kristján claimed that his memory was poor that evening because he had taken a sleeping tablet (the story had shifted from buying to selling Geirfinnur alcohol, which matched Saevar's changed story).

On 8 November, Saevar requested an interview with Karl Schütz, as he wanted to tell the truth about where Geirfinnur's body was hidden, claiming it was hidden in Álftanes, which was a peninsular town in the eastern part of Reykjanes, located within Iceland's capital region. Saevar made a drawing and said he could definitely point to the location. The following day, detectives took Saevar to Álftanes to the place he had drawn, but Saevar was then unsure it was the right place. In an interview on 5 October, Albert Skaftason had pointed to Álftanes in connection with the location of Gudmundur Einarsson's body, which was not found.[18] This strongly suggests a cross-case contamination from the Gudmundur to the Geirfinnur case one month apart.

On 9 November, Kristján admitted having Erla's coat, stating that he had on 20 November 1974 taken it in from the car in which they had travelled to Keflavík the previous evening. He said Gudjón had not driven the passenger car to Keflavík, but thought he had driven the delivery van. According to this version of events, Kristján and Saevar had been driven to the Harbour Café, Kristján telephoned Geirfinnur, and when he arrived they drove to the slipway. He identified the 'chubby' man as Sigurbjörn Eiríksson and was sure he was on the slipway. A fight broke out between Geirfinnur, Saevar, Gudjón, and Sigurbjörn. Kristján prevented Geirfinnur from leaving and hit him in self-defence. Sigurbjörn held Geirfinnur by the head and Kristján hit Geirfinnur with a piece of wood on the shoulder. Gudjón then hit Geirfinnur with the piece of wood.

## GUDJÓN'S ARREST AND SUBSEQUENT INTERROGATIONS

12 November 1976, Gudjón was arrested in the early hours and interrogated between 07.25 and 13.10, using Schütz's 'Indian technique' (see Chapter 10). He was told for the first time that he was a suspect in

---

[17] Evidence Book XV, pp. 793–794. My italics. There was always the underlying threat that Erla could be charged with a criminal offence if she made any accusations against the investigators or retracted her previous statements.

[18] ICCRC Report, 2017, Albert Skaftason, Paragraph 238.

the Geirfinnur case, but he asserted that he had no knowledge of the disappearance of Geirfinnur. He was taken to Sídumúli Prison, where Karl Schütz interviewed Gudjón the following day. He now said that he had never heard Saevar talk about the Gudmundur and Geirfinnur cases, apart from once when Saevar claimed he knew everything about the Geirfinnur case (they were in the company of others at the time). Gudjón still denied having been at Vatnsstígur with Saevar and Erla, which he had been questioned about the previous May when he was not officially a suspect.

Gudjón's wife, Gudrún, was interviewed on 15 November for almost four hours. They had been married for nine years and separated in August 1975. During 1968–1972 the couple were teachers at Reykjanessskóli at Ísafjardardjúp. She knew Saevar as a pupil there for a short while: Gudjón was his teacher. They moved to Reykjavík in 1972, where Gudjón attended university. After separating in August 1975 she and Gudjón travelled abroad in the Citroen car, including several countries in Europe. She left Gudjón in Paris. After Gudjón was taken into custody in December 1975, 'he was not the same man'. By 1976 he had become temperamental – she thought the drug smuggling with Saevar had ruined his life.

Erla tentatively identified Gudjón Skarphédinsson as the 'fourth man' on 15 November.

On 16 November, Gudjón was interviewed and told Detective Grétar Saemundsson that he had taken a ferry to Norway on 20 August 1975 with his wife and daughter. Saevar was on the ferry. In early November, Saevar contacted Gudjón via a telegram while he was in France and they met in Luxembourg. Gudjón went home by ferry with Saevar and Ásgeir Ebenezer and his car was transported home separately with hidden drugs.

Schütz interviewed Gudjón on 18 November and told him he should tell them what he knew about the case, pointing out the accusations that Kristján, Saevar, and Erla had made against him. Gudjón said he would do his best to help, pointing out that he thought he had a good memory. Schütz told Gudjón that he seemed to have had an interest in the case, because he had made notes about it in his diary, which the police had found during a house search on the day he was arrested. Schütz pointed to further accusations that had been made against him regarding the Geirfinnur case. Gudjón said this was all fantasy and Schütz told him that he was not being helpful.

Saevar was interviewed on 25 November about the removal of Geirfinnur's body from Grettisgata 82. Saevar and Kristján had allegedly removed the body, and Erla had driven them in her and Saevar's Land Rover to Álftanesvegur and hidden the body in the lava field. Saevar said that the men who went to Keflavík were not pleased with the hiding place and therefore they moved the body to the Álftanes beach. Saevar was evasive about who had wanted the body removed but eventually gave two completely different names to those he had given previously. This suggests that about seven months after the 'four wrongly accused' were released he was still implying there had been some other men behind Geirfinnur's death.

On 28 November, Gudjón was taken to Vatnsstígur, the Keflavík slip-way, and the Harbour Café. He could not recall anything about Vatnsstígur and was reminded that he had earlier mentioned a Volkswagen car connected to Vatnsstígur. He replied: 'Yes I once went to Keflavík in a Volkswagen car.' He said he was the driver but could not give the date in November 1974 when it took place.

Gudjón gave his first confession on 29 November. The purpose of the interview was to ask him about what he had remembered after being taken to Vatnsstígur and Keflavík the previous day. Gudjón said he could not recall any meeting at Vatnsstígur, but he remembered that Erla came to his house in a Land Rover, but he drove Erla, Saevar, and Kristján to Keflavík in a Volkswagen, possibly a hire car. Gudjón explained his poor memory in terms of not having been mentally well at the time: 'In the spring of 1974 I was very excitable, irritable and fretful. In July I was traumatized when my father died in a road traffic accident and my daughter was injured. Around that time I had several nervous breakdowns. In the autumn I became depressed, apathetic and weak-minded'.[19]

Gudjón gave another statement the following day and said that on 19 November 1974 he drove a Fiat car, belonging to his mother-in-law, to Lambhól. He met Saevar there, who asked him to drive to Keflavík. He vaguely recalled a Volkswagen, which Saevar may have had. It was possible that he drove to Vatnsstígur and thought Erla and Saevar were with him. Gudjón said that he could have driven to the slipway, although he did not recognize it. In any case, it was dark and he had problems seeing things from a distance because of eyesight problems. He did not recall a fight, but on the way back to Reykjavík, Saevar had mentioned that he was now an 'accessory to murder', commenting 'Didn't you see it when we killed the man?'.

On 30 November, Erla appeared in Court before Örn Höskuldsson and informed him that Saevar had told her to mention the names of Magnús, Sigurbjörn, Valdimar, Einar, and others if implicated in the case, in order to draw attention away from the truly guilty persons (i.e. Saevar, Kristján, and Gudjón). This alleged collusion led to perjury charges (i.e. giving false statements against the 'four wrongly accused').

---

[19] Evidence Book XV, p. 850.

On 3 December, Erla claimed that she had driven her Land Rover to Gudjón's home on 19 November 1974 where the car was left because of electrical failure. In view of this, she and Saevar went to the Geysir car hire at Laugavegur in Reykjavík and got a light blue Volkswagen and drove to Vatnsstígur where she met Kristján and Gudjón. Gudjón drove them in the Volkswagen to Keflavík. (The police checked all car hire companies in Reykjavík but failed to find the names of the accused.)

It was pointed out to Gudjón on 6 December that it was a criminal offence to implicate people wrongly. He was then asked if he knew whether the four released men had anything to do with the case. Gudjón said the others had wrongly implicated them. They were now finally out of the case, after having been released from custody the previous May.

Saevar informed the police on 8 December that Sigurdur Óttar Hreinsson had driven a van to Keflavík on 19 November 1974 to collect the smuggled alcohol. He later became an important prosecution witness against Saevar, Kristján, and Gudjón.

Saevar gave a long statement on 9 December 1976. He had heard Geirfinnur's name in relation to the smuggling of alcohol. On Sunday 17 November 1974 he and Kristján met Geirfinnur in Klúbburinn. Saevar pretended he was interested in buying the alcohol, but his real motive was to find out where it was kept and steal it. Geirfinnur wrote down his name and address but not his telephone number. Saevar later asked Gudjón to get involved, and Erla and Saevar hired a light blue Volkswagen car. They paid the car hire receptionist kr. 5,000 and asked him not to make a formal contract. After the film show at Kjarvalsstadir, they changed cars (from Land Rover to Volkswagen) and went to Gudjón's house.

They then drove to Vatnsstígur and from there to Keflavík. Saevar had with him kr. 70,000, which he was prepared to pay Geirfinnur for information.[20] Saevar and Kristján went into the Harbour Café. Geirfinnur was not there. They did not immediately make a phone call from the Harbour Café. They drove around, went into a nearby petrol station to make the phone call, but it was too busy so went back to the Harbour Café, and Saevar gave Kristján the piece of paper with Geirfinnur's telephone number on it. Geirfinnur soon arrived and got into the car and Saevar showed him the kr. 70,000 and asked him to tell him where the alcohol was kept. Geirfinnur took the money but then said he thought he was buying alcohol from us and threw the money on the floor in the car, stating 'I know Sigurbjörn and you and the others in Klúbburinn'. They later started fighting in the slipway

---

[20] Evidence Book XV, pp. 926–936.

and Gudjón joined in. Kristján put his arm around Geirfinnur's neck from behind. Saevar hit Geirfinnur's legs with a piece of wood, followed by Gudjón hitting him with the wood. They put Geirfinnur's body upright in the back of the car. Erla looked scared so Saevar gave her kr. 5,000 for a taxi to Reykjavík.

On 13 December, Erla, who was still in custody, told police that a few days after Geirfinnur was killed in the slipway and his body hidden in the Red Hills (*Rauðhólar*), Saevar told her in the company of Kristján and Gudjón that if anybody asked, then tell them the Klúbburinn men were responsible, suggesting a conspiracy to pervert the course of justice.[21]

## THEMATIC ANALYSIS OF THE SUCCESSIVE ACCOUNTS

I used thematic analysis (Braun & Clarke, 2006) to identify, analyse, and report pertinent themes within the statements, using a 'bottom up' approach (i.e. themes derived from the data rather than theory).

### Early general themes

The general themes that emerged from the early interviews were: (a) At least one car and a delivery van had gone to Keflavík. (b) The purpose of the trip was to purchase smuggled alcohol from Geirfinnur (this was to change later). (c) The car driver was variously referred to as either Einar or Magnús, driving a Fiat. (d) The delivery van driver was not identified, although in his second statement Kristján thought it was Valdimar. (e) Geirfinnur was seen as being uncooperative and needed to be dealt with firmly. (f) There were several people said to be present on the slipway. This included Jón Ragnarsson and Ásgeir Eiríksson and many others who were not arrested or interviewed in relation to what had allegedly happened there. Ásgeir was interviewed under caution on 8 March 1976 in connection with being suspected of having been in possession of smuggled alcohol and his association with Einar, Magnús, Valdimar, and Sigurbjörn). (g) Some people, including Geirfinnur, had gone on board a boat to collect the smuggled alcohol from the sea. (h) Geirfinnur had fallen into the sea, either by accident or during a fight, as a result of which he had died. (On 20 April 1976, Kristján gave a statement claiming that he had seen a group of people surrounding a person [Geirfinnur] on the slipway, who looked frightened

---

[21] Evidence Book XV, pp. 957–961.

and had blood on their face – the crime scene had now moved to the shore, supported by Erla's confession statement on 4 May that she had shot Geirfinnur there).[22]

It is evident from the early statements that the focus was on implicating Einar, Magnús, Valdimar, and Sigurbjörn. Once they were released from custody, and particularly in the autumn of 1976, the focus shifted on to Saevar, Kristján, and Gudjón implicating themselves and each other in the murder of Geirfinnur, with the support of Erla and Sigurdur Óttar.

There was one surprising omission in the early statements of Erla, Saevar, and Kristján: none of the suspects referred to the Harbour Café and having made a phone call to Geirfinnur's home. This was first mentioned in a statement on 7 September 1976, after detectives had taken Kristján to the Harbour Café, which he then thought he had recognized. From then onward the Harbour Café featured as a key theme.

**Note:** If this event did take place, why did none of the suspects volunteer this pertinent information in their many early statements? This omission undermines the credibility of the entire story.

Another important omission is the general absence in the suspects' statements of the lighting conditions on the slipway. There are vague references to darkness and some light, but no proper description of the fact that the slipway is likely to have been very dark with poor visibility. In spite of this the suspects gave descriptions of people, actions, and even facial expressions.

The final story was that Erla, Saevar, and Gudjón had picked up Kristján at Vatnsstígur in a hired Volkswagen. Gudjón was the driver and Sigurdur Óttar accompanied them in a Mercedes-Benz van. The Volkswagen picked up Geirfinnur from the Harbour Café, and then went to the slipway, where the delivery van was parked: Sigurdur Óttar's role was to transport the smuggled alcohol to Reykjavík.

### The Clay Head

The general theme was that the stranger who entered the Harbour Café shortly after 22.00 on 19 November to make a phone call was involved in Geirfinnur's disappearance. During the Keflavík investigation (Chapter 7), the clay head was thought to resemble Magnús Leópoldsson, and had allegedly been made from a picture of him (Jónasson, 1996), but once he was out of the case for good, a new person had to be identified and Karl Schütz decided that Kristján was the person portrayed by the clay head. The Supreme Court decided that either Kristján or

---

[22] Evidence Book XII, pp. 192–195.

Saevar had made the phone call to Geirfinnur from the Harbour Café (Supreme Court Judgement, p. 24), which was surprising, given the two men differed greatly in their appearance and stature: Kristján was exceptionally tall (190 cm or six feet and three inches), and Saevar was very short (165 cm or five feet and five inches), and neither were positively identified by witnesses as having been in the Harbour Café.

## Motive

Kristján, Saevar, and Gudjón allegedly attacked Geirfinnur on the Keflavík slipway. The motive was said to be to force him to reveal the location of smuggled alcohol, which they intended to steal and transport back to Reykjavík. In later statements, Kristján and Saevar eventually admitted that they had met Geirfinnur in Klúbburinn on 17 November 1974, and discussed the purchase of alcohol, but somehow Geirfinnur had misunderstood this and wanted to purchase alcohol from them. Thus, Geirfinnur's death resulted from a misunderstanding.

## Death

How Geirfinnur allegedly died always remained vague: even during the re-enactment, Erla and the three suspects could not agree. The early stories variously focused on Geirfinnur falling overboard, accidentally or during a fight, or in an incident on the shore, where he was variously, shot, strangled, hit, or beaten with a club. At one point, Kristján gave a statement saying that Geirfinnur had accidentally fallen over a cliff by the slipway. The vagueness and lack of a consistent and coherent story about what happened to Geirfinnur on the slipway undermines the confessions' credibility.

## Memory Problems

Kristján and Gudjón repeatedly complained of memory problems. The development of Gudjón's memory problems over time is well documented from the interview statements and his personal diaries (see Chapter 17).

## THE KEFLAVÍK SLIPWAY RE-ENACTMENT

On 23 January 1977, shortly before Karl Schütz completed his investigation, there was a staged re-enactment at the Keflavík slipway of what had allegedly taken place there on 19 November 1974. The purpose appears to have been to 'wrap up' the Geirfinnur investigation by getting the witnesses and suspects together at the slipway to re-enact what each of them believed had taken place in order to synchronize their testimony. This was without legal representation and hazardous with regard to potential contamination of evidence. Re-enactments are more common in inquisitorial than adversarial investigations and have come under criticism, for example in Thailand.[23] The chief justice of the Supreme Court in Thailand described re-enactments as 'an imaginative model of how crime is committed'.[24]

According to the District Court Judgement, those present during the re-enactment were the defendants: Saevar, Kristján, Gudjón, and Erla, and a witness, Sigurdur Óttar. The police report described the re-enactment as revealing major inconsistencies in the details provided by the defendants. The position of the individual cars was also determined. Sigurdur Óttar described the location of the van he had supposedly driven to Keflavík to collect the merchandise for Kristján, but the location was inconsistent with those mentioned by the defendants. Sigurdur Óttar said he had not observed or directly witnessed what had happened on the slipway.

The BBC journalist, Simon Cox, revealed in 2014 the most dramatic photograph of the re-enactment:[25]

> The first few are negatives of the harbour but then an astounding image appears. It's an A5 black and white photo of one of the suspects, Kristján Vidarsson, pretending to strangle a middle-aged policeman who is playing the part of Geirfinnur. Crime reconstructions are common but getting the suspected killers to re-enact an offence they can't remember shows how desperate the police had become in their struggle to find any evidence.

## THE OVERLAP WITH GUDMUNDUR AGNARSSON'S 'FALSE' CONFESSION

Table 9.2 shows the considerable overlap between the confessions of Erla, Saevar, and Kristján with those of Gudmundur Agnarsson, who in October 1975 had confessed to seeing Geirfinnur drown in the sea off

---

[23] *Phuket Gazette*, 14 June 2013.
[24] http://www.nationmultimedia.com/news/national/aec/30208456 (last accessed 24 January 2018).
[25] *The Reykjavik Confessions*, BBC 15 May 2014 (http://www.bbc.co.uk/news/special/2014/ newsspec_7617/index.html, last accessed 24 January 2018).

**Table 9.2**    Gudmundur Agnarsson's confessions in October 1975
and a comparison with the suspects' subsequent statements

1. Gudmundur Agnarsson went to Keflavík slipway at the request of
   Sigurbjörn Eiríksson. The purpose was to collect smuggled alcohol from the
   sea off the Keflavík harbour.
       **Note:** In his first statement, Saevar referred to Magnús Leópoldsson and
   Einar Bollason inviting him to go with them to Keflavík to collect alcohol
   from the sea. Saevar, Kristján and Erla later referred to Sigurbjörn Eiríksson.
2. Gudmundur Agnarsson and Magnús were due to meet Geirfinnur at the
   Harbour Café, but they were late so Magnús telephoned Geirfinnur from
   the Harbour Café.
       **Note:** On 7 September 1976, Kristján was taken to the Harbour Café and
   recalled having made a phone call from there to Geirfinnur.
3. Gudmundur Agnarsson went in a boat with Geirfinnur to collect the
   merchandise from the sea.
       **Note:** In his first statement, Saevar referred to Geirfinnur collecting
   smuggled alcohol by boat off the Keflavík harbour.
4. Gudmundur Agnarsson mentioned several men were on the slipway when
   he arrived, including Sigurbjörn Eiríksson and Magnús Leópoldsson, but
   he provided no details of the other men.
       **Note:** In his first statement, Saevar referred to Magnús Leópoldsson.
5. Two cars are specified: a hospital car and a Range Rover driven by Magnús
   Leópoldsson.
       **Note:** In her first statement, dated 23 January 1974, Erla refers to a car
   and a large delivery van. Magnús was the car's driver. On the same day,
   Kristján gave a statement referring to a large Mercedes-Benz delivery van
   being driven to Keflavík harbour.
6. Geirfinnur dived into the sea to get the alcohol, but on the third trip down
   did not return. Gudmundur Agnarsson said he waited four hours for
   Geirfinnur to return from the sea, but he did not.
       **Note:** In his first statement, Saevar referred to Geirfinnur having fallen
   overboard from a boat by accident and drowned.
7. Only Sigurbjörn Eiríksson was left on the slipway when Gudmundur
   Agnarsson returned from the sea without Geirfinnur.
       **Note:** In his first statement, Saevar referred to only Magnús Leópoldsson
   being at the harbour when he and Einar Bollason returned there (i.e. as in
   Gudmundur Agnarsson's statement, only one person remained there).
8. Gudmundur Agnarsson had done a similar previous trip before and was
   paid kr. 70,000, with Geirfinnur diving into the sea.
       **Note:** In a statement dated 9 December 1976, Saevar offered Geirfinnur
   kr. 70,000 for the smuggled merchandise and showed him the money.

Keflavík harbour while collecting smuggled alcohol (see Chapter 7).
The consistent themes from the two sets of statements were:
• The references to the slipway and Harbour Café;
• The presence of the two people from Klúbburinn, Sigurbjörn
  Eiríksson and Magnús Leópoldsson;
• Geirfinnur going out to sea to collect the smuggled alcohol;

- Geirfinnur not being at the Harbour Café at the pre-arranged time, and a phone call being made from the Harbour Café to Geirfinnur's home;
- There being an accident at sea regarding Geirfinnur;
- The reference to kr. 70,000 (about £580 at the time).

The reasons for these similarities are not clear. Gudmundur Agnarsson claimed that he had made up details from public rumours at the time, and of course, Erla, Saevar, and Kristján may have done the same. However, the Reykjavík Team were aware of Mr Agnarsson's 1975 confession, and indeed interviewed him about it in February 1976. Research demonstrates that investigators do sometimes communicate, either wittingly or unwittingly, salient case details to suspects (Garrett, 2011; Gudjonsson, 2003a).

The most suspicious detail is the amount of money connected to the smuggling, which was not in the public domain at the time; it seems unlikely that Saevar would have guessed the precise amount of kr. 70,000 so correctly.

There were some salient differences in the defendants' accounts, including who was meant to receive the kr. 70,000 (Gudmundur Agnarsson versus Geirfinnur) and Erla, Saevar, and Kristján did not make any reference in their statements to Geirfinnur diving into the sea for the alcohol. Mr Agnarsson did not make a reference to an altercation on the slipway, which featured in the later statements of the convicted persons.

It is also important to note that in Agnarsson's confession he was an active participant in the events (i.e. arranged a boat and took Geirfinnur out to sea to collect the contraband). In contrast, in their early statements Saevar and Kristján appear to have been present merely as passive bystanders of the dealings of the 'four wrongly accused' with Geirfinnur, their role being primarily to help bring back the contraband to Reykjavík and distribute it.

## THE PRESS CONFERENCE: THE OFFICIAL VERSION OF WHAT HAPPENED

In January 1977, Schütz completed his final report in the Geirfinnur case and concluded:

> There are no grounds for doubting that the deed and antecedents, as described in the confessions, are correct. With this in mind it can be assumed that the outcome of the investigation approached certainty.
> (Working Group Report, 2013, p. 123)

On 2 February 1977, Karl Schütz had completed his investigation and he and members of his Task Force attended a press conference where Schütz outlined his investigative strategy and the key findings over two and a half hours. These were reported in detail the following day in Iceland's leading newspaper, *Morgunbladid* (pp. 20, 21, 24, and 25). Schütz announced that the investigation had produced good results and the Geirfinnur case was now solved, although the outcome was not 100% successful due to the failure to find the body or any forensic evidence to link the suspects to Geirfinnur's disappearance. The evidence was based on the confessions of five people: three suspects (Saevar, Kristján, and Gudjón) and two witnesses (Erla and Sigurdur Óttar):

> From our side, there is no doubt; we are completely certain that these people are telling the truth in their confessions.
> *(Morgunbladid,* 3 February 1977, p. 25)

> We criminal specialists are satisfied when cases have been successfully solved, the guilty persons found, and wrongly accused men are cleared.
> *(Morgunbladid,* 3 February 1977, p. 25)

Schütz pointed out that when he started work in the summer of 1976 he set up a Task Force of 12 people, which focused primarily on the Geirfinnur case. A special card reference system had been set up with the names of 1,200 people, which investigative judge Örn Höskuldsson arranged to be computerized along with all case documents.

In terms of investigative strategy, Schütz explained that for the first two months, the Task Force focused on finding witnesses who could help explain what had happened to Geirfinnur. This proved unsuccessful for two reasons. Firstly, it was now almost two years since Geirfinnur's disappearance and people recalled little of relevance from that period, and secondly, the friends and associates of the suspects were, for various reasons, considered unreliable informants, in my view because they did not provide information that fitted the police investigators' hypotheses at any given point in time.

For these reasons the focus had shifted onto the suspects, using methods that Schütz had used in Germany, including the 'Indian technique' he had taught the Icelandic investigators (see Chapter 10). According to Schütz, they now found some solid points, but the investigators had to be very vigilant, because Saevar, Kristján, and Erla were allegedly cunning and repeatedly lied.

Schütz said that when Gudjón Skarphédinsson was arrested in November 1976 after Saevar had implicated him, the Task Force had their 'first reliable witness' (*Morgunbladid,* 3 February 1976, p. 25). This was in spite of the fact that over many days Gudjón denied any involvement in the case. Once he began to incriminate himself and Saevar and Kristján, he never had a clear recollection of what supposedly took place on the slipway. His credibility appears to have been due to his being seen as cooperative, not actively lying, but reluctant to reveal the full truth of what had happened to Geirfinnur. It probably also helped that he was well educated, spoke German, and was always respectful to the investigators.

There is evidence that Schütz did not believe that Gudjón's memory gaps were genuine. In his report on 7 January 1977, which on 12 January Chief Judge Halldór Thorbjörnsson forwarded to the Minister of Justice, Ólafur Jóhannesson, Schütz wrote:

> But this 'interrogation' is in sharp contrast with the previous – successful – tactic used by the Commission [Task Force] to convince the accused that it would be best to tell the whole truth and that his supposed 'memory gaps' are not at all credible.

The 'interrogation' Schütz was referring to was the lie detector test I had given Gudjón on 31 December 1976, which made him doubt his involvement in the case (see Chapter 17).

According to Schütz, the second solid lead in the case came in December 1976 when Saevar implicated Kristján's cousin, Sigurdur Óttar Hreinsson, whose role was to collect the smuggled alcohol from the Keflavík slipway:

> And later we found Sigurdur Óttar Hreinsson, the delivery van driver, and now the investigation gained momentum.
> (*Morgunbladid*, 3 February 1977, p. 25)

At the press conference Schütz described in detail the sequence of events regarding Geirfinnur's disappearance, which is as follows:

On Sunday 17 November 1974, Saevar and Kristján went to Klúbburinn to steal the wallets of intoxicated men, and met Geirfinnur, who was there with two of his friends. When Geirfinnur said his name, Saevar realized that he was the man from Keflavík who was known for selling smuggled alcohol. Saevar introduced himself as Magnús Leópoldsson, Klúbburinn's managing director. He offered to purchase alcohol, but Geirfinnur may have thought that he was offering to sell him alcohol. Saevar's intention was to steal the alcohol after Geirfinnur had revealed its location.[26] Geirfinnur gave Saevar his address so he could contact him.

---

[26] It is surprising that Karl Schütz should have believed and relied on such an unlikely story.

The following day, Saevar got Geirfinnur's telephone number from the national telecommunication service and later that day phoned him from Gudjón's home. A child answered and said that Geirfinnur was not at home. Saevar had told Gudjón that he had to meet somebody in Keflavík for business and asked Gudjón to go with him. Saevar then contacted Kristján and also asked him to come along the following day to Keflavík to steal alcohol but needed him to arrange a delivery van for the merchandise. Kristján contacted Sigurdur Óttar, who had access to a light coloured Mercedes-Benz van.

At around dinner time on 19 November Saevar spoke to Geirfinnur on the telephone and arranged to meet him later that evening by the Harbour Café. Geirfinnur did not seem very interested on the phone and Saevar thought they might need to be tough with him if he started wasting their time. After the phone call, Erla drove Saevar and his mother to a film show at Kjarvalsstadir in her Land Rover. When the festival ended, Erla dropped Saevar's mother off at her home and then drove to Hjallavegur where Erla lived. Parked outside was a light blue Volkswagen car that Saevar and Erla had hired the day before from Geysir car hire company at Laugavegur. There was allegedly no contract for the car hire because Erla promised to clean the assistant's flat and gave him kr. 5,000 (about £40.00 at the time) in total, which was allegedly for his own use.[27]

Erla drove the Volkswagen car to Gudjón's place, but he was not at home and they found him visiting friends at Lambhól in Reykjavík. From there they drove to Vatnsstígur to pick up Kristján. The Mercedes-Benz van arrived there at about the same time and they all headed for Keflavík to meet Geirfinnur, having told Sigurdur Óttar to meet them on the slipway and wait for them. Gudjón drove the Volkswagen with Erla, Saevar, and Kristján as passengers. They stopped at the Harbour Café and Saevar and Kristján went inside to look for Geirfinnur but could not find him.[28] They then drove to the slipway to make sure Sigurdur Óttar was there and he was. Saevar then went into a small café nearby to phone Geirfinnur but it was too busy so they drove back to the Harbour Café and Kristján made the phone call. Geirfinnur's son answered and called his father, who told Kristján he had already been to the Harbour Café but would go there again; it was only a few minutes' walk away.[29]

---

[27] This story emerged after the police had failed to find any contract to support the car hire story. Gudjón had introduced the Volkswagen in one of his interviews and this is the story the police believed.

[28] Schütz was surprised that nobody in the Harbour Café had noticed the two men together because Kristján was exceptionally tall and Saevar was very short. Schütz said this demonstrated how much people forgot things over time. The most likely explanation is that neither of them went into the Harbour Café that night.

[29] Schütz and Örn Höskuldsson had identified Kristján as the 'clay head' (*Leirfinnur*).

When Geirfinnur arrived he got into the back of the Volkswagen and they drove to the slipway. It was around 22.30 and a misunderstanding had emerged. Saevar wanted to buy the smuggled alcohol, but so did Geirfinnur. Saevar thought Geirfinnur was bluffing and handed him kr. 70,000, which Geirfinnur threw over the front seat. When they arrived at the slipway they all left the Volkswagen and Geirfinnur walked away. Gudjón tried to stop him and a fight broke out, which escalated. It was dark and the suspects did not give a consistent story of what occurred, but Kristján held Geirfinnur by the neck from behind and Saevar hit Geirfinnur's legs and stomach with a club. Kristján then hit Geirfinnur in the chest and on the chin. When this happened all three suspects and Erla were present, but Sigurdur Óttar was in the van parked some distance away and did not see what had happened. Geirfinnur was lying dead on the ground and Sigurdur Óttar was told to leave. Saevar told Erla to 'hitch hike' back home, because they needed the back seat for Geirfinnur's body. Instead, Erla stayed overnight in a nearby empty house, later identified as the Red Mill, and went back the following day. Geirfinnur's head was propped up in the back seat by Erla's coat, which she had left behind in the Volkswagen car. Geirfinnur's body was then transported to Kristján's home at Grettisgata in Reykjavík where they hid it for a day and a half in a washroom in the basement, which was not in regular use. On Thursday 21 November, Saevar, Erla, and Kristján met and moved the body in the Land Rover to the Red Hills where they dug a grave, poured petrol over Geirfinnur's body, burned it, and then covered it up.

At the press conference, Örn Höskuldsson said that there was evidence from Saevar, Kristján, and Erla that they had colluded to implicate the 'four wrongly accused' (Sigurbjörn Eiríksson, Magnús Leópoldsson, Einar Bollason, and Valdimar Olsen) if any of them were picked up by police. According to Saevar, this agreement first took place at the end of 1974 when rumours were spreading about the involvement of Sigurbjörn Eiríksson and Magnús Leópoldsson in Geirfinnur's disappearance. Örn Höskuldsson pointed out that falsely implicating the four people was a criminal offence.

## THE CONVICTIONS

Verbal submissions were heard in the District Court between 3 and 7 October 1977 with the guilty verdicts being announced on 19 December. At the trial, Saevar, Kristján, and Erla gave speeches. Both men proclaimed their innocence in the cases and Erla said that her sincere hope was that 'the truth would come out'. Saevar's final words about

**Table 9.3**  The Supreme Court's version of the facts in the Geirfinnur Einarsson case

On 17 November, two days before Geirfinnur's disappearance, Kristján and Saevar met Geirfinnur at Klúbburinn. Geirfinnur had agreed to sell them black market alcohol.

On the evening of 19 November, Kristján, Saevar, Erla, and Gudjón drove to Keflavík in a hired Volkswagen. Kristján's cousin, Sigurdur Óttar Hreinsson, accompanied them in a delivery van for the purpose of transporting the alcohol.

It was either Kristján or Saevar who made the phone call to Geirfinnur from the Harbour Café, at about 22.15.

Kristján, Saevar, and Gudjón attacked Geirfinnur on the Keflavík slipway. The motive was said to be to force him to reveal the location of his own smuggled alcohol, which they intended to steal and transport back to Reykjavík.

Geirfinnur was killed. Saevar, Kristján, and Gudjón took his body to Kristján's home at Grettisgata 82, Reykjavík, and kept it in the basement for two days. Erla returned home from Keflavík in the early hours of 20 November, after hitching lifts from two different drivers.

Saevar, Kristján, and Erla later transferred the body to another location – possibly the 'Red Hills' lava field on the southeastern outskirts of Reykjavík. Geirfinnur's body has never been found.

The Court concluded that Erla, Saevar, and Kristján had agreed soon after Geirfinnur's murder to implicate the 'four falsely accused' (Sigurbjörn Eiríksson, Magnús Leópoldsson, Einar Bollason, and Valdimar Olsen) if they were apprehended in the Geirfinnur case.

Erla, Saevar, Kristján, and Sigurdur Óttar all retracted their confession statements, but the Court did not accept their retractions.

the conduct of his case were: 'This is brainwashing, this is mental torture' (Sigtryggur Sigtryggsson, *Morgunbladid*, 9 March 2017).[30]

Verbal submissions were heard in the Supreme Court between 14 and 23 January 1980. The Judgement was announced on 22 February 1980.

Table 9.3 gives the Supreme Court version of what happened to Geirfinnur. It is very similar to the version given at the press conference on 2 February 1977. Table 9.4 shows the convictions and sentences. The sentences were given jointly in the Gudmundur and Geirfinnur cases. Saevar and Kristján were found guilty of killing both men. Tryggvi was found guilty of killing Gudmundur, and Gudjón of killing Geirfinnur. Erla Bolladóttir was convicted of giving false testimony with regard to the 'four wrongly accused' in the Geirfinnur

---

[30] http://www.mbl.is/frettir/innlent/2017/03/09/thetta_er_andleg_pining/ (last accessed 24 January 2018).

**Table 9.4**   The convictions and sentences in the Gudmundur Einarsson and
Geirfinnur Einarsson cases (Supreme Court Judgement, 22 February 1980)

**Saevar Ciesielski**. Convicted of manslaughter in the Gudmundur and
   Geirfinnur cases, and for perjury with regard to the 'four wrongly accused'.
   Sentenced to 17 years in prison.
**Kristján Vidarsson**. Convicted of manslaughter in the Gudmundur and
   Geirfinnur cases, and for perjury with regard to the 'four wrongly accused'.
   Sentenced to 16 years in prison.
**Tryggvi Leifsson**. Convicted of manslaughter in the Gudmundur case and
   sentenced to 13 years in prison.
**Gudjón Skarphédinsson**. Convicted of manslaughter in the Geirfinnur case
   and sentenced to 10 years in prison.
**Erla Bolladóttir**. Convicted of perjury with regard to the 'four wrongly
   accused' and sentenced to three years in prison.
**Albert Skaftason**. Convicted of participating in interfering with the crime
   scene and sentenced to 12 months in prison.

case (i.e. perjury), along with Saevar and Kristján. Albert was found
guilty of participating in interfering with the crime scene in the
Gudmundur case.

## CONCLUSIONS

It is evident from this review that the Reykjavík Team were interested
in Saevar's possible knowledge about the Geirfinnur case soon after
Erla was released from custody on 20 December 1975, following her
implicating Saevar and Kristján in the Gudmundur case.

On 30 December 1975, Erla was taken to Sídumúli Prison where she
was kept for about five hours. The following day senior prosecutor
Hallvardur Einvardsson requested the papers in the Geirfinnur case
from the Keflavík Sheriff's Department and received them on 5 January
1976. This sequence of events is unlikely to be a coincidence and suggests that the police and prosecutor were taking an interest in the
Geirfinnur case prior to Erla complaining of the frightening phone calls.

The early recorded interrogations focused on establishing who had
been on the Keflavík slipway on the evening of 19 November 1974. The
investigators showed Erla, Saevar, and Kristján a large number of photos of men who might have been on the slipway, but they were selective
in whom they arrested. For example, apart from Magnús Leópoldsson,
Einar Bollason, Valdimar Olsen, and Sigurbjörn Eiríksson, Jón
Ragnarsson was mentioned very early on as having been on the slipway, but he was not arrested or even interviewed as far as one can

gather from the case papers. The implication is that the investigators were focusing on specific individuals that supported their working hypothesis. I strongly suspect that their focus was primarily on Sigurbjörn Eiríksson and Magnús Leópoldsson, but others were needed to bridge the gap between Saevar/Kristján and the two 'club men'. Einar Bollason and Valdimar Olsen served that important function (see Chapter 12).

The pressure to solve the case was building up as the investigators failed to find corroborative evidence to link the 'four wrongly accused' to Geirfinnur's disappearance, which led Erla on 3 May 1976 to be brought to Sídumúli Prison for interrogation, and the following day giving a written statement confessing to shooting Geirfinnur. On 5 May the suspects' face-to-face confrontation meeting was arranged between Erla, Saevar, and Kristján, which went disastrously wrong, leading three years later to a duress investigation.

On 9 May the 'four wrongly accused' were released from custody. Erla, Saevar, and Kristján often gave inconsistent accounts, repeatedly changing their version of events and the details: the police had a very hard time trying to corroborate anything they said. The investigation was truly in crisis and Karl Schütz was brought in from Germany to assist with the case and set up the Reykjavík Task Force, which focused principally on the Geirfinnur case.

It is noteworthy that in the autumn of 1976, Sigurbjörn Eiríksson's name still featured in the suspects' statements, suggesting that he remained 'a person of interest' long after he had been released from custody. This changed after Gudjón stated on 8 December that the four released men had nothing to do with the case. The four men were now finally out of the case, leading Erla and Saevar to give statements claiming that they had agreed to implicate the four men if any of the three of them were caught, leading to perjury charges and convictions.

A consistent feature of the statements from Erla, Saevar, Kristján, and Gudjón, is their vagueness, changeability, and lack of tangible detail and completeness. The story was clearly obtained piecemeal, and the accounts twist and turn to fit the latest police theories and information. The absence of expected salient information is also worrying. This includes there being no reference to the Harbour Café until the suspects were taken there many months after giving their first confession statements, and apparently the general absence of any reference to the lighting conditions on the slipway. Taken together, these factors cast doubt on the credibility of the suspects' stories and suggest that they were describing a hypothetical, rather than a real-life event.

I have not come across a reference to the 'Indian technique' in the literature, and have never heard of its use, apart from in the Gudmundur and Geirfinnur investigation. According to Karl Schütz, it began to be used once the Task Force had shifted their focus from seeking witnesses to Geirfinnur's disappearance, which had proved fruitless, to breaking down the suspects' resistance and 'lies', using methods that Schütz had previously used in Germany with success.

The Task Force allegedly found some 'solid points', which Schütz said could be tested during the formal face-to-face confrontation meetings between the suspects, which functioned as police pressure by proxy. These face-to-face confrontations were numerous and I have seen no evidence that they were effective in eliciting the truth, although they may have played a role in harmonizing the suspects' contradictory statements. The final focus was on finding the drivers of the passenger car and the delivery van referred to by Erla, Saevar, and Kristján, which eventually led to the arrest of Gudjón and an incriminating witness statement from Sigurdur Óttar Hreinsson. These were the two key witnesses in the eventual convictions of Saevar, Kristján, and Gudjón.

At the end of his investigation, Karl Schütz outlined the 'evidence' at a press conference on 2 February 1977, claiming the case was solved and expressing confidence in the guilt of the three suspects. It is clear that both the District Court and the Supreme Court relied substantially on Mr Schütz's investigative hypotheses, bias, and flimsy findings.

I will now turn to what is known about Karl Schütz and his methods.

# 10

# Misguiding Force

*Meanwhile it had been discovered that Judge Birgir Thormar, in collaboration with the young former police officer and currently a psychology student, Gisli Gudjonsson, had devised a so-called psychological test that he had previously applied to the accused*[1]

In this chapter I discuss the background, role, and character of Karl Schütz, who dominated the Gudmundur and Geirfinnur investigation after his arrival in Iceland on 28 July 1976. He came from Germany to work full-time on the cases over a six-month period. I had a number of interactions with him in the summer of 1976 and we worked on the same enquiry team for a short while during the investigation into the murder of Lovísa Kristjánsdóttir on 26 August 1976, which was unrelated to the other two cases. Schütz's forceful character and methods set the tone for the Gudmundur and Geirfinnur investigation and its conclusion.

---

[1] Karl Schütz's reaction to finding out at the beginning of January 1977 that I had administered a lie detector test to Gudjón while he had been on a Christmas vacation in Germany (see Chapter 17).

---

*The Psychology of False Confessions: Forty Years of Science and Practice*, First Edition.
Gisli H. Gudjonsson.
© 2018 John Wiley & Sons Ltd. Published 2018 by John Wiley & Sons Ltd.

## KARL SCHÜTZ'S PROFESSIONAL BACKGROUND

Little is known about Karl Schütz's career during the Second World War. According to his book with journalist Jürgen Neven-du Mont (*Kleinstadtmörder: Spur 1081*), he had been held in a British prisoner of war camp in Italy (Neven-du Mont & Schütz, 1977).[2] I have no information about his military record. He would have been in his late twenties at the beginning of the Second World War.

In an interview with the Icelandic *Tíminn* newspaper, published on 5 February 1977 (pp. 1–3), Schütz said that he began to work as an ordinary policeman in the northern part of West Germany (Slésvík-Holstein) in 1946. While in the police he studied police science and after completing his studies he moved to criminal investigations. He was later appointed to the Federal Criminal Police Office (Bundeskriminalamt; BKA) to investigate major crimes and espionage cases. The *Tíminn* journalist who interviewed Schütz asked him to mention his most memorable cases. These included: (a) a criminal investigation against the *Spiegel* magazine for treason; (b) the shooting of five soldiers at an armoury in Lebach; (c) espionage cases; and (d) the investigation into the members of the Baader-Meinhof group, who were a group of extremist socialists in the late sixties and early seventies who rebelled against capitalistic society with attacks on individuals and companies having a Nazi past (Smith & Moncourt, 2009). Karl Schütz said in the *Tíminn* article on 5 February 1977 (pp. 1–3) that he had spent a long time on the Baader-Meinhof investigation. I will briefly discuss three of these investigations, because they give a good insight into Schütz's status in Germany, as well as his investigative methods and demeanour.

## THE *SPIEGEL* INVESTIGATION

On the 21 September 2012, *Spiegel Online* published an article in English about the '50th Anniversary of the "SPIEGEL Affair": A Watershed Moment for West German Democracy'.[3] The case involved *Der Spiegel's* alleged betrayal of state secrets in a previously published

---

[2] The book by Jürgen Neven-du Mont and Karl Schütz was first published by Hoffmann u. Campe, Hamburg 1971, ISBN 3-455-05610-5. An Icelandic translation of the book was published in Reykjavík by Setberg in 1977, titled *Sakamál 1081*.

[3] http://www.spiegel.de/international/germany/50th-anniversary-of-the-spiegel-affair-a-857030-2.html (last accessed 24 January 2018).

article (i.e. a treasonable offence). The case had serious political repercussions, with the head of the Defence Ministry, Franz Josef Strauss, having to resign, and Konrad Adenauer almost losing his chancellorship. Karl Schütz played a big role in the investigation:

> At 9:30 p.m. that day [26 October 1962], police led by Karl Schütz stormed SPIEGEL headquarters in Hamburg as the editorial team was working on the new issue. Police vans surrounded the building. Before long, the 117 rooms and 3,000 square meters (32,000 square feet) of office space were occupied. Phone calls were prohibited, and the magazine's work came to a halt. All the rooms were supposed to be vacated and sealed off. The journalists were cut off from the outside world.[3]

Strauss's downfall was that he had interfered with the criminal investigation by telephoning the German military attaché in Madrid during the night and demanding that he immediately arrest Ahlers, the lead author of the alleged treasonable article in *Der Spiegel*, falsely claiming that he had been acting on behalf of Chancellor Adenauer. He lied to parliament about his actions.

The *Spiegel* magazine did not appear to have been damaged in the scandal:

> On the contrary, the publication ultimately benefited from the affair: Its circulation soared, and SPIEGEL suddenly became famous internationally. In his obsession with power, Strauss had gambled away any chance he had of becoming chancellor[3]...

## THE MURDER OF FOUR SOLDIERS IN LEBACH

This is the case that features in Karl Schütz's book, *Kleinstadtmörder: Spur 1081*. I have read the Icelandic translation of the book, *Sakamál 1081 (Criminal Case 1081* – Neven-du Mont & Schütz, 1977), which was published by the Icelandic publisher Setberg after Schütz had completed the Gudmundur and Geirfinnur investigations in 1977 and returned to Germany.

According to the book, on 20 January 1969, Karl Schütz was the head of the security investigation department within the BKA when five soldiers were shot in Lebach, four of whom died. Two men had attacked and shot the soldiers who were guarding an armoury. In view of the nature and seriousness of the case, Schütz was put in charge. In his book, Schütz described his approach to work and said his given nickname was *Kugelblitz*, or 'Ball of lightning' (I have also seen it referred to in English as 'Bullet flash'). Schütz explained how he got this nickname. He was in charge of over 80 specialist police and his method of working was not comfortable for his staff. He often worked in the evenings and at night and next morning he would arrive at the office 'glowing with energy' and full of 'new ideas'. The description in the book suggests an impatient and demanding person, who became surprised when his orders were not followed immediately. He became irritated when the phone rang; he said he only wanted the phone for making calls and would slam down the receiver repeatedly when the phone rang to make it clear that he did not want to be disturbed. When telling the story, Schütz appeared to take pride in this type of behaviour. He said he liked to be surrounded by colleagues who admired him and made him the centre of attention, suggesting strong narcissistic personality traits. He boasted that he was the boss and that everybody knew it.

The two main culprits in the Lebach attack were professional men: a court stenographer (Ditz) and a banker (Fuchs). The man who assisted them with four murders, robbery, one attempted murder, and black-mail, was a dental technician, named Wenzel. Wenzel became a key witness against the other two and only received a six-year prison sentence, whereas Ditz and Fuchs received life sentences.

The three men, according to Schütz, were all motivated by greed, intending to steal weapons from the armoury. The three suspects in the Lebach case required persuasive questioning to confess, having spun a web of lies, but they were educated men and Schütz expressed a certain amount of respect for them. After repeated denials, but vague hints that he had been out for walks with Fuchs and Ditz, Schütz said he took Wenzel out for a long Sunday walk in the woods, accompanied by three other policemen, and applied heavy pressure on him to confess and implicate the key culprits and disclose the location of the stolen weapons. Schütz briefly described the nature of the pressure applied to break down Wenzel's denials and resistance, which consisted of direct confrontation and persuasive interviewing. Schütz's efforts during the walk paid off and the case was solved, perhaps using his 'Indian technique' discussed below.

## THE BAADER-MEINHOF GROUP

When Horst Herold became the Chief Commissioner of the BKA in September 1971, he set up a 'Baader-Meinhof Special Commission' and his 'utmost priority' was to hunt down members of the Red Army Faction (Smith & Moncourt, 2009, p. 116). Karl Schütz, according to his own account, was actively involved in this investigation over a long period of time (*Tíminn*, 6 February 1977, p. 2).

Within a few years, almost all of the original members of the group were either dead or captured, yet the harsh treatment that the latter received as prisoners garnered them a degree of public sympathy, and their own unflagging resistance earned them the respect of many (Smith & Moncourt, 2009, p. xxi).

One of the survivors of the Baader-Meinhof group, Margrit Schiller, has written her memoirs regarding her radicalization into the movement, and her arrest and imprisonment (Schiller, 2009). She was arrested and imprisoned by the German government first for two years and then for another five, for a murder she denies committing. This book is Margrit's own story of political radicalization in the 1960s, her integration into the German urban guerrilla movement (Baader-Meinhof) before her arrest, the terror of solitary confinement, and the mysterious deaths of four of her colleagues in prison (Schiller, 2009).

Margrit Schiller described her arrest as follows:

> The plainclothes men did a body search to look for further weapons. After they had put me in handcuffs, they pushed me into the back seat of the car and took me to the next police station. I was taken into a room and watched over by two policemen with their pistols drawn. One of them searched me again, and when I protested he said: 'Here you have absolutely no say whatsoever.'
>
> (p. 5)

It seems that the approach of the police to the Baader-Meinhof group members was to exercise complete power and control. Karl Schütz and his Reykjavík Task Force investigators did have a great deal of power and control over the suspects and witnesses in the Gudmundur and Geirfinnur cases: there was always the underlying threat of almost unlimited solitary confinement if interviewees were not seen to cooperate with the police, even if it was not explicitly stated. At least on two occasions with Schütz, Erla tried to retract her confession in the Geirfinnur case, claiming she had not been to Keflavík on 19 November 1974. The records show that Schütz's strategy was to confront Erla with her previous admissions, not being prepared to listen to her claims of innocence, and confronting her with the consequences of lying (e.g. a possible criminal charge of perjury).

Two interpreters, Pétur Eggerz and Audur Gestsdóttir, have described Karl Schütz as being polite when interrogating suspects and witnesses and using logic to challenge them rather than threats (Supreme Court Judgement, p. 312). However, it is evident from his interactions with Erla, highlighted in Chapter 9, that he was capable of using threats and intimidation, even in front of his interpreter, Pétur Eggerz. He spoke no Icelandic and his interrogations were conducted through interpreters, which according to one defence lawyer was legally questionable (Working Group Report, 2013).

When Simon Cox interviewed Erla and Gudjón for the BBC in 2014 (*The Reykjavík Confessions*[4]), they described Karl Schütz's interrogation tactics in the following terms:

> He [Schütz] leaned over [the] desk and told me: 'If you sign [the] report you have a chance of being released.' I lost control at one point. Ashtrays and coffee cups and books – I threw everything and went berserk until they held me.
>
> (Erla)

> The main thing with a good questioner like Karl Schütz is he was both a priest and a psychologist. You should confess because you will feel better afterwards. There's a burden taken off your shoulder if you confess. Tell us the truth and you will feel better forever. And God will look upon you with a blessing. It was his philosophy and he got very far with it.
>
> (Gudjón[5])

These comments suggest that Schütz tailored his interrogation techniques to manipulate the vulnerabilities of the interviewee. Erla was vulnerable because she desperately wanted to be released from custody in order to see and be with her infant daughter and had an extremely compliant temperament (see Chapter 14). Gudjón's father had been a priest and Gudjón put all his faith in God, leaving himself vulnerable to psychological manipulation involving clearing his conscience of a crime the police had persuaded him he had committed (see Chapter 17).

## APPOINTED TO THE CASE

According to the Icelandic documentary *Aðför að Lögum* (*Execution According to the Law*)[6], the Minister of Justice, Ólafur Jóhannesson, asked Ambassador Pétur Eggerz to act as an intermediary in finding an experienced German police detective to assist with the Gudmundur

---

[4] http://www.bbc.co.uk/news/special/2014/newsspec_7617/index.html (last accessed 24 January 2018).

[5] Gudjón Skarphédinsson had been persuaded by Karl Schütz and the Task Force detectives that he was guilty of participating in the murder of Geirfinnur Einarsson, although he had no actual memory of being involved.

[6] *Aðför að Lögum*. 'The most controversial criminal case in Iceland's history'. Sigursteinn Málsson and Einar Magnús Magnússon wrote and produced the documentary in 1996. Its two parts were subsequently combined into a film and shown in Bíó Paradís in Reykjavík.

and Geirfinnur investigation. Mr Jóhannesson was allegedly getting very tired of the constant criticism levelled against the judiciary for not being able to solve the cases. Ambassador Pétur Eggerz happened to be in Athens at the beginning of June 1976 on behalf of the foreign office, and Jóhannesson knew that he was due to meet Dr Siegfried Fröhlich, the German Director of the Ministry of the Interior. It was during a supper in the Citadel of Athens that Eggerz and Fröhlich discussed Jóhannesson's request. Dr Fröhlich recommended Karl Schütz, a recently retired 'secret service policeman'.

Schütz was employed by the Ministry of Justice from 29 June 1976 as a 'special adviser/consultant to the Reykjavík Criminal Court regarding the investigation of the disappearance of Gudmundur Einarsson and Geirfinnur Einarsson' when he spent a few days in Iceland, leaving Iceland on 5 July (*Tíminn*, 5 February 1977, p. 6). Ólafur Jóhannesson must have been impressed with Schütz during his week in Iceland, because on 7 July he wrote a letter to Dr Fröhlich thanking him for recommending such an able and experienced man to assist and provide advice to the Reykjavík Criminal Court and the Office of State Prosecution in connection with the investigation into complicated suspected murder cases (Working Group Report, 2013). In the same letter it was requested that Karl Schütz had access to the forensic laboratory in Wiesbaden for forensic investigations. The head of the BKA agreed. On 21 July 1976, the *Dagbladid* journalist Bolli Hedinsson, based in Wiesbaden, wrote an article about the excellent facilities at the BKA (*Dagbladid*, 21 July 1976, p. 9).

When Schütz returned to Iceland on 28 July to work full-time on the cases, he was accompanied by Örn Höskuldsson, the investigative judge, in day-to-day charge of the Gudmundur and Geirfinnur cases. According to an article on the front page of *Vísir* newspaper, dated 29 July, Örn Höskuldsson had spent a few days in Germany but refused to answer questions about his trip there (*Vísir*, 29 July 1976, p. 1). It is likely that after Schütz returned to Germany on 5 July, he was preparing for the work in Iceland, having been provided with essential papers to study. The papers would have needed to be translated into German since Schütz did not read or speak Icelandic. His appointed interpreter during his work in Iceland was Pétur Eggerz, the man who had assisted with finding Schütz in the first place, who was an eminent man in his own right (see Chapter 9).

According to Chief Judge Halldór Thorbjörnsson:

His [Schütz's] work does not only involve giving advice regarding the investigation. He has on occasions interrogated suspects and witnesses with the assistance of an interpreter. He regularly provides me with reports and asks my advice when he considers it necessary. In other respects I don't supervise the investigation beyond that of other criminal cases.

(*Tíminn*, 5 February 1977, p. 6)

(This detailed explanation was provided in the context of Chief Judge Halldór Thorbjörnsson having to justify why the judiciary had agreed to provide Karl Schütz with an 'official public servant' status, in accordance with section 108 of the Icelandic Criminal Code, in his fight against *Morgunbladid*, which had published two cartoons implying his background was associated with the Gestapo.)

Halldór Thorbjörnsson said Schütz had worked continuously on the investigation since 28 July 1976 apart from a short trip to Germany in September. He stayed away over the Christmas period of 1976 and came back to Iceland at the beginning of January 1977.

In October 1976 information obtained in the Geirfinnur case was being prepared for data entry on a computer[7], which was a real innovation in Iceland inspired by Karl Schütz. Prior to the computerization of data, Schütz had introduced an index card system to record and coordinate information in the Geirfinnur case. This was unheard of in Iceland at the time and I was impressed when I heard about it in 1976 from members of the Reykjavík Task Force.

## CAMERA SHY

According to the *Dagbladid*, on 18 August 1976, a journalist from the newspaper, Berglind Ásgeirsdóttir, and photographer, Árni Páll Jóhannsson, were 'arrested' at lunchtime in the canteen of the Reykjavík Criminal Investigation Police and the Court.[8] Árni Páll had taken a few photographs of Karl Schütz when Örn Höskuldsson turned up and took the photographer into the offices of the Court and demanded to have the camera and film. The photographer refused and requested permission to call his lawyer, but Örn Höskuldsson ordered police officers to take the camera and film from him by force. The photographer and the journalist accompanying him were detained separately, for over an hour. Neither was allowed to have any external contact and the reason for their detention was not explained. No statement was taken from either the photographer or the journalist.

---

[7] *Althýdubladid*, 16 October 1976, p. 1.
[8] *Dagbladid*, 19 August 1976, pp. 1 and 8.

The canteen was also used by other organizations within the building. It was not exclusively for the police and Court.

Over time, Karl Schütz became less camera shy and subsequently many photographs of him appeared in the newspapers and he appeared at a press conference on 2 February 1977 when the Gudmundur and Geirfinnur investigation was ready for prosecution and trial.

## THE CARTOONS AND LEGAL ACTION

A cartoon by 'Sigmund', a famous Icelandic cartoonist, in *Morgunbladid* newspaper, appeared on 8 August 1976 (p. 6) depicting a Nazi official under the heading 'A German is employed to work with the Criminal Court'. The cartoon showed a person in uniform, wearing a Nazi insignia on his left arm, pistol holder, a whip, with a barking dog on a lead. There was another similar cartoon of him on 2 September. It showed the statue of a person, apparently in Nazi uniform, being unveiled, under the heading:

> 'We can now breathe more easily dear comrades. We have managed to do a clay likeness of the police's latest secret weapon.'

The plinth of the statue was engraved with the name 'Karl Schütz'.

Karl Schütz made a formal complaint about the cartoons on 3 September to the Reykjavík Criminal Court, stating that they were defamatory and implied that he had been involved with the Gestapo and the SS, which he denied. He demanded a penalty for the perpetrators and compensation for the damage to himself. Normally such a complaint would be treated as a civil matter, since Schütz was not an Icelandic citizen or an Icelandic public servant, but in his case the Reykjavík Criminal Court made an exception and determined it was a criminal matter. Schütz was treated as if he was an Icelandic government official, having been appointed to work on the Gudmundur and Geirfinnur cases.[9] This shows the power and status Schütz held within the Icelandic judiciary.

The editors of *Morgunbladid* were fined and in addition had to pay Schütz compensation, and this was confirmed by the Supreme Court on appeal.[10] The cartoonist, who had drawn 2,400 cartoons for the newspaper was acquitted. Karl Schütz ferociously fought any perceived insults to his character.

---

[9] *Tíminn*, 5 February 1977, p. 6.
[10] *Morgunbladid*, 21 March 1978, p. 12.

## THE 'INDIAN TECHNIQUE'

In his book (Neven-du Mont & Schütz, 1977), Schütz described his fascination with the technique of the Native American Indians in catching the enemy by surprise. He applied this to interrogation and taught the members of the Reykjavík Task Force the 'Indian technique', which was referred to in several of the interrogation reports (Working Group Report, 2013). For example, Detective Haraldur Árnason in an interrogation of Kristján on 1 November 1976 specifically states that he used the 'Indian technique' in the Geirfinnur case.

The technique involved investigators asking suspects or witnesses questions from unexpected perspectives and not in a particular time sequence (i.e. not following the temporal order of events). The basic assumption was that when this technique is used, suspects and witnesses would find it very difficult to persist with their lies. The questions were few but were organized according to whether they were based on the investigator's genuine or misleading information (Working Group Report, 2013, p. 121). Task Force investigators that the Working Group interviewed were not in agreement about the effectiveness of the technique.

The basic principles of the 'Indian technique', as described in the above paragraph, show that it is guilt presumptive and relied on trickery. It was likely to confuse suspects and witnesses and would have been in breach of sections 39 and 40 of the Icelandic code of legal practice that was in operation at the time of the Gudmundur and Geirfinnur investigation (see Chapter 6, Box 6.2). The code emphasized transparency and accountability, stipulating that questions should be 'clear, short and unequivocal' and not in any way attempts to confuse a person with lies or in other ways. The Reykjavík Criminal Court, which was in charge of the investigation, and subsequently the Supreme Court, apparently raised no concerns about the use of this technique.

## SCHÜTZ'S FOREWORD TO HIS BOOK
### KLEINSTADTMÖRDER: SPUR 1081

In the Foreword to his book (Neven-du Mont & Schütz, 1977), Schütz gave an account of his work on the Geirfinnur case, which provides an insight into his approach. He praised Ambassador Pétur Eggerz for his outstanding work with the Task Force. According to Schütz, Pétur Eggerz liaised between Schütz and various organizations and the administration and helped solve problems that arose: 'He was my personal interpreter during many difficult interrogations, in discussions and on committees' (p. 6).

Schütz contrasted the suspects in the Geirfinnur case with those responsible for the murders of soldiers in Lebach. He praised the murderers in the Lebach case for their good family background, their intellect, and the fact that unlike the suspects in the Geirfinnur case, they all confessed fully once the proof of their involvement was revealed.

He stated: 'Those involved in the Keflavík case focused on delaying the investigation and misleading the police' (p. 7).

Schütz said that the first job of the Task Force was to try to sort out the muddle that the case was in. This took up the first three months of the Task Force's work. He said that it did not help that the suspects were always pointing to new locations where Geirfinnur's body had been hidden. He found it particularly helpful that basic case information was recorded on index cards and analysed on computers. This had not been done in Iceland before. Schütz pointed out that the newest technology was used with the investigation and interrogation. He described the Task Force unfolding the web of lies produced by the suspects.

In the Foreword to his book, Karl Schütz commented that he had difficulty judging the temperament of the suspects in the Geirfinnur case. In Germany he had found it easy to determine whether people were telling lies or not, but in Iceland he found people were lying for reasons he did not understand. Even witnesses not implicated in the case were giving the wrong story and looked suspicious. He stated: 'I found this tendency to conceal the most innocent parts very novel and curious' (p. 8).

The most likely reason for Schütz's failure to understand the Icelandic people is that he failed to come to terms with the context. He assumed from the start that the suspects were involved in Geirfinnur's disappearance and were reluctant to tell the truth. The reality is that they probably did not know what had happened to Geirfinnur and were repeatedly pressured for information they did not possess. When they proclaimed their innocence they were not believed and were given further solitary confinement and restrictions within the prison. Schütz made a fundamental investigative and attribution error, because he failed to approach the suspects with an open mind and see the broader context.

At the end of his Foreword Schütz states the following:

I will always be grateful to Ólafur Jóhannesson, Minister of Justice, and Halldór Thorbjörnsson, Chief Judge. They enabled me to work within my own responsibility in Iceland and without disturbance or interference.

(p. 9)

It is apparent from the above quote that Ólafur Jóhannesson and Halldór Thorbjörnsson gave Schütz full authority to behave independently and they seem to have set him no boundaries. Schütz was able to do what he wanted and he used it to his full advantage, including applying the Indian technique, which was not consistent with the spirit and letter of the relevant Icelandic legislation at the time.

Schütz's greatest frustration and disappointment was undoubtedly not being able to find any forensic evidence to link the suspects with Geirfinnur's disappearance. Importantly, Schütz failed to ask himself the most fundamental question in the Geirfinnur case: Were the suspects possibly innocent?

## THE *DER SPIEGEL* 1979 ARTICLE[11]

The main focus of the article, which was published on 24 September 1979 (Issue 39), was on the growing number of foreign investigators and politicians visiting the BKA because of its state-of-the-art technology.

With regard to Schütz's work in Iceland, the magazine reports:

...the BKA has become so international that sometimes personal administrative assistance is granted to friendly countries. When in about 1976 the Icelandic government was facing a crisis after influential friends of the then Justice Minister Ólafur Jóhannesson were suspected by the opposition of being schnaps smugglers and the brains behind the unexplained murder of construction worker Geirfinnur Einarsson, the island's government searched for a top independent detective.

Thanks to a tip-off from Wiesbaden it found him in Karl Schütz, 64, the head of department of the Bonn security group, who had just retired. A man with a reputation: colleagues gave him the nickname 'Commissioner ball lightning' because of his successful detection of: [...], the murder of the soldiers in Lebach, the earlier Baader-Meinhofs and the GDR agents Sütterlin and Guillaume.

In investigations on the ground that lasted 166 days, Schütz caught the real smugglers; they had buried Einarsson's body in the 'Red Hills' [*Rauðhólar*], a wild lava landscape. Incidentally, the German on-loan criminal investigator revealed Iceland's TV announcer Ásgeir Ingólfsson as the killer of a cleaning lady.

---

[11] I had the article officially translated into English.

'You have taken away a nightmare from the Icelandic people', Jóhannesson praised the retired 'Ball of lightning' when saying goodbye. And for the forensic assistance of the BKA, Reykjavík awarded the head of the BKA, Horst Herold, the Order of the Silver Crane.[12]

According to the records of the Icelandic presidential website[13], Horst Herold received the *stórriddarakross med stjörnu* medal on 15 July 1977. Horst Herold had been appointed as the Chief Commissioner of the BKA in September 1971 and was 'an expert on the new methods of using computerized data processing as a law enforcement tool. Under Herold's leadership, the BKA was transferred from a relatively unimportant body into the West German equivalent of the FBI' (Smith & Moncourt, 2009, p. 115). He had generously offered laboratory facilities to the Icelandic authorities during the Gudmundur and Geirfinnur investigation at the discretion of Karl Schütz. At the time, Iceland had limited forensic laboratory facilities.[14]

Not mentioned in the *Der Spiegel* article is the fact that on the same day five other Germans associated with the Geirfinnur investigation also received an 'Order of the Falcon' award (*Fálkaorða*). Four were awarded the *stórriddarakross* medal. These were the head of the BKA science department, Driesen Horst-Hilmar, Chrisfried Leszeynski (dean), Ekkehard Kissling (manager), and Karl Schütz, described as a previous BKA dean. Dr Siegfried Fröhlich (Ministry of the Interior), who had recommended Karl Schütz to Ólafur Jóhannesson in early June 1976, was awarded the *stórkross*.

The significance of the medals is that the President of Iceland at the time, Dr Kristján Eldjárn, the highest official in the land, was showing his gratitude to Karl Schütz, members of the BKA, and the German official who had recommended Karl Schütz in June 1976 during a meeting in Athens.

On 13 March 1977, four months before the medals were presented, the front page of the German *Abendpost zum Sonntag* (night edition) newspaper read:[15]

'A German spy hunter rescues Iceland's government'.

---

[12] The website of the President of Iceland shows five levels of order: (1) *riddarakrossinn*, which is most commonly awarded, (2) *stórriddarakross*, (3) *stórriddarakross með stjörnu*, (4) *stórkross*, and (5) *keðja ásamt stórkrossstjörnu*, which is only awarded to heads of state. For an English translation of the different awards see https://grapevine.is/mag/articles/2011/08/24/the-fellowship-of-the-order-of-the-falcon/ (last accessed 24 January 2018).

[13] http://www.forseti.is/falkaordan/orduhafaskra/#/ (last accessed 24 January 2018).

[14] *Tíminn*, 2 September 1976, p. 1.

[15] This was a German Sunday evening newspaper in the 1970s that no longer exists.

## PERSONAL IMPRESSION OF KARL SCHÜTZ

My general impression of Schütz is that he was on a single-minded mission to achieve consistency in the confessions (i.e. get a coherent story) and locate the bodies of the two missing men. He was determined to solve the cases; claims of innocence were never an option for the suspects. Problems arose when none of the six suspects were able to assist with the discovery of the men's bodies and the Task Force had problems corroborating their stories. The suspects' mission was to get the investigators 'off their back'; they had no story to tell but the investigators would not accept that. The suspects were in a hopeless situation, their claims of innocence were not believed, neither were their vague and unconvincing changing stories. Schütz, the investigators, the judges, and the lawyer representing the prosecution, grew increasingly frustrated. The juggernaut journey had gathered momentum and there was no turning back. Once Schütz had become involved in the case at the end of July 1976, convictions were probably inevitable. He came with an excellent recommendation, was an extremely experienced German investigator, had a forceful and dominant personality that broke down denials and resistance, and the Icelandic judiciary apparently had complete confidence in him and his tactics.

From my interactions with Schütz and observations of his behaviour with others, he spoke in a loud and authoritative voice, he seemed very driven and determined, was overzealous, became easily irritated when things did not go his way, and liked to be surrounded by an entourage. Pétur Eggerz, his official interpreter, who followed him everywhere, was a kind and gentle man, physically towering over Schütz, who was a much shorter man of a plump build.

## CONCLUSIONS

Karl Schütz was resourceful and methodical in his work. He dominated the investigation, leaving no one in any doubt that he was in charge of the day-to-day management of the cases (Working Group Report, 2013). His approach early on was to focus primarily on the Geirfinnur case, which was strategically more important than the Gudmundur case (i.e. it was of greater political importance and had a greater mystery surrounding it, linking it to smuggling). Once the Geirfinnur investigation was considered solved, it had a ripple effect on the Gudmundur case (Saevar and Kristján were implicated in both cases).

Schütz had set up an impressive index card system, which was subsequently computerized, and he had access to the state-of-the-art forensic laboratory within the BKA. It seems that this facility was of limited practical use because there was no crime scene that led to forensic evidence to investigate. As a result, the two cases depended on the results from interrogations, at least in part using the 'Indian technique' that Schütz used and taught to the Task Force investigators. Everything centred on obtaining confessions that would be accepted by the judiciary.

It seems that Ólafur Jóhannesson and Halldór Thorbjörnsson gave Schütz full authority to behave independently, and they seem to have set no boundaries. Schütz was able to do what he wanted and he used it to his full advantage, including applying the Indian technique, which was not consistent with the spirit and letter of the relevant Icelandic legislation at the time. In addition, the head of the Reykjavík Criminal Court gave him full support when Schütz made a complaint to the Criminal Court about the cartoons published in the *Morgunbladid* newspaper in August and September 1976, shortly after his arrival in Iceland. What seemed to be a civil matter was treated by the Courts as a criminal matter, suggesting that Schütz was accorded a special status within the Icelandic judiciary.

The political importance of the case is best illustrated by the announcement of Ólafur Jóhannesson in February 1977 with thanks to Schütz and the comment 'The nation has been unburdened of a nightmare'. In addition, on 15 July 1977 Karl Schütz, four of his colleagues from the BKA, and the person who recommended Karl Schütz to Pétur Eggerz in June 1976 at a meeting in Athens, were all awarded decorations by the President of Iceland. This demonstrates how much Ólafur Jóhannesson and the judiciary needed to solve the Gudmundur and Geirfinnur cases, and the Icelandic head of state rewarded Schütz and his colleagues handsomely for their efforts. The German press referred to Karl Schütz as a German spy hunter who 'rescued Iceland's government'. Schütz appears to have been perceived as a hero both in Iceland and Germany.

In my view, Schütz's work in Iceland misguided the police and judiciary. He claimed to have obtained a credible story from three of the suspects in the Geirfinnur case that left him in no doubt about their guilt.

# 11

# The Return of the Gudmundur and Geirfinnur Cases

*A diary kept by an innocent man because of a big case! A man who is wrongly accused! But the truth always comes out in the end, even if late*[1]

In this chapter, I discuss the circumstances under which I became involved as an expert witness in the Gudmundur and Geirfinnur cases. I never envisaged that I would become involved, after having left my country of birth permanently in the autumn of 1976, at a time when the investigation was reaching its final stages under the leadership of Karl Schütz. That was all to change because of a telephone conversation at the end of September 2011 with Icelandic journalist Helga Arnardóttir.

## HELGA ARNARDÓTTIR'S TELEPHONE CALL AND THE DIARIES

On the morning of 27 September 2011, I received an important phone call. The person at the other end of the phone identified herself as Helga Arnardóttir from the Channel 2 television station in Iceland, who had the previous week contacted my Icelandic colleague Jón

---

[1] Written by Tryggvi Leifsson on the front page of his personal diary while in Síðumúli Prison, dated 19 March 1977.

*The Psychology of False Confessions: Forty Years of Science and Practice*, First Edition.
Gisli H. Gudjonsson.
© 2018 John Wiley & Sons Ltd. Published 2018 by John Wiley & Sons Ltd.

Fridrik Sigurdsson about Tryggvi's diaries. Jón Fridrik contacted me and asked whether I was prepared to speak to Helga and I agreed.[2]

Helga told me that she had been shown three diaries written by the late Tryggvi while he was in police custody in the mid- to late 1970s in connection with the Gudmundur case. In 2011 she had begun to investigate the cases following Saevar's death, and a publication of the biography of the first detective investigating Geirfinnur's disappearance, Haukur Gudmundsson, who believed that innocent people had been convicted (Jónsdóttir, 2010).

Helga had discovered the existence of the diaries when attending an interview with Tryggvi's widow, Sjöfn Sigurbjörnsdóttir. Sjöfn had a daughter, Kristín, who was born eight months before the arrest of Tryggvi on 23 December 1975. He later became her adoptive father. Sjöfn had told Kristín about the interview with Helga and invited her to be present. Kristín turned up at her mother's house on her way home from work and showed Helga the diaries.

Helga told me during our telephone conversation that she thought the diaries might help to throw a new light on the cases. Helga wanted me to comment on extracts from the diaries and later that morning she emailed me the extracts. Towards the end of the day Helga emailed me some general questions about false confessions and some questions about the diaries. She asked whether I would like to answer the questions on the telephone or on Skype. She interviewed me over the telephone about false confessions and I made some general comments about the diaries. I said that I needed to see the diaries to be able to properly comment on them rather than reviewing selected extracts.

Helga discussed the telephone interview with her two editors at Channel 2. They said this was a very important interview and wanted me interviewed on camera. Helga then asked whether I would come to Iceland that weekend and look at the diaries and give my comments on national television. My initial reaction was not to get involved. I already felt overburdened with work, which had to be completed prior to my retirement from King's College London on 1 January 2012 and did not have time to go to Iceland at such short notice. Helga sensed my reluctance and politely and compassionately argued that having my views on the diaries would be important. This was new material that had not previously featured anywhere in the cases. Helga wanted an expert

---

[2] Helga later told me that she had been reluctant to contact me in the first instance because the producer of *Aðför að Lögum* had told her about my reluctance in the 1990s to get involved in the cases due to my association with the Reykjavík police at the time of the investigation.

view on the diaries. After all, I was one of the world's leading and most experienced experts on the evaluation of cases of disputed confessions, I had met five of the convicted persons at the time of the Gudmundur and Geirfinnur investigation in the 1970s, and I knew most of the officers involved through my service with the police and some of the conditions under which the suspects had been detained for questioning. I had the unique advantage that I could read all the material in Icelandic. When entering university in England in the early 1970s, I had a strong ambition to bring back scientific knowledge to the benefit of Iceland. Now almost 40 years later, this was my chance to do so.

After accepting that I was not able to visit Iceland immediately, Helga offered to investigate whether she could obtain funding from her TV station to bring the diaries to my home in England for me to review them. She said she would call me back. Within a few hours Helga phoned me again and said that she had managed to obtain funding for her to come to England, but Kristín would not hand over the diaries. She had to come too but had to fund the flight herself. These were hard financial times in Iceland.

When I spoke to Helga on the telephone I was impressed by her determination, resourcefulness, and commitment to the cases. I said I would be prepared to read the diaries and comment on them, but I said I could not promise anything about the outcome of the review, but Helga accepted this.

## MEETING WITH HELGA AND KRISTÍN

The date for our meeting was set for Saturday 1 October 2011. Helga and Kristín landed at Heathrow at 11.30. I collected them from the airport and we arrived at my house in Surrey shortly after 13.00. Their return flight back to Iceland was due to depart at 20.35 that same evening. I did not have much time to read the diaries and comment on them. The pressure was on, and I felt it.

At the time Helga and Kristín brought the diaries to my home, I did not know the full circumstances behind the diaries, nor did I know their significance. All I knew was that these were the three surviving diaries of about a dozen that Tryggvi Rúnar had written while in custody in connection with the Gudmundur case in 1976 and 1977.

After brief introductions and coffee, we agreed a plan. Kristín would hand over the diaries, which she had been guarding with her life, and I would take them into another room and read each in turn. Kristín handed over the diaries but seemed reluctant to leave them out of her sight. For Kristín, the diaries were very precious: a link to her father's past, her love for him, and complete faith in his innocence. This was a big day for her and she came across as apprehensive. She had never met me before, did not know whether she could trust me, and my findings from this preliminary review of the diaries might not be favourable to her father's case. She later told me that at the time her mind kept oscillating between positive and negative thoughts regarding the outcome of our meeting. There had been so many disappointments about the case over the years and she was too scared to expect much from our meeting. Kristín was even concerned that I would not turn up at the airport: she took nothing for granted.

## THE CONTENT OF THE DIARIES

Each diary was close to 100 pages, about 300 pages in all. I knew I could not read the diaries in full in the time available. I decided to focus on extracts where there was a reference made to Tryggvi's mental state and the confessions. The diaries were all written in Icelandic, and I have translated the most relevant extracts into English. These were as follows:

### Diary 1: 25 October 1976 – 6 February 1977

This diary was labelled on the front page as 'Diary No IV', indicating that there were three previous diaries. By the time Tryggvi commenced writing the fourth diary, he had been in custody for over 10 months. Those three previously written diaries might have been helpful in providing information about Tryggvi's mental health and confessions during the early period of the detention, including periods of memory distrust and confusion. My approach to it at the time was, 'we've got to make do with what we have and see how far it takes us'.

The first entry in this diary reads[3]:

> In this diary I write everything that happens to me, here inside the walls, so we can call this the diary of my life inside Síðumúli! The time is dragging on, 10 ½ months in solitary confinement. Alone in a cell. Yes it's a long time in one's life and to be innocent of the allegations made against

---

[3] The ICCRC Report (2017) (Tryggvi Leifsson) dates the first diary entry to 2 October 1976 (Paragraph 292), but this is a mistake. The front page of the diary clearly states that it begins on 25 October 1976.

me [...] I hope that soon the facts will emerge so that I and my family will be cleared of this dreadful event [...] my name has been well aired in the media and exaggerated so the situation is not good at present.

There was a great deal in this diary about trivial events, such as leaving the cell to go to the toilet, there being no toilet or washing facilities within the cells in the prison, having his morning and afternoon coffee, details of his rigorous physical exercises, and his daily prescribed medication, taken in the morning, mid-afternoon, and at night, typically around midnight. He particularly enjoyed being allowed out of his cell and into the small prison back yard some afternoons where he ran around for 10–20 minutes, at one point commenting that he needed at least 15 minutes for effective exercise, which he could not always achieve, because a prison officer had to stay in the yard with him and one was not always available.

The general theme was that Tryggvi was doing his best to cope with his predicament; it was all about survival. Once he had been implicated in the Gudmundur case, he knew he was going nowhere for a long time: Örn Höskuldsson and other judges made sure of that with their apparently unlimited judicial power to detain the suspects in solitary confinement, over and over again.

I knew from my work as a detective in 1976 that the suspects in the Gudmundur and Geirfinnur cases were sedated while in custody and therefore, this did not come as a surprise to me when I read the diaries. Tryggvi made a reference to chloral hydrate and nitrazepam being taken at night because he had serious problems sleeping. On 29 January 1977 he wrote that his chloral hydrate had been increased from 15 mg to 30 mg and he was coming off nitrazepam. There were indications that Tryggvi was addicted to the medication. For example, there is a reference to him becoming agitated on 1 November 1976 when his afternoon medication had not arrived on time and did not arrive until 17.40.

Throughout this diary there were references to him proclaiming his innocence ('I'm innocent'), referring to his having told this to the investigators, prison officers, and judges.

### Diary 2:19 March 1977 – 1 May 1977

On the front page of this diary Tryggvi had written:

'A diary kept by an innocent man because of a big case! A man who is wrongly accused! But the truth always comes out in the end, even if late', signed 'Tryggvi Leifsson'.

This diary began with Tryggvi meeting the prison doctor, Gudsteinn Thengilsson, and asking him for anabolic steroids for building up his muscles. Dr Thengilsson did not think he needed the steroids, pointing out his muscular physique, and he encouraged Tryggvi to keep up with his fitness regime, but he promised he would consider his request.

Extracts from the second diary on Tuesday 29 March written the day before he formally retracted his confession:

> Yes now the time has come to achieve my aim to tell the truth in Court. But it has taken time. I never expected 15 ½ months! If I had anticipated this I would never have confessed myself into the case […] I believed that by incriminating myself, I would be given bail until the case went to Court. I did not want the two years in solitary confinement that Örn Höskuldsson threatened me with if I did not confess. And that I would not be let out, that was certain. Now Örn Höskuldsson's time is up. I'm afraid that he will be sent packing with a kick in the backside as a leaving present. He and Eggert [Bjarnason], conducted illegal interrogations all the time they were getting confessions […] One can be driven crazy by being innocent and implicated in this kind of case. I always thought about my family.

An extract from 18 April 1977 shows that Tryggvi was hopeful that the investigators would believe his innocence:

> Well, I'm entitled to a trip abroad for this awful lot here. What's more, I will enjoy the sunshine in Spain as well! I need it after all this incarceration! And all this time of torment [kveljast] and suffering [þjást], fighting for my innocence! It's such a pressure on a normal man that he has a nervous breakdown, which has happened to me here more often than others realize, since if that was not the case that man would be abnormal.

An extract dated 29 April 1977 shows a changing attitude towards him in the prison: 'I have noticed that most of the prison guards are treating me like an outcast [úrhrak]. At least, their attitude towards me is not the same as before'.

Tryggvi then tried to figure out when there was a change in attitude towards him and related it to his being allowed to meet with his lawyer for a private consultation the day before.

It is evident from this entry that Tryggvi had hoped that his statement of innocence would be believed when the case went to Court. His thoughts of his family kept him going. He kept himself physically fit by doing body building and having a rigorous exercise regime. He viewed himself as a tough and resilient guy coping with intolerable circumstances.

## Diary 3: *8 June 1977 – 5 December 1977*

The entries show how Tryggvi had become increasingly agitated about being detained and uncertainties about his future as it got closer to the trial. On 24 October 1977 he revealed that he had not spent so much time completing his diary: 'The reason is that I have been so busy with my physical exercises during the previous three months'.

He was spending up to three hours a day exercising and it had apparently become an obsession in order to cope with the intolerable stress. He refers to having spent 22 months in custody as an innocent man and the effect it had on him: 'Locked away from everybody. I have not been allowed to see my family all this time, except for a brief time when I was in the "East" [Litla-Hraun Prison]'.

As in the previous diaries, Tryggvi reiterated numerous times that he was innocent. After spending about two and a half hours reading the essential parts of the diaries, I formed these initial views:

- The diaries were without doubt written at the time he was in custody (i.e. contemporaneous material).
- They were probably written for 'his eyes only', a way of keeping his sanity while in his cell on his own, day after day, week after week, and month after month.
- He only became neglectful of the diaries when his trial approached. He had also become obsessed with his fitness routine, aiming to spend three hours a day on physical exercise.
- Throughout the diaries he proclaims his innocence. The general theme is his frustration at being detained for a crime he had not committed and his belief that the truth would eventually emerge, even if it was going to take a long time. He had faith in his innocence being believed in Court, but his confidence in the criminal justice system oscillated between hope and a state of despair, depending on what was happening in the case at any given time.
- It was the sincerity of the content of the diaries that impressed me, and the entries were written with passion and conviction.

Tryggvi's diaries opened my eyes to aspects of the conditions in custody and his predicament which I had been oblivious to when I visited the custody area on a number of occasions during the summer of 1976. I had met Tryggvi for one and a half hours on 12 July 1976 when he was a participant in my lie detection experiment, and we did not discuss his case or his suffering.

The content in the diaries all made sense to me. I knew that the diaries represented important new material. Yes, offenders commonly go on to deny offences they have truly confessed to as the reality of the deleterious consequences hits home, particularly after speaking to their lawyer. They know they are in serious trouble, because most courts admit and rely on confession evidence, even in the absence of good corroborative evidence (Gudjonsson, 2003a). This means that denials are not by themselves proof of innocence, but in some cases they are good pointers. In the case of Tryggvi's diaries, I was confident that they gave a new insight into the case that was relevant to all six persons convicted in the Gudmundur and Geirfinnur cases. Of course, by themselves they were no proof of Tryggvi's innocence, but they called for a review into the cases. I was in no doubt about that and was prepared to say so on Icelandic national television.

## THE FILMING

I walked into the kitchen where Helga and Kristín were with my wife Julia. They had been looking at the clock ticking away and wondered when I would come and what I would say. Julia sensed the tension in the kitchen increasing over time; it must have been a dreadful wait for Kristín, particularly. I asked them to join me in the sitting room. I said I would not prejudge Tryggvi's factual guilt or innocence, but the 'voice' coming through from the diaries was from a person who believed in his innocence and thought justice would eventually prevail. I told them I thought the diaries were genuine and Tryggvi was being sincere. I said this was, in my view, important new material. Kristín turned her face aside, having become overwhelmed by emotion.

Helga had set the camera up in our conservatory where the interview took place. I stated on national television that there was a problem with the Gudmundur and Geirfinnur cases and that I would be prepared to assist with a review.

When Helga and Kristín were preparing to leave our house for Heathrow Airport, I reassured Kristín that her father's diaries appeared genuine, were important new evidence in the case, and that her father had been right about what he had written on the front of one of his diaries that 'the truth always comes out in the end, even if late'. My saying this made Kristín become tearful and I sensed that she felt greatly relieved. It had been a highly emotionally charged day for all of us, particularly Kristín, who strongly believed in her father's innocence.

## A CALL FROM THE MINISTER OF THE INTERIOR

I was not in Iceland to see the TV news programme on 3 October 2011 where I commented on the need to review the case and had not foreseen the consequences of the broadcast. Within a few days of the programme being broadcast, I was in my office at the Institute of Psychiatry in Camberwell, London, when I had a call from an assistant to the Icelandic Minister of the Interior, Ögmundur Jónasson, saying the Minister wanted to speak with me. I accepted the call with trepidation: what did the Minister of the Interior wish to speak to me about? I suspected that it might have something to do with the TV broadcast.

The conversation with Ögmundur was short and formal. He told me that there was a public demand for a review of the Gudmundur and Geirfinnur cases and that he had decided to set up a Working Group to review the cases. He said he had been looking into the convictions for a while and was going to appoint a young team of lawyers with no past links to the investigations. He wanted me to act as an expert to the Working Group. I said I would accept this task provided there was no perception of conflict of interest due to my having worked as a detective in the Reykjavík Criminal Investigation Police at the time of the investigations in the summer of 1976. My main concern was with how the convicted persons and their families would feel about my involvement. Did they have confidence that I would work dispassionately, knowing about my past links with the investigators? As things turned out, I need not have worried.

On 7 October 2011, Ögmundur appointed the Working Group. He stated that he had received a petition from 1,190 individuals who had demanded an investigation and review of the Gudmundur and Geirfinnur cases because of the general perception that the criminal justice system had failed to ensure the integrity of the convictions of the six individuals. There had always remained a lurking doubt about the convictions due to the lack of any tangible evidence, beyond the confessions.

## CONCLUSIONS

Tryggvi clearly viewed the diaries as personal and had apparently failed to recognize their potential legal significance: they were not produced at either the District Court or the Supreme Court. Unfortunately, only three out of about a dozen diaries survived. In spite of this, the surviving diaries provide a good insight into Tryggvi's mental state during his solitary confinement and how he tried to cope with his predicament. They demonstrate his desperate hope that his innocence would be believed, 'even if late'. As far as I am concerned, meeting Kristín and Helga, and viewing the diaries, was a pivotal event. It made me realize that in 1976 I had been unaware of what was really happening in the interrogation room at Síðumúli Prison. Once I had read the diaries I knew that there was no turning back, the Gudmundur and Geirfinnur cases had to be reviewed afresh.

In the next chapter I explain the work of the Working Group and my testimony before the Icelandic Court Cases Review Commission at the Reykjavík District Court on 28 January 2016, where I answered detailed questions about the background, method, and results of our enquiries. I also discuss and comment on the outcome of the Commission reports, which were published on 24 February 2017.

# 12

# The Findings From the Working Group, Special Prosecutor, and Icelandic Court Cases Review Commission

*Having opened Pandora's Box there will be no closure until the Angel of Hope rises up as Greek mythology would have it*[1]

In this chapter I discuss the methodology and findings of the Working Group, key elements of the testimony in the District Court on 28 January 2016, and the critique and recommendations of the Icelandic Court Cases Review Commission, which I refer to as the Commission.

Table 12.1 provides a timeline of the salient events, including the involvement and recommendation of the special prosecutor, David Björgvinsson, who was appointed after the Director of Prosecution had to disqualify herself from reviewing the appeal applications because of a conflict of interest. According to the Faculty of Law, University of Copenhagen, where David Björgvinsson was appointed as a professor of law on 1 January 2014, his background was described as follows:

David Thór [Björgvinsson] is born in Reykjavik, Iceland 9 April 1956. He studied history, philosophy and law at the University of Iceland and legal philosophy at Duke University School of Law in the USA. He is a

---

[1] A comment made by Michael Mansfield QC in a Foreword to a book highlighting the failure to fully confront a miscarriage of justice (Sekar, 2012).

*The Psychology of False Confessions: Forty Years of Science and Practice*, First Edition.
Gisli H. Gudjonsson.
© 2018 John Wiley & Sons Ltd. Published 2018 by John Wiley & Sons Ltd.

**Table 12.1**  A brief summary of the key events relating to the Working Group, special prosecutor, and the Icelandic Court Cases Review Commission

| Date | Event |
| --- | --- |
| 7 October 2011 | The Working Group is set up. Arndís Sigurdardóttir is appointed as the Chairperson. She is assisted by two lawyers, Haraldur Steinthórsson and Valgerdur Sigurdardóttir, and a professor of psychology, Jón Fridrik Sigurdsson. |
| 28 November 2011 | Gisli Gudjonsson is appointed as an expert to the Working Group. |
| 30 January 2012 | Gisli Gudjonsson has his first meeting with the Working Group and commences his work on the two cases. |
| 21 March 2013 | The Working Group completes its report. |
| 26 June 2014 | The lawyer representing Gudjón Skarphédinsson and Erla Bolladóttir formally requests an appeal. |
| 3 October 2014 | David Björgvinsson is appointed as a special prosecutor to review the applications of Gudjón and Erla. |
| 12 March 2015 | The lawyer representing the descendants of Saevar Ciesielski and Tryggvi Leifsson formally requests an appeal. |
| 31 March 2015 | The lawyer representing Albert Skaftason formally requests an appeal. |
| 15 April 2015 | David Björgvinsson is appointed as a special prosecutor to review the applications of Saevar and Tryggvi. |
| 6 May 2015 | David Björgvinsson is appointed as a special prosecutor to review the application of Albert. |
| 1 June 2015 | David Björgvinsson completes his reports on the applications of Gudjón Skarphédinsson and Erla Bolladóttir. He supported Gudjón's appeal against killing Geirfinnur, but rejected Erla's application regarding the conviction for giving false evidence against the 'four wrongly accused'. |
| 2 July 2015 | David Björgvinsson completes his reports on the applications of Saevar, Tryggvi, and Albert supporting the appeal against their convictions (i.e. Saevar for killing Gudmundur and Geirfinnur, Tryggvi for killing Gudmundur, and Albert for participating in interfering with the crime scene in the Gudmundur case). |
| 25 August 2015 | The Commission requests that the special prosecutor takes a position regarding Kristján, who had not appealed against his convictions regarding the killing of Gudmundur and Geirfinnur. |
| 30 September 2015 | The lawyers of the five appellants provide comments on the special prosecutor's reports. |

**Table 12.1**   (*Continued*)

| Date | Event |
| --- | --- |
| 17 December 2015 | The special prosecutor requests that Kristján's case should be considered for an appeal along with those of the other convicted persons. |
| 28 January 2016 | Members of the Working Group, Gisli Gudjonsson, and the three members of the Reykjavík Team testify in the District Court. |
| 5 September 2016 | The special prosecutor and the appellants' lawyers are invited to present their arguments and comments verbally before the Commission. Mr Björgvinsson has now changed his position regarding Erla's false evidence convictions against the 'four wrongly accused', recommending that her conviction should also be considered for appeal. |
| 24 February 2017 | The Commission completes its reports with regard to the convicted persons' merit for appeal. It recommends the appeal of the four men's manslaughter convictions and Albert's conviction for participating in interfering with the crime scene, but rejects the applications of Erla, Saevar, and Kristján for giving false evidence against the 'four wrongly accused'. The Commission makes no reference to David Björgvinsson having changed his mind about Erla's application on 5 September or to Gisli Gudjonsson's and Jón Fridrik Sigurdsson's evidence in the District Court on 28 January 2016 where they addressed the issues and arguments in detail at the Commission's request. |
| 21 August 2017 | The appeal applications supported by the Commission are received and registered in the Supreme Court. |
| 22 December 2017 | David Björgvinsson has about 20,000 pages of documents in the Gudmundur and Geirfinnur case delivered to the Supreme Court. He is currently preparing prosecution submissions to the Supreme Court. |
| 21 February 2018 | David Björgvinsson demands an acquittal with regard to the manslaughter convictions of Saevar, Kristján, Tryggvi and Gudjón, and an acquittal of Albert's conviction for participating in interfering with the crime scene in the Gudmundur case. |

doctor of international law from Strasbourg University. He has done research in his field at the University of Edinburgh in Scotland, Rand Afrikaans Universiteit in Johannesburg in South Africa, University of Copenhagen, Max Planck Institute in Heidelberg, Germany and Oxford University in England [...] David Thór was a judge at the European Court of Human Rights in respect of Iceland 2004-2013.[2]

---

[2] http://jura.ku.dk/english/news/2014/david-thor-bjorgvinsson/.

David Björgvinsson was well qualified to undertake the task of the special prosecutor. He recommended that there were grounds for appeal in relation to the manslaughter convictions in the Gudmundur and Geirfinnur cases, and Albert Skaftason's conviction in the Gudmundur case for participating in interfering with the crime scene (e.g. transportation of Gudmundur's body from the crime scene). In contrast, he did not support the applications regarding the false allegations made against Einar Bollason, Magnús Leópoldsson, Sigurbjörn Eiríksson, and Valdimar Olsen, which left Erla Bolladóttir out of the appeal loop (i.e. the Supreme Court had only convicted her of perjury).

However, on 5 September 2016, Mr Björgvinsson[3] told the Commission at a prearranged meeting that he had changed his mind and now also supported Erla's application.[4] How was the Commission going to respond to this change of opinion? To Erla's lawyer, Ragnar Adalsteinsson, Member of Parliament Ögmundur Jónasson, and Working Group Chairperson Arndís Sigurdardóttir, the outcome was not what they had expected.[5]


## THE WORKING GROUP

Mr Ögmundur Jónasson served as a member of the Icelandic Parliament (MP) between 1995 and 2016. He was the Minister of the Interior between 2011 and 2013 and was instrumental in setting up the Working Group in October 2011, having become actively involved in the cases after Saevar Ciesielski's death in Denmark on 12 July 2011. Erla Bolladóttir has told me that Ögmundur arranged funding for Saevar's body to be brought back to Iceland and Ögmundur has confirmed this in an email to me, dated 11 April 2017.

Erla said that she had met Ögmundur early one morning at his office before Saevar's funeral and spent an hour with him. She told him a little about herself and her background, her experience of solitary confinement in the cases, and what she thought needed to be done (i.e. the cases being reviewed and justice done). After the meeting, Ögmundur reassured her 'that something will be done'. Sometime later

---

[3] For the purpose of this chapter I am avoiding using his academic title in order not to confuse his role in the cases.

[4] http://www.mbl.is/frettir/innlent/2016/09/05/rok_fyrir_endurupptoku_a_mali_erlu/ (last accessed 24 January 2018).

[5] http://www.mbl.is/frettir/innlent/2017/03/02/undrast_nidurstodu_nefndarinnar/ (last accessed 24 January 2018).

he told her that he was setting up the Working Group. Ögmundur was a man of his word.

All my interactions with Ögmundur have been cordial and respectful. I am impressed by his compassion, drive, determination, persistence, and support for human rights. He is a genuine fighter for justice and has the confidence to stand up for what he believes in.

Ögmundur appointed Arndís Sigurdardóttir as the Chairperson of the Working Group. She had completed police training in 2000, served as a police officer in Reykjavík for three years, then worked part-time with the police while studying law at the University of Iceland (2002–2006). She qualified as a lawyer in 2008 and has worked in that capacity since. She was a 'member' (*Varaþingmaður*) of parliament between 2009 and 2013.

In addition, Arndís runs Hotel Fljótshlíd, a very successful three star country hotel on the Farm of Smáratún, situated in the lee of Eyjafjallajökull, which erupted in 2010, causing major travel chaos in Europe.

I perceived Arndís as a natural leader, an immensely talented and affable person with a strong sense of ethics. It is remarkable how she was able to combine the committee work with all her other duties.

The two other members of the Working Group were Haraldur Steinthórsson, a lawyer, and Professor Jón Fridrik Sigurdsson, a psychologist. I did not have the opportunity of getting to know Haraldur well, but he clearly had a sound understanding of relevant points of law and excellent judgement. He came across as being conscientious and meticulous. He has BA and MA degrees in law from the University of Iceland, his final dissertation being on the 'Use and assessment of evidence as part of the right to a fair trial in the meaning of Article 6 ECHR' [European Convention on Human Rights]. He has worked at the Icelandic Ministry of Finance since 2007 and was seconded to work part-time on the Working Group between 2011 and 2013.

I first met Jón Fridrik in 1989 when he came to visit the secure unit at the Bethlem Royal Hospital in England as part of his professional development. At the time he worked at the Icelandic Prison and Probation Administration, where he was employed between 1988 and 2001, following which he spent many years as the Head of Clinical Psychology Services at the National University Hospital of Iceland.

In 1992 Jón Fridrik registered for a PhD at the Institute of Psychiatry and I supervised his dissertation. He successfully completed his PhD in 1998 and we published a number of papers together in the area of false confession. He achieved an astonishing record in the percentage of prisoners participating in research: some 96%. He is a Professor of Psychology both at the University of Iceland and Reykjavík University.

In view of his academic, clinical, and prison psychology background, Jón Fridrik was an ideal professional to be appointed to the Working Group. He had served on other similar committees, including those investigating abuse in care homes in Iceland (Spano et al., 2016). Jón Fridrik is meticulous in his work, well organized, and resourceful.

Valgerdur Sigurdardóttir, a lawyer, was already employed by the Ministry of the Interior and was commissioned to assist the Working Group with practical matters related to its work. She received and recorded all case file material that the Ministry had received from the National Archives of Iceland and other sources. She read every single document and set out a timeline in an Excel spreadsheet file, summarizing the relevant pieces of information relating to the Gudmundur and Geirfinnur cases. Her role, skills, and contribution were essential to the Working Group.

Valgerdur qualified as a lawyer from the University of Iceland in 2008 and had originally worked for the Ministry of Justice before she moved to the Ministry of the Interior. Her MA dissertation was titled: 'Schengen Area of Freedom, Security and Justice'. Throughout my work in Iceland she was always very helpful, had a cheerful and charming demeanour, and efficiency that was exemplary.

Arndís appointed me as an expert to the Working Group in a letter dated 28 November 2011. My terms of reference were to provide advice and work with the Group on the evaluation of the confessions and evidence of persons who were investigated in connection with the Gudmundur and Geirfinnur cases in the 1970s. I spent 39 days in Iceland between 30 January 2012 and 7 February 2013 working on the cases. After that, Jón Fridrik sent me several emails with questions or material he wanted me to comment on before the publication of the Working Group Report on 21 March 2013.

It took the Working Group over a year to obtain 'all' the documents in the Gudmundur and Geirfinnur cases because of a lack of cooperation by the Supreme Court, the Office of Public Prosecution, and the National Archives. The National Commissioner of the Icelandic Police and the Reykjavík District Court proved more cooperative with gaining access to documents. Documents were still being discovered two months before the Report was due to be completed. The poor access to the documents hampered the work of the Group.

The Working Group had no investigative powers and all witnesses attended interviews voluntarily.[6]

---

[6] ICCRC Report, 2017, Saevar Ciesielski, Paragraph 1967.

## The Methodology

After meeting with the Working Group on 30 January 2012, it was agreed that Jón Fridrik and I would work jointly on the psychological evaluation of the reliability of the convicted persons' confessions and incriminating statements to the police and court. This was partly due to the amount of work required for the psychological evaluation, but it also allowed Jón Fridrik and me to combine our strengths and resources in order to maximize the efficacy and quality of the chapter we jointly wrote in the Working Group Report.

Valgerdur provided us with the case file material, the Sídumúli Prison diaries, the Reykjavík Penitentiary diaries, and copies of the diaries of Gudjón Skarphédinsson and Tryggvi Leifsson, which they had written during their period in custody. We checked many of the entries in the diaries with those in Sídumúli Prison custody record (diaries) and this provided important confirmation that these personal diaries had been written contemporaneously. We were in no doubt that the two diaries provided important new material, in addition to many highly revealing entries in the Sídumúli Prison log.

We decided to write a timeline entry for each of the six convicted persons from the Sídumúli Prison Daily Diary Log during their solitary confinement. We did the same for the 'four wrongly accused' (Einar Bollason, Magnús Leópoldsson, Sigurbjörn Eiríksson, and Valdimar Olsen) for comparison purposes, but because of pressure of time we were not able to include this in the Working Group Report. However, a brief comparison of the custody records and reports of interrogations showed that the 'four wrongly accused' had been treated much more favourably than the other suspects, both in terms of access to lawyers and being subjected to fewer, shorter, and less harsh interrogation sessions.

In general terms, I dictated to Jón Fridrik the relevant information from the Sídumúli Prison diaries and police reports and he entered it onto the computer, compiling a timeline for each person. This included information about access to legal advice, pertinent telephone calls or messages, time spent with the investigators and visitors, suspects' face-to-face confrontations[7], and visits to Court or crime scene visits, many of which involved looking for the bodies of Gudmundur and Geirfinnur. Jón Fridrik calculated the hours and number of

---

[7] This is where two or more suspects were put together in a room, supervised by police, in order to improve consistency in their accounts of what had happened in the Gudmundur and Geirfinnur cases. This sometimes consisted of one suspect putting pressure on another suspect to change his/her account – functioning like police pressure by proxy.

interrogations and other relevant categories, including meetings with lawyers and suspects' face-to-face confrontations.

Jón Fridrik and I met with convicted persons Erla, Gudjón, and Kristján, with me leading the interviews. Albert refused to meet with the Working Group but agreed to talk to me alone. No formal psychological tests were administered because of the length of time since the interrogation (i.e. about 36 years). All the interviews were electronically recorded.

When all the data had been entered into the database, we used it as the foundation for writing our chapter in the Report (i.e. Chapter 19, Sections 19.2 and 19.3), along with a timeline that Valgerdur had produced, which unlike ours, included statements from the court. We jointly drafted the psychological evaluation of each of the six convicted persons. Our chapter was entitled 'Psychological evaluation of the testimony of the convicted persons in the Gudmundur and Geirfinnur cases' (my translation). Preceding this chapter was a comprehensive review of the science of false confessions, which I had written alone. It included an outline of the approach we used in the psychological evaluation using the framework I had developed, in part with Dr James MacKeith in the 1990s, and illustrated in Gudjonsson (2003a).

The key components that I would typically focus on in my evaluation are:

- *Context* (e.g. the nature and seriousness of the offence, pressure on the police to solve the crime, and the special circumstances of the suspect, such as a mother being separated from her young baby, or an interviewee suffering from bereavement).
- *Custody* (i.e. the nature and duration of the confinement).
- *Interrogation* (i.e. the nature and duration of the interrogation).
- *Physical and mental health* (e.g. health problems, lack of access to prescribed medication, history of substance misuse, intellectual disability, attention deficit hyperactivity disorder – ADHD).
- *Personality* (e.g. suggestibility, compliance, dependency, low intelligence).
- Support (e.g. access to a lawyer, or 'appropriate adult' where required).
- *Relationships and interactions* between the suspect, interviewers, and others present during the interview.

### Caveats

In our report, Jón Fridrik and I put forward three caveats regarding our findings. Firstly, nearly 40 years had elapsed since the Gudmundur and Geirfinnur investigations and during that time the memories of the four surviving convicted persons, and the prison and police officers were likely to have deteriorated, particularly regarding peripheral detail. Salient central detail would be likely to have been better preserved.

Secondly, caution needed to be exercised when relying exclusively on the accounts given by convicted persons in cases of disputed confessions, because of their potential self-serving focus (Gudjonsson, 2003a). In view of this, Jón Fridrik and I tried, as far as possible, to corroborate accounts with established records, including the Síðumúli Prison diaries. Of course, the retrospective accounts given by police and prison officers could also be self-serving, but this is rarely raised by the court because of the assumed inherent credibility of these professional groups.

Thirdly, we relied substantially on documents that had been entered into the two separate timeline files produced by Valgerdur, and Jón Fridrik and me, respectively. We did not always cite in our chapter the sources of the information entered.

I would add one further caveat. The number of interrogations and how long they took was based on incomplete records and is an underestimate. In addition, we did not enter data from the Reykjavík Penitentiary (*Hegningarhúsið*) where diary entries were available from January 1977. We relied on diary entries at Síðumúli Prison and officially recorded interrogations.

## THE GENERAL FINDINGS OF THE WORKING GROUP

In its comprehensive review of the Gudmundur and Geirfinnur cases, the Working Group Report (2013) identified and discussed a number of weaknesses with the investigation, including the following:

- There were no bodies and there was a complete absence of forensic evidence.
- The two men had disappeared between one and two years previously, which hampered the investigation.
- The six convicted persons all repeatedly changed their version of events in major respects.
- The investigation relied almost exclusively on information gathered from suspects, witnesses, and informants.
- The circumstantial, corroborative, and identification evidence was weak or non-existent.
- All attempts by the police to find tangible evidence, including a coat, shovel, and knife, failed.
- The length of solitary confinement with regard to some of the suspects is the longest ever seen in Icelandic cases in modern history.

- Over a year into the investigation, the police discovered that the telephone at Hamarsbraut 11, the alleged murder scene, had been disconnected at the time of Gudmundur's disappearance, which meant that the suspects could not have telephoned Albert from the flat, as claimed.
- No tangible evidence was found from any of the alleged crime scenes.
- Fourteen months after the suspects were arrested, Saevar suddenly identified a new witness (Gunnar Jónsson).
- Extensive searches in a large number of locations were conducted in an attempt to find the bodies of Gudmundur and Geirfinnur. All proved unsuccessful.
- In the Geirfinnur case, the police checked evidence provided by psychics.

While the suspects were in solitary confinement, the investigators' most recent theories and information were communicated between them by:

- The evidence of other suspects being introduced to an interviewee for comment.
- Suspects' versions of events being communicated to one another during their face-to-face confrontations.
- Prison officers communicating police theories and information to suspects.
- The police indirectly communicating what other suspects had said through the nature of the questions asked during interrogation.

The Working Group found that the convicted persons had been held in solitary confinement for between 87 and 655 days. Based on more or different information, the Commission found that the figures ranged between 88 and 741 days (Table 12.2). Table 12.2 also shows the total

**Table 12.2** Days in detention and proportion spent in solitary confinement, according to the Icelandic Court Cases Review Commission Report

| Convicted person | Days in detention* | Days in solitary confinement (%) |
|---|---|---|
| Saevar | 1,533 | 741 (48.3) |
| Kristján | 1,522 | 682 (44.8) |
| Tryggvi | 1,522 | 627 (41.2) |
| Erla | 241 | 241 (100.0) |
| Gudjón | 1,197 | 412 (34.4) |
| Albert | 88 | 88 (100.0) |

*In the cases of Saevar, Kristján, Tryggvi, and Gudjón this refers to the date from which they were detained until the judgement in the Supreme Court on 22 February 1980.

number of days in custody prior to conviction in the Supreme Court in February 1980 – from 88 to 1,533 days. The percentage of time they were held in solitary confinement also varied. Erla and Albert spent all of their time in solitary confinement, whereas Saevar, Kristján, Tryggvi, and Gudjón spent 48.3%, 44.8%, 41.2%, and 34.4% of their time there, respectively.

## THE FINDINGS FROM THE PSYCHOLOGICAL EVALUATION

Our findings were unequivocal. The confessions of the convicted persons to the police and in court were unreliable, and in the case of Gudjón we went further and stated that his confessions were false, because his diaries had clearly shown that he was confessing to something of which he had no memory. (A detailed model of each of the six persons' confessions is presented in Chapters 13–18.) We listed nine factors that both individually and together cast doubts on the confessions. These were:

1. Long periods of solitary confinement, combined with many and lengthy interrogations.
2. Individual vulnerability factors, which were evident among all six persons.
3. Many informal contacts between the suspects and the investigators, which included visits to their cells or taking them out of the prison, often on unspecified visits.
4. The frequency of direct suspects' face-to-face confrontations, which increased the risk of contamination.
5. Visits outside the prison to help look for the bodies of Gudmundur and Geirfinnur.
6. Limited access to lawyers and commonly not being able to see their clients in private.
7. Fear that custody would be extended if the investigators were not satisfied with their statements (i.e. Örn Höskuldsson had enormous power and freedom to remand suspects in solitary confinement, or extend their existing detention, and used it frequently and coercively).
8. On occasions, prison officers interrogated the suspects and assisted in looking for the bodies of Gudmundur and Geirfinnur. This shows how prison officers exceeded their role and remit.
9. The investigators had tunnel vision, guilt-presumption, and negative attitudes towards the suspects, particularly Saevar and Kristján.

**Table 12.3**  Number of police interviews, hours of police interactions with the suspect, number of suspects' face-to-face confrontations, number of outside visits, and presence of lawyer

|                              | Erla | Saevar | Kristján | Tryggvi | Gudjón | Albert |
|------------------------------|------|--------|----------|---------|--------|--------|
| Number of police interviews  | 105  | 180    | 160      | 95      | 75     | 26     |
| Hours of interviews          | 120  | 340    | 215      | 124     | 160    | 17     |
| Face-to-face confrontations  | 11   | 20     | 18       | 16      | 5      | 16     |
| Outside visits               | 9    | 36     | 22       | 3       | 9      | 11     |
| Presence of lawyer           | 3    | 49     | 28       | 25      | 27     | 4      |

Content taken from Gudjonsson et al. (2014).

Table 12.3 shows the number of police interviews, total number of hours the interviewers spent with each of the convicted persons, the number of face-to-face confrontation sessions between suspects, the number of times each person was taken out of the police custody area (i.e. 'crime scene' visits, taking them out 'for a drive', and medical visits), and the number of meetings with a lawyer, which were often not in private. The figures were derived from the Sídumúli Prison Detention Daily Diary Log ('diaries') and police reports.

The total number of interrogations for the six convicted persons was 641 (range 26–180), stretched over 976 hours (range 17–340). Saevar and Kristján had the largest number of interrogations (180 and 160) and hours of interrogation (340 and 215), respectively.[8]

Saevar and Kristján had the largest number of suspects' face-to-face confrontations, 20 and 18, respectively, followed by Tryggvi and Albert (16 each) and Erla (11). These were particularly common in May, June, and July 1976 after the release of the 'four wrongly accused' on 9 May 1976.[9]

Visits out of Sídumúli Prison most commonly occurred with Saevar and Kristján, followed by Albert, Gudjón, Erla, and Tryggvi. Many of these visits appear to have involved visits to alleged crime scenes or unsuccessful searches for the bodies of Gudmundur and Geirfinnur.

In terms of access to lawyers, Erla and Albert had the fewest visits, and Saevar the most. Erla only saw her lawyer on three occasions and Albert on four occasions. Access to lawyers, when it occurred, was

---

[8] The Commission draws attention to the fact that this calculation may be an underestimate, because it did not cover the period between 7 October and 12 December 1977, the latter date referring to the end of verbal submissions in the District Court (ICCRC Report, 2017, Saevar Ciesielski, Paragraph 2386).
[9] ICCRC Report, 2017, Saevar Ciesielski, Paragraph 2300.

generally ineffective because over a long period of time they were not allowed to speak to their client in private (i.e. police officers were present during consultations) and the lawyers were rarely present during interrogations.

## THE TESTIMONY IN THE REYKJAVÍK DISTRICT COURT

On 22 December 2015, I received an email from the assistant of the special prosecutor David Björgvinsson, summoning me to attend the Reykjavík District Court on 28 January 2016 and answer questions concerning my qualifications, professional experience, association with the convicted persons in 1976, memory distrust syndrome, conclusions, and the methodology Jón Fridrik and I had used when evaluating the reliability of the confessions in the Gudmundur and Geirfinnur cases for the Working Group. My testimony was in Icelandic and lasted almost three hours without a break. The authors of the Working Group Report – Arndís, Haraldur, Jón Fridrik, and Valgerdur – were also required to testify but had fewer questions to answer. They all testified in the morning. Valgerdur testified via a telephone call from Brussels where she worked and lived at the time. I testified in the afternoon.

Following me in the witness box were the three members of the Reykjavík Team, Örn Höskuldsson, Sigurbjörn Vídir Eggertsson, and Eggert Bjarnason, who testified in that order. Eggert testified by telephone apparently because of health issues. Ragnar Adalsteinsson, the lawyer representing Erla and Gudjón, had requested their attendance to answer questions about why the Gudmundur Einarsson investigation had started in December 1975.[10]

### My Testimony[11]

It was helpful to have the questions in advance of my testifying. Many of these were complicated questions that required considerable preparation. They appeared to have been substantially based on comments that the special prosecutor David Björgvinsson had made in his observations of the convicted persons' applications for appeal.

I saw my testimony as an opportunity to advance some of the arguments Jón Fridrik and I had made in the Working Group Report,

---

[10] ICCRC Report, 2017, Gudjón Skarphédinsson, Paragraph 1426.
[11] I have not discussed Jón Fridrik Sigurdsson's testimony due to the overlap between our testimonies.

particularly those relating to Erla and Albert being brought as 'witnesses' into Sídumúli Prison for questioning, which was intimidating and coercive.

The Court was situated right in the centre of Reykjavík, in Laekjartorg Square, a place I knew well and loved. The courtroom was packed full of interested parties, including Erla, the grown-up children of Saevar, and journalists. The atmosphere was tense; this was uncharted territory for the Commission, special prosecutor, judiciary, and defence lawyers. David Björgvinsson asked the questions and cross-examined me. This was followed by questions from defence lawyers Lúdvík Bergvinsson (for Saevar and Tryggvi), Ragnar Adalsteinsson (for Gudjón and Erla), and Snaedís Agnarsdóttir (for Albert). There was no representation for Kristján, because he had not formally appealed his conviction. This was not an indication of his guilt and had to do with his personal/ health issues.[12]

After I had answered the special prosecutor's numerous questions, the three defence lawyers asked me questions. Lúdvík Bergvinsson and Ragnar Adalsteinsson asked a large number of the questions: they were well prepared and formidable defence lawyers. Snaedís Agnarsdóttir was impressive too. She was substituting for Albert's appointed lawyer, Gudjón Ólafur Jónsson, who could not attend.

Early in my testimony I was asked about a possible conflict of interest regarding my involvement in the cases, because as a young detective in 1976, I had administered lie detector tests to Saevar and Gudjón. In a biography that Anna Hildur Hildibrandsdóttir had written about me in 2001, I, too, had expressed concerns about a possible conflict of interest. However, I did not think this disqualified me from taking on the cases for the Working Group. I put forward two arguments: firstly, that nearly 40 years had elapsed since I had worked in the police and I was no longer tainted by the guilt-presumptive attitude of many of my police colleagues in the 1970s, and secondly, I had learned from experience that I could work objectively and dispassionately on cases, even under difficult circumstances.

The reality is that the Gudmundur and Geirfinnur cases were exceptionally complex and I was probably the best qualified 'confession expert' to evaluate them. In addition, I could read all the documents in Icelandic and my experience with the police in the 1970s gave me a unique context from which to work (e.g. I was aware of the

---

[12] On 17 December 2015, the special prosecutor had requested that Kristján's case be considered for an appeal (see Table 12.1). Kristján Vidarsson was notified in a letter dated 7 January 2016 and given the status of an appellant (ICCRC Report, 2017, Kristján Vidarsson, Paragraph 1).

guilt-presumptive attitude against the six convicted persons and the pressure to solve the cases, and I knew the facilities well, including those in Síðumúli Prison, and the social and police culture).

In response to a question from David Björgvinsson, I explained that in relation to suspects' thinking processes and expectations in detention, I differentiated between those who had committed a serious crime, such as murder, and suspects who were genuinely innocent. The former may deny any involvement of the crime in order to avoid detention and conviction, but detention will generally not come as a surprise to them after arrest, and eventually they usually accept it. In contrast, innocent suspects are typically surprised at being arrested and detained and believe that the truth will somehow prevail. Their focus is on avoiding custody, and if in custody, they will often do their best to cooperate with the police in the hope that they will be released as soon as possible. I explained that problems arise when the interrogators do not accept their claims of innocence and interview them in a guilt-presumptive fashion.[13]

I expressed concerns about the Gudmundur and Geirfinnur cases where the suspects were readily given solitary confinement when they were not seen to be providing the police with the information they wanted (e.g. making denials, not going along with the police investigative hypothesis or scenario, or retracting a confession). This could extend over many months to over two years, during which time the suspects would be repeatedly interrogated. Under those circumstances and conditions, suspects arrested in serious cases are often more focused on the short-term benefit of providing incriminating information against themselves or others (i.e. either attempting to avoid custody or hoping to be released, if already in custody) than the potential long-term consequences (e.g. being convicted for the crime or for giving false statements against others).

I explained that the situation had been more straightforward in England in the 1970s because suspects in serious cases were typically kept in custody for only three days at most, after which they had to be charged or released. If they were charged, no further interrogation would take place. This provided a possible safety net with regard to false confessions, because suspects knew that they only had to cope with the confinement and interrogation for a limited number of days, after which they would either be released or charged. Even under those more favourable conditions, false confessions still occurred, highlighting

---

[13] The essence of good police interviewing is open-mindedness, which was well embedded in Icelandic law at the time, but unfortunately it was not practiced by the investigators or enforced by the court.

the point that even short periods of solitary confinement, involving a few hours or days, combined with interrogative pressure, can sometimes result in a false confession.

The Commission was interested in the phenomenon of memory distrust syndrome and whether it is the result of pre-existing vulnerabilities or develops in response to contextual factors. A good question indeed, I thought. I testified that it could be either, or a combination of both. Memory problems, lack of confidence in one's memory, suggestibility, compliance, and trust in the police certainly accelerate the development of the condition, while circumstances such as long and intense guilt-presumptive interviewing and solitary confinement can lead to profound memory distrust without significant pre-existing vulnerabilities. As an example of the latter, I mentioned Einar Bollason, Erla's half-brother, who had developed memory distrust during his period in custody but had the resilience to overcome it and did not make a false confession (Karlsson, 1994).

I was asked about the difference between Erla's statements given in and out of custody. On 20 December 1975 she had implicated Saevar and Kristján in the Gudmundur case prior to her release from one week in solitary confinement at Síðumúli Prison. According to police statements, on 23 January 1976 Erla had implicated Einar Bollason and Magnús Leópoldsson in the Geirfinnur case, and about two weeks later she formally implicated Sigurbjörn Eiríksson.[14]

On 4 May 1976 Erla gave a confession statement to shooting Geirfinnur, having been brought the previous evening to Síðumúli Prison as a witness and interrogated and then kept there overnight. I argued that there were no differences in the reliability between the in and out of custody statements, considering all as being unreliable. My reasoning in court was as follows.

The investigators were in contact with Erla following her release from custody on 20 December. They brought her to Síðumúli Prison on 21 and 23 January and interrogated her there.[15] Questioning her in the prison where she had been held in custody for over a week the previous month was intimidating and coercive. The investigators had much better interviewing facilities at their nearby offices. I testified that their procedure was bizarre, particularly considering that they were

---

[14] Erla never properly implicated Valdimar Olsen but was nevertheless convicted of doing so (see Ragnar Adalsteinsson's letter to the special prosecutor, dated 22 May 2017, outlined later in this chapter).

[15] Further evidence has emerged to show that she was also brought to the prison on 30 December and 22 January for a total of almost seven hours without a proper record of what went on (see Chapter 9).

interviewing an extremely vulnerable young woman, who had a young baby and allegedly had the status of a witness. Her vulnerabilities were evident from her reaction after being brought to Sídumúli Prison for interrogation on the evening of 3 May 1976, and after a night in custody gave a statement that she had murdered Geirfinnur (see Chapters 9 and 14). I concluded with regard to Erla:

> I'm convinced that when Erla was not in custody she was dependent on the police officers, was mentally weak, feared custody, wanted to be with her baby, and did everything she could to please them.
> (Court testimony transcript, p. 65)

Following this I was asked about the difference in reliability between Albert's first confession, when he was officially interviewed as a witness, and his subsequent confessions as a suspect in solitary confinement. The Commission and the prosecutor seemed concerned that Albert had apparently confessed quite readily during his first police interview on 23 December 1975. I testified that there was no difference in the reliability in the two circumstances: the confessions in both circumstances were unreliable. The reasons I gave were as follows.

The day before Christmas Eve (i.e. on 23 December), Albert was brought from Seydisfjördur (a town in the far Easten Region of Iceland) during the night, arriving in Sídumúli Prison at 05.00, where he stayed locked in until he was interviewed the following afternoon, about eight hours later. In spite of being given the status of a witness, which meant that he was not entitled to consult with a lawyer, which worked to the advantage of the police, by the way he was treated he must have realized the seriousness of the situation. This was a most unusual way of treating a witness. He could have been taken to the offices of the police where witnesses were interviewed in a more comfortable setting. He was left with his own thoughts and uncertainties in prison for many hours, which undoubtedly functioned as a 'softening up' process and would have weakened his resistance during subsequent police questioning. At the time, Albert had general memory problems, little self-confidence, and was extremely compliant. I pointed out that he had tolerated solitary confinement poorly, because four days after being brought to Sídumúli Prison he became extremely agitated and his feet were shackled. The essence of my conclusions was:

> I think that from the beginning, when he was collected and taken to Sídumúli Prison and kept waiting there, he had become susceptible to believing what he was alleged of knowing about the case [...] I'm not evaluating guilt or innocence, that's for the court to decide. I'm evaluating the circumstances and vulnerabilities, and how much reliance can

be placed on the confessions. I'm convinced that Albert was from the beginning very vulnerable and the risk of his giving an unreliable confession was very high.

(Court testimony transcript, p. 67)

I testified that the reason for the strong conclusions in our chapter in the Working Group Report regarding the reliability of the confessions was due to the nature, extent, and severity of the risk factors involved. I also pointed out that nothing tangible or credible had emerged from the confessions.

I was pleased that I had the opportunity to introduce new and important evidence regarding Saevar's ADHD, although surprisingly the Commission did not refer to it in its Report. In March 2015, Saevar's son, Hafthór, had provided me with social services records from Denmark, which showed that two years prior to his death, Saevar had been diagnosed with ADHD, a condition he undoubtedly had in childhood (see Chapter 13), and was given Ritalin. I introduced this in court and Saevar's lawyer, Lúdvík Bergvinsson, followed this up in questions. I stated that Saevar's ADHD would have increased the risk of his giving a false confession.

Ragnar Adalsteinsson skilfully questioned me regarding Erla, Saevar, and Kristján making false allegations against the 'four wrongly accused'. He wanted to know whether the conclusions Jón Fridrik and I had come to in the Working Group Report also included those false allegation statements. I said that they did. I testified that it was not credible that Erla and Saevar had decided after allegedly murdering Geirfinnur to implicate the four men if she or Saevar happened to be arrested in connection with Geirfinnur's disappearance. This was the foundation for the false allegation (perjury) charges. Strictly speaking, the issue was not about reliability, it was about whether or not the false allegation statements were obtained voluntarily. One had to look at the circumstances under which they were obtained, and this is why I focused on this in my testimony.

Ragnar also asked me questions about Erla's motivation on 4 May 1976 to confess to shooting Geirfinnur. I explained that at the time she was undoubtedly in a state of 'despair', found herself under intolerable pressure, and 'wanted to be left alone' (Court testimony transcript, p. 91). Jón Fridrik Sigurdsson gave a similar explanation in his testimony.

## The Testimony of the Reykjavík Team

The testimony of the three original investigators in the Gudmundur and Geirfinnur cases lasted for about an hour and 40 minutes. The Commission and the special prosecutor had no questions for these three retired investigators, which is surprising since they were the only people who really knew why they had started the Gudmundur and Geirfinnur investigations.

Defence lawyer Ragnar Adalsteinsson had requested their attendance and asked most of the questions. The lawyer representing Saevar and Tryggvi, and the lawyer representing Albert, followed with their questions. The most striking and consistent feature of the retired investigators' evidence was their claimed inability to recollect why they had started the Gudmundur investigation in the first place or to name the informant who had brought the suspects to their attention. They also claimed to have very poor memory of the investigation generally and the methods they had employed, which was surprising since this was the most high profile murder investigation in their entire careers. None of them were able or willing to explain why they had brought witnesses to Sídumúli Prison for questioning, rather than using the much more comfortable and convenient facilities at the nearby police and court headquarters. All three witnesses were very vague about the interactions they had had with Erla between her release from custody on 20 December 1975 and when she gave her first statement on 23 January 1976.

Sigurbjörn Vídir Eggertsson went as far as to agree that Erla had been visited at home in connection with the Gudmundur and Geirfinnur cases (Court testimony transcript, p. 108). This was probably the most useful aspect of his evidence. The other two witnesses were less forthcoming about visits to Erla's home, claiming memory lapses.

Örn Höskuldsson claimed not to remember taking part in any of the interrogations but said he might have been present on occasions. He claimed that the two detectives, whom he described as 'very experienced' had led the investigation, apparently trying hard to distance himself from the cases. He denied giving the detectives instructions. In contrast, in their testimony the two officers insisted that Örn Höskuldsson had been in charge of the investigation and had given them instructions.

Örn Höskuldsson said that the Chief Judge sometimes allocated cases to the legal representatives but did not interfere in investigations. In the Gudmundur and Geirfinnur cases, the referral had come directly from the police. The main role of the legal representative was to remand suspects in custody and he/she could only do so if the alleged offence carried more than a two-year prison sentence. Their role did not include questioning witnesses or suspects. The evidence available in the Sídumúli Prison diaries showed that he went well beyond his role as a legal representative / investigative judge in the cases.

Ragnar Adalsteinsson asked Örn Höskuldsson about informant SSA in connection with the cases (Court testimony transcript, pp. 99–100). Örn Höskuldsson claimed not to remember anything about it.

Snaedís Agnarsdóttir asked Örn Höskuldsson about an entry at 22.35 on 22 December 1975 in the Sídumúli Prison diary stating: 'Sheriff Erlendur Björnsson from Seydisfjördur telephoned and spoke to Eggert Bjarnason and refused to arrest the man [Albert] unless there was a warrant or a telegram' (Court testimony transcript, p. 103). Since this was not possible, a senior person from the Ministry of Justice was asked to speak to the Sheriff. Mr Höskuldsson was asked whether he had known about this, whether a telegram was necessary in order to arrest Albert, and whether a warrant should have come from him. His answer was: 'I assume so, but I can't remember this, no' (p. 103).

This was a different jurisdiction and a warrant was probably required, but once back in Reykjavík the police could have arrested Albert if they had sufficient grounds for doing so. The fact that a request had been made to arrest him indicates that he was treated as a suspect but nevertheless given the status of a witness, which meant that he was not entitled to consultation with a lawyer.

In their testimony, Sigurbjörn Vídir and Eggert Bjarnason also claimed not to recall the circumstances behind Albert being collected from Seydisfjördur.

## THE FINDINGS OF THE ICELANDIC COURT CASES REVIEW COMMISSION

Following the Working Group Report in March 2013, the Icelandic Court Cases Review Commission – *Endurupptökunefnd* – Law Number 15/2013) was created. It is an independent administrative organization that has the power to decide whether there are sufficient grounds to authorize the rehearing of cases. The Commission is made up of three people, appointed for five years at a time. The three members reviewing the Gudmundur and Geirfinnur cases were Björn L Bergsson (Foreman), Ásgerdur Ragnarsdóttir, and Sigurdur Tómas Magnússon.

The Commission produced separate reports for each of the six convicted persons (ICCRC Report, 2017). The reports are very lengthy and detailed, ranging between 566 (Albert) and 1,271 (Saevar) pages. Inevitably, there is considerable duplication between the basic materials presented in the different reports.

The reports were extremely informative and the arguments in favour of appeal with regard to the manslaughter convictions and Albert's conviction of participating in interfering with the crime scene are cogent and compelling. The amount of work that went into these reports was enormous and the clarity of the Commission's findings impressive. Unfortunately, the same level of attention and quality does not hold true for its approach regarding the perjury conviction applications.

The Commission relied heavily on the new evidence discovered by the Working Group Report and its findings, but it also reviewed all the documents and discovered further important previously undisclosed material.

The Commission's key findings are presented below.

### Problems With the Investigation and Evidence

The Commission highlighted three general summary points:[16]

- There now exist firm conclusions from scholars that the confessions of all six convicted persons were unreliable, which undermines the foundation of their convictions. No such evaluation of the confessions' reliability had been conducted previously. At the time of the Working Group, all of the six persons had retracted their confessions and some have fought publicly for a long time to have their name cleared.
- Evidence has emerged that the investigation was seriously flawed. There are examples of numerous unrecorded lengthy and detailed interrogations, crime scene visits, and suspects' face-to-face confrontations. There were many lengthy interactions taking place between the suspects and the investigators of which the court was unaware, giving a misleading impression of how the confession statements developed and progressed over time. In addition, the suspects were subjected to coercive interviews, were kept in custody for an extremely long time, and given drugs that had the effects of making them drowsy and impairing their resistance.
- Some of the witnesses who appeared in court had stated that their evidence was untrue (referred to as 'SÓH', 'EJR', and 'SM' in the Commission Report – SÓH refers to Sigurdur Óttar Hreinsson, a key witness in the Geirfinnur case; the other two persons were witnesses to Gudmundur being seen outside the dance hall in Strandgata, in the early hours of 27 January 1974, in the presence of another man, assumed to be Kristján Vidarsson).

---

[16] ICCRC Report, 2017, Saevar Ciesielski, Paragraphs 2041–2043.

The Commission considered that in view of the above, the outcome in the Supreme Court might have been different if this new information had been available at the time of the court hearing.

The Commission also pointed out in the reports that the convicted persons were not given the benefit of reasonable doubt, which clearly existed with regard to their incriminating testimony before the police and in court.

## Arguments for Appeal

The Commission viewed the Working Group Report as 'fresh evidence' – 'It is evident that the Report contains much new information which would have made a real difference regarding the case's outcome'.[17]

## The Confessions

The convictions of the six persons were almost exclusively dependent on confession evidence, which Saevar, Kristján, Tryggvi, and Erla had retracted prior to the Supreme Court hearing in February 1980.[18] In view of the court's reliance on the confessions, the Commission's report discussed in detail the confessions, their reliability, the antecedents, and the context within which the suspects gave their confessions. I have translated key paragraphs regarding the Commission's findings (i.e. it does not represent an official translation).

The Commission concluded that there is a substantial likelihood that the exceptionally long and harsh solitary confinement, the investigative methods, the imprecise recording of statements, the limited access to defence lawyers, and the breach of police codes of practice had all impacted on the reliability of the convicted persons' testimony, which had been wrongly determined by the Supreme Court. In addition, the Commission thought that the Supreme Court had been inaccurate and in some instances given the wrong evaluation of the development of the confessions, the dates when the confessions were retracted, the trustworthiness of the retractions, and changed testimony of witnesses:

> The findings of the psychologists Gísli H Gudjónsson and Jón Fridrik Sigurdsson regarding the reliability of the convicted persons' testimony in the Minister of the Interior Working Group Report, support the view of the Commission that various important factors that substantially

---

[17] ICCRC Report, 2017, Saevar Ciesielski, Paragraph 2115.
[18] Erla later also retracted her statement in the Gudmundur case.

reduced the evidential value [*sönnunargildi*] of the confessions of all the convicted persons had been ignored.[19]

## Saevar Ciesielski's Confessions

The Commission makes an interesting observation of the confessions and retractions that Saevar and Kristján gave. It concluded that a careful analysis of all the documents in the case suggested that the two men had given credible explanations of the reasons why they had confessed and of their retractions. The convicted persons were not given the benefit of the doubt associated with their confessions:

> The findings of the psychologists Gísli H Gudjónsson and Jón Fridrik Sigurdsson regarding the reliability of the convicted persons' testimony in the Minister of the Interior Working Group Report support the Commission's view in this respect.[20]

## Kristján Vidarsson's Confessions

The Commission considered it very likely that Kristján's mental state had been so poor during the last few months in 1976 and early 1977 because of long solitary confinement and psychological vulnerabilities that it was doubtful that his statements to the police and evidence in court had any validity at all.[21] During this period, Kristján made confessions to two further murders and implicated his grandmother in helping him cut up the body of one of the men. As examples of his poor mental state, Kristján made suicide attempts in late December 1976 and early January 1977. The Commission expressed doubts about his fitness for interview during this period.

The Supreme Court made no reference to the many contradictory and improbable testimonies and how this and Kristján's poor mental state may have impacted on the trustworthiness of his testimony. He was not allowed the benefit of doubt that surrounded his confessions:

> The finding of the psychologists Gísli H Gudjónsson and Jón Fridrik Sigurdsson, in the Minister of the Interior Working Group Report, that the appeal applicant's testimony both to police and in court had been found to be unreliable support this conclusion of the Commission.[22]

---

[19] ICCRC Report, 2017, Saevar Ciesielski, Paragraphs 3119 and 3120.
[20] ICCRC Report, 2017, Saevar Ciesielski, Paragraphs 3052 and 3053.
[21] ICCRC Report, 2017, Kristján Vidarsson, Paragraph 2074.
[22] ICCRC Report, 2017, Kristján Vidarsson, Paragraph 2955.

## Tryggvi Leifsson's Confessions

The Commission believed that Tryggvi's diaries give an indication that his confessions to the police and in court early in the investigation had come about because he thought it sensible under the circumstances to confess falsely and trust that a fair court process would ascertain the truth. This created reservations about the reliability of his confessions, which typically included only points that had already been given by the other convicted persons, and he contributed little to the course of events at Hamarsbraut 11:

> The finding of the psychologists Gísli H Gudjónsson and Jón Fridrik Sigurdsson that the appeal applicant's evidence both to police and in court had been unreliable support this conclusion of the Commission.[23]

## Gudjón Skarphédinsson's Confessions

The Commission considered it a 'real possibility' [raunhæfan möguleika] that the investigative methods used under the direction of Karl Schütz, after Gudjón had been implicated by others in the case, 'stopped him trusting his memory and caused him to confess to participating in the assault on Geirfinnur'. It concluded:

> Statements of the appeal applicant to police and particularly in court, and his diaries while in Sídumúli Prison, support the finding of psychologists Gísli H Gudjónsson and Jón Fridrik Sigurdsson, in the Minister of the Interior Working Group Report, that he had made false confessions. It is inevitable but to conclude that the fact the convicted person [Gudjón] did not retract his confession before a court carried great weight in the Supreme Court's evaluation of evidence regarding the guilt of all the convicted persons.[24]

## Albert Skaftason's Confessions

The Commission noted that even though Albert had been very cooperative with the police, he had serious problems recalling what had allegedly taken place. In fact, he was very unsure throughout of his real memories and his testimony changed in substantial ways in accordance with the police investigative hypothesis at any given time, which I believe is strong evidence of his high level of suggestibility and compliance. His memory problems were not referred to in court and he

---

[23] ICCRC Report, 2017, Tryggvi Leifsson, Paragraphs 1813–1814.
[24] ICCRC Report, 2017, Gudjón Skarphédinsson, Paragraph 2406.

appears not to have been given the benefit of doubt that surrounded his confession:

> The finding of the psychologists Gísli H Gudjónsson and Jón Fridrik Sigurdsson that the appeal applicant's evidence both to police and in court had been unreliable support this conclusion of the Commission.[25]

### Erla Bolladóttir's Confessions

In a discussion of the Geirfinnur case, the Commission commented on Erla's testimony in relation to the trip to Keflavík and the burial of Geirfinnur's body in the 'Red Hills'.[26] It concluded that when Erla's testimony is viewed as a whole, it must be considered very unreliable and a long way from being proven beyond reasonable doubt:

> The findings of the psychologists Gísli H Gudjónsson and Jón Fridrik Sigurdsson regarding the reliability of the convicted person Erla's testimony in the Minister of the Interior Working Group Report support the Commission's view.[27]

## Why Did the Gudmundur Investigation Start?

The Commission is in possession of evidence that strongly indicates that SSA, a serving prisoner at Litla-Hraun Prison, implicated the convicted persons in causing the death of Gudmundur in exchange for leniency regarding his own offences. SSA was brought to Sídumúli Prison at 15.00 on 18 December 1975, presumably in connection with information regarding the Gudmundur case, and the following day he was collected by police, who said he would not be returning to prison. At 15.30 he was due to fly to Egilsstadir with his brother, now being a free man. At the time that SSA was in Sídumúli Prison, Erla was confessing to the Post and Telecommunication fraud and she was then asked questions about Gudmundur's disappearance.

Importantly, SSA had in early December 1975 informed the police that Saevar and Erla were responsible for the Post and Telecommunication fraud, as a result of which Kristján was brought to Sídumúli Prison on 10 December for questioning. Sigurdur and Kristján

---

[25] ICCRC Report, 2017, Albert Skaftason, Paragraph 1512.
[26] In view of the fact that Erla was not convicted in the Supreme Court of killing Geirfinnur, the unreliability of her testimony is only referred to in the reports of the other convicted persons.
[27] ICCRC Report, 2017, Saevar Ciesielski, Paragraph 3021.

were at the time fellow inmates at Litla-Hraun Prison. SSA was released that time from Litla-Hraun Prison on 12 December, the same day Saevar was arrested and placed in custody at Sídumúli Prison.

In June 2016, SSA, along with another man, were arrested and interrogated in connection with the disappearance of Gudmundur Einarsson. They did not confess and the case was dropped.[28] When asked about his association with the police in 1975, SSA said he had been in the habit at the time of telling them fabricated stories [sífellt verið að ljúga í þá sögum].[29]

The background to this is as follows. In October 2014 a woman had reported to police that she had been a passenger in a car with Sigurdur Almarsson and another man in the early hours of 27 January 1974 when the car hit Gudmundur and apparently injured him. Gudmundur was brought into the car and taken away. The witness, who was dropped off at her home with Gudmundur still being in the car, was Sigurdur Almarsson's partner at the time. She also said that she had been present when Sigurdur met with the police and investigative judge to implicate Saevar and Kristján in the disappearance of Gudmundur in exchange for Sigurdur being released from prison. One of the detectives and the investigative judge were questioned about this during the police investigation into this matter, said they could not remember.[30]

### Weather Conditions in the Gudmundur Case

The Commission pointed out that while the convicted persons were allegedly driving around Hafnarfjördur in the early hours of 27 January 1974 in a small Volkswagen car, which included going to the nearby lava field with Gudmundur's body, heavy snow had been falling and the weather conditions were ferocious. It is known that after midnight, taxi drivers had stopped working due to the bad conditions.[31] In my view, if the convicted persons had been out that night, it is surprising that they did not mention the bad weather conditions to the police when interviewed, nor were they apparently asked about it.[32] Neither the Criminal Court nor Supreme Court addressed this important factor.[33]

---

[28] ICCRC Report, 2017, Saevar Ciesielski, Paragraph 1972.
[29] ICCRC Report, 2017, Saevar Ciesielski, Paragraph 2396.
[30] ICCRC Report, 2017, Saevar Ciesielski, Paragraph 1972.
[31] ICCRC Report, 2017, Saevar Ciesielski, Paragraph 2350.
[32] ICCRC Report, 2017, Saevar Ciesielski, Paragraph 2958.
[33] ICCRC Report, 2017, Saevar Ciesielski, Paragraph 2959.

In addition, the Commission considered it unlikely that Kristján and Tryggvi had met Gudmundur in Hafnarfjördur as claimed and gone with him to Hamarsbraut 11 when witnesses had seen Gudmundur at Reykjavíkurvegur, heading towards Reykjavík.[34]

## The Yellow Toyota Car

In their statements in December 1975, Albert and Kristján had referred to a yellow Toyota car being used to transport Gudmundur's body to the Hafnarfjördur lava field. Saevar had allegedly telephoned Albert from Hamarsbraut 11 and asked him to come. Albert arrived in his father's Toyota car and opened the boot and observed through the back mirror how Saevar, Kristján, and Tryggvi had placed bags in the boot of the car. There is a record of the police having discovered that Albert's father had not owned a Toyota car in January 1974, but a Volkswagen car, which had the boot in the front.[35] According to the Commission, this rendered the statements of Albert, Kristján, and Tryggvi meaningless. However, Albert's father did purchase a Toyota car later that year so the ownership of such a car was not fictitious, but the timing was wrong.

## The Beginning of the Reykjavík Investigation into Geirfinnur's Disappearance

When did the Reykjavík investigation into the disappearance of Geirfinnur begin? According to Detective Eggert Bjarnason's progress report of 10 March 1976, this happened around the middle of January and followed Erla complaining of threatening telephone calls. The Commission, justifiably, argued that there were 'strong indications' [sterkar vísbendingar] that the Reykjavík Criminal Court had received all the case papers around the turn of the year 1975/1976, following an initial request from the prosecution. The Criminal Court had in their possession some information that led to the request for the entire case file.[36]

I strongly suspect this related to information that Erla had given to the investigators after Detective Sigurbjörn Vídir took her to her sealed flat at Thverbrekka 4 and started questioning her about Saevar's knowledge about the Geirfinnur case (see Chapter 14).

It is also noteworthy that Erla was taken to Sídumúli Prison on four occasions between 30 December 1975 and 23 January 1976, for about

---

[34] ICCRC Report, 2017, Saevar Ciesielski, Paragraphs 2952 and 2957.
[35] ICCRC Report, 2017, Saevar Ciesielski, Paragraphs 2348 and 2489.
[36] ICCRC Report, 2017, Saevar Ciesielski, Paragraph 2529.

14 hours (see Chapter 9, Table 9.1), showing that the investigators were taking a keen interest in her prior to her first official statement in the Geirfinnur case (i.e. 11 hours at the prison prior to her giving her first written statement).

## Gudmundur Agnarsson – The First False Confession

The Commission accepted that there were striking similarities between the accounts of Gudmundur Agnarsson to his family in October 1975 and the accounts given by the convicted persons in the Geirfinnur case, suggesting the police used Mr Agnarsson's confession as their initial investigative hypothesis.[37] I provided a detailed discussion of this confession in Chapter 7.

## Solitary Confinement

The Commission expressed great concern about the nature and duration of the solitary confinement.[38] It pointed to the general consensus among psychologists, discussed in the Working Group Report, that solitary confinement tends to weaken detainees' resistance to interrogation due to sleep disturbance and increased suggestibility and compliance, in addition to specific individual differences effects.[39] The longer the confinement, generally the higher the risk of unreliable testimony.

The Commission's scrutiny of the evidence suggested that decisions to detain the convicted persons in solitary confinement were in many instances due to how cooperative they were seen to be in providing new information that confirmed the police investigative hypothesis at a given time.

## Interrogation

The Commission described the police investigative methods used during the Gudmundur and Geirfinnur investigation as 'primitive' (frumstæðar). It noted that the primary focus of the interrogations was to obtain confessions, and often long solitary confinement was used to coerce confessions.[40]

---

[37] ICCRC Report, 2017, Saevar Ciesielski, Paragraphs 2528 and 3141.
[38] ICCRC Report, 2017, Saevar Ciesielski, Chapters VII.6.3.d and VIII.3.2.
[39] ICCRC Report, 2017, Saevar Ciesielski, Paragraph 2281.
[40] ICCRC Report, 2017, Saevar Ciesielski, Paragraph 2833.

The Commission raised an important point about the way interrogations were recorded at the time of the Gudmundur and Geirfinnur investigation. This relates to police officers recording the accounts given by suspects and witnesses, in varying detail and fashion, without it generally being disclosed what questions were asked and the specific context. It was evident from some of the answers given that the questions were leading. The Supreme Court was not aware of the extent of the unrecorded conversations between the suspects and the investigators, and the Commission emphasized the importance of three sets of diaries:

> The inaccurate explanations provided by the police officers and representative of the chief judge concerning these contacts seemed to have been accepted as good and valid. The Commission considers that the comprehensive information that is now available from the Síðumúli Prison diaries and the diaries of Tryggvi and Gudjón throws a new light on the unrecorded associations between the convicted persons and the investigators.[41]

### Karl Schütz

According to the Commission there was no legal foundation for appointing Karl Schütz to work in the Gudmundur and Geirfinnur investigation and no appointment letter has been discovered. When he arrived, the investigation became better focused and statements more precise. It pointed out that Schütz's approach to his work was principally to 'standardize the statements' (samræma framburði) and find points that 'support the confessions' (styrkja játningar), ignoring the legal requirement for a balanced investigation.[42] The investigators avoided asking further questions about the chain of events where consistencies had been achieved.

Furthermore, the points that supposedly supported the confessions produced no tangible evidence, and little or nothing emerged in this regard from the evidence of witnesses. Indeed, Schütz distorted or misrepresented the evidence to support his views, which the Commission thought was well illustrated in relation to the employee of the car hire company (Geysir) who had made it clear that he could not remember whether he had lent Erla's Volkswagen car or not without the necessary paperwork, but if he had it would not have been until spring 1975 (i.e. many months after the alleged trip to Keflavík). The Commission argued that Schütz's bias was also evident by how he

---

[41] ICCRC Report, 2017, Saevar Ciesielski, Paragraph 2293.
[42] ICCRC Report, 2017, Gudjón Skarphédinsson, Chapter VII.5.2.d.5.

responded to Gudjón having had second thoughts about his involvement in the Geirfinnur case after I had given him the lie detector test on 31 December 1976 (see Chapter 17 for details of the test and Schütz's reaction).

According to the Commission:

> Karl Schütz thought his role was not to prepare a case that was accurate and balanced in a criminal justice sense, but rather solve criminologically an unsolved crime.[43]

It was also highly critical of Schütz's unfounded derogatory comments about Saevar and Kristján in a document attached to his final report.

The Commission thought it likely that the state prosecutor had Schütz's final report when he was preparing the charges in the Geirfinnur case.

## Medication in Custody

The Commission reviewed in detail the drugs given to the convicted persons while in custody at Sídumúli Prison, which included various psychotropic drugs, sleeping medication, and tranquilizers.[44] The type of drugs referred to include chlorpromazine, chloral hydrate, nitrazepam, and diazepam. Gudjón and Tryggvi made frequent references to these drugs in their personal diaries that were discovered in 2011. The diaries of the two men suggest that the effects of the drugs were to reduce their concentration and clarity of thought. The Commission concluded that the combination of drugs and long solitary confinement would have deleteriously impacted on the detained persons' physical and mental state and adversely affected the reliability of their statements at the time. As an example, the Commission refers to Kristján, on 19 September 1976, confessing in a vivid fashion to stabbing Geirfinnur and killing a Faroese man and cutting up his body.

## Abreaction

The Commission stated that on 12 October 1976, Erla, Tryggvi, and Kristján were individually brought before a psychiatrist and injected with an undisclosed drug, aimed to help them recall events that they

---

[43] ICCRC Report, 2017, Gudjón Skarphédinsson, Paragraph 1870.
[44] ICCRC Report, 2017, Saevar Ciesielski, Chapter VII.5.2.c.

had hitherto been unable to recall.[45] Their cooperation with this procedure, and Albert's with the hypnosis sessions, suggests that they were trying their best to recall what had allegedly happened and assist with the investigation. These procedures reduced the credibility of their subsequent testimonies. It is unlikely that the convicted persons would have participated in these procedures if they were genuinely trying to conceal their guilt.

## The Trip to Keflavík

The Commission considered the convicted persons' evidence that was accepted in court regarding their trip to Keflavík, the preparation, and timing as highly improbable. This includes the type and colour of the cars that went to Keflavík eventually agreed on, after numerous previous contradictory descriptions. Witnesses reported having seen these or similar cars by the Harbour Café on 19 November 1974, but their testimony appeared to eliminate the convicted persons as the drivers or passengers.[46]

In addition, the Commission noted that in order to drive from Reykjavík to Keflavík within the known time constraint, the convicted persons would have had to substantially exceed the speed limit while driving through Reykjavík, Kópavogur, Gardabaer, and Hafnarfjördur at an average speed of 84 km (52.2 miles) per hour without stopping. This is highly unlikely, and the Commission considered this to be one of the most important factors where the Supreme Court wrongly interpreted the evidence.[47]

A similarly unrealistic travel plan was presented by the prosecution in the case of Carole Richardson, one of the 'Guildford Four', with regard to her car journey from London to Guildford in 1974. A police driver who ignored the speed limit just made the journey in the time and this was used as prosecution evidence (Gudjonsson & MacKeith, 2003).

## Erla's Hitch-hiking From Keflavík

The Commission reviewed the evidence regarding Erla's alleged lifts from two drivers on the morning of 20 January 1974.[48] After the Keflavík police failed to find the alleged drivers, the Reykjavík police

---

[45] ICCRC Report, 2017, Saevar Ciesielski, Chapter VII.5.2.d.1 and Paragraphs 2335 and 2568. On 26 October 1976, the newspaper *Vísir* (p. 1) had an article stating that Erla and Kristján had recently been injected with drugs for memory enhancement, but this had been unsuccessful and the Commission referred to this article.

[46] ICCRC Report, 2017, Saevar Ciesielski, Paragraphs 3088–3091.

[47] ICCRC Report, 2017, Saevar Ciesielski, Paragraphs 3089–3091.

[48] ICCRC Report, 2017, Kristján Vidarsson, Paragraphs 2912–2919.

advertised for the drivers in the media. Two drivers came forward, one of whom gave evidence in court.[49] The Supreme Court relied heavily on these two witnesses, although by that time Erla had retracted her statement, including her claim of hitch-hiking from Keflavík to Hafnarfjördur. The Commission found some problems with the evidence of the two drivers (e.g. the drivers only came forward in March/April 1976 after the police had advertised for the drivers, one driver failed to identify Erla, and the other seemed tentative in his identification) but said it was a 'clue' (*vísbending*) that she might have made the trip as given in her police statements. In spite of this possibility, the evidence did not throw light on what had happened to Geirfinnur on the slipway.

## Special Knowledge – Contamination

The Commission considered that caution should be exercised when interpreting the alleged special knowledge that the convicted persons gave (e.g. Saevar correctly giving two digits of Geirfinnur's home telephone number and Gudjón the correct colour of the delivery van bumper) because of the risk of contamination. There were indications that much information reportedly provided independently by the convicted persons had originated from the investigators (i.e. they were merely reiterating details that the police had introduced).[50]

## Clues

The Commission's view was that there were 'strong clues' (*sterkar vísbendingar*) from the convicted persons that they were responsible for Gudmundur's disappearance.[51] This relates to it generally being considered improbable that so many persons would confess wrongly to an assault upon a man that resulted in his death and that three witnesses would give a false testimony in the same way. However, the Commission rightly pointed out that the false confession of several defendants within a single case had been reported in other countries.

On the face of it, having several suspects confess to the same crime in a similar fashion, supported by witness testimony, appears highly incriminating and convincing to the triers of fact. However,

---

[49] One of the drivers had died before his evidence could be heard in the Criminal Court. He had failed to identify Erla in an identification parade involving five women.

[50] ICCRC Report, 2017, Saevar Ciesielski, Paragraph 3098.

[51] ICCRC Report, 2017, Saevar Ciesielski, Paragraph 2971. See Paragraph 3108 for similar arguments in the Geirfinnur case.

understanding the dynamics involved in such miscarriage of justice cases makes it easy to see why it occurs. In some cases, the real perpetrator may be a prosecution witness or even a co-defendant, aiming to shift the responsibility of the crime on to others (Garrett, 2011).

More commonly, one suspect's testimony is used to break down the resistance of another, and in extreme instances the police may fabricate a confession from one suspect to get a confession from another, which happened in the Carl Bridgewater case (Gudjonsson, 2003a).

My reading of the suspects' statements shows very clearly that one suspect's confession statement was used to extract a confession from another. The earliest example of this is in relation to Saevar's first confession in the Gudmundur case on 22 December 1975. Saevar was repeatedly asked about his knowledge of Gudmundur's disappearance. After persistently denying any knowledge of it, he confessed after a part of Erla's witness statement was read out to him. Such was the pressure he was under and power of his relationship with Erla.

In the well-documented 'Central Park jogger' case of 1989, the confessions coerced by police were so powerful that almost nobody questioned the suspects' guilt, in spite of there being no tangible corroborative evidence (Kassin, 2005, 2015; Sullivan, 1992):

> In many cases, what may or may not have actually happened at the crime scene, or in the interrogation room, will never objectively be known [...] In the Central Park case, for example, there were so many contradictions among the defendants' accounts that it is impossible to know conclusively what occurred.
>
> (Sullivan, 1992, p. 314)

In December 2002, DNA evidence linked to a serial rapist exonerated the five young men.[52] None of the five confessed that they themselves actually raped the jogger, but each pointed the finger at the others and minimized their own role in the offence.[53]

What the Commission probably did not know is that over 30% of false confession cases involve more than one false confessor (Drizin & Leo, 2004). It is also well known that confession evidence can have corruptive effects on other evidence, including that of witnesses to facts and expert witnesses, known as *forensic confirmation bias* (Kassin, 2015, p. 40). This is what undoubtedly happened in the Gudmundur

---

[52] Kassin, S. False confessions and the jogger case. *New York Times*, 1 November 2002: http://www.nytimes.com/2002/11/01/opinion/false-confessions-and-the-jogger-case.html (last accessed 24 January 2018).

[53] http://thepsychreport.com/conversations/coerced-to-confess-the-psychology-of-false-confessions/ (last accessed 24 January 2018).

and Geirfinnur cases regarding the repeatedly changing stories of the witnesses and suspects as they were presented with the latest investigative hypothesis.

## Gudmundur's Body

The convicted persons gave various locations where Gudmundur's body was hidden, but regardless of this it was never found:

> In view of the fact that all the convicted persons had confessed to killing Gudmundur it seems difficult to find a reasonable explanation that they, one or more, did not disclose exactly how Gudmundur's body was taken from Hamarsbraut 11, when one can assume that such an event is memorable.[54]

The reason, of course, is most likely due to the fact that they did not know exactly how the body was moved, whether it had been moved, and its ultimate burial place and were merely appeasing the police, who would not accept that they did not know.

> The explanation that the convicted persons had wanted to avoid the discovery of the body seems highly improbable since they had all confessed to having attacked Gudmundur and hidden his body.[55]

The Commission pointed out that none of the suspects had made a reference to the harsh weather conditions on the night of Gudmundur's disappearance.

## Geirfinnur's Body

Considerable effort was made to find Geirfinnur's body, and the convicted persons were repeatedly asked about it, particularly after Saevar and Kristján began in the autumn of 1976 to confess to having killed Geirfinnur. By that time, they had been in custody for nearly a year, the 'four wrongly accused' were more or less out of the case, and soon Gudjón was implicated.

The Commission stated that it could not exclude the possibility that the convicted persons had tried to deliberately confuse the investigators about the location of Geirfinnur's body, but it was considered equally likely that they had had no real memory of where the body

---

[54] ICCRC Report, 2017, Saevar Ciesielski, Paragraph 2962.
[55] ICCRC Report, 2017, Saevar Ciesielski, Paragraph 2963.

was located.[56] By pointing to new locations or agreeing with the testimony of the other convicted persons about where the body was to be found, they were basically giving in to pressure from the investigators.

The Commission's careful analysis of confession statements found considerable contamination in the ways in which new information from one person was passed on to another, who then gave a similar story. It concluded that uncertainties about the trustworthiness of the convicted persons' testimony regarding the location of Geirfinnur's body cast doubt on their entire testimony in the Geirfinnur case.

## Access to Legal Advice and Support

The Commission pointed out that the convicted persons had very limited access to lawyers while in custody.[57] Over long periods of time, lawyers were prevented from speaking privately to their clients. In addition, they were not kept informed of developments, or invited to be present when key witnesses were giving statements or to ask them questions in court, which importantly included the extensive questioning and testimony of Gunnar Jónsson (see section below).

In order to put the Commission's concerns in context, it is helpful to compare the convicted persons' access to lawyers with those of the 'four wrongly accused'. Our data entry for the Working Group showed a huge difference between these two groups of suspects in having access to lawyers, favouring the latter, although we did not use this information in the Working Group Report because of time constraints in completing the report.

Daníelsson (2016) has produced a useful comparison from the Síðumúli Prison diaries for the six-week period between 26 January and 9 March 1976 and the differences are striking. During this period, Saevar, Kristján, Tryggvi, and Albert each saw their lawyer only once or twice, whereas Einar Bollason, Magnús Leópoldsson, Sigurbjörn Eiríksson, and Valdimar Olsen met with their lawyers on average twice a week (8–12 times during this period): seven times more often than the other detainees. It is also important that unlike the other detainees, the 'four wrongly accused' met with their lawyers soon after their arrest and frequently thereafter. This undoubtedly provided important social and emotional support, as well as legal advice, reducing the risk of a false confession:

---

[56] ICCRC Report, 2017, Saevar Ciesielski, Chapter VIII.5.7.
[57] ICCRC Report, 2017, Saevar Ciesielski, Paragraph 2345.

*Magnús Leópoldsson:*

> Hafsteinn Baldvinsson, lawyer, came in the evening [...] explained my position. Custody is strict and that would not change, I would receive no visits apart from his and would have to accept it [...] He asked me to stay calm [...] Hafsteinn said he would soon be back, he gave me huge support, was fatherly in all respects and reassured me that he would do all he could for me.
>
> (Jónasson, 1996, pp. 37–38)

*Einar Bollason:*

> My friend Ingvar Björnsson, lawyer, visited me in the cell and he was the first and only person allowed to visit me while I was in custody.
>
> (Karlsson, 1994, p. 94)

## How the Court Evaluated Chaotic and Inconsistent Testimony

The Commission described two approaches at the court's disposal for interpreting the chaotic and inconsistent accounts given by the convicted persons in the Gudmundur and Geirfinnur cases. The first involves the court viewing the statements as deliberate attempts, or even collusion of the co-accused, to mislead the investigators. This appears to have been the approach taken by both the Criminal Court and Supreme Court.

The other option was to view the chaotic and inconsistent accounts as being due to the absence of real memories, casting doubts about their involvement in the two cases. Strong support for this alternative was found in the fact that the convicted persons appeared to have major problems recalling the central details of the alleged crimes they were questioned about and never provided tangible evidence that could be corroborated. On the contrary, they provided different and inconsistent peripheral details that were impossible to corroborate. It was typical that the accounts changed either in minor or major ways from one interrogation to another.

The Commission pointed out that the diaries of Tryggvi and Gudjón, as well as the convicted persons' statements, suggested that they were genuinely trying to remember what had happened but were unable to do so.

It concluded:

> Even though substantial harmony [conformity] was eventually achieved in the convicted persons' testimony, the Commission views it so contradictory and wandering that taken together it cannot be viewed as trustworthy. The Commission therefore thinks that it is very doubtful

that their testimony about alleged criminal activity was based on their own recollection.[58]

## Gunnar Jónsson's Witness Testimony – Gudmundur Case

From December 1975 and until the end of February 1977 the testimony of the convicted persons had been that Saevar had telephoned Albert from Hamarsbraut 11 in the early hours of 27 January 1974 and that he soon arrived there in his father's car to assist with the disposal of Gudmundur's body in the Hafnafjördur lava field. Over 14 months later, and after charges had been laid in the Gudmundur case, it emerged that Saevar could not have phoned Albert from Hamarsbraut 11 because at the time the telephone was disconnected because of failure of payment. Saevar now introduced a new story, later confirmed by Albert and Kristján, which led to the introduction of a new person, Gunnar Jónsson, who allegedly had been present with Albert at the time Gudmundur was killed in the basement flat. Two police officers were sent to Spain to collect Gunnar and he accepted during lengthy questioning in court that he had been at Hamarsbraut 11 at the time of Gudmundur's death (see Chapter 8, Box 8.1). He was now a key pros-ecution witness in the case.[59]

The Commission pointed out that the Supreme Court put weight on Gunnar's evidence on the basis that he had been able to describe rooms and conditions at Hamarsbraut 11 (i.e. was in possession of special knowledge), mistakenly claiming that he had not been to the flat prior to his first statement in the Criminal Court in 1977. This mistake was due to the Supreme Court having misinterpreted the evidence that the two police officers who had collected Gunnar from Spain had given in 1977 (i.e. both officers denied in evidence that they had themselves taken Gunnar to Hamarsbraut 11 prior to his first statement in court on Monday 2 May 1977; however, other officers had taken Gunnar there two days before his testimony (i.e. on Saturday 30 April).

The Supreme Court also failed to mention that it was only after five hours of face-to-face confrontation (*samprófun*) with Albert in Court on 3 May 1977 that Gunnar began to 'remember' the event. The Commission pointed out that Gunnar had been placed under great pressure to cooperate with the court in order to avoid a deterioration in his (legal) position. Gunnar's witness statement was coerced by the Criminal Court and the convicted persons' lawyers had not been informed or invited to attend his giving evidence that was going to be used against their clients.

---

[58] ICCRC Report, 2017, Saevar Ciesielski, Paragraph 2880.
[59] ICCRC Report, 2017, Saevar Ciesielski, Chapter VIII.4.1.f.

Gunnar was undoubtedly left in a position where he foresaw no alternative but to accept the prosecution scenario. The court summons made it clear that he was a crucial witness to the events that led to Gudmundur's death. His being accompanied from Spain by two detectives and then placed under police guard ensured that he understood the seriousness of the situation. Continued denial under those circumstances would have been futile. If his denials were not accepted he could, as a witness, be charged with perjury. Gunnar compromised. He accepted that he had been with Albert at Hamarsbraut 11 and witnessed Saevar, Kristján, and Tryggvi being involved in a fight with a man, who could have been Gudmundur Einarsson.

I have reviewed Gunnar's testimony in court and found it to be vague, tentative, and incomplete. He may have been persuaded that he was present at Hamarsbraut 11, even if he could not remember it. Unfortunately, we do not have an account from him about his mental process during and after making the incriminating admissions in court, which would have informed us whether or not this was a case of memory distrust syndrome, but I suspect it was.

### Sigurdur Óttar Hreinsson's Witness Testimony – Geirfinnur Case

Cars were central to the alleged trip to Keflavík on 19 November 1974. Saevar and Kristján did not have driving licences and there was no indication that Erla had been the driver to Keflavík, although she was in possession of a Land Rover car and had a valid driving licence at the time. After the 'four wrongly accused' were released from custody in May 1976, two drivers were needed, according to the accounts given by the convicted persons: a passenger car and a delivery van to collect the smuggled alcohol. Erla, Saevar, and Kristján were pressured to provide names, and Gudjón was eventually mentioned as the driver of the passenger (Volkswagen) car.

Saevar and Erla first mentioned Sigurdur Óttar as a possible driver of the delivery van on 9 and 13 December 1976, respectively. He was interrogated on 13 December and presented with Saevar's claims. Sigurdur Óttar said there was no truth in the allegations, after which he was placed in custody overnight at Sídumúli Prison in spite of having the status of a witness. After a night in solitary confinement he was interrogated and confessed to having been the delivery van driver. On 25 May 1977 he confirmed this in Court. In October 1977 he retracted his confession. The prosecution responded by charging (*kærði*) Sigurdur Óttar with having given false testimony in Court the previous May. On 12 October he was remanded in custody at Sídumúli Prison and the following day the three (trial) judges in the case informed the lawyers

of Saevar, Gudjón, and Kristján that they 'must not under any circumstances speak with their client'.[60] Sigurdur Óttar claimed to have given
a false statement because of pressure from the police and the investigative judge.

It appeared to the Commission that the custody was aimed at getting
him to withdraw his retraction, but fortunately, Sigurdur Óttar now
had the resilience to stick to his original story: that he was not
the driver. He was kept in custody for about four weeks. The Supreme
Court did not accept Sigurdur Óttar's retraction and used his evidence
to support the convictions of Saevar, Gudjón, and Kristján in
the Geirfinnur case.

The Commission found Sigurdur Óttar's retraction credible (i.e. they
believed his story of non-involvement) and found that the statements
of the convicted persons regarding his presence in Keflavík lacked
credibility. It was very critical of the treatment that he received from
the police, prosecution, and court, which it described as 'farcical'
(farsakennd). It showed the ferocity with which the authorities treated
witnesses if they were not seen to be going along with the police investigative hypothesis.

The problem for the Supreme Court was that it was confronted with
information that when initially speaking to his lawyer, family, friends,
and work mates, Sigurdur Óttar was in two minds over 'whether he
had done those things'. I have reviewed the relevant documents and
consider it likely that the interrogation had resulted in Sigurdur Óttar
developing memory distrust syndrome, which the Supreme Court
judges misinterpreted as evidence of his having been the van driver
(see Appendix 1).

## Critique of the Psychological Report

My overall impression of the Commission's reports is that they marginalize our work, particularly in relation to the perjury convictions.

In spite of having relied heavily on the psychological report in their
conclusions, the Commission pointed out that the work that Jón Fridrik
and I completed for the Working Group was not without its limitations.
There were two main criticisms, the first one being that we had used a
'broad brush' approach when evaluating the reliability of the confessions in the two cases, and the second being that we had not focused on
the fact that in the Supreme Court, Erla had only been convicted of
giving false statements in the Geirfinnur case. With regard to this second point, the Commission claims that the value of our psychological

---

[60] ICCRC Report, 2017, Saevar Ciesielski, Chapter VIII.5.2.e, Paragraph 3027.

report is compromised by a mistake in the Working Group Report that is of no relevance to our psychological findings. The mistake was that in our chapter in the Working Group Report we cited Erla's convictions in the Criminal Court rather than the reduced conviction in the Supreme Court, where only the perjury conviction remained.

It is true that the Working Group did not specifically consider Erla's false allegations against the four innocent men. In retrospect this was unfortunate, but Jón Fridrik and I were given the opportunity of addressing Erla's incriminating statements against the four men when she was not in custody in our testimony on 28 January 2016.

It is correct that we did not conduct a discriminative analysis of the different confessions in terms of the weight of their unreliability. This would have required substantially more time than we had at our disposal. Nor did we consider it essential with regard to our terms of remit (i.e. with regard to each convicted person we focused on the overall reliability of their confessions). I still think this was the right approach.

As an example of their criticism, the Commission noted that the suspects in the Gudmundur case confessed relatively quickly, whereas in the Geirfinnur case, Saevar and Kristján did not confess to participation in his murder until 27 October and 9 November 1976, respectively, about 10 months after having first implicated the 'four wrongly accused'. This is not to forget that on 3–4 May 1976 Erla confessed to shooting Geirfinnur, after having been brought into Sídumúli Prison for questioning after it had become apparent that justification for further detention of the 'four wrongly accused' was in doubt.

The explanation, in my view, lies at least in part in the different circumstances surrounding the two cases. In the Gudmundur case, the convicted persons were friends; they were not implicating outsiders in his death and were under no investigative pressure to do so. They had acted together, although they pointed the finger at one another, like the wrongly convicted persons in the 'Central Park jogger' case, discussed earlier in this chapter. The covert investigative hypothesis from the beginning, apparently based on the informant Sigurdur Almarsson, was that Saevar, Kristján, and Tryggvi had murdered Gudmundur.

In the Geirfinnur case, the early covert investigative hypothesis, in my view, focused on the two people from Klúbburinn – Sigurbjörn Eiríksson and Magnús Leópoldsson – and as discussed above and in Chapter 9, this may have been in part based on the confession statement of Gudmundur Agnarsson to his family in October 1975. It is evident from reading the statements of Saevar and Kristján that the police investigative hypothesis shifted once the 'four wrongly accused' had been released from custody on 9 May 1976, putting Saevar and

Kristján directly into the centre of the investigation, followed later in the year by Gudjón officially joining the list of suspects.

### Giving False Statements (Perjury) Against the 'Four Wrongly Accused'

With regard to the convictions of Saevar, Erla, and Kristján for giving false statements, the Commission pointed out the 'long way between accepting the investigating hypotheses of the police, if this was what happened, and during interrogation people being named as culprits like the appeal applicant did repeatedly' (the Commission is referring to each of the three –Saevar, Erla, and Kristján).[61]

The Commission rejected Erla's claim of a close and frequent contact with the investigators between 20 December 1975 and 23 January 1976, which included them allegedly visiting Erla at her mother's home, on the basis that: 'No documents exist to support her story, nor have the investigators said anything about it.'[62] It noted only three recorded contacts: on 28 December 1975 and 6 and 25 January 1976. In that case, why did the Commission not make an effort to seek the relevant information? It did not even ask the investigators a single question when they gave evidence in the District Court on 28 January 2016. Instead, the Commission used the investigators' silence, poor record keeping, and lack of cooperation to challenge Erla's claims. This  suggests that the Commission was poorly motivated to seek out the truth regarding the perjury convictions.

The Commission placed considerable weight on the fact that all three persons admitted having made false statements against the four men, which is of course a serious criminal offence. The real issue is whether or not these confessions were coerced by the investigators, not that the convicted persons made them (i.e. it was the circumstances under which they were elicited and maintained that should have been given a greater focus).

While Erla was not in custody at the time of implicating the four men, Saevar and Kristján were and had been in solitary confinement for about a month, a sufficient length of time to cause them considerable distress and make them vulnerable to police pressure. Both men have claimed that they were kept awake at night in order to extract a confession (see Chapters 13 and 15). In addition, there were breaches of the existing laws and police codes of practice from the beginning (e.g. lengthy unrecorded interrogations, and leading questions).

---

[61]  ICCRC Report, 2017, Erla Bolladóttir, Paragraph 2512.
[62]  ICCRC Report, 2017, Erla Bolladóttir, Paragraph 2443.

As far as Erla's appeal application is concerned, the Commission observed that:[63]

- Erla does not dispute the fact that she implicated the 'four wrongly accused'.
- No documents exist to show that Erla had been 'forced or encouraged' (*knúin eða hvött*) by police or others to give those false accusations.

The Commission emphasized the fact that the names of Einar Bollason and Valdimar Olsen first appeared in the statements of Erla and Saevar.[64] Unlike the names of Sigurbjörn Eiríksson and Magnús Leópoldsson, the other two men had never been previously connected to the Geirfinnur case. References to Einar Bollason and Valdimar Olsen may not have originated from the police, but it does not mean to say that their names did not emerge within a coercive process. Why did Erla and Saevar incorporate them into their story to the police? Having read the relevant statements, I agree with Jón Daníelsson (2016) that Erla only vaguely referred to Valdimar Olsen in her statement on 3 February 1976, and she said Saevar had referred to him in her statement on 1 September 1976.

Einar and Valdimar had no direct links to Klúbburinn. However, according to Magnús Leópoldsson, Valdimar was a single man who worked in the offices of another club, Thórskaffi. After work he frequently visited Klúbburinn and was acquainted with Magnús, who thought Valdimar's employment in a club may have been used against him, because at the time key people working in the entertainment business were linked via gossip to being gangsters (Jónasson, 1996, p. 12).

Erla was well acquainted with Valdimar (see Chapter 14). She was a good friend of his younger sister and sometimes stayed in their flat at Framnesvegur and attended parties there. According to Erla, the investigators became particularly interested when she mentioned that her brother Einar had attended parties at Framnesvegur and when she made a reference to having heard that he had been selling smuggled whisky (Bolladóttir, 2008). According to the Commission, Erla's personal links with Einar and Valdimar probably increased the credibility of her story as a passive observer of events on the slipway.

---

[63] ICCRC Report, 2017, Erla Bolladóttir, Paragraph 2524.

[64] Jón Daníelsson has rightly criticized the Commission by pointing out that Erla never positively identified Valdimar Olsen but was nevertheless convicted of falsely accusing him of being involved in the Geirfinnur case. See: http://stundin.is/pistill/erla-bar-aldrei-sakir-valdimar-olsen/.

There is at least a *real possibility* that the investigators' early investigative hypothesis focused on finding incriminating evidence against Sigurbjörn Eiríksson and Magnús Leópoldsson in the Geirfinnur case, but Erla did not know these men personally and there was therefore a missing link between them and the young persons (i.e. Erla, Saevar, and Kristján). Erla had never met Sigurbjörn Eiríksson, but she had met Magnús Leópoldsson when Valdimar took her and Hulda one evening to Thórskaffi (Bolladóttir, 2008). Erla and Hulda were good friends at the time (see Chapter 14).

Erla's half-brother had attended parties at Framnesvegur and had been involved in selling smuggled alcohol, which the police took seriously[65], combined with Valdimar having links with Magnús Leópoldsson, which provided a circumstantial link, even if it was tenuous. It was the best link the police were going to get, and they went along with it. The names of many other men were mentioned, but they appear to have received less police attention. It is essential to understand this broader context within which the names of Einar and Valdimar came to be associated with the Geirfinnur case.

A good description of Erla's interactions with the investigators between 20 December 1975 and 23 January 1976 is provided in her account to Saevar's lawyer at the time, Ragnar Adalsteinsson, whom she met on 19 November 1996.[66]

The Commission makes much of the fact that Erla had been out of solitary confinement for 34 days when she formally implicated Einar Bollason and Magnús Leópoldsson on 23 January, and 44 days when she implicated Valdimar Olsen and Sigurbjörn Eiríksson on 3 February. It stated that arguments concerning the impact of solitary confinement and lack of access to a lawyer would therefore not apply to Erla's application.

The Commission put weight on the fact that Erla implicated the men on more than one occasion, which in its view added to its seriousness. Not acknowledged is the likelihood that once Erla had implicated these four people and they had been arrested and detained, she would have been under huge pressure to maintain the story or face being placed in solitary confinement and possibly charged with perjury, like Sigurdur Óttar had been when he retracted his testimony.

What the Commission did not take sufficiently into account was that Erla and the investigators had been in regular contact since her release from custody on 20 December 1975, and crucially she had been brought

---

[65] They found substance in the allegation that Einar Bollason had been selling smuggled alcohol (e.g. see Evidence Book XII, pp. 158–163).

[66] ICCRC Report, 2017, Saevar Ciesielski, Paragraph 1949.

to Sídumúli Prison as a potential witness on three separate occasions between 30 December 1975 and 22 January 1976 for a total of about 11 hours prior to giving her first written statement (see Chapter 9, Table 9.1). In the absence of documented records, the Commission did not wish to rely on Erla's claims that the investigators had visited her at her home and questioned her.

Unfortunately, when questioned about this by defence counsels in Court on 28 January 2016, the three investigators claimed 'memory lapses'. However, as discussed earlier in this chapter, Sigurbjörn Vídir did at least acknowledge that there had been visits to Erla's home in connection with the Gudmundur and Geirfinnur cases.

There was always the underlying implicit threat that Erla could be detained in solitary confinement for an almost 'unlimited' time if she was not seen to be cooperating with the investigators. This was a consistent theme seen during the investigation, with Örn Höskuldsson apparently being willing to use his judicial power to 'soften up' witnesses and break down their resistance to fit in with the latest flimsy investigative hypothesis.

Erla's extreme psychological vulnerabilities, when technically not in custody, are probably best illustrated by her reaction to being taken to Sídumúli Prison on the evening of 3 May 1976 as a witness, during which time she falsely confessed to shooting Geirfinnur, illustrating her capacity for extreme self-blame and feelings of helplessness when placed under interrogative pressure. She became very distressed after not being allowed to go home to her infant, and had to receive the support of the prison chaplain and be sedated in order to be able to sleep (see Chapter 14). How could the Commission ignore such an important indicator of her susceptibility to intimidation and coercion?

It was very clear that the police and prosecution had taken a keen interest in the Geirfinnur case very soon after Erla had spoken to Detective Sigurbjörn Vídir on 28 December 1975. This is unlikely to be a coincidence. There is a clear and compelling sequence of events from the records, as shown in Chapter 9 (Table 9.1), which gives some credence to Erla's account of what took place after she met with the officer at the end of December (Bolladóttir, 2008).

Unfortunately, the investigators were extremely bad at keeping records of their interactions with Erla, including those in Sídumúli Prison, and this along with their claimed lack of recollection regarding these crucial interactions undoubtedly hindered Erla's appeal application against her perjury conviction. The Commission made no comment regarding the 'memory lapses' of the three members of the Reykjavík Team, including that seen during their testimony before the Commission in the District Court in 2016. I find this surprising.

In my testimony on 28 January 2016, instigated by the Commission's questions, I stated that taking a witness to Síðumúli Prison for questioning was intimidating and coercive, especially for Erla, given her idiosyncratic vulnerabilities and special circumstances (see Chapter 14). I find it curious that the Commission chose to ignore my evidence with regard to this issue as if I had not given it, and perhaps more importantly, it failed to comment on the possible impact of the investigators repeatedly bringing Erla to Síðumúli Prison for lengthy periods, a place where she had shortly before been detained in solitary confinement for eight days and coerced into implicating Saevar and Kristján in the Gudmundur case.

The statements that Saevar and Erla made in December 1976 admitting conspiracy to implicate the 'four wrongly accused' and others, if caught, are farcical. For example, in his statement on 9 December, Saevar claims that in July 1975 he, Erla, and Gudjón met Kristján at his Grettisgata home and decided that if any of them were arrested they would complicate the case by implicating the two men from Klúbburinn and bootleggers in Reykjavík. Saevar said Erla had suggested the names of her half-brother Einar, Valdimar Olsen, and Jón Ragnarsson because they were connected to Klúbburinn and this would be corroborated during a police investigation.

In her statement on 13 December 1976, Erla told police that a few days after Geirfinnur was killed on the slipway and his body hidden in the Red Hills, Saevar told her that if anybody asked, to tell them the Klúbburinn men were responsible. This was allegedly before the names of Magnús Leópoldsson and Sigurbjörn Eiríksson were linked with the case through rumours during the Keflavík investigation.

At the time of giving those statements, Saevar had been in solitary confinement for almost a year and Erla for more than seven months. According to the Commission's own logic, this would have increased the likelihood of them giving unreliable statements.

The Commission referred to an interview in a newspaper (*Helgarpósturinn*) on 18 January 1980, in which Erla described the reasons she had implicated the four men. These included her saying that she falsely implicated her half-brother Einar because of family disputes, Magnús because of his resemblance to the clay head, and Sigurbjörn and Valdimar were linked to entertainment clubs and had a bad reputation among people with whom she associated.[67] While I cannot exclude these reasons, I suggest two equally plausible alternative hypotheses: (a) at the time, Erla was feeling guilty about implicating the four men and was prone to self-blame, not an unreasonable

---

[67] ICCRC Report, 2017, Erla Bolladóttir, Paragraph 2519.

assumption in my experience[68], and (b) she was aware that her blaming the investigators for her having implicated the four men, even if justi-fied, risked arrest and prosecution for making false accusations against them. The authority's approach to Sigurdur Óttar's retraction and alle-gations against police showed the ferocity with which witnesses were treated if they were not seen to be cooperating. It would have been Erla's testimony against the investigators', without her having availa-ble corroborative evidence to back it up. She would not have stood a chance and she undoubtedly knew it. She had to take the blame entirely on herself. Blaming it on the police, even if true, was not a viable option at the time.

It is important to remember that the three investigators who elicited the false allegation statements from Erla, Saevar, and Kristján against four innocent men have never been forthcoming about their investiga-tive methods or actions. On 28 January 2016, all three retired investi-gators claimed in court 'memory lapses' regarding key aspects of the Gudmundur and Geirfinnur investigation and disagreed about who had been in charge.

This was not the first time they had claimed a 'memory lapse'. When questioned in 1979 in connection with Saevar's duress investigation, Eggert Bjarnason said that he could not recall chief prison officer Gunnar Gudmundsson slapping Saevar in the face on 5 May 1976, Sigurbjörn Vídir claimed that he was not aware that the incident had taken place, and Örn Höskuldsson said that it must have taken place when he was out of the room attending to a phone call. He did not recall the incident ever having been mentioned. Neither did he recall who was in charge of the meeting but accepted that it was either he or Hallvardur Einvardsson.[69] According to Mr Einvardsson's witness statement, the investigation was at a crucial stage and Mr Höskuldsson had requested the confrontation meeting.

Fortunately, senior prosecutor Hallvardur Einvardsson and Chief Inspector Njördur Snaehólm, who had also witnessed the incident, remembered it clearly and were prepared to give statements against the prison officer.[70]

---

[68] Kristján made a similar self-blame accusation when he retracted his first confession in the Geirfinnur case on 2 March 1976 ('I basically made up the entire story in my mind about how I had gone to Keflavík and what happened there. I did this entirely on my own initiative, and as I have said before, I don't know why' – Evidence Book XII, p. 110).

[69] Witness statements taken in September and October 1979 (Duress Investigation Report, pp. 140–142).

[70] Witness statements taken in September 1979 (Duress Investigation Report, pp. 124–128).

The three investigators' credibility as reliable witnesses is in doubt. In view of this, when considered in tandem with Sídumúli Prison diaries, should Erla, Saevar, and Kristján not be believed when they claim that the perjury convictions were obtained from them by coercion? Furthermore, if they are genuinely innocent of killing Geirfinnur the convicted persons would not have had any motivation in the first place to implicate the 'four wrongly accused'.


## RAGNAR ADALSTEINSSON'S LETTER
## TO THE SPECIAL PROSECUTOR

Erla's lawyer, Ragnar Adalsteinsson, is very unhappy with the decision of the Commission to reject his client's appeal application regarding the perjury conviction and he has very good grounds for concern.

No defence lawyer has greater knowledge and insight into the Gudmundur and Geirfinnur cases than Ragnar. He worked on Saevar's application for appeal in the 1990s, which unfortunately was unsuccessful. The judiciary was not ready at the time to accept Ragnar's compelling arguments. In 2014 he began to work on the Geirfinnur case again, now representing Erla and Gudjón. Ragnar is one of the most dignified, hard-working, and committed lawyers I have ever known and he should be listened to.

On 22 May 2017, Ragnar wrote a 21-page letter to special prosecutor David Björgvinsson, whose current role is to present the Commission's appeal recommendations regarding the manslaughter convictions before the Supreme Court. Ragnar's letter makes compelling arguments as to why the prosecutor should use his legal authority to include the perjury convictions in the forthcoming appeals in the Supreme Court.

Does David Björgvinsson have the courage and motivation to do so? After all, on 5 September 2017 he had given his support for doing so, although the Commission completely ignored his changed position in their reports on Erla, Saevar, and Kristján. This will be a test of his resolve. My impression is that he is a man of good integrity and professionalism.

In his letter, Ragnar identified a number of serious flaws in the Commission's report regarding its rejection of Erla's perjury conviction appeal application. He thought some of these were of such a serious nature that they amount to either 'gross neglect' or 'intent' (*stórkostlegri vanrækslu* or *ásetningi*), the latter implying that the Commission had deliberately sidestepped the issue because it was not on its agenda.

Ragnar's key points are as follows:

- The investigators concealed from the suspects, their lawyers, and the Supreme Court the real reason behind the commencement of the investigation, which began on a false footing. This resulted in wrongful convictions, including those for perjury. Ragnar suggests that Saevar's and Erla's arrest and detention in connection with the fraud offences had been carried out under false pretences as a prelude for questions about Gudmundur's disappearance.

- Erla was interviewed as a witness in the Gudmundur and Geirfinnur cases, but the evidence shows that the investigators viewed her as a suspect (e.g. taking her on several trips to look for a body or bodies when she was not in custody, and ordering a psychiatric evaluation), thereby preventing her from having legal advice and assistance. If the investigators had followed the law and appointed her a lawyer, the outcome would have been different.

- The Commission relied extensively on the expert psychological evidence in relation to the manslaughter convictions and Albert's conviction for participating in interfering with the crime scene in the Gudmundur case, but it completely ignored the detailed evidence that Jón Fridrik and I had given in the District Court on 28 January 2016 that focused heavily on Erla's statements to the police when she was not in custody. It addressed specifically the concerns the Commission had expressed regarding a limitation in our Working Group Report chapter (i.e. not focusing specifically on the perjury convictions). According to Ragnar, none of the three members of the Commission attended court to listen to our evidence under oath, which they had specifically requested. Ragnar's view is that the Commission tried to marginalize the impact of our work in relation to the perjury convictions by petty criticisms and their use of 'amateur common sense' psychology (*Leikmannshyggjuvit*) rather than relying on expert testimony.

- The Commission ignored Ragnar's concern, which he had first addressed to the Commission on 30 September 2015, that the records show that Erla had not implicated Valdimar Olsen in the Geirfinnur case and should therefore not have been charged with that offence or convicted. This alone is in his view sufficient grounds for appeal.

## CONCLUSIONS

The Working Group and the Commission opened a Pandora's box. Out sprang crucial evidence that the Supreme Court had not been aware of in 1980, failed to ask or follow up the right questions about, and misinterpreted or misrepresented some of the evidence from. The Working Group Report and the psychological evaluation had introduced 'fresh evidence'. The Commission, rightly in my view, placed considerable weight on the contemporaneous content of the diaries of Tryggvi and Gudjón.

The Commission's criticisms of the investigation, the police methods, Karl Schütz, the Reykjavík Criminal Court, and the Supreme Court will make it hard for the judiciary to uphold these convictions, but we cannot take their decision for granted. David Björgvinsson will continue as the special prosecutor and will decide what steps should be taken to present the appeals before the Supreme Court (*Morgunbladid*, 2 March 2017, p. 2).

The sting in the tail is that surprisingly the Commission did not support Erla's application regarding her false allegation conviction against the 'four wrongly accused'. It appears to have ignored the surrounding circumstances behind how the perjury allegations of Erla, Saevar, and Kristján were elicited.

I have argued in this chapter that there are good grounds for arguing that Erla, Saevar, and Kristján had a defence of duress. The false allegations against the 'four wrongly accused' and the false confessions of the convicted persons being on the slipway, and in later statements taking part in Geirfinnur's murder, are so intertwined that it is not helpful to separate them. Surprisingly, within this context, the Commission failed to consider Jón Fridrik's and my detailed expert evidence before the District Court on 28 January 2016, evidence that it had itself requested but then completely ignored (i.e. making no reference to it at all in their reports).

The motivation behind the Commission's failure to support the perjury conviction appeal applications is curious, but Erla's lawyer has gone as far as to suggest either 'gross neglect' or 'intent'. The consequence of the Commission's decision is that the authorities will continue to place the blame for implicating innocent people on Erla, Saevar, and Kristján rather than on the investigators. This is known as the 'blame game' (Sekar, 2017).

# Part III

# A Psychological Analysis of the Confessions of the Six Convicted Persons

# 13

# Did Saevar Ciesielski Have Undiagnosed ADHD?

*A person fleeing from an animal does not ask for directions*[1]

## SALIENT POINTS

- On 22 February 1980 the Supreme Court convicted Saevar of manslaughter in the Gudmundur and Geirfinnur cases and perjury with regard to the 'four wrongly accused'. He received a 17-year prison sentence.
- Saevar had a history of being a victim of bullying from an early age and had adjustment problems.
- The evidence reviewed in this chapter indicates that Saevar had undiagnosed attention deficit hyperactivity disorder (ADHD) in childhood/adolescence and that it left him additionally vulnerable to making false confessions.
- He coped poorly with his solitary confinement, at least in part because of his ADHD symptoms.
- The investigators, the prosecutor, and the prison officers had no insight into his condition and appear to have misinterpreted his symptoms, functional impairments, and denials as his being obstructive.

---

[1] Saevar's description of his confession in the Gudmundur case (Unnsteinsson, 1980, p. 53). This sentence is also referred to in one of Saevar's letters of complaint to the trial court judges in 1977 (ICCRC Report, 2017, Saevar Ciesielski, Paragraph 1224).

---

*The Psychology of False Confessions: Forty Years of Science and Practice*, First Edition.
Gisli H. Gudjonsson.
© 2018 John Wiley & Sons Ltd. Published 2018 by John Wiley & Sons Ltd.

- Saevar fought hard to prove his innocence but died tragically at the age of 56 in an accident. Alcohol was a contributory factor.
- With regard to the perjury conviction, Saevar was interrogated for a total of about 22 hours, unrecorded, during the three days leading up to his first Geirfinnur statement. He was not in good psychological and physical health at the time. It is probable that his confessions were coerced by the investigators.

Saevar Ciesielski was born in Árnessýsla, Iceland, on 6 July 1955. His mother was Icelandic but his father, Michael Ciesielski, was an American, who worked for a while at the American naval base at Keflavík Airport. His father was reportedly educated in business studies. Saevar's parents married in 1951 and lived in the USA until 1955 when they moved to Iceland. Michael had problems with adjusting to living in Iceland because of the language barrier, and he became a heavy drinker. The marriage broke up in 1967. Michael Ciesielski went back to America and two years later died in a road traffic accident.

Saevar was the second of four children to the couple. He was always physically small and developmentally slow. At the time of his arrest in 1975 he was 165 cm (five feet and five inches) in height and weighed less than 50 kg (eight stone). He experienced learning difficulties at school, was bullied, and when about 10 years of age started truanting from school and fell into bad company. He started offending and engaged in substance misuse. When Saevar was 11 years of age, the Reykjavík Social Services sent him to a residential home, Jadar, at the request of his mother who was no longer able to control him. He spent one school year at Jadar. The following winter he stayed with his maternal grandparents away from Reykjavík. When aged 13 he returned to school in Reykjavík and was again found to be truanting and his behaviour was beyond his mother's control. He was sent to a psychiatrist who diagnosed 'maladaptive adolescence'. The following year, Saevar was sent to another residential home, called Breidavík, where he completed his mandatory education. Breidavík has special relevance to this book and will be discussed below.

## SAEVAR'S INTERROGATION

According to the Commission, Saevar remained in solitary confinement for 741 days, of which 647 days were in Sídumúli Prison.[2] He was questioned by the police on 180 occasions for a total of 340 hours, and

---

[2] ICCRC Report, 2017, Saevar Ciesielski, Paragraph 2276.

participated in 20 suspects' face-to-face confrontations (Gudjonsson et al., 2014). In spite of this there were only 45 formal statements taken from him. The length of his interrogations repeatedly exceeded the six-hour legal limit, his lawyer was rarely invited to be present, and the light in his cell was kept on 24 hours a day over a two-month period, commencing at the beginning of January 1976 (Working Group Report, 2013). His recorded interrogations and confessions in the Gudmundur and Geirfinnur cases are described in Chapters 8 and 9, respectively. Saevar was released from prison on licence on 28 April 1984.

Saevar appealed his convictions twice to the Supreme Court, on 23 November 1994 and 2 February 1999, and these appeals were rejected on 15 July 1997 and 18 March 1999, respectively.[3]

## RETRACTIONS

Saevar formally retracted his confessions on eight occasions between 1 April 1976 and 13 September 1977. Six of the retractions were in the form of interrogation statements, one was during a face-to-face confrontation with Albert (30 April 1976), and one was in the form of a letter (5 September 1977). Typically, after a retraction Saevar would confess again during a subsequent interrogation. He did not give any confessions after his final retraction on 13 September 1977 and proclaimed his innocence thereafter.

Saevar reiterated his innocence in the Geirfinnur case in a police report, dated 22 October 1976, but a few days later he broke down again and gave a detailed confession. On 28 October he admitted for the first time an involvement in Geirfinnur's death. He had now been in continuous solitary confinement for 333 days.[4]

When questioned in connection with Saevar's 1979 duress investigation, Örn Höskuldsson wished to point out:

> Saevar complained to me about having been coerced to confess in the Gudmundur case. I did not do anything about Saevar's complaint, because I knew it was wrong. When Saevar first confessed about his part in the Gudmundur case, I was present and also his lawyer, Jón Oddsson.[5]

---

[3] ICCRC Report, 2017, Saevar Ciesielski, Paragraphs 1961 and 1963.
[4] ICCRC Report, 2017, Saevar Ciesielski, Paragraph 2997.
[5] Duress Investigation Report (Case Number 2875/79), pp. 141–142. Saevar had alleged that he had retracted his confession on 11 January 1976 when he met with Örn Höskuldsson (see his letter of complaint, Duress Investigation Report, pp. 57–58).

In his letter of complaint to Thórir Oddsson, the person in charge of the duress investigation, Saevar wrote that he had confessed in front of Örn Höskuldsson and Jón Oddsson, because Detective Eggert Bjarnason had promised that he would be released from custody if he confessed, and then added: 'I had been involved in long and harsh interrogations when I signed the report'.

An inspection of the Sídumúli Prison diary log shows that Detectives Eggert Bjarnason and Sigurbjörn Vídir had interrogated Saevar for over 10 hours the previous day (21 December 1975) with a one-hour lunch break. No records are available of this extremely long interrogation.[6] Saevar was interrogated for two hours the following morning (11.00–13.00), which was also unrecorded. There was then a five-hour interrogation (14.00–19.00) at the end of which Saevar gave a confession statement.[7] At 15.30 Örn Höskuldsson and Jón Oddsson arrived at the prison and entered the interrogation room. Undoubtedly, by that time Saevar's resistance had been substantially broken down, leaving him very vulnerable to making a false confession.

Therefore, Örn Höskuldsson's refusal to accept Saevar's retraction on 11 January was based on his failure to consider the full context within which Saevar had given his confession statement. This is a common mistake in cases of miscarriage of justice (Gudjonsson, 2003a). Merely uttering the confession in his presence was no proof of its veracity.

## KARL SCHÜTZ'S VIEW OF SAEVAR

In his final report in the Geirfinnur case, Schütz concluded:

> At the end of October [1976], Jónas Bjarnason took over Saevar's inter-rogation. Saevar tried as before to confuse the case and pretended to have nothing to do with it. Saevar was much on the alert during inter-rogation and tried repeatedly to discover what the other accused had said and requested suspects' face-to-face confrontation to find out what they had said. On the other hand, he generally answered all questions and seemed in a good mood. In particular, he repeatedly gave wrong information regarding the body's hiding place and this caused much work and cost [...] The investigator often talked to Saevar about his views of himself and his interests. It was obvious that he suffered from an inferiority complex, which is probably due to his being strikingly small and unsightly. He speaks very superficially and is keen to imply that he knows important public figures [...] The solitary confinement seems to have affected him badly.

---

[6] ICCRC Report, 2017, Saevar Ciesielski, Paragraph 58.
[7] ICCRC Report, 2017, Saevar Ciesielski, Paragraph 59.

## SAEVAR'S SPEECH BEFORE THE DISTRICT COURT

An extract from Saevar's speech in the District Court in the autumn of 1977 has become available (Sigtryggur Sigtryggsson, *Morgunbladid*, 9 March 2017):[8]

> What happened in this case is something that is happening and has occurred all over the world. Innocent people are made to confess to crimes they did not commit and are then rejected by society. This happened in Russia in 1937 and this has happened widely elsewhere. This is altogether a cunning and strange case and the charges laid against me are heavy. The prosecution demands life imprisonment. It can demand what it likes. I have said from the beginning that I was innocent and I stand by that statement [...] I have been locked up for 700 days in a cell, which is only 2 × 2.5 metres. We, the charged persons in this case have been physically assaulted. The police have assaulted us for no reason, I have often seen this over the years, and these men are now interrogating us. What came out of our mouth is nothing but confession chatter. This is brainwashing, this is mental torture [...] Dignified judges, it is yours to judge, be sensible.

The trial and Supreme Court judges took no notice of Saevar's elegant and powerful speech, but in February 2017 the three members of the Icelandic Court Cases Review Commission were listening, but unfortunately only to parts of the story (see Chapter 12).

## BREIDAVÍK

Breidavík was a farm and fishing base in the West Fjords of Iceland. In 1952 it became a government residential establishment for boys with serious behavioural problems. In 1972 it also began to admit girls. Breidavík was closed in 1979 and it is estimated that it housed a total of 158 children over that period (Spano et al., 2016). The place is of relevance to this book in two respects.

Firstly, Saevar was one of its ex-residents and in the 1970s became Iceland's most notorious murder suspect. He was sent to Breidavík when he was 14 years of age. The second reason for discussing Breidavík in this book is its relevance to science. In 1974, I was completing a six-month university 'work placement' at the Reykjavík Social Services Department. I was employed as an assistant social worker to work

---

[8] http://www.mbl.is/frettir/innlent/2017/03/09/thetta_er_andleg_pining/ (last accessed 24 January 2018).

with young offenders and their families. I learned how dysfunctional families were having problems managing their children and as a result adolescent boys were often sent to Breidavík, a place I was told was producing good results. At the time I was looking for a suitable project for my BSc dissertation. I wondered whether this perception of a successful outcome could be empirically tested and it became the topic of my BSc dissertation in England (Gudjonsson, 1975, 1982). My supervisor was Dr Keith Devlin, a Reader in Law at Brunel University, who in the early 1990s became a resident judge at Luton Crown Court.[9]

I followed up 71 boys who had been sent from Reykjavík to Breidavík between 1953 and 1970. I had access to all relevant reports, including psychology reports, and obtained up-to-date copies of their criminal records. The study showed that being in trouble with the police was the most common reason for referral to Breidavík, followed by difficult home circumstances (i.e. the child being beyond the parents' control). In 20% of cases, the parents had asked for the child to be temporarily removed from the home because of their inability to cope with the child's behavioural and emotional problems. Truancy from school was very common in the sample but was never the main reason for referral to Breidavík.

Reflecting on the study 40 years on, I am in no doubt that many of those boys had ADHD, which was not generally a well-recognized condition at that time. Placing this in context, in a recent meta-analysis of the prevalence of ADHD in incarcerated populations, Young, Moss, et al. (2015) found a rate of 30% in youths, which represented a fivefold increase in comparison with prevalence in the general population. The rate of ADHD among the Breidavík residents is likely to have been even higher because of their young age, (i.e. mean age 11.2 years, range 8–15, Gudjonsson, 1975), but symptoms remit with age in adolescence (Faraone, Biederman, & Mick, 2006; Young & Gudjonsson, 2008).

A vivid description of what Breidavík was like is provided by one of its residents, who spent over three years there in the 1960s (Elíson & Jónsson, 2007). His background and behavioural problems were typical of the boys sent to Breidavík. He was sent to Breidavík when only 10 years of age, along with his older brother, and reported being subjected to both physical and sexual abuse.

Saevar has also discussed in detail his experience in Breidavík and the regular physical abuse he endured (Unnsteinsson, 1980). In addition to the harsh physical discipline, he described another form of discipline, being locked in his bedroom and starved for three days at a time.

---

[9] http://www.feltmakers.co.uk/his-honour-keith-devlin-phd-1933-2012 (last accessed 24 January 2018).

The findings from my research were unfavourable regarding subsequent offending and suggested that residing in Breidavík caused damage to the boys' future behaviour in terms of subsequent criminal convictions (Gudjonsson, 1975, 1982). The Social Services printed and bound 20 copies of my report, three of which I kept: one for myself and two for Brunel University submitted as my BSc dissertation.

The results shocked the Reykjavík Social Services Department. The Director of Social Services, Sveinn Ragnarsson, who had been very supportive of my research and was a lovely man to work for, gently requested that I did not disclose the findings in a public forum. All remaining 17 copies of my BSc dissertation were apparently stamped 'Confidential' on the front page and lay dormant in Iceland for over 30 years when the report finally was made public and became an influential document in an official enquiry into allegations of physical and sexual abuse in the Breidavík home (Spano et al., 2016). Saevar Ciesielski was one of the youngsters I reviewed for my dissertation.

Within a year of completing my BSc dissertation in 1975, Saevar and I met face to face in Sídumúli Prison: he was a murder suspect and I was a detective and a clinical psychology trainee. The date was 5 September 1976. Saevar had just participated in my MSc dissertation on lie detection. I remember that he was very chatty and expressed great interest in lie detection.

I am in no doubt that the closure of Breidavík in 1979 was at least in part due to the unfavourable findings from my BSc research. What I learned from the Breidavík study was the importance of research; merely relying on people's perceptions of a successful outcome is not always valid and needs to be empirically tested. This important lesson has stayed with me throughout my professional career as a clinical forensic psychologist.

## BREIDAVÍK'S PUBLIC ENQUIRY

On 19 October 2007, a documentary film, *Synir feðranna* (*Sons of the Fathers*), was released in Reykjavík's Háskólabíó cinema about the fate of the boys sent to Breidavík and their families, highlighting extensive emotional, physical, and sexual abuse in Breidavík. It was prior to the making of this movie that my 'confidential' BSc dissertation finally surfaced. It was now in the public domain: I was interviewed and appeared in the documentary.

In early 2007, a number of reports in the Icelandic media provided accounts of individuals who had been placed as children in Breidavík, alleging that they had suffered ill treatment during their stay there. On 13 February 2007 the government of Iceland submitted a Bill to Parliament providing for a comprehensive enquiry into the running of the children's home from 1952 to 1979 (Spano et al., 2016).

The Breidavík Enquiry was announced by the Prime Minister of Iceland on 2 April 2007, which became Act No. 26/2007, promulgated by the Icelandic Parliament. A committee of experts was set up, consisting of a professor of law, as chairman, two professors of psychology, and a professor of social work. Breidavík's ex-residents and a selected sample of former employees were interviewed. The committee interviewed 80 (51%) of the 158 ex-residents. It discovered that 33 (21%) were deceased, which is an astonishingly high figure. A recent Danish nationwide cohort study found that ADHD was significantly associated with decreased life expectancy, mainly due to accidental causes (Dalsgaard, Østergaard, Leckman, Mortensen, & Pedersen, 2015). The risk was highest when ADHD was only diagnosed in adulthood, probably reflecting the more severe form of the disorder. Dalsgaard and colleagues concluded: 'Our results also showed that comorbid oppositional defiant disorder, conduct disorder, and substance use disorder increased the risk of death in individuals with ADHD' (p. 2194).

The committee decided on an independent external evaluation of the individual accounts given by witnesses before reaching its final conclusions. I was appointed to carry out this evaluation. I was asked to evaluate in general terms the credibility of the accounts given by the former residents and employees in order to assist the committee in deciding whether or not ill treatment and physical and sexual violence had occurred at some point in the history of Breidavík. I also conducted a review of the most recent scientific literature on the credibility of witness accounts, which guided the committee's work and conclusions. By this approach, the committee believed that the overall assessment of the accounts and its final conclusions were as far as possible founded on solid grounds (Spano et al., 2016).

The committee concluded that during certain periods, some children placed in Breidavík were ill-treated by other residents and/or by the staff members, particularly between 1964 and 1972.

## YES, SAEVAR DID HAVE UNDIAGNOSED ADHD

In the afternoon of 3 March 2015, I met Saevar's son, Hafthór Saevarsson, a law student, at the bar in the Hotel Holt, in the centre of Reykjavík. I had arranged to meet Hafthór to discuss my interest in writing a book chapter on his father. During our conversation, Hafthór mentioned that he had his father's 'social journal' from Lærkehøj, which was a shelter for homeless people in Frederiksberg, Denmark. We arranged to meet a couple of days later in a coffee house in Reykjavík. Soon after we had sat down in the basement of the coffee bar, which was very busy in the late afternoon, he handed me a pocket folder and said I could keep the journal and use it in this current book.

After we had had our coffee, Hafthór briefly interviewed me for his law studies about my work on cases of miscarriage of justice. I got back to my car and opened the folder but read it in more detail when I got home. The first entry was 9 January 2008 and the final entry on 1 July 2011, 12 days before Saevar died from head injuries. Reading through the 'social journal', I came across an entry on 25 February 2010 that he had screened positive for ADHD and had been prescribed Ritalin. The initials 'BF' were next to the entry. I later telephoned Hafthór and told him of my discovery. He said the initials BF stood for Birgitte Falck-Jensen, a social worker, and he gave me her telephone number in Denmark and consented to my speaking with her. I spoke to Birgitte on 27 July 2015. She said she had first met Saevar in the autumn of 2007 when he arrived at one of their shelters in Copenhagen where he stayed for a year. At the time he was consuming a lot of vodka but would not accept that he was an alcoholic. He then moved to Lærkehøj, another shelter where he lived for the last three years of his life. His alcohol consumption was reduced, but it was still of concern to staff. According to Birgitte, on 6 July 2011 Saevar had been celebrating his 56th birthday at the shelter but while intoxicated fell, dying a week later from his injuries.

Birgitte described Saevar as a 'very nice' and 'interesting' person and enjoyed her work with him. In contrast, many of her colleagues found Saevar difficult to work with because of his extreme anger and bitterness regarding his manslaughter convictions in the Gudmundur and Geirfinnur cases. He became easily agitated and emotionally unstable, which frightened some people. Emotional instability is a very common feature of ADHD (Skirrow et al., 2014).

In our recent meta-analysis of adult prisoners with ADHD, we found that co-morbidity of substance use disorder, anxiety disorder, and mood disorder increased by 74%, 68%, and 66%, respectively, in comparison with other prisoners (Young, Sedgwick, et al., 2015).

During our telephone conversation, Birgitte Falck-Jensen informed me that a doctor and his team had diagnosed Saevar with ADHD in February 2010 while at Lærkehøj. This was apparently the first time that he had been diagnosed with ADHD. The diagnosis of ADHD in adulthood has become increasingly common in recent years

(Asherson et al., 2013). What is known is that about 15% of children diagnosed in childhood retain full ADHD symptoms at the age of 25, with a further 50% remaining in partial remission, with persistent symptoms associated with significant functional impairments (Faraone et al., 2006). Unfortunately, ADHD goes largely undetected within the criminal justice system (González, Gudjonsson, Wells, & Young, 2016; Young et al., 2011).

After speaking to Birgitte on 27 July, I wrote a short report for Saevar's family appeal lawyer, Lúdvík Bergvinsson, informing him of the diagnosis and the implications for the case. On 28 January 2016, I testified at the Reykjavík District Criminal Court and at the end I referred to Saevar's ADHD. It was now formally a part of the appeal process and in the public domain. In my view, this was important new evidence.

The tragic story of Saevar Ciesielski is best illustrated by the final paragraph in an article published in Iceland's *Grapevine* on 29 July 2011:

> Ultimately, Saevar had no country. It is reported that in the end he was not registered as an Icelandic citizen. A group of Icelanders met him in Christiania a few days before he died. Saevar was staying in a tree house. He introduced himself, but of course they instantly recognised him despite the dirt and the years of hard living. 'I was made an outlaw from Iceland', Saevar told them. 'We know, Saevar, we know,' was the interlocutor's feeble answer. 'But anyway, Iceland has sunk,' Saevar added.[10]

## EVIDENCE SUPPORTIVE OF ADHD DURING CHILDHOOD AND ADOLESCENCE

A diagnosis of ADHD in adulthood requires that the symptoms of ADHD were present before the age of 12 years (American Psychiatric Association, 2013). I do not know the full details of Saevar's ADHD diagnosis in Denmark, but there is a great deal from his early records to support that he had childhood ADHD (i.e. he displayed characteristics commonly seen in children with ADHD). Stefán Unnsteinsson's (1980) detailed description of Saevar's early life is particularly helpful. Stefán, a sociology student, got to know Saevar well from the autumn of 1972. Stefán was 22 and Saevar was 17. Saevar's full pretrial psychiatric/psychological evaluation is detailed in the book. In addition, Saevar provided an excellent insight into his early psychological problems and vulnerabilities. One of Saevar's childhood

---

[10] http://grapevine.is/mag/articles/2011/07/29/the-tragic-story-of-saevar-ciesielski/.

teachers was interviewed for Unnsteinsson's book, as well as some of his contemporaries. Table 13.1 provides some key features that together provide strong evidence that Saevar had childhood ADHD. These can be briefly summarized as follows:

- Early developmental delays and reading problems. ADHD and reading disabilities tend to co-occur and arise primarily through shared genetic influences (Stevenson et al., 2005). ADHD in childhood is associated with poorer educational outcome (Barkley, Murphy, & Fischer, 2008), which was certainly the position regarding Saevar.
- Saevar vividly described feeling very bored at school, which made him disinterested in his studies. This is a common feature of young persons with ADHD (Shaw et al., 2012).
- Sleep disturbance is commonly associated with ADHD both in childhood and adulthood (Snitselaar, Smits, van der Heijden, & Spijker, 2017; Young & Bramham, 2007). Lack of sleep is known to significantly increase the susceptibility to interrogative pressure (Blagrove, 1996; Blagrove & Akehurst, 2000; Blagrove et al., 1994; Gudjonsson, 2003a). Sleep problems would be exacerbated in solitary confinement and there is evidence that prison officers deliberately kept him awake at night to break down his resistance (Working Group Report, 2013).
- Saevar described being bullied by other children at school and this appears to have distressed him greatly. ADHD status significantly increases the likelihood of his being bullied at school (Unnever & Cornell, 2003). Having a history of being a bully victim increases the risks of false confession over four times (Gudjonsson, Sigurdsson, Sigfusdottir, & Young, 2012a).
- Truancy and conduct problems are commonly found in children with ADHD (Gudjonsson, Sigurdsson, Sigfusdottir, & Young, 2012a; Waschbusch, 2002) with a common genetic influence (Martin, Levy, Pieka, & Hay, 2006; Thapar, Harrington, & McGuffin, 2001). ADHD also commonly co-occurs with oppositional defiant disorder and reading disability (Levy, Hay, Bennett, & McStephen, 2005), with a strong shared genetic variance (Martin et al., 2006).
- Saevar described not getting on with other children and being oppositional in his behaviour. The core combined symptoms are associated with angry and irritable mood, argumentative behaviour, and vindictiveness (American Psychiatric Association, 2013).
- Saevar said that in childhood/adolescence he was addicted to tobacco and that 'nothing could be done about it'. In our large Icelandic epidemiological study we found that children who screened positive for ADHD in adolescence were over six times more likely to report currently smoking than the non-ADHD group (Gudjonsson, Sigurdsson, Sigfusdottir, & Young, 2012b).

**Table 13.1** Problems and behaviour suggesting childhood ADHD (extracts from Unnsteinsson, 1980)

There was some developmental delay in that Saevar was physically clumsy and slow to learn to talk. He had learning difficulties at school, including problems with reading, and had to be moved to another school.

In an interview with a psychiatrist, Saevar's mother described him in childhood as 'restless' and 'fidgety' with an 'irregular sleep pattern'.

He was bullied at school and started truanting when aged nine.

Aged 11 he spent a year at Jadar boarding school.

Helga Saemundsdóttir was Saevar's teacher in the year 10 class (age 10). 'Saevar was in a bad situation that autumn, nowhere near literate in terms of reading and writing. By spring he read stutteringly. I don't think this was due to lack of intelligence, more due to long-standing lack of interest'. (p. 72)

At age 13 a psychiatrist diagnosed Saevar with 'maladaptive adolescence' and when aged 14 he was sent to Breidavík because of behavioural problems and truancy, where he completed his mandatory education. The following school year he went to a school at Reykjanes at Ísafjardardjúp, where Gudjón Skarphédinsson was working as a teacher. Saevar was expelled after the first term for behavioural problems.

According to Saevar, when the psychiatrist asked him why he did not want to attend school, he replied: 'In school you are only taught to be confrontational. The teacher tells me to shut up when I try to talk and throws me out of class. What is in the books is rubbish'. (p. 31)

During the psychological evaluation in 1976, Saevar was described as manipulative and garrulous, exhibiting oppositional behaviour. He did anything to avoid taking psychological tests, including getting another person to complete one of the questionnaires.

The psychiatrist described Saevar's demeanour during the pretrial evaluation: 'Collaboration was rather difficult, because he was prone to jump from one topic to another in a superficial manner and often out of context'.

In Saevar's biography, Stefán Unnsteinsson described Saevar as 'very funny, but he could also be tiring, especially when he talked only for the sake of talking'. (p. 6)

Saevar's own perception of his childhood problems was as follows:
1. He got easily bored at school, did not like being told what to do, and became oppositional.
2. 'I truanted a lot. There was some devil in me as a child, I had problems sleeping, was startled easily or could not go to sleep. Nightmares. So in the mornings I was sleepy, and then it was convenient not to go to school, especially if the curriculum was boring'. (p. 21)
3. 'I soon ended up in opposition with both other children and the teachers. I irritated them, I don't know why, but I felt the same. I was often blamed for things I had not done, so I gave up and continued truanting from school' (p. 23) 'I had a different mindset to these people and was somehow completely different. I was addicted to tobacco and nothing could be done about it'. (p. 29)
4. The last words that Saevar's father said to him before he left for America for good in 1967 were: 'Grow up and be a man'. (p. 29)

- Saevar talked for the sake of talking, jumping from one topic to another, and often talking out of context. In a police interview on 1 May 1976, Gudjón Skarphédinsson described Saevar in the following terms: 'It was common that Saevar would talk about some issue or incident for no apparent reason and out of context', which corroborates the observation of Saevar's biographer and the pretrial psychiatrist. These kinds of conversational problems are very common in people with ADHD (Young & Bramham, 2007). People with ADHD also have a tendency to blurt things out without thinking of the consequences, which can get them into trouble with the police (Gudjonsson & Young, 2006).
- ADHD is associated with mortality in children, adolescents, and adults (Dalsgaard et al., 2015).

### Functional Impairment

Saevar did have a number of functional impairments associated with his ADHD. These were evident in a number of different domains including: educational (e.g. reading and learning difficulties at school), occupational (i.e. he had no work when jobs were readily available and he had fanciful ideas about becoming a film producer and this title was noted as his occupation in some of his police statements), interpersonal relationships (some of which were superficial and manipulative), emotional (i.e. feelings of anger, frustration, and irritability), poor self-concept (Saevar compensated by bluffing and boasting), risk-taking behaviour (i.e. he acted impulsively and took chances), and offending (i.e. he was involved in drug smuggling).

Important in relation to the Gudmundur and Geirfinnur cases, Saevar never obtained a driving licence or drove a car. He encouraged Erla Bolladóttir, who became his girlfriend in November 1973, to get a driving licence, which she did in 1974 and they purchased a car from Kristján's cousin (Bolladóttir, 2008). According to Erla, Saevar admired successful criminals like Al Capone and his ambition in life was to commit a big crime and get away with it, leading to his involving Erla in the Post and Telecommunication fraud so he could satisfy his desire to become a film producer.

Saevar was in the habit of boasting and given the opportunity he would pretend that he knew more about crime than anybody else. This included his boasting to people that he knew something about Geirfinnur's disappearance. The case was very much discussed within the public domain and there was a saying in Iceland at the time that people should look inside their cupboards for Geirfinnur. Erla described in her autobiography how Saevar was from the beginning of their relationship in 1973 being persecuted by the police, particularly by Kristján Pétursson from Keflavík Customs, who apparently kept Saevar under surveillance, even on the evening of Geirfinnur's disappearance (Bolladóttir, 2008).


## THE PRETRIAL PSYCHOLOGICAL/PSYCHIATRIC EVALUATION

The outcome of the pretrial evaluation in 1976 is described in detail in the Working Group Report (2013) and Saevar's biography (Unnsteinsson, 1980). The psychologist found Saevar difficult to assess, because he was garrulous, manipulative, and tried to avoid taking the tests.

On 24 May 1976, the psychologist left the Minnesota Multiphasic Personality Inventory for Saevar to complete, but Saevar tried to get another prisoner to complete it for him; it comprised over 500 items and required fifth grade (age about 10) reading skills (Pope, Butcher, & Seelen, 1993). The incident was discovered and Saevar had his feet shackled for 11 days as punishment. His duvet was also taken away from him and he was given a blanket instead, and he was not allowed any reading material or tobacco for two to three months.[11] The reason for the 'cheat' was undoubtedly seen as devious and manipulative, but there is another possible reason. Erla has told me that during that period of solitary confinement, Saevar would have had problems completing the questionnaire because of his reading problems and may have been reluctant to tell the psychologist about it. Erla had met Saevar in August 1973 and they started living together at the beginning of 1974. Erla spent a lot of time teaching him to read and write but his reading ability was still limited in 1976 when he took the test. Such a long questionnaire would also have been taxing to complete for a person who was symptomatic for ADHD. It is likely that Saevar's motive for getting another prisoner to complete the test was misunderstood.

Saevar obtained an IQ score in the low average range, which the psychologist thought was an underestimate and I agree. ADHD symptoms can suppress IQ scores (Gudjonsson & Young, 2006). His personality was described as 'deeply disturbed', involving irresponsibility, poor

---

[11] The two men had also been sending letters and tobacco between them (ICCRC Report, 2017, Saevar Ciesielski, Paragraph 2469). They were at the time in opposite cells on the same corridor and there was a gap between the cell door and the floor, which allowed prisoners to toss letters between the cells (Working Group Report, 2013).

judgement, low self-esteem, insecurity, and antisocial behaviour. The psychiatrist diagnosed Saevar with antisocial personality disorder.

## THE IMPACT OF SAEVAR'S ADHD ON HIS FUNCTIONING DURING THE CASES

Figure 13.1 provides a model of Saevar's coerced confessions in the Gudmundur and Geirfinnur cases. It describes the antecedents and processes involved. The context provided the 'trigger' for breaking down Saevar's resistance regarding the alleged murders of Gudmundur and Geirfinnur. The three key components were confinement and social isolation, the investigators' guilt-presumption and persuasive interrogation, and high emotional intensity. The emotional intensity was related to the notoriety and seriousness of the cases and the ferocity of the investigation.

It is apparent from the records that Saevar did not cope well with solitary confinement and there is evidence that he was deliberately kept awake at night in order to break down his resistance, confess, and reveal the location of the bodies of Gudmundur and Geirfinnur (Working Group Report, 2013). The pressure on Saevar to confess in both the Gudmundur and Geirfinnur cases was immense.

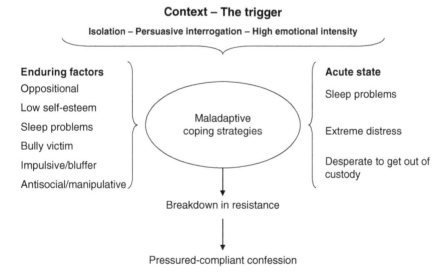

**Figure 13.1**   A model of Saevar Ciesielski's confessions in the two cases

Saevar described his solitary confinement in the following terms (Antonsson, 1991):

> I had nothing to do, nothing to read, nothing to scatter my thoughts. I calmed myself by listening to my breath and sometimes I managed to do so. And to break away from the solitary confinement I ruminated about the past [...] Sometimes I relieved the suffering by composing a film script.
>
> (p. 354)

The three 'contextual' triggers fed directly into Saevar's cognitive appraisal of the situation and impacted on his pre-existing vulnerabilities, labelled 'enduring factors', which were:
- Oppositional behaviour (i.e. getting into arguments with the investigators, which typically backfired and resulted in more police coercion – it is evident that Saevar had distrust of the investigators and the investigators / prison officers had little respect for him and did not treat him well).
- Low self-esteem.
- Sleep problems.
- Bully victim (Saevar had a history of being bullied from a young age).
- Impulsive and erratic behaviour, with Saevar trying to bluff his way out of tricky situations.
- Antisocial and manipulative behaviour (e.g. Saevar acted irresponsibly and on occasions manipulated others into criminal activities).

The contextual risk factors also activated 'acute state' factors. The key ones were:
- Sleep problems made worse by prison officers deliberately keeping him awake at night.
- Feelings of extreme distress and despair (e.g. at the beginning of January 1976 Saevar was complaining of nose bleeds and chest pains).
- Saevar desperately wanted to get out of custody and was prepared to say anything he thought the investigators wanted to hear.

On 15 February 1976 Saevar tried to run away outside Síðumúli Prison when Örn Höskuldsson and Eggert Bjarnason were taking him out for a 'drive'. Örn ran after him, caught him, and as punishment Saevar had his hands and feet shackled and prison officers were instructed to provide him with 'as little service as possible'. In 1979, during a duress investigation, Saevar claimed that his feet were shackled for three weeks, but his hands for only 24 hours.

The contextual, enduring, and acute factors made it impossible for Saevar to cope constructively with his predicament. He utilized maladaptive coping strategies typical of people with ADHD, namely fruitless confrontation and escape-avoidance (Young & Bramham, 2007). This only made his situation worse as it was met with harsh confrontation with police / prison officers, resulting in the breakdown of resistance, pressured-compliant confession and subsequent retraction, more police confrontation, and further confessions. This was a repeated pattern during his solitary confinement. Saevar kept alternating between confessing and retracting the confession. His lawyer was ineffective in supporting him due to him rarely being allowed to see his client in private.

Custodial confinement is likely to be particularly distressing for people with ADHD and impair their ability to cope with police questioning and lengthy detention (Young et al., 2009; Young et al., 2013). There is evidence that they are two to three times more likely than their peers to give a false confession during police questioning (Gudjonsson, Sigurdsson, Bragason et al., 2008; Gudjonsson, Sigurdsson, Sigfusdottir, & Young, 2012a; Gudjonsson, Sigurdsson, et al., 2016).

## WAS SAEVAR COERCED TO IMPLICATE INNOCENT PEOPLE?

In their report on Saevar, the Commission referred to only one period when Saevar was subjected to coercion. This was during the period from 25 April 1976 until the autumn that year when there were increased restrictions in solitary confinement, allegedly because he was 'lying one person out and another in' during interrogation.[12] On 7 May, Saevar had separate face-to-face confrontations with Erla and Kristján Vidarsson, lasting 135 and 75 minutes, respectively. Saevar gave a highly improbable statement the following day. On 9 May the 'four wrongly accused' were released from custody. Saevar was then repeatedly interrogated and subjected to more suspects' face-to-face confrontations without written reports.

There is compelling evidence that Saevar was subjected to coercion leading up to his statement on 23 January 1976 when he wrongly implicated Einar Bollason, Magnús Leópoldsson, and Valdimar Olsen. In a later statement he also implicated Sigurbjörn Eiríksson, leading to their arrest and detention in Sídumúli Prison.

In February 2017, the National Archives of Iceland discovered previously undisclosed documents in the Gudmundur and Geirfinnur cases, which included letters that Saevar had written in 1977 to the three newly appointed trial judges, apparently in the hope that they would

---

[12] ICCRC Report, 2017, Saevar Ciesielski, Paragraph 2996.

listen to his complaints of the extensive mental and physical abuse he had suffered at the hands of the investigators and prison officers at Síðumúli Prison. The letter was typed from the Skólavörðustígur Penitentiary from early 1977.

Particularly relevant sections from his letters are the following:

- On 14 January 1976, investigative judge Örn Höskuldsson spoke to Saevar (confirmed by inspection of the custody record). Saevar described this date as the beginning of his being asked questions about Geirfinnur's disappearance.
- Saevar wanted to consult his lawyer and get his prescribed heart medication from Dr Gudsteinn Thengilsson (i.e. for irregular heart beat and heart pain – there is independent evidence that Saevar had had long-standing concerns about his heart, including a witness statement from his mother).
- His tobacco and writing utensils had been taken away from him.
- Saevar complained that the light in his prison cell (number 22 – see Chapter 6) was left on all night for one and a half months from soon after Christmas 1975, a matter that had been referred to in the Working Group Report (2013). This was undoubtedly an attempt to keep him awake and break down his resistance, and it worked. There is independent evidence to support this (Working Group Report, 2013). Saevar has described elsewhere how the continuous light in his cell 22 made him lose all sense of time (Unnsteinsson, 1980, p. 54). In addition, the windows had non-transparent glass and the air-conditioning was noisy and erratic in terms of heating (i.e. blowing either hot or cold).
- After the investigators stopped interrogations, prison officers continued to question him and get him to confess.
- Saevar alleged that he was physically assaulted by police and prison officers. On one occasion a prison officer forced his head under water during the early part of his detention (Working Group Report, 2013).
- Detective Sigurbjörn Víðir told Saevar during one of these January 1976 interrogations that he had proof that Saevar had gone to Keflavík on 19 November 1974 with Einar Bollason.
- Detective Eggert Bjarnason informed Saevar that Erla had had a murder threat via a phone call and that he should know why.
- Saevar's letters described a buildup of immense pressure to confess in the Geirfinnur case prior to the official statement that he gave on 21 January 1976: 'When I returned to my cell after these so-called interrogations, the prison officers took over; this continued over four days [...] When I asked the prison officers to call for the night doctor they laughed and said that there was nothing wrong with me except fantasy [...] I had palpitations and terrible sharp pain and fainted a few times, but the prison officers laughed'.

Saevar has described his health in custody as follows:

> My health was dreadful, all my muscles ached and my heart seemed disconnected at times. Often I could not sleep for days and if I went to sleep I always woke up after a little while and thought I was dying. The prison officers sometimes told me that it was easy to kill me and make it look like suicide, so I had to stay constantly vigilant. But I was determined not to give up and argued with them, my body was so numb that I had stopped feeling the beatings.
>
> (Unnsteinsson, 1980, p. 55)

Table 13.2 shows the buildup of pressure during the three weeks leading to him implicating innocent people in the disappearance of Geirfinnur. It starts from 2 January 1976 when Saevar was complaining of 'heart pain'.[13] After a car journey late at night on 4 January, after almost five hours of interrogation that day, in the early hours of that night Saevar ended up vomiting, had a nose bleed, and complained of heart pain. It appears that he was not in good mental or physical health, raising concerns about his fitness to be interviewed.

On 9 January Örn Höskuldsson apparently did not find Saevar cooperative and the interview was quickly terminated. Four days later the three Reykjavík Team investigators took Saevar out for a two-hour 'sightseeing tour', late at night when it was pitch-dark. It is unknown what this outing was about.

On 11 January Saevar was interrogated for almost four hours in connection with the Post and Telecommunication fraud and the Gudmundur case, and a statement was taken (Working Group Report, 2013). Afterwards, his detention was extended for a further 60 days and a psychiatric evaluation ordered.

Örn Höskuldsson interrogated Saevar for 35 minutes on 14 January, and again for a very 'short while' on 16 January, when the two men appeared to be in dispute over something, suggesting that Saevar was not happy, which is confirmed from his own account above. Saevar's distress after this brief interview can be seen from his immediately ringing the cell bell and wanting to speak to Örn Höskuldsson on his own.

## THE 'REAL-LIFE' LIE DETECTOR TEST

The prison custody record shows that I conducted the card task experiment on Saevar on the afternoon of 5 September 1976; the entire session was conducted between 14.20 and 16.15. I am described as a

---

[13] This is not an exhaustive list of all interrogations during those three weeks.

**Table 13.2**  Key entries in the Sídumúli Prison diary leading up to Saevar's confession regarding the false allegations against the 'four wrongly accused'

| | |
|---|---|
| 2 January 1976 | It is recorded that at 23.45 Saevar's medication was taken to him in his cell, but he refused to take it because he had a pain in the heart. At 02.15 Saevar rang the bell and had a nose bleed. |
| 3 January 1976 | Dr Gudsteinn Thengilsson speaks to Saevar and takes him off diazepam. |
| 4 January 1976 | Saevar was interrogated for about five hours that day. After the last interrogation, which ended at 23.00, Örn Höskuldsson, Eggert Bjarnason, and Sigurbjörn Vídir took Saevar for a 'drive' and returned at 00.10. At 01.50 Saevar rang the cell bell and was found to have vomited, had a nose bleed, and complained of heart pain. |
| 6 January 1976 | At 16.15 Saevar's brother brought him some oranges, but they were thrown away by the prison officer (recorded by chief prison officer Gunnar Gudmundsson). |
| 9 January 1976 | At 10.30 Örn Höskuldsson interviewed Saevar, but the interview was terminated after 15 minutes and described as 'unsuccessful'. |
| 11 January 1976 | Saevar was interrogated for almost four hours (13.40–17.30) and his detention was extended for a further 60 days and a psychiatric evaluation ordered. |
| 13 January 1976 | Örn Höskuldsson, Eggert Bjarnason, and Sigurbjörn Vídir took Saevar for a 'sightseeing tour', which lasted two hours (21.40–23.50) at the darkest time of the year. |
| 14 January 1976 | Örn Höskuldsson took Saevar for interrogation (13.45–14.20). Saevar claims this was the beginning of the interrogation in the Geirfinnur case. |
| 16 January 1976 | At 16.30 'Saevar was taken for an interview in the "corner room" [interrogation room], the interview was very short and Saevar was moved quickly to his cell again. He immediately rang the bell and asked for an interview with Örn on his own, which took place, but it was very short.' |
| 18 January 1976 | Örn Höskuldsson talked to Saevar in his cell at the end of the day. |
| 19 January 1976 | Saevar was taken for interrogation, which lasted for almost six hours (14.50–20.40). There is no report of this interview. |
| 20 January 1976 | Saevar was taken for interrogation, which lasted for almost six hours (09.05–14.55). That same day it was noted in the diary at 20.10 that the interrogation of Saevar had finished, but there was no record of when it started. There are no reports of these two interviews. |

**Table 13.2**    (*Continued*)

| | |
|---|---|
| 21 January 1976 | Eggert Bjarnason and Sigurbjörn Vídir took Saevar for interrogation at 10.35, and at 10.50 Örn Höskuldsson joined them. The interview ended at 13.45 (three hours and 10 minutes), which shows that it lasted just over three hours. Another interrogation started at 16.25 and lasted until 18.45 (two hours and 20 minutes). The third interrogation started at 20.15 and ended at 01.10 (four hours and 55 minutes). |
| | This shows a total of over 10 hours of interrogation in one day, all unrecorded, with the exception of some handwritten points showing that Saevar was being questioned about the Geirfinnur case and suggesting that Erla was probably frightened of Einar Bollason, Jón Ragnarsson, and Magnús Leópoldsson. |
| | There was also a reference to 'Valdimar' in the notes, who had worked in Klúbburinn and might, according to Saevar, have gone with the others to Keflavík (ICCRC Report, 2017, Saevar Ciesielski, Paragraph 114).    ⎰ |

psychology student and it is recorded that the experiment had nothing to do with the case. Four days later I was visiting Sídumúli Prison to speak to a detainee, unrelated to the Gudmundur and Geirfinnur cases, when Saevar wanted to see me in his cell, having heard that I was in the prison. He wanted to know the results of the card tests and expressed an interest in lie detector machines in real-life cases. Soon thereafter I was approached by a detective and it was suggested to me that it would be interesting to try out the lie detector on Saevar in relation to the Gudmundur and Geirfinnur cases. I had not expected this request and hesitated because I had had no training in the forensic use of lie detectors in real-life cases and my research only focused on simple, non-crime related, card tasks. At the time I did not think it would do any harm and thought it would be a useful experience. I was full of enthusiasm and had the thirst to learn, never wasting an opportunity to do so.

My understanding at the time of agreeing to the real-life test on Saevar was that this was being done primarily for my own learning experience and that the findings would not be used as evidence in the case. It is possible that Saevar asked for the test after he participated in the card test experiment rather than the idea having come from the police.

Jónas Bjarnason, a detective from Schütz's Task Force, collected Saevar from Sídumúli Prison at 19.55 on 13 September to take him the few minutes' drive to the Headquarters of the Criminal Investigation

Police in Borgartún 7, where the testing took place in the presence of Saevar's lawyer at the time, Jón Oddsson. I asked Saevar a number of questions about the disappearance of both Gudmundur and Geirfinnur and some 'control questions'. Saevar firmly denied any involvement in the cases.

In early 1997, Saevar contacted me about the results of the real-life lie detector test from 13 September 1976, which he wanted to use for his attempted appeal. He believed the findings had been favourable to him. I met with Saevar in Iceland and advised him not to use the findings for his appeal, because they were not straightforward. He accepted this but then tried to persuade me to take on his case as an expert witness. When I declined, mainly because of existing work pressures, Saevar smiled and stated: 'But it would be a great honour for you'.

Saevar did have charm and a good sense of humour!

## CONCLUSIONS

Having carefully reviewed the evidence, I am confident that Saevar had ADHD in childhood and was still symptomatic when he died at the age of 56. One of the effects of ADHD is that suspects' resilience to resist pressure from the police is weakened (Gudjonsson, Sigurdsson, Sigfusdottir, & Young, 2012a) and this undoubtedly happened in Saevar's case. The investigators, the prosecutor, and the prison officers did not know how to manage Saevar while he was in solitary confinement in Sídumúli Prison. They had no insight into his condition, nor did the psychologist and psychiatrist who assessed him pretrial. His undiagnosed ADHD affected Saevar's ability to cope both with the solitary confinement and the lengthy interrogations and significantly increased the likelihood that he would give a false confession under pressure. His ADHD also explains why Saevar's resistance after retracting his confessions could quite readily be broken down again. Saevar's history of being a victim of bullying from an early age further increased the risk of his giving a false confession in the Gudmundur and Geirfinnur cases (Gudjonsson, Sigurdsson, & Sigfusdottir, 2010).

On a personal note, my recollection is that in 1976 the investigators and the prosecutor became increasingly frustrated by the fact that Saevar never gave any tangible piece of information that could be corroborated. His behaviour was construed as his playing games with the police and being manipulative. He was subjected to maltreatment and cruelty from January 1976 in custody (e.g. keeping him awake at night, ignoring his request for heart medication, and his feet being shackled on two separate occasions over a long period of time), aimed to punish him, break down his resistance, and make him more compliant and cooperative.

It did not help that Saevar was confrontational with people in authority, had eluded the narcotics police over a long time regarding his drug dealing offences, was cunning, and could be manipulative. He had no credibility in the eyes of the investigators and was a thorn in their side. He appears to have been viewed as some master criminal, who was capable of the most hideous of crimes. He was not treated with respect. The four times I met Saevar, he was polite and respectful. He had a certain charm about him and was likeable.

Saevar's skills were his ability to engage people and persuade them to do what he wanted them to do, but this did not work with the police because they did not trust him or accept his claims of innocence. His weakness was that he was a garrulous and boastful man. He boasted to Kristján about the 1974 Post and Telecommunication fraud with Erla, which Kristján told another fellow prisoner about, leading to Saevar's arrest on 12 December 1975. Saevar had also boasted about knowing what had happened to Geirfinnur, because the mystery over his disappearance was the talk of the town. When the police learned about this they took a keen interest in him.

There is no evidence that memory distrust and heuristic failure are relevant to Saevar's confessions in the two cases. The evidence shows that the process of his confessions involved the gradual breakdown of resistance to the police and custodial pressure over time, during intensive interrogation, and that the mechanism involved maladaptive coping. The evidence of maladaptive coping is well illustrated by Saevar's repeated attempts to retract his confessions and then breaking down again (i.e. he kept alternating between a confession and denials), suggesting pressured-compliant confession. The most likely reason why Saevar did not develop memory distrust syndrome is that he did not trust the police; as discussed in Chapters 3 and 4, trust is an essential prerequisite for the development of memory distrust and suggestibility.

With regard to the perjury conviction, on 19, 20, and 21 January 1976, Saevar was interrogated for a total of 22 hours, which included 10 and a half hours on the 21st. The following day he implicated Einar Bollason, Magnús Leópoldsson, and Valdimar Olsen, subsequently leading to their arrest, followed two weeks later by the arrest of Sigurbjörn Eiríksson. Unfortunately, we do not know what happened during those 22 hours. The investigators failed to keep an official record of what took place behind the closed doors in the interrogation room at Sídumúli Prison.

By the time Saevar gave his first signed statement in the Geirfinnur case, he had been in solitary confinement for 41 days, and his persistent denials regarding the fraud allegations and involvement in Gudmundur's death had been broken down, undoubtedly draining his psychological resources and resilience. Furthermore, during the three days leading up to his first Geirfinnur statement, he had been interrogated for 22 hours, he had been kept awake in his cell, he was not in a good psychological or physical state, and he had no access to a lawyer. Under these circumstances his ADHD would have significantly aggravated his distress and further reduced his resilience.

In spite of us not knowing what went on during Saevar's interrogations, merely considering the above factors strongly suggests coercion and casts serious doubts on the voluntariness of Saevar's statements in the Geirfinnur case. Why did the Commission not consider these factors, which are listed but not discussed in their report, before rejecting the perjury aspect of the appeal application?

# 14

# Erla Bolladóttir – A Vulnerable Young Woman

*Cherchez la femme*[1]

## SALIENT POINTS

- On 22 February 1980 the Supreme Court convicted Erla of perjury in the Geirfinnur case and she was sentenced to three years in prison.
- Erla was indecently assaulted as a child and in adolescence she was raped.
- When her baby was 11 weeks old she was held in solitary confinement for eight days, intensively interrogated, and pressured to implicate people in Gudmundur's disappearance, followed a month later by her making false allegations against people in the Geirfinnur case.

---

[1] From *Les Mohicans de Paris* (Alexandre Dumas, 1854), where police officer Joseph Fouch announces: 'There's a woman in every case; as soon as someone reports a crime to me, I say, "Look for the woman"'. In her usage notes Laura Lawless explains: 'In other words, whenever a man does something wrong, it's always the woman's fault. Her greed, jealousy, anger or spite forced the poor innocent man to commit the crime, so once you figure out who she is, case closed' (http://www.lawlessfrench.com, last accessed 24 January 2018).

---

*The Psychology of False Confessions: Forty Years of Science and Practice*, First Edition. Gisli H. Gudjonsson.

- All she wanted was to be with her newborn baby.
- She was no match for the determination and ferocity of the police, Karl Schütz, and judiciary.
- She was only 20 years old and her life became a living nightmare.
- This chapter shows the importance of situational as well as dispositional factors in producing unreliable confessions.
- It is probable that while not in custody, Erla was used and manipulated, and coerced into giving false statements against the 'four wrongly accused' in order to go along with the investigative hypothesis of the police.

Erla Bolladóttir was born in Reykjavík on 19 July 1955. Her father, Bolli, was originally a radio operator with Loftleidir Icelandic, known internationally as Icelandic Airlines, and he later worked for Pan American Airways. Bolli had two boys from a previous marriage, one being Einar, who Erla later implicated in the Geirfinnur case. Einar was 12 years older than Erla, and she was not brought up with her half-brothers.

Erla was the third eldest of five biological siblings. During the psychiatric evaluation in 1976 she reported normal development. Her parents moved with her to the USA when she was two and a half years old and returned five years later to Reykjavík. Erla reported a poor relationship with her mother, Thóra, who she described as strict, and Erla could not easily confide in her. She describes in her autobiography their turbulent relationship (Bolladóttir, 2008). Her parents argued a lot and separated in 1971. After this, Erla's academic performance deteriorated substantially and she got into conflict with her teachers.

In her autobiography, Erla reported being indecently assaulted by a farmer when she was nine years of age. This incident affected her greatly in her teenage years. She described being sent to a farm in Djúpavík, a small village in northwest Iceland, to help look after a couple's children. One day the farmer asked Erla to follow him to the chicken shed to collect eggs. While in the shed he grabbed hold of her, touched her all over her body, and forced his tongue into her mouth. She managed to escape from him and he told her not to tell anybody. Afterwards the farmer's wife sensed that something was wrong and pressured Erla to tell her what had happened, which she did. The woman told her she would speak to her husband and make sure this did not happen again. She also asked Erla not to tell anybody about the incident. Erla had no way of leaving the isolated farm, felt trapped, and refused to return to the farm the following summer. She felt unable to confide in anybody about this incident. Years later she told her mother something of what had happened.

In 2016, Erla told me that she was raped when aged 17 and that this had further damaged her psychologically. She had tried hard to resist the assault but eventually had to submit and it left her with bruises. This incident is described in the pretrial psychiatric report and in detail in her book. She felt ashamed and frightened and did not want to report the incident to the police, even though her close friend Hulda encouraged her to do so. She had met the man at Hulda's home at Framnesvegur, where she was a frequent visitor. Hulda was living at Framnesvegur with her half-brother Valdimar Olsen. In February 1976, Erla partly implicated him in the Geirfinnur case. Erla and Hulda were close friends at that time and were the same age. Valdimar Olsen was seven years their senior (Daníelsson, 2016).

Importantly in relation to Erla, it is known from our research that young persons who are sexually assaulted in childhood show increased immediate and delayed suggestibility (Vagni et al., 2015). It is their ability to cope with interrogative pressure that is most adversely affected, a consistent feature seen in Erla during interrogation in 1975 and 1976.

Following the incident on the isolated farm in Djúpavík, Erla began to show behavioural problems, including stealing money from her father and smoking cigarettes. Her mother found out and 'the interrogation commenced immediately' (Bolladóttir, 2008, p. 29). Erla tried to deny stealing the money, but eventually confessed. She felt a strong sense of relief after confessing to the thefts, which surprised her. She felt better than she had done for a long time. Confessing produced a sense of relief and comfort in her, which is something we have confirmed from our own research (Gudjonsson & Sigurdsson, 1999).

Soon afterwards, Erla's mother interrogated her again over a lost family allowance book. Erla did not know what had happened to the book and repeatedly denied having taken it, but her mother did not believe her, eventually pressuring Erla into confessing falsely that she had hidden the book somewhere but could not recall where. Rather than telling her off, her mother praised her for her honesty and gave her a glass of milk as a reward, then barred her from going out over the weekend. This upset Erla greatly because her father had just bought a new car and was taking the family out for a drive, while she had to stay in her bedroom. Erla was also very upset that her mother would not believe her when she was telling the truth and her mind was eventually overborne by the pressure. She described her mother as being very controlling, which Erla tried to fight. When the police interviewed Erla's mother on 5 April 1976, she described Erla as having been more stubborn than her other daughters and prone to fantasy. She had disapproved of Erla's relationship with Saevar and said that Erla had appeared to be completely under his control.[2]

Erla describes in her autobiography how, over 10 years later, she was reminded of this experience in early May 1976 after confessing to murdering Geirfinnur by shooting him. Afterwards, prosecutor Hallvardur Einvardsson rewarded her with praise and bought her an ice cream (i.e. 'positive reinforcement'). Erla was subsequently remanded in solitary confinement at Sídumúli Prison where she stayed for almost eight months.

## THE RELATIONSHIP WITH SAEVAR

Erla met Saevar at her friend Hulda's home at Framnesvegur in 1973, where there were frequent parties, sometimes annoying the neighbours to the extent that the police were called (Bolladóttir, 2008). Erla stayed there frequently at the time, and when Hulda brought Saevar home, she introduced them.[3] Erla did not think he looked attractive, but he came across as being generous and kind. She later met him in a café for a chat and he disclosed a lot of personal information about her and her family (which she already knew) after claiming that he knew everything about her. Saevar liked to give the impression to people that he was knowledgeable about others, including claiming that he knew something about the Geirfinnur case.

In November 1973, Erla's father had bought a basement flat at Hamarsbraut 11. Erla felt uncomfortable staying there when her father was away, and so she spent a lot of time at Framnesvegur, where Saevar was by now a frequent guest. Erla and Hulda planned a trip to America that autumn and Saevar wanted to go with them, having relatives there. As it turned out, Valdimar Olsen, who was responsible for his sister's welfare, banned Hulda from going. Erla and Saevar went to America together in November 1973 and during the visit a relationship developed between them. Saevar told her that the Icelandic police were persecuting him and at one time they had Interpol arrest him in Denmark for suspected drug offences, and he was extradited to Iceland.

When Erla and Saevar returned from the USA they were stopped by customs officers at Keflavík Airport and Erla was strip searched.

---

[2] Evidence Book XII, pp. 168–172.
[3] According to Hulda's witness statement dated 5 May 1976, Saevar, Kristján, and Albert came to vist her at Framnesvegur at the beginning of August 1973 and Erla was there at the time (Evidence Book XII, p. 213).

She was released after a while but Saevar was detained. She went to Hamarsbraut 11 in Hafnarfjördur with her father, who had waited for her at the airport while she attempted to find out when Saevar was going to be released. This did not leave her father with a good impression of Saevar. Her association with Saevar caused difficulties in her relationship with her father and half-brother Einar. Then Erla's father became seriously ill and Hamarsbraut 11 was later sold. Erla now had to find her own accommodation and establish her independence. Her relationship with Saevar was turbulent: several times they broke up and got back together again (Bolladóttir, 2008).

In her book, Erla described an incident in about September 1974 when Saevar physically beat her after having lost his temper in a jealous rage. Saevar soon apologized and the relationship started again.

In November 1974, Erla had learned from a friend at work that she was being linked to the Post and Telecommunication fraud and would soon be arrested. As a result she and Saevar decided to escape to Copenhagen, where they knew people. Erla went ahead and Saevar followed two weeks later. Erla returned home on her own in April 1975, three and a half months' pregnant. Their relationship in Copenhagen had been turbulent and at one point, while Erla was pregnant, Saevar lost his temper and kicked her. She now wanted to leave him for good.

Erla told me in 2016 that when she returned from Copenhagen she at first went to live with Saevar's mother, then moved from one accommodation to another, trying to avoid Saevar. She found a small flat at Grundastígur and felt safe. In about July or August, Saevar found out where she lived and persuaded her to get back together again. She was unable to resist his pressure and they moved into a small flat at Thverbrekka 4, in Kópavogur, on the outskirts of Reykjavík. When her family discovered that she and Saevar were once more together they terminated contact and Erla was now on her own. Her only contact was now Saevar, who throughout their relationship had successfully isolated her from her friends and other social contacts, making her heavily dependent on him. Saevar was frequently not at home and Erla felt 'depressed', 'extremely lonely', and 'lost'. He was very derogatory about her friends and family, commonly calling them 'idiots'.

On 24 September 1975 Erla and Saevar's daughter, Julia, was born. She breastfed the baby but stopped after more than two months on the advice of the midwife. On 13 December 1975, she was arrested in connection with the Post and Telecommunication fraud. Saevar had been arrested the previous day. Her daughter had now become the only person she loved and adored and for the first time in her life Erla felt like she had a sense of purpose, but she was worried about the future, having no stability in her life or financial security.

In November 1975, the couple had agreed to separate for good, and Saevar had signed a letter allowing Erla to keep all their domestic possessions after their intended separation in January 1976. Shortly after Saevar signed the declaration, they were arrested and detained in custody. The police discovered the letter when they searched the flat and this made it easier to get Erla to incriminate Saevar in the Gudmundur and Geirfinnur cases.

## ERLA'S INTERROGATION

Erla remained in solitary confinement for a total of 241 days during two separate periods, of which she spent 142 days in Síðumúli Prison.[4] She was questioned by the police on 105 occasions for a total of 120 hours, and participated in 11 suspects' face-to-face confrontations in relation to the Gudmundur and Geirfinnur cases (Gudjonsson et al., 2014). Her statements and confessions are thoroughly documented in Chapters 8 and 9. According to Erla's autobiography, after implicating Saevar and Kristján in the Gudmundur case and leaving Síðumúli Prison on 20 December 1975, she had to move in with her mother in Stóragerði because her own flat at Thverbrekka had been sealed by the police and she could not return. (This is confirmed in the case papers). She did not feel comfortable living at her mother's flat but had nowhere else to go. Her relationship with her mother at the time was strained. She felt very much on her own and isolated from people, apart from the investigators who were in contact with her.

Around 23 December 1975, Erla was alone at home with her daughter, when Detective Sigurbjörn Vídir telephoned her to enquire how she was and to remind her of her promise to continue to help them with their investigation. He offered to provide her with assistance in practical matters, such as an application for child maintenance. He told her that Saevar's confession statement in the Gudmundur case matched hers, which persuaded her that the material events at Hamarsbraut 11 had really happened.

According to Erla, she telephoned Sigurbjörn Vídir between Christmas and the New Year, because she urgently needed personal possessions kept at her Thverbrekka flat. (There is a record in the Síðumúli Prison diary of Sigurbjörn Vídir having taken a telephone call from Erla at 13.35 on 28 December 1975.) Sigurbjörn soon collected her from Stóragerði and took her to her home at Thverbrekka

---

[4] ICCRC Report, 2017, Erla Bolladóttir, Paragraph 2319.

and they started chatting. While they were in the flat standing by the window in the sitting room, where she had been arrested two weeks previously, the conversation focused on a comment Saevar had made a year previously about his theory of the Geirfinnur case. Sigurbjörn then suggested that perhaps Saevar knew something about the case. He started questioning Erla about it, but she was reluctant to comment. He then took her back to Stóragerdi, stopped the car outside the block of flats and asked her directly whether she thought Saevar knew anything. She hesitated in her answer, as she did not want to upset him:

> I feared that I might upset him, which could mean he would not want anything to do with me. I could not tolerate that thought. The three investigators [Sigurbjörn Vídir, Örn Höskuldsson, and Eggert Bjarnason] were the only people from whom I could seek assistance.
>
> (Bolladóttir, 2008, p. 199)

The following morning, the investigators turned up at her mother's flat without warning and started questioning her. Örn Höskuldsson told her that they knew her very well by now and thought that she was going through something similar to that she had experienced in the Gudmundur case (i.e. a traumatic life event regarding Geirfinnur's disappearance and she had suppressed it deeply in her subconscious). She was frightened to deny it completely in case it upset the investigators and she ended up in custody again, and she felt she needed their support. After a long and difficult morning the investigators left and said they would be in contact. Very soon thereafter she was taken to Sídumúli Prison where the Reykjavík Team questioned her at length about her views of Saevar's possible involvement in the Geirfinnur case and asked whether she knew Magnús Leópoldsson and Sigurbjörn Eiríksson, the two people from Klúbburinn. She said she had met Magnús once at Thórskaffi restaurant with Hulda and her brother Valdimar Olsen. The investigators were particularly interested in hearing that her half-brother Einar had been referred to in connection with smuggled alcohol. 'From my ambiguous answers the investigators let their minds wander and gave a free rein to their imagination' (Bolladóttir, 2008, p. 203).

Erla refers in her book to some unrecorded interrogations in Sídumúli Prison before her recorded interview on 23 January 1976. Her recollection is that the focus of these interrogations was on her having been so traumatized by Geirfinnur's fate that she had problems remembering it. The investigators suggested various scenarios, including one unknown to her, that Saevar and her half-brother Einar had had some business relationship. Erla noted that the rumours in the community regarding Magnús Leópoldsson and Sigurbjörn Eiríksson seemed to give the investigators an inspiration in the storytelling and the first confession she gave had some similarities to the confessions three months earlier of Gudmundur Agnarsson, discussed in Chapter 7. According to Erla, many years later she learned how her story had been shaped by Mr Agnarsson's confession.

According to Erla, the investigators told her that there were dangerous people connected to the case, asked her to be careful, and said that she should contact them immediately if something untoward happened or if she was being disturbed. Shortly after, the telephone rang and a man's voice asked whether she 'had not said enough' and terminated the call. Erla became terrified and she telephoned Sídumúli Prison, the only telephone number she had for the investigators, and Detective Sigurbjörn Vídir answered. Very soon the police arrived at her mother's flat, including armed officers. She was informed that it had not been possible to trace the threatening phone call. It was never established who had made that threatening call, and suggestions have been made that the investigators engineered it to frighten Erla into compliance (Antonsson, 1991; Daníelsson, 2016).

In the police version of events, on 25 January 1976 two armed police officers kept guard on Erla overnight at her mother's home for fear of revenge after the arrest of three men in the Geirfinnur case.[5] According to the prison custody diary, Erla had telephoned the prison at 14.40 on 25 January and spoken to one of the detectives in the case, which appears to have led to the armed officers arriving at her home later that day. It is also known that Erla had made a call on 6 January 1976 to the prison wishing to speak urgently to either Sigurbjörn Vídir or Eggert Bjarnason, but the purpose of this call is unknown. According to Detective Bjarnason's retrospective notes on 10 March 1976, Erla had telephoned around the middle of January regarding threatening phone calls.[6]

### Confessing to Geirfinnur's Murder

The custody record shows that Erla was booked in at Sídumúli Prison at 20.30 on 3 May 1976. She was interrogated until 23.40, and 38 minutes later she was locked in a cell overnight. Shortly afterwards she became emotional, and the prison chaplain was called at her request and spent over two hours with her. She was then given chloral hydrate to help her sleep. The prosecutor Hallvardur Einvardsson telephoned

---

[5] ICCRC Report, 2017, Erla Bolladóttir, Paragraph 2468.
[6] Evidence Book XII, p. 126.

the prison at 01.05 to enquire whether the chaplain had seen Erla and reiterated that Erla must be 'very carefully supervised'.

Erla's account of this is as follows (Bolladóttir, 2008). The Geirfinnur investigation was in crisis. The 'four wrongly accused' had not confessed after about three months in solitary confinement and their custody would shortly need to be extended. This could not be done unless there was more evidence discovered against them. Erla was brought to Síðumúli Prison for interrogation before Hallvardur Einvardsson, Örn Höskuldsson, and Detective Eggert Bjarnason, all of whom looked serious. They wanted to know more about what had happened to Geirfinnur and began to ask her leading questions. As the interrogation progressed, Erla sensed that they wanted her to confess to killing Geirfinnur, which she did, eventually. Afterwards, Hallvardur rewarded her with an ice cream. She was told that in view of what she had said she would have to remain in the prison. Detectives Eggert Bjarnason and Sigurbjörn Víðir then took her to her mother's home, which was no more than about a five minute drive away, to collect some essentials and inform her mother that she would not be returning home that night. The following day the investigators typed out her confession from the previous evening and she was given a 60-day detention on remand.

There was no statement taken of Erla's confession during the three-hour interrogation on the evening of 3 May 1976, but she was further interrogated the following day and then a statement was taken. Officially, she confessed to shooting Geirfinnur on 4 May. However, I find her account of a confession the previous evening credible.

## Hypnosis and Abreaction

In her autobiography Erla describes how during the summer of 1976 the investigators were getting very impatient with her, accusing her of a lack of cooperation and attempts to confuse or delay the investigation. She was allegedly told that this could result in a heavier penalty and that her child could be taken away from her. She was told to try harder to remember what had happened on the slipway. The psychiatrist who was doing the pretrial evaluation came to the prison shortly after Erla had given a confession statement regarding shooting Geirfinnur, injected her with a relaxant, and hypnotized her. He asked her questions about the case and when the investigators thought she had said enough he withdrew the needle and helped her 'wake up'.

These kinds of abreactions were commonly used in the UK in the early 1980s and I was present during some of them, but they never seemed to produce any useful results (Gudjonsson, 1992a) and were likely to confuse suspects (Gudjonsson et al., 1999).

## ERLA'S ATTEMPTS TO RETRACT HER CONFESSIONS

Table 14.1 shows that Erla made a number of unsuccessful attempts to retract her confessions in the Geirfinnur case. The only retraction that was ultimately accepted was that she had not killed Geirfinnur herself. Her withdrawal of her retraction letter to judge Örn Höskuldsson on 14 August 1976 shows her dependence on him and fear of making him angry. The key to the hold he had over her lay in his power to deny her access to her infant daughter, born the previous September, and keep her in solitary confinement. The method that Karl Schütz used to persuade her to withdraw her retraction was to forcefully confront her with her previous statements and apparent special knowledge regarding Geirfinnur's disappearance.

In her book (Bolladóttir, 2008), Erla describes a meeting with Schütz when she told him that her confession was false. She saw this as an opportunity to tell the truth to somebody who was independent of the Reykjavík police in the hope that she might be listened to, and it made her emotional. Schütz was not impressed by her retraction:

> I recovered my composure and the German looked at me for a while before he replied. He broke the silence by asking me if I thought he was an idiot. He said he had not come to Iceland at the invitation of the authorities to play games with me. I had over several months robbed these good investigators of their private life by talking nonsense and should consider my position.
>
> (p. 236)

> The meeting with Schütz had broken me down and all my attempts to convince the investigators were powerless after that.
>
> (p. 237)

> After I had given up and agreed to cooperate again with the investigation, it was his first job to ensure that I was allowed to see my daughter again.
>
> (p. 238)

## THE PRETRIAL PSYCHIATRIC EVALUATION

Erla was referred for a psychiatric evaluation on 23 April 1976 (Working Group Report, 2013) when she had the status of a witness; at the time, only suspects were legally referred for a psychiatric evaluation, which suggests that in reality she was viewed by the investigators as a suspect. Her witness status meant that she was not entitled to legal advice and assistance, making her even more dependent on

**Table 14.1**   Erla's attempts to retract her confession in the Geirfinnur case

---

**14 August 1976**
Erla handed investigative judge Örn Höskuldsson a letter retracting her confession of killing Geirfinnur, claiming she had made it all up.
The following day she withdrew her retraction, claiming her letter had been a 'mistake', declaring:
'I withdraw the retraction in the hope that you forgive me and I can imagine how angry the letter must have made you feel […] I hope you will forgive me and that we can have a conversation in connection with my child, who I live for'.
**Note:** Within half an hour of Mr Höskuldsson receiving Erla's retraction letter on 14 August he had advised the prison staff to increase the restrictions in solitary confinement (see ICCRC Report, 2017, Erla Bolladóttir, Paragraph 564).

**1 September 1976**
Erla appeared before judge Örn Höskuldsson, wishing to retract her confession regarding shooting Geirfinnur, after which he remanded her to a further 90 days in custody. Later that day she retracted for good her confession to killing Geirfinnur during a police interview, but accepted that she had been in Keflavík when Geirfinnur disappeared.

**15 October 1975**
Erla handed Karl Schütz a letter insisting that she had not been to Keflavík. Schütz would not accept her retraction. He placed her under pressure to explain her apparent special knowledge, resulting in Erla becoming 'hysterical and repeatedly banging the table, shouting out crying', stating: 'Nobody here believes me'.

**30 October 1976**
Karl Schütz and Sigurbjörn Víðir interrogated Erla, who insisted that she had not gone to Keflavík and that she could prove it. She was directed to her previous testimony and eventually admitted that she had been on the trip, along with Saevar, Kristján, and another man, who became known as 'the fourth man').

**11 January 1980**
Erla appeared in court and retracted her confession in the Geirfinnur case. This was three days before the proceedings commenced in the Supreme Court.

---

the investigators. According to the Icelandic Court Cases Review Commission, the alleged reason for the referral was due to her having memory problems with regard to the Geirfinnur case.[7]

According to the custody record, the psychiatrist first interviewed Erla on the evening of 4 May (21.30–23.25), after Erla had given her statement about shooting Geirfinnur. A few days later she was seen by a psychologist. The psychological evaluation, which included an IQ and personality assessment, showed that Erla was of average intelligence, had a 'hysterical personality', and was extremely 'passive' and

---

[7] ICCRC Report, 2017, Erla Bolladóttir, Paragraph 2307.

'compliant', to the point of 'masochism'. She was also described as being 'imaginative', having impaired 'reality monitoring' and 'confused thinking', and there was a considerable likelihood of her experiencing a 'dissociative state' and 'associated memory loss' (Working Group Report, 2013, p. 356). Erla also told the psychologist that all she cared about was her baby Julia's welfare: she was preoccupied with the thought of her baby.

The psychiatrist diagnosed Erla with 'psychopathy', 'passivity', and a strong need to be controlled by others. The reference to 'psychopathy' is curious, because there is insufficient evidence to support it. I have come across many cases where a diagnosis of psychopathy has been influenced by what the suspect is alleged to have done, referred to as 'forensic confirmation bias' (Kassin, 2015), and I think this happened in Erla's case.

### Erla's Extreme Compliance

In 2016 I met with Erla and she completed the Gudjonsson Compliance Scale (GCS). She completed the scale twice, firstly with reference to her current personality, and again in relation to herself in 1975.

Erla proved to be currently of low average compliance, obtaining a score of 7 (about 20th percentile rank). She said that she no longer does things merely to please others and is now well able to stand up to people in authority.

As far as Erla's compliance in 1975, she obtained a score of 20, which is the maximum possible score, falling in the 98th percentile rank. She described feeling 'like a mouse in a corner' and 'being caught between a rock and a hard place' – as soon as her resistance was broken down in relation to the fraud case, she began to implicate people in the two murder cases. Erla attributed her malleability to her history of sexual abuse, which destroyed her self-respect. It is of course possible that Erla's high compliance score was to a certain extent artificially inflated by the police pressure she experienced and her inability to cope with it. Nevertheless, the score corroborates the findings from the psychological and psychiatric evaluations from 1976.

### KARL SCHÜTZ'S VIEW OF ERLA

In his final report in the Geirfinnur case, Schütz concluded:

> Erla's testimony in the case has been very confusing. She says one thing today and another tomorrow and made up substantial stories connected

to her versions. For example, she confessed to shooting Geirfinnur Einarsson. Her testimony looked very weird, but she has said that her confession was due to her suffering from a pang of conscience for wrongly implicating the aforementioned men. [...] Erla is of average intelligence, considerably impressionable, seems 'hysterical' and often careless. She also seems impertinent.

## ERLA'S INTERVIEW FOR THE WORKING GROUP

Working Group member Jón Fridrik and I interviewed Erla on 6 February 2012 (Working Group Report, 2013). The most relevant findings were as follows. Erla said that she had not been involved or witnessed anything to do with the disappearances of Gudmundur and Geirfinnur. Prior to her being questioned about the Gudmundur case in December 1976, she had known nothing about the case. After telling the police about a dream she had had on the night of Gudmundur's disappearance, Örn Höskuldsson interpreted this as her having witnessed a serious event at Hamarsbraut 11, which she had repressed, and that they would help her remember what she had witnessed. This idea of trauma and repression was based on the investigators' misunderstanding of memory processes that was common everywhere at the time. This psychodynamic model of memory is widely discredited by psychologists (Barden, 2016; Sabbagh, 2009). It is known that investigators do sometimes take advantage of the popular belief in the repression of memories for criminal acts and use it against suspects who claim not to remember committing the crime (Laney & Takarangi, 2013; McNally, 2003; Ofshe & Watters, 1994).

The story that emerged was based on her dream, the investigators' suggestions, and her own imagination. She had soon realized that she would be kept in custody if she did not cooperate with the investigators. Her focus was to get out of Sídumúli Prison, where she had been in custody for a week, and to be with her baby. I find Erla's explanation credible.

Erla reported that she had been 100% sure that she knew nothing about the Gudmundur case when first questioned about it, but after being persuaded that her dream was a real event, she began to doubt her own memory (i.e. the confidence in her own memory went down from 100% to 30%, based on a rating scale).

After the investigators later told her that her statement was corroborated by the accused, she became more confident that they had been involved in Gudmundur's disappearance (i.e. she was by now 60%–70% sure they were involved, based on a rating scale).

Importantly, at the time Erla was in custody she had no actual memory of what had happened at Hamarsbraut 11, and it was a few years later that she became fully confident that Saevar, Kristján, and Tryggvi were all innocent. This was the reason she gave Jón Fridrik and I for not officially retracting her incriminating statements in the Gudmundur case.

Erla said that the position was very different in the Geirfinnur case. She never believed that any of the suspects were involved in the Geirfinnur case but went along with the investigators' suggestions because she had formed a close 'friendship' with them and become dependent on them. She wanted to avoid upsetting them, feared their rejection, and was terrified that she would be locked up and her daughter taken away from her if she did not go along with them. She felt under their control and at their mercy.

Erla said that Detective Sigurbjörn Vídir had been particularly helpful and she had viewed him like a special confidant.

In her book and in interviews with the Working Group, Erla had reported that in July 1976 one of the investigators had sexually abused her in her cell at Sídumúli Prison. She said that for a long time afterwards she blamed herself for this incident and it broke down her fighting spirit when this investigator was present during subsequent interrogations.

## MODELS OF ERLA'S CONFESSIONS

Figures 14.1 and 14.2 provide a model for understanding Erla's confessions in the Gudmundur and Geirfinnur cases, respectively. The enduring or pre-existing vulnerability factors were the same but differences existed with regard to the contextual triggers, acute state, and psychological mechanism.

Figure 14.1 provides a heuristic model of memory distrust that describes the antecedents and processes involved in producing Erla's confession in the Gudmundur case. The context provided the 'trigger' for altering her belief systems regarding the alleged offence. The three key components were confinement, the investigators' persuasive interrogation, and high emotional intensity. The emotional intensity was related to the potential seriousness of the case she was questioned about, the buildup of stress during Erla's solitary confinement, her desperate need to be with her infant daughter, and the intensity of the questioning.

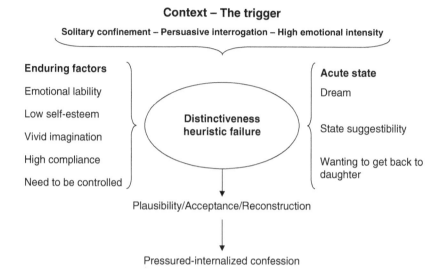

**Figure 14.1**   A model of Erla's pressured-internalized confession in the Gudmundur case

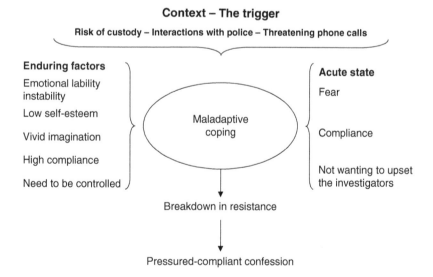

**Figure 14.2**   A model of Erla's pressured-compliant confession in the Geirfinnur case

The three contextual triggers fed directly into Erla's cognitive appraisal of the situation and impacted on her pre-existing vulnerabilities, labelled as 'enduring factors':
- Emotional lability.
- Low self-esteem and proneness to self-blame.
- Vivid imagination.
- High compliance.
- Need to be controlled (i.e. she described a very controlling mother, was emotionally dependent on Saevar and allowed him to control her, she became dependent on the investigators, and according to the pretrial psychological/psychiatric evaluation, she reached a point where her need for control reached a 'masochistic' proportion).

The contextual risk factors also activated 'acute state' factors. The key ones were:
- Her dream of hearing people whispering outside her window at Hamarsbraut 11, which turned into her describing an incident inside the flat involving Saevar, Kristján, and a 'third man' (Tryggvi).
- High state suggestibility (i.e. her gradually believing what the investigators told her about witnessing a traumatic event).
- Erla desperately wanted to get back to her baby, from whom she had been separated for a week.

The enduring and acute state factors made Erla unable to critically scrutinize the police scenario and its origin, leading to distinctiveness heuristic failure (i.e. she was unable to stick to her original belief that this was just a dream, creating a fundamental source monitoring error). With continued interrogation she *accepted* that the three men were involved and engaged in reconstruction of what may have taken place (i.e. Gudmundur's body being moved about in her flat), resulting in her pressured-internalized confession.

Figure 14.2 provides a model of Erla's confession in the Geirfinnur case. The three main contextual factors were risk of custody, close interactions with the investigators after she was released from custody on 20 December 1975 (she viewed one of them as a special confidant), and nuisance phone calls – the last call was threatening and frightened her. This built up considerable pressure on Erla to cooperate as much as she could with the police and she showed considerable dependency on them (i.e. they had her under their influence and control).

The three acute factors were her fear of custody and for her safety, not wanting to upset the investigators, and state compliance (i.e. avoidance of conflict and confrontation with the investigators and eagerness to please them). Gudjonsson and Sigurdsson (2003) argue that although compliance is generally construed as a relatively stable dispositional characteristic, it can also be viewed as a behavioural response to a given situation.

As discussed in Chapter 4, a high level of compliance may occur in both personal and impersonal relationships and is correlated with general compliance as measured by the GCS (Gudjonsson, Sigurdsson, Einarsson, & Einarsson, 2008). The authors conclude that fear of emotional rejection and/or abandonment may contribute to vulnerability in personal relationships, such as Erla's close relationship with the investigators. This suggests that an existing interpersonal relationship produces an additional pressure on the coerced person.

The contextual, enduring, and acute factors made it impossible for Erla to cope constructively with her predicament. She utilized maladaptive coping strategies, which consisted of mental and behavioural disengagement (i.e. she switched off from resisting the investigators' assertions and suggestions), she was in a state of denial about the real implications of what she was agreeing with and making up (i.e. naming innocent people), and she focused primarily on her own emotions (i.e. attempts to reduce conflict and stress). She had a desperate need to be with her infant daughter and this was the linchpin to her confession.

## CONCLUSIONS

Erla was an extremely vulnerable young woman when she gave her incriminating statements in the Gudmundur and Geirfinnur cases. She had a history of sexual abuse, low self-esteem and self-blame, a compliant temperament, and was susceptible to allowing others to control her. In addition to these pre-existing (enduring) vulnerabilities, the two cases show the importance of situational factors (i.e. context and acute state).

Relevant to both cases is the fact that Saevar and Erla were having serious difficulties in their relationship, which the police knew about, making it easier for her to implicate him in the disappearance of the two men. In addition, Erla had heard Saevar boast that he knew about Geirfinnur's disappearance. According to Erla, once she had mentioned this to the investigators, they zoomed in on her as a potential witness in the Geirfinnur case and there was no turning back once she began to implicate people. In Erla's own words, at the time of the Gudmundur and Geirfinnur investigations, she felt 'like a mouse in a corner' and 'being caught between a rock and a hard place'. Her resistance was broken down and her mind was overborne. Her statements were involuntary.

This chapter shows that when Erla tried to retract her confessions in the Geirfinnur case, she was not listened to and was quickly made to withdraw her retractions. The only retraction that the investigators and court ultimately accepted was that she had not shot Geirfinnur as she had claimed on 4 May 1976.

At the time of their arrest in December 1975, the couple had an 11-week-old daughter, to which Erla was very attached, and she feared losing her if she did not cooperate with the investigators. This was a real fear due to the fact that she had committed a serious fraud with Saevar, to which she had just confessed and knew she would be charged and sentenced for. All she wanted was to be with her baby. There is evidence from the records, discussed in Chapter 9, that the investigators used her baby to encourage her to cooperate with them in the Geirfinnur case. Throughout the investigation, access to her daughter and her fear of losing her became the investigators' trump card. She was under their control; they knew it and used it to manipulate her.

Erla makes it clear in her book that the circumstances of her confessions with regard to the Gudmundur and Geirfinnur cases were very different. In the Gudmundur case, it was the dream and her being misleadingly questioned about it as if it represented a trauma that she had witnessed, which made her vulnerable to distrust her own memory and begin to confabulate, leading in turn to her implicating Saevar, Kristján, and later Tryggvi. It is likely that at the time, Erla suffered from memory distrust syndrome, which was brought about by intensive and persuasive interrogation, her enduring vulnerabilities, and a number of situational factors, including her desperately wanting to get out of solitary confinement and be with her baby. Her confidence in the suspects' guilt was reinforced when she was told the accused had corroborated her story. The psychological mechanism with regard to Gudmundur's confession was distinctiveness heuristic failure, in which Erla had become unable to activate her critical thinking faculty (i.e. effective 'reality monitoring') to rule out the idea that her dream represented a traumatic real-life event that she had forgotten (i.e. a source monitoring error).

Of importance in Erla giving an internalized confession in the Gudmundur case is that she thought the police suggestions contained *plausibility*. This was not the position in the Geirfinnur case, in which she found the investigators' suggestions highly implausible and she therefore never accepted them.

The psychological mechanism with regard to the Geirfinnur case was maladaptive coping. This was a gradual process, commencing soon after she was released from custody on 20 December 1975, when the investigators were in frequent contact with her, having befriended her, and she in turn had become dependent on them because of her social isolation. She came to view Detective Sigurbjörn Vídir as her trusted confidant and during subtle questioning told him that Saevar had previously boasted that he knew about the Geirfinnur case, leading her to inadvertently agree that he might be involved. Then the real interrogation started; Erla claims that she was brought for interrogation in Sídumúli Prison on several occasions before her first confession statement was taken on 23 January 1976 (see Chapter 9). Importantly, the prison diary records show that Erla was brought to Sídumúli Prison on 30 December 1975, and 21, 22, and 23 January 1976, and kept there for about five, four, two, and three hours, respectively.[8] A statement was only taken on her last visit to the prison, but we know from the records that she was extensively interviewed about the Geirfinnur case on 21 January, providing the basis for her subsequent statement two days later. I am in no doubt that she would also have been questioned on the other occasions, which is something Erla has claimed in my interviews with her; otherwise her being taken to the prison as a witness and kept there for hours would have been nonsensical. Questioning her in Sídumúli Prison carried an implicit threat of what might happen if she did not fully cooperate with the investigators (she had been there in solitary confinement for eight days during the previous month).

There were far better interviewing facilities at the police headquarters, Borgartún 7, with each detective having his/her own interrogation room. The most probable reason for interviewing Erla in Sídumúli Prison was to create a coercive environment where she would be more malleable to accept the police investigative hypothesis. The only advantage to Erla's case is that it left a paper trail in the prison log of the date and her time of entry and departure each time she was brought there.

In early January 1976, prosecutor Hallvardur Einvardsson had the Keflavík investigation papers in the Geirfinnur case delivered to him, at his request. This showed that the Reykjavík authorities were taking an interest in the case, having requested the papers at the end of December 1975 (see Chapter 9). The sequence of events is apparently as follows. On 28 December Erla met with Detective Sigurbjörn Vídir; two days later Erla was taken to Sídumúli Prison for five hours, and the following day the prosecutor requested the papers in the Geirfinnur case.

The above supports Erla's claim that the investigators were extensively questioning her before the frightening phone calls, which puts a different perspective on the sequence of events that led to her implicating innocent people. It should not be held against Erla's defence that the investigators failed to keep records of their interactions with Erla

---

[8] ICCRC Report, 2017, Erla Bolladóttir, Paragraphs 74, 114, 116, 119, and 120.

and then when questioned about it in court on 28 January 2016 conveniently claimed 'memory loss'.

While not in custody, was she used, manipulated, and coerced into giving false statements against the 'four wrongly accused' in order to go along with the investigative hypothesis of the police? Certainly on the balance of probabilities, this is likely to have been the case. It is the only scenario that makes sense, and there is evidence to support it. Erla should not be made the scapegoat.

# 15

# Kristján Vidarsson's Memory Distrust Syndrome and Confession

*I thought I had experienced the worst of what the police could do to you, but I was seriously mistaken*[1]

## SALIENT POINTS

- On 22 February 1980 the Supreme Court convicted Kristján of manslaughter in the Gudmundur and Geirfinnur cases and perjury with regard to the 'four wrongly accused'. He received a 16-year prison sentence.
- Kristján had a disturbed and traumatic childhood with his father being killed in a trawler accident when he was four years of age. He did not get on with his stepfather and was brought up by his maternal grandmother, who had little control over him.
- In adolescence he became addicted to alcohol and drugs. He was highly impulsive and restless, and was diagnosed with antisocial personality disorder.
- Kristján coped poorly with solitary confinement and twice attempted suicide.

---

[1] An answer Kristján gave to a question when the author interviewed him for the Working Group on 6 February 2012.

---

*The Psychology of False Confessions: Forty Years of Science and Practice*, First Edition.
Gisli H. Gudjonsson.
© 2018 John Wiley & Sons Ltd. Published 2018 by John Wiley & Sons Ltd.

- There are three sources of evidence that support the view that Kristján's confessions were the result of memory distrust syndrome (i.e. very poor recollection during interrogation, findings from the pretrial psychiatric evaluation, and an interview with the current author in 2012).
- With regard to the perjury conviction, considering the circumstances under which his statements were obtained there are good grounds for arguing that these were coerced by the investigators.

Kristján Vidarsson was born in Reykjavík on 21 April 1955. His father was a fisherman and died when his trawler sank in February 1959. His mother had mental health issues and the marriage was turbulent because of the husband's heavy drinking when at home. Kristján was brought up by his maternal grandmother, a divorced woman. When he was seven years old his mother married an Egyptian man and they had one child together. The marriage did not last long and Kristján continued to live with his grandmother at Grettisgata 82. According to the pretrial psychiatric report, Kristján was stubborn and difficult to manage. There was little discipline and he did what he liked, with his grandmother minimizing his difficulties to others. He lacked a positive male role model and engaged in substance misuse from the age of 11. Age 13, he was expelled from school for truancy and arguing with a teacher. In adolescence he was seen by a psychiatrist and a psychologist, but this had no long lasting beneficial effect. When age 17 his grandmother moved out of their home at Grettisgata. Kristján continued to live there and provided accommodation to some homeless people, who provided him with drugs. He was later admitted to hospital for alcohol and drug addiction. His first criminal conviction was in August 1972 for assault, burglary, and theft. By the time Kristján was arrested in the Gudmundur case he had already served prison sentences.

## KRISTJÁN'S INTERROGATION AND CONFINEMENT

Kristján remained in solitary confinement for a total of 682 days, of which 508 days were in Sídumúli Prison.[2] During that period he was questioned by the police on 160 occasions for a total of 215 hours, and participated in 18 face-to-face confrontations (Gudjonsson et al., 2014). His recorded interrogations and confessions in the Gudmundur and Geirfinnur cases are described in Chapters 8 and 9, respectively.

Kristján was released from prison on licence on 30 June 1983.

---

[2] ICCRC Report, 2017, Kristján Vidarsson, Paragraph 2088.

The general content of Kristján's confessions in the Gudmundur and Geirfinnur cases showed that he was vague and hesitant in his replies to questions, which he blamed on memory problems, caused by his extensive history of substance misuse (see Chapters 8 and 9).

Initially Kristján denied any involvement in the Gudmundur and Geirfinnur cases, but then confessed.

## KRISTJÁN'S MENTAL STATE IN SOLITARY CONFINEMENT

On 10 December 1975 Kristján was brought temporarily to Síðumúli Prison as a potential witness in the Post and Telecommunication fraud, having implicated Saevar. The prison doctor, Gudsteinn Thengilsson, expressed concerns about the quantity of medication he was being given but did not want to alter it if Kristján was only staying for one or two days.[3] The following day Kristján was interviewed for four hours in the afternoon, but because of his behavioural disturbance, the police delayed taking a statement from him until the evening. According to the Commission, the Síðumúli Prison diary described Kristján being 'wound up' and 'rather rude' (e.g. attempting to call out to other prisoners and making 'song screams' – söngvein). After giving his statement he was said to have informed on a rather big case and as a reward he was immediately transported back to Litla-Hraun Prison, where he was serving a sentence, and arrived there at 02.45.[4]

Kristján was brought back to Síðumúli Prison on 23 December 1975 as a suspect in the Gudmundur case. At about 10.00 on 6 January 1976, Dr Thengilsson arrived at Síðumúli Prison to obtain a urine sample from Kristján, who was unable to provide one and the doctor left empty handed. Kristján's inability to give a urine specimen may have been caused by stress in custody (Gudjonsson & Sartory, 1983).

On the morning of 10 January 1976, Dr Thengilsson made some changes to his medication. On 17 January the doctor returned to examine Kristján and examined him on a number of subsequent occasions.

On 24 December 1976, Kristján attempted suicide by cutting his wrist and on 5 January he set fire to a mattress in his cell. At the time, Kristján's mental state was said to be poor: he showed little resistance to stress and was unpredictable.[5] His mental state appeared to have deteriorated in the autumn of 1976 and he remained in a poor

---

[3] ICCRC Report, 2017, Kristján Vidarsson, Paragraph 49.
[4] ICCRC Report, 2017, Kristján Vidarsson, Paragraph 50.
[5] ICCRC Report, 2017, Kristján Vidarsson, Paragraph 1065.

state until May 1977. During that period Kristján confessed to two other murders and implicated his grandmother in one of them. The Commission expressed serious reservations about his fitness for interview during this period.[6] Fitness for interview is a concept that has been incorporated into police codes of practice in the UK, following our research (Gudjonsson, 1995a, 2003a, 2016; Gudjonsson, Hayes, & Rowlands, 2000), in order to ensure fairness and justice.

As a result of his two suicide attempts, Kristján was heavily medicated for about four months and this apparently caused him to develop manic symptoms and feelings of depersonalization, further undermining the reliability of his statements to the police.[7]

Kristján was placed on 'suicide watch' at Skólavördustígur Penitentiary in Reykjavík between 6 January and 17 May 1977 due to his having set fire to the mattress in his cell (Working Group Report, 2013), after which he was transferred to Litla-Hraun Prison, and his mental state appeared better once he came off his heavy medication there.[8]


## RETRACTIONS

Kristján retracted his confessions on several occasions. The first retraction was on 2 March 1976 when he said he had not been in Keflavík on the evening of 19 November 1974 and was not implicated in the case. He confessed again on 9 March after being told that Erla had stated that he had entered the car at Vatnsstígur in Reykjavík on the night of Geirfinnur's disappearance, which allegedly brought back his memory of the journey.

On 31 March 1976, Kristján gave a statement in court and claimed that his statements of the previous 23 and 27 January were fabricated due to his wanting peace and quiet from prison and police officers, claiming that the continuous and intensive interrogations in the Gudmundur case had badly affected him mentally (Working Group Report, 2013, p. 389). He said he recalled little about the Geirfinnur case and could not confirm anything for certain. The following day he claimed that overnight he had begun to remember more and described observing a fight on the slipway (i.e. he was a witness to it and not a perpetrator).

---

[6] ICCRC Report, 2017, Kristján Vidarsson, Paragraph 2074.
[7] ICCRC Report, 2017, Kristján Vidarsson, Paragraph 2073.
[8] ICCRC Report, 2017, Kristján Vidarsson, Paragraph 2073.

His subsequent retractions were between 6 July and 29 September 1977, after which he never gave another confession in the Gudmundur or Geirfinnur cases and has repeatedly proclaimed his innocence ever since. At the time of retracting his confession on 6 July, Kristján had been in Litla-Hraun Prison since mid-May and was apparently improving considerably (e.g. he had come off his medication). However, after retracting his confession in the Geirfinnur case, he was immediately returned to solitary confinement at Síðumúli Prison.[9] Retractions were not tolerated and had severe consequences for those who dared to do so.

## KARL SCHÜTZ'S VIEW OF KRISTJÁN

In his final report in the Geirfinnur case, Schütz concluded:

> Kristján Vidar Vidarsson is very suspicious of others, particularly and specifically against the authorities. He had a strong tendency to protect his relatives. This was clearly evident during the investigation against his cousin Óttar [Sigurdur Óttar was the alleged delivery van driver in the Geirfinnur case, discussed in Chapter 9 and Appendix 1]. Kristján tried hard to keep him out of trouble. He often gave his statements with this in mind.

> Kristján Vidar also had a strange relationship between honesty and distorted morality. His sense of hopelessness regarding his future is very common and there is much self-accusation. He had more than once commented that he finds it unbearable to think of the grief he has caused others.

## THE PRETRIAL EVALUATION

The psychiatric evaluation report was completed on 30 July 1976, and included within it a detailed psychological evaluation, which included psychometric testing. It revealed the following:
- Psychometric testing showed Kristján to be of low average intelligence. The Minnesota Multiphasic Personality Inventory suggested poor emotional development, impulsivity, restlessness, and antisocial tendencies.
- The psychiatric evaluation diagnosed Kristján with 'alcohol addiction', 'drug dependence', and 'antisocial personality disorder'.

---

[9] ICCRC Report, 2017, Kristján Vidarsson, Paragraph 2073.

It was noted during the evaluation that he was restless, had problems with attention and memory, was suspicious, and was found to become easily agitated and angry.

- In the psychiatric interviews, Kristján was rather unclear about what had happened regarding the Gudmundur and Geirfinnur cases. He claimed memory problems but apparently tried hard to remember what had happened. He seemed to remember more detail in the Gudmundur case. However, in both cases 'there are descriptions which suggest that reality and fantasy merge', for example, ideas and imagination are presented as reality. The psychiatrist thought that his long-term alcohol and drug problems had adversely affected his memory.

## KRISTJÁN'S INTERVIEW FOR THE WORKING GROUP

Working Group member Jón Fridrik and I met Kristján on 6 February 2012 (Working Group Report, 2013). Kristján arrived with his lawyer, who was present during the interview, which I conducted. Kristján looked very anxious, suspicious, and emotionally fragile, which limited the amount of probing that could be done in relation to the confessions. (I thought it might upset him unduly if I asked him to complete a rating scale measuring the extent of his memory distrust during his interrogation, a measure I had been able to administer to Erla, Gudjón, and Albert.)

The most relevant findings from the interview were as follows:

- When Kristján arrived at Sídumúli Prison on 23 December 1975 there were many prison and police officers there and they formed a circle around him and kept pushing him between them. After a while, investigative judge Örn Höskuldsson signalled for them to stop.
- Kristján said he was innocent of both the Gudmundur and Geirfinnur disappearances. From the beginning, prison officers kept him awake at night in Sídumúli Prison. In addition, they forced him to crawl on his hands and knees and arms when he needed to go out of his cell to the toilet. Kristján said the reason was that they wanted to torment him and break down his resistance. He experienced it as a form of torture.
- He found the solitary confinement very difficult and it was made worse by his suffering from asthma. 'These were fierce conditions and were very bad for me. It alternated between being hot and cold. I always felt sickly'.

  He said he became confused during the interrogations and could not distinguish between what was real and imaginary. He did not differentiate between the Gudmundur and Geirfinnur cases, experiencing it like 'one big case'. He began to 'dream this nonsense'.

- He said that Detective Sigurbjörn Vídir was particularly imaginative in coming up with different scenarios about what had allegedly taken place, including the idea that Kristján had stabbed Gudmundur at Hamarsbraut 11.

- I asked Kristján how the custody in the Gudmundur and Geirfinnur cases differed from his other detentions, because he had had substantial previous experience of solitary confinement. He replied: 'I thought I had experienced the worst of what the police could do to you, but I was seriously mistaken [...] This was complete horror, really disgusting. I often contemplated whether or not I would get through this alive'.

- Kristján said that while in custody he had kept diaries but Örn Höskuldsson had taken them away from him in August 1976.

- He said that while the chief judge was reading out the beginning of the Court Judgement on 19 December 1977 he temporarily lost his hearing, which is likely to have been caused by the stress he experienced at the time.

A similar psychogenic phenomenon in court was found in the case of Barry George, who allegedly murdered BBC *Crimewatch* broadcaster Jill Dando on 26 April 1999 but was subsequently acquitted after an appeal eight years later. During legal arguments at the Old Bailey at the end of April 2001, Mr George claimed to have lost his eyesight. On 1 May, I brought back his eyesight by the use of hypnosis in a cell in the basement at the Old Bailey, and the trial continued (Gudjonsson & Young, 2015). This type of use of hypnosis is very different to its more common use for memory enhancement, which occurred in the case of Albert. The use of hypnosis for memory enhancement is very problematic in terms of potential contamination of memory (Gudjonsson, 1992a).

## A HEURISTIC MODEL OF KRISTJÁN'S CONFESSION

Figure 15.1 provides a heuristic model of memory distrust that describes the antecedents and processes involved in producing Kristján's pressured-internalized confession. The context provided the 'trigger' for altering his belief system regarding the alleged offence. The three key components were confinement and social isolation, the investigators' guilt presumption and persuasive interrogation, and high emotional intensity.

These three contextual factors – isolation, persuasive interrogation, and high emotional intensity – fed directly into Kristján's cognitive

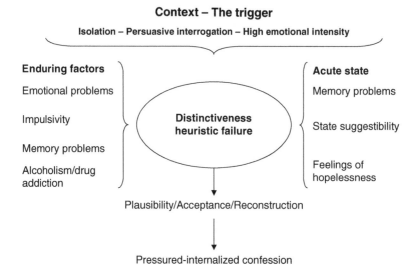

**Figure 15.1**    Heuristic model of Kristján's pressured-internalized confession

appraisal of the situation and impacted on his pre-existing vulnerabilities, labelled as 'enduring' factors:
• Emotional lability (i.e. the pretrial psychiatric/psychological evaluation refers to his being emotionally unstable (i.e. becoming easily agitated and angry).
• Impulsivity.
• Attentional and memory problems.
• Long-standing alcoholism and drug addiction.
According to the memory distrust syndrome model (Gudjonsson & MacKeith, 1982), Kristján's alcoholism made him a prime candidate for developing memory distrust syndrome when his memory of events was challenged by the police.

The contextual risk factors also activated 'acute state' factors. The key ones were:
• Memory problems (i.e. a breakdown in reality monitoring).
• This increased his delayed suggestibility.
• Feelings of hopelessness, which eventually resulted in his making two suicide attempts while in custody.
The enduring and acute state factors made Kristján unable to critically scrutinize the police scenario and its origin. With continued interrogation during the first two weeks of his detention, he gradually accepted that he may have been involved in the Gudmundur case, while having no clear memory of the alleged event. Soon thereafter, he

was questioned about his alleged knowledge in the Geirfinnur case and gradually gave in to the pressure from the investigators.

## CONCLUSIONS

Kristján had an unhappy and unsettled childhood and adolescence. He had poor behavioural control, extensive history of substance misuse from an early age, and memory problems. It is possible that he had childhood attention deficit hyperactivity disorder (ADHD), but there is insufficient information to argue this point.

In spite of his height, strong physique, and macho image, he was emotionally brittle and vulnerable to giving unreliable statements under pressure. It is mental (cognitive and emotional) strength not physical power that helps suspects resist pressures in police interviews and solitary confinement.

In the light of the current analysis, it is reasonable to describe Kristján's confession as a *pressured-internalized confession*. He was confessing to something that he thought might have happened, but it was not based on an actual memory. He could not distinguish between what was real and imaginary and saw the two cases as 'one big case'. His substance misuse history made him vulnerable to distrusting his own memory. It was easy to manipulate him into believing that he had had some knowledge about the Gudmundur and Geirfinnur cases and over time, implicating himself increasingly in the two cases. The fact that he retracted his confessions on a number of occasions from 2 March 1976 onward, suggests that his belief in his *possible involvement* in the cases fluctuated over time (i.e. it was fragile and unstable) but was never expressed with a great deal of certainty. On 6 July 1977, after his mental state apparently improved having spent almost two months in less restrictive surroundings at Litla-Hraun Prison, he retracted his confessions for good. The pressure was off and he was sufficiently robust mentally to persist with his retraction, even after being transferred back to Sídumúli Prison, undoubtedly as punishment for his retraction.

The Commission accepted that there were indications that Kristján had been treated harshly in solitary confinement, but it did not think there were sufficient grounds for an appeal with regard to the perjury conviction, especially since the police and prison officers had given evidence in court denying Kristján's claims of duress.[10]

---

[10] ICCRC Report, 2017, Kristján Vidarsson, Paragraph 2985.

In my experience of similar cases, police and prison officers invariably deny allegations of harassing or coercing suspects, even when substantiated. Their denials do not always represent the truth, and their perceived inherent credibility as witnesses in this respect is overrated. Defendants are rarely believed when it is their word against that of the authorities. Unfortunately, police misconduct is hard to substantiate or study (Garrett, 2011).

Occasionally there is a 'breach in the wall of silence', but attempts may be made to discredit such witnesses (e.g. see the case of the Birmingham Six; Mullin, 1989, pp. xv and xvi). The Working Group was to a certain extent able to break 'the wall of silence' and found evidence that prison officers had treated some of the suspects harshly, in spite of persistent denials by others.

Kristján's comment that the Gudmundur and Geirfinnur cases merged into 'one big case' shows how intertwined the two cases were in his mind. After giving his confession statement in the Gudmundur case on 3 January 1976, he was questioned for over 11 hours, during a dozen occasions, before giving his first statement in the Geirfinnur case on 23 January.

The fact that Kristján did not actively seek to appeal his convictions along with the other convicted persons and their families shows how psychologically damaged he had become. This is supported from my observations of him when I interviewed him in the presence of his lawyer in February 2012. According to the Commission, in January 2016 he even declined his entitlement to be legally represented at his appeal.[11] This supports the strong clinical impression of Grounds (2004, 2005) of irreversible damage to persons wrongfully convicted. Grounds found that the key deleterious impact relates to two separate events: (a) psychological trauma at the time of the initial arrest and custody, the principal emotion being an experience of an overwhelming fear of what was happening; and (b) chronic psychological trauma due to years of notoriety and isolation.

I believe there are good grounds for believing that Kristján's confessions were coerced by the investigators, including those relating to the perjury conviction. He now has a formidable counsel, Jón Steinar Gunnlaugsson, who is a former Supreme Court judge (Gunnlaugsson, 2014).

---

[11] ICCRC Report, 2017, Kristján Vidarsson, Paragraph 3.

# 16

# Tryggvi Leifsson's Memory Distrust Syndrome and Confession

*Now Örn Höskuldsson's time is up. I'm afraid that he will be sent packing with a kick in the backside as a leaving present[1]*

## SALIENT POINTS

- On 22 February 1980 the Supreme Court convicted Tryggvi of manslaughter in the Gudmundur case and he received a 13-year prison sentence.
- Due to the immense stress associated with his arrest and detention, he was unable to sleep for four nights and had to be medically sedated by an injection.
- There are four sources of evidence that support the view that Tryggvi's confession was the result of memory distrust syndrome (i.e. very poor recollection during interrogation, letters to the police, pretrial psychiatric evaluation, and a comment in his personal diary while in custody).
- It is probable that Tryggvi had attention deficit hyperactivity disorder (ADHD), which would have impacted negatively on his

---

[1] An entry in Tryggvi's diary on 29 March 1977, the day before he retracted his confession, showing his strong faith in the Icelandic criminal justice system, which was misguided.

*The Psychology of False Confessions: Forty Years of Science and Practice*, First Edition.
Gisli H. Gudjonsson.
© 2018 John Wiley & Sons Ltd. Published 2018 by John Wiley & Sons Ltd.

ability to cope with the custodial interrogation and confinement and substantially further increased the risk of false confession.

- Tryggvi had apparently on a previous occasion given a false confession to burglary in order to avoid custody.
- An interview with Tryggvi's widow and daughter in 2015 shows the hugely deleterious impact that his conviction had on his quality of life following his release from prison.

Tryggvi Leifsson was born in Reykjavík on 2 October 1951. At the time, his father was a City of Reykjavík employee, a married man who was having an affair with Tryggvi's mother. They later married, but Tryggvi was largely brought up by his maternal grandmother and his grandfather Tryggvi Gunnarsson, who was the Icelandic Glíma (Nordic self-defence technique) champion in 1919 and 1920. He had two younger brothers. Tryggvi described strict religious discipline within the family. His grandmother took the main responsibility for his upbringing. He was in regular contact with his parents, who were both heavy drinkers, and his father was violent towards his mother, which angered Tryggvi greatly. The records show that prior to his detention at Síðumúli Prison on 23 December 1975, Tryggvi had been in custody there for 11 days in the autumn of 1974. He had a list of previous convictions dating back to 1968 for serious traffic violations, alcohol-related offences, and theft offences. He had served prison sentences. In January 1970, he was disqualified from driving for life.

## HISTORY OF FALSE CONFESSION?

On 5 December 1975, less than three weeks before he was arrested in the Gudmundur case, Tryggvi was acquitted of burglary.[2] According to the detective in the case, Tryggvi had 'volunteered' a confession to a burglary. A co-accused denied the offence and there was no evidence against them, apart from Tryggvi's confession, which he had retracted when the case went to court, claiming that he had falsely confessed in order to avoid being remanded in custody.

His acquittal in the burglary case may have given him hope that the same strategy would also work in the Gudmundur case, an explanation the Commission thought was likely.[3] According to the Commission, Tryggvi retracted his confession on 30 March 1977, which was his first opportunity after the court proceedings started. Tryggvi's explanation

[2] ICCRC Report, 2017, Tryggvi Leifsson, Paragraph 30.
[3] ICCRC Report, 2017, Tryggvi Leifsson, Paragraph 1755.

for the confession was related to the methods of interrogation, his distress at the beginning of his solitary confinement, and because the investigators had threatened him that he might have to 'rot in Sídumúli Prison for two years' and that he would in any case be convicted because the others had implicated him.

## EVIDENCE FOR MEMORY DISTRUST SYNDROME

There are four sources of evidence that support the view that Tryggvi's confession to involvement in the death of Gudmundur Einarsson was the result of memory distrust syndrome and involved a pressured-internalized confession.

## TRYGGVI'S INTERROGATION AND CONFESSION

Tryggvi arrived in Sídumúli Prison at 14.15 on 23 December 1975 and was interviewed at 18.50 for 10 minutes. He denied any knowledge of Gudmundur's disappearance.

In the early hours of 27 December, it was recorded in the Sídumúli Prison diary that Tryggvi had been periodically talking to himself in his cell from 20.00 the previous evening. At 11.05 the following morning he was taken for interrogation. At 12.25 Dr Gudsteinn Thengilsson, the prison physician, was contacted and by 14.00 he had injected Tryggvi with chlorpromazine to help him sleep. This does not appear to have been sufficient because at 16.55 that same day Tryggvi was given 70 mg of diazepam.[4] It was then reported in the diary that Tryggvi had slept from approximately 19.45 until midday the following day (i.e. over 16 hours). After lunch he went back to bed. Later that day he was interrogated for two and a half hours. Considering the likely deleterious effect of the sedation on his capacity to give a coherent account of events, it is unlikely that he would have been 'fit for interview' (Lader, 1999).

On 9 January 1976, Tryggvi was interrogated at Sídumúli Prison about Gudmundur's disappearance and gave a two page statement. He had by then been in solitary confinement for 17 days and interrogated for 21 hours, but no statements had been taken and there were no

---

[4] ICCRC Report, 2017, Tryggvi Leifsson, Paragraph 34.

notes produced from those interviews.[5] At the beginning of the first recorded interview, Tryggvi said he had thought a lot about the case since his interrogation on 23 December 1975, and he now wanted to give a statement. His confession was vague, hesitant, lacked some essential details, and was the product of the many previous unrecorded interviews. What happened during those interviews has never been explained. Tryggvi's lawyer wrote to the court on 14 September 1977 requesting an explanation of why Tryggvi was interviewed on over 30 occasions without reports, but he never received a satisfactory response from the authorities.

On 27 September 1977 the two lead detectives appeared in court. Detective Eggert Bjarnason said he doubted that Tryggvi had been interrogated so often, but could not challenge it. He said it had been mainly at Tryggvi's request. Detective Sigurbjörn Víðir replied, 'It's not customary during interrogations to take notes/statements unless something new comes up or the interviewee wishes to add something to his testimony'.[6]

It seems that it was only when Tryggvi gave a confession that a statement was taken and then allegedly at his own request. It is unfortunate that the two detectives did not provide a detailed explanation about what happened during these unrecorded interviews. For example, on 7 January, two days before the confession, Tryggvi was interrogated for over five hours by the two detectives, and also part of the time by the investigative judge, Örn Höskuldsson. We know nothing about what happened during those five hours, but what emerged from the interrogation on 9 January lacked substance.

In two letters to the chief trial judge Gunnlaugur Briem, dated 22 and 27 September 1977, Örn Höskuldsson explained that he sometimes entered Tryggvi's detention cell because Tryggvi wanted to show him pictures that he had drawn or painted.[7] In the second letter, Örn Höskuldsson said he could not explain why Tryggvi was interrogated 30 times without reports. He said that Tryggvi often requested to speak to the officers about matters that had nothing to do with the case, for example messages to relatives.[8]

Tryggvi remained in solitary confinement for 627 days in Síðumúli Prison[9], during which time he was questioned by the police on 95 occasions for a total of 124 hours, and participated in 16 suspects'

---

[5] ICCRC Report, 2017, Tryggvi Leifsson, Paragraph 1756.
[6] Evidence Book IV, p. 160.
[7] Evidence Book III, p. 61.
[8] Evidence Book III, p. 62.
[9] ICCRC Report, 2017, Tryggvi Leifsson, Paragraph 1398.

face-to-face confrontations (Gudjonsson et al., 2014) in which he was confronted with other suspects and their version of what had happened as a way of harmonizing their statements. He was released from prison on licence on 24 December 1981.

### Tryggvi's Letters to Detective Sigurbjörn Vídir Eggertsson

From 21 March 1976, Tryggvi wrote a number of 'confession reports', addressed to Detective Sigurbjörn Vídir, which included his describing fights he had been involved in, arson, cheque fraud, burglary, and having stolen wallets from people with Saevar and Kristján. One of the reports started with the words: 'Dear Vídir. Confession. Complete surrender. Yes, it's right that there is no point in waiting any longer with what I have to say'.[10]

In June and July 1976, Tryggvi wrote letters to Sigurbjörn Vídir, much of which does not appear relevant to the Gudmundur case. However, on 13 June, he wrote a letter addressed to the detective, which is highly informative of his possible memory distrust syndrome:

> What I recollect and write down, as a reminder, and will hopefully be of benefit to this tedious case, which we can call 'my memory problem case', and I think it can be claimed that Kristján, but there was another, as we know, who knows more, and can say how it happened and I assert that he can point to the location. But we must have the belief that this will come.[11]

Tryggvi then listed the questions he wanted the detective to ask Kristján:
1. 'Whether it is possible that we went to Hafnarfjördur by bus?'
2. 'As far as I recall, I saw us two strolling by the Kópavogur Hospital. I also think I recall that we were looking for Saevar.'
3. 'Is it possible that we took a taxi to Kópavogur Hospital and then a bus to Hafnarfjördur?'
4. 'What is more important is whether we went with Viggó [a taxi driver that Saevar frequently used, who went with Saevar to Denmark the week before Gudmundur Einarsson disappeared] to Kópavogur Hospital and then back into town.'

Tryggvi was apparently trying hard to remember the journey from Reykjavík to the staff accommodation at Kópavogur Hospital, where Saevar's friend, Helga, worked and lived. From there they went to Hafnarfjördur where Gudmundur was allegedly picked up in the centre

---

[10] ICCRC Report, 2017, Tryggvi Leifsson, Paragraphs 125, 127, and 129.
[11] Evidence Book V, p. 68.

of town in the early hours of 27 January 1974 and taken to Hamarsbraut 11. There, he was allegedly killed by Kristján, Tryggvi, and Saevar after an argument over money.

Tryggvi then made the following comments in further documents attached to the letters:[12]

- He had the feeling that they had at some point gone to Hafnarfjördur by bus, sitting at the back of the bus.
- He also had the feeling or a vague recollection that they were looking for Saevar's home. He refers to being reminded of the house when he went there with police on 13 June 1976 (i.e. on the day the letter to Sigurbjörn Vídir was written). The Sídumúli Prison log shows that on 13 June 1976 at 15.45 Sigurbjörn Vídir and Örn Höskuldsson took Tryggvi for a drive and returned at 18.20, which supports his recollection that he was being taken to the alleged crime scene.[13]
- He thought they were impatiently looking for Saevar's house.
- He said he did not know whether Gudmundur was with him and Kristján, 'but it feels as if it was not just the two of us. That somebody was close to us, I can't picture it, but perhaps not surprisingly, because I didn't know this man, as far as I know, so would not have noticed him'.[14]

Tryggvi's reference to 'my memory problem case' and his vague descriptions about the journey to Hafnarfjördur on 27 January 1974 and what happened when they arrived at Hamarsbraut 11, provide support for the presence of memory distrust syndrome.

On 2 July 1976, Tryggvi wrote letters to Sigurbjörn Vídir about the clothes he was wearing on the material day (26/27 January 1974): 'The only thing I can imagine is that I was wearing the leather jacket, which I received from taxi driver Viggó, or bought from him'.[15] 'As I have said before, I can imagine that I was wearing a leather jacket and a stripy jumper … and the built up shoes I mentioned before.'[16]

Following this letter (Evidence Book V, pp. 84–85), there is an undated letter in which Tryggvi apologized for not having written sooner. He asked for greetings to be given to prison officers Hlynur, Högni, and Jóhann, and requested that Sigurbjörn Vídir ask Örn Höskuldsson whether there was any news on the purchase of state bonds that Örn was going to enquire about on his behalf. He was intending to purchase kr. 200,000 (about £1,700 at the time) worth of

---

[12] Evidence Book V, pp. 69–70.
[13] Evidence Book III, p. 47.
[14] Evidence Book V, p. 70.
[15] Evidence Book V, p. 80.
[16] Evidence Book V, p. 83.

government bonds. He signed the letter as follows: 'Well, dear friend. With greetings to you and your family. Your friend. Tryggvi Rúnar'.[17]

These comments suggest that Tryggvi had formed a close personal relationship with both Sigurbjörn Víðir and Örn Höskuldsson, presumably because at the time he accepted that he was involved in the Gudmundur case, was on his best behaviour, and was trying to find a way out of his predicament. This close rapport between Tryggvi and the investigators facilitated his cooperation with the case and maintained his memory distrust syndrome.

On 16 July 1976, Tryggvi was transferred to Litla-Hraun Prison and stayed there for about two months, with the exception of occasions when he was temporarily brought back to Síðumúli Prison for blood tests and investigative purposes.[18] It was during his time at Litla-Hraun Prison, where there was less pressure and more freedom, that his memory distrust syndrome appears to have been resolved. He was working in Litla-Hraun Prison, was able to practice his hobbies, and associated with other prisoners.[19]

On 15 September 1976, there was an article in the *Dagbladid* newspaper, drawing attention to the fact that Tryggvi had been given freedom and privileges at Litla-Hraun Prison for two months while Saevar and Kristján were still in solitary confinement at Síðumúli Prison (this included him being able to make phone calls and receive visitors).[20] The following day it was reported in *Tíminn* newspaper that Tryggvi was now back in solitary confinement. Örn Höskuldsson was quoted as saying that the purpose of sending Tryggvi to Litla-Hraun Prison was to give him respite from solitary confinement.[21]

On 28 September 1976, it is reported in the Síðumúli Prison diary that Sigurbjörn Víðir 'had taken Tryggvi for questioning' in the evening, but Tryggvi had not eaten that day because he was 'unhappy with the system'.[22]

It is recorded in the Síðumúli Prison diary, dated 16 October 1976, that Tryggvi was interrogated by 'Karl Schütz and Co.', but we can assume that nothing of importance to the Gudmundur case emerged during this session, because no records were kept of it.[23] Following this,

---

[17] Evidence Book V, pp. 84–85. It seems this letter was written shortly after Tryggvi was transferred to Litla-Hraun Prison on 16 July 1976, because he referred to having been in custody for seven months (ICCRC Report, 2017, Tryggvi Leifsson, Paragraph 229).

[18] ICCRC Report, 2017, Tryggvi Leifsson, Paragraphs 216, 226, and 243.

[19] ICCRC Report, 2017, Tryggvi Leifsson, Paragraph 1445.

[20] ICCRC Report, 2017, Tryggvi Leifsson, Paragraph 254.

[21] ICCRC Report, 2017, Tryggvi Leifsson, Paragraph 256.

[22] ICCRC Report, 2017, Tryggvi Leifsson, Paragraph 284.

[23] ICCRC Report, 2017, Tryggvi Leifsson, Paragraph 320.

Detective Sigurbjörn Vídir interrogated Tryggvi on many occasions, but again nothing was recorded from these sessions.

## The Pretrial Psychiatric Evaluation

The psychiatric evaluation was commissioned at the end of May 1976 and included within it a detailed psychological evaluation (i.e. psychometric testing). The report was not dated but was submitted to the court on 7 September 1976. It revealed the following:

- Low average intellectual functioning.[24] The psychologist concluded that on the basis of an uneven pattern of scores that the Full Scale IQ score was likely to be much below his potential. Tryggvi's general knowledge was particularly bad and thought to reflect his lack of education due to truancy. Symptoms of ADHD are also known to suppress IQ scores due to inattention and high impulsivity (Gudjonsson & Young, 2006).
- Poor judgement, insensitivity, shallow emotion, impulsivity, and an inferiority complex.
- The psychiatrist described Tryggvi during his assessment as quick in his movements, restless, and tense. He tried very hard to be polite and cooperative to the point of exaggeration. He was a poor informant about his life history, lacked confidence in his general memory, was hesitant, and made a number of linguistic errors. This was in spite of him trying very hard to do his best during the evaluation. He described himself as fidgety, indecisive, and drifting through life (i.e. lacking a plan and focus, which is a common feature of ADHD – Gudjonsson, Wells, & Young, 2012).
- He told the psychiatrist that he had possibly started substance abuse to rebel against his grandmother's harsh discipline.
- Tryggvi told the psychiatrist that he had been taken by surprise when he was placed in custody on 23 December 1974 in the Gudmundur case, because he did not think he was involved or knew anything about it. He said he became extremely distressed, thought he was being tricked, could not sleep for four nights, and experienced confusion and hallucinations (e.g. hearing his friends' voices), the hallucinations disappearing a few days after he was sedated. The prison's custody record confirms that he had to be sedated by injection after four days in custody. He said he was then interrogated

---

[24] Tryggvi's IQ was 83. When tested in 1968 in relation to unrelated cases, it was 75, showing an improvement over time (ICCRC Report, 2017, Tryggvi Leifsson, Paragraph 28). In 1968, Tryggvi's borderline IQ was seen as his principal vulnerability in relation to his persistent offending.

in the Gudmundur case, and he could not remember anything about the case until he had been in custody for about 30 days.[25] What he did recall was unclear and fragmented, but he thought he clearly recalled now that he got into a fight with Gudmundur, with two other men, and one of them had kicked Gudmundur in the face when he was lying on the floor.

On 29 August 1976, Tryggvi talked about having been with Saevar and Kristján to a place called Fjárborg.[26] The police photographed it on 8 March 1977 and placed the photograph in the court papers, which suggests that the police viewed it as a credible location for Gudmundur's body.[27]

## TRYGGVI'S DIARIES

As discussed in Chapter 11, Tryggvi kept diaries of his thoughts and events while in Síðumúli Prison. Only three of the diaries have survived, the first entry being 25/26 October 1976, and they showed his feelings of distress and despair while in custody. Tryggvi's consistent belief, expressed so clearly in the diaries, that truth and justice will prevail in the end, show how his naivety put him at increased risk of false confession (Kassin, 2015).

According to the Síðumúli Prison diary, around midday on 27 October 1976, Tryggvi talked to his lawyer, Hilmar Ingimundarson, with Sigurbjörn Víðir listening to the conversation. That day Tryggvi wrote in his diary that he had told his lawyer that he was innocent and had lied about the 'fight' [at Hamarsbraut 11].[28] He continued:

Regarding the transportation [of Gudmundur's body], which I have never informed on, simply because I could not remember it and did not want to muddle it further by making up a story about it from their [the investigators'] suggestions, i.e. go along with what I had heard.[29]

---

[25] The memory distrust syndrome (i.e. his considering the plausibility that he had been at Hamarsbraut 11 when Gudmundur Einarsson was allegedly killed) is likely to have commenced during the period 23 December 1975 to 8 January 1976, when he was extensively interrogated and taken on crime scene visits.

[26] ICCRC Report, 2017, Tryggvi Leifsson, Paragraph 599.

[27] Evidence Book II, pp. 193–195.

[28] ICCRC Report, 2017, Tryggvi Leifsson, Paragraph 331.

[29] This is a direct translation from Tryggvi's diary.

394 The Psychology of False Confessions

This suggests that Tryggvi had privately believed that *he might* have been involved in the case (i.e. it was *plausible*) but was not willing to commit himself to accepting what the police were suggesting to him concerning the transportation of the body, presumably based on the story of the co-accused, Saevar and Kristján, because of the absence of any specific memory of it. In his statement on 9 January 1976 he had vaguely accepted that he had been at Hamarsbraut 11 when an altercation broke out. He had been there previously with Saevar and Kristján (Bolladóttir, 2008, p. 187), which undoubtedly made it easier for him to accept that part of the story.

It seems that Tryggvi did not recall what he was doing at the time of the alleged offence, two years previously, which weakened his resistance to police suggestions because of the *absence of a memory trace* to guide him. He had become unable to insist: 'I didn't do it' and 'If I had done it I would remember it'.


## DID TRYGGVI HAVE ADHD?

There are a number of factors that taken together provide evidence that Tryggvi was probably symptomatic for ADHD at the time of his detention in Síðumúli Prison. The evidence for this comes from the pretrial psychiatric evaluation and my interview with his widow, Sjöfn Sigurbjörnsdóttir, and daughter, Kristín Tryggvadóttir, on 14 May 2015 (see extracts from the interview at the end of this chapter). Sjöfn had known Tryggvi since adolescence and described him at that time as very active, impulsive, and as someone who had got into bad company with older boys who had led him astray. He was apparently compliant in his temperament and began to smoke cigarettes and drink alcohol at an early age.

The pretrial psychiatric evaluation addressed his restlessness, impulsivity, memory problems, and dependence on alcohol, all symptoms that are commonly seen in people with ADHD (Young & Bramham, 2007). Tryggvi had become an alcoholic by the age of 16 and drug dependent by age 17.

When Tryggvi was released from prison in December 1981 and until his death, he displayed traits and symptoms commonly seen in people with adult ADHD:

- He was always very active, driven, and impulsive.
- He had serious sleep problems.
- He was always 'on the go' and found it difficult to sit down and relax. He could only watch a television programme if it was of special

interest to him, such as football, which he loved playing and watching on television. Otherwise he became easily bored and restless.
• Tryggvi explained his early offending to Sjöfn in terms of his being 'impressionable and impulsive'.
If Tryggvi had ADHD at the time of his arrest and detention then it would have significantly increased the risk of him giving a false confession due to reduced capacity to cope with his predicament, lack of confidence in his memory, and the intolerable distress of a restless and physically active man locked in a small cell. Tryggvi was more physically driven and active than the other detainees, which would have made his solitary confinement particularly difficult and exacerbated by the high emotional intensity associated with the case. Tryggvi was proud of his muscular physique and engaged in body building while in detention, perhaps wanting to emulate his grandfather's physical prowess as a national champion in Glíma.

## A HEURISTIC MODEL OF TRYGGVI'S CONFESSION

Figure 16.1 provides a heuristic model of memory distrust that describes the antecedents and processes involved in producing Tryggvi's pressured-internalized confession. The context provided the 'trigger'

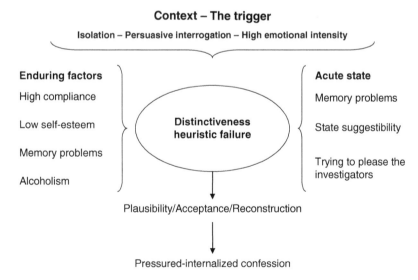

**Figure 16.1**  Heuristic model of Tryggvi's pressured-internalized confession

for altering Tryggvi's belief systems regarding the alleged offence. The three key components were confinement and social isolation, the investigators' guilt presumption and persuasive interrogation (i.e. the explicit or implicit communication from investigators about the seriousness of Tryggvi's predicament), and high emotional intensity. The high emotional intensity is evident from the Síðumúli Prison Custody Record, where he could not sleep for the first four nights and had to be sedated by the prison doctor by an injection. The psychiatrist who assessed him for a pretrial report noted his distress and how Tryggvi had tried to be polite and cooperative to the point of exaggeration. A similar demeanour of exaggerated eagerness to please was noted in his letters to Detective Sigurbjörn Víðir in June 1976, one of the two detectives responsible for eliciting his confession on 9 January 1976 after more than two weeks of intensive interrogation, none of which was recorded. In view of Detective Sigurbjörn Víðir's answer in court when asked about these unrecorded confessions, that statements were only recorded when new information emerged, it is reasonable to assume that these interrogations, which the two detectives maintained were mainly at Tryggvi's own request, consisted of denials.

Another possibility is that Tryggvi was giving some admission during interrogations prior to his confession statement on 9 January 1976 but considering the vagueness and incompleteness of his initial confession statement, the investigators may have delayed taking a statement until the confession had a more coherent content. It is likely that during those early unrecorded interrogations, persuasive and guilt-presumptive interrogation took place, which resulted in Tryggvi gradually accepting in principle his involvement in the disappearance of Gudmundur Einarsson rather than the sudden realization of his role. It seems from Tryggvi's diaries and correspondence that he viewed investigative judge Örn Höskuldsson and Detective Eggert Bjarnason as the 'hard' men ('Mr Nasty'), pressuring him to falsely confess, whereas Detective Sigurbjörn Víðir was 'Mr Nice': good at establishing rapport with suspects so that they dropped their defences.

The three contextual factors – isolation, persuasive interrogation, and high emotional intensity – fed directly into Tryggvi's cognitive appraisal of the situation and impacted on his pre-existing vulnerabilities, labelled as 'enduring' factors:
• High compliance, particularly his eagerness to please others.
• Low self-esteem.
• Poor memory.
• Long-standing alcoholism and drug addiction.
According to the memory distrust syndrome model (Gudjonsson & MacKeith, 1982), Tryggvi's alcoholism made him a prime candidate for

developing memory distrust syndrome when his memory for events was challenged.

The contextual risk factors activated 'acute state' factors. The key ones were:

- Tryggvi gradually began to distrust his memory of not being involved in the Gudmundur case.
- This increased his state suggestibility.
- Tryggvi was trying to please the investigators, which is evident from his correspondence with Detective Sigurbjörn Vídir in June–July 1976.

The enduring and acute state factors made Tryggvi unable to critically scrutinize the police scenario and its origin. With continued interrogation during the first two weeks of his detention, he gradually 'accepted' that he might have been involved (i.e. considered it plausible), while having no clear memory of the alleged event. His reference to 'my memory problem case' in his correspondence to Detective Sigurbjörn Vídir in June 1976 is revealing of his vulnerable mental state at the time. It suggests that he had accepted that he might somehow be involved, but could not recall exactly what had happened and tried hard to help the police solve the case, including providing the police with questions to ask his co-accused Kristján. At that time he was apparently on good terms with the investigators, even referring in one of his letters to Detective Sigurbjörn Vídir as his friend, and believing that investigative judge Örn Höskuldsson would assist him in purchasing government bonds on his behalf, and he asked Sigurbjörn Vídir to chase it up. This was no ordinary relationship between a suspect and investigators. It had become personal rather than professional, making Tryggvi more susceptible to manipulation.

Tryggvi's lawyer, Hilmar Ingimundarson, was apparently ineffective in supporting him because of his rarely being allowed to see his client in private. In fact, on 14 September 1977, Hilmar requested that trial judge Gunnlaugur Briem be removed from the case for refusing to allow him access to his client, despite Tryggvi requesting to speak to his lawyer. Hilmar's complaint was heard both in the District and Supreme Court to no avail. The judge's reason for the refusal was that granting Tryggvi access might at that point have interfered with the investigation. We know that Tryggvi formally retracted his confession on 30 March 1977 and never made any further admissions. The reason and date for the resolution of Tryggvi's memory distrust syndrome is unknown, although there are some credible pointers (see Conclusions). He died in May 2009 and unfortunately his first three private diaries written while in custody had been destroyed.

The circumstances behind the retraction can be seen from an entry in his second diary, dated 29 March 1977, discussed in Chapter 11.

Having formally retracted his confession in court, and showing no signs of getting back into confession mode, he was faced with the wrath of the establishment (in his diary he describes prison officers treating him differently – see Chapter 11), a common reaction in the Gudmundur and Geirfinnur cases to retracted confessions. After that Tryggvi became increasingly agitated about being detained and the uncertainties about his future as it came closer to the trial, with the gradual realization that his claim of innocence was not being accepted, no matter how hard he fought.

## CONCLUSIONS

Tryggvi initially denied any involvement in the disappearance of Gudmundur Einarsson. Even though he had been in custody at Sídumúli Prison the previous year for a few days on an unrelated matter, the intensity surrounding the Gudmundur investigation seriously derailed his mental state.

It seems that Tryggvi did not recall what he was doing at the time of the alleged offence, two years previously. This weakened his resistance to police suggestions due to the *absence of a memory trace* to guide him. He had become unable to insist: 'I didn't do it' and 'If I had done it I would remember it'. He differed from the other suspects in that he was unwilling to engage in extensive provoked confabulation and hence gave only a very limited account of what he thought might have happened in relation to Gudmundur's disappearance. He was able to give a reasonable account of the interior at Hamarsbraut 11 because he had been taken there by the police, suggesting a contamination effect.[30] The Commission noted that his accounts of the sequence of events inside the basement flat merely echoed those of the other suspects and changed over time to fit in with their latest story.

Tryggvi's early history of alcoholism and drug dependence left him vulnerable to memory distrust syndrome. When first incarcerated for the Gudmundur case, his poor mental state was evident. He was unable to sleep for four nights and needed heavy sedation. There were 21 hours of interrogation between 23 December 1975 and 8 January 1976, when he apparently steadfastly denied any involvement in the case. Once admitting involvement, his story was hesitant, unclear, and lacked comprehensive detail.[31]

---

[30] ICCRC Report, 2017, Tryggvi Leifsson, Paragraph 1753.
[31] ICCRC Report, 2017, Tryggvi Leifsson, Paragraph 1756.

The content of the recorded interrogations and his letters to Detective Sigurbjörn Vídir in June and July 1976 suggest that he was suffering from memory distrust syndrome, which had apparently gone by October when he started writing his fourth diary.

This is supported by a comment in Tryggvi's diary dated 27 October, where he uses a past rather than a present tense: 'Regarding the transportation [of Gudmundur's body], which I have never informed on, simply because I could not remember it and did not want to muddle it further by making up a story about it from their [the investigators'] suggestions, i.e. go along with what I had heard'.

A likely explanation for the reduction in memory distrust is that in about the middle of July he had been transferred to Litla-Hraun Prison for two months where he had much more freedom and less contact with the interrogators, giving him the time and opportunity to challenge his memory distrust and regain his complete belief in his innocence. As discussed in Chapter 4, once the interrogation stops and the pressure no longer exists, the state of confusion associated with memory distrust is typically resolved.

It is probable that Tryggvi had childhood ADHD, which would have impacted negatively on his ability to cope with the custodial interrogation and confinement and substantially further increased the risk of memory distrust syndrome and false confession.

With regard to the heuristic model of Tryggvi's confession, there are two caveats. Firstly, unfortunately his three diaries for the first 10 months in custody have been destroyed and they might have provided important information about the subtle psychological factors that led to his giving a confession in the Gudmundur case. The subsequent diaries do not provide evidence of memory distrust syndrome from October 1976 onward and suggest that Tryggvi principally confessed in an attempt to avoid custody. He had apparently on a previous occasion falsely confessed to burglary in order to avoid custody. It is possible that he later began to believe that he was involved in the Gudmundur case (i.e. the confession changed from pressured-compliant to pressured-internalized over time), which is supported by the pretrial psychiatric report. This is what happened in the case of Carole Richardson, one of the 'Guildford Four' (see Chapter 2).

Another possibility is that Tryggvi was from the beginning very focused on being released from custody, which was undoubtedly the case, but soon became confused about whether or not he had been involved in the case, gradually developing memory distrust syndrome over time, and peaking in June 1976, when he wrote his letter to Sigurbjörn Vídir, describing his 'memory problem case'. This is the most likely scenario.

The second caveat is that at the time of the Working Group, Tryggvi had died and could not be interviewed about his 'memory problem' while in solitary confinement. He died on 1 May 2009 from cancer.

Tryggvi's poor capacity for provoked confabulation suggests that he was reluctant to incorporate suggestions (post-event information) from the interrogators into his memory. He was agreeing with their suggestions, believing at the time that they might be true (i.e. seeing it as plausible rather than fully accepting it and incorporating suggestions over time into his recollection). This shows a high level of immediate suggestibility, but a low level of delayed suggestibility. These two different types of suggestibility, discussed in detail in Chapter 3, are poorly correlated.

## AN INTERVIEW WITH TRYGGVI'S WIDOW AND DAUGHTER

I visited Kristín Tryggvadóttir's home in Reykjavík on 14 May 2015 for an interview with her mother, Sjöfn Sigurbjörnsdóttir. I had previously interviewed Kristín about her father's diaries and she was present during the interview with her mother and contributed to the conversation.

What immediately impressed me was the warmth and elegance of their welcome, with a beautifully laid out table in the sitting room, laden with pancakes of two traditional varieties, flatbread and smoked lamb, and pastries. The coffee served was excellent too. Throughout the interview both Sjöfn and Kristín spoke of Tryggvi with such affection, there remained no doubt in my mind about their love for and dedication to him.

The focus of the interview was on Sjöfn's relationship with Tryggvi, what had happened to the diaries that he had written while in solitary confinement after his arrest in December 1975, and how he had adjusted to home life after his release on 24 December 1981, exactly six years after his arrest in the Gudmundur case.

Sjöfn was a year younger than Tryggvi and she had known him since the age of 13. They were then acquaintances rather than friends. She liked his bubbly personality; she found him charming and full of life. He was very active, impulsive, had a strong temper, and in his teens had got into bad company with older boys who had led him astray. He began to drink alcohol and got into trouble with the police. His main weakness was his dependence on alcohol.

Sjöfn told me that she had little to do with Tryggvi during their teenage years; she went to live in Australia for a while and had her daughter, Kristín Anna, who was born in April 1975. Tryggvi later adopted her. When Sjöfn returned to Iceland in the late 1970s, Tryggvi had heard through another prisoner that Sjöfn was back in Iceland. He telephoned Sjöfn and invited her to visit him at Litla-Hraun Prison for 'coffee and a chat'. She visited him soon afterwards and there was an instant attraction and they became romantically involved. Sjöfn subsequently visited him regularly in prison and they married on 26 December 1978, while Tryggvi was serving his prison sentence at Litla-Hraun. The ceremony took place at Eyrarbakkakirkja, which is a very old church in a small fishing village located near Litla-Hraun Prison. Afterwards there was a reception at the prison. According to Sjöfn, Tryggvi was a very popular person, and the wedding and reception were attended by family and prison officers.

'It was a lovely occasion,' Sjöfn said, with a warm smile.

Early on in the interview, when asked about her relationship with Tryggvi, Sjöfn declared in a firm voice: 'I've no regrets about marrying Tryggvi Rúnar. He was a very kind and sensitive person.'

Kristín, who was present during the interview, interjected: 'He was a brilliant dad.'

Sjöfn admitted that the early years of their marriage were difficult. When Tryggvi was released from prison in December 1981 he moved in with Sjöfn and Kristín in Meistaravellir. However, at first he experienced adjustment problems and he was finding it difficult to cope with day-to-day living. He was particularly bitter towards Erla and Saevar for having 'dragged him into the case'. He was suspicious and distrusting of people (apart from his family whom he trusted implicitly), started drinking again, was irritable, bad tempered, and moody.

'He had some very dark days, even when sober,' Sjöfn said.

'This was very true in the early years after his release, but not at the end.'

'He kept asking, himself, how this could have happened.'

'He did not walk out of prison the same man as he had been when he went in.'

When I asked Sjöfn how he had changed, she replied:

'He was very suspicious of people generally' and did not trust anybody, 'except his family'.

'He was terrified of being led into a trap again.'

'He had some paranoia about the police, but at the beginning they had him under surveillance.'

Sjöfn said that Tryggvi had always been a hard-working man, even during the dark days in the 1980s. While always remaining very active, driven, and impulsive, his mood and temper improved greatly after he successfully completed a substance misuse treatment programme in the early 1990s for his long-standing alcoholism. Sjöfn and Kristín enjoyed many happy years together.

'He found an inner peace,' Sjöfn said.

Sjöfn described Tryggvi as having serious sleep problems. He tried various things to improve his sleep, including attending relaxation classes and yoga.

Tryggvi explained his early offending to Sjöfn in terms of his being 'impressionable and impulsive'.

While serving his sentence at Litla-Hraun Prison Tryggvi had learned a trade and became a welder, which proved to be a useful skill and was a good achievement. Sjöfn and Tryggvi later ran a car washing and polishing company. It was first operated by Sjöfn's brother-in-law Hilmar, but she and Tryggvi took over the business. One of the men they employed was Gudmundur Einarsson's youngest brother, 'Bói', who according to Sjöfn believed that Gudmundur had died from exposure and disappeared.

'He did not believe his brother had been murdered', Sjöfn said.

'Tryggvi would go to work in the early morning, work late, then go after work to the gym or play football. He would be home late.'

He was always 'on the go' and found it difficult to sit down and relax. He could only watch a television programme if it was of special interest to him, such as football, which he loved playing and watching on television. Otherwise he became easily bored and restless.

Tryggvi always remained bitter and resentful about his arrest and imprisonment and on his death bed in April 2009, about a week before he died, he begged Sjöfn's forgiveness for not having been able to get his conviction for the murder of Gudmundur Einarsson overturned.

'There is nothing to forgive,' she replied.

'Do you believe me?' he asked.

'The whole of Iceland believes you,' Sjöfn replied.

Tryggvi sighed with relief. All he had ever wanted was for his family to believe him and for the authorities to acknowledge that he was an innocent man. At the time of his death he knew his family believed him, but unfortunately he did not live to see the authorities acknowledge his innocence.

Sjöfn and Kristín became determined to make sure that his name was cleared. This was now their mission.

'I want to see the case completed before I die,' Sjöfn stated.

'So do I,' I uttered and the three of us burst out laughing.

During his solitary confinement Tryggvi had written diaries. Sjöfn learned of the diaries when she visited Tryggvi in prison. He was worried that the diaries would be taken away from him by the authorities and asked Sjöfn to smuggle them out of the prison, which she did, removing three or four diaries at a time for safe keeping. Sjöfn estimated that there were over a dozen diaries. She read all the diaries with his consent but Tryggvi did not want anybody else to read them. He viewed the diaries as 'private', having only written them for his own benefit while in solitary confinement.

I think it is likely that the diaries helped him keep track of time and his mind occupied, hence reducing the intolerable distress and boredom he was experiencing at the time. It is also likely that writing the diaries gave him some sense of control over his oppressive environment.

Sjöfn said that when he was not released after confessing, Tryggvi strongly believed that his lawyer would get him out, but this did not happen. He was full of hope until the day he was convicted. It was his belief in fairness and justice that gave him the strength to cope with solitary confinement. It was only after his conviction on 19 December 1977 that the reality of his predicament really set in. He was now a convicted murderer. He felt ashamed that he allowed himself to be manipulated by investigators and prison officers. He also felt very angry about it and was determined not to fall into the same trap again.

'He was determined never to give a false confession again.'

'He was particularly angry about the false promise Örn Höskuldsson had given him about being released from custody if he confessed, Örn didn't keep his promise.'

'His aim was to prove his innocence but he did not know how to go about it. He was very dependent on his lawyer. He saw Saevar struggling with his appeal, and he couldn't face going through it himself.'

'He felt sorry for Saevar and forgave him in the end, but he couldn't forgive Erla'.

Sjöfn said Tryggvi was furious about the mental torture he had been subjected to by the investigators and prison officers during his confinement, including being tricked and pressured to give a false confession, prison officers at times keeping him awake at night by walking on the roof of the building and taping his mouth shut and hands together at night, claiming that he was shouting in his sleep and kept ringing the buzzer, which Tryggvi did not remember doing. He thought the prison officers were playing with his mind, trying to make him think he was 'going mad'.

'The solitary confinement was hell for him,' Sjöfn said.

About 10 years after leaving prison Tryggvi wanted to destroy the diaries, but Sjöfn tried to persuade him to keep them. Tryggvi eventually decided that he wanted the diaries destroyed and he and Sjöfn tore them up, put them in plastic bags, and took them to the Reykjavík rubbish dump where they disappeared for ever. Unknown to either of them, in her teens Kristín had found the diaries and had kept three in her possession when the remaining diaries were destroyed. This is Kristín's story:

In about 1991 Kristín had found a briefcase containing the diaries in a store room in the basement of their block of flats at Grýtubakki 10, Breidholt, where she happened to be looking through things, not for any particular reason. She was about 16 years of age at the time. She thinks there were over a dozen diaries. She took two or three diaries out of the briefcase at any one time and hid them in her bedroom where she read them. One time she took three diaries and when she went into the store room sometime later to return them, the briefcase with the diaries had disappeared; Kristín assumed her father had thrown them away or destroyed them. She kept the three remaining diaries and one day when visiting her father at the hospice where he was dying, she told him that she had read the diaries and had kept three of them. He seemed pleased and told her:

'You will know what to do with them.'

# 17

# Gudjón Skarphédinsson's Memory Distrust Syndrome and Confession

*I see no reason why I should not try to remember the case to the best of my abilities*[1]

## SALIENT POINTS

- On 22 February 1980 the Supreme Court convicted Gudjón of manslaughter in the Geirfinnur case and sentenced him to 10 years in prison.
- Ten months into the Geirfinnur investigation, Gudjón was identified as the alleged driver to Keflavík.
- In spite of Gudjón's high intelligence and good education, there had been disappointments in his life and he had mental health issues.
- There is evidence that Gudjón had a compliant temperament, poor self-esteem, and possessed a vivid imagination.
- While in solitary confinement he kept a detailed diary, which showed how his mind gradually became overborne by the investigators' suggestions and his eagerness to assist the police.
- A thematic analysis of his diary showed that he was too trusting of the investigators, was unable to assert himself, internalized his

---

[1] An extract from Gudjón's diary, dated 28 November 1976, after the police had persuaded him that he was involved in the Geirfinnur case.

*The Psychology of False Confessions: Forty Years of Science and Practice*, First Edition.
Gisli H. Gudjonsson.
© 2018 John Wiley & Sons Ltd. Published 2018 by John Wiley & Sons Ltd.

distress, had a defeatist and self-sacrificing attitude, and appealed to God for help, rather than relying on himself.

• Gudjón did not have the psychological resources or resilience to effectively mitigate his memory distrust, leading to a pressured-internalized false confession.

• His memory distrust syndrome was not temporary in that it lasted several years.

Gudjón was born in Vatnsdalur, Austur-Húnavatnsskýsla, on 19 June 1943. His father was a practicing Minister of Religion. Gudjón was the oldest of seven children and was brought up by his maternal grandparents, whereas his younger siblings were brought up by his parents.

Gudjón was academically bright and went to university in 1966 to study theology, but dropped out after a while. He married in the summer of 1967 and within two months they had a daughter. During 1968–1972 the couple were teachers at Reykjanesskóli in Ísafjardardjúp and it was there that Gudjón first met Saevar, who was his pupil for a term.


## DETERIORATION IN MENTAL STATE

The couple moved to Reykjavík in 1972 and Gudjón went back to university to study social sciences but did not complete his studies. He left university in the spring of 1974 and his functioning began to deteriorate. His wife became very concerned about his mental health, but Gudjón refused to see a psychiatrist. After his father's death in July 1974 in a road traffic accident, Gudjón's mental state deteriorated further and from the description of the symptoms he gave when I interviewed him in 2015, he was probably depressed; he showed a lack of interest in life, poor drive and motivation, and had no sense of purpose or direction. His marriage, too, was in serious difficulties, there were financial problems, and he was not functioning well at work.

In late summer 1975, Gudjón travelled in Europe, part of the time with his wife, and then he met up with Saevar, who persuaded him to smuggle cannabis into Iceland in his car. Gudjón returned to Iceland at the end of November 1975 and was arrested two weeks later after the drugs were discovered when his car arrived by ship from Holland. He was detained in custody for five days. According to his wife, who was interviewed as a part of Gudjón's psychiatric examination in 1977, Gudjón had difficulties coping with solitary confinement in 1975 and felt frightened and depressed afterwards.

Gudjón's mental state appeared to deteriorate further during the spring of 1976 and at the request of his mother, he saw a doctor, who found him hyperactive and unrealistic. The doctor offered him admission to a psychiatric ward, but Gudjón declined. Gudjón could talk continuously for 24 hours without a break, showing manic symptoms. His brother, who was a doctor, examined him and prescribed him chlorpromazine – an antipsychotic medication – which Gudjón took irregularly.

A psychiatric/psychological evaluation of Gudjón in late December 1976 and early 1977 concluded that he was highly intelligent, introverted, sensitive, proud, dependent, and impulsive. He had poor self-esteem, and possessed a vivid imagination and unrealistic ambitions. He was also described as having a manic-depressive disorder, which at times made him hyperactive, highly imaginative, and prone to anger and sleep disturbance.

When interviewing Gudjón in 2015, I asked him to describe his personality and behaviour prior to his arrest in 1976. He described himself as 'lazy', 'avoidant', 'carefree', 'easily bored', 'gave in easily to people', had 'no stamina or strength', and 'drifted a lot'. He described a man with low self-esteem, who had lost his focus in life. He said that these characteristics developed in his late teens, but before that he was more able to focus on his studies and had had greater interest in life.

## THE ARREST AND CUSTODY

The police first interviewed Gudjón about the Geirfinnur case in February 1976, and again in May 1976 when he gave a witness statement. He was interviewed because he knew the prime suspect (Saevar). Gudjón denied any special knowledge about the case, but it is evident from the Court records that the Reykjavík Team were investigating Gudjón as a potential suspect in the Geirfinnur case as early as May 1976 (see Chapter 9).

On 28 October 1976 Saevar implicated Gudjón in the case and he was arrested on 12 November and taken into custody, where he remained in solitary confinement for 412 days (12 November 1976 to 29 December 1977)[2] during which time he was questioned by the police on 75 occasions for a total of 160 hours, and participated in five suspects' face-to-face confrontations (Gudjonsson et al., 2014).

---

[2] ICCRC Report, 2017, Gudjón Skarphédinsson, Paragraph 1534.

Very early on 12 November 1976, four policemen went to Gudjón's home to arrest him. He was interrogated between 07.25 and 13.10 and when told he was a suspect in the Geirfinnur case, he stated:

> I assert that I have no knowledge of the disappearance of Geirfinnur Einarsson, or anything in connection with that beyond that which I have read in the newspapers.

The following day, and while detained in solitary confinement, Gudjón was interviewed by Karl Schütz through an interpreter. Gudjón again denied any involvement in the case. He was extensively interviewed on 15 and 16 November and still denied his involvement. He continued to be interrogated and on 23 November, on the 11th day in solitary confinement, his resistance was beginning to break down. The records show that Karl Schütz interrogated Gudjón that day in a guilt-presumptive fashion. When asked directly whether he was involved in the case, Gudjón said that as far as he knew he was not, but he could not be sure. This was the first indication from the police records that Gudjón was beginning to accept the possibility that perhaps he was involved but could not recall it (i.e. he was beginning to distrust his own memory, and *plausibility* had set in). By this time, he had been interrogated for about 25 hours.

The interrogations continued and on 28 November, having been in solitary confinement for just over two weeks, he gave his first self-incriminating admission during a trip with the investigators to the alleged crime scene in Keflavík. He described in vague terms the car journey to Keflavík on the day of Geirfinnur's disappearance in 1974, but could not recall any altercation there with Geirfinnur. When asked why he could not recall such an important event, Gudjón explained that he became depressed following the death of his father on 5 July 1974. He had failed to activate the distinctiveness heuristic, which should have told him 'If I had done it, I would have remembered it'.

The interrogation continued, and on 8 December he told the investigators:

> I intend to tell the truth in this case to the best of my recollection. Some aspects of the case are unclear in my memory, but may come to me later.

On this day, Gudjón admitted that he had been involved with Saevar and Kristján in an attack on Geirfinnur that resulted in his death on the slipway. This was the account accepted both by the District Court and Supreme Court and used as the foundation for convicting all three men. Subsequent interrogations focused on trying to locate Geirfinnur's body, but all locations Gudjón identified were only 'possibilities' (i.e. he had no actual recollection of what had happened to the body and was only guessing possible locations).

Gudjón did not retract his confession until 1996, when this was reported in Iceland's largest national newspaper, *Morgunbladid*. I asked Gudjón why he had not retracted the confession earlier. He said that until he began to read the court papers after his conviction in December 1977, and noticed that there was no evidence against him apart from his confession, he thought he was involved in Geirfinnur's murder, but this was not with full conviction. In fact, he always remained unsure about his involvement in the case and never had a clear memory of the event taking place. When I interviewed him for the Working Group in 2012, he said that at the time of making the confession he was 50% sure he had been involved, but this had gone down to 0% by 2012. When the case went to the Supreme Court for appeal in February 1980, Gudjón was beginning to seriously doubt his involvement in the case, but he did not think retracting his confession would make any difference (i.e. nobody would believe him, suggesting strong passivity and lack of confidence).

When I interviewed Gudjón in 2012 for the Working Group, he named three people who were instrumental in persuading him that he was involved in the Geirfinnur case. The first was Birgir Thormar, allocated judicial supervision of Gudjón at the time, who encouraged him from the time of his arrest to tell everything he knew about the case, while Örn Höskuldsson still remained in overall charge of the Geirfinnur case. The assumption communicated to Gudjón was that he was involved in the case, even if he could not remember it. According to Gudjón's diary, he liked Birgir Thormar very much and trusted him ('a super man and a good man' – see Appendix 2).

On 18 November 1976, six days after his arrest, Gudjón was visited in custody by a Sheriff Jón Ísberg from the northwest part of Iceland, who was a relative of his (he was married to Gudjón's aunt). Sheriff Ísberg suggested to Gudjón that he was involved in the case and that it was important for the Icelandic nation that the case be solved. Helping the nation to solve the case appealed to Gudjón and appears to have given him a sense of purpose and self-worth (Gudjón's description of his mental state was that prior to his arrest he was low in mood, had poor self-esteem, and lacked focus).

The third person was Detective Grétar Saemundsson, who conducted most of the interviews with Gudjón. They were of the same age. Gudjón described Grétar as a very logical and persuasive man – a description I entirely agree with, having come to know Grétar quite well in 1976.

According to Gudjón, Karl Schütz dominated the investigation and became increasingly frustrated and angry that Gudjón was not able to help him locate Geirfinnur's body.

Gudjón was released from prison on licence on 12 October 1981.

## KARL SCHÜTZ'S PERCEPTION OF GUDJÓN

In his final report in the Geirfinnur case, Schütz concluded:

> Gudjón seems on alert during interrogation and continuously complains of amnesia. On the other hand, he has more than once shown that he remembers very well various details. It must be said though that he has never tried to hinder the investigation by deliberately telling lies [...] He has a strong tendency to avoid explaining the key aspects of the case e.g. how Geirfinnur died, what happened regarding the body [...] He has remained emotionally stable during interrogation, but has said that he can become furious for a short while and then unaware of what he says and does.

## THE 'LIE DETECTION'

When leaving Iceland for England on 18 September 1976 after an eventful summer with the Reykjavík police, I continued with my clinical psychology training at the University of Surrey in England. I returned to Iceland on 20 December for a Christmas vacation with my parents and brother Gudmundur, who was a police officer. One of the detectives from Schütz's Task Force had left a message at my parents' house asking me to urgently contact him, which I did. I met with Birgir Thormar, who had been allocated judicial supervision of Gudjón. He asked whether I was prepared to give Gudjón a lie detector test. I did not have the lie detector machine with me in Iceland but thought of a compromise: I would tape-record Gudjón's replies to the questions and ask Alan Smith to analyse the stress in Gudjón's voice using the Psychological Stress Evaluator (PSE) when I returned to England.[3] I had met Alan earlier in the year and knew that this was possible. At the time I did not know whether Alan would be willing to analyse the tape, but I took a chance that he would. He had been very helpful

---

[3] Alan Smith's work on the PSE was discussed in Chapter 1.

to me in the past and I was confident that he would assist. I contacted him when I returned to England in early January 1976 and he agreed to analyse the tape with Gudjón's replies.

The lie detector test took place on 31 December 1976, by which time Gudjón had been in custody for 50 days. My recollection of the reason for the test was that Gudjón had problems remembering what had happened to Geirfinnur on the slipway and had been unable to help the police find the body. Gudjón's investigative judge in the case, Birgir Thormar, and the police thought that a lie detector test might help him focus his mind and it did, but not in the direction they wanted.

Detective Gunnlaugur Sigurdsson and I collected Gudjón from Sídumúli Prison at 12.20. We took him to Borgartún 7 for the test and he returned to the prison at 15.35. I had written out the proposed questions and these were discussed with Gudjón's lawyer prior to the test. He was asked all the questions twice and changed his answer from 'Yes' to 'No' regarding the question 'Do you know who is behind Geirfinnur's disappearance?', suggesting that he was unsure who was involved, while accepting that somehow he was implicated. He responded consistently to all the other questions and answered affirmatively the questions: 'Were you involved in Geirfinnur's disappearance?', 'Did you go to Keflavík on 19 November 1974?', and 'Have you told the police all you remember about the Geirfinnur case?'. My impression at the time was that Gudjón was passive and compliant during the procedure and was trying hard to do his best on the test. I was in no doubt that he was making a genuine effort and was struggling to make sense of his alleged involvement in the case.

Gudjón's lawyer, Benedikt Blöndal, and investigative judge, Birgir Thormar, were present during the testing.

## The Outcome

Alan Smith analysed Gudjón's responses to the questions and wrote to me on 25 February 1977, concluding:

> Using my criterion of a 25 point difference in scores being at the 95% significance level, there are some reliable differences in the subject's responses. You might be able to link this with the meaning of some of the questions.

The single greatest level of stress was in Gudjón responding affirmatively to the question 'Were you involved in Geirfinnur's disappearance?' Assuming the PSE was giving reliable results, one interpretation is that accepting that he was involved in the disappearance of Geirfinnur, the question caused him a great deal of distress. This may have been caused by the agony of his not being able to remember anything about his alleged involvement in the case, and perhaps more importantly, contemplating the possibility that he had been involved in Geirfinnur's murder, but was unable to remember the details.

## The Aftermath

Karl Schütz had gone back to Germany during the Christmas festivities in 1976 and returned to Iceland on 4 January 1977. Upon his return he had a meeting with the Task Force and was updated on any progress made while he was away. He was told that following a lie detector test on 31 December, Gudjón had been experiencing problems providing further evidence in the case. Prior to the lie detector test, he had been able to give a vague account of the journey to Keflavík, which was allegedly consistent with the accounts given by his co-accused. He was now telling members of the Task Force 'that he didn't really know exactly if he had been in Keflavík or not' and was considering retracting his confession (i.e. 'First of all I must now think about everything. Should I perhaps take back everything that I have said?').

This was potentially a serious setback to the investigation. In Schütz's report on 7 January, which Chief Judge Halldór Thorbjörnsson forwarded to the Minister of Justice, Ólafur Jóhannesson, he commented regarding the impact of the lie detector test on Gudjón:[4]

> I feel obliged to refer to the above-mentioned obstacles to the investigation, since they could have dramatically jeopardized the further progress of the findings, which are not yet fully completed. In particular, Gudjón could have been expected to provide the answer to the final questions. The entire investigation tactics following his arrest were organized with this objective.

*Comment:* This paragraph shows Schütz's view that the lie detector test may have dramatically jeopardized further progress with the Geirfinnur investigation. The entire investigation had focused on Gudjón providing answers to the final questions and disputes, which I suspect involved greater certainties about the alleged murder of

---

[4] Karl Schütz wrote his report in German and it had been translated into Icelandic. In order to preserve the authenticity of its content and tone I had the report professionally translated from German into English.

Geirfinnur (i.e. getting the 'story straight') and ultimately the discovery of his body.

> But this 'interrogation' [lie detector test] is in sharp contrast with the previously – successful – tactic used by the Commission [Task Force] to convince the accused that it would be best to tell the whole truth and that his supposed 'memory gaps' are not at all credible.

*Comment:* This shows that the Task Force did not believe that Gudjón's 'memory gaps' were genuine, were convinced he was involved in the Geirfinnur case (presumption of guilt), thought their interrogation tactics had been 'successful' so far, and were intending on persuading him 'to tell the whole truth', meaning implicating himself and the others further in the case and disclosing the location of the body.

It is clear from Schütz's report that he did not approach the case with an open mind.

> At the request of the undersigned [Karl Schütz], Judge Birgir has released the documents on this test. It is not clear at present if these are complete; at least the answers of the accused were not submitted. While I was away, Mr Birgir concealed his plan from the Commission [Task Force] and refused to release the test questions to the Commission.

*Comment:* During the lie detector test I wrote down Gudjón's answers as well as tape-recording my questions and his answers. I had the only copy, but Gudjón's lawyer and Birgir Thormar had copies of the questions, which had been agreed with Gudjón's lawyer in advance. I think Birgir Thormar was correct in not releasing the list of questions to the Task Force, because they were confidential to Gudjón and his lawyer. It looks like Karl Schütz pressured Birgir Thormar to release the list of questions to the Task Force. Karl Schütz was not concerned about professional etiquette, confidentiality, and ethics. His approach appears to have been heavy-handed. The allegation that Birgir Thormar had 'concealed' his plan from the Task Force is incorrect. Some of the detectives in the Task Force knew about the lie detector test and I suspect that the initiative for the test came from one of them. I was in regular contact with them from the time I arrived in Iceland before Christmas and was assisting the police (e.g. on Christmas Eve, 24 December, Grétar Saemundsson and I collected Gudjón from Sídumúli Prison to meet with his wife at Borgartún 7 and I was present during their meeting). It is more likely that the members of the Task Force were too scared of Karl Schütz to tell him the truth about the lie detector test. Schütz was an intimidating and punitive figure, who would not take kindly to Task Force members facilitating or knowing about the lie detector test. I am in no doubt that if Schütz had known, he would not have hesitated to remove one or more of them from the Task Force. Instead, Judge Birgir Thormar became a convenient scapegoat and had to pay the price.

> Through an instruction by the head of the Icelandic Criminal Court, senior criminal judge Halldór Thorbjörnsson, the further judicial supervision of the accused has been transferred to Mr Örn Höskuldsson.

*Comment:* As a result of Schütz's wrath, the judicial supervision of Gudjón was transferred back to the original Reykjavík investigative judge, Örn Höskuldsson. I felt saddened when I read about this in 2012. I had found Birgir Thormar congenial and a man of integrity. I think he genuinely believed in Gudjón's involvement in the case. All my interactions with Birgir Thormar were respectful and professional.

Police reports show that after the lie detector test, attempts were made to try to 'consolidate the confessions'. On 10 January 1977, Gudjón refused to sign the statement taken from him. He had become less cooperative after the lie detector test, but his temporary resistance was soon broken down again and he remained in a 'confession mode' until the trial and subsequent Supreme Court Judgement.

### Follow-Up Query

On 1 November 1979, I received a letter from Gunnlaugur Briem, the senior judge involved in the Gudmundur and Geirfinnur cases, which suggested that Birgir Thormar never had Gudjón's answers to the lie detector questions in his possession. An English translation of the letter reads as follows:

> I enclose photocopies of documents regarding an investigation that you and judge Birgir Thormar conducted on Gudjón Skarphédinsson in 1976. These documents were not used in the case, but Benedikt Blöndal, the lawyer of the accused, has requested access to the documents. While inspecting the documents, I cannot find the answers that Gudjón gave to the questions he was asked, and Birgir cannot find them among his papers. I request that you provide me with the answers, if you still have the documents.

I forwarded the answers to Gunnlaugur Briem on 14 November 1979.[5] That was the last communication I had about the lie detection test of Gudjón until 2012, when I came across Karl Schütz's report of 7 January 1977.

---

[5] It is documented that Gunnlaugur Briem received the letter and relevant material on 22 November 1979 (ICCRC Report, 2017, Gudjón Skarphédinsson, Paragraph 1381).

## GUDJÓN'S DIARY

Gudjón kept a detailed diary of key events and his experiences while in solitary confinement in 1976 and 1977. The existence of the diary was not known until November 2011 when he mentioned it during an interview with the Working Group. There is no reference to the diary in the court papers, and Gudjón had kept it safe after he was released from prison on licence on 12 October 1981. Remarkably, either the investigators did not know of its existence or chose not to interfere. It seems from the case papers that Gudjón was treated with more respect than the other suspects in the Geirfinnur case and was seen as a crucial witness against the other suspects. Both Kristján and Erla have told me that they also wrote personal diaries while in solitary confinement, but the investigators took these away from them.

The first diary entry is dated 16 November 1976, four days after his arrest (see Appendix 2). The last entry is 27 December 1977, three days before he was sent to Kvíabryggja Prison to serve his prison sentence, unlike Saevar and Kristján, in an open prison. The most crucial entries regarding the development of Gudjón's memory distrust syndrome and confession are found for the period between 16 November 1976 and 12 January 1977 and are presented in Appendix 2. I have completed a thematic analysis of his diary entries during this period and the key themes are shown in Figure 17.1. The figure shows the relationship of four key themes to a central idea.

The central idea (Level 1) encompasses the main task that Gudjón was struggling to achieve, namely, to help the police find Geirfinnur's body. Both Saevar and Kristján had been unable to help the police locate the body, and my impression from my association with the investigators in late December 1976 was that Gudjón's arrest had given the investigators fresh hope of a solution to the case. According to Gudjón's diary, he was repeatedly asked about the location of the body, and on 7 December asked himself: 'Where is the body? It is strange that it doesn't show up'.

23 December 1976: 'Slept little and bad. [...] Grétar came. We discussed the body, location and other things. [...] The question is whether I'm the only one who knows where the body is?'

30 December: 'Then Eggert and Grétar arrived and now around 20.00 we have discussed constantly about where Geirfinnur's body is? Do I know it or not and it's taking a long time [...] A lot of things indicate that I am coming closer to the solution to the case, including that I was shaking so much that I could hardly eat. [...] A long interrogation with Eggert which ended with a visit to Kópavogur football stadium, where I think Geirfinnur's body is hidden. Judge Örn, Grétar and Eggert all went with me. It was terribly cold outside.'

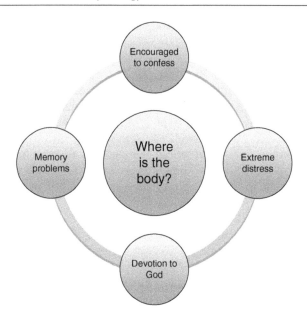

**Figure 17.1**   A thematic analysis of the relevant content of Gudjón's diary

During our interviews in 2012 and 2015, Gudjón told me that he had given the police numerous possible locations where Geirfinnur's body might be hidden, including a football stadium, but these were not based on an actual memory, but on places he had visited and treated as 'possibilities'.

Level 1 corresponds to the outer ring of four key theme circles, labelled 'Encouraged to confess', 'Memory problems', 'Extreme distress', and 'Devotion to God'. I will discuss each of these in turn.

### Encouraged to Confess

The diary shows that after his arrest, Gudjón denied any special knowledge in the Geirfinnur case, but the police did not believe him and kept breaking down his resistance. They wanted a confession and the location of Geirfinnur's body. Within six days of Gudjón's arrest, his aunt's husband, Sheriff Jón Ísberg, visited him in Síðumúli Prison and Gudjón commented that it was 'Good to see Jón Ísberg'. The custody records show that the sheriff and Detective Grétar interviewed Gudjón together for 15 minutes in the interrogation room on 19 November 1976.

Within two weeks of his arrest, Gudjón noted: 'Grétar [Detective Grétar Saemundsson] came and implied many things and thinks I'm in a bad position in the case. He even wants me to get used to the thought of being a murderer. I find that a bit much'.

The diary entry dated 28 November 1976, shows that Gudjón thought he could help the police solve the case: 'I see no reason why I should not try to remember the case to the best of my abilities. It's a pity that I remember so little. I slept well on the diazepam, much, good and long. Went on a car journey to Keflavík with Grétar, Schütz and Pétur [Schütz's interpreter], little to gain from that, we drove around town, even less to gain from that. I want to solve the case right away. And receive a long and heavy sentence. I am finished.'

**Note:** Gudjón seemed very easily influenced by external sources, was keen to assist the investigators, trusted them, and treated them with respect.

## Memory Problems

Gudjón's diary shows that from 17 November, five days after his arrest, memory distrust was setting in: 'Interrogation tomorrow. Now the matter will become clearer. But I cannot remember any link between me and the Geirfinnur case. But something is brewing.'

The following day Gudjón commented: 'Sometimes I feel guilty but I cannot remember what has happened.'

On 23 November, Gudjón wrote in his diary: 'Intensively encouraged to confess, which I can't do because I can't remember anything.'

29 November: 'Had a long conversation with Grétar today. I try to remember all about that trip to Keflavík. Not going too well but I am feeling better than before. I am tired after this. I wish I could remember it all better. Grétar says I can't go easy on myself, it needs courage he says. I tell him I find it hard to remember.'

30 November: 'I find it difficult to remember what happened and how [...] But the case is progressing and I hope God gives me energy, courage and memory to tell truthfully and correctly what happened so that there will be an answer and conclusion to the case soon [...] Tomorrow I need to try to remember what cars were on the trip, but it has been difficult to remember. I'm very uncertain about this, maybe it will clear up soon.'

3 December: 'Many things are still unclear, I have to try to remember and use my next evenings for just that. It will be difficult, but will happen with prayer and concentration.'

8 December: 'Woke up late and started discussing with Grétar, we discussed for a long time until dinner time. Continued after dinner until almost five this morning. Then I had confessed to being involved in the

murder of G. Einarsson [Geirfinnur Einarsson] and had given a third report regarding the most unfortunate trip to Keflavík I have ever gone on in my entire life. Hopefully the body of the man will be found in the next few days and this nation can relax, even though I will not be among those people, but my conscience should be better now than before [...] I'm no longer in a state of despair, don't want to die, but this will be difficult. I will go to sleep now. Now something will happen.'

27 December: 'Now lawyer, judge, psychologist and investigators arrive and ask me questions and I recall less now than I did before Christmas. [...] I was woken up about 1 pm and Grétar wanted to ask me some questions and left me in abeyance. The position is complicated regarding the Keflavík trip and now the psychologist [Gísli Gudjonsson], Birgir and lawyer Benedikt. The truth test will be conducted on Thursday or Friday and I have nothing to lose and everything to win.'

31 December: 'After a lot of crying, I feel better, but still I am miserable. The voice tests [lie detector test] took place today, but I feel like I made some mistakes there. The recent interrogations and that stadium issue have affected my nerves. Örn, G and E [Grétar and Eggert] were here today and wanted to discuss the case even further. [...] I'm all breaking down and hardly recognize my name with certainty. [...] I wish God would take me to Him, I am about to give up, amnesia. Where are these bodies? How should I know? I have a headache. Feel terrible.'

1 January 1977: 'I hope and pray that I will never again live such a horrible New Year's Eve. Can't sleep nor stay awake. The headache felt like blowing my eyes out. [...] Reverend Jón [Bjarman] came and it is always good to see him. Calm and in good control. Asked his advice on the case and Örn and Birgir. Don't make any deals, he said. Will discuss it all with my lawyer and Birgir, he is the judge responsible for my aspect of the case. But I'm losing my mind that is for sure. This ends by my no longer knowing my own name. They are trying to arrange a deal under the table. Try to trick information from me that I don't even have. What is Örn up to? Why has he suddenly appeared? [...] I will speak to Grétar tomorrow. What about? My reservations concerning the location and the outcome of the interrogation the other day.'

2 January 1977: 'I feel tangled up in some absurd web of lies, no breaks, no glimpse of clear sky. Success is harder to swallow than failure. It will be great when they have solved this Geirfinnur case. There is something not right about this case. I find this amnesia especially odd, it has never happened to me when I am sober, not to remember anything. What was happening, did I never go to Keflavík on 19/11/74 but some other night? What important business do Benedikt and Birgir

have with me tomorrow? And Örn, Eggert, Grétar? Is something brewing? Has something new emerged?'

## Extreme Distress

Gudjón's diary shows that he became increasingly distressed as he struggled with his memory regarding his alleged involvement in the Geirfinnur case.

22 November 1976: 'For two years I have had the belief that I did not know anything about this case but now I am supposed to have been very much involved. In fact most of it has not yet come to light. [...] What game is God playing with me? Am I mentally ill, or have been? I would admit to that. Many of the things I have done in the recent years were madness.'

23 November: 'The nights are the worst. I wait desperately to fall asleep but it is slow in coming and I have intrusive thoughts [...] If I only knew if I had participated in this or not. I deceive people; that's the way it is. I am always acting, I am an ill man [...] Only if I had not smuggled cannabis. It ruined my life.'

24 November: 'I have problems breathing, feel terrible. [...] My mental illness is now evident.'

7 December: 'I feel so bad right now, I am so tired, cannot remember anything, have difficulties talking, cannot think, dread tomorrow, know that it will all be the same, don't remember, know nothing, then I will be deprived of my sanity. I am totally exhausted.'

13 December: 'I'm always thinking about suicide. I could do it. I have the means. I'm a bit ambivalent about it but it will not take much if things go wrong for me to do it.'

18 December: 'I'm always thinking about suicide, a rather ugly word suicide, know how I would do it, could not go wrong. [...] What in the world has happened to Grétar? I have not heard from him in a long time. Doesn't really matter but I am not entirely content, something is not right.'

4 January 1977: 'What is it that keeps me alive? I'm able to end it, why don't I? Is it that I can see some future? Is it the belief in life and that one should not go against God's wishes?'

8 January 1977: 'Are they now coming harder at me. Breaking me down by not talking to me, forbid the priest to come, stalling letters and packages etc. No, paranoid talk. You can get so paranoid and full of hate being isolated like this. I try to keep my mood stable. Be patient and calm, have inner vision. Review incidents from life.'

**Note:** It is evident that Gudjón's distress was very much internalized. He did not act out his distress, apparently feeling passive and helpless. He had a defeatist and self-sacrificing attitude.

### Devotion to God

Gudjón makes frequent references to God in his diary:

22 November: 'What game is God playing with me?'

27 November: 'Dear Lord, give me the strength to admit my guilt and admit my responsibility.'

30 November: 'I hope God gives me energy, courage and memory to tell truthfully and correctly what happened so that there will be an answer and conclusion to the case soon.'

1 December: 'I only hope that God helps me tell everything I know to be right and true.'

31 December: 'I wish God would take me to Him, I am about to give up.'

**Note:** Gudjón is pleading to God for help and his faith seemed to have taken away his personal resource and resilience (i.e. he stopped being self-reliant, instead relying heavily on God for guidance and support).

## A HEURISTIC MODEL OF GUDJÓN'S CONFESSION

Figure 17.2 provides a heuristic model of memory distrust that describes the antecedents and processes involved in producing Gudjón's pressured-internalized false confession. The context provided the trigger for altering Gudjón's belief systems regarding the

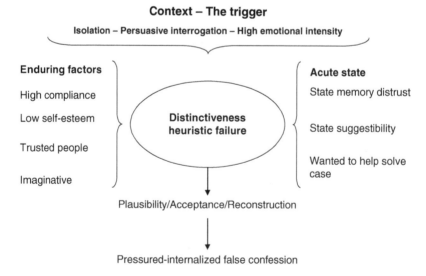

**Figure 17.2**   Heuristic model of Gudjón's pressured-internalized false confession

alleged offence. The three key components were confinement and social isolation, the investigators' guilt presumption and persuasive interrogation (i.e. the explicit or implicit communication from investigators about the seriousness of Gudjón's predicament, the investigator not believing his memory gaps, and the futility of his continued denials), and high emotional intensity. The high emotional intensity is well documented in Gudjón's diary, including his having found a way of killing himself if he felt he had no alternative. He had become confused, utterly exhausted, and had no resilience to resist the investigators' suggestions.

These three 'contextual' factors fed directly into Gudjón's cognitive appraisal of the situation and impacted on his pre-existing vulnerabilities, labelled as 'enduring factors':

• High compliance, particularly his eagerness to please, lack of direction in life, and defeatist attitude.
• Low self-esteem, which was well documented.
• Great trust and respect for people in authority.
• Vivid imagination, which made it easier for him to confabulate after he began to confess to involvement in Geirfinnur's murder.

His lawyer was apparently ineffective in supporting him because of his rarely being allowed to see Gudjón in private. There was also a strong self-destructive component in Gudjón's personality.

The contextual risk factors also activated 'acute state' factors. The key ones were:

• Gudjón gradually had begun to distrust his memory that he was not involved in the Geirfinnur case.
• This increased his delayed suggestibility.
• Gudjón's faith in the investigators and the investigative judge Birgir Thormar, and a sense of being valued if he could possibly help solve the case.

After the meeting with Sheriff Jón Ísberg six days after his arrest, Gudjón began to entertain the idea that perhaps he could help the police solve the case, and this gave him a sense of purpose in life, something he had lacked. A similar internal motivation of people with low self-esteem has been reported in a British case of memory distrust, unreliable confession, and confabulation involving Andrew Evans (Gudjonsson et al., 1999).

The enduring and acute state factors led to a distinctiveness heuristic and source monitoring failures, beautifully described in his diary on the first day of his tentative confession (i.e. 'I see no reason why I should not try to remember the case to the best of my abilities. It's a pity that I remember so little' – his having been persuaded that he was involved and not being able to insist: 'If I had done it I would remember it').

With continued guilt-presumptive interrogation, within a few days Gudjón accepted that it was *plausible* that he was involved and had knowledge about Geirfinnur's disappearance. Then he gradually *accepted* that he probably was involved, while having no clear memory of his being involved. With the help of the investigators, he tried to *reconstruct* what had allegedly happened, using his imagination and creativity, resulting in speculative self-incriminating statements and guess work (confabulation) regarding what had happened to Geirfinnur and the location of his body. There was pre-existing evidence that Gudjón had a compliant temperament and may have been vulnerable to suggestion.

Gudjón's diary shows that after a few days in custody he began to accept the investigators' suggestion that he was involved and could provide important information to help solve the case. The uncertainty about not knowing whether or not he was involved caused him distress, which was further exacerbated by his inability to produce any tangible memories that assisted with locating Geirfinnur's body. His distress reached the point of his seriously considering committing suicide.

After the lie detector test on 31 December 1976, seven weeks into his solitary confinement, Gudjón's belief in his involvement in the Geirfinnur case diminished and he was thinking of retracting his confession. This was met with fierce resistance by the investigators and he was brought back into a 'confession mode', which lasted until trial. The Court emphasized the fact that Gudjón had 'steadfastly stuck to his testimony' (Supreme Court Judgement, p. 22).

The *resolution* to Gudjón's belief in his innocence was a gradual process during his prison sentence, and he did not retract his confession until 19 years after his conviction. At the time I interviewed him in 2012, he stated he was now 100% convinced of his innocence and never had any clear memory of murdering Geirfinnur, but at the time of his confessions he was giving the investigators details (with their assistance) about what he thought might have happened, largely accepting the stories of his co-accused and the investigators' working 'hypothesis' of what had happened to Geirfinnur. However, there still appear to be occasions when doubts come temporarily into his mind.

## AFTER RELEASE FROM PRISON

Gudjón was released from prison on licence on 12 October 1981. According to an interview in *Morgunbladid* on 24 February 2017, following the positive outcome of the Icelandic Court Cases Review

Commission (see Chapter 12), he went to Denmark in the autumn of 1981 to study theology and returned to Iceland 15 years later and was elected as a priest in Snaefellsnes in western Iceland. Escaping to Denmark and then working in the rural part of Iceland helped him cope with the trauma of his arrest, solitary confinement, and conviction. He was responsible for a number of different churches over the years and had a successful career (Latham & Gudjonsson, 2016).


## CONCLUSIONS

In spite of Gudjón's high intelligence and good educational background, there had been disappointments in his life, and there probably had been untreated periods of depression. His high level of compliance led him into drug smuggling in the autumn of 1975, which had devastating effects on him. His diary shows that he explained his possible involvement in the Geirfinnur case as being due to his disturbed mental state ('Many of the things I have done in the recent years were madness'), lowering his threshold for plausibility of involvement in the case, and there appears to have been an underlying need to help the police ('I want to solve the case right away'). His memory distrust, source monitoring problems, and confabulation were made worse by his determination to help assist the investigation and the fact that he totally engrossed himself, day and night, in trying to remember what had happened to Geirfinnur and the location of the body, even spending many days attempting to write down for the investigators what he thought had happened. In spite of this, he never managed to come up with a credible story of what had happened to Geirfinnur on the slipway and the location of his body. He was not able to devise a strategy of daily distraction activities that could curtail his memory distrust, nor did he have the psychological resources or resilience to effectively mitigate his memory distrust.

A thematic analysis of his diary showed that he was too trusting of the investigators, was unable to assert himself, internalized his distress, had a defeatist and self-sacrificing attitude, and appealed to God for help rather than relying on himself. His diary describes well how his mind gradually became overborne and self-destructive. According to the heuristic model, he was a passive recipient of his coercive environment. Furthermore, his memory distrust provoked confabulation was not temporary and lasted several years.

In view of the overwhelming evidence that Gudjón was confessing to involvement in the Geirfinnur case without his having any memory of it, it is justified to describe his confession as a pressured-internalized false confession (see Chapter 4). His detailed and contemporaneous diary provided a unique insight into the process (i.e. gradual break-down in resistance to police suggestions and pressure) and mechanism (i.e. distinctiveness heuristic failure) that produces this type of false confession.

# 18

# Albert Skaftason's Memory Distrust Syndrome and Confession

*I'll help you boys as much as I can*[1]

## SALIENT POINTS

- On 22 February 1980 the Supreme Court convicted Albert of participating in interfering with the crime scene and sentenced him to 12 months in prison.
- It was alleged and accepted in Court that Albert was the driver in the Gudmundur case.
- He was the only one of the convicted persons not to undergo a pre-trial psychiatric/psychological evaluation.
- In childhood he had literacy, attentional, and sleep problems, and poor behavioural control, suggesting childhood attention deficit hyperactivity disorder (ADHD).
- During the investigation, Albert had serious problems remembering what had allegedly happened at Hamarsbraut 11 and where Gudmundur's body was hidden.

---

[1] A quote from a real-life case showing how eagerness to please can result in a false confession (Gudjonsson, 1995b).

---

*The Psychology of False Confessions: Forty Years of Science and Practice*, First Edition.
Gisli H. Gudjonsson.
© 2018 John Wiley & Sons Ltd. Published 2018 by John Wiley & Sons Ltd.

- Albert was extremely eager to assist the police. A psychologist and psychiatrist were hired to enhance his memory.
- His main vulnerabilities at the time of his interrogation were profound distrust of his memory and extreme compliance, leading to his giving a pressured-internalized false confession.
- His memory distrust syndrome has persisted since his solitary confinement in December 1975 and he is permanently left with the dread that one day he may remember what allegedly happened at Hamarsbraut 11.

Albert Skaftason was born in Reykjavík on 16 February 1955. He is the youngest of six siblings. His father was a musician. Albert was the only defendant for whom the court did not order a pretrial psychiatric evaluation, the reason for this omission being unknown. Therefore, little is known about his background history, personality, and mental state at the time of his detention in December 1975. Saevar brought him into the case during interrogation on 22 December 1975. He mentioned that on the night in question Gudmundur Einarsson, Kristján, and Tryggvi came to Hamarsbraut 11 and a fight broke out. Saevar said that he telephoned Albert after Gudmundur's death and he arrived later in his father's car, which was allegedly used to transport Gudmundur's body to a lava field south of Hafnarfjördur where the body was hidden.

With this information, the police immediately sought to collect Albert, who was visiting Seydisfjördur, a small town in the Eastern Region of Iceland, and bring him to Sídumúli Prison for questioning. The Sheriff in Seydisfjördur had refused to arrest Albert unless there was a warrant issued, neither of which happened. Instead two Reykjavík detectives, Eggert Bjarnason and Jón Gunnarsson, travelled overnight by a small private aeroplane to collect Albert from nearby Egilsstadir Airport and bring him to Reykjavík on a voluntary basis to assist the police with their enquiries. Albert was intending to spend the Christmas holiday with his wife at the time and her family in Seydisfjördur.

Albert was clocked in at Sídumúli Prison at 05.00 on 23 December. At the time, he had the status of a witness, but he was undoubtedly aware of the seriousness of the situation. He was not technically under arrest, but he would undoubtedly have been arrested if he had refused to accompany the detectives to Reykjavík. The fact that he was brought to Reykjavík overnight and then locked up in Sídumúli Prison emphasized the seriousness of the situation. It was a harsh way of treating a witness. Albert had no criminal convictions, but the police knew that he was a close friend of Saevar and Kristján, and the three of them were old school friends.

In the middle of February 1974, the Reykjavík police were looking for Albert and Kristján, who were suspected of drug-related offences.[2] As I will discuss below, Albert's weakness was alcohol and drugs, and these are relevant to how quickly he developed memory distrust syndrome while in custody at Síðumúli Prison in December 1975, which continued throughout the case.

## ALBERT'S INTERROGATION

Albert was kept in Síðumúli Prison for over eight hours before he was questioned. Detective Eggert Bjarnason questioned him between 13.55 and 17.10. He was informed that Saevar had given a statement concerning what had happened at Hamarsbraut 11 in the early hours of 27 January 1974. Albert referred to frequently keeping company with Saevar, Kristján, and Tryggvi and at the time he had access to his father's yellow Toyota. The four of them had often been in the car together.

After four days in solitary confinement, Albert went berserk in his cell and broke a chair. He was handcuffed and his legs shackled until he had calmed down. This showed the extreme stress he was under in custody and his inability to cope with his predicament.

On 7 March 1976, Albert appeared before Örn Höskuldsson in a virtual court at Síðumúli Prison and reported that he was now certain that there were two separate trips with Gudmundur's body (implying it was moved after the first burial), accompanied by Saevar, Kristján, and Tryggvi. He said he could not remember where it was taken the first time but thought it might have been subsequently moved south to Kúagerdi, in Reykjanes. The reason for Albert referring to the body being removed arose because of a fundamental problem with Albert's original statement. At the time of Gudmundur's disappearance, Albert's father had a Volkswagen and only purchased a Toyota later that year. In view of this mistake, Albert is said to have requested an interview with the police to correct this mistake.[3] After giving his statement on 19 March 1976, he was released from custody.

Albert remained in solitary confinement for 88 days (23 December 1975 to 19 March 1976) in Síðumúli Prison.[4] During this time he was

---

[2] Evidence Book II, p. 203.
[3] Evidence Book I, pp. 92–94.
[4] ICCRC Report, 2017, Albert Skaftason, Paragraph 1105.

428    The Psychology of False Confessions

questioned by police on 26 occasions for a total of 17 hours, and participated in 16 suspects' face-to-face confrontations (Gudjonsson et al., 2014). He was released from prison on licence on 12 March 1981.

## MEMORY ENHANCEMENT

In view of Albert's serious memory problems, the police hired a psychologist, Geir Vilhjálmsson, 'to facilitate recovery of his memory regarding the details of the car trip with his companions Saevar, Kristján, and Tryggvi' (Working Group Report, 2013, p. 418). After an initial assessment interview on 9 March, four memory enhancement sessions took place at Síðumúli Prison – on 11, 13, 15, and 19 March 1976. In all, the five sessions lasted for a total of 10 hours.[5] These were labelled *sefjunarfundir*, which implies mental relaxation and suggestive induction akin to hypnosis.[6] Two hours after the last psychological session, the police interrogated Albert and he gave a crucial statement, now claiming that he had carried Gudmundur's body in a Volkswagen in the early hours of 27 January 1974, not a Toyota as he had said in his first statement. Albert was then released from custody, which had lasted from 23 December 1975 to 19 March 1976.

Immediately after the session on 13 March the psychologist went with Albert, Detective Sigurbjörn Víðir, and investigative judge Örn Höskuldsson on an 'expedition', presumably to identify the route taken with Gudmundur's body and the location of his burial site.

A psychiatrist, Dr Jakob Jónasson, attempted to hypnotize Albert, but with limited success: he was not particularly responsive to the hypnotic induction procedure. I remember Dr Jónasson well from the 1970s when he was one of Iceland's leading experts on hypnosis.

Geir Vilhjálmsson's memory enhancement sessions were not labelled as hypnosis, but they appear to have involved similar components, such as altering Albert's state of consciousness through induction and suggestion and having him 'relive' what had allegedly taken place at the time of Gudmundur's disappearance. According to the Commission, such a procedure inevitably affects the potential credibility of the information obtained.[7]

---

[5] ICCRC Report, 2017, Albert Skaftason, Paragraph 1131.
[6] ICCRC Report, 2017, Albert Skaftason, Paragraph 1128.
[7] ICCRC Report, 2017, Albert Skaftason, Paragraph 1132.

Geir Vilhjálmsson concluded in his report:

> It is without doubt that the above-mentioned procedure was effective in activating Albert's memory potential considerably, showing from the tests carried out, that he obtained results of just over 50% in correctly arranging week days and months between one and a half and two and a half years back in time, in contrast to the 14% expected by chance. This 50% error margin shows on the other hand of course that we can expect errors in his testimony in the hypnotic state and in view of this, information elicited during the sessions must be treated with similar caution to that of other testimony.
>
> (Working Group Report, 2013, p. 419)

With regard to the trip to the aquarium, the psychologist advised the police:

> If a thorough search between this road and the aluminium factory was unsuccessful then it may be worth searching on the other side of the Keflavíkurvegur between the aluminium factory and the aquarium. [...] If this search was unsuccessful it would be possible to induce in Albert an even deeper calming state in order to attempt to elicit further information from him.
>
> (Working Group Report, 2013, p. 419)

We know that nothing useful emerged from these *sefjunarfundir* (hypnotic induction-related sessions) to advance the case and they are likely to have confused Albert even more. The Commission was very critical of the use of this procedure. In Geir Vilhjálmsson's defence, he was doing his best to assist with a difficult case. Neither should the police be criticized for hiring Mr Vilhjálmsson and Dr Jónasson.

In the 1970s, hypnosis was often used in the UK to facilitate memory in witnesses (Gudjonsson, 1992a; Gudjonsson & Young, 2015). In the 1980s, the use of hypnosis to enhance memory came under close scrutiny (Gudjonsson & Young, 2015) and the British Psychological Society advised psychologists that its use for this purpose 'should be treated with the utmost caution' (British Psychological Society, 2001, p. 8).

## ALBERT'S ACCOUNT OF EVENTS, AND HIS PERSONALITY

Albert repeatedly refused to meet with the Working Group in 2012, but agreed to meet me alone and that the Working Group could then use the information he gave to me in that interview. He said that Erla had encouraged him to speak to me and he agreed because he trusted me.

This interview took place on 7 February 2012. I asked him to describe the antecedents to his arrest on 23 December 1975. He told the story as follows:

• When first contacted by the police he was not told why they wanted to speak to him, but he suspected it was in connection with some offences. When onboard the plane from Egilsstadir to Reykjavík he was told that it concerned a serious case. When he arrived in Sídumúli Prison he was informed that it involved the Gudmundur Einarsson case. At the time he did not know who Gudmundur was and knew nothing about his disappearance. The detectives had explained to him the involvement of the others, all of whom he knew well. He was also told that this was a very serious matter and that he would not be released from Sídumúli Prison until he had given a confession statement about what had happened (i.e. an explicit threat of solitary confinement, a common feature in the Gudmundur and Geirfinnur cases).

• Initially, Albert repeatedly told the police that he could not be involved, because he could not remember anything about it. As the interrogation progressed he gradually thought that it was possible that he might have been present at Hamarsbraut 11 on the night in question (i.e. *plausibility*). He had been there before and thought it possible that Kristján and Tryggvi were involved, because he had seen them get into fights before. He found it more difficult to believe that Saevar was directly involved, but he sometimes used Kristján and Tryggvi to do the dirty work for him, such as threatening people or beating them up to extract money from them. Albert had often driven Saevar around and thought Saevar, Kristján, and Tryggvi might be involved in Gudmundur's disappearance.

• Over time, his testimony caused major problems, because he could never remember what had actually happened. His statements were built on suggestions from the investigators. They told him that his memory loss was due to his having experienced something he did not want to remember.[8] The investigators sought the assistance of a psychologist and psychiatrist, but nothing useful came out of this.

• After about three months in solitary confinement, Albert was about 50% sure he was involved, but still could not recall what had actually happened. He could not give the investigators a detailed and coherent story, because he could not remember anything.

• On 3 May 1977, Albert attended court for a confrontation with a new witness in the Gudmundur case, Gunnar Jónsson. Albert told me

---

[8] Erla also claimed a similar suggestion from the investigators (see Chapter 14).

that his role was to convince Gunnar that he had been with him at Hamarsbraut 11 in the early hours of 27 January 1974, but Gunnar insisted that he could not remember being at Hamarsbraut 11 at the time.

Towards the end of our interview in 2012, I asked Albert to describe his personality. He said he was a good and obliging person, who often got into difficulties because he had problems saying no to people. He described himself as a big 'yes man', implying an extremely high level of compliance. He said he had always been like that. He said that all his life he had had a poor memory, with no confidence in it. He said his greatest fear in life after being interrogated by the police and kept in solitary confinement in Síðumúli Prison was that he had committed a crime or witnessed something and that the memory of it would eventually emerge.

I interviewed Albert again on 15 May 2015 and 6 March 2017 at his favourite coffee house, Cafe Retro, on the west side of Reykjavík over-looking the harbour. He said he still lived with the fear that perhaps he had witnessed something at Hamarsbraut 11, although he still had no memory of actually being involved in Gudmundur's disappearance. He said that after meeting me in 2012 his fear was substantially reduced, but not eliminated altogether.

Albert said that at the time of the Gudmundur investigation he had been heavily involved in substance misuse, which included alcohol and drugs (mainly cannabis and LSD) from his early teens onward. He had problems coping with school work due to attentional and literacy problems. He truanted a lot and described himself as 'impressionable' and had poor self-esteem. He described poor behavioural control, including high levels of impulsivity, and felt his mind was rushing all the time (he described having problems stopping his flight of ideas). He had slept poorly from the age of about eight. He had always lacked confidence in his memory. At one point he commented that he thought he had ADHD but said he now had better control over his symptoms than when he was younger. When I asked Albert to describe his current symptoms it was evident that he was still experiencing symptoms of ADHD, remaining inattentive, impulsive, and hyperactive. He felt habitually restless and had to keep himself constantly occupied. He became bored easily and could not rest and keep still while on holiday; sunbathing in Spain was not for him, he commented. He advised me that when we arranged to meet again I should telephone him 15 minutes before the appointment in case he had forgotten it!

Albert said the investigators told him he would not be released from Síðumúli Prison until he 'confessed'. He saw no alternative but to try to cooperate and agree with their suggestions, which he considered *plausible* at the time (i.e. he thought Saevar, Kristján, and Tryggvi were capable of attacking Gudmundur as the police had suggested), but the investigators were very concerned about his poor memory and therefore brought in the psychologist and psychiatrist, which did not help. According to Albert, the interrogation was subtle from the beginning and he gradually accepted the scenarios the investigators presented to him, while having no actual memory of the night of Gudmundur's disappearance. The investigators kept telling him: 'It's possible that you were there, isn't it?'

## A HEURISTIC MODEL OF ALBERT'S CONFESSION

Figure 18.1 provides a heuristic model of memory distrust that describes the antecedents and processes involved in producing Albert's pressured-internalized false confession. Having conducted further work on the case since the Working Group Report (i.e. interviewing Albert again, studying all the relevant documents in the case in more detail, and reading the detailed ICCRC Report), I was persuaded that Albert's confession was highly likely to be 'false' (i.e. not due to a real memory).

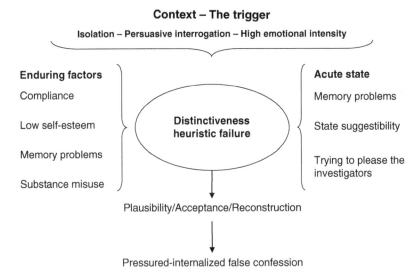

**Figure 18.1**    Heuristic model of Albert's pressured-internalized false confession

The context provided the 'trigger' for altering Albert's belief systems regarding the alleged offence. The three key components were confinement (i.e. isolation in Síðumúli Prison for several hours), the investigators' guilt presumption and persuasive interrogation (i.e. the explicit or implicit communication from investigators about the seriousness of Albert's predicament and that he would not be released until he confessed), and high emotional intensity.

With regard to the confinement, there are two issues that need to be addressed. Firstly, according to the police, Albert was brought to Síðumúli Prison as a witness and he was technically not under arrest. Whether Albert was technically not under arrest was of no importance to his frame of mind. He would have known that he had no choice but to accompany the police to Reykjavík for questioning. Once he was on the plane he knew the offence was serious, which was confirmed when he arrived at Síðumúli Prison to be told that it involved the disappearance of Gudmundur Einarsson. At the time, the police had excellent facilities at their Headquarters for interviewing witnesses and suspects. Taking a witness to the prison was coercive. The implicit message communicated to Albert was the seriousness of his predicament and this ensured his maximum compliance and cooperation. He was also allegedly threatened that he would be locked up in Síðumúli Prison if he did not 'confess'.

The second issue was that Albert's memory distrust syndrome developed within hours of his being brought to Síðumúli Prison, and he confessed later the same day, after being questioned for over three hours (his statement was taken between 13.55 and 17.10). Síðumúli Prison custody record shows that Albert was taken out of the building at 14.25 for an 'expedition', which probably involved a trip to the alleged crime scene to refresh his memory. By the time Albert was interviewed he had been waiting in the prison for over eight hours. In our early research on the vulnerability of people detained at police stations, we found that waiting and not knowing what was going on, even if only for a short while, was extremely distressing for many detainees (Gudjonsson et al., 1993). Waiting for over eight hours to be interviewed, as in Albert's case, would have been particularly distressing. Even among mentally healthy and high functioning adults, under certain circumstances, memory distrust syndrome may develop within hours in police custody (e.g. Hain, 2012).

The high emotional intensity associated with Albert's detention is evident from the Síðumúli Prison custody record, where after four days in solitary confinement Albert went 'berserk' in his cell and had to be restrained.

The important thing to remember about Albert's logged interrogations is that he remained very vague, tentative, and hesitant in his accounts, often giving conflicting accounts over time (Working Group Report, 2013), providing evidence that he was reporting an event that was not based on any real memory.

The three contextual triggers fed directly into Albert's cognitive appraisal of the situation and impacted on his pre-existing vulnerabilities, labelled as 'enduring factors':

- High compliance, particularly his eagerness to please others.
- Low self-esteem.
- Poor memory.
- Long-standing substance misuse.

According to the model, Albert's substance abuse made him particularly vulnerable to developing memory distrust syndrome when his memory for events was challenged (Gudjonsson & MacKeith, 1982).

The contextual risk factors also activated 'acute state' factors. The key ones were:

- Albert had begun to distrust his belief that he was not involved in the Gudmundur case and this happened quite quickly.
- This increased his delayed suggestibility.
- Albert was trying hard to cooperate fully with the investigators.

The enduring and acute state factors resulted in Albert not being able to critically scrutinize the police scenario and its origin. His key vulnerability was that he had a long-standing general distrust of his memory, which appears to have developed early in life (e.g. his reported attentional, memory, and dyslexia difficulties in childhood), and this became exacerbated by subsequent substance misuse. When Albert's memory was challenged he could not exclude the possibility that the event had occurred, even though he could not remember it, because he lacked confidence both in his memory and in himself. This combined with his high level of compliance speeded up the distinctiveness heuristic failure and explains why it happened so early during his detention. Importantly, he never properly incorporated the police scenario of what happened at Hamarsbraut 11 into his recollection, but merely accepted it. However, on occasions he added details to the story that had the ring of plausibility (e.g. during his first interview he reported feeling the car rock a little as something heavy was put in the boot of his car).

In summary, the shock of being brought to Sídumúli Prison, being told that he would not leave the prison until he 'confessed', his habitual distrust of his memory and high compliance, his belief that Saevar, Kristján, and Tryggvi were capable of vicious assaults on people, and poor recollection of what he was doing at the time of Gudmundur's disappearance (i.e. weak memory trace) quickly set the memory distrust syndrome in full motion. He soon accepted that it was plausible that he was a witness to Gudmundur's disappearance, and then accepted that he probably was involved, while having no clear memory of his role. He never fully accepted his involvement, but at its peak after three months in custody, he said he was about 50% sure the event had occurred.

Albert did not retract his confession until 1997, when he did so in the course of Saevar's attempts for appeal.[9] However, he has never been completely sure he had not witnessed something at Hamarsbraut 11. When I interviewed him in May 2015, he said he was now over 90% sure that he was not involved, but the remaining 10% uncertainty is uncomfortably high for him to live with, especially when his greatest fear is that memories of what may have taken place at Hamarsbraut 11 may flood back into consciousness at some time in the future. This is something he has had to live with for over 40 years. It is unlikely that Albert's fear can ever be completely dispelled, unless the real facts about Gudmundur's disappearance can be ascertained.

## CONCLUSIONS

In the light of the current analysis, it is reasonable to describe Albert's confession as a pressured-internalized false confession. I have discovered nothing to suggest that Albert's confession represented a genuine memory of an observed event. His 88 days in solitary confinement, 26 police interviews, and 11 crime scene visits produced no evidence that could be independently corroborated. The seriousness of Albert's memory problems can be seen from his police interviews and the fact that the police hired a psychologist and a psychiatrist in an attempt to enhance his memory about what had happened to Gudmundur.

Albert's descriptions were consistently vague, tentative, and hesitant. In his first interview he made the basic error of saying he had gone to Hamarsbraut 11 in his father's Toyota, rather than the Volkswagen car his father actually owned at the time. This in turn led to a necessary change in his story of the body not fitting in the boot, given that in the Volkswagen Beetle, storage space was in the front

---

[9] In an interview with Saevar's defence lawyer Ragnar Adalsteinsson on 19 January 1997, Albert gave a very good description of his memory distrust syndrome and stated that he could not claim (fullyrt) that he had been at Hamarsbraut 11 in the early hours of Sunday 27 January 1974 (see ICCRC Report, 2017, Albert Skaftason, Paragraph 792).

rather than the back of the car. Instead, he now said the body had to be put on the floor in the back of the car with Kristján and Tryggvi sitting with their feet on it. Albert had now made two trips with his comrades, one to the Hafnarfjördur lava field in the Volkswagen on the night of Gudmundur's death and again later in the summer of 1974 when the body was removed from the lava field in the Toyota car to some unidentified place. Various places were mentioned, including two graveyards, one in Reykjavík and another one in Hafnarfjördur, but nothing was ever found. The Supreme Court wisely decided not to rely on Albert's and his comrades' testimony regarding the specific location of Gudmundur's body.

I am in no doubt that at the time of his arrest in the Gudmundur case, Albert was extremely vulnerable to police suggestions and pressure. From his description of himself as having serious attentional and memory problems in childhood, difficulties with sleep, dyslexia, truancy, and poor behavioural control, it is likely that he had childhood ADHD, whose primary symptoms were still present to some extent in adulthood. His early involvement in substance misuse (i.e. excessive alcohol consumption and illicit drugs) undoubtedly exacerbated his pre-existing memory and confidence difficulties. According to Albert, ADHD has been found in members of his family.

Albert's refusal to meet members of the Working Group in 2012 shows the seriousness of his residual memory distrust syndrome. Albert had trusted the police in the 1970s, accepted their suggestions, and complied with their requests for information about something he could not recall, only to find himself convicted of a criminal offence and having to serve a prison sentence. He has been permanently left with the dread that one day he might suddenly remember what happened at Hamarsbraut 11. Albert's memory distrust syndrome regarding the Gudmundur case now appears to be a lifelong condition, adversely affecting his quality of life. His nightmare is never ending.

# Conclusions

*Deep down, I knew it didn't happen*[1]

## SCIENCE AND PRACTICE – THE BEGINNING

Until the 1980s little was known about the psychology of false confessions, including how they were elicited, the mechanism and processes involved, and how they could be identified. This is well illustrated by Barrie Irving's comment in 1980 that 'At present it is not even possible to be certain about how a confession which is known to be false came to be made' (Irving & Hilgendorf, 1980, pp. 25–26).

At the time, there was general reluctance to accept that suspects would confess falsely to serious crimes that they had not committed, unless they suffered from a mental disorder, such as mental illness or intellectual disability. Dr James MacKeith and I became aware of this scepticism among some colleagues when we presented a paper on false confessions at The Stockholm Symposium on Witness Psychology in September 1981 and introduced the concept of 'memory distrust syndrome'. Memory distrust syndrome occurs when people develop

---

[1] A comment Erla Bolladóttir made in an interview with the *Guardian* newspaper, 4 August 2017.

*The Psychology of False Confessions: Forty Years of Science and Practice*, First Edition.
Gisli H. Gudjonsson.
© 2018 John Wiley & Sons Ltd. Published 2018 by John Wiley & Sons Ltd.

profound distrust of their own memory, usually under intensive interrogation, that may cause them to confess to a crime they did not commit, in spite of having no distinct memory of it.

Whether or not memory distrust syndrome results in a false confession depends on a number of interacting factors. According to the
*heuristic model* developed in this book, custodial risk factors may
activate both enduring and state vulnerability factors, which under
certain circumstances lead to failure in the 'distinctiveness heuristic'
(i.e. a state of mental confusion and self-doubt where the person is no
longer able to recall that he/she had not committed or witnessed the
crime). Once there has been failure in the 'distinctiveness heuristic',
this is usually followed by thoughts of *plausibility* (i.e. it could
have happened), leading to *acceptance* (i.e. an admission) and crime
*reconstruction* (i.e. an internalized false confession).

The concept of memory distrust syndrome has proved extremely
helpful in the evaluation of cases involving pressured-internalized
false confessions, which is vividly illustrated throughout the book. It is
most typically associated with interrogation-induced false confessions
but can in exceptional circumstances be self-induced such as in the
case of Andrew Evans whose false confession was elicited by a dream
(Gudjonsson et al., 1999).

High profile cases of disputed confessions in the UK in the mid-
1970s, late 1980s, and early 1990s led the way to more receptive attitudes among the police and judiciary following the successful appeals
of three young persons in the Confait case (October 1975), the 'Guildford
Four' (October 1989), the 'Birmingham Six' (March 1991), in the Judith
Ward case (one person appealing) (May 1992), the 'Tottenham Three'
(November 1992), and the 'Cardiff Three' (December 1992).

These six landmark cases broadened the legal, police practice, and
scientific landscape. The Confait case led to the setting up of the Royal
Commission on Criminal Procedure and the creation of the Police and
Criminal Evidence Act and its Codes of Practice. The new legislation
and police practice were based in part on an impressive research
evidence base from the late 1970s. The acquittals of the Guildford Four
raised awareness of police impropriety, psychological vulnerabilities
during questioning, and false confessions. It opened the way to justice
in other cases, including the Birmingham Six. Following the acquittal
of the Birmingham Six, the Home Secretary set up the Royal
Commission on Criminal Justice, and the creation of the Criminal
Cases Review Commission followed.

In the case of Engin Raghip, expert psychological evidence was admitted on appeal and proved influential in overturning a conviction in a
case of disputed confession. The judgement broadened the criteria for

the admissibility of psychological evidence to cases involving the personality of the defendant(s), more specifically interrogative suggestibility and compliance measures and implied that the lower courts should not confine admissibility to an arbitrary IQ point of 69. This landmark judgement has influenced successful appeals in a large number of other cases. It was a major victory for clinical forensic psychology.

In response to these miscarriages of justice, the PEACE Model was developed as a collaborative project across the disciplines of policing, psychology, and law. It has been in continuous use in the UK since 1993, when it was rolled out as part of a national training package for police officers. It consists of an information-gathering approach that focuses on establishing rapport with interviewees, and uses open-ended questions to elicit information and establish evidence of either guilt or innocence. It is a science-based, fact-finding approach with an emphasis on professionalism, transparency, and accountability. In view of this it is better described as *investigative interviewing* rather than *interrogation* (Oxburgh, Fahsing, et al., 2016).

In 1976 important developments were taking place in the USA with Peter Reilly being cleared of murdering his mother three years previously. The case provides an excellent example of the *coerced-internalized* type of false confession, which is one of the three types identified by Saul Kassin and Lawrence Wrightsman in their groundbreaking work.[2] The other two types are *voluntary* and *coerced-compliant* types. Their threefold classification was partly inspired by Hugo Münsterberg's (1908) early work. In spite of some criticisms, their classification has been hugely influential in stimulating research and providing a framework for practice. The theoretical developments of Richard Ofshe and Richard Leo in the late 1990s have also added considerably to understanding the psychology of police-coerced false confessions. Their model shows the complexities of false confessions and the potential overlap with true coerced confessions.

## THE DEVELOPMENT OF THE SCIENCE

### Interrogation

Research into interrogation tactics and false confessions has increased exponentially since the 1990s, following Irving's (1980) pioneering observational study at Brighton Police Station and early attempts to

[2] I prefer the use of the terms *pressured-internalized* and *pressured-compliant*, because there may be stress and pressure without coercion.

understand the psychological approaches to interrogation and confession (Irving & Hilgendorf, 1980), and Leo's (1994, 1996) observational study of interrogation tactics in the USA. These studies set the scene for the large number of studies that have followed and continue to the present day. Most of the influential studies have been conducted in the UK and USA (Kelly et al., 2013). Much less is known about investigative interviewing and interrogation in other countries, especially in the Middle and Far East (Walsh, Redlich, et al., 2016). The two dominant approaches in the Western countries are the Reid Technique, practiced in the USA and parts of Canada, and the PEACE Model, practiced in England (Oxburgh, Fahsing, et al., 2016).

The electronic recording of police interviews, now mandatory in the UK, and greater access to such recordings for research purposes has hugely improved our understanding of the dynamics of interrogation, and underlined the risk of certain tactics producing false confessions. In the late 1980s and early 1990s, police officers in the UK sometimes used aspects of the Reid Technique to break down resistance in serious cases, which provided an opportunity for a unique scientific analysis of the dynamics of coercive interrogation.

In the first study of its kind, Pearse and Gudjonsson (1999, 2003), used factor analysis to identify the tactics used by police to break down resistance and obtain confessions in serious criminal cases, and the suspects' reactions to these tactics. This study clearly showed how tactics and reactions interact and vary over time. It was the first to demonstrate empirically the dynamic and interactive nature of police interviews. It showed that it is not merely a question of what tactics are used, but when and how they are used also matters. This methodology allowed us to discriminate between the tactics used, distinguishing between 'overbearing' tactics (e.g. intimidation, psychological manipulation, and exaggeration of evidence) and a more 'sensitive' style of interviewing (e.g. appeal and soft challenges). The greater the number and frequency of 'overbearing' tactics, the more likely it was that the outcome resulted in acquittal, which occurred in 50% of the cases. The findings suggested, for example, that what legitimately breaks down resistance in sex offences cases is reassurance and shame reduction, delivered in a low tone, yet firmly emphasizing the 'true' evidence in the case.

A proper evaluation of coercive tactics involves having an electronic recording of the entire interrogation, because tactics involving *minimization* and *maximization*, which are the two most commonly used tactics in the Reid Technique, are typically communicated through subtle but influential use of language (Gudjonsson & MacKeith, 1994; Ofshe & Leo, 1997a).

Recently, a taxonomy of interrogation tactics has been developed, reflecting their dynamic nature (Kelly et al., 2013). This has been followed up by empirical research, showing the importance of subtle presentation of evidence and good rapport-building as a way of maximizing cooperation and increasing the likelihood of a confession (Kelly et al., 2016). The taxonomy has yet to be applied specifically to false confessions.

What is now needed is research that focuses more explicitly on the dynamics (i.e. the interplay between the interrogator and the suspect) that cause different types of false confession during interrogation. Ofshe and Leo (1997a, 1997b) argue that similar coercive techniques break down resistance in guilty and innocent suspects, but they differ in terms of the post-event information they are able to provide. The two groups may also differ in the duration of interrogation and the amount of pressure needed to get them to confess (Redlich et al., 2011).

Interrogations involving false confessions tend to be of long duration, mostly over six hours (Drizin & Leo, 2004; Perske, 2008), but may be considerably shorter, especially when suspects are psychologically vulnerable (Gudjonsson, 2003a). For example, in the Confait case, all three suspects confessed to murder within two and a half hours of their detention (Irving & McKenzie, 1989).

In the UK, the presence of a legal representative during interrogation does not always provide satisfactory protection against false confession (Ede & Shepherd, 2000; Pearse & Gudjonsson, 2003). The situation for suspects is complicated by the fact that adverse inferences can be drawn from their silence, which means they are encouraged to answer questions (Gudjonsson, 2003a; Morgan & Stephenson, 1994).

The position is different in the USA, because no adverse inferences are drawn from silence and the presence of a lawyer typically results in no interview taking place (Leo, 2008). In theory this provides a stronger protection against self-incrimination, but in practice is of little benefit in cases of false confessions because of the high proportion of suspects who waive their Miranda rights (Leo, 1998, 2008).

Bull and Soukara (2010) have shown that the implementation of the PEACE Model in the UK has substantially reduced coerced interrogations and the risk of false confession, while not adversely affecting the confession rate. They recommend that police organizations around the world consider adopting this information gathering approach and its associated training programmes as a way of improving fairness and justice. This is a legitimate recommendation considering that the UK information gathering approach has proved superior to the American accusatorial approach in terms of eliciting more accurate information and fewer false confessions (Meissner et al., 2010, 2012, 2014; Vrij et al., 2014).

Pearse and Gudjonsson (2016) have emphasized the need for inter-viewers to maintain an open mind and be aware of their own cognitive biases and emotional reactions to the interviewee and the process itself.

## Miscarriage of Justice

False confessions occur in about 14% to 25% of cases of miscarriage of justice in the USA (Drizin & Leo, 2004). DNA exonerations in the USA since 1989 have shown that about 25% of those involved false admis-sions or confessions. These comprised almost exclusively murder and rape cases, where DNA evidence is most readily available and only represent the 'tip of the iceberg' of overall false confessions. This means they are likely to give a misleading picture of the overall pattern of false confessions within the criminal justice system.

Drizin and Leo (2004) analysed 125 cases of proven interrogation-induced false confessions in the USA, showing that false confessions are more common than previously thought, corroborating what I had argued previously (Gudjonsson, 1992a, 2003a). The false confessions obtained were so powerful that they resulted in convictions in 81% of disputed cases that went for trial. In addition, many other defendants had pleaded guilty, mainly in order to avoid a more severe penalty. The authors concluded that 'virtually all false confessions in America occur because of psychologically coercive interrogation methods and strategies, police overreaching and/or police misconduct' (Drizin & Leo, 2004, p. 995). Drizin and Leo point to the added vulnerabilities of suspects with intellectual disabilities and juveniles, who were both construed as vulnerable because of their eagerness to please people in authority, impulsivity, immaturity, and impaired decision-making.

The main limitation of this study is that it does not discuss the vulnerabilities of those who were neither juveniles nor intellectually disadvantaged. Borchard (1932) puts the essence of psychological vulnerabilities during interrogation in a nutshell when he states: 'The influence of the stronger mind upon the weaker often produces, by persuasion or suggestion, the desired result' (p. xviii). Both situational and personal risk factors are relevant, highlighted by my own work (Gudjonsson, 2003a, 2010a) and that of Davis and Leo (2012, 2013). A detailed analysis of 34 miscarriage of justice cases in the UK, which were successfully appealed between 1989 and 2009, showed that rather than mental disorders per se, the principal reason for the confession was the inability to cope with the interrogation and custodial pres-sures, often caused by high suggestibility and compliance.

It is a mistake to assume that false confessions are primarily con-fined to people with intellectual disabilities and juveniles, although these are salient risk factors. There is now considerable evidence that suspects with other conditions, such as attention deficit hyperactivity disorder (ADHD), are also at heightened risk of giving a false confession. Even normal individuals, in certain circumstances, as Münsterberg (1908) argued over 100 years ago, can be manipulated into giving a false confession to serious crimes such as murder. Most people have some vulnerability, which if known to police, can be manipulated to induce a false confession.

Studies have generally not separated out the various types of false confession, which is probably due to the lack of relevant information in news reports and case files.

The *pressured-compliant* type is undoubtedly most common in cases of miscarriage of justice, followed by the *pressured-internalized* type, which from my case files of 46 successful appellants in 34 UK cases, involved six (13.0%) individuals (Gudjonsson, 2010a).

In our study of 62 false confessors among Icelandic prisoners, nine (14.5%) were of the *internalized* type, associated with heightened suggestibility and confabulation (Sigurdsson & Gudjonsson, 1996a).

Ofshe (1989) argues on the basis of four case studies that the primary mechanism of the *pressured-internalized* type consists of inducing self-doubt and confusion in the mind of suspects, which permits the alteration in their perception of reality. This provided an excellent early framework for understanding this type of false confession, which I have developed further in this book and briefly discuss at the end of this chapter after reviewing the Gudmundur and Geirfinnur cases.

## False Confessions

Most investigations and surveys of false confessions have been conducted in Iceland because of my collaborative work with Jón Fridrik Sigurdsson and other colleagues at Reykjavík University. Nine studies conducted among pupils in their final three years of compulsory schooling and those in further education show that the rate of reported false confession of those interrogated by the police was on average over 9%. This figure represents a lifetime prevalence rate among young persons; many reported more than one false confession.

A consistent finding from anecdotal and research studies is that young persons, particularly juveniles, are more likely to confess falsely than older suspects. The main reason appears to be that they are less robust in resisting police pressure because of their relative immaturity and inexperience. It is also known that juveniles are more susceptible to interrogative pressure than older persons (Gudjonsson, 2003a). Young persons are also particularly likely to 'take on a case' for a peer, and these cases are 'hidden' within the criminal justice system because they are rarely retracted.

There have been four prison studies: three in Iceland and one in Scotland, where the lifetime prevalence rates among prisoners of reported false confessions have ranged between 11.8% and 33.4% with many reporting more than one false confession. A similar American study among mentally ill 'offenders' found a lifetime prevalence rate of 22%, or 4.4% per interrogation. There was also a high rate of false pleas in this study, corroborating Drizin and Leo's (2004) and Garrett's (2011) findings that innocent defendants sometimes plead guilty to crimes because of plea bargaining or because they could see no other way out of their predicament than to accept a guilty plea.

The reasons given for those false confessions across the community and prison studies typically consist of protecting the real perpetrator, which do not feature in studies of wrongful convictions, and succumbing to police pressure. It is also evident from our research that both the base rate of guilt and false confessions varied considerably across countries. Avoidance of custody was commonly reported in Iceland as a reason for the false confession, but not so much in other countries, where the focus was more on terminating the interrogation. This undoubtedly relates to the ready availability of solitary confinement of suspects in Iceland, which the European Committee for the Prevention of Torture and Inhuman or Degrading Treatment or Punishment has strongly criticized.

There is now extensive evidence that many people detained at police stations for questioning are psychologically vulnerable to giving false confessions, under certain circumstances, because of low IQ, ADHD, a history of substance misuse, past trauma, and disturbed mental state, which typically increase their level of suggestibility and/or compliance. I have identified 17 areas of situational and personal vulnerabilities in this book that increase the risk of false confession. Innocence itself may be a risk factor when suspects focus primarily on the immediate effect of confessing (e.g. completing the interrogation, being released from custody) and naively waiving any legal (e.g. Miranda) rights, believing that truth and justice will always prevail and their lawyer will sort it out for them.

The presence of personal vulnerabilities needs to be interpreted within the context of the totality of evidence in the case, particularly the situational factors associated with the interrogation and confinement. The fact that the suspect has a low IQ, a history of trauma, and is suggestible does not by itself necessarily undermine the reliability of the confession.

When there is little or no tangible evidence against the suspect, the interrogation techniques found to be successful in breaking down resistance among guilty suspects are similar to those that are associated with eliciting false confessions. The risks of false confession are greatest when the police are guilt-presumptive and use psychological manipulation, deception, and coercive techniques to break down denials in psychologically vulnerable suspects.

The post-admission narrative is a potentially powerful discriminant between true and false confessions, provided the police have not either wittingly or unwittingly communicated the 'special knowledge' to the suspect. Unfortunately, cases of proven false confession show that they typically include salient details that must have originated from the police, something the police invariably deny at trial. The most powerful special knowledge is when the suspect reveals information that the police did not know, such as the location of the murder weapon or the body of the victim.

There are no definitive markers of false confession that can be applied across all cases. Each case needs to be considered on its own merit. The larger the number of risk factors involved, and the greater their salience, the higher the risk of false confession.

A great deal has been learned about the psychology of false confessions over the past three decades, particularly with regard to salient risk factors, but we still need to learn more about the dynamic and interactive processes that provide the causal link between context, situational and personal risk factors, and false confessions. The current evidence suggests that these are different for *voluntary*, *pressured-internalized*, and *pressured-compliant* false confessions. These are best investigated by the use of case-study methodology, which I have discussed in this book.

Finally, once false confessions are extracted, they typically contaminate other evidence and are very difficult to correct during the criminal justice process. The focus should be on preventing false confessions happening in the first place (Gudjonsson, 1992b). Based on my own work and the suggestions of Meissner and Lassiter (2010) and others, the best ways of reducing false confessions in the early stages of an investigation are as follows:

1. There should be electronic recording of all investigative interviews throughout.
2. Psychologically manipulative interrogation techniques that have been shown to produce false confessions should be prohibited. The PEACE Model should replace the Reid Technique and other similar confrontational and guilt-presumptive methods.
3. Investigative interviewers should be trained in 'ethical' interviewing, apply and practice these skills in the workplace, and be aware of the risk of false confessions, including familiarity with all three types – *voluntary*, *pressured-internalized*, and *pressured-compliant*.

The false confessions that are most likely to go unnoticed are voluntary false confessions where young persons admit responsibility for an offence to protect a peer.

4. Police should be aware that false confessions do sometimes occur without any undue police pressure in interviews because of contextual factors and idiosyncratic vulnerabilities (e.g. drug addiction, disturbed mental state) where suspects feel under great pressure to terminate the interview and be released from custody.

5. Suspects must be appropriately administered their legal (Miranda) rights prior to an interview and their understanding of their rights ensured.

6. Many suspects are psychologically vulnerable during questioning and detention and should be provided with appropriate protection to ensure the integrity of the statement taken (e.g. ensuring they understand the questions asked and the implications of their answers).

7. Investigators should not take advantage of the popular belief in the repression of memories for criminal acts and use it against suspects who claim not to remember committing the crime (Laney & Takarangi, 2013; McNally, 2003; Ofshe & Watters, 1994).

8. Vulnerabilities should never be manipulated or exploited to extract a confession.

9. 'Appropriate adults' should be provided in all cases of juveniles (i.e. under the age of 18 in England and Wales) and where the police have reasonable grounds to suspect that one is needed (e.g. in cases in which there may be mental health issues or comprehension difficulties).

10. Investigators must follow the law and their codes of practice, which the investigators in the Gudmundur and Geirfinnur cases failed to do, with disastrous consequences.

11. In the 1980s Dr MacKeith and I found that educating lawyers and judges about false confessions was important in changing attitudes among members of the judiciary, leading up to the release of the Guildford Four and Birmingham Six. Raising public and judicial awareness of the risks of false confessions is essential to reforms to policy and practice (Kassin, 2017).

## THE GUDMUNDUR AND GEIRFINNUR CASES

Gudmundur and Geirfinnur disappeared without a trace on 27 January and 19 November 1974 respectively. Their bodies have never been found, there are no independently corroborated crime scenes, and no credible witnesses to what happened to these two men. Having carefully scrutinized many thousands of pages of documents, including the confessions of the six suspects and the circumstances under which they were obtained, and having interviewed the four surviving convicted persons, I consider it highly probable that the confessions were coerced by the investigators, are unreliable, and most probably false.

Nothing of any substance came out of the confessions. I used thematic analysis to identify, analyse, and report pertinent themes within the confession statements. Reading the statements within the context of the numerous unrecorded interviews and police arranged face-to-face confrontations between suspects, documented in the prison custody diary, it is evident that the accounts twist and turn to fit the latest police theories and information. There was considerable cross-suspect contamination, as interviewees were presented with the latest evidence of a co-accused, rather than representing a free narrative of their uncontaminated recollections.

There were no reasonable grounds for commencing the investigations. Indeed, one of the most striking features is the repeated reluctance of the three original and key investigators to disclose why they commenced the Gudmundur investigation, which was soon followed by questions about Geirfinnur's disappearance. When testifying in the District Court on 28 January 2016, the investigators claimed memory lapses. It is now strongly suspected that the case started with information from a prison informant, who has subsequently admitted that he often gave police false information in exchange for favours. After his apparent incriminating information in the Gudmundur case, which was never officially recorded or disclosed, he was indeed released from prison. Therefore, the Gudmundur case apparently commenced on the basis of information provided by an unreliable informant, who had something to gain from telling lies. The repeated failure of the investigators to disclose the circumstances surrounding the decision to start the Gudmundur case suggests that they were not confident in the credibility of the informant, or for some reason did not wish to be transparent, but nevertheless decided to proceed with a murder investigation that turned out to be the largest and most controversial in Iceland's history.[3] This strongly suggests an overzealous attitude and motivation.

The police claimed that the reason for commencing the investigation in the Geirfinnur case was that Erla Bolladóttir had complained of nuisance phone calls around the middle of January 1976, after having

---

[3] Erla's lawyer, Ragnar Adalsteinsson has suggested that Saevar's and Erla's arrest and detention in connection with the fraud offences had been carried out under false pretences as a prelude for questions about Gudmundur's disappearance (see Chapter 12).

been held less than a month previously for eight days in solitary confinement at Sídumúli Prison, initially for suspected fraud and then the unexpected questioning regarding Gudmundur's disappearance. Erla was taken as a witness to Sídumúli Prison on three separate occasions for about 11 hours in total before a statement was taken from her on 23 January 1976 about Geirfinnur's disappearance. If Erla was giving a voluntary witness statement, as the police claim, why did it take all that time for her to tell her story? Studying the case files and interviewing Erla, I consider it more likely that the investigators were 'grooming' her to implicate 'persons of interest' linked to Klúbburinn.

And why did the investigators repeatedly take Erla to Sídumúli Prison for interviews, while she technically had the status of a witness? Irrespective of whether this was done wittingly or unwittingly, it carried the implicit threat of what might happen if she did not fully cooperate with the investigators (i.e. she could be placed in solitary confinement for a long time and kept away from her baby daughter whom she was looking after). When the three key investigators were asked in the District Court on 28 January 2016 why Erla was not interviewed at the offices of the criminal investigation police, which was standard procedure at the time, they claimed memory lapses.

In the Gudmundur case, the suspects were implicating themselves and their friends, but in the Geirfinnur case Erla, Saevar, and Kristján implicated a large number of men for his disappearance, before settling on four, who were arrested in early 1976 and kept in solitary confinement until 9 May 1976, which resulted in Erla, Saevar, and Kristján being charged with perjury and subsequently being convicted of that offence.

It was not until the autumn of that year that Saevar and Kristján began to implicate themselves and Gudjón. The circumstances behind the confessions in the Gudmundur and Geirfinnur cases were very different, as I emphasized in Chapter 12.

## The Interrogations and Solitary Confinement

The Icelandic Court Cases Review Commission, referred to as the Commission in this book, was set up in 2013 to review the appeal applications in the Gudmundur and Geirfinnur cases, following the findings of a Ministry of the Interior Working Group that the confessions of all six convicted persons were without doubt unreliable. The Commission calculated that the six persons had been kept in solitary confinement for between 88 and 741 days during the Gudmundur and Geirfinnur investigation and were interrogated 641 times (range 26–180 per suspect), stretched over 976 hours (range 17–340). Saevar and Kristján, viewed by police and the court as the main perpetrators, had the largest number of interrogations (180 and 160) and hours of interrogation (340 and 215), and longest prison sentences (17 and 16 years), respectively. This officially stated number and duration of interrogations is undoubtedly an underestimate because many interrogations were not logged by the police, and in the ones not logged, no statements were taken: these had to be estimated by entries in the Síðumúli Prison diary.

Where statements were available, they consisted almost exclusively of narratives that did not indicate the questions asked by the police. It is therefore impossible to know properly what took place during those interrogations. The convicted persons claimed extensive and prolonged coercion. Their stories, as described in detail in this book, are credible and compelling.

In the Gudmundur and Geirfinnur cases the suspects were readily given solitary confinement when they were not seen to be providing the police with the information they required (e.g. making denials, not going along with the police investigative hypothesis or scenario, or retracting a confession). This was extended over many months, during which time the suspects were repeatedly interrogated. If placed in solitary confinement, the suspects never knew for certain how long they would remain there, but at the time this could last for up to two years in serious cases. There is no doubt that the uncertainty would have been intolerable, which is evidenced by records of the suspects' extreme distress and use of heavy sedation. Under such circumstances and conditions, suspects arrested in serious cases are often more focused on the short-term benefits (e.g. terminating the interrogation, release from custody) than the potential long-term consequences (e.g. conviction, a charge of perjury).

The situation was more straightforward in England and Wales in the 1970s as suspects in serious cases were typically only being kept in custody for up to three days, after which they had to be charged or released. If they were charged, no further interrogation could take place. This provided a possible safety net with regard to false confessions, because suspects knew that they only had to cope with the confinement and interrogation for a limited amount of time, after which they would either be released or charged. Even under those more favourable conditions, false confessions still occurred, highlighting the point that even short periods of solitary confinement, involving a few hours or days, combined with interrogative pressure, can sometimes result in a false confession.

While in solitary confinement, the Icelandic suspects were given various psychotropic drugs, sleeping medication, and tranquilizers. The type of drugs referred to include chlorpromazine, chloral hydrate, nitrazepam, and diazepam. These drugs appear to have been given to help the suspects cope with the intolerable stressors associated with solitary confinement. The main effect of these drugs would have been to impair the suspects' clarity of thought and decision-making. The Commission concluded that the combination of drugs and long solitary confinement would have had a deleterious impact on their physical and mental well-being and adversely affected the reliability of their statements at the time.

The Commission also concluded that the six suspects had very little access to lawyers while in custody. Over long periods of time, lawyers were prevented from speaking privately to their clients. In addition, the lawyers were not kept informed of developments, or invited to be present when key witnesses were giving statements or to ask them questions in court. Importantly, this included the extensive questioning and testimony of Gunnar Jónsson, a key witness in the Gudmundur case, who was in my view coerced in the Reykjavík Criminal Court to provide incriminating testimony against Saevar, Kristján, and Tryggvi, resulting in their convictions for manslaughter.

## The Suspects' Personal Diaries

A unique feature of the Icelandic cases is that Tryggvi Leifsson and Gudjón Skarphédinsson had kept diaries[4] while in solitary confinement and these revealed fascinating insights into what was going on around them, their intense and prolonged emotional suffering, and their thinking processes. The existence of the diaries was not known until 2011. Unfortunately, only three of Tryggvi's diaries have survived, covering the period October 1976 to December 1977. Throughout this period he expressed the belief that truth and justice would eventually prevail, showing how his naivety put him at increased risk of false confession. Tryggvi's account corroborates Saul Kassin and colleagues' elegant experimental demonstration of how innocence and naivety can put some suspects at risk of false confession (Kassin & Norwick, 2004). I have come across many cases where suspects did not think they needed a lawyer because they were innocent. This is a naive perspective to take and mostly these suspects did not have an

---

[4] Erla and Kristján also claim that they kept diaries but the investigators took these away from them.

intellectual disability. In fact, short-sighted decision-making is a common reason suspects give for having made a false confession (Gudjonsson, 2003a).

It was the discovery of Tryggvi's diaries and my being asked by a television journalist to comment on them that caused me to review the cases for the Working Group as a 'confession expert'.

The Commission concluded that Tryggvi's diaries gave an indication that his confessions to the police and in court early in the investigation had come about because he thought it sensible under the circumstances to confess falsely and trust that a fair court process would ascertain the truth. I agree with this interpretation of the content of his diaries.

Gudjón also kept detailed diaries of key events and his experiences while in solitary confinement between November 1976 and December 1977. The existence of the diaries was not known until November 2011 when he mentioned them during an interview with the Working Group. There is no reference to the diaries in the court papers, and Gudjón had kept them safe after he was released from prison on licence on 12 January 1981. A thematic analysis of his diaries showed that he was too trusting of the investigators, was unable to assert himself, internalized his distress, had a defeatist and self-sacrificing attitude, and appealed to God for help. His diaries show how his mind gradually became overborne and self-destructive, and importantly they give a unique insight into the gradual development of his memory distrust syndrome and the risk factors involved. According to the heuristic model applied in this book, Gudjón, a highly intelligent man, was a passive recipient of his coercive environment, leading to his providing a false confession of involvement in Geirfinnur's death. Importantly, his provoked confabulation was not temporary and lasted several years, supporting Kassin's (2007) view regarding the potentially enduring deleterious impact of intensive interrogation on memory processes in some cases of coerced-internalized false confession.

## What Went Wrong?

The reasons for the convictions of the six defendants in the Gudmundur and Geirfinnur cases are similar to those found in cases of wrongful convictions in the UK and USA, with some additional unique factors, such as the extreme use of solitary confinement and intensive interrogation, lack of separation between the police and the criminal court, the hiring of Karl Schütz, and the unprecedented media frenzy once the investigation had developed a momentum. Looking at the case as a whole, there were systemic failures across various organizations, particularly the police, Sídumúli Prison, the prosecution, the Reykjavík Criminal Court, and the Supreme Court. The key problems were as follows:

1. *An unreliable prison informant?* This apparently started the Gudmundur murder investigation, and then shortly afterwards led to some of the same people being asked questions about Geirfinnur's disappearance. Known in the USA as 'jailhouse informants', they are responsible for a large number of miscarriages of justice, particularly in murder cases (Garrett, 2011; The Justice Project, 2007).

2. *Overzealous investigators and prosecutor.* This was an extremely important factor in both the Gudmundur and Geirfinnur cases. Kennedy (1986) considered 'overzealousness' on the part of the police to be the most important cause of false confessions, which commences with some circumstantial piece of evidence connecting the person to the alleged crime. The police then allow their suspicions to harden into certainty and presumption of guilt, 'browbeat' the suspect to give a confession, pressure witnesses to say what they want them to say, suppress or ignore exculpatory evidence, and 'lose' documents that could help prove the suspect's innocence. Most of these factors are pertinent to the Gudmundur and Geirfinnur investigations.

3. *Presumption of guilt.* The strength of the police and judiciary's belief in the suspects' guilt was such that there was apparently no consideration of the fact that the failure to produce credible statements and discover the bodies of the two men was most probably due to their having no involvement in the two men's disappearance. This was a serious attribution error in the collection and evaluation of evidence.

4. *Media and political pressure.* Vilmundur Gylfason, an Icelandic history teacher and journalist, wrote an article in the *Vísir* newspaper on 10 October 1975 attacking Ólafur Jóhannesson in relation to his alleged interference in the reopening of Klúbburinn in 1972 after the police had closed it.[5] This was 10 days before Gudmundur Agnarsson made his voluntary false confession in the Geirfinnur case, which had crime scene content that featured in the confessions of the suspects three months later, suggesting contamination. Once the investigators had elicited confessions in the Gudmundur case during the latter part of December 1975, within a week the prosecutor requested the case file in the Geirfinnur case from the Keflavík

---

[5] This was followed by another similar article on 30 January 1976, a few days after the arrest of three of the 'four wrongly accused'. The background to Vilmundur's articles and his subsequent political career is discussed in his biography (Halldórsson, 1985).

police, who had done the original investigation, and on 9 January the media began to link the two cases, suggesting a leak of information from the police. The Gudmundur and Geirfinnur cases then developed such momentum and media frenzy that there was no turning back to consideration of innocence.

5. *Interrogations and solitary confinement.* Drizin and Leo (2004) argue that coercive interrogation is the primary psychological cause of most false confessions. In the Gudmundur and Geirfinnur cases, the number of interrogations, their duration, and the extensive use of solitary confinement, are unique in terms of criminal cases that I have come across in my 40-year career as a clinical forensic psychologist, having evaluated almost 500 cases of disputed confessions internationally. Neither have I come across similar cases in the literature on false confessions. Even in George Bush's 'war on terror', US Secretary of Defense Donald Rumsfeld commented in relation to Guantánamo Bay that solitary confinement had 'not been generally used for interrogation purposes for longer than thirty days', although ominously there was no upper limit (Rose, 2004, p. 100; see also Fallon, 2017). The six suspects in the Gudmundur and Geirfinnur cases were in solitary confinement for between 88 and 741 days for interrogative purposes. Under those conditions, the risk of false confession would have been extremely high.

6. *Breaches of the code of legal (police) practice in criminal cases.* In the 1970s the Icelandic police had excellent laws (codes of practice) regarding interrogations, which required that all investigations should be approached with an open mind (i.e. focusing on evidence of innocence as well as that of guilt), offering inducements and lying to suspects was illegal, and the questions asked should be 'clear, short and unequivocal' and not likely to confuse suspects. Interrogations must not last more than six hours and suspects should be allowed sufficient sleep and rest. Each time a suspect was interviewed it should be logged when the questioning started and the interview concluded. This legal framework dated back to the early 1950s and for its time showed a remarkably advanced police code of practice, with its emphasis on open-mindedness and fairness. The risk of false confession would have been substantially reduced, provided the codes were properly applied and enforced. Unfortunately, in the Gudmundur and Geirfinnur cases, they were not and both the Criminal and Supreme Court ignored the numerous and serious breaches by the police. This shows the importance of following up police breaches with sanctions. Police codes of practice are there for good reasons and need to be followed. If not followed, this may lead to catastrophic consequences for fairness and justice.

7. *The hiring of Karl Schütz.* By the end of July 1976 the Minister of Justice had hired Karl Schütz, a retired high profile investigator with the German Federal Criminal Police Office. He dominated the Geirfinnur investigation in the summer and autumn of 1976 and helped the Icelandic judiciary to convict the six defendants by his strong presumption of guilt, forthright assertions, and misguided investigation. According to the Commission, there was no legal foundation for appointing Karl Schütz to work in the Gudmundur and Geirfinnur investigation and no appointment letter has been discovered. When he arrived, the investigation became better focused and statements more precise. However, his approach was principally to 'eliminate inconsistencies in statements' and finding points that 'support the confessions', ignoring the legal requirement for a balanced investigation.

8. *Error pathways.* Leo and Drizin's (2010) three error pathways to false confession and wrongful convictions certainly apply to the Gudmundur and Geirfinnur cases. These are: (a) *misclassification* (i.e. the police erroneously decided that innocent people were guilty); (b) *coercion* (i.e. the investigators induced confessions by using pressure, psychological manipulation, and persuasive questioning, involving subtle threats and inducements); and (c) *contamination* (i.e. the police assisted the suspects with constructing confessions with incriminating details). Garrett (2011) has shown from American exonerees' criminal trials that 'once central evidence is contaminated in the early stages of a case, the damage cannot be easily discovered or reversed' (p. 272). The two cases were riddled with *forensic confirmation biases* (Kassin, 2015). Therefore, good police practice is the most important step to take in order to prevent wrongful convictions caused by false confessions.

9. *Limited understanding of psychological vulnerabilities.* Saevar, Erla, Kristján, Tryggvi, and Gudjón all underwent a comprehensive psychological/psychiatric evaluation. None of the vulnerabilities identified were addressed in relation to the potential unreliability of the suspects' statements. In addition, I provide evidence in this book that Saevar, Tryggvi, and Albert were probably symptomatic for ADHD, which is an important vulnerability to giving a false confession during interrogation and confinement. No psychiatric evaluation was made of Albert, who at the time was undoubtedly extremely vulnerable to giving a false confession.

10. *Lack of separation between the police and the judiciary.* Until 1 July 1977, criminal investigations were under the control of the Reykjavík Criminal Court. The lack of separation between the police and Criminal Court had created problems during the

Gudmundur and Geirfinnur investigation, which led to the establishment of the State Criminal Investigation Police (SCIP). The
SCIP was abolished 20 years later and its work was transferred to
local police commissioners and the newly established Office of the
National Commissioner (Gudjónsson [Gudmundur], 2004). This
lack of separation in the 1970s may explain why the Criminal
Court apparently turned a blind eye to breaches of the police code
of practice, and the investigative judge taking part in interrogations, which according to his own testimony on 28 January 2016
was not a part of his job description.

11. *The Supreme Court.* The Supreme Court convicted all six defendants in February 1980. According to the Commission, the Supreme
Court was not aware of the extent of the unrecorded conversations
between the suspects and investigators. The Commission also
emphasized the importance of three sets of diaries in providing
new information – those from Síðumúli Prison, Tryggvi Leifsson,
and Gudjón Skarphéðinsson. The Supreme Court had ignored and
misinterpreted crucial evidence, and did not give the suspects the
benefit of the doubt when warranted.

12. *The Criminal and Supreme Court largely ignored the circumstances
under which the confessions were obtained, the vulnerabilities of
the suspects, and their serious memory problems.* I have written
detailed individual chapters on the six convicted persons, the intensive pressure they were under, and I provide evidence that five of
them suffered from memory distrust syndrome, which was relevant
to their confessions.

## Guilt or Innocence

According to Drizin and Leo (2004), once suspects have made a false
confession it is impossible for them to 'prove' 'beyond any reasonable
doubt' their innocence (p. 953), unless it can be objectively established
that the crime did not happen (e.g. the victim assumed dead turns up
alive), the suspect could not have physically committed it (e.g. has a
solid alibi), the true perpetrator is apprehended and his or her guilt
proven, or scientific evidence, most commonly DNA, establishes the
false confessor's innocence.

The Commission's view is that there were 'strong clues' from the
convicted persons that they were responsible for the two men's death.
This relates to it generally being considered improbable that so many
persons would confess wrongly to an assault upon a man that resulted
in his death and that witnesses would give a false testimony in the
same way. What the Commission probably did not know is that over

30% of false confession cases, predominantly murder cases, involve more than one false confessor (Drizin & Leo, 2004). This is typically due to one or more suspects' testimony being used to put pressure on other suspects to confess (Gudjonsson, 2003a). My reading of the suspects' statements in the Gudmundur and Geirfinnur cases shows very clearly that one suspect's confession statement was used to extract a confession from another. The earliest example of this is in relation to Saevar's first confession in the Gudmundur case on 22 December 1975. Saevar was repeatedly asked about his knowledge of Gudmundur's disappearance. After persistently denying any knowledge of it, he confessed after a part of Erla's witness statement was read out to him.

Gunnar Jónsson and Sigurdur Óttar Hreinsson, key witnesses in the Gudmundur and Geirfinnur cases, respectively, were also subjected to coercive pressure to corroborate the confessions of the suspects. The Commission described the treatment that Sigurdur Óttar had received from the police, prosecution, and court as 'farcical'. Gunnar Jónsson's testimony was coerced over several days in court when he was confronted with the 'evidence' of the suspects involving his presence at Hamarsbraut 11 when Gudmundur was murdered. I have presented compelling evidence that Sigurdur Óttar's coerced statement involved memory distrust syndrome, and the same appears to have happened in Gunnar's case. This shows that because of the nature of interrogation and presumption of guilt by the investigators and trial judges, both the suspects and witnesses developed memory distrust syndrome, suggesting a pervasive problem in the cases.

Having carefully considered the evidence in the Gudmundur and Geirfinnur cases, I think it is probable that they are all innocent of any involvement in the disappearances of the two men. The key factors are as follows:

1. An analysis of the content of the confessions reveals huge inconsistencies both within and between suspects, despite Karl Schütz's determined effort to 'eliminate inconsistencies in statements'. There was considerable cross-suspect contamination, as interviewees were presented with the latest evidence of a co-accused through hypothesis-driven, rather than evidence-based, investigations.
2. Nothing tangible emerged from those interviews (i.e. they completely lacked substance, and where there appeared to be corroboration, the evidence was dubious due to probable contamination).
3. While the convicted persons were allegedly driving around Hafnarfjördur in the early hours of 27 January 1974 in a small Volkswagen car, which included going to the nearby lava field with Gudmundur's body, heavy snow had been falling and the weather conditions were ferocious. It is unlikely that this trip happened.

4. The Commission considered the convicted persons' evidence that was accepted in court regarding their trip to Keflavík, together with the preparation and timing of it, and concluded that it was highly improbable. This included the type and colour of the car and van that went to Keflavík, which had been eventually agreed upon, after numerous previous contradictory descriptions. Witnesses reported having seen these or a similar car and van by the Harbour Café on 19 November 1974, but their testimony appeared to eliminate the convicted persons as the drivers or passengers. In addition, the Commission noted that in order to drive from Reykjavík to Keflavík within the known time constraints, the convicted persons would have had to substantially exceed the speed limit while driving through Reykjavík, Kópavogur, Gardabaer, and Hafnarfjördur at an average speed of 84 km (52.2 miles) per hour without stopping. This is highly unlikely, and the Commission considered this to be one of the most important factors where the Supreme Court wrongly interpreted the evidence in the Geirfinnur case.

5. Daníelsson (2016) has discovered credible evidence that Saevar had an alibi for the evening of 19 January 1974 when Geirfinnur disappeared.

6. It is unlikely that Erla, Tryggvi, and Kristján would have participated in the abreaction injection procedures, administered by a psychiatrist, if they were genuinely trying to conceal their guilt. Similarly, Albert's compliance with hypnosis sessions suggests that he was trying his best to recall what had allegedly happened and assist with the investigation.

7. Crucially, none of the six suspects were able to point to the locations of the two men's bodies, which one or more of them probably would have been able to if they had been involved in the disposal of the bodies. In addition, no crime scene was independently corroborated and no forensic evidence found that the two men had been murdered. The reason, of course, is most likely due to the fact that they did not murder Gudmundur and Geirfinnur and were merely appeasing the police who would not accept that they did not know where the bodies were hidden.

8. The extent of the interrogations and solitary confinement, accompanied by the circumstances under which the confessions were obtained, resulted in a state of helplessness and despair from which the suspects could not escape.

9. In Chapters 13–18, I have given detailed descriptions of the psychological vulnerabilities of each of the six suspects and present compelling evidence that their confessions were wholly unreliable.

## The Perjury Convictions

With regard to the perjury convictions of Saevar, Erla, and Kristján, the Commission pointed out the 'long way between accepting the investigating hypotheses of the police, if this was what happened, and during interrogation people being named as culprits like the appeal applicants did repeatedly'. The Commission placed considerable weight on the fact that all three persons admitted having made false statements against the four innocent men, which is of course a serious criminal offence. The real issue is whether or not these confessions were coerced by the investigators, not that the convicted persons made them (i.e. it was the circumstances under which they were elicited and maintained that should have been given a greater focus). I have strongly argued in this book that there are good grounds for appeal regarding the perjury convictions. The false allegations against the 'four wrongly accused' and the false confessions of the convicted persons said to have been on the Keflavík slipway, and in later statements taking part in Geirfinnur's murder, are so intertwined that it is not helpful to separate them. Surprisingly, the Commission failed to consider Jón Fridrik Sigurdsson's and my detailed expert evidence on those issues before the District Court on 28 January 2016, evidence that the Commission had itself requested from us, but then completely ignored (i.e. making no reference to it at all in their reports). The Commission appears to have used the investigators' claims of memory lapses and appalling record keeping to challenge Erla's claims of frequent contact with them when not in 'custody', which is in fact supported by three visits with Erla to Sídumúli Prison where she spent about 11 hours before giving her first incriminating witness statement in the Geirfinnur case. Ragnar Adalsteinsson, Erla's lawyer, has gone as far as to suggest either 'gross neglect' or 'intent'. The consequence of the Commission's decision is that the authorities will continue to place the blame for implicating innocent people on Erla, Saevar, and Kristján rather than on the investigators.

## Memory Distrust in the Gudmundur and Geirfinnur Cases

The Gudmundur and Geirfinnur cases are unique in terms of the number of people who developed interrogation-induced memory distrust syndrome. I present evidence in this book that five out of the six suspects, Saevar being the exception, developed a profound distrust of their memory that was instrumental in their giving incriminating statements against themselves and/or others. It was the combination of intense interrogations, accompanied by solitary confinement and psychological vulnerabilities that led to their giving false statements to the police.

I have presented a *heuristic model* for the internalized confessions of Erla, Kristján, Tryggvi, Gudjón, and Albert (Chapters 14–18). The basic mechanism (i.e. state of mental confusion and self-doubt where the person is no longer able to distinctively recall that he/she had not committed or witnessed the crime) and processes (i.e. context/trigger, decision-making, plausibility, acceptance, reconstruction) are similar, but there is some variability across the suspects in the enduring and acute state factors. The most common *enduring factors* were high compliance, low self-esteem, and memory problems.

As far as *acute state* factors are concerned, mental confusion, self-doubt, trying to please the investigators and suggestibility were the typical factors. In the case of Gudjón, he had been persuaded that he could help the police solve the case, which gave him a sense of purpose. Gudjón's detailed diaries describe well the process whereby a highly intelligent and educated man gradually began to accept that he had been involved in Geirfinnur's disappearance.

In Erla's case, as far as Gudmundur's alleged death was concerned, it all started with a dream she had had around the time of his disappearance. She was in an acute anxiety state because after giving a full and frank confession to fraud after seven days in solitary confinement, she was expecting to be allowed to go home to her infant daughter when the investigators started asking her questions about Gudmundur, resulting in her implicating Saevar, Kristján, and a 'third' man, later identified as Tryggvi, in Gudmundur's death. At the time, Erla was an extremely vulnerable young woman who was easily manipulated by the investigators into agreeing with their investigative hypothesis.

In addition to trust of the police, negative-related cognitions of self and others (e.g. perceptions of 'bad character') are likely to increase the risk of false memories for criminal acts (Laney & Takarangi, 2013).

What protected Saevar from developing memory distrust syndrome was his lack of trust and confidence in what the investigators were telling him. He had a suspicious cognitive set towards the investigators, which is known to reduce suggestibility (Gudjonsson & Clark, 1986). In the *heuristic model* of internalized false confession, trust in the interviewer is an essential component. Police persuasion involves interviewees accepting and believing that they may have been involved in the crime or witnessed it. Saevar never did, as far as I can tell from the documented evidence, including an insightful book about him (Unnsteinsson, 1980). His confessions in the Gudmundur and Geirfinnur cases were of the pressured-compliant type as a way of his attempting to escape from an intolerable predicament after his truthful denials were not believed.

The extent to which the suspects were able to engage in provoked confabulation during the reconstruction of what had allegedly taken place varied considerably, emphasizing the importance of individual differences. Erla was particularly imaginative, which was a feature of her personality, being prone to vivid imagination and delayed suggestibility. Albert and Tryggvi struggled. The police commissioned a psychiatrist and psychologist to facilitate Albert's memory, which included hypnosis. Tryggvi gave very few written statements, because he was reluctant to engage in imaginative reconstruction, which is well illustrated by a comment he made in his diary after 10 and a half months in solitary confinement when he had eventually come to believe in his innocence:

> Regarding the transportation [of Gudmundur's body], which I have never informed on, simply because I could not remember it and did not want to muddle it further by making up a story about it from their [the investigators'] suggestions, i.e. go along with what I had heard. (See Chapter 16.)

One way of interpreting Tryggvi's relative absence of provoked confabulation is that he had low delayed suggestibility. The distinction between immediate and delayed suggestibility is crucial in relation to *pressured-internalized* false confessions. Delayed suggestibility is more directly relevant to *provoked confabulation* during the crime reconstruction process than immediate suggestibility, but there is evidence that how the person responds to leading questions (e.g. in terms of hesitancy, vagueness, and the number of 'Don't know' and 'Not sure' answers) during a test of immediate suggestibility indicates a proneness to memory distrust. On occasions it leads to pressured-internalized false confession.

The duration of the memory distrust syndrome varied considerably across the suspects. The resolution was quickest in the case of Kristján, who never seemed entirely confident about what he was telling the police, and repeatedly kept retracting his confessions without success, after further persuasion from the police. It took Gudjón several years to regain the belief and confidence that he had not been involved in the Geirfinnur case, which he had held at the beginning of his interrogation and solitary confinement.

A similar duration occurred with regard to Erla's memory distrust syndrome in the Gudmundur case. Albert's memory distrust syndrome has persisted since his solitary confinement in December 1975 and he is permanently left with the dread that one day he may remember what allegedly happened at Hamarsbraut 11. There has been a permanent belief change.

These findings suggest that contrary to Ofshe and Leo's (1997b) conclusion, in exceptional circumstances, like in the cases Gudjón, Erla, and Albert, the influences and pressures of interrogation on memory distrust can continue for several years after making the confession. Gudjón, Erla, and Albert had important traits in common at the time of their interrogation: they were all extremely compliant in temperament, trusted the police, and tried hard to cooperate with them. All three with the assistance of the investigators had constructed a story, which they thought might be true, but to them it did not feel like a complete memory. Nor did any of them have full confidence in the story, which was reminiscent of a 'screenplay' rather than a real event. These internalized confessions and their duration have much in common with those in the Norwegian Birgitte Tengs case, whose defendant I evaluated in 1998. Again it was the combination of intense and lengthy interrogation and solitary confinement that had the most damaging effect on the belief system of the defendant in the Birgitte Tengs case and on his trust in his own memory.

Rather than internalized false confessions necessarily comprising genuinely held false memories, in some cases the process may be limited to 'constructive imagination and thinking' (Bartlett, 1932). In the Gudmundur and Geirfinnur cases this comprised 'false information' from the investigators and co-accused and 'imagination inflation' without full confidence in the accounts they accepted and produced in evidence. (For a discussion of similar issues in laboratory experiments see Brewin & Andrews, 2016, McNally et al., 2004, and Schacter & Loftus, 2013.)

It was principally the lack of confidence in their memory and the deleterious impact on their autobiographical belief system that led to their confessions. This is a component of memory where reflective experiences have not been demonstrated with full confidence and are probably best described as 'partial memories' (Brewin & Andrews, 2016).

It seems that Erla's memory was badly affected, having been elicited in the Gudmundur case by a discussion of a dream, similar to that in the case of Andrew Evans (Gudjonsson et al., 1999). It lasted several years and was only resolved after a thorough discussion of the evidence in the case with a friend. In Erla's case, a dream was turned through manipulative interrogation into her having witnessed a murder. Meaningful beliefs are easier to incorporate into memory than those that have a low level of plausibility (Horselenberg et al., 2006).

## LESSONS LEARNED

There is evidence from the UK (Hain, 2012, pp. 97–98) and Iceland (Karlsson, 1994) that solitary confinement without lengthy and intensive interrogation can result in the development of memory distrust in healthy and intelligent suspects to the extent that they begin to believe that they may have been involved in the alleged offence. For example, in January 1976 Erla implicated her half-brother Einar Bollason in the disappearance of Geirfinnur. He was arrested and kept in solitary confinement for 105 days. After a week in custody, Mr Bollason was about to 'break down' (*bugast*). He describes what appears to be the development of memory distrust syndrome regarding his innocence:

> At a particular time I had become so confused that I seriously contemplated whether I had got mixed up in some case, or been a witness to some dreadful event and become so shocked that I could not recall precisely what had happened. My belief in criminal justice was so strong that I was beginning to believe that I was even guilty because I had been kept in custody so long.
>
> (Karlsson, 1994, p. 96)

His vulnerability was his strong belief in the police and criminal justice system, which in my experience was the prevalent attitude among the general public in Iceland in the 1970s. But he was not interrogated as intensively as Erla, Saevar, Gudjón, Tryggvi, Kristján, and Albert, and unlike them was allowed regular access to his lawyer. However, he might have made a false confession if he had not decided to devise a system of activities for getting him through each day. This involved his taking a bath in the custody suite every day and for as long as he could; he read all books available to him in custody; he physically exercised in his small cell three times a day; and he prayed to God. It worked. Mr Bollason was a resourceful man, which may have stopped him making a false confession, but according to his own account he was left traumatized by the experience for years to come. The case brings into focus the vulnerabilities of people, even strong and healthy individuals, to seriously doubt their memory under certain interrogative and custodial conditions, which could result in a false confession and a heavy prison sentence.

The abuse of solitary confinement was a serious problem with regard to the suspects in the Gudmundur and Geirfinnur cases. More than 40 years on, solitary confinement is apparently still used excessively by the Icelandic police for interrogative purposes.[6] On 16 March 2017 the

---

[6] http://www.ruv.is/frett/kastljos-i-kvold-einangrun-mannrettindabrot.

Supreme Court of Iceland ruled that the Icelandic State had violated a clause in the constitution that bans any sort of torture or humiliation of citizens (Mál nr. 345/2016).

Another lesson from the Gudmundur and Geirfinnur cases is that good law and codes of practice are of no use if they are not followed and the court ignores the police breaches. If the Reykjavík investigators had followed the existing law regarding investigative interviewing, I very much doubt that the six suspects would have been convicted. Justice was severely compromised by the absence of professionalism, humanity, transparency, and accountability.

# Appendix 1

**09 December 1976**
Detective Jónas Bjarnason interviewed Saevar for six hours. Saevar reported
  having asked Kristján Vidarsson the day before Geirfinnur's disappearance
  to obtain a delivery van to carry the smuggled alcohol from Keflavík.
  Kristján allegedly asked his cousin Sigurdur Óttar Hreinsson for access to
  such a van and he agreed. According to Saevar's statement, Sigurdur Óttar
  parked the van in the slipway on the day of Geirfinnur's disappearance, but
  may not have witnessed the assault (Evidence Book XV, pp. 926–936).

**13 December 1976**
Sigurbjörn Vídir interviewed Erla for over four hours. She said that the
  delivery van she had seen at Vatnsstígur was similar to the van Sigurdur
  Óttar used to move her belongings in August 1974. She said she was sure
  the van had been in the slipway along with a small boat in the harbour. She
  said it was a Mercedes-Benz car (Evidence Book XV, pp. 957–961).

**13 December 1976**
After Erla completed her statement, Eggert Bjarnason interviewed Sigurdur
  Óttar for over five hours at the Police Headquarters at Borgartún 7
  (17.20–22.30). He denied any knowledge of Geirfinnur's disappearance, said
  he had never been to the slipway, and that Saevar was not telling the truth.
  He had a vague recollection of removing Erla's belongings when she moved
  house, but could not recall what car he was driving at the time (Evidence
  Book XV, pp. 962–963).

(Continued)

*The Psychology of False Confessions: Forty Years of Science and Practice*, First Edition.
Gisli H. Gudjonsson.
© 2018 John Wiley & Sons Ltd. Published 2018 by John Wiley & Sons Ltd.

**Appendix 1**  *(Continued)*

**13 December 1976**
At 22.55 Eggert Bjarnason and Ívar Hannesson transported Sigurdur Óttar
to Sídumúli Prison where he was placed in custody overnight (referred to
as *geymsla* or 'overnight stay'). (Evidence Book XXII, p. 33).

**14 December 1976**
The records show that Sigurdur Óttar was collected from Sídumúli Prison at
10.30 and returned there at 20.04, then having been remanded in custody
(Evidence Book XXII, p. 33).

Karl Schütz interviewed Sigurdur Óttar through an interpreter at the Police
Headquarters at Borgartún 7. The interview commenced at 11.00 in the
morning and the end time is not recorded but may have been close to 20.00
when he was returned Sídumúli Prison. There had been a long
interrogation before this 'admission' statement was taken, because at the
beginning of the statement Sigurdur Óttar says:
'After a long conversation, I will tell the truth.'
The details of this conversation and how long it lasted are not recorded.
The statement he gave is accompanied in the papers by handwritten notes
Sigurdur Óttar had made about the sequence of events leading to his
going to the slipway on 19 November 1974.

His subsequent admission is vague and tentative in language.
He could not recall the precise date but said it could have been on 19
November 1974 that Kristján asked him to go to Keflavík in the van 'to
collect something'. Sigurdur Óttar drove the borrowed yellow Mercedes-
Benz van to Keflavík. He met Kristján there, who directed him to the
slipway. He parked about 10–12 metres from the harbour and waited.
After about 30 minutes Kristján turned up and told him:
'It's ok, the trip is off, you can go and you know nothing about this.'
He drove back to Reykjavík on his own, only having seen Kristján in the
slipway and did not notice any fight.
In reply to a direct unrecorded question, Sigurdur Óttar said:
'I can't tell for sure if I went to Keflavík on 19.11.74, but I'm sure it was around
that time. I did not know that events connected to Geirfinnur happened that
night, until Kristján was arrested and the newspapers wrote about it. I want
to make it clear that I didn't know of any alcohol smuggling, nor that
Geirfinnur was involved before I went on this trip. I didn't know anything, I
was just told to go [to Keflavík].' (Evidence Book XV, pp. 964–966)

**14 December 1976**
At 22.55 Eggert Bjarnason interviewed Sigurdur Óttar who had now been placed
in custody at Sídumúli Prison. He wanted to add to and change certain things
from his earlier statement. He had spoken to the van's owner on 18 November
1974, who said it was fine for him to use the car if the prison officer was not
using it. Sigurdur Óttar took the car, without the prison officer's knowledge,
from a road near the Reykjavík Penitentiary at Skólavördustígur, where the
prison officer had parked it while at work. Sigurdur Óttar said that while in the
slipway he did not see anybody, but 'on the other hand I could hear indistinct
voices as if several people were talking' (Evidence Book XV, p. 971–973).
After this interview, Sigurdur Óttar was released from custody at 23.40
(Evidence Book XXII, p. 33).

**23 January 1977**
The police attempted a reconstruction of the murder of Geirfinnur Einarsson
at the Keflavík slipway. Present were Saevar Ciesielski, Kristján Vidarsson,
Gudjón Skarphédinsson, Erla Bolladóttir, and Sigurdur Óttar Hreinsson.

**Appendix 1** *(Continued)*

Due to inconsistencies among the suspects in describing the chain of events relating to the assault on Geirfinnur, the focus was on the location of the vehicle (Volkswagen car and Mercedes-Benz van) and people. Sigurdur Óttar placed the van 30 metres further east than the others.

**02 February 1977**
At a press conference that day, Karl Schütz stated that Gudjón Skarphédinsson had become 'the first reliable witness' … 'And later we found Sigurdur Óttar Hreinsson, the delivery van driver, and the investigation really moved on. And you will hear the results here today.' (*Morgunbladid*, 3 February 1977, p. 25)
**Note:** Karl Schütz's declaration at the press conference showed the importance of Sigurdur Óttar's testimony in the Geirfinnur case.

**12 May 1977**
Following some negative publicity in the media of Sigurdur Óttar's name in connection with the Geirfinnur case, his lawyer, Róbert Árni Hreidarsson, made an announcement in *Morgunbladid*, declaring that there was no evidence that his client knew what had happened in the Keflavík slipway, and that he was only questioned in the case as a witness (Evidence Book XXII, p. 123).

**12 October 1977**
The Deputy Director of the Office of State Prosecution, Bragi Steinarsson, attended the offices of the State Criminal Investigation Police, which had recently been created, at 13.00 and explained that two lawyers (Jón Oddsson and Páll A Pálsson, representing defendants in the Geirfinnur case) had come to his office that morning and explained that the previous Monday (10 October 1977) they had been summoned to a meeting with Sigurdur Óttar's lawyer, Róbert Árni Hreidarsson, and they spoke with Sigurdur Óttar for about two hours, who claimed that he had not gone to Keflavík on 19 November 1974 and had given a false statement due to the threat of custody and intimidation (Evidence Book XXII, pp. 6–7).

**12 October 1977**
Sigurdur Óttar gave a statement to Detective Ívar Hannesson (14.15–17.00), in the presence of a lawyer (Sigurdur Georgsson). He said his first statement to police was correct and pointed out that his other statements and testimony in court were wrong. He gave the following reasons (Evidence Book XXII, pp. 8–12):
1. 'After I was first taken I was interrogated for a long time and then placed in custody overnight, and when subsequent reports were taken I was threatened with custody if I did not give the right statement. The investigators had led me into the case and I made up or filled in the gaps'.
2. 'I was released from Sídumúli Prison around midnight on 14 December 1976 and the following morning I went to meet Róbert Árni Hreidarsson, lawyer … I explained to him that I had been pressured to admit to the trip to Keflavík on 19 November 1974, which I had never made. I sought advice from Róbert in connection with this and told him about the treatment I had received. His advice was that I should immediately correct this, but I was reluctant to do this then, both because of doubts I had about whether I could have gone on the trip and also due to fear of the police.'

**Appendix 1** *(Continued)*

At 18.02 Sigurdur Óttar and Róbert Árni Hreidarsson were interviewed together. The following emerged, which strongly suggests that Sigurdur Óttar developed memory distrust syndrome during the interrogations:
Róbert Árni remembered well when Sigurdur Óttar came to see him in December 1976. He described him as having been 'very upset and agitated' due to the three interrogations he had to endure: 'Óttar said that eventually he was beginning to doubt the trustworthiness of his first statement and began to believe the description of the incident that he was given and had to agree with. I recall that Óttar said if he did not recognise that description of events he would be remanded in custody for up to 30 days. I asked Óttar repeatedly if he had gone on the Keflavík trip in question and he said verbatim that he could not distinguish after the interrogations what was real and what was not, and said it was like a bad dream. He said he could not make sense of the chain of events and his role in it. I asked Óttar if he wanted me to revoke his statements, but he answered "no", because he was so confused about the case, that he did not understand his position' (Evidence Book XXII, pp. 17–20).

**13 October 1977**
Sigurdur Óttar appeared in court with his lawyer. The prosecution requested that Sigurdur Óttar be placed in custody for up to 30 days while his changed testimony was being investigated. The judge reserved her judgement until 13.00 the following day.

**14 October 1977**
Sigurdur Óttar appeared in court with his lawyer. He said he did not want to change the retraction he gave in court the previous day. The judge remanded Sigurdur Óttar into custody for 26 days.
Sigurdur Óttar's lawyer raised an objection:
'I was neither yesterday nor today given the opportunity in court to object to the prosecutor's request for custody over Sigurdur Óttar Hreinsson' (ICCRC Report, 2017, Erla Bolladóttir, Paragraphs 1672 and 1673).

**17 October 1977** (Evidence Book XXII, pp. 24–31)
Detective Grétar Saemundsson interviewed Sigurdur Óttar in relation to being suspected of having given false testimony in court under oath.
His lawyer was present and the interrogation lasted three and a half hours. He was asked 27 questions. The following questions are particularly relevant to his giving an explanation for his false testimony (the questions Detective Grétar Saemundsson asked are summarized, but the answers were translated verbatim):
**Question.** When did the fear of police and custody begin?
Answer: 'After I was put into custody.'
**Question.** What was the nature of this fear?
Answer: 'I was afraid of confinement and constant pressure from the police officers, who were always accusing me of lying, and if I did not say what they wanted I would be remanded in custody for 30 days.'
**Question.** When and which police officers threatened you with custody?
Answer: 'When I had given my first statement, Eggert Bjarnason telephoned Örn Höskuldsson, and from what I heard was that I could expect 30 days in custody, if I did not say what they wanted. I then asked the police officers whether I would be put in custody. They replied that if I did not tell the truth, I would be put into custody. I particularly remember that Sigurbjörn Vídir Eggertsson said it.'

**Appendix 1** *(Continued)*

**Question.** Were you threatened with custody while giving your first statement?
Answer: 'Not until I had given the statement.'
**Question.** Can you explain how the second interrogation [14 December 1976, commenced at 11.00] was conducted?
Answer: 'My memory is that Eggert Bjarnason, Ívar Hannesson, and Sigurbjörn Vídir Eggertsson started the interrogation, and around midday Karl Schütz came and participated in the interrogation into the afternoon. I think up to 10 men took part in this interrogation. They alternated in asking the questions, but sometimes several were asking questions at the same time. These men kept asking questions. They had some papers to read from and eventually persuaded me that I had gone on this trip. In this connection I want to mention that when Örn Höskuldsson entered the room he had a coat hanger in his hands and hit his palm and thigh with it. He walked up to me and asked me about the case and I found him threatening. I also remember that Karl Schütz had a safety pin [*bendipinna*], which he thrust into his palm while he interrogated me.'
**Question.** What was the reason you did not want your lawyer to withdraw your confession when you saw him on 15 December 1976, after being released from custody the previous night?
Answer: 'I told Róbert Árni that the Criminal Investigation Police had pressured me to admit the trip, which I thought I had not undertaken. Róbert Árni wanted to act immediately and correct this, but I was not ready and asked him not to do anything immediately.'
**Question.** What was the reason you did not want to act immediately?
Answer: 'The doubt I was experiencing and fear that the police would lock me up.'
**Question.** Can you explain further the reason for the doubt you experienced?
Answer: 'The doubt involved me not knowing what I was doing on the day in question and I had admitted to things that I was not sure I had done.'
**Question.** Did the fear of the police continue from the time you were released from custody on 14 December 1976 and until you changed your testimony in court (13 October 1977)?
Answer: 'The fear is in reality the same, but I now have the courage to tell the truth.'
**Question.** In your statement of 24 January 1977, after attending the re-enactment the previous day, you gave the same story as you had in your confession statements. What was the reason you did not change your testimony then?
Answer: 'Same reason as before, fear of police locking me up.'
**Question.** You said you were led by police, but why did you then place the van 30 metres further east than the defendants?
Answer: 'I placed the car where I thought it should have been.' When further questioned about this, he said: 'I can't give an answer except that I thought the car should have been there.'
Detective Grétar Saemundsson asked Sigurdur Óttar why he had on 25 May 1977, while in court, added to his previous account about what he heard in the slipway.
Answer: 'The reason was me fantasizing.'
**Question.** Who else apart from the police, lawyers, and judges have you told that you did not make that trip (i.e. gave a false statement)?
Answer: I told my fiancée immediately after I was released on 14.12.1976. As I said before, I told Róbert Árni the following day. The same day I also told my employer... The day after that I went to work and told my work colleagues.'

(Continued)

**Appendix 1**   (*Continued*)

**24 October 1977**
Sigurdur Óttar's lawyer appealed the Criminal Court's decision on 14 October
to remand Sigurdur Óttar in custody. The Supreme Court upheld the
original ruling and pointed out that Sigurdur Óttar had given inconsistent
witness statements in a serious case where his testimony was potentially
important.

**22 February 1980** (Supreme Court Judgement)
In spite of Sigurdur Óttar's retraction of his witness statement the court
ruled:
'It is proved that the delivery van that Sigurdur Óttar drove at the request of
Kristján, arrived at Vatnsstígur on the evening of 19 November 1974, and
Sigurdur Óttar drove it to Keflavík. When he arrived there Kristján spoke
to Sigurdur Óttar and requested that he park the van close to the slipway'
(p. 23).
The court pointed out that witnesses who were present when Karl Schütz
interviewed Sigurdur Óttar did not see any coercion and he was described
as 'calm and normal' during the interrogation (p. 22).
Importantly, the court noted that when Sigurdur Óttar discussed the trip
with lawyers, family, friends, and workmates, he was in two minds over
'whether he had done those things' (p. 22).
As an example of Sigurdur Óttar's doubts on 19 October 1977, a statement
was taken from a friend of his, Ágúst Jakobsson, who said that he had
repeatedly asked him about the case soon after Sigurdur Óttar was
released from custody after making his admission. Sigurdur Óttar 'always
gave the same answer, that he could not remember going on this trip to
Keflavík' (Evidence Book XXII, pp. 43–44). This means he could not exclude
its *plausibility*, leading to temporary *acceptance* of the police investigative
hypothesis.

# Appendix 2

**16 November 1976**: 'Short interrogation concerning cannabis in Citroen [car from Rotterdam] 12/12/75. Interrogation so far not aimed directly at Geirfinnur's disappearance [...] but various things hinted at.'

**17 November 1976:** 'Interrogation tomorrow. Now the matter will become clearer. But I cannot remember any link between me and the Geirfinnur case. But something is brewing.'

**18 November 1976:** 'Good to see Jón Ísberg [a sheriff, who was married to Gudjón's aunt and encouraged him to tell the police all he knew about the case and this conversation was apparently critical in Gudjón beginning to think that perhaps he was involved]. Interrogated by Birgir Thormar [a Criminal Court lawyer who had been allocated judicial supervision of Gudjón] [...] I had a panic attack last night. Sometimes I feel guilty but I cannot remember what has happened. This waiting is so difficult and I think about all the people who care about and have cared about me. I must be ill and have been for a long time. This is mental illness. My will is lacking all strength.'

**22 November 1976:** 'For two years I have had the belief that I did not know anything about this case but now I am supposed to have been very much involved. In fact most of it has not yet come to light. The next week will probably be decisive. [...] What game is God playing with me? Am I mentally ill, or have been? I would admit to that. Many of the things I have done in the recent years were madness.'

(Continued)

*The Psychology of False Confessions: Forty Years of Science and Practice*, First Edition.
Gisli H. Gudjonsson.
© 2018 John Wiley & Sons Ltd. Published 2018 by John Wiley & Sons Ltd.

**Appendix 2** *(Continued)*

**23 November 1976:** 'The nights are the worst. I wait desperately to fall asleep but it is slow in coming and I have intrusive thoughts [...] If I only knew if I had participated in this or not. I deceive people; that's the way it is. I am always acting, I am an ill man [...] Only if I had not smuggled cannabis. It ruined my life. Interrogated by Schütz [...] Intensively encouraged to confess, which I can't do because I can't remember anything. The Supreme Court has confirmed my solitary confinement. Impatience among all those working on the case and they wanted to conclude the case.'

**24 November 1976:** 'I have problems breathing, feel terrible. [...] I'm writing a report on the relationship between Saevar and I. Horrible job, but I deserve it. Have completed nine pages and much left. My mental illness is now evident.'

**25 November 1976:** 'Had a visit from Reverend Jón Bjarman today. We discussed a lot about the case and other things. He is content and believes in my innocence. Grétar [Detective Grétar Saemundsson] came and implied many things and thinks I'm in a bad position in the case. He even wants me to get used to the thought of being a murderer. I find that a bit much [...] If they think I am going to confess to the stories of S [Saevar] and Erla, then there is a misunderstanding.'

**26 November 1976:** 'I have completed 11 pages on the relationship between Saevar and me and a horrible description from my point of view [...] I should have been dead a long time ago. It would have been better than this, particularly if I'm involved in the Geirfinnur case, although I don't know how [...] 23.20. It has been a long day until the evening and I have heard little good news today. Grétar has been and said I was in a bad position regarding the case.'

**27 November 1976:** 'Dear Lord, give me the strength to admit my guilt and admit my responsibility [...] Best I speak to Grétar. Nobody believes me any longer.'

**28 November 1976:** 'I see no reason why I should not try to remember the case to the best of my abilities. It's a pity that I remember so little. I slept well on the diazepam, much, good and long. Went on a car journey to Keflavík [alleged murder scene] with Grétar, Schütz and Pétur [Schütz's interpreter], little to gain from that, we drove around town, even less to gain from that. I want to solve the case right away. And receive a long and heavy sentence. I am finished.'

**29 November 1976:** 'Had a long conversation with Grétar today. I try to remember all about that trip to Keflavík. Not going too well but I am feeling better than before. I am tired after this. I wish I could remember it all better. Grétar says I can't go easy on myself, it needs courage he says. I tell him I find it hard to remember. Will try again tomorrow. Later there will be a psychiatric assessment. Hopefully I will not be found criminally insane and locked up for the rest of my life.'

**30 November 1976:** 'Slept well, am reasonably fit, but soon get tired after long interrogations. I find it difficult to remember what happened and how [...] But the case is progressing and I hope God gives me energy, courage and memory to tell truthfully and correctly what happened so that there will be an answer and conclusion to the case soon [...] Tomorrow I need to try to remember what cars were on the trip, but it has been difficult to remember. I'm very uncertain about this, maybe it will clear up soon.'

**Appendix 2**   *(Continued)*

**1 December 1976:** 'I did not wake up until after midday and then spoke with judge Birgir, a super man and a good man. B. Blöndal [Gudjón's defence lawyer] was present but he can't be in court tomorrow, but the solitary confinement will be extended, how long we don't know, we will see [...] I only hope that God helps me tell everything I know to be right and true.'

**2 December 1976:** 'It is now evening and the case was taken up in court at 2 o'clock. The trip to Keflavík was brought up and afterwards Grétar and I tried to understand the case better. Later this evening my solitary confinement was extended for a further 60 days.'

**3 December 1976:** 'Grétar came, optimistic as always, saying that soon I would be transferred to Skólavördustígur [Penitentiary] where I could get some visitors [...] Many things are still unclear, I have to try to remember and use my next evenings for just that. It will be difficult, but will happen with prayer and concentration.'

**4 December 1976:** 'Wake up late, long after midday and did not want to wake up again. Reverend Jón came. It was good to see him and hope to see him again next week.'

**5 December 1976:** 'I was woken up to speak with Pétur and Schütz [...] Schütz wanted me to speak to a psychiatrist [...] I was asked again about the location of the body.'

**6 December 1976:** 'Got out of bed 18.00 [...] Woke up from a dream where told "You are finished".'

**7 December 1976:** 'Went for a ride with G [Grétar] and Eggert [Detective Eggert Bjarnason]. Tomorrow is some kind of final hearing about the case. They probably want everything cleared up before Christmas. [...] The question is, where is the body? It is strange that it doesn't show up. [...] I feel so bad right now, I am so tired, cannot remember anything, have difficulties talking, cannot think, dread tomorrow, know that it will all be the same, don't remember, know nothing, then I will be deprived of my sanity. I am totally exhausted.'

**8 December 1976:** 'Woke up late and started discussing with Grétar, we discussed for a long time until dinner time. Continued after dinner until almost five this morning. Then I had confessed to being involved in the murder of G. Einarsson and had given a third report regarding the most unfortunate trip to Keflavík I have ever gone on in my entire life. Hopefully the body of the man will be found in the next few days and this nation can relax, even though I will not be among those people, but my conscience should be better now than before [...] I'm no longer in a state of despair, don't want to die, but this will be difficult. I will go to sleep now. Now something will happen.'

**9 December 1976:** 'Reverend Jón [Bjarman] came and we talked for a while.'

**10 December 1976:** 'I have slept an awful lot, really all day [...] Grétar is in the building, intended to speak to me last night, but did not do it. I don't know what he wants to do this evening.'

**11 December 1976:** 'Long conversation with Eggert and Grétar. Eggert makes me tired, makes me morose and annoyed, I couldn't talk to him for long [...] Asked the doctor today for medication which would help me write what I need to write. I have had three doses today and slept most of the day so not written much.'

**12 December 1976:** 'I have slept so much and the time was 5 pm when I woke, had more medication and am about to go back to sleep. I'm feeling fine. I feel so sleepy. There will be little of my report writing if this carries on.'

**13 December 1976:** 'Grétar came and woke me up, walked around and said that this was urgent and he seemed very disappointed that I had not written anything. [...] I'm always thinking about suicide. I could do it. I have the means. I'm a bit ambivalent about it but it will not take much if things go wrong for me to do it. [...] Grétar came and asked me about my writings, of which there were none, gave me the chance to hand them over in the morning or else I would have to answer in court about what I knew, what I remembered etc. We discussed suicide and how much courage it takes [...] He pointed out to me that I had to come clean, go to Hraunið [Litla-Hraun, Iceland's largest prison] and start writing.'

**14 December 1976:** 'This has been a big day. I have written almost 12 pages for Grétar. We had a long conversation, many things discussed.'

**15 December 1976:** 'I was expecting Grétar this evening but I have not heard from him.'

**16 December 1976:** 'I got up late, got dressed just before lunch and then had a visit from Judge Birgir and Ingvar Kristjánsson, a psychiatrist. I was shown a letter regarding a psychiatric evaluation.'

**17 December 1976:** 'Today nothing has happened.'

**18 December 1976:** 'I'm always thinking about suicide, a rather ugly word suicide, know how I would do it, could not go wrong. [...] What in the world has happened to Grétar? I have not heard from him in a long time. Doesn't really matter but I am not entirely content, something is not right.'

**20 December 1976:** 'I'm terribly fed up with the Geirfinnur case and all the problems. To hell with it all. I have been here for nearly two months. Poor Saevar, he is entering his second year in solitary confinement.' [Gudjón makes a reference to taking his chlorpromazine].

**21 December 1976:** 'Slept badly last night, was writing a letter in my mind to the psychologist about my life and childhood.' [This refers to the forthcoming psychiatric evaluation]. 'Talk about relieving the restrictions of the custody, I say that I am fine here. He wants to know a little more but I just remember so little. But something is going on now that Óli Jóh [Minister of Justice] and the court cases were on the news [*Kastljós* current affairs TV programme] tonight'.

**22 December 1976:** 'Woke up lunchtime. Later Grétar came and wanted answers, which I could not give him. I then went for my dinner, ate much, and wanted to go to sleep. Then Judge Birgir arrived with a psychologist [Gisli Gudjonsson between 21.10 and 21.40] who wants to give me a lie detector test. Physiological stress detector. I asked for precedents but there is none. I wanted to discuss this with Benedikt and that will be tomorrow. Otherwise I gave my consent. This relates to the police not believing in my innocence, rather they think I am covering up. I have no problem this being investigated with the newest technology.'

**Appendix 2**   *(Continued)*

**23 December 1976:** 'Slept little and bad. [...] Grétar came. We discussed the body, location and other things. [...] The question is whether I'm the only one who knows where the body is?'

**24 December 1976:** 'Benedikt and I will meet after Christmas and decide on the voice stress test [lie detector test], how it should be conducted, and it has to be completed by 3 January at the latest' [because Gisli Gudjonsson who conducted the test was leaving Iceland for England on 4 January where he was in his second year of clinical psychology training].

**25 December 1976:** 'I'm like a new man, have slept well and long.'

**26 December 1976:** 'Interrogations, psychological assessment and the truth test. I'm feeling better about these now than before.'

**27 December 1976:** 'Now lawyer, judge, psychologist and investigators arrive and ask me questions and I recall less now than I did before Christmas. [...] I was woken up about 1 pm and Grétar wanted to ask me some questions and left me in abeyance. The position is complicated regarding the Keflavík trip and now the psychologist [Gisli Gudjonsson between 17.45 and 18.35], Birgir and lawyer Benedikt. The truth test will be conducted on Thursday or Friday and I have nothing to lose and everything to win. Judge Birgir asked me various complicated questions, which I found difficult to answer, but it is evident that this will cost me a few years in Litla-Hraun.'

**28 December 1976:** 'Grétar full of questions, no answers. Was intending to come back later but didn't.'

**29 December 1976:** 'Örn [Höskuldsson, investigative judge] came and talked to me about this and that, it was nice to see him and talk with him. He wants me to feel good and said wise things about the future and the present. He especially wanted to point out to me to toughen up, let my pride go and tell everything. Then Birgir and I spoke for a while. [...] Long and demanding interrogation with Grétar after dinner.' [The custody log shows that this interrogation lasted between 21.00 and 03.00].

**30 December 1976:** 'Then Eggert and Grétar arrived and now around 20.00 we have discussed constantly about where Geirfinnur's body is? Do I know it or not and it's taking a long time [...] A lot of things indicate that I am coming closer to the solution to the case, including that I was shaking so much that I could hardly eat. [...] A long interrogation with Eggert which ended with a visit to Kópavogur football stadium, where I think Geirfinnur's body is hidden. Judge Örn, Grétar and Eggert all went with me. It was terribly cold outside.'

**31 December 1976:** 'After a lot of crying, I feel better, but still I am miserable. The voice tests [lie detector test] took place today, but I feel like I made some mistakes there. The recent interrogations and that stadium issue have affected my nerves. Örn, G and E were here today and wanted to discuss the case even further. [...] I'm all breaking down and hardly recognize my name with certainty. [...] I wish God would take me to Him, I am about to give up, amnesia. Where are these bodies? How should I know? I have a headache. Feel terrible.'

(Continued)

**Appendix 2** (*Continued*)

**1 January 1977:** 'I hope and pray that I will never again live such a horrible New Year's Eve. Can't sleep nor stay awake. The headache felt like blowing my eyes out. [...] Reverend Jón [Bjarman] came and it is always good to see him. Calm and in good control. Asked his advice on the case and Örn and Birgir. Don't make any deals, he said. Will discuss it all with my lawyer and Birgir, he is the judge responsible for my aspect of the case. But I'm losing my mind that is for sure. This ends by my no longer knowing my own name. They are trying to arrange a deal under the table. Try to trick information from me that I don't even have. What is Örn up to? Why has he suddenly appeared? [...] I will speak to Grétar tomorrow. What about? My reservations concerning the location and the outcome of the interrogation the other day.'

**2 January 1977:** 'I feel tangled up in some absurd web of lies, no breaks, no glimpse of clear sky. Success is harder to swallow than failure. It will be great when they have solved this Geirfinnur case. There is something not right about this case. I find this amnesia especially odd, it has never happened to me when I am sober, not to remember anything. What was happening, did I never go to Keflavík on 19/11/74 but some other night? What important business do Benedikt and Birgir have with me tomorrow? And Örn, Eggert, Grétar? Is something brewing? Has something new emerged?'

**3 January 1977:** 'Squabble with Eggert from 3–7 but also have major conversations with Judge B and B lawyer [after the lie detector test Gudjón was considering retracting his confession, which caused a problem for the investigators]. Birgir is a judge and will remain so. He is in charge of my case. Told them about Örn and his offer. B lawyer will possibly ask Örn about that. Otherwise they have confused me and I asked E [Eggert] today if I could read my statement over again. Judge B said I should come to him personally.'

**4 January 1977:** 'What is it that keeps me alive? I'm able to end it, why don't I? Is it that I can see some future? Is it the belief in life and that one should not go against God's wishes?'

**5 January 1977:** 'What is my name and where am I going or coming. [...] Not heard from anybody today.'

**6 January 1977:** 'Not motivated to do anything.'

**7 January 1977:** 'Grétar is on the premises but has not asked for an interview. [...] Have not done much today. [...] All these days ahead.'

**8 January 1977:** 'Are they now coming harder at me. Breaking me down by not talking to me, forbid the priest to come, stalling letters and packages etc. No, paranoid talk. You can get so paranoid and full of hate being isolated like this. I try to keep my mood stable. Be patient and calm, have inner vision. Review incidents from life.'

**9 January 1977:** 'Not seen or heard from anybody today.'

**12 January 1977:** 'Woken up at 17 [pm] to go out. Brought before the Chief Judge, Halldór Thorbjörnsson. He said Judge Birgir is no longer the Judge in my case' [after Karl Schütz's fury over Gudjón's reaction to the lie detector test, Judge Birgir Thormar was replaced by Örn Höskuldsson as Gudjón's investigative judge].

# References

Aebi, M. F., & Campistol, C. (2013). 'Voluntary' false confessions as a source of wrongful convictions: The case of Spain. In C. R. Huff, & M. Killias (Eds.), *Wrongful convictions and miscarriages of justice* (pp. 193–208). New York: Routledge.

American Psychiatric Association. (2013). *Diagnostic and statistical manual of mental disorders* (5th ed.). Washington, DC: Author.

Antonsson, Þ. (1991). *Aminntur um sannsögli*. Reykjavik: Bókaútgáfan Skjaldborg.

Appleby, S. C., Hasel, L. E., & Kassin, S. M. (2013). Police-induced confessions: An empirical analysis of their content and impact. *Psychology, Crime and Law, 19,* 111–128.

Appleby, S. C., & Kassin, S. M. (2016). When self-report trumps science: Effects of confessions, DNA, and prosecutorial theories on perceptions of guilt. *Psychology, Public Policy, and Law, 22,* 127–140.

Asherson, A., Young, S., Adamou, M., Bolea, B., Coghill, D., Gudjonsson, G. H., ... Thome, J. (2013). *Handbook for attention deficit hyperactivity disorders in adults*. London: Springer HealthCare.

Ayers, M. S., & Reder, L. M. (1998). A theoretical review of the misinformation effect: Predictions from an activation-based memory model. *Psychonomic Bulletin & Review, 5,* 1–21.

Baddeley, A. D. (1995). The Psychology of memory. In A. D. Baddeley, B. A. Wilson, & F. N. Watts (Eds.), *Handbook of Memory Disorders* (pp. 3–25). Chichester: John Wiley & Sons Ltd.

Baldwin, J. (1992). *Videotaping police interviews with suspects: A national evaluation. Police Research Series Paper 1*. London: Home Office Police Department.

Baldwin, J. (1993). Police interviewing techniques. Establishing truth or proof? *The British Journal of Criminology, 33,* 325–352.

*The Psychology of False Confessions: Forty Years of Science and Practice*, First Edition.
Gisli H. Gudjonsson.
© 2018 John Wiley & Sons Ltd. Published 2018 by John Wiley & Sons Ltd.

Barden, R. C. (2016). Memory and reliability: Developments and controversial issues. In P. Radcliffe, G. Gudjonsson, A. Heaton-Armstrong, & D. Wolchover (Eds.), *Witness testimony in sexual cases. Evidential, investigative and scientific perspectives* (pp. 343–359). Oxford: Oxford University Press.

Barkley, R. A., Murphy, K. R., & Fischer, M. (2008). *ADHD in adults. What the science says.* London: Guilford Press.

Barthel, J. (1976). *A death in Canaan.* New York: Congdon.

Bartlett, F. C. (1932). *Remembering. A study in experimental and social psychology.* Cambridge: Cambridge University Press.

Bedau, H. A., & Radelet, M. L. (1987). Miscarriages of justice in potentially capital cases. *Stanford Law Review, 40,* 21–179.

Bem, D. J. (1966). Inducing belief in false confessions. *Journal of Personality and Social Psychology, 3,* 707–710.

Bem, D. J. (1967). When saying is believing. *Psychology Today, 1,* 22–25.

Berggren, E. (1975). *The psychology of confessions.* Leiden: Brill.

Binet, A. (1900). *La suggestibilite.* Paris, France: Doin et Fils.

Blackburn, R. (1996). What is forensic psychology? *Legal and Criminological Psychology, 1,* 3–16.

Blagrove, M. (1996). Effects of length of sleep deprivation on interrogative suggestibility. *Journal of Experimental Psychology: Applied, 2,* 48–59.

Blagrove, M., & Akehurst, L. (2000). Effects of sleep loss on confidence–accuracy relationships for reasoning and eyewitness memory. *Journal of Experimental Psychology: Applied, 6,* 59–73.

Blagrove, M., Cole-Morgan, D., & Lambe, H. (1994). Interrogative suggestibility: The effects of sleep deprivation and relationship with field dependence. *Applied Cognitive Psychology, 8,* 169–179.

Blair, J. P. (2007). The role of interrogation, perception, and individual differences in producing compliant false confessions. *Psychology, Crime & Law, 13,* 173–186.

Bolladóttir, E. (2008). *Erla, góða Erla.* Reykjavík: Vaka-Helgafell.

Borchard, E. M. (1932). *Convicting the innocent: Sixty-five actual errors of criminal justice.* Garden City, NY: Doubleday.

Brandon, R., & Davies, C. (1973). *Wrongful imprisonment.* London: Allen and Unwin.

Braun, V., & Clarke, V. (2006) Using thematic analysis in psychology. *Qualitative Research in Psychology, 3,* 77–101.

Brewin, C. R., & Andrews, B. (2016). Creating memories for false autobiographical events in childhood: A systematic review. *Applied Cognitive Psychology, 31,* 2–23.

British Psychological Society. (2001). *The nature of hypnosis.* Leicester: British Psychological Society.

British Psychological Society. (2004). *A review of the current scientific status and fields of application of polygraphic deception detection.* Leicester: British Psychological Society.

Brown, N. N., Gudjonsson, G. H., & Connor, P. (2011). Suggestibility and fetal alcohol spectrum disorders: I'll tell you anything you want to hear. *Journal of Psychiatry & Law, 39,* 39–72.

Bull, R. (1999). Police investigative interviewing. In A. Memon, & R. Bull (Eds.), *The psychology of interviewing* (pp. 279–292). Chichester: John Wiley & Sons.

Bull, R. (2013). What is 'believed' or actually 'known' about characteristics that may contribute to being a good/effective interviewer? *Investigative Interviewing: Research and Practice, 5,* 128–143.

Bull, R., & Soukara, S. (2010). Four studies of what really happens in police interviews. In G. Daniel Lassiter & Christian A. Meissner (Eds.), *Police interrogations and false confessions* (pp. 81–95). Washington, DC: American Psychological Association.

Bull, R., Valentine, T., & Williamson, T. (2009). *Handbook of psychology of investigative interviewing.* Chichester: Wiley-Blackwell.

Cain, A., Westera, N. J., & Kebbell, M. (2016). Interviewing suspects in Australia and New Zealand. In D. Walsh, G. E. Oxburgh, A. D. Redlich, & T. Myklebust (Eds.), *International developments and practices in investigative interviewing and interrogation. Volume 2: Suspects* (pp. 71–81). London: Routledge.

Chrobak, Q. M., & Zaragoza, M. S. (2013). The misinformation effect: Past research and recent advances. In A. M. Ridley, F. Gabbert, & D. J. La Rooy (Eds.), *Suggestibility in legal contexts* (pp. 21–44). Chichester: Wiley-Blackwell.

Cialdini, R. B. (1993). *The psychology of persuasion.* New York: Quill William Morrow.

Clare, I. C. H., & Gudjonsson, G. H. (1993). Interrogative suggestibility, confabulation, and acquiescence in people with mild learning difficulties (mental handicap): Implications for reliability during police interrogation. *British Journal of Clinical Psychology, 32,* 295–301.

Clare, I. C. H., & Gudjonsson, G. H. (1995). The vulnerability of suspects with intellectual disabilities during police interviews: A review and experimental study of decision-making. *Mental Handicap Research, 8,* 110–128.

Clare, I. C. H., Gudjonsson, G. H., Rutter, S. C., & Cross, P. (1994). The interrater reliability of the Gudjonsson Suggestibility Scale (Form 2). *British Journal of Clinical Psychology, 33,* 357–365.

Clarke, C., & Milne, R. (2016). Interviewing suspects in England and Wales. In D. Walsh, G. E. Oxburgh, A. D. Redlich, & T. Myklebust (Eds.), *International developments and practices in investigative interviewing and interrogation. Volume 2: Suspects* (pp. 101–118). London: Routledge.

Cohen, J. (1992). A power primer. *Psychological Bulletin, 112,* 1304–1313.

Connery, D. S. (1977). *Guilty until proven innocent.* New York: Putman.

Connors, E. F., Lundregan, T., Miller, N., & McEwen, J. T. (1996). *Convicted by juries, exonerated by science: Case studies in the use of DNA evidence to establish innocence after trial.* Washington, DC: US Department of Justice, National Institute of Justice.

CPT. (1993). *Report to the Icelandic Government on the visit to Iceland carried out by the European Committee for the Prevention of Torture and Inhuman or Degrading Treatment or Punishment (CPT) from 6 to 12 July 1993.* Strasbourg/Reykjavík: Author.

Dalsgaard, S., Østergaard, S. D., Leckman, J. F., Mortensen, P. B., & Pedersen, M. G. (2015). Mortality in children, adolescents, and adults with attention deficit hyperactivity disorder: A nationwide cohort study. *The Lancet, 385,* 2190–2196.

Daníelsson, J. (2016). *Sá sem flýr undan dýri.* Reykjavík: Mýrún.

Davis, D., & Leo, R. A. (2012). Interrogation-related regulatory decline: Ego depletion, failures of self-regulation, and the decision to confess. *Psychology, Public Policy, and Law, 18,* 673–704.

Davis, D., & Leo, R.A. (2013). Acute suggestibility in police interrogation: Self-regulation failure as a primary mechanism of vulnerability. In A. M. Ridley, F. Gabbert, & D. J. La Rooy (Eds.), *Suggestibility in legal contexts. Psychological research and forensic implications* (pp. 45–61). Chichester: Wiley-Blackwell.

Davison, S. E., & Forshaw, D. M. (1993). Retracted confessions: Through opiate withdrawal to a new conceptual framework. *Medicine, Science and the Law, 33,* 285–290.

DeClue, G. (2005). *Interrogations and disputed confessions. A manual for forensic psychological practice.* Sarasota, Florida: Professional Resource Press.

DeClue, G. (2010). Oral *Miranda* warnings: A checklist and a model presentation. In G. D. Lassiter, & C. A. Meissner (Eds.), *Police interrogations and false confessions* (pp. 179–190). Washington, DC: American Psychological Association.

Drake, K. E. (2010). Interrogative suggestibility: Life adversity, neuroticism and compliance. *Personality and Individual Differences, 48,* 493–498.

Drake, K. E. (2014). The role of trait anxiety in the association between the reporting of negative life events and interrogative suggestibility. *Personality and Individual Differences, 60,* 54–59.

Drake, K. E., Bull, R., & Boon, J. C. (2008). Interrogative suggestibility, self-esteem, and the influence of life adversity. *Legal and Criminological Psychology, 13,* 299–307.

Drake, K. E., Gonzalez, R. A., Sigurdsson, J. F., Sigfusdottir, I. D., & Gudjonsson, G. H. (2017). A national study into temperament as a critical susceptibility factor for reported false confessions amongst adolescents. *Personality and Individual Differences, 111,* 220–226.

Drake, K. E., Gudjonsson, G. H., Sigfusdottir, I. D., & Sigurdsson, J. F. (2015). An investigation into the relationship between the reported experience of negative life events, trait stress-sensitivity and false confessions among further education students in Iceland. *Personality and Individual Differences, 81,* 135–140.

Drake, K. E., Sigfusdottir, I. D., Sigurdsson, J. F., & Gudjonsson, G. H. (2016). Investigating the interplay between the reported witnessing and experiencing of physical violence within the home, the death of a parent or sibling, stress-sensitivity, and reported false confessions in males. *Personality and Individual Differences, 88,* 114–119.

Drizin, S. A., & Leo, R. A. (2004). The problem of false confessions in the post-DNA world. *North Carolina Law Review, 82,* 891–1007.

Ede, R., & Shepherd, E. (2000). *Active defence.* London: Law Society Publishing.

Eggerz, P. (1971). *Minningar ríkisstjóraritara.* Reykjavík: Skuggsjá.

Einarsson, Þ. B. (2007). *Morðið á Laugalæk.* Reykjavík: Skrudda ehf.

Elíson, P. R., & Jónsson, B. R. (2007). *Breiðavíkurdrengur. Brotasaga Páls Elísonar.* Reykjavík: Mál og Menning.

Ewing, C. P., & McCann, J. T. (2006). *Minds on trial. Great cases in law and psychology.* Oxford: Oxford University Press.

Eysenck, H. J., & Eysenck, S. B. G. (1975). *Manual of the Eysenck Personality Scales (Junior and Adult).* London: Hodder & Stoughton.

Fahsing, I. A., Jakobsen, K. K., & Öhr, J. (2016). Investigative interviewing of suspects in Scandinavia. In D. Walsh, G. E. Oxburgh, A. D. Redlich, & T. Mykelburts (Eds.), *International developments and practices in investigative interviewing and interrogation. Volume 2: Suspects* (pp. 180–192). London: Routledge.

Fallon, M. (2017). Unjustifiable means. *The inside story of how the CIA, Pentagon, and US Government conspired torture.* New York: Regan Arts.

Faraone, S. V., Biederman, J., & Mick, E. (2006). The age-dependent decline of attention deficit hyperactivity disorder: A meta-analysis of follow-up studies. *Psychological Medicine, 36,* 159–165.

Feld, B. C. (2006). Police interrogations of juveniles: An empirical study of policy and practice. *Journal of Criminal Law & Criminology, 97,* 219–316.

Feld, B. C. (2013). *Kids, cops, and interrogation: Inside the interrogation room.* New York: New York University Press.

Fenner, S., Gudjonsson, G. H., & Clare, I. C. H. (2002). Understanding of the current police caution (England & Wales) among suspects in police detention. *Journal of Community and Applied Social Psychology, 12*, 83–93.

Fitzgerald, E. (1987). Psychologists and the law of evidence: Admissibility and confidentiality. In G. Gudjonsson, & J. Drinkwater (Eds.), *Psychological evidence in court. Issues in criminological and legal psychology, Number 11* (pp. 39–48). Leicester: British Psychological Society.

Forst, B. (2013). Wrongful convictions in a world of miscarriages of justice. In C. R. Huff, & M. Killias (Eds.), *Wrongful convictions and miscarriages of justice* (pp. 15–43). New York: Routledge.

Frumkin, I. B. (2016). The role of suggestibility in personal injury claims. *Psychological Injury and Law, 9*, 97–101.

Frumkin, I. B., Lally, S. J., & Sexton, J. E. (2012). A United States forensic sample for the Gudjonsson Suggestibility Scales. *Behavioral Sciences and the Law, 30*, 749–763.

Fulero, S. M., & Everington, C. (2004). Mental retardation, competency to waive *Miranda* rights, and false confessions. In C. Lassiter (Ed.), *Interrogations, confessions and entrapment* (pp. 163–179). New York: Kluwer Academic/Plenum Publishers.

Gale, A. (1988). Introduction. The polygraph test, more scientific investigation. In A. Gale (Ed.), *The polygraph test. Truth, lies and science* (pp. 1–9). London: Sage Publication.

Gallo, D. A., Meadow, N. G., Johnson, E. L., & Foster, K. T. (2008). Deep levels of processing elicit a distinctiveness heuristic: Evidence from the criteria recollection task. *Journal of Memory and Language, 58*, 1095–1111.

Garrett, B. L. (2011). *Convicting the innocent. Where criminal convictions go wrong.* London: Harvard University Press.

González, R., Gudjonsson, G. H., Wells, J., & Young, S. (2016). The role of emotional distress and ADHD on institutional behavioral disturbance and recidivism among offenders. *Journal of Attention Disorders, 20*, 368–378.

Granhag, P.A. & Hartwig, M. (2008). A new theoretical perspective on deception detection: On the psychology of instrumental mind-reading. *Psychology, Crime & Law, 14*, 189–200.

Granhag, P.A., & Hartwig, M. (2015). The strategic use of evidence technique: A conceptual overview. In P. A. Granhag, A. Vrij, & B. Verschuere (Eds.), *Detecting deception. Current challenges and cognitive approaches* (pp. 231–251). Chichester: Wiley Blackwell.

Griffiths, A., & Milne, R. (2006). Will it all end in tiers? Police interviews with suspects in Britain. In T. Williamson (Ed.), *Investigative interviewing: Rights, research, regulation* (pp. 167–189). Cullompton, Devon: Willan Publishing.

Grisso, T. (1980). Juveniles' capacities to waive Miranda rights: An empirical analysis. *California Law Review, 68*, 1134–1166.

Grisso, T. (1986). *Evaluating competencies. Forensic assessments and instruments.* New York: Plenum Press.

Gross, S. (2013). How many false convictions are there? How many exonerations are there? In C. R. Huff, & M. Killias (Eds.), *Wrongful convictions and miscarriages of justice* (pp. 45–59). New York: Routledge.

Gross, S. R., Jacoby, K., Matheson, D. J., Montgomery, N., & Patil, S. (2005). Exonerations in the United States, 1989 through 2003. *Journal of Criminal Law and Criminology, 95*, 523–553.

Grounds, A. T. (2004). Psychological consequences of wrongful conviction and impris-onment. *Canadian Journal of Criminology and Criminal Justice*, *46*, 165–182.

Grounds, A. T. (2005). Understanding the effects of wrongful imprisonment. In M. Tonry (Ed.), *Crime and justice: A review of research, Volume 32* (pp. 1–58). Chicago: University of Chicago Press.

Gudjónsson, Gudmundur (Ed.) (2004). *The Icelandic Police. A historical sketch*. Reykjavík: The National Commissioner of Police.

Gudjonsson, G. H. (1975). *Delinquent boys in Reykjavik: A follow-up study of boys sent to an approved school*. BSc dissertation, Brunel University (UK).

Gudjonsson, G. H. (1977). *The efficacy of the galvanic skin response in experi-mental lie detection: Some personality variables*. MSc dissertation, University of Surrey (UK).

Gudjonsson, G. H. (1979). Electrodermal responsivity in Icelandic criminals, clergymen and policemen. *British Journal of Social and Clinical Psychology*, *18*, 351–353.

Gudjonsson, G. H. (1982). Delinquent boys in Reykjavik: A follow-up study of boys sent to an institution. In J. Gunn, & D. P. Farrington (Eds.), *Abnormal offenders, delinquency, and the criminal justice system* (pp. 203–212). Chichester: John Wiley & Sons.

Gudjonsson, G. H. (1983). Suggestibility, intelligence, memory recall and personality: An experimental study. *British Journal of Psychiatry*, *142*, 35–37.

Gudjonsson, G. H. (1984a). A new scale of interrogative suggestibility. *Personality and Individual Differences*, *5*, 303–314.

Gudjonsson, G. H. (1984b). Interrogative suggestibility: Comparison between 'false confessors' and 'deniers' in criminal trials. *Medicine, Science and the Law*, *24*, 56–60.

Gudjonsson, G. H. (1987). A parallel form of the Gudjonsson Suggestibility Scale. *British Journal of Clinical Psychology*, *26*, 215–221.

Gudjonsson, G. H. (1988). Interrogative suggestibility: Its relationship with assertiveness, social-evaluative anxiety, state anxiety and method of coping. *British Journal of Clinical Psychology*, *27*, 159–166.

Gudjonsson, G. H. (1989a). Compliance in an interrogation situation: A new scale. *Personality and Individual Differences*, *10*, 535–540.

Gudjonsson, G. H. (1989b). The effects of suspiciousness and anger on suggest-ibility. *Medicine, Science and the Law*, *29*, 229–232.

Gudjonsson, G. H. (1989c). The psychology of false confessions. *The Medico-Legal Journal*, *57*, 93–110.

Gudjonsson, G. H. (1990). One hundred alleged false confession cases: Some normative data. *British Journal of Clinical Psychology*, *29*, 249–250.

Gudjonsson, G. H. (1992a). *The psychology of interrogations, confessions and testimony*. Chichester: John Wiley & Sons.

Gudjonsson, G. H. (1992b). The psychology of false confessions and ways to improve the system. *Expert Evidence*, *1*, 49–53.

Gudjonsson, G. H. (1995a). 'Fitness for interview' during police detention: A conceptual framework for forensic assessment. *Journal of Forensic Psychiatry*, *6*, 185–197.

Gudjonsson, G. H. (1995b). 'I'll help you boys as much as I can': How eagerness to please can result in a false confession. *Journal of Forensic Psychiatry*, *6*, 333–342.

Gudjonsson, G. H. (1997). *The Gudjonsson Suggestibility Scales manual*. Hove: Psychology Press.

Gudjonsson, G. H. (2003a). *The psychology of interrogations and confessions. A handbook*. Chichester: John Wiley & Sons.

Gudjonsson, G. H. (2003b). Psychology brings justice. The science of forensic psychology. *Criminal Behaviour and Mental Health, 13*, 159–167.

Gudjonsson, G. H. (2006a). Disputed confessions and miscarriages of justice in Britain: Expert psychological and psychiatric evidence in the court of appeal. *Manitoba Law Journal, 31*, 489–521.

Gudjonsson, G. H. (2006b). Sex offenders and confessions: How to overcome their resistance during questioning. *Journal of Clinical Forensic Medicine, 13*, 203–207.

Gudjonsson, G. H. (2006c). The psychological vulnerabilities of witnesses and the risk of false accusations and false confessions. In A. Heaton-Armstrong, E. Shepherd, G. Gudjonsson, & D. Wolchover (Eds.), *Witness testimony. Psychological, investigative and evidential perspectives* (pp. 61–75). Oxford: Oxford University Press.

Gudjonsson, G. H. (2010a). Psychological vulnerabilities during police interviews. Why are they important? *Legal and Criminological Psychology, 15*, 161–175.

Gudjonsson, G. H. (2010b). Interrogative suggestibility and false confessions. In J. M. Brown, & E. A. Campbell (Eds.), *The Cambridge handbook of forensic psychology* (pp. 202–207). Cambridge: Cambridge University Press.

Gudjonsson, G. H. (2010c). The psychology of false confessions: A review of the current evidence. In G. D. Lassiter, & C. A. Meissner (Eds.), *Police interrogations and false confessions* (pp. 31–47). Washington, DC: American Psychological Association.

Gudjonsson, G. H. (2012). False confessions and correcting injustices. *New England Law Review, 46*, 689–709.

Gudjonsson, G. H. (2013). Interrogative suggestibility and compliance. In A. M. Ridley, F. Gabbert, & D. J. La Rooy (Eds.), *Suggestibility in legal contexts. Psychological research and forensic implications* (pp. 45–61). Chichester: Wiley-Blackwell.

Gudjonsson, G. H. (2014). Mental vulnerabilities and false confession. In M. St-Yves (Ed.), *Investigative interviewing. The essentials* (pp. 191–222). Toronto: Carswell.

Gudjonsson, G. H. (2016). Detention: fitness to be interviewed. In J. Payne-James, & R. W. Byard (Eds.), *Encyclopaedia of forensic and legal medicine. Volume 2* (2nd ed.) (pp. 214–219). Oxford: Elsevier.

Gudjonsson, G. (2017). Memory distrust syndrome, confabulation and false confession. *Cortex, 87*, 156–165.

Gudjonsson, G. H., & Clare, I. C. H. (1994). The proposed new police caution (England & Wales): How easy is it to understand? *Expert Evidence, 3*, 109–112.

Gudjonsson, G. H., Clare, I., Rutter, S., & Pearse, J. (1993). *Persons at risk during interviews in police custody: The identification of vulnerabilities*. Royal Commission on Criminal Justice. Research Study No. 12. London: HMSO.

Gudjonsson, G. H., & Clark, N. K. (1986). Suggestibility in police interrogation: A social psychological model. *Social Behaviour, 1*, 83–104.

Gudjonsson, G. H., González, R. A., & Young, S. (in preparation). The risk of making false confessions: The role of developmental disorders, conduct disorder, psychiatric symptoms, and compliance.

Gudjonsson, G. H., & Gunn, J. (1982). The competence and reliability of a witness in a criminal court. *British Journal of Psychiatry, 141,* 624–627.

Gudjonsson, G. H., Hannesdottir, K., Petursson, H., & Tyrfingsson, T. (2000). The effects of alcohol withdrawal on memory, confabulation, and suggestibility. *Nordic Journal of Psychiatry, 54,* 213–220.

Gudjonsson, G. H., & Haward, L. R. C. (1998). *Forensic psychology: A guide to practice.* London: Routledge.

Gudjonsson, G. H., Hayes, G. D., & Rowlands, P. (2000). Fitness to be interviewed and psychological vulnerability during police detention. A survey of the views of doctors, lawyers and police officers. *Journal of Forensic Psychiatry, 11,* 4–92.

Gudjonsson, G. H., & Joyce, T. (2011). Interviewing adults with intellectual disabilities. *Advances in Mental Health and Intellectual Disabilities, 5,* 16–17.

Gudjonsson, G. H., Kopelman, M. D., & MacKeith, J. A. C. (1999). Unreliable admissions to homicide: A case of misdiagnosis of amnesia and misuse of abreaction technique. *British Journal of Psychiatry, 174,* 455–459.

Gudjonsson, G. H., & Lebegue, B. (1989). Psychological and psychiatric aspects of a coerced-internalized false confession. *Journal of the Forensic Science Society, 29,* 261–269.

Gudjonsson, G. H., & MacKeith, J. A. C. (1982). False confessions. Psychological effects of interrogation. A discussion paper. In A. Trankell (Ed.), *Reconstructing the past: The role of psychologists in criminal trials* (pp. 253–269. Deventer, The Netherlands: Kluwer.

Gudjonsson, G. H., & MacKeith, J. A. C. (1990). A proven case of false confession: Psychological aspects of the coerced-compliant type. *Medicine, Science and the Law, 30,* 329–335.

Gudjonsson, G. H., & MacKeith, J. A. C. (1994). Learning disability and the Police and Criminal Evidence Act 1984. Protection during investigative interviewing: A video-recorded false confession to double murder. *Journal of Forensic Psychiatry, 5,* 35–49.

Gudjonsson, G. H., & MacKeith, J. A. C. (1997). *Disputed confessions and the criminal justice system.* Maudsley Discussion Paper No. 2. London: Institute of Psychiatry.

Gudjonsson, G. H., & MacKeith, J. A. C. (2003). The 'Guildford Four' and the 'Birmingham Six'. In G. H. Gudjonsson, *The psychology of interrogations and confessions. A handbook* (pp. 445–457. Chichester: John Wiley & Sons.

Gudjonsson, G. H., Murphy, G. H., & Clare, I. C. H. (2000). Assessing the capacity of people with intellectual disabilities to be witnesses in court. *Psychological Medicine, 30,* 307–314.

Gudjonsson, G. H., & Pearse, J. (2011). Suspect interviews and false confessions. *Current Directions in Psychological Science, 20,* 33–37.

Gudjonsson, G. H., & Petursson, H. (1982). Some criminological and psychiatric aspects of homicide in Iceland. *Medicine, Science and Law, 22,* 91–98.

Gudjonsson, G. H., & Petursson, H. (1990). Homicide in the Nordic countries. *Acta Psychiatrica Scandinavica, 82,* 49–54.

Gudjonsson, G. H., & Petursson, H. (1991). Custodial interrogation: Why do suspects confess and how does it relate to their crime, attitude and personality? *Personality and Individual Differences, 12,* 295–306.

Gudjonsson, G. H., Petursson, H., Sigurdardottir, H., & Skulason, S. (1991). Overcontrolled hostility among prisoners and its relationship with denial and personality scores. *Personality and Individual Differences, 12,* 17–20.

Gudjonsson, G. H., Rutter, S. C., & Clare, I. C. H. (1995). The relationship between suggestibility and anxiety among suspects detained at police stations. *Psychological Medicine*, *25*, 875–878.

Gudjonsson, G. H., & Sartory, G. (1983). Blood-injury phobia: A "reasonable excuse" for failing to give a specimen in a case of suspected drunken driving. *Journal of the Forensic Science Society*, *23*, 197–201.

Gudjonsson, G. H., & Sigurdsson, J. F. (1994). How frequently do false confessions occur? An empirical study among prison inmates. *Psychology, Crime and Law*, *1*, 21–26.

Gudjonsson, G. H., & Sigurdsson, J. F. (1999). The Gudjonsson Confession Questionnaire-Revised (GCQ-R). Factor structure and its relationship with personality. *Personality and Individual Differences*, *27*, 953–968.

Gudjonsson, G. H., & Sigurdsson, J. F. (2003). The relationship of compliance with coping strategies and self-esteem. *European Journal of Psychological Assessment*, *19*, 117–123.

Gudjonsson, G. H., Sigurdsson, J. F., Asgeirsdottir, B. B., & Sigfusdottir, I. D. (2006). Custodial interrogation, false confession and individual differences. A national study among Icelandic youth. *Personality and Individual Differences*, *41*, 49–59.

Gudjonsson, G. H., Sigurdsson, J. F., Bragason, O. O., Einarsson, E., & Valdimarsdottir, E. B. (2004). Confessions and denials and the relationship with personality. *Legal and Criminological Psychology*, *9*, 121–133.

Gudjonsson, G. H., Sigurdsson, J. F., Bragason, O. O., Newton, A. K., & Einarsson, E. (2008). Interrogative suggestibility, compliance and false confessions among prisoners and their relationship with attention deficit hyperactivity disorder (ADHD) symptoms. *Psychological Medicine*, *38*, 1037–1044.

Gudjonsson, G. H., Sigurdsson, J. F., & Einarsson, E. (2004). The role of personality in relation to confessions and denials. *Psychology, Crime and Law*, *10*, 125–135.

Gudjonsson, G. H., Sigurdsson, J. F., Einarsson, E., & Einarsson, J. H. (2008). Personal versus impersonal relationship compliance and their relationship with personality. *Journal of Forensic Psychiatry and Psychology*, *19*, 502–516.

Gudjonsson, G. H., Sigurdsson, J. F., & Sigfusdottir, I. D. (2009a). Interrogations and false confessions among adolescents in seven countries in Europe. What background and psychological factors best discriminate between false confessors and non-false confessors? *Psychology, Crime and Law*, *15*, 711–728.

Gudjonsson, G. H., Sigurdsson, J. F., & Sigfusdottir, I. D. (2009b). False confessions among 15- and 16-year-olds in compulsory education and their relationship with adverse life events. *Journal of Forensic Psychiatry and Psychology*, *20*, 950–963.

Gudjonsson, G. H., Sigurdsson, J. F., & Sigfusdottir, I. D. (2010). Interrogation and false confessions among adolescents. Differences between bullies and victims. *Journal of Psychiatry and Law*, *38*, 57–76.

Gudjonsson, G. H., Sigurdsson, J. F., Sigfusdottir, I. D., & Asgeirsdottir, B. B. (2008). False confessions and individual differences. The importance of victimization among youth. *Personality and Individual Differences*, *45*, 801–805.

Gudjonsson, G. H., Sigurdsson, J. F., Sigfusdottir, I. D., Asgeirsdottir, B. B., González, R., & Young, S. (2016). A national epidemiological study investigating risk factors for police interrogation and false confession among juveniles and young persons. *Social Psychiatry and Psychiatric Epidemiology, 51,* 359–367.

Gudjonsson, G. H., Sigurdsson, J. F., Sigfusdottir, I. D., & Young, S. (2012a). False confessions to police and their relationship with conduct disorder, ADHD, and life adversity. *Personality and Individual Differences, 52,* 696–701.

Gudjonsson, G. H., Sigurdsson, J. F., Sigfusdottir, I. D., & Young, S. (2012b). An epidemiological study of ADHD symptoms among young persons and the relationship with cigarette smoking, alcohol consumption, and illicit drug use. *Journal of Child Psychiatry and Psychology, 53,* 304–312.

Gudjonsson, G. H., Sigurdsson, J. F., Sigurdardottir, A. S., Steinthorsson, H., & Sigurdardottir, V. M. (2014). The role of memory distrust in cases of internalised false confession. *Applied Cognitive Psychology, 28,* 336–348.

Gudjonsson, G. H., Sigurdsson, J. F., Sveinsdottir, B., Arnardottir, H., & Jonsson, A. (2010). Psychiatric and psychological evidence in the Supreme Court of Iceland—2001 to 2007. *Nordic Journal of Psychiatry, 64,* 283–287.

Gudjonsson, G. H., Sigurdsson, J. F., & Tryggvadottir, H. B. (2011). The relationship of compliance with a background of childhood neglect and physical and sexual abuse. *Journal of Forensic Psychiatry and Psychology, 22,* 87–98.

Gudjonsson, G. H., & Singh, K. K. (1984). The relationship between criminal conviction and interrogative suggestibility among delinquent boys. *Journal of Adolescence, 7,* 29–34.

Gudjonsson, G. H., & Singh, K. K. (1989). The revised Gudjonsson blame attribution inventory. *Personality and Individual Differences, 10,* 67–70.

Gudjonsson, G. H., Vagni, M., Maiorano, T., & Pajardi, D. (2016). Age and memory related changes in children's immediate and delayed suggestibility using the Gudjonsson Suggestibility Scale. *Personality and Individual Differences, 102,* 25–29.

Gudjonsson, G. H., Wells, J., & Young, S. (2012). Personality disorders and clinical syndromes in ADHD prisoners. *Journal of Attention Disorders, 16,* 305–314.

Gudjonsson, G. H., & Young, S. (2006). An overlooked vulnerability in a defendant: Attention deficit hyperactivity disorder and a miscarriage of justice. *Legal and Criminological Psychology, 11,* 211–218.

Gudjonsson, G. H., & Young, S. (2009). Suboptimal effort and malingering. In S. Young, M. Kopelman, and G. Gudjonsson (Eds.), *Forensic neuropsychology in practice. A guide to assessment and legal processes* (pp. 267–299). Oxford: Oxford University Press.

Gudjonsson, G. H., & Young, S. (2015). Forensic clinical psychology. In J. Hall, D. Pilgrim, & G. Turbin (Eds.), *Clinical psychology in Britain. Historical perspectives* (pp. 309–322). Leicester: The British Psychological Society.

Gudjonsson, G. H., Young, S., & Bramham, J. (2007). Interrogative suggestibility in adults diagnosed with attention-deficit hyperactivity disorder (ADHD). A potential vulnerability during police questioning. *Personality and Individual Differences, 43,* 737–745.

Gunnlaugsson, H. S. (2014). *Í krafti sannfæringar. Saga lögmanns og dómara.* Reykjavík: Almenna bókafélagið.

Hain, P. (2012). *Outside in.* London: Biteback Publishing Ltd.

Halldórsson, J. O. (1985). *Löglegt en siðlaust. Stjórnmálasaga Vilmundar Gylfasonar.* Reykjavík: Bókhlaðan.

Hammersley, R., & Read, J. D. (1986). What is integration? Remembering a story and remembering false implications about the story. *British Journal of Psychology*, 77, 329–341.

Haraldsson, G. (1993). *Lögfræðital 1736-1992*. Reykjavík: Iðunn.

Haward, L. R. C. (1981). *Forensic psychology*. London: Batsford Academic and Educational Ltd.

Hayes, S., Shackell, P., Mottram, P., & Lancaster, R. (2007). The prevalence of intellectual disability in a major UK prison. *British Journal of Learning Disabilities*, 35, 162–167.

Henkel, L. A., & Coffman, K. J. (2004). Memory distortions in coerced false confessions: A source monitoring framework analysis. *Applied Cognitive Psychology*, 18, 567–588.

Hildibrandsdóttir, A. H. (2001). *Réttarsálfræðingurinn. Saga Gísla H. Guðjónssonar*. Reykjavík: Mál og Menning.

Hilgendorf, E. L., & Irving, B. (1981). A decision-model of confessions. In S. M. A. Lloyd-Bostock (Ed.), *Psychology in legal contexts. Applications and limitations* (pp. 67–84). London: Macmillan Press Ltd.

Holmberg, U., & Christianson, S. A. (2002). Murderers' and sexual offenders' experiences of police interviews and their inclination to admit or deny crimes. *Behavioural Sciences and the Law*, 20, 31–45.

Holmberg, U., Christianson, S. A., & Wexler, D. (2007). Interviewing offenders: A therapeutic jurisprudential approach. In S. A. Christianson (Ed.), *Offenders' memories of violent crimes* (pp. 259–278). Chichester: John Wiley & Sons.

Home Office. (1985). *Police and Criminal Evidence Act 1984*. London: HMSO.

Home Office. (2017). *Police and Criminal Evidence Act 1984 (PACE). Code C. Revised Code of Practice for the detention, treatment and questioning of persons by Police Officers*. London: Author.

Horgan, A. J., Russano, M. B., Meissner, C. A., & Evans, J. (2012). Minimization and maximization techniques: Assessing the perceived consequences of confessing and confession diagnosticity. *Psychology, Crime & Law*, 18, 65–78.

Horselenberg, R., Merckelbach, H., & Josephs, S. (2003). Individual differences and false confessions: A conceptual replication of Kassin and Kiechel (1996). *Psychology, Crime & Law*, 9, 1–8.

Horselenberg, R., Merckelbach, H., Sweets, T., Franssens, D., Peters, G.-J. Y., & Zeles, G. (2006). False confessions in the lab: Do plausibility and consequences matter? *Psychology, Crime & Law*, 12, 61–75.

Huff, C. R., Rattner, A., & Sagarin, E. (1996). *Convicted but innocent: Wrongful convictions and public policy*. London: Sage.

ICCRC (Icelandic Court Cases Review Commission) Report. (2017). *Úrskurður Enduruppökunefndar í máli nr. 15/2015*. Reykjavík, 24 February 2017.

Inbau, F. E., Reid, J. E., & Buckley, J. P. (1986). *Criminal interrogation and confessions* (3rd ed.). Baltimore: Williams & Wilkins.

Inbau, F. E., Reid, J. E., Buckley, J. P., & Jayne, B. C. (2013). *Criminal interrogation and confessions* (5th ed.). Burlington: Jones and Bartlett Learning.

Irving, B. (1980). *Police interrogation: A case study of current practice*. Royal Commission on Criminal Procedure. Research Study No. 2. London: HMSO.

Irving, B. (1987). Interrogative suggestibility: A question of parsimony. *Social Behaviour*, 2, 19–28.

Irving, B., & Hilgendorf, E. L. (1980). *Police interrogation: The psychological approach*. Royal Commission on Criminal Procedure. Research Study No. 1. London: HMSO.

Irving, B. L., & McKenzie, I. K. (1989). *Police interrogation: The effects of the Police and Criminal Evidence Act 1984*. London: The Police Foundation.

Jahr, B. O. (2015). *Hvem drepte Birgitte Tengs?* Trondheim, Norway: Gyldendal Norsk Forlag.

Janoson, M., & Frumkin, B. (2007). Gudjonsson Suggestibility Scales. In K. F. Geisinger, R. A. Spies, J. F. Carlson, & B. S. Plake (Eds.), *The seventeenth mental measurement yearbook*. Lincoln, NE: Buros Institute of Mental Measurements, University of Nebraska Press.

Johnson, M. K., Hashtroudi, S., & Lindsay, D. S. (1993). Source monitoring. *Psychological Bulletin, 114*, 3–28.

Johnson, M. K., & Raye, C. L. (1981). Reality monitoring. *Psychological Review, 88*, 67–85.

Jóhannesson, Ó. (2013). *Forystumaður úr Fljótum. Æviminningar Ólafs Jóhannessonar prófessors og forsætisráðherra*. Sauðarkróki: Sögufélag Skagfirðinga.

Jónasson, J. (1996). *Saklaus í klóm réttvísinnar*. Reykjavík: Vaka-Helgafell.

Jónsdóttir, F. (2010). *19. Nóvember. Æviminningar Hauks Gudmundssonar fyrrverandi rannsóknarmanns*. Reykjavík: Sögur ehf.

Jónsson, Þ., & Gudjónsson, Gudmundur (1997). *Lögreglan á Íslandi. Stéttartal og saga*. Reykjavík: Byggðir og bú ehf.

Karlsson, H. (1994). *Ridid á vadid. Thaettir úr lífi Einars Bollasonar*. Reykjavík: Fródi HF.

Kassin, S. M. (1997). The psychology of confession evidence. *American Psychologist, 52*, 221–233.

Kassin, S. M. (2005). On the psychology of confessions: Does innocence put innocents at risk? *American Psychologist, 60*, 215–228.

Kassin, S. M. (2007). Internalized false confessions. In M. Toglia, J. Read, D. Ross, & R. Lindsay (Eds.), *Handbook of eyewitness psychology: Volume 1, Memory for events* (pp. 175–192). Mahwah, NJ: Erlbaum.

Kassin, S. M. (2015). The social psychology of false confessions. *Social Issues and Policy Review, 9*, 24–49.

Kassin, S. M. (2017). False confessions: How can psychology so basic be so counterintuitive? *American Psychologist, 72*, 951–964.

Kassin, S. M., Drizin, S. A., Grisso, T., Gudjonsson, G. H., Leo, R. A., & Redlich, A. P. (2010a). Police-induced confessions: Risk factors and recommendations. *Law and Human Behavior, 34*, 3–38.

Kassin, S. M., Drizin, S. A., Grisso, T., Gudjonsson, G. H., Leo, R. A., & Redlich, A. P. (2010b). Police-induced confessions, risk factors, and recommendations: Looking ahead. *Law and Human Behavior, 34*, 49–52.

Kassin, S. M., & Gudjonsson, G. H. (2004). The psychology of confessions. A review of the literature and issues. *Psychological Science in the Public Interest, 5*, 33–67.

Kassin, S.M., & Kiechel, K. L. (1996). The social psychology of false confessions: Compliance, internalization, and confabulation. *Psychological Science, 7*, 125–128.

Kassin, S. M., Leo, R. A., Meissner, C. A., Richman, K. D., Colwell, L. H., Leach, A-M., & La Fon, D. (2007). Police interviewing and interrogation: A self-report survey of police practices and beliefs. *Law and Human Behavior, 31*, 381–400.

Kassin, S. M., & McNall, K. (1991). Police interrogations and confessions: Communicating promises and threats by pragmatic implication. *Law and Human Behavior, 15*, 233–251.

Kassin, S. M., Meissner, C. A., & Norwick, R. J. (2005). "I'd know a false confession if I saw one": A comparative study of college students and police investigators. *Law and Human Behavior*, *29*, 211–227.

Kassin, S. M., & Norwick, R. J. (2004). Why people waive their *Miranda* rights: The power of innocence. *Law and Human Behavior*, *28*, 211–221.

Kassin, S. M., & Wrightsman, L. S. (1985). Confession evidence. In S. M. Kassin, & L. S. Wrightsman (Eds.), *The psychology of evidence and trial procedures* (pp. 67–94). London: Sage.

Kee, R. (1989). *Trial and error*. London: Penguin Books.

Kelly, C. E., Miller, J. C., & Redlich, A. D. (2016). The dynamic nature of interrogation. *Law and Human Behavior*, *40*, 295–309.

Kelly, C. E., Miller, J. C., Redlich, A. D., & Kleinman, S. M. (2013). A taxonomy of interrogation methods. *Psychology, Public Policy, and Law*, *19*, 165–178.

Kelman, H. C. (1950). The effects of success and failure on "suggestibility" in the autokinetic situation. *Journal of Abnormal and Social Psychology*, *46*, 267–285.

Kelman, H. C. (1958). Compliance, identification, and internalization: Three processes of attitude change. *Journal of Conflict Resolution*, *2*, 51–60.

Kennedy, L. (1986). Foreword. In N. Fellows (Ed.), *Killing time* (pp. 6–8). Oxford: Lion.

Kennedy, L. (1988). *10 Rillington Place*. London: Grafton.

Kissinger, H. (2011). *Henry Kissinger. Years of upheaval. Volume 2*. London: Simon & Schuster.

Kopelman, M. D. (1987). Two types of confabulation. *Journal of Neurology, Neurosurgery, and Psychiatry*, *50*, 482–1487.

Kopelman, M. D. (2010). Varieties of confabulation and delusion. *Cognitive Neuropsychiatry*, *15*, 14–37.

Lader, M. (1999). The influence of drugs upon testimony. *Medicine, Science and the Law*, *39*, 99–105.

Laney, C., & Takarangi, M. K. T. (2013). False memories for aggressive acts. *Acta Psychologica*, *143*, 227–234.

Lassiter, G. D., Ware, L. J., Lindberg, M. J., & Ratcliffe, J. J. (2010). Videotaping custodial interrogations: Toward a scientifically based policy. In G. D. Lassiter & C. A. Meissner (Eds.), *Police interrogations and false confessions* (pp. 143–160). Washington, DC: American Psychological Association.

Latham, J., & Gudjonsson, G. H. (2016). *Sugar Paper Theories*. London: Here Press.

Lee, K. (2004). Age, neuropsychological, and social cognitive measures as predictors of individual differences in susceptibility to the misinformation effect. *Applied Cognitive Psychology*, *18*, 997–1019.

Leo, R. A. (1994). *Police interrogation in America: A study of violence, civility and social change*. PhD thesis, University of California at Berkeley.

Leo, R. A. (1996). Inside the interrogation room. *Journal of Criminal Law and Criminology*, *86*, 266–303.

Leo, R. A. (1998). *Miranda* and the problems with false confessions. In R. A. Leo, & G. C. Thomas (Eds.), *The Miranda debate. Law, justice and policing* (pp. 271–182). Boston: Northeastern University Press.

Leo, R. A. (2008). *Police interrogation and American justice*. Cambridge, MA: Harvard University Press.

Leo, R. A., & Drizin, S. A. (2010). The three errors: Pathways to false confession and wrongful conviction. In G. D. Lassiter, & C. A. Meissner (Eds.), *Police interrogations and false confessions* (pp. 9–30). Washington, DC: American Psychological Association.

References

Leo, R. A., & Ofshe, R. J. (1998). The consequences of false confessions: deprivations of liberty and miscarriages of justice in the age of psychological interrogation. *Journal of Criminal Law and Criminology, 88*, 429–496.

Lepper, M. R. (1983). Social control processes and the internalization of social values: An attributional perspective. In E. T. Higgins, D. N. Ruble, & W. W. Hartup (Eds.), *Social cognition and social development* (pp. 294–330). New York: Cambridge University Press.

Levey, A. B. (1988). *Polygraph. An evaluative review*. London: HMSO.

Levy, F., Hay, D. A., Bennett, K., & McStephen, M. (2005). Gender differences in ADHD subtype comorbidity. *Journal of the American Academy of Child and Adolescent Psychiatry, 44*, 368–376.

Leósdóttir, J. (2013). *Við Jóhanna*. Reykjavík: Mál og Menning.

Loftus, E. F. (1979). *Eyewitness testimony*. Cambridge, MA: Harvard University Press.

Loftus, E. F. (1991). Made in memory: Distortions in recollection after misleading information. *Psychology of Learning and Motivation, 27*, 187–215.

Loftus, E. F. (2005a). Searching for the neurobiology of the misinformation effect. *Learning and Memory, 12*, 1–2.

Loftus, E. F. (2005b). Planting misinformation in the human mind: A 30-year investigation of the malleability of memory. *Learning and Memory, 12*, 361–366.

Loftus, E. F., & Hoffman, H. G. (1989). Misinformation and memory: The creation of new memories. *Journal of Experimental Psychology: General, 118*, 100–104.

Loftus, E. F., Miller, D. G., & Burns, H. J. (1978). Semantic integration of verbal information into a visual memory. *Journal of Experimental Psychology: Human Memory & Learning, 4*, 19–31.

Mansfield, M. (2009). *Memoirs of a radical lawyer*. London: Bloomsbury.

Martin, N. C., Levy, F., Pieka, J., & Hay, D. A. (2006). A genetic study of attention deficit hyperactivity disorder, conduct disorder, oppositional defiant disorder and reading disability: Aetiological overlaps and implications. *International Journal of Disability, Development and Education, 53*, 21–34.

Mastroberardino, S., & Marucci, F. S. (2013). Interrogative suggestibility: Was it just compliance or a genuinely false memory? *Legal and Criminological Psychology, 18*, 274–286.

Mazzoni, G. A. L., Loftus, E. F., & Kirsch, I. (2001). Changing beliefs about implausible autobiographical events: A little plausibility goes a long way. *Journal of Experimental Psychology: Applied, 7*, 51–59.

McCann, J. T. (1998). A conceptual framework for identifying various types of confessions. *Behavioral Sciences and the Law, 16*, 441–453.

McKee, G., & Franey, R. (1988). *Time bomb*. London: Bloomsbury.

McKenzie, K., Michie, A., Murray, A., & Hales, C. (2012). Screening for offenders with an intellectual disability: The validity of the Learning Disability Screening Questionnaire. *Research in Developmental Disabilities, 33*, 791–795.

McKenzie, K., Sharples, P., & Murray, A. L. (2015). Validating the Learning Disability Screening Questionnaire against the Weschler Adult Intelligence Scale, Fourth Edition. *Intellectual and Developmental Disabilities, 53*, 301–307.

McNally, R. J. (2003). *Remembering trauma*. Cambridge, MA: Harvard University Press.

McNally, R. J., Lasko, N. B., Clancy, S. A., Macklin, M. L., Pitman, R. K., & Orr, S. P. (2004). Psychophysiological responding during script-driven imagery in people reporting abduction by space aliens. *Psychological Science, 15,* 493–497.

Medford, S., Gudjonsson, G. H., & Pearse, J. (2000). *The identification of persons at risk in police custody. The use of appropriate adults by the Metropolitan Police.* London: Institute of Psychiatry and New Scotland Yard.

Medford, S., Gudjonsson, G. H., & Pearse, J. (2003). The efficacy of the appropriate adult safeguard during police interviewing. *Legal and Criminological Psychology, 8,* 253–266.

Meissner, C.A., & Kassin, S. M. (2002). "He's guilty!": Investigator bias in judgments of truth and deception. *Law and Human Behavior, 26,* 469–480.

Meissner, C. A., & Lassiter, G. D. (2010). Conclusion: What have we learned? Implications for practice, policy, and future research. In G. D. Lassiter & C. A. Meissner (Eds.), *Police interrogations and false confessions: Current research, practice, and policy recommendations* (pp. 225–229). Washington, DC: American Psychological Association.

Meissner, C. A., Redlich, A. D., Bhatt, S., & Brandon, S. (2012). Interview and interrogation methods and their effects on true and false confessions. *Campbell Systematic Reviews, 13,* 1–53.

Meissner, C. A., Redlich, A. D., Michael, S. W., Evans, J. R., Camilletti, C. R., Bhatt, S., & Brandon, S. (2014). Accusatorial and information-gathering interrogation methods and their effects on true and false confessions: A meta-analytic review. *Journal of Experimental Criminology, 10,* 459–486.

Meissner, C. A., Russano, M. B., & Narchet, F. M. (2010). The importance of laboratory science for improving the diagnostic value of confession evidence. In G. D. Lassiter, & C. A. Meissner (Eds.), *Police interrogations and false confessions: Current research, practice, and policy recommendations* (pp. 111–126). Washington, DC: American Psychological Association.

Mikulincer, M., Babkoff, H., Caspy, T., & Sing, H. (1989). The effects of 72 hours of sleep loss on psychological variables. *British Journal of Psychology, 80,* 145–162.

Moore, T. E., & Keenan, K. (2013). What is voluntary? On the reliability of admissions arising from Mr. Big undercover operations. *Investigative Interviewing: Research and Practice, 5,* 45–46.

Morgan, D., & Stephenson, G. M. (1994). Introduction: The right to silence in criminal investigations. In D. Morgan, & G. Stephenson (Eds.), *Suspicion and silence. The right to silence in criminal investigation* (pp. 91–106). London: Blackstone Press Ltd.

Moston, S., & Stephenson, G. M. (1993a). The changing face of police interrogation. *Journal of Community and Applied Social Psychology, 3,* 101–115.

Moston, S., & Stephenson, G. M. (1993b). *The questioning and interviewing of suspects outside the police station.* Royal Commission on Criminal Justice. Research Study No. 22. London: HMSO.

Moston, S., Stephenson, G. M., & Williamson, T. M. (1992). The effects of case characteristics on suspect behaviour during questioning. *British Journal of Criminology, 32,* 23–40.

Mullin, C. (1989). *Error of judgement. The truth about the Birmingham bombings.* Dublin: Poolbeg Press Ltd.

Münsterberg, H. (1908). *On the witness stand: Essays on psychology and crime.* Garden City, NY: Doubleday.

Narchet, F., Meissner, C. A., & Russano, M. B. (2011). Modeling the influence of investigator bias on the elicitation of true and false confessions. *Law and Human Behavior*, *35*, 452–465.

Nash, R. A., & Wade, K. A. (2009). Innocent but proven guilty: Eliciting internalized false confessions using doctored-video evidence. *Applied Cognitive Psychology*, *23*, 624–637.

Neven-du Mont, J., & Schütz, K. (1977). *Sakamál 1081*. Reykjavík: Setberg.

Norris, R. J. (2017). *Exonerated. A history of the innocence movement*. New York: New York University Press.

North, A. S., Russell, A. J., & Gudjonsson, G. H. (2008). High functioning autism spectrum disorders: An investigation of psychological vulnerabilities during interrogative interview. *Journal of Forensic Psychiatry and Psychology*, *19*, 323–334.

Ofshe, R. (1989). Coerced confessions: The logic of seemingly irrational action. *Cultic Studies Journal*, *6*, 1–15.

Ofshe, R. J. (1992). Inadvertent hypnosis during interrogation: False confession due to dissociative state; mis-identified multiple personality and the satanic cult hypothesis. *International Journal of Clinical and Experimental Hypnosis*, *XL*, 125–156.

Ofshe, R. J., & Leo, R. A. (1997a). The decision to confess falsely: Rational choice and irrational action. *Denver University Law Review*, *74*, 979–1122.

Ofshe, R. J., & Leo, R. A. (1997b). The social psychology of police interrogation: The theory and classification of true and false confessions. *Studies in Law, Politics and Society*, *16*, 189–251.

Ofshe, R., & Watters, E. (1994). *Making monsters. False memories, psychotherapy, and sexual hysteria*. New York: Charles Scribner's Sons.

Okado, Y., & Stark, C. E. L. (2005). Neural activity during encoding predicts false memories created by misinformation. *Learning and Memory*, *12*, 3–11.

Oxburgh, G., Fahsing, I., Haworth, K., & Blair, J. P. (2016). Interviewing suspected offenders. In G. Oxburgh, T. Myklebust, T. Grant, & R. Milne, *Communication in investigative and legal contexts* (pp. 135–157). Chichester: Wiley Blackwell.

Oxburgh, G., Myklebust, T., Grant, T., & Milne, R. (2016). Communication in investigative and legal settings: Introduction and contexts. In G. Oxburgh, T. Myklebust, T. Grant, & R. Milne (Eds.), *Communication in investigative and legal contexts* (pp. 1–13). Chichester: Wiley Blackwell.

Pearse, J. J. (1997). *Police interviewing: An examination of some of the psychological, interrogative and background factors that are associated with a suspect's confession*. Doctoral thesis, King's College London.

Pearse, J., & Gudjonsson, G. H. (1996). Police interviewing techniques at two south London police stations. *Psychology, Crime and Law*, *3*, 63–74.

Pearse, J., & Gudjonsson, G. H. (1999). Measuring influential police interviewing tactics: A factor analytic approach. *Legal and Criminological Psychology*, *4*, 221–238.

Pearse, J., & Gudjonsson, G. H. (2003). The identification and measurement of 'oppressive' police interviewing tactics in Britain. In G. H. Gudjonsson, *The Psychology of interrogations and confessions. A handbook* (pp. 75–129). Chichester: John Wiley & Sons.

Pearse, J., & Gudjonsson, G. H. (2016). Forensic psychiatry and forensic psychology: Forensic interviewing. In J. Payne-James, & R. W. Byard (Eds.), *Encyclopaedia of forensic and legal medicine. Volume 2* (2nd ed.) (pp. 603–609). Oxford: Elsevier.

Pearse, J., Gudjonsson, G. H., Clare, I. C. H., & Rutter, S. (1998). Police interviewing and psychological vulnerabilities: Predicting the likelihood of a confession. *Journal of Community and Applied Social Psychology*, *8*, 1–21.

Perske, R. (2008). False confessions from 53 persons with intellectual disabilities: The list keeps growing. *Intellectual and Developmental Disabilities*, *46*, 468–479.

Petursson, H., & Gudjonsson, G. H. (1981). Psychiatric aspects of homicide. *Acta Psychiatrica Scandinavica*, *64*, 363–372.

Pérez-Sales, P. (2017). *Psychological torture. Definition, evaluation and measurement*. London: Routledge.

Pétursson, K. (1994). *Þögnin er rofin*. Reykjavík: Bókaútgáfan Skjaldborg HF.

Polak, M., Dukala, K., Szpitalak, M., & Polczyk, R. (2016). Toward a non-memory misinformation effect: Accessing the original source does not prevent yielding to misinformation. *Current Psychology*, *35*, 1–12.

Pope, H. S., Butcher, J., & Seelen, J. (1993). *The MMPI, MMPI-2 and MMPI-A in court. A practical guide for expert witnesses and attorneys*. Washington, DC: American Psychological Association.

Powers, P. A., Andriks, J. L., & Loftus, E. F. (1979). Eyewitness accounts of females and males. *Journal of Applied Psychology*, *64*, 339–347.

Price, C., & Caplan, J. (1977). *The Confait confessions*. London: Marion Boyars.

Raven, J. C. (1960). *Guide to the Standard Progressive Matrices*. London: Lewis.

Redlich, A. D., & Goodman, D. S. (2003). Taking responsibility for an act not committed: The influence of age and suggestibility. *Law and Human Behavior*, *27*, 141–156.

Redlich, A. D., Kulish, R., & Steadman, H. J. (2011). Comparing true and false confessions among persons with serious mental illness. *Psychology, Public Policy, and Law*, *17*, 394–418.

Redlich, A. D., Summers, A., & Hoover, S. (2010). Self-reported false confessions and false pleas among offenders with mental illness. *Law and Human Behavior*, *34*, 79–90.

Reid, J. E., & Inbau, F. E. (1977). *Truth and deception. The polygraph ("lie detector") technique* (2nd ed.). Baltimore: The Williams & Wilkins Co.

Reik, T. (1959). *The compulsion to confess: On the psychoanalysis of crime and punishment*. New York: Farrar, Straus and Cudahy.

Richardson, G. (1991). *A study of interrogative suggestibility in an adolescent forensic population*. MSc dissertation, University of Newcastle.

Ridley, A. M., & Gudjonsson, G. H. (2013). Suggestibility and individual differences: Psychosocial and memory measures. In A. M. Ridley, F. Gabbert, & D. J. La Rooy (Eds.), *Suggestibility in legal contexts* (pp. 85–106). Chichester: Wiley-Blackwell.

Rose, D. (2004). *Guantánamo. America's War on Human Rights*. London: Faber and Faber.

Rosenblad, E., & Sigurdardottir-Rosenblad, R. (1993). *Iceland from past to present*. Reykjavík: Mál og Menning.

Russano, M. B., Meissner, C. A., Narchet, F. M., & Kassin, S. K. (2005). Investigating true and false confessions within a novel experimental paradigm. *Psychological Science*, *16*, 481–486.

Sabbagh, K. (2009). *Remembering our childhood. How memory betrays us*. Oxford: Oxford University Press.

Schacter, D. L. (2007). *How the mind forgets and remembers*. London: Souvenir Press.

Schacter, D. L., & Loftus, E. F. (2013). Memory and law: What can cognitive neuroscience contribute? *Nature Neuroscience*, *16*, 119–123.

Schatz, S. J. (2018). Interrogated with intellectual disabilities. The risks of false confessions. *Stanford Law Review, 70*, 643–690.

Scheck, B., Neufeld, P., & Dwyer, J. (2000). *Actual innocence.* New York: Doubleday.

Schiller, M. (2009). *Remembering the armed struggle.* Hamburg: Zidane Press.

Schooler, J. W., & Loftus, E. F. (1986). Individual differences and experimentation: Complementary approaches to interrogative suggestibility. *Social Behaviour, 1*, 105–112.

Scoboria, A., Mazzoni, G., Kirsch, I., & Milling, L. S. (2002). Immediate and persisting effects of misleading questions and hypnosis on memory reports. *Journal of Experimental Psychology: Applied, 8*, 26–32.

Sekar, S. (1997). *Fitted in. The Cardiff 3 and the Lynette White Inquiry.* London: The Fitted In Project.

Sekar, S. (2012). *The Cardiff Five. Innocent beyond any doubt.* Hook, Hampshire: Waterside Press.

Sekar, S. (2017). *Trials and tribulations: Innocence matters?* London: The Fitted In Project.

Shalev, S. (2008). *A sourcebook on solitary confinement.* London: Mannheim Centre for Criminology, London School of Economics. Available online at www.solitaryconfinement.org/sourcebook.

Shaw, J., & Porter, S. (2015). Constructing rich false memories of committing crime. *Psychological Science, 26*, 291–301.

Shaw, M., Hodgkins, P., Caci, H., Young, S., Kahle, J., Woods, A. G., & Arnold, L. E. (2012). A systematic review and analysis of long-term outcomes in attention deficit hyperactivity disorder: Effects of treatment and non-treatment. *BMC Medicine, 10*, 99.

Shawyer, A., Milne, B., & Bull, R. (2009). Investigative interviewing in the UK. In T. Williamson, B. Milne, & S. P. Savage (Eds.), *International developments in investigative interviewing* (pp. 24–37). Cullompton, Devon: Willan Publishing.

Shepherd, E., & Griffiths, A. (2013). *Investigative interviewing: The conversation management approach* (2nd ed.). Oxford: Oxford University Press.

Sigurdsson, J. F. (1998). *Alleged false confessions among Icelandic offenders: An examination of some psychological, criminological and substance use factors that are associated with the reported false confessions.* Doctoral thesis, King's College London.

Sigurdsson, J. F., & Gudjonsson, G. H. (1994). Alcohol and drug intoxication during police interrogation and the reasons why suspects confess to the police. *Addiction, 89*, 985–997.

Sigurdsson, J. F., & Gudjonsson, G. H. (1996a). The psychological characteristics of 'false confessors'. A study among Icelandic prison inmates and juvenile offenders. *Personality and Individual Differences, 20*, 321–329.

Sigurdsson, J. F., & Gudjonsson, G. H. (1996b). The relationship between types of claimed false confession made and the reasons why suspects confess to the police according to the Gudjonsson Confession Questionnaire (GCQ). *Journal of Criminological and Legal Psychology, 1*, 259–269.

Sigurdsson, J. F., & Gudjonsson, G. H. (2001). False confessions: The relative importance of psychological, criminological and substance abuse variables. *Psychology, Crime and Law, 7*, 275–289.

Sigurdsson, J. F., Gudjonsson, G. H., Einarsson, E., & Gudjonsson G. (2006). Differences in personality and mental state between suspects and witnesses immediately after being interviewed by the police. *Psychology, Crime and Law, 12*, 619–628.

Sigurdsson, J. F., Gudjonsson, G. H., & Peersen, M. (2001). Differences in the cognitive ability and personality of desisters and re-offenders: A prospective study among young offenders. *Psychology, Crime and Law, 7*, 33–43.

Skirrow, C., Ebner-Priemer, U., Reinhard, I., Malliaris, Y., Kuntsi, J., & Asherson, P. (2014). Everyday emotional experience of adults with attention deficit hyperactivity disorder: Evidence for reactive and endogenous emotional lability. *Psychological Medicine, 44*, 3571–3583.

Smith, G. A. (2011). *From tests to therapy. A personal history of clinical psychology*. Leicester: Matador.

Smith, J., & Moncourt, A. (2009). *The Red Army Faction: A documentary history. Volume 1. Projectiles for the people*. Montreal, Canada: Kersplebedeb.

Smith, S. M., Stinson, V., & Patry, M. W. (2009). Using the "Mr. Big" technique to elicit confessions: Successful innovation or dangerous development in the Canadian legal system? *Psychology, Public Policy, & Law, 15*, 168–193.

Snaehólm, N. (1949). *Á kafbáta veiðum. Íslendingur í her og lögreglu Bandamanna*. Reykjavík: Ísafoldarprentsmiðja H.F.

Snitselaar, M. A., Smits, M. G., van der Heijden, K. B., & Spijker, J. (2017). Sleep and circadian rhythmicity in adult ADHD and the effect of stimulants: A review of the current literature. *Journal of Attention Disorders, 21*, 14–26.

Snook, B., Luther, K., & Barron, T. (2016). Interviewing suspects in Canada. In D. Walsh, G. E. Oxburgh, A. D. Redlich, & T. Mykelburts (Eds.), *International developments and practices in investigative interviewing and interrogation. Volume 2: Suspects* (pp. 229–239). London: Routledge.

Softley, P. (1980). *Police interrogation: An observational study in four police stations*. Home Office Research Study No 61. London: HMSO.

Soukara, S., Bull, R., Vrij, A., Turner, M., & Cherryman, C. (2009). A study of what really happens in police interviews with suspects. *Psychology, Crime, and Law, 15*, 493–506.

Spano, R. E., Sigurdsson, J. F., & Gudjonsson, G. H. (2016). Institutional abuse inquiries. In P. Radcliffe, G. Gudjonsson, A. Heaton-Armstrong, & D. Wolchover (Eds.), *Witness testimony in sexual cases. Evidential, investigative and scientific perspectives* (pp. 193–204). Oxford: Oxford University Press.

Steingrimsdottir, G., Hreinsdottir, H., Gudjonsson, G. H., Sigurdsson, J. F., & Nielsen, T. (2007). False confessions and the relationship with offending behaviour and personality among Danish adolescents. *Legal and Criminological Psychology, 12*, 287–296.

Stephenson, G., & Moston, S. (1994). Police interrogation. *Psychology, Crime & Law, 1*, 151–157.

Stern, W. (1939). The psychology of testimony. *Journal of Abnormal and Social Psychology, 34*, 3–20.

Stevenson, J., Langley, K., Pay, H., Payton, A., Worthington, J., Ollier, W., & Tapar, A. (2005). Attention deficit hyperactivity disorder with reading disabilities: Preliminary genetic findings on the involvement of the ADRA2A gene. *Journal of Child Psychology and Psychiatry, 46*, 1081–1088.

Stukat, K. G. (1958). *Suggestibility: A factor and experimental analysis*. Almgvist & Wiksell: Stockholm.

Styron, W. (1996). Introduction. In D. S. Connery (Ed.), *Convicting the innocent*. Cambridge, MA: Brookline Books.

St-Yves, M. (2009). Police interrogation in Canada: From the quest for confession to the search for the truth. In T. Williamson, B. Milne, & S. P. Savage (Eds.), *International developments in investigative interviewing* (pp. 92–110). Devon, UK: Willan Publishing.

St-Yves, M. (2014). Rapport in investigative interviews. Five fundamental rules to achieve it. In M. St-Yves (Ed.), *Investigative interviewing. The essentials* (pp. 1–19). Toronto: Carswell.

Sullivan, T. (1992). *Unequal verdicts. The Central Park trials.* New York: Simon & Schuster.

Szpitalak, M. (2017). The indirectly generated tainted truth effect: Warning is not necessary to worsen the testimony of non-misled persons. *Psychology, Crime & Law, 23,* 323–341.

Szpitalak, M., & Polczyk, R. (2016). Reinforced self-affirmation and interrogative suggestibility. *Psychiatry, Psychology and Law, 23,* 512–520.

Thapar, A., Harrington, R., & McGuffin, P. (2001). Examining the comorbidity of ADHD-related behaviours and conduct problems using a twin study design. *British Journal of Psychiatry, 179,* 224–229.

The Justice Project. (2007). *Jailhouse snitch testimony. A policy review.* Washington DC: Author.

Thorley, C. (2013). Memory conformity and suggestibility. *Psychology, Crime & Law, 17,* 565–575.

Tousignant, J. P., Hall, D., & Loftus, E. F. (1986). Discrepancy detection and vulnerability to misleading post-event information. *Memory and Cognition, 14,* 329–338.

Unnever, J. D., & Cornell, D. G. (2003). Bullying, self-control, and ADHD. *Journal of Interpersonal Violence, 18,* 129–147.

Unnsteinsson, S. (1980). *Stattu þig drengur.* Reykjavík: Iðunn.

Vagni, M., Maiorano, T., Pajardi, D., & Gudjonsson, G. H. (2015). Immediate and delayed suggestibility among suspected child victims of sexual abuse. *Personality and Individual Differences, 79,* 129–133.

Valsson, P. (2017). *Minn tími. Saga Jóhönnu Sigurdardóttur.* Reykjavík: Mál og Menning.

Van Bergen, S. (2011). *Memory distrust in the legal context.* Doctoral thesis, University of Maastricht.

Van Bergen, S., Horselenberg, R., Merckelbach, H., Jelicic, M., & Beckers, R. (2010). Memory distrust and acceptance of misinformation. *Applied Cogntivie Psychology, 24,* 885–896.

Van Bergen, S., Jelicic, M., & Merckelbach, H. (2008). Interrogation techniques and memory distrust. *Psychology, Crime & Law, 14,* 425–434.

Van Bergen, S., Jelicic, M., & Merckelbach, H. (2009). Are subjective memory problems related to suggestibility, compliance, false memories, and objective memory performance? *American Journal of Psychology, 122,* 249–257.

Victory, P. (2001). *Justice and truth. The Guildford Four and Maguire Seven.* London: Christopher Sinclair-Stevenson.

Viljoen, J. L., Klaver, J., & Roesch, R. (2005). Legal decisions of preadolescent and adolescent defendants: Predictors of confessions, pleas, communication with attorneys, and appeals. *Law and Human Behavior, 29,* 253–277.

Vrij, A. (2008). *Detecting lies and deceit. Pitfalls and opportunities* (2nd ed.). Chichester: John Wiley & Sons, Ltd.

Vrij, A., Granhag, P. A., Mann, S., & Leal, S. (2011). Outsmarting the liars: Towards a cognitive lie detection approach. *Current Directions in Psychological Science, 20,* 28–32.

Vrij, A., Hope, L., & Fisher R. P. (2014). Eliciting reliable information in investigative interviews. *Policy Insights from Behavioral and Brain Sciences (PIBBS)*, *1*, 129–136.

Wachi, T., Watanabe, K., Yokota, K., Otsuka, Y., & Lamb, M. E. (2016). The relationship between police officers' personalities and interviewing style. *Personality and Individual Differences, 97*, 151–156.

Walkley, J. (1987). *Police interrogation. A handbook for investigators*. London: Police Review Publishing.

Walsh, D., Oxburgh, G. E., Redlich, A. D., & Myklebust, T. (Eds.), (2016). *International developments and practices in investigative interviewing and interrogation. Volume 2: Suspects*. London: Routledge.

Walsh, D., Redlich, A. D., Oxburgh, G. E., & Myklebust, T. (2016). Conclusion. In D. Walsh, G. E. Oxburgh, A. D. Redlich, & T. Myklebust (Eds.), *International developments and practices in investigative interviewing and interrogation. Volume 2: Suspects* (pp. 267–270). London: Routledge.

Ward, J. (1993). *Ambushed*. London: Vermilion.

Waschbusch, D. A. (2002). A meta-analytic examination of comorbid hyperactive-impulsive-attention problems and conduct problems. *Psychological Bulletin, 128*, 118–150.

Wechsler, D. (1999). *Wechsler abbreviated scale of intelligence*. New York: The Psychological Corporation, Harcourt Brace & Company.

Williamson, T. (1994). Reflection on current practice. In D. Morgan, & G. Stephenson (Eds.), *Suspicion and silence. The right to silence in criminal investigation* (pp. 107–116). London: Blackstone Press Ltd.

Williamson, T. (2006). Towards greater professionalism: Minimizing miscarriages of justice. In T. Williamson (Ed.), *Investigative interviewing: Rights, research, regulation* (pp. 147–166). Cullompton, Devon: Willan Publishing.

Williamson, T. (2007). Psychology and criminal investigation. In T. Newburn, T. Williamson, & A. Wright (Eds.), *Handbook of criminal investigation* (pp. 68–91). Abingdon: Willan Publishing.

Woody, W. D., & Forrest, K. D. (2009). Effects of false-evidence ploys and expert testimony on jurors' verdicts, recommended sentences, and perceptions of confession evidence. *Behavioral Sciences and the Law, 27*, 333–360.

Working Group Report. (2013). *Skýrsla starfshóps um Gudmundar – og Geirfinnsmál til innanríksráðherra*. Reykjavik: The Ministry of the Interior.

Wright, K., & Gudjonsson, G. H. (2007). The development of a scale for measuring offence-related feelings of shame and guilt. *Journal of Forensic Psychiatry and Psychology, 18*, 307–316.

Wrightsman, L. S., & Kassin, S. M. (1993). *Confessions in the courtroom*. Newbury Park: Sage.

Young, S., Absoud, M., Blackburn, C., Branney, P., Colley, B., Farrag, E., Fleisher, S., … Mukherjee, R. (2016). Guidelines for identification and treatment of individuals with attention deficit/hyperactivity disorder and associated fetal alcohol spectrum disorders based upon expert consensus. *BMC Psychiatry, 16*, 324.

Young, S., Adamou, M., Bolea, B., Gudjonsson, G. H., Müller, U., Pitts, M., Thome, J., & Asherson, P. (2011). The identification and management of ADHD offenders within the criminal justice system: A consensus statement from the UK Adult ADHD Network and criminal justice agencies. *BMC Psychiatry, 11*, 116.

Young, S., & Bramham, J. (2007). *ADHD in adults. A psychological guide to practice*. Chichester: John Wiley & Sons, Ltd.

Young, S., Gonzalez, R. A., Mutch, L., Mallet-Lambert, I., O'Rourke, L., Hickey, N., Asherson, P., & Gudjonsson, G. H. (2016). Diagnostic accuracy of a brief screening tool for attention deficit hyperactivity disorder in UK prison inmates. *Psychological Medicine, 46*, 1449–1458.

Young, S., Goodwin, E. J., Sedgwick, O., & Gudjonsson, G. H. (2013). The effectiveness of police custody assessments in identifying suspects with intellectual disabilities and attention deficit hyperactivity disorder. *BMC Medicine, 11*, 248.

Young, S., & Gudjonsson, G. H. (2008). Growing out of ADHD: The relationship between functioning and symptoms. *Journal of Attention Disorders, 12*, 162–169.

Young, S., Gudjonsson, G. H., Wells, J., Asherson, P., Theobald, D., Oliver, B., Scott, C., & Mooney, A. (2009). Attention deficit hyperactivity disorder and critical incidents in a Scottish prison population. *Personality and Individual Differences, 46*, 265–269.

Young, S., Moss, D., Sedgwick, O., Fridman, M., & Hodgkins, P. (2015). A meta-analysis of the prevalence of attention deficit hyperactivity disorder in incarcerated populations. *Psychological Medicine, 45*, 247–258.

Young, S., Sedgwick, O., Fridman, M., Gudjonsson, G. H., Hodgkins, P., Lantigua, M., & González, R. (2015). Co-morbid psychiatric disorders among incarcerated ADHD populations: A meta-analysis. *Psychological Medicine, 45*, 2499–2510.

# Author Index

*The Psychology of False Confessions: Forty Years of Science and Practice*, First Edition.
Gisli H. Gudjonsson.
© 2018 John Wiley & Sons Ltd. Published 2018 by John Wiley & Sons Ltd.

# Subject Index

10 Rillington Place murder, 69–70

absence of support during custody and interviews, 116
activation-based model of memory, 53
ADHD
  and custodial confinement, 347
  diagnosis, 338–40
  and discrepancy detection, 61
  'don't know' replies in interrogations, 61
  evidence for, 340–3
  and false confessions, 347
  functional impairment, 343–4
  incidence at Breidavík residential home, 336
  and IQ scores, 344, 392
  and life expectancy, 338
  risk of false confessions, 131–2
Agnarsson, Gudmundur, voluntary false confession in Geirfinnur case, 170–4

alcohol
  abuse, 150–2
  memory blackouts, 2
  memory distrust syndrome, 382, 396
  risk of false confessions, 116
  smuggling, 234–8
  voluntary false confessions, 173–4
antisocial conduct and personality, false confession risk factor, 116
attention deficit hyperactivity disorder *see* ADHD

Baader-Meinhof Special Commission, 256–8
'bad company', false confession risk factor, 116
base rate of guilt, 103–8
behavioural analysis interview (BAI) *see* Reid Technique
Berggren, Eric, psychoanalytic model of confession, 91

*The Psychology of False Confessions: Forty Years of Science and Practice*, First Edition.
Gisli H. Gudjonsson.
© 2018 John Wiley & Sons Ltd. Published 2018 by John Wiley & Sons Ltd.